PEARSON mysocialworklab

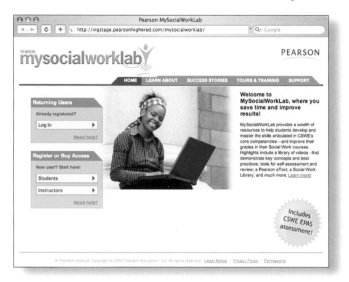

Save time and improve results!

MySocialWorkLab is a dynamic website that provides a wealth of resources geared to help students develop and master the skills articulated in CSWE's core competencies—and improve their grades in their social work courses.

MySocialWorkLab is available at no extra cost when bundled with any text in the **Connecting Core Competencies Series.** Visit **www.mysocialworklab.com** to learn more.

MySocialWorkLab offers:

- A complete **Pearson eText** of the book
- A wealth of engaging **videos**
  - **Brand-new videos**—organized around the competencies and accompanied by interactive assessment—that demonstrate key concepts and practices
  - **Career Exploration videos** that contain interviews with a wide range of social workers
- Tools for **self-assessment and review**—chapter specific quizzes tied to the core competencies, many written in the same format students will find on the licensing exam
- A **Gradebook** that reports progress of students and the class as a whole
- **MySocialWorkLibrary**—a compendium of articles and case studies in social work, searchable by course, topic, author, and title
- **MySearchLab**—a collection of tools that aid students in mastering research assignments and papers
- And much more!

> **"I would require [MySocialWorkLab]—especially if there were a way to harvest the results for program assessment."**
>
> —Jane Peller, *Northeastern Illinois University*

In recent years, many Social Work departments have been focusing on the CSWE Educational Policy and Accreditation Standards (EPAS) to guide their accreditation process. The current standards, issued in 2008, focus on mastery of the CSWE's ten core competencies and practice behaviors. Each of the ten core competencies now contains specific knowledge, values, skills, and the resulting practice behaviors as guidance for the curriculum and assessment methods of Social Work programs.

In writing this text, we have used the CSWE core competency standards and assessment recommendations as guidelines for structuring content and integrating the pedagogy. For details on the CSWE core competencies, please see www.cswe.org.

For the core competencies highlighted in this text, see page iv.

CSWE EPAS 2008 Core Competencies

Professional Identity

2.1.1 Identify as a professional social worker and conduct oneself accordingly.

Necessary Knowledge, Values, Skills

- Social workers serve as representatives of the profession, its mission, and its core values.
- Social workers know the profession's history.
- Social workers commit themselves to the profession's enhancement and to their own professional conduct and growth.

Operational Practice Behaviors

- Social workers advocate for client access to the services of social work;
- Social workers practice personal reflection and self-correction to assure continual professional development;
- Social workers attend to professional roles and boundaries;
- Social workers demonstrate professional demeanor in behavior, appearance, and communication;
- Social workers engage in career-long learning; and
- Social workers use supervision and consultation.

Ethical Practice

2.1.2 Apply social work ethical principles to guide professional practice.

Necessary Knowledge, Values, Skills

- Social workers have an obligation to conduct themselves ethically and engage in ethical decision-making.
- Social workers are knowledgeable about the value base of the profession, its ethical standards, and relevant law.

Operational Practice Behaviors

- Social workers recognize and manage personal values in a way that allows professional values to guide practice;
- Social workers make ethical decisions by applying standards of the National Association of Social Workers Code of Ethics and, as applicable, of the International Federation of Social Workers/International Association of Schools of Social Work Ethics in Social Work, Statement of Principles;
- Social workers tolerate ambiguity in resolving ethical conflicts; and
- Social workers apply strategies of ethical reasoning to arrive at principled decisions.

Critical Thinking

2.1.3 Apply critical thinking to inform and communicate professional judgments.

Necessary Knowledge, Values, Skills

- Social workers are knowledgeable about the principles of logic, scientific inquiry, and reasoned discernment.
- They use critical thinking augmented by creativity and curiosity.
- Critical thinking also requires the synthesis and communication of relevant information.

Operational Practice Behaviors

- Social workers distinguish, appraise, and integrate multiple sources of knowledge, including research-based knowledge, and practice wisdom;
- Social workers analyze models of assessment, prevention, intervention, and evaluation; and
- Social workers demonstrate effective oral and written communication in working with individuals, families, groups, organizations, communities, and colleagues.

Adapted with the permission of Council on Social Work Education

Diversity in Practice

2.1.4 Engage diversity and difference in practice.

Necessary Knowledge, Values, Skills

- Social workers understand how diversity characterizes and shapes the human experience and is critical to the formation of identity.
- The dimensions of diversity are understood as the intersectionality of multiple factors including age, class, color, culture, disability, ethnicity, gender, gender identity and expression, immigration status, political ideology, race, religion, sex, and sexual orientation.
- Social workers appreciate that, as a consequence of difference, a person's life experiences may include oppression, poverty, marginalization, and alienation as well as privilege, power, and acclaim.

Operational Practice Behaviors

- Social workers recognize the extent to which a culture's structures and values may oppress, marginalize, alienate, or create or enhance privilege and power;
- Social workers gain sufficient self-awareness to eliminate the influence of personal biases and values in working with diverse groups;
- Social workers recognize and communicate their understanding of the importance of difference in shaping life experiences; and
- Social workers view themselves as learners and engage those with whom they work as informants.

Human Rights & Justice

2.1.5 Advance human rights and social and economic justice.

Necessary Knowledge, Values, Skills

- Each person, regardless of position in society, has basic human rights, such as freedom, safety, privacy, an adequate standard of living, health care, and education.
- Social workers recognize the global interconnections of oppression and are knowledgeable about theories of justice and strategies to promote human and civil rights.
- Social work incorporates social justice practices in organizations, institutions, and society to ensure that these basic human rights are distributed equitably and without prejudice.

Operational Practice Behaviors

- Social workers understand the forms and mechanisms of oppression and discrimination;
- Social workers advocate for human rights and social and economic justice; and
- Social workers engage in practices that advance social and economic justice.

Research Based Practice

2.1.6 Engage in research-informed practice and practice-informed research.

Necessary Knowledge, Values, Skills

- Social workers use practice experience to inform research, employ evidence-based interventions, evaluate their own practice, and use research findings to improve practice, policy, and social service delivery.
- Social workers comprehend quantitative and qualitative research and understand scientific and ethical approaches to building knowledge.

Operational Practice Behaviors

- Social workers use practice experience to inform scientific inquiry; and
- Social workers use research evidence to inform practice.

Human Behavior

2.1.7 Apply knowledge of human behavior and the social environment.

Necessary Knowledge, Values, Skills

- Social workers are knowledgeable about human behavior across the life course; the range of social systems in which people live; and the ways social systems promote or deter people in maintaining or achieving health and well-being.
- Social workers apply theories and knowledge from the liberal arts to understand biological, social, cultural, psychological, and spiritual development.

Operational Practice Behaviors

- Social workers utilize conceptual frameworks to guide the processes of assessment, intervention, and evaluation; and
- Social workers critique and apply knowledge to understand person and environment.

Policy Practice   2.1.8 Engage in policy practice to advance social and economic well-being and to deliver effective social work services.

Necessary Knowledge, Values, Skills	Operational Practice Behaviors
• Social work practitioners understand that policy affects service delivery and they actively engage in policy practice. • Social workers know the history and current structures of social policies and services; the role of policy in service delivery; and the role of practice in policy development.	• Social workers analyze, formulate, and advocate for policies that advance social well-being; and • Social workers collaborate with colleagues and clients for effective policy action.

Practice Contexts

2.1.9 Respond to contexts that shape practice.

Necessary Knowledge, Values, Skills	Operational Practice Behaviors
• Social workers are informed, resourceful, and proactive in responding to evolving organizational, community, and societal contexts at all levels of practice. • Social workers recognize that the context of practice is dynamic, and use knowledge and skill to respond proactively.	• Social workers continuously discover, appraise, and attend to changing locales, populations, scientific and technological developments, and emerging societal trends to provide relevant services; and • Social workers provide leadership in promoting sustainable changes in service delivery and practice to improve the quality of social services.

Engage, Assess, Intervene, Evaluate   2.1.10 Engage, assess, intervene, and evaluate with individuals, families, groups, organizations, and communities.

Necessary Knowledge, Values, Skills	Operational Practice Behaviors

• Professional practice involves the dynamic and interactive processes of engagement, assessment, intervention, and evaluation at multiple levels.
• Social workers have the knowledge and skills to practice with individuals, families, groups, organizations, and communities.
• Practice knowledge includes
  - identifying, analyzing, and implementing evidence-based interventions designed to achieve client goals;
  - using research and technological advances;
  - evaluating program outcomes and practice effectiveness;
  - developing, analyzing, advocating, and providing leadership for policies and services; and
  - promoting social and economic justice.
	(a) Engagement
	• Social workers substantively and effectively prepare for action with individuals, families, groups, organizations, and communities;
	• Social workers use empathy and other interpersonal skills; and
	• Social workers develop a mutually agreed-on focus of work and desired outcomes.
	
	(b) Assessment
	• Social workers collect, organize, and interpret client data;
	• Social workers assess client strengths and limitations;
	• Social workers develop mutually agreed-on intervention goals and objectives; and
	• Social workers select appropriate intervention strategies.
	
	(c) Intervention
	• Social workers initiate actions to achieve organizational goals;
	• Social workers implement prevention interventions that enhance client capacities;
	• Social workers help clients resolve problems;
	• Social workers negotiate, mediate, and advocate for clients; and
	• Social workers facilitate transitions and endings.
	
	(d) Evaluation
	• Social workers critically analyze, monitor, and evaluate interventions.

CONNECTING CORE COMPETENCIES Chapter-by-Chapter Matrix

Chapter	Professional Identity	Ethical Practice	Critical Thinking	Diversity in Practice	Human Rights & Justice	Research Based Practice	Human Behavior	Policy Practice	Practice Contexts	Engage Assess Intervene Evaluate
1		✔		✔	✔		✔			
2				✔	✔	✔				
3		✔					✔		✔	✔
4			✔	✔						✔
5					✔		✔	✔	✔	
6				✔	✔		✔	✔		
7	✔			✔					✔	
8	✔	✔		✔						✔
9		✔	✔		✔			✔		
10	✔				✔					
Total Chapters	3	4	2	6	6	1	4	3	3	3

FIFTH EDITION

Human Behavior and the Social Environment

Shifting Paradigms in Essential Knowledge for Social Work Practice

Joe M. Schriver
University of Arkansas, Fayetteville

Allyn & Bacon

Boston Columbus Indianapolis New York San Francisco Upper Saddle River
Amsterdam Cape Town Dubai London Madrid Milan Munich Paris Montreal Toronto
Delhi Mexico City Sao Paulo Sydney Hong Kong Seoul Singapore Taipei Tokyo

Editor in Chief: Dickson Musslewhite
Executive Editor: Ashley Dodge
Editorial Assistant: Carly Czech
Director of Development: Sharon Geary
Development Editor: Deb Hanlon
Director of Marketing: Brandy Dawson
Senior Marketing Manager: Wendy Albert
Marketing Assistant: Kyle VanNatter
Advertising Director: Kate Conway
Advertising Manager: Sara Sherlock
Design Specialist: Robert Farrar-Wagner

Copywriter: Jonathan Andrew
Senior Media Editor: Melanie MacFarlane
Senior Production Project Manager: Pat Torelli
Editorial Production and Composition Service:
  Laserwords, Maine
Manager of Design Development:
  John Christiana
Interior Design: Joyce Weston Design
Cover Design: Joel Gendron
  Kristina Mose-Libon
Manufacturing Buyer: Debbie Rossi

Credits appear on page 542, which constitutes an extension of the copyright page.

Library of Congress Cataloging-in-Publication Data

Schriver, Joe M.
  Human behavior and the social environment : shifting paradigms in
essential knowledge for social work practice / Joe M. Schriver. — 5th ed.
    p. cm.
  Includes bibliographical references and index.
  ISBN-13: 978-0-205-52097-8
  ISBN-10: 0-205-52097-9
  1. Social psychology. 2. Behavioral assessment. 3. Social interaction.
  4. Social systems. 5. Paradigms (Social sciences) 6. Social service. I.
  Title.
  HM1033.S373 2010
  302—dc22

                              2009050682

10 9 8 7 6 5 4 3   BRR 14 13 12 11

Allyn & Bacon
is an imprint of

www.pearsonhighered.com

ISBN 10: 0-205-52097-9
ISBN 13: 978-0-205-52097-8

Contents

Preface

Human Behavior and the Social Environment begins with a presentation of the basic purposes and competencies of social work. Principles and fundamental concepts necessary for acquiring and organizing knowledge about human behavior and the social environment (HBSE) are also presented. Next, a conceptual framework for thinking about both traditional and alternative ways in which knowledge is created and influenced is outlined. This conceptual framework is accompanied by discussion of some widely used approaches and fundamental themes guiding social workers in the selection, organization, and use of knowledge about human behavior and the social environment. The book then uses the notions of traditional and alternative paradigms to organize and present a variety of models, theories, and concepts concerning HBSE.

At least one full chapter (two chapters are included on individual behavior and development) is devoted to content about each of the social system levels required of professional social work education by the Educational Policy and Accreditation Standards (EPAS) of the Council on Social Work Education. Knowledge for practice with individuals, families, groups, organizations, communities, and global contexts as well as content on the interaction among these systems are presented.

Throughout the book, a series of "Illustrative Readings" is provided to give additional depth and perspective in a variety of areas. These readings are also intended to extend content in the text, emphasizing the importance of including the widest possible range of different human voices and experiences in our efforts to understand HBSE.

A Note about Bias and the Author

I should make explicit that I am biased. I recognize the contributions of traditional perspectives and approaches to creating and valuing knowledge, but I believe that we as humans will not realize our collective (and individual) potential for well-being as long as we do not embrace alternative perspective and worldviews such as those described in this book. Therefore, while traditional perspectives and paradigms are presented in this book, the reader should keep in mind that the author generally finds these perspectives lacking. This author believes that the perspectives used to define and describe "normal" or "optimal" human behavior and experiences too often represent the beliefs and realities of only a privileged few. This privileged few too often includes only those who have the power, the good fortune, the gender, the color, the wealth, or the sexual orientation consistent with and reflected in traditional perspectives and worldviews.

The reader should also be aware that, though in many respects this book is a critique of traditional paradigm thinking, this author is a product of the traditional institutions that create and enforce those traditional perspectives and worldviews. This author also shares many of the characteristics of the "privileged few." Therefore, writing this book has been an effort to question, to examine, and to expand my own worldview.

Connecting Core Competencies Series

The new edition of this text is now a part of Pearson Education's new *Connecting Core Competencies* series, which consists of five foundation-level texts that make it easier than ever to ensure students' success in learning the ten core competencies as stated in 2008 by the Council on Social Work Education. This text contains:

- ▶ **Core Competency Icons** throughout the chapters, directly linking the CSWE core competencies to the content of the text. **Critical thinking questions** are also included to further students' mastery of the CSWE's standards. Check out the table of contents and chapter-opening outlines to see where the icons are located throughout the text. For easy reference, page iv also displays which icons are used in each chapter, in a chapter-by-chapter matrix.
- ▶ **An end-of-chapter Practice Test,** with multiple-choice questions that test students' knowledge of the chapter content and mastery of the competencies. These questions are constructed in a format that will help prepare students for the **ASWB Licensing exam.**
- ▶ **Additional information pertaining to the videos found on the new MySocialWorkLab** at the end of each chapter to encourage students to access the site and explore the wealth of available materials. If this text did not come with an access code for MySocialWorkLab, you can purchase access at: www.mysocialworklab.com.

Acknowledgments

Those friends and colleagues from around the country listed in the second edition remain a supportive community for me. That community is ever expanding, and for that I am most grateful. Special thanks to reviewers for all editions: Leslie Ann Gentry, The University of North Carolina at Chapel Hill; Kim Haynes, Lipscomb University; Larry Icard, University of Washington; Ameda Manetta, Winthrop University; Mark Schmitz, Rutgers University; and Maria Zuniga, San Diego State University.

I noted in the first edition that my son, Andrew, then almost two years old, had taught me more about human behavior and the social environment than anyone else. Andrew, now at an amazing 17 years old and off to college next year, you continue to be the best of teachers as you share your curiosity and wonder about humans and our worlds.

Executive Editor, Ashley Dodge, and Development Editor, Deb Hanlon, Editorial Assistant, Carly Czech, and my Production Editor, Pat Torelli, have had to endure with me the challenges of changing to an entirely new editorial team in "midstream" in the completion of this edition. In addition, it would be unfair not to recognize my previous editor, Pat Quinlin, for her support over many years and some hard times. Pat and I discussed, several years ago, the idea of a "foundation series" such as this one of which my book is now a part. I'm sure she regrets she is not among the team that brought the "series" idea to fruition. Thanks for everything, Pat.

Cathy Owens Schriver, as with the other editions—I could not have done it without you.

1

Human Behavior and the Social Environment (HBSE) and Paradigms

CONNECTING CORE COMPETENCIES *in this chapter*

| Professional Identity | Ethical Practice | Critical Thinking | Diversity in Practice | Human Rights & Justice | Research Based Practice | Human Behavior | Policy Practice | Practice Contexts | Engage Assess Intervene Evaluate |

1

Who should use this book and how should it be used? Instructors in both undergraduate and graduate social work education programs can use this book to help their students gain HBSE content. The book is designed to meet the requirements of the Council on Social Work Education for HBSE foundation content at either the undergraduate or graduate level. At the undergraduate level, the book may work best in programs with a two-course HBSE sequence designed to provide content on HBSE from a multisystems perspective (individual, family, group, organization, community, and global systems). At the foundation graduate level, the book can be effectively used as the text in a single HBSE course or a two-course sequence designed to provide basic content across system levels and, in the case of graduate programs, prior to delivering advanced HBSE content. In addition, this book integrates content from the other CSWE required competencies into the HBSE area.

The purpose of human behavior and the social environment content within the social work curriculum is to provide us with knowledge for practice. We need to continually look at this content for how to apply what we are learning about human behavior and the social environment to social work practice and to our lives. As we move through the material in this book, we will struggle to integrate what we are learning here with what we have learned and are learning from our own and others' life experiences, from our other social work courses, and from our courses in the liberal arts and sciences. We will try to weave together all these important sources of knowing and understanding into an organic whole that can help us become life-long learners and guide us in our social work practice.

PURPOSES, FOUNDATIONS, AND ASSUMPTIONS

Diversity in Practice

Social workers are expected to understand how diversity characterizes and shapes the human experience and is critical to the formation of identity. Why is it important that, as social workers, we must recognize the influences of our own diversity and culture in order to be competent practitioners?

Moving through the content of this book can be compared to a journey. Before we begin our journey we will place the content and purposes of this human behavior and the social environment (HBSE) book within the context of the purposes and foundations of social work education as they have been defined by the Council on Social Work Education (CSWE). The **Council on Social Work Education** is the organization responsible for determining and monitoring the accreditation standards for undergraduate and graduate (MSW) social work education programs in the United States.

Assumptions

Your journey through this book will be guided by several very basic assumptions:

1. How we view the world and its people directly affects the way we will practice social work.

2. The way we view the world and its people already affects the way we behave in our daily lives.

3. Our work as social workers and our lives are not separate from each other.

4. Our lives are not separate from the lives of the people with whom we work and interact.

5. While our lives are interconnected with the lives of the people with whom we work and interact, we differ from each other in many ways. As social workers we must respect these differences and learn from them. Our differences can be celebrated as rich, positive, and mutual sources of knowledge, growth, and change for all concerned.

6. The assumptions we make about ourselves and others are strongly influenced by our individual and collective histories and cultures.
7. Change is a constant part of our lives and the lives of the people with whom we work.

Such assumptions as these are reflected in what we will come to conceptualize as an alternative paradigm for thinking about social work. Before we discuss alternative paradigms further, we will explore the more general concept of paradigm.

PURPOSE OF THE SOCIAL WORK PROFESSION

According to the Council on Social Work Education:

> The purpose of the social work profession is to promote human and community well-being. Guided by a person and environment construct, a global perspective, respect for human diversity, and knowledge based on scientific inquiry, social work's purpose is actualized through its quest for social and economic justice, the prevention of conditions that limit human rights, the elimination of poverty, and the enhancement of the quality of life for all persons. (CSWE 2008: 1)

The purpose of social work will guide us throughout our journey to understand HBSE content. The purpose emerges from the history of the social work profession and its continuing concern for improving quality of life, especially for vulnerable populations.

Core Competencies

Ethical Practice

Social workers are expected to be knowledgeable about the value base of the profession. How might the fundamental values of the social work profession be reflected in and guide our efforts to gain knowledge about human behavior and the social environment?

Social work education programs (BSW and MSW) are required to prepare all students to demonstrate mastery of ten core competencies. These competencies, along with the knowledge, values, and skills necessary to achieve competence, and examples of practice behaviors that provide evidence of mastery of the competencies are summarized in Table 1.1.

While achieving competence in human behavior and the social environment (see Table 1.1, Core Competency #7) is the focus of this book, significant attention is also given to integrating the other nine core competencies with knowledge, values, and skills you gain in HBSE (see Table 1.1). In addition, Competency #9, "respond to contexts that shape practice," is an integral element related to HBSE, since so much of what we will address in this book is intertwined with the "contexts" or "environments" (i.e., Human Behavior and the social **environment**) that both influence and are influenced by human behavior. The competencies acquired as you move through the book and your HBSE course(s) are clearly linked with the competencies you are acquiring in your other social work courses including field education.

It is difficult to imagine that competence in HBSE can be achieved without including content related to the other core competencies:

- ▶ The development of your professional identity as a social worker
- ▶ Ethical behaviors and dilemmas
- ▶ Critical thinking skills
- ▶ Human diversity
- ▶ Human rights and social and economic justice
- ▶ Research-informed practice and practice-informed research
- ▶ Social policy practice
- ▶ The processes involved in *doing* social work

It is difficult as well to imagine that achieving competence in the nine areas listed above could be accomplished without HBSE content. In essence, this book is intended to be an integral and interdependent part of your overall social work education.

In addition, the content of this book is grounded in the basic and fundamental values of the social work profession as identified by the CSWE: *service, social justice, the dignity and worth of the person, the importance of human relationships, competence, human rights, and scientific inquiry* (CSWE 2008). These values are and have historically been the underpinning for all of social work education and practice.

Table 1.1   EPAS 2008 Core Competencies, Definitions, Operational Practice Behaviors

Competency	Necessary Knowledge, Values, Skills	Operational Practice Behaviors
1. Identify as a professional social worker and conduct oneself accordingly.	1. Social workers serve as representatives of the profession, its mission, and its core values. 2. Social workers know the profession's history. 3. Social workers commit themselves to the profession's enhancement. 4. Social workers commit themselves to their own professional conduct and growth.	1. Advocate for client access to the services of social work; 2. Practice personal reflection and self-correction to assure continual professional development; 3. Attend to professional roles and boundaries; 4. Demonstrate professional demeanor in behavior, appearance, and communication; 5. Engage in career-long learning; and 6. Use supervision and consultation.
2. Apply social work ethical principles to guide professional practice.	5. Social workers have an obligation to conduct themselves ethically. 6. Engage in ethical decision-making. 7. Social workers are knowledgeable about the value base of the profession, its ethical standards, and relevant law.	7. Recognize and manage personal values in a way that allows professional values to guide practice; 8. Make ethical decisions by applying standards of the National Association of Social Workers Code of Ethics and, as applicable, of the International Federation of Social Workers/International Association of Schools of Social Work Ethics in Social Work, Statement of Principles; 9. Tolerate ambiguity in resolving ethical conflicts; and 10. Apply strategies of ethical reasoning to arrive at principled decisions.
3. Apply critical thinking to inform and communicate professional judgments.	8. Social workers are knowledgeable about the principles of logic, scientific inquiry, and reasoned discernment. 9. They use critical thinking augmented by creativity and curiosity. 10. Critical thinking also requires the synthesis and communication of relevant information.	11. Distinguish, appraise, and integrate multiple sources of knowledge, including research-based knowledge, and practice wisdom; 12. Analyze models of assessment, prevention, intervention, and evaluation; and 13. Demonstrate effective oral and written communication in working with individuals, families, groups, organizations, communities, and colleagues.

Competency	Necessary Knowledge, Values, Skills	Operational Practice Behaviors
4. Engage diversity and difference in practice.	11. Social workers understand how diversity characterizes and shapes the human experience and is critical to the formation of identity.	14. Recognize the extent to which a culture's structures and values may oppress, marginalize, alienate, or create or enhance privilege and power;
	12. The dimensions of diversity are understood as the intersectionality of multiple factors including age, class, color, culture, disability, ethnicity, gender, gender identity and expression, immigration status, political ideology, race, religion, sex, and sexual orientation.	15. Gain sufficient self-awareness to eliminate the influence of personal biases and values in working with diverse groups;
	13. Social workers appreciate that, as a consequence of difference, a person's life experiences may include oppression, poverty, marginalization, and alienation as well as privilege, power, and acclaim.	16. Recognize and communicate their understanding of the importance of difference in shaping life experiences; and
		17. View themselves as learners and engage those with whom they work as informants.
5. Advance human rights and social and economic justice.	14. Each person, regardless of position in society, has basic human rights, such as freedom, safety, privacy, an adequate standard of living, health care, and education.	18. Understand the forms and mechanisms of oppression and discrimination;
	15. Social workers recognize the global interconnections of oppression and are knowledgeable about theories of justice and strategies to promote human and civil rights.	19. Advocate for human rights and social and economic justice; and
	16. Social work incorporates social justice practices in organizations, institutions, and society to ensure that these basic human rights are distributed equitably and without prejudice.	20. Engage in practices that advance social and economic justice.

continued

Table 1.1   Continued

Competency	Necessary Knowledge, Values, Skills	Operational Practice Behaviors
6. Engage in research-informed practice and practice-informed research.	17. Social workers use practice experience to inform research, employ evidence-based interventions, evaluate their own practice, and use research findings to improve practice, policy, and social service delivery. 18. Social workers comprehend quantitative and qualitative research and understand scientific and ethical approaches to building knowledge.	21. use practice experience to inform scientific inquiry and 22. use research evidence to inform practice.
7. **Apply knowledge of human behavior and the social environment.**	19. **Social workers are knowledgeable about human behavior across the life course;** 20. **The range of social systems in which people live; and** 21. **The ways social systems promote or deter people in maintaining or achieving health and well-being.** 22. **Social workers apply theories and knowledge from the liberal arts to understand biological, social, cultural, psychological, and spiritual development.**	23. **utilize conceptual frameworks to guide the processes of assessment, intervention, and evaluation; and** 24. **critique and apply knowledge to understand person and environment.**
8. Engage in policy practice to advance social and economic well-being and to deliver effective social work services.	23. Social work practitioners understand that policy affects service delivery and they actively engage in policy practice. 24. Social workers know the history and current structures of social policies and services; 25. Social Workers know the role of policy in service delivery; and 26 Social Workers know role of practice in policy development.	25. analyze, formulate, and advocate for policies that advance social well-being; and 26. collaborate with colleagues and clients for effective policy action.
9. Respond to contexts that shape practice.	27. Social workers are informed, resourceful, and proactive in responding to evolving organizational, community, and societal contexts at all levels of practice. 28. Social workers recognize that the context of practice is dynamic, and use knowledge and skill to respond proactively.	27. continuously discover, appraise, and attend to changing locales, populations, scientific and technological developments, and emerging societal trends to provide relevant services; and 28. provide leadership in promoting sustainable changes in service delivery and practice to improve the quality of social services.

Competency	Necessary Knowledge, Values, Skills	Operational Practice Behaviors
10. Engage, assess, intervene, and evaluate with individuals, families, groups, organizations, and communities	29. Professional practice involves the dynamic and interactive processes of engagement, assessment, intervention, and evaluation at multiple levels. 30. Social workers have the knowledge and skills to practice with individuals, families, groups, organizations, and communities. 31. Practice knowledge includes: a. Identifying, analyzing, and implementing evidence-based interventions designed to achieve client goals; b. Using research and technological advances; c. Evaluating program outcomes and practice effectiveness; d. Developing, analyzing, advocating, and providing leadership for policies and services; and e. Promoting social and economic justice.	**Engagement** 29. substantively and affectively prepare for action with individuals, families, groups, organizations, and communities; 30. use empathy and other interpersonal skills; and 31. develop a mutually agreed-on focus of work and desired outcomes. **Assessment** 32. collect, organize, and interpret client data; 33. assess client strengths and limitations; 34. develop mutually agreed-on intervention goals and objectives; and 35. select appropriate intervention strategies. **Intervention** 36. initiate actions to achieve organizational goals; 37. implement prevention interventions that enhance client capacities; 38. help clients resolve problems; 39. negotiate, mediate, and advocate for clients; and 40. facilitate transitions and endings. **Evaluation** 41. Social workers critically analyze, monitor, and evaluate interventions.

Source: CSWE, 2008 455:3-7

HUMAN BEHAVIOR AND THE SOCIAL ENVIRONMENT

So, specifically what does the CSWE expect of us in order to attain the required competence in HBSE? In order to become competent in applying "knowledge of human behavior and the social environment," we are expected to be knowledgeable about:

- Human behavior across the life course
- The range of social systems
- The ways social systems promote or deter people in maintaining or achieving health and well-being

In addition, we are expected to be able to:

- Apply theories and knowledge from the liberal arts to understand biological, social, cultural, psychological, and spiritual development

We will know we have achieved these expectations when we can:

- ❯ Utilize conceptual frameworks to guide the processes of assessment, intervention, and evaluation
- ❯ Critique and apply knowledge to understand person and environment. (CSWE 2008:6)

In addition to being guided by the requirements of CSWE regarding HBSE, our journey through this book will be guided by a several very basic assumptions.

PARADIGMS AND SOCIAL WORK

A **paradigm** "is a world view, a general perspective, a way of breaking down the complexity of the real world" (Lincoln and Guba 1985:15). Paradigms constitute "cultural patterns of group life" (Schutz 1944). More specifically, Kuhn (1970 [1962]:175) defines a paradigm as "the entire constellation of beliefs, values, techniques, and so on shared by the members of a given community." Paradigms shape and are shaped by values, knowledge, and beliefs about the nature of our worlds. The values, knowledge, and beliefs about the world that make up paradigms are often so "taken for granted" that we are virtually unaware of their existence or of the assumptions we make because of them. For social workers the notion of paradigm is particularly important, because if we can become conscious of the elements that result in different world views, this awareness can provide us with tools to use to think about and to understand ourselves, others, and the environments we all inhabit. The notion of paradigm can help us understand more completely the past perspectives, current realities, and future possibilities about what it means to be human. Furthermore, the notion of paradigm can help us understand our own and others' roles in creating and re-creating the very meaning of humanness.

Specifically, thinking in terms of paradigms can provide us with new ways of understanding humans' behaviors in individual, family, group, organizational, community, and global contexts. The concept of paradigm can serve us very well to order and to increase our awareness of multiple theories, models, and perspectives about human behavior and the social environment. The notion of paradigm can help us understand the way things are, and, equally important for social workers, it can help us understand the way things *might* be.

Two Types of Paradigms: Traditional and Alternative

In this book we are concerned with exploring two quite different but not mutually exclusive kinds of paradigms. One of these we refer to as traditional or dominant paradigms. The other we will call alternative or possible paradigms. We explore in some detail the characteristics of both of these kinds of paradigms in Chapter 2. For now, when we refer to **traditional or dominant paradigms,** we simply mean the paradigms or world views that have most influenced the environments that make up our worlds. When we refer to **alternative or possible paradigms,** we mean world views that have had less influence and have been less prominent in shaping our own and others' views about humans and their environments. For example, the belief that quantitative and objective approaches provide the most dependable (or the most accurate) avenues to understanding the world around us reflects two core elements of the traditional and dominant paradigm.

An example of quantitative and objective elements of traditional or dominant paradigm thinking related to social work can be illustrated through the following approach to assessing and identifying community needs in order to design and implement services to meet those needs. According to the traditional or dominant approach, we assume that we can best understand the needs of the people in the community through use of a survey. We distribute a questionnaire to a random sample of community residents. We design the questionnaire using a list of specific possible needs from which the community respondents can select. We ask the respondents to make their selections by completing the questionnaire we have designed and returning it to us. Once the questionnaires are returned, we do a statistical analysis of the responses. Based on the frequency of responses to our questions we determine the community's needs. We then set about bringing into the community the resources and people we believe are necessary to design and implement services to meet the needs determined through the survey.

The belief that we can learn as much or more about the world around us from qualitative and subjective, as from quantitative and objective, approaches to understanding reflects an alternative and nondominant view of the world. Using the same social-work-related example as above, let's take an alternative approach to understanding the needs of a particular community in order to design and implement services to meet those needs. Our alternative approach will have us not simply asking community members to answer questions about typical community needs we have previously devised and listed in a questionnaire. We will instead first go into the community and involve as many different people representing as many diverse groups (not a random sample) as possible. We will involve these community members not primarily as respondents to predetermined questions but as partners in determining what the questions should be, how the questions should be asked (individual or group face-to-face meetings, perhaps), and who should do the asking (the community members themselves, rather than outside "experts," for example) (Guba and Lincoln 1989; Reason 1988). We are primarily interested in finding and understanding needs emerging from the real-life experiences of community people. We seek articulation of needs described in the language of the community members themselves. As this process is carried out, we continue to work as partners with community members in gathering resources and connecting people together to address the needs they have articulated. This process focuses on involving the community members directly in creating resources and in delivering services in their community.

The two processes described above represent quite different approaches to doing the same thing. Though the two approaches are not necessarily mutually exclusive, they do operate from very different assumptions about us as social workers, about the appropriate level of involvement of a community's citizens, and about our relationships with one another. Traditional approaches see the two groups of people—those doing the studying and intervening ("us") and those being studied and to whom interventions are directed ("them")—as separate from each other, with very different roles to play. Alternative approaches see the parties involved as interconnected partners in a mutual and emergent process.

Paradigm Analysis, Critical Thinking, and Deconstruction

Paradigm analysis is a helpful process for becoming more aware, constructively critical, and analytical in our interactions inside and outside the formal context of our education—in our work and in our interpersonal relationships.

Put simply, **paradigm analysis** is learning to "think paradigm." It is a process of continually asking questions about what the information, both spoken and unspoken, that we send and receive reflects about our own and others' views of the world and its people, especially people different from ourselves. It is a process of continually "thinking about thinking." Paradigm analysis requires us to continually and critically evaluate the many perspectives we explore for their consistency with the core concerns of social work. It is important to recognize that such critical thinking as that required of paradigm analysis is a helpful, positive, and constructive process, rather than a negative or destructive one.

Paradigm Analysis

Paradigm analysis involves first of all asking a set of very basic questions about each of the perspectives we explore in order to determine its compatibility with the core concerns of social work. These questions are:

1. Does this perspective contribute to preserving and restoring human dignity?
2. Does this perspective recognize the benefits of, and does it celebrate, human diversity?
3. Does this perspective assist us in transforming ourselves and our society so that we welcome the voices, the strengths, the ways of knowing, the energies of us all?
4. Does this perspective help us all (ourselves and the people with whom we work) to reach our fullest human potential?
5. Does the perspective or theory reflect the participation and experiences of males and females; economically well-off and poor; white people and people of color; gay men, lesbians, bisexuals, and heterosexuals; old and young; temporarily able-bodied and people with disabilities?

The answers we find to these questions will tell us generally if the perspective we are exploring is consistent with the core concerns of social work. The answer to the final question will tell us about how the paradigm came to be and who participated in its development or construction. Both critical thinking and "deconstruction" are required to do paradigm analysis.

Critical Thinking

In debating the importance and possibility of teaching critical thinking in social work education, Gibbs argues that it is an essential part of the education process for social workers. A general definition of **critical thinking** is "the careful and deliberate determination of whether to accept, reject, or suspend judgment about a claim" (Moore and Parker in Bloom and Klein 1997:82). How does one engage in the process of critical thinking? Gibbs et al. describe the perspective and processes necessary to "do" critical thinking:

1. A predisposition to question conclusions that concern client care and welfare;
2. Asking "does it work?" and "how do you know?" when confronted with claims that a method helps clients, and also questioning generalizations about treatment methods;

3. Weighing evidence for and against assertions in a logical, rational, systematic, data-based way; and

4. Analyzing arguments to see what is being argued, spotting and explaining common fallacies in reasoning, and applying basic methodological principles of scientific reasoning. (1995:196)

Deconstruction

Deconstruction is a process of analyzing "texts" or perspectives "that is sensitive . . . to marginalized voices" (Sands and Nuccio 1992:491) and "biased knowledge" (Van Den Bergh 1995:xix). Through deconstruction "biased knowledge can be altered by reconstructing truth through inclusion of the voices of disempowered people. Knowledge that had previously been marginalized can then be centered" (hooks 1984 in Van Den Bergh 1995:xix). Deconstruction requires that we do "not accept the constructs used as given; instead [we look] at them in relation to social, historical, and political contexts. The deconstructionist identifies the biases in the text, views them as problematic, and 'decenters' them. Meanwhile, the perspectives that are treated as marginal are 'centered' " (Sands and Nuccio 1992:491). Through this process of moving marginal voices to the center, more inclusive understandings of reality emerge. Missing or marginalized voices begin to be heard and begin to become a significant part of the paradigm creation process.

SEHB or HBSE?: A Critical Thinking Deconstructive Example

A critical thinking and deconstructive approach can and should be applied to your thinking about the subject of this book and the CSWE requirement that content on "human behavior and the social environment" be included as one of the foundations of your social work education. For example, we might question the very name of this foundation area—Human Behavior and the Social Environment. Why is "human behavior" first in the name and "social environment" second? How might the perspectives and content of this book and this course change if the course or the foundation area were referred to as "Social Environment and Human Behavior?" One might argue that if this were the name, a significant shift in both perspective and content would need to take place. The very order of the chapters in this book might need to be reversed. If the social environment is primary and human behavior is secondary in the name, rather than trying to understand individual human behavior (human development) first, we might focus first on the impact of larger systems on the individual human. We might begin by trying to understand the important influences of the larger social environment—global issues for example—on the individual's development. As a result, you might explore Chapter 10—the "global" chapter—before you read Chapters 4 and 5—the chapters concerned with individual development. There might also be only one chapter focused on individual behavior and development rather than two.

To think critically about this question requires asking questions about more than this book or this course. It requires thinking about the priorities of social work education and practice. Should social work be primarily concerned with understanding and intervening at the level of the individual, or should our primary focus be understanding and intervening in the larger social environment in order to fulfill the purposes of social work? This is a question members of the profession have struggled with throughout much of our history.

It is an issue we will struggle with and will return to as we move through the chapters in this book. One way that we will do so is by including discussion of content from the perspective of the "social environment and human behavior" in a number of the remaining chapters. For example, with such a shift in perspective, would the priority given of the profession and commitment to poverty reduction change?

Poverty Reduction

Perhaps such a change in perspective would result in a return in the profession to a primary focus on poverty reduction that many in the profession believe has become underemphasized. If we look at a central purpose of social work— "to promote human and community well-being," which is "actualized through its quest for social and economic justice" and "the elimination of poverty" (CSWE 2008:7)—we see poverty elimination as a prominent component. If we look at the current required competencies for social work education, we see one competency focused on "human rights and social and economic justice." This competency is listed as #5 of the 10 competencies (see page 4 and Competency #5 in Table 1.1, "advance human rights and social and economic justice"). As we look at the various system levels of concern to us, we will consistently see that poverty status is closely associated with how well one does on virtually all social, educational, and health indicators at all system levels. Poverty is directly linked to barriers to attaining a good education, to maintaining health throughout the life course, to family and community well-being, to access to and use of technological resources, to violence and abuse, and to infant mortality and low-birthweight babies. Low birthweight is a predictor of many health and developmental risks in children. Rank and Hirschl argue, "whether the discussion revolves around welfare use, racial inequalities, single-parent families, infant mortality, economic insecurity, or a host of other topics, poverty underlies each and every one of these subjects" (Rank and Hirschl 1999: 201).

Poverty and Oppression

Perhaps most important as we proceed on our journey is to attend to the intertwining of oppression and poverty. For example, we need to carefully examine why being a member of an oppressed group—a person of color, a woman, a person with a disability—makes one so much more likely to be poor in U.S. society and globally than a member of the dominant group (white male of European heritage).

SEHB: A Global Context

Perhaps one of the most dramatic examples of the need to consider the social environment at least equally, if not first, in attempts to understand human behavior is the increasingly global and interdependent context in which we live. For people in the United States and to a large extent around the world, the events of September 11, 2001, and those unfolding since that tragedy brought a sense of urgency to consistently including the global context as an important sphere of the social environment. As you proceed through the chapters in this book, you will regularly explore individual, family, group, organizational, community, social, economic, and policy issues through a global lens.

Technological Poverty: Social Work and HBSE/SEHB

As we will see in the chapters that follow, constantly evolving technology continues to reshape our ability to communicate locally and globally, and it is also a major social and environmental influence on human behavior at individual, family, group, organizational, and community levels. As technology continues to play an increasingly influential role in our lives both at the individual and collective levels, it is essential that we become increasingly better able to assess and understand the impact of technology in multiple areas of human behavior and the social environment. We must learn to use technology as one of the important tools to assist us in achieving the purposes of social work.

However, we must approach technology and the changes it brings from a critical perspective. In order to accomplish this, we must think about both the benefits of technology and its limits. For social workers, it is especially important to recognize the potential of technology to increase rather than decrease the gap between the "haves" and the "have-nots" in the United States and more importantly in a global context. This increasing gap in access to technology and its benefits is referred to as the **digital divide.** As we proceed through coming chapters we will attend to the benefits and limitations of technology for increasing human well-being, alleviating poverty and oppression, and increasing our understanding of human behavior and the social environment at multiple levels. We will also explore policy and practice implications surrounding technology.

Paradigms and History

To help us apply a critical thinking approach to explore either traditional or alternative paradigms, we need to acquire a historical perspective about the contexts out of which these world views emerged. Neither the traditional nor their alternative counterparts came about in a historical vacuum. They instead emerged as points along a historical continuum marked by humans' attempts to understand their own behaviors, the behaviors of others, and the environments in which they lived.

Pre-modern/Pre-positivism

A historical perspective can help us appreciate that the paradigms we will explore as traditional and currently dominant were considered quite alternative and even radical at the times of their emergence. For example, the emergence of **humanism**—a belief in the power of humans to control their own behaviors and the environments in which they lived—in Europe at the opening of the Renaissance (mid-1400s) and at the ending of the Middle Ages (the early 1400s) was an alternative, and for many a radical, paradigm at that time. Humanism was considered by many, especially those in power, to be not only alternative but also dangerous, wrong, and heretical. Humanism was considered an affront to scholasticism, the traditional paradigm or worldview that had been dominant throughout much of Europe in the Middle Ages (approximately A.D. 476–mid-1400s). **Scholasticism** (approximately A.D. 800–mid-1400s) was a worldview that saw a Christian god, represented by the Roman Catholic Church, as the sole determiner and judge of human behavior. This Christian god was the controller of the entire natural world or environment in which humans existed. Similarly, **Protestantism** was a worldview placed in motion by Martin Luther during the early 1500s. It questioned the absolute authority of the Roman Catholic Church and the Pope as the sole representative of God, and was seen as another radical alternative affronting the existing worldview. The emergence of both humanism and Protestantism were alternative ways of viewing humans and their environments that called into question, and were seen as significant threats to, the then existing dominant and traditional ways of viewing the world (Manchester 1992; Sahakian 1968).

Modernism/Positivism

Another important perspective from which to get a sense of the historical continuum out of which paradigms emerge is that of the birth of worldviews explaining human behavior and the environments we inhabit through science. The emergence of worldviews that explained the world through science were in some ways extensions of the humanistic paradigm. Science was a powerful tool through which humans could gain control of their behaviors and of the universe they inhabited. **Science** allowed humans to understand the world by directly observing it through the senses and by carefully measuring, experimenting, and analyzing of what was observed. The emergence of scientific thinking or positivism during the period called the Enlightenment or the "Age of Reason" in the 17th and 18th centuries, however, was also a significant challenge to humanism and represented an alternative paradigm itself. Scientific thinking questioned humanism's central concern for gaining understanding through such expressions as art, literature, and poetry. A scientific world view saw humanism and its reflection in the humanities as a traditional and insufficient way of viewing the world.

Science sought to extend, if not replace, humanism's ways of knowing and understanding the world with a more reliable and comprehensive perspective that was *cosmos centered* rather than *[hu]man centered* (Sahakian 1968:119). The humanities raised questions and sought answers by looking to and rediscovering the great ideas and expressions of humans from the past, such as the classic works of the Romans and Greeks. Science offered keys to unlocking the secrets of the universe and the future through new ways of asking and answering questions. Science promised not only new questions and new ways of posing them but also answers to questions both new and old (Boulding 1964).

The empirical observations of Galileo Galilei in the first half of the 1600s confirming the earlier findings of Copernicus in the early 1500s, for example, literally provided a new view of the world (Manchester 1992:116–117). This new and alternative view moved the earth from the stable and unmoving center of the universe to one in which the earth was but one of many bodies revolving around the sun. The threat posed by such a dramatically different view of the world as that of Copernicus to the traditional Roman Catholic theology-based paradigm is captured eloquently by Manchester in his book *A World Lit Only by Fire:*

> The Scriptures assumed that everything had been created for the use of man. If the earth were shrunken to a mere speck in the universe, mankind would also be diminished. Heaven was lost when "up" and "down" lost all meaning—when each became the other every twenty-four hours. (1992:229)

According to Manchester, it was written in 1575 that "No attack on Christianity is more dangerous . . . than the infinite size and depth of the universe" (1992:229).

Much about the traditional paradigms that we explore in the next chapters has its roots in science and scientific ways of thinking that we virtually take for granted today. These approaches to understanding our worlds are centered in empirical observation and rational methods of gaining knowledge. So, science offers us a current example of what was, in a historical sense, an alternative paradigm becoming a traditional paradigm today. As has historically been the case, changes in paradigms currently taking place— what we will call *alternative paradigms*—call into question, challenge, and seek to extend our world views beyond those that have science and a scientific approach as the central tool for understanding human behavior and the social environment.

Postmodernism/Post-positivism

Berman (1996), for example, notes that the basic methods and assumptions of the traditional scientific paradigm that emerged during the 17th-century Enlightenment have not solely resulted in progress for people and the earth. Berman (1996:33) argues that the scientific, also referred to as "the mechanical paradigm sees the earth as inert, as dead, or at best as part of the solar system, which is viewed as a kind of clockwork mechanism . . . and one consequence of [this view] was the opening of the door to the unchecked exploitation of the earth." In addition Berman suggests that science leaves little room for the spiritual and subjective elements of the world and its mechanistic tendencies leave little motivation for seeing the world as a living system. He makes an important observation that: "As a tool, there is nothing wrong with the mechanistic paradigm. But for some reason, we couldn't stop there; we had to equate it with all of reality and so have arrived at a dysfunctional science and society at the end of the twentieth century" (Berman 1996:35). We will explore in more detail both the elements of scientific method and alternatives to the scientific paradigm in the next two chapters.

For now we simply need to recognize that today there is considerable discussion and considerable disagreement as well, about whether we have moved or are moving in history to the point that we live in a post-positivist or postmodern world in which science and scientific reasoning are less likely to be considered the only, the best, or even the most accurate means for understanding the world around us.

Historical periods in summary

Before we proceed to look at social work in the context of history it may be helpful for us to try to get an overview (though a very incomplete and oversimplified view) of some basic periods of history. Below is another different perspective on the past that can help us do this. The perspective is provided by Lather (1991) and uses the notion of modernism as central to looking at the past and the present in terms of knowledge production, views of history, and the economy.

Three historical eras profiled by Lather:

1. Premodern: Centrality of church/sacred basis of determining truth and knowledge; feudal economy; history as divinely ordered.
2. Modern: Centrality of secular humanism, individual reason, and science in determining truth; the industrial age, capitalism, and bureaucracy as bases of economic life; history as linear in the direction of constant progress driven by human rationality and science. Ideal of ignorance to enlightenment to emancipation of human potential as the "inevitable trajectory of history."

3. Postmodern: Existing/traditional knowledge and knowledge creation processes intensely questioned. Emphasis on multiple ways of knowing through processes that are non-hierarchical, feminist influenced, and participatory; economy more and more based on information, technology, and global capitalism; view of history as non-linear, cyclical, continually rewritten. "Focus on the present as history, the past as a fiction of the present." (Lather 1991:160–161)

Social Work History: Science and Art

That we should wonder about alternative approaches to those based solely on a scientific approach to understanding HBSE is significant and timely for us as social workers (and soon-to-be social workers). A scientific approach to doing social work has been a major avenue used by social workers to attempt to understand and intervene in the world during the short history of social work as a field of study and practice. Although we have claimed allegiances to both art and science, many of us have preferred that science guide our work. This is not surprising, given the power and faith in the scientific approach that has pervaded the modern world of the nineteenth and twentieth centuries. The period of the late nineteenth and twentieth centuries coincides with the birth and development of social work as an organized field of knowledge and practice.

Many of the historical arguments and issues concerning traditional and alternative paradigms—humanism, science, religion—for understanding our worlds and ourselves have parallels in the history of social work. The mission, concerns, and purposes of social work all reflect beliefs about the nature of the world and people. The concern of social work with individuals, families, and communities in interaction and interdependence, as well as its concern for social reform to bring about improvements in individual and collective well-being, reflects important beliefs about the nature of the world and its inhabitants.

Goldstein (1990:33–34) reminds us that social work has followed two quite distinct tracks to put its mission into practice. These two distinct tracks parallel in a number of ways the two quite different world views or paradigms represented by humanistic and scientific perspectives. Goldstein reminds us that, while social work adopted a scientific approach to pursuing its mission, it did not discard completely its humanistic inclinations. These divergent paths have led us to multiple approaches to understanding humans' behaviors and the environments they inhabit and within which they interact. These paths have at times and for some of us led to "Freudian psychology, the empiricism of behavioral psychology, and the objectivity of the scientific methods of the social sciences" (1990:33). At other times we have followed much different paths in "existential, artistic, and value-based" alternatives (1990:35). Goldstein found social workers today (as he found the social sciences generally) turning again toward the humanistic, subjective, or interpretive paths. This is a direction quite consistent with the alternative paradigms for understanding human behavior and the social environment that we will explore in the chapters to come. This alternative path allows social workers "to give more serious attention to and have more regard for the subjective domain of our clients' moral, theological, and cultural beliefs, which . . . give meaning to the experiences of individuals and families" (England 1986 in Goldstein 1990:38).

Evidence-Based Practice (EBP)

More recently this ongoing debate has focused on what is referred to as evidence-based practice. **Evidence-based practice** (EBP) is "the conscientious, explicit, and judicious use of current best evidence in making decisions about the care of individuals" (Sackett, Richardson, Rosenberg, and Haynes, 1997, in Gambrill 1999). According to Gambrill:

> It involves integrating individual practice expertise with the best available external evidence from systematic research as well as considering the values and expectations of clients. Hallmarks of evidence-based practice (EPB) include: (1) an individualized assessment; (2) a search for the best available external evidence related to the client's concerns and an estimate of the extent to which this applies to a particular client; and (3) a consideration of the values and expectations of clients (Sackett et al., 1997). Skills include identifying answerable questions relating to important practice questions, identifying the information needed to answer these questions, tracking down with maximum efficiency the best evidence with which to answer these questions, critically appraising this evidence for its validity and usefulness, applying the results of this appraisal to work with clients and, lastly, evaluating the outcome. Evidence-based practice requires an atmosphere in which critical appraisal of practice-related claims flourishes, and clients are involved as informed participants. A notable feature of EBP is attention to clients' values and expectations. (1999)

Witkin and Harrison (2001) question the shift to evidence-based practice. They argue that "social workers see the heart of their practice as 'person in situation,' in expanding problem understanding to include social and environmental elements. Social work practice involves seeing people as much for their differences as for anything that links them to classifiable problems or diagnoses. It values the often subjugated perspectives of the people we serve and attempts to understand their individual and collective narratives of their situations and conditions" (Witkin 2001: 294). Witkin suggests that too much reliance on an evidence-based practice approach limits social work practice and aligns it too closely with dominant paradigms. He suggests that the "person and environment" perspective requires social workers to individualize their work and use multiple lenses to focus on the actual lived experiences of persons in interaction with groups and communities. He points out, for example, that "these interactive accounts of people in their situations are not just tools for understanding, but the essential components of the individual's experience of social problems, medical conditions, and behavior. We learn to listen for discrepancies between the public discourse of disadvantaged people dealing with more powerful systems and the internal discourse within groups and individuals that frequently offer different understandings. In this sense, social workers often are cultural bridges, able to deal in multiple worlds of understanding" (Witkin and Harrison 2001:294). It is clear that the historic debate in social work over the proper balance of art and science in effective practice is alive and well and will continue.

Both/and not either/or

Much of the emphasis in this book is on shifting to alternative paradigms and transcending the limits of traditional and dominant paradigm thinking. It is important to realize, though, that our journey to understanding Human

Behavior and the Social Environment (referred to as HBSE throughout this book) is not to *either* one *or* the other worldview. Our journey will take us to *both* traditional *and* alternative destinations along the way. After all, traditional scientific worldviews have revealed much valuable knowledge about ourselves and our worlds.

We will try in this book to learn about alternative paradigms and to challenge and extend ourselves beyond traditional paradigms in which science is the single source of understanding. However, in order to understand alternative paradigms, we need to be cognizant of traditional theories about human behavior and development. We will challenge traditional paradigms as incomplete, as excluding many people, and as reflecting biases due to the value assumptions and historical periods out of which they emerged. These inadequacies, however, render traditional theories nonetheless powerful in the influences they have had in the past, that they currently have, and that they will continue to have on the construction and application of knowledge about human behavior and the social environment. Traditional approaches provide important departure points from which we may embark on our journey toward more complete, more inclusive, and less-biased visions (or at least visions in which bias is recognized and used to facilitate inclusiveness) of HBSE. Many of the alternative paradigms we will visit began as extensions or reconceptualizations of existing traditional worldviews.

There is another very practical reason for learning about theories that emerge from and reflect traditional paradigms. The practice world that social workers inhabit and that you will soon enter (and we hope transform) is a world constructed largely on traditional views of human behavior and the social environment. To survive in that world long enough to change it, we must be conversant in the discourse of that world. We must have sufficient knowledge of traditional and dominant paradigms of human behavior and development to make decisions about what in those worldviews we wish to retain because of its usefulness in attaining the goal of maximizing human potential. Knowledge of traditional and dominant paradigms is also necessary in deciding what to discard or alter to better serve that same core concern of social work.

Understanding the historical flow or continuum out of which differing world views emerged over time is an important means of recognizing the changes in perspectives on the world that at any given moment are likely to seem stable, permanent, and unchangeable. Even the changes occurring over time in the Western worldviews illustrated in the examples above give us a sense that permanency in approaches to understanding our worlds is less reality than perspective at a particular point in time. One way to conceptualize these fundamental changes occurring over time is to think in terms of paradigm shift.

Paradigm Shift

A **paradigm shift** is "a profound change in the thoughts, perceptions, and values that form a particular vision of reality" (Capra 1983:30). To express the fundamental changes required of a paradigm shift, Thomas Kuhn (1970) uses the analogy of travel to another planet. Kuhn tells us that a paradigm shift "is rather as if the professional community had been suddenly transported to another planet where familiar objects are seen in a different light and are joined by unfamiliar ones as well" (p. 111). The elements of this analogy— travel, another planet or world, viewing both familiar and new objects in a different light—are consistent with our efforts in this book to travel on a journey toward a more complete understanding of HBSE. Our journey will take us to other people's worlds and it will call upon us to view new things in those worlds and familiar things in our own worlds in new ways and through others' eyes. As we continue on our journey we should try to appreciate that the process of taking the trip is as important and enlightening as any final destination we might reach.

Paradigms are not mysterious, determined for all time, immovable objects. Paradigms are social constructs created by humans. They can be and, in fact, have been changed and reconstructed by humans throughout our history (Capra 1983:30). Kuhn ([1962] 1970:92), for example, discusses scientific and political revolutions that result in paradigm shifts and changes. Such changes, Kuhn suggests, come about when a segment of a community, often a small segment, has a growing sense that existing institutions are unable to adequately address or solve the problems in the environment—an environment those same institutions helped create. The actions taken by the dissatisfied segment of the community can result in the replacement of all or parts of the older paradigm with a newer one. However, since not all humans have the same amount of influence or power and control over what a paradigm looks like and whose values and beliefs give it form, efforts to change paradigms involve conflict and struggles (Kuhn [1962] 1970:93).

Use of the notion of paradigm shift will enable us to expand our knowledge of human behavior and the social environment and to use this additional knowledge in our practice of social work. It can free us from an overdependence on traditional ways of viewing the world as the only ways of viewing the world. It can allow us to move beyond these views to alternative possibilities for viewing the world, its people, and their behaviors.

The concept of paradigm shift allows us to make the transitions necessary to continue our journey to explore alternative paradigms and paradigmatic elements that represent the many human interests, needs, and perspectives not addressed by or reflected in the traditional and dominant paradigm. The concept of paradigm shift is also helpful in recognizing relationships between traditional and alternative paradigms and for tracing how alternative paradigms often emerge from traditional or dominant ones. Traditional or dominant paradigms and alternative or possible paradigms for human behavior are often not necessarily mutually exclusive.

As we discussed in our exploration of paradigms and history, different paradigms can be described as different points in a progression of transformations in the way we perceive human behavior and the social environment. The progression from traditional and dominant to alternative and possible that we envision here is one that reflects a continuous movement (we hope) toward views of human behavior more consistent with the core concerns and historical values of social work and away from narrow perspectives that include only a privileged few and exclude the majority of humans. In some cases, this progression will mean returning to previously neglected paradigms. Such a progression, then, does not imply a linear, forward-only movement. It might more readily be conceived as a spiral or winding kind of movement. The worldviews illustrated in our discussion of history, for example, represented the perspectives almost exclusively of Europeans. Very different world views emerged in other parts of the world. Myers (1985:34), for example, describes an Afrocentric worldview that emerged over 5,000 years ago among Egyptians that posited the real world to be both spiritual and material at once. This holistic perspective found God manifest in everything. The self included "ancestors, the yet unborn, all of nature, and the entire community" (Myers 1985:35). Many scholars suggest that this paradigm continues to influence the worldviews of many people of African descent today. This Afrocentric paradigm clearly offers an alternative to European humanist or scientific paradigms that emerged during the Renaissance. Such an alternative emphasizing the interrelatedness of individuals and community and their mutual responsibility for one another encompasses much that is valuable and consistent with the core concerns of social work. The notion of a continuum helps us to understand the importance and usefulness of knowing about dominant paradigms at the same time that we attempt to transcend or shift away from the limits of traditional paradigms and move toward ones that are more inclusive and that more fully reflect the core concerns of social work.

Paradigm Shift, Social Work, and Social Change

The concept of paradigm change has significant implications for us as social workers. If you recall from earlier discussion, the basic purposes of social work include social change or social transformation in their call for us to be involved in social and political action to promote *social and economic justice.* Social change is also required in our call to enhance human well-being and to work on behalf of oppressed persons denied access to opportunities and resources or power. When we as social workers become a part of the processes of changing paradigms and the institutions that emerge from them, we are, in essence, engaging in fundamental processes of social change and transformation.

We can use the information we now have about paradigms and paradigm analysis to change or replace paradigms that create obstacles to people meeting their needs and reaching their potential. Since paradigms are reflected throughout the beliefs, values, institutions, and processes that make up our daily lives, we need not limit our thinking about paradigms only to our immediate concerns here about human behavior and the social environment. We can apply what we know about paradigms and paradigm change throughout our education and practice. For us as students of social work, that means we must become aware of the nature of the paradigms reflected throughout all areas of our studies in social work necessary to achieve the 10 core competencies required of professional social workers (see Table 1.1). We certainly also must begin to analyze the nature and assumptions of the paradigms we encounter through our course work in the arts and humanities (music, theater, visual arts, philosophy, literature, English, languages, religious studies), social sciences (economics, political science, psychology, sociology, anthropology, history), and natural sciences (biology, physics, chemistry, geology, geography) as well as through our own personal histories and life experiences.

Socialization is the process of teaching new members the rules by which the larger group or society operates. Socialization involves imparting to new members the knowledge, values, and skills according to which they are expected to operate. For example, the social work education process in which you are currently involved is a process for socializing you to the knowledge, values, and skills expected of professional social workers. (We will explore the concept of socialization further in a later section.)

In a more general sense, we are socialized to and interact with others in the social environment from paradigmatic perspectives. These perspectives are not only imparted to us through formal education in the schools but also through what we are taught and what we learn from our families, religious institutions, and other groups and organizations as well. We are influenced by worldviews and we reflect the worldviews to which we have been socialized. The worldview likely to have influenced us most if we were socialized through the educational system in the United States is the traditional or dominant paradigm. The influence of this paradigm is pervasive, even if the worldviews of our families or cultures are in conflict with parts or all of the traditional or dominant paradigm. Because of the power accorded thinking consistent with the traditional paradigm, it is extremely difficult for alternative paradigms to be accorded legitimacy. It is not, however, impossible. As we shall see, it is quite possible through understanding traditional and alternative paradigms and the dynamics of paradigm change that we can exercise choice in the paradigms or worldviews through which we lead our lives. We suggest here that social changes resulting from shifts in worldviews inherently and inextricably flow from changes in the way we as individuals view our worlds. This position is consistent with the suggestion of much alternative paradigm thinking, in particular that of feminism, that *the personal is political.*

In order to use our understanding of paradigms to support processes of social change/transformation we must first engage in the process of paradigm analysis we described earlier. Paradigm analysis, you might recall, requires us to ask a set of questions that can guide us, in our education and practice, toward adopting and adapting approaches to understanding human behavior and the social environment that incorporate perspectives consistent with the core concerns of social work.

As we suggested earlier, a significant responsibility for us as social workers is assisting people whose needs are not met and whose problems are not solved by the institutions and processes in the social environment that emerge from and reflect the dominant/traditional paradigms. Much of what social work is about involves recognizing, analyzing, challenging, and changing existing paradigms. An essential step in fulfilling this important responsibility is learning to listen to, respect, and effectively respond to the voices and visions that the people with whom we work have to contribute to their own well-being and to the common good. In this way paradigms that too often have been considered permanent and unchangeable can be questioned, challenged, altered, and replaced. More important, they can be changed to more completely include the worldviews of persons previously denied participation in paradigm-building processes.

Such a perspective on knowledge for practice allows us to operate in partnership with the people with whom we work. It allows us to incorporate their strengths, and it provides us an opportunity to use social work knowledge, skills, and values in concert with those strengths in our practice interactions.

The possible or alternative paradigms of human behavior with which we will be concerned are those that enrich, alter, or replace existing paradigms by including the voices and visions—values, beliefs, ways of doing and knowing—of persons who have usually been left out of the paradigm building that has previously taken place. It is interesting, but not coincidental, that the persons who have usually been left out of paradigm-building processes are often the same persons with whom social workers have traditionally worked and toward whom the concerns of social workers have historically been directed.

Much of our work as we proceed through the remaining chapters of this book will involve understanding, critiquing, and analyzing traditional or dominant paradigms as well as alternative, more inclusive paradigms. We will engage in these processes as we explore theories and information about individual human behavior in the contexts of families, groups, organizations, communities, and globally. Central to understanding, critiquing, and analyzing paradigms is consideration of the concepts of culture, ethnicity, and race in relation to paradigms.

PARADIGMS, CULTURE, ETHNICITY, AND RACE

A paradigm, as the concept is used here, encompasses a number of different but interrelated elements. Among the elements that can help us understand the complexities and variations of worldviews or paradigms held by different people are culture, ethnicity, and race. Even though, as Helms (1994:292) notes these terms "are often used interchangeably . . . neither culture nor ethnicity necessarily has anything to do with race, as the term is typically used in U.S. society." Each of these terms include a variety of meanings and are used in different ways depending on the context of their use and the worldview held by their users. For example, each of these concepts, in the hands of their users, can either be a very strong and positive force for unity and cooperation or an equally strong and negative force for divisiveness and domination. We will examine some of the interrelated meanings of these concepts next.

Culture and Society: Multiple Meanings

A very basic and traditional definition of **culture** is that it is the "shared values, traditions, norms, customs, arts, history, folklore, and institutions of a group of people" (NCCC, 2004). Even more basic is the definition offered by Herskovits that culture is "the human-made part of the environment" (Lonner 1994:231). **Society** can be defined as a "group of people who share a heritage or history" (Persell 1987:47–48). Lonner (1994:231) suggests that culture is "the mass of behavior that human beings in any society learn from their elders and pass on to the younger generation." This definition links the concepts culture and society as converging on or uniting with one another and adds the suggestion that culture is learned from others in the society. The transmission of culture can happen in two ways. It can occur through **socialization**, which is the teaching of culture by an elder generation to a younger one very explicitly through formal instruction and rules. This transmission process can also occur through **enculturation** by "implicitly or subtly" teaching the culture to the younger generation "in the course of everyday life" (Lonner 1994:234).

These definitions reflect the sense that culture is constructed by groups of people (societies), is made up of beliefs, practices, and products (artifacts), and is passed from one generation to another. However, many people would argue that culture is considerably more complex and varied than is implied by the definitions above.

Helms (1994) suggests, for example, that culture might be thought of as at least two very different entities or types: "a macroculture (symbolized here as CULTURE) and a variety of subsidiary cultures identified with particular collective identity groups (symbolized here as 'culture')." Helms' definition of *culture* as "the customs, values, traditions, products, and sociopolitical histories of the social groups" seems quite similar to the traditional definitions given above, however, her reference to these cultures as "subsidiary" and existing "within a CULTURE, where CULTURE refers to the dominant society or group's [belief system] or worldview" (1994:292) provides a significantly alternative perspective. Helms has added the dimension of dominance and power to the concept of culture. As we will see later the notion of power differences is an important element necessary for understanding differences between traditional or dominant and alternative paradigms.

The definitions above all emphasize similarities and commonalties among the people who make up cultures and societies. It is very important for us as social workers to be careful not to overgeneralize about these similarities. We need to recognize that "culture does not simply make people uniform or homogenize them: It rather sets trends from which in some cases it allows, and

How might the people in this photo and their activity reflect the concepts of culture, ethnicity, and race? How might the meaning differ depending on whether the people in the photo or others (you, for example) provide the definitions?

in other case even encourages, deviation: be it by attributing differentiating roles, or simply by encouraging individual differences in fashion, imagination, or style. In other words, a culture seems to need both uniformity and individuality" (Boesch 1991 in Lonner 1994:233).

Ethnicity

Ethnicity is "socially defined on the basis of cultural criteria. . . . Thus, customs, traditions, and values rather than physical appearance per se define ethnicity" (Van Den Berghe in Helms 1994:293). Helms (1994:293) suggests that ethnicity might "be defined as a social identity based on the culture of one's ancestors' national or tribal groups as modified by the demands of the CULTURE in which one group currently resides." As with her definitions of culture, Helms includes the impact of dominant or more powerful groups on other groups in her definition of ethnicity. She notes that the social identity that is ethnicity may be adapted or altered by groups as a result of demands of dominant or more powerful groups. However, she is careful to note the limits of a more powerful group in determining ethnicity for another group. She does this by differentiating between ethnic classification and ethnic identity. **Ethnic classification** is defined "from the outside in" and it "may be inferred from external criteria such as physical characteristics or symbolic behaviors (for example, ethnic dress)." **Ethnic identity**, on the other hand is "defined from the inside (of the person) out (to the world)" and is "self-defined and maintained because it 'feels good' rather than because it is necessarily imposed by powerful others" (Helms 1994: 293–294).

Multiple Meanings of Race

The word **race** has historically had a variety of meanings. These meanings have varied over time. Consistently, though, the very term *race* in U.S. society is highly charged emotionally and has different meanings and very different consequences for different people. We will explore race here as a multifaceted concept and as a concept that must be considered contextually. We will also find that the meaning of race is consistently used in U.S. society as an arena for power struggle. Racial distinctions are often used as a means of attaining and holding power by dominant group members over less powerful groups. At this point, we address the concept of race in terms of its cultural and social meanings and we give some attention to misconceptions that race is primarily a biological rather than primarily a social construction with biological elements only secondary. We briefly explore the uses of racial designations for oppression and for solidarity and liberation. Chapter 2 addresses the dimensions of traditional and alternative paradigms dealing with whiteness, diversities, and oppressions.

RACE: BIOLOGY, CULTURE, OR BOTH

There has been ongoing argument in this society over what we mean by "races." Spickard (1992:13–14) suggests that "the most common view has been to see races as distinct types. That is, there were supposed to have been at some time in the past four or five utterly distinct and pure races, with physical features, gene pools, and the character qualities that diverged entirely one from another." The biological terms related to this purist view of races as types are **genotype**, which means genetic structure or foundation, and **phenotype**, which means physical characteristics and appearance.

Spickard (1992:15) also stresses that:

> in the twentieth century, an increasing number of scientists have taken exception to the notion of races as types. James C. King (1981), perhaps the foremost American geneticist on racial matters, denounces the typological view as "make-believe" (p. 112). Biologists and physical anthropologists are more likely to see races as subspecies. That is, they recognize the essential commonality of all humans, and see races as geographically and biologically diverging populations. . . . They see all human populations, in all times and places, as mixed populations. There never were any 'pure' races.

Most scientists today have concluded, "that race is primarily about culture and social structure, not biology . . . [and that] while it has some relationship to biology . . . [it] is primarily a sociopolitical construct. The sorting of people into this race or that in the modern era has generally been done by powerful groups for the purposes of maintaining and extending their own power" (Spickard 1992:13–14).

RACE AND POWER

Spickard (1992:19) argues, "from the point of view of the dominant group, racial distinctions are a necessary tool of dominance. They serve to separate the subordinate people as 'Other.' Putting simple, neat racial labels on dominated peoples—and creating negative myths about the moral qualities of those peoples—makes it easier for the dominators to ignore the individual humanity of their victims. It eases the guilt of oppression." For example, in U.S. society "the typological view of races developed by Europeans arranged the peoples of the world hierarchically, with Caucasians at the top, Asians next, then Native Americans, and African at the bottom—in terms of both physical abilities and moral qualities" (Spickard 1992:14).

While race is often used as a tool of domination, it

is by no means only negative, however. From the point of view of subordinate peoples, race can be a positive tool, a source of belonging, mutual help, and self-esteem. Racial categories . . . identify a set of people with whom to share a sense of identity and common experience. . . . It is to share a sense of peoplehood that helps locate individuals psychologically, and also provides the basis for common political action. Race, this socially constructed identity, can be a powerful tool, either for oppression or for group self-actualization. (Spickard 1992:19)

Race: Biology, culture, power

As we noted earlier the concepts of culture, society, ethnicity, and race are closely intertwined. Helms and Gotunda (in Helms 1994) argue that race as it is used in the United States has three types of definitions that reflect this intertwining of multiple concepts:

1. Quasi-biological race: based on visible aspects of a person that are assumed to be racial in nature, such as skin color, hair texture, or physiognomy [facial features]. "Group-defining racial characteristics generally are selected by the dominant or sociopolitically powerful group. . . . Thus, in the United States, White people specify the relevant racial traits and use themselves as the standard or comparison group." For example, "Native Americans are considered 'red' as compared to Whites; Blacks are black in contrast to Whites."

2. Sociopolitical race: "efforts to differentiate groups by means of mutually exclusive racial categories also imply a [hierarchy] with respect to psychological characteristics, such as intelligence and morality, with gradations in skin color or other relevant racial-group markers determining the group's location along the hierarchy. On virtually every socially desirable dimension, the descending order of superiority has been Whites, Asians, Native American, and Africans."

3. Cultural race: the customs, traditions, products, and values of (in this instance) a racial group. (Helms 1994:297–299)

Social Work and Cultural Competence

It is not enough for social workers to simply understand the abstract complexities that make up definitions of culture, society, ethnicity, or race. Because respect for diversity is so central to social work values and practice and because culture is such an important tool for understanding human diversity, social workers are beginning to make considerations about culture and cultural differences central to what we consider to be competent social work practice. The notion of culturally competent social work practice and what it involves has been described for multiple levels and areas of practice including individual practitioners and clients, families and agencies.

Cultural Competence is a set of cultural behaviors and attitudes integrated into the practice methods of a system, agency, or its professionals, that enables them to work effectively in cross cultural situations (National Center for Cultural Competence 2004). According to the National Center for Cultural Competence (NCCC), cultural competence comprises two dimensions:

▶ **Surface Structure:** Use people, places, language, music, food, and clothing familiar to and preferred by the target audience.
▶ **Deep Structure:** Involves socio-demographic and racial/ethnic population differences and the influence of ethnic, cultural, social, environmental, and historical factors on behaviors (National Center for Cultural Competence 2004).

The NCCC also suggest three major characteristics of culturally competent service delivery (see box below).

Culturally competent social work practice—its meaning and its application— is emerging as one of the most critical aspects of social work practice. It is especially important as the diversity of the U.S. population continues to increase. Culturally competent practice is also increasingly important as we become more and more interrelated with other people in the world as a result of the rapid shifts toward ever more global economics, communication, and transportation. Culturally competent social work practice is addressed in more detail in Chapter 3 as one of the "Tools for Social Work Practice."

Paradigms, Culture, and Society

Paradigms or worldviews simultaneously shape and reflect the institutions and processes shared by people in a society. However, there is a great deal of variation in the specific paradigmatic elements—the parts that constitute a paradigm— and the degree to which these parts are shared by different persons in the same society. This is especially true in the United States, although it is often unrecognized. Paradigmatic elements include the processes, beliefs, values, and products that make up cultures and give multiple meanings to such concepts as ethnicity and race. They include and are reflected in such varied expressions of cultures as art, music, science, philosophy, religion, politics, economics, leisure, work, and education. As Logan (1990:25) suggests, "culture must be viewed in the sense of the spiritual life of a people as well as material and behavioral aspects." As in the case of the concept of society, there is tremendous variation in the nature of the paradigmatic elements that constitute different cultures and the degree to which these elements are shared by the peoples of the United States and the world. It is contended here that this variation, this diversity, is a rich and essential, although underutilized, resource for understanding human behavior and the social environment.

Characteristics of Culturally Competent Service Delivery

Available: Availability of services refers to the existence of health services and bicultural/bilingual personnel

Accessible: Accessibility is contingent on factors such as cost of services, the hours of service provision, and the geographic location of a program.

Acceptable: Acceptability is the degree to which services are compatible with the cultural values and traditions of the clientele. (National Center for Cultural Competence 2004)

Social Work and the Liberal Arts

Social workers apply theories and knowledge from the liberal arts to understand biological, social, cultural, psychological, and spiritual development. Why do you think this is a necessary component of education for competent social work practice?

In order to help prepare us for culturally competent social work practice, we will search for ways to become aware of the many paradigmatic elements that influence our day-to-day lives and the ways we experience our worlds. Because paradigmatic elements are so interwoven with the many expressions of cultures and societies, it is essential for social workers to have as wide a range of opportunities as possible to learn and to think about these important elements and expressions. One way this is accomplished is through requirements that all social work education be based on a foundation of studies in a wide range of multidisciplinary liberal arts and sciences courses. Our studies in these courses can provide us new avenues to understand our own cultures and the cultures of others.

Social workers have recognized these valuable avenues to understanding human behavior and the social environment for a long time. They are considered so important in the overall education of social workers that content in the liberal arts and sciences disciplines is part of the knowledge required to achieve competence in applying knowledge of human behavior and the social environment in your social work pratice (CSWE 2008).

As we proceed we will try, through this book, to connect what we are thinking and learning about human behavior and the social environment with the experiences and knowledge we have (we all have a great deal!) and are continually gaining through the liberal arts and sciences.

Lather suggests a helpful way of thinking about the liberal arts and sciences as "human sciences" which encompass social, psychological, and biological sciences as they relate to humans. The definition of "human science" she puts forth suggests a broader, more inclusive approach to understanding human behavior through the liberal arts and sciences. **Human science** "is more inclusive, using multiple systems of inquiry, a science which approaches questions about the human realm with an openness to its special characteristics and a willingness to let the questions inform which methods are appropriate" (Polkinghome quoted in Lather 1991:166). This more inclusive and open approach to achieving understanding is consistent with the perspective or stance we take in this book toward alternative paradigms for understanding HBSE.

Howard Goldstein (1990), a social worker, suggests that broad knowledge from the liberal arts (the humanities) can help us do better social work. He suggests that much understanding about the continuously unfolding and complex nature of the lives of the people with whom we work (and of our own lives) can be achieved through study in the liberal arts. According to Goldstein, this broad range of knowledge includes art, literature, drama, philosophy, religion, and history.

Creative thinking that helps us ask questions that lead us toward understanding the experiences and the worlds of the people with whom we work, as well as our own, is central to what social work practice is all about.

Paradigms, Power, and Empowerment

Examination of the paradigms that simultaneously shape and are reflected in cultures and societies such as those in the United States can tell us much about power relations and the differential distribution of resources. Concerns about power, inequality, and resource distribution are, we must remember, core concerns for social workers. Our study of paradigms can help us understand a number of things about inequality and differences in power and resources.

Social workers under-
stand the forms and
mechanisms of oppres-
sion and discrimination,
advocate for human
rights and social and
economic justice, and
engage in practice to
advance social and
economic justice. How
can understanding the
concept of power and its
inequitable distribution
help us achieve these
expectations?

Power: Social and economic justice

Of major concern to social workers are power and resource differences (social
and economic justice) that result from one's gender, color, sexual orientation,
religion, age, ability, culture, income, and class (membership in populations-
at-risk). These differences have resulted in the exclusion of many persons from
having a place or a voice in dominant or traditional paradigms that guide decision making in this society. Differences such as those listed above have
resulted in the worldviews of some individuals and groups having much more
influence than others on the institutions and processes through which human
needs must be met and human potential reached. It is the contention in this
book that when some of us are denied opportunities to influence decision-
making processes that affect our lives we are all hurt. We all lose when the
voices and visions of some of us are excluded from paradigms and paradigm-
building processes. By listening to the voices and seeing the world through the
eyes of those who differ from us in gender, color, sexual orientation, religion,
age, ability, culture, income, and class we can learn much about new paradigms or worldviews that can enrich all our lives. Close attention to, and inclusion of the voices and visions of, persons different from us can greatly expand,
with exciting new possibilities, our understanding of human behavior and the
social environment—and our understanding of what it means to be human.

Empowerment

Empowerment is a concept helpful to us as we think about the importance of
power for understanding paradigms and its role in achieving the basic purposes of social work. Empowerment involves redistributing resources so that
the voices and visions of persons previously excluded from paradigms and
paradigm-building processes are included. Specifically, **empowerment** is the
process through which people gain the power and resources necessary to shape
their worlds and reach their full human potential. Empowerment suggests an
alternative definition of power itself. A very useful alternative definition of
power has been suggested by African American feminists. This definition
rejects the traditional notion of power as a commodity used by one person
or group to dominate another. It instead embraces "an alternative vision of
power based on a humanist vision of self-actualization, self-definition, and
self-determination" (Lorde 1984; Steady 1987; Davis 1989; hooks 1989, cited in
Collins 1990:224). This alternate vision seems much more consistent with the
purposes and foundations of social work than traditional conceptualizations of
power that define power as "power over" someone else.

   As social workers we are especially concerned, in our explorations of alternative visions of power, with the empowerment of those persons who differ
from the people whose voices and visions are represented disproportionately
in the traditional and dominant paradigms. The persons most disproportionately represented in traditional paradigms are "male, white, heterosexual,
Christian, temporarily able-bodied, youthful with access to wealth and
resources" (Pharr 1988:53). Our alternative vision seeks the empowerment of
women, people of color, gay men and lesbians, non-Christians, non-young, persons with disabilities, non-European descended, low-income, and non-middle-
or non-upper-socioeconomic-class persons.

   The purpose of **empowerment is in essence the purpose of social work:** *to
preserve and restore human dignity, to benefit from and celebrate the diversities of humans, and to transform ourselves and our society into one that welcomes and supports the voices, the potential, the ways of knowing, the energies
of us all.* "Empowerment practice in social work emerged from efforts to

develop more effective and responsive services for women and people of color" (Gutierrez et al. 1995:534). Empowerment focuses on changing the distribution of power. It "depicts power as originating from various sources and as infinite because it can be generated in the process of social interaction" (Gutierrez et al. 1995:535). As we proceed through this book and consider a variety of perspectives on individuals, families, groups, organizations, communities, and the world, we need to keep in mind their potential for empowering all persons and for facilitating social change or social transformation. As we proceed we will continually weigh what we discover about any of the paradigms and perspectives we explore against the historic mission and core concerns of social work—"[the] quest for social and economic justice, the prevention of conditions that limit human rights, the elimination of poverty, and the enhancement of the quality of life for all persons" (CSWE 2008:1). The tasks we set for ourselves as we continue our journey toward more complete understanding of HBSE are certainly challenging ones. However, like the assumptions of interconnectedness and interdependence we made at the beginning of this chapter about social work, ourselves, and the people with whom we work, the topics and tasks we take on as we proceed through this book are interconnected and interdependent.

SUMMARY/TRANSITION

This chapter has presented you with information and perspectives in a number of areas. It has introduced you to the place and importance of human behavior and the social environment content in the social work curriculum. It has described HBSE content as required content for all accredited social work education programs that, in concert with a wide range of content from the liberal arts and sciences, builds a foundation of knowledge upon which to base social work practice. The chapter has presented a number of guiding assumptions about the interrelationships among ourselves, others, and social work practice.

Definitions of the concept of paradigm or worldview have been presented, along with discussions of the related notions of paradigm analysis and paradigm shift and their significance for social workers and social change. This chapter has introduced the notions of traditional or dominant paradigms and alternative or possible paradigms. These concepts have been placed in context through discussion of their emergence and change over time within a historical continuum. Attention has been given in this chapter to the purposes and foundations of social work that form its historic mission to enhance human and community well-being and alleviate poverty and oppression. Issues of power and empowerment as they relate both to understanding paradigms and to the core concerns of social work have been discussed. The exclusion of many diverse persons from traditional and dominant paradigms has been introduced. In addition, the complexities and multiple definitions of culture, ethnicity and race were introduced. The concepts and issues in this chapter present the basic themes that will guide us throughout our journey to understanding human behavior and the social environment in the chapters that comprise this book. The concepts and issues presented in this chapter are intended to provide a base from which to explore in more detail dimensions of traditional and alternative paradigms in the next chapter.

Succeed with **mysocialworklab**

Log onto **www.mysocialworklab.com** to watch videos on the skills and competencies discussed in this chapter. (If you did not receive an access code to **MySocialWorkLab** with this text and wish to purchase access online, please visit www.mysocialworklab.com.)

Diversity in Practice   Ethical Practice   Human Behavior   Human Rights & Justice

PRACTICE TEST

1. Which of the following statements is inconsistent with social work values?
   a. Social worker's professional relationships are built on regard for individual worth and dignity.
   b. Social workers respect people's right to make independent decisions.
   c. Social workers require clients to follow their instructions.
   d. Social workers are responsible for their own ethical conduct.

Critical Thinking

2. A social worker who weighs evidence for and against assertions in a logical, rational, systematic, data-based way and asks "does it work?" and "how do you know?" about treatment methods is using:
   a. the scientific method
   b. evidence based practice thinking
   c. critical thinking
   d. empirical thinking

3. A profound change in the thoughts, perceptions, and values that form a particular vision of reality is called a(n)_____.
   a. paradigm shift
   b. paradigm analysis
   c. thinking paradigm
   d. alternative paradigm

4. The process of gaining understanding about ourselves through art, literature and poetry can be referred to as _____
   a. secularism
   b. humanism
   c. empericism
   d. post modernism

5. _____ is an example of what was originally an alternative paradigm and is today considered a traditional paradigm.
   a. scholasticism
   b. premodernism
   c. science
   d. critical thinking

6. Two divergent worldviews influencing social work are scientific and _____ perspectives.
   a. positivistic
   b. interpretive
   c. hedonistic
   d. deterministic

7. _____ is a social identity based on the culture of one's ancestor's national or tribal group as modified by the demands of the CULTURE in which one group currently resides.
   a. ethnicity
   b. society
   c. enculturation
   d. socialization

Diversity in Practice

8. The _____ of a group is "defined from the inside (of the person) out (to the world)" and is "self-defined and maintained because it 'feels good'".
   a. culture
   b. ethnic identity
   c. race
   d. ethnic classification

9. Kuhn defines _____ as "the entire constellation of beliefs, values, techniques, and so on shared by the members of a given community".
   a. paradigm
   b. culture
   c. community identity
   d. social thinking

10. Which of the examples listed below is NOT a characteristic of Lather's Postmodern Era?
    a. importance of individual reason in determining truth
    b. emphasis on multiple ways of knowing
    c. history is viewed as non-linear
    d. importance of participatory, feminist-influenced, non-hierarchical means of truth seeking

Log onto **MySocialWorkLab** once you have completed the Practice Test above to take your Chapter Exam and demonstrate your knowledge of this material.

Answers

1) c 2) c 3) a 4) b 5) c 6) b 7) a 8) b 9) b 10) a

Social Work Education in the Homeland: *Wo'Lakota Unglu'su'tapi.*[1]
EPAS or Impasse? Operationalizing Accreditation Standard 6.0

Richard W. Voss
West Chester University

Albert White Hat, Sr.
Sinte Gleska University
Rosebud Sioux Tribe

Jim Bates
Eastern Washington State University
Yankton Sioux Tribe

Margery Richard Lunderman
Ring Thunder Ti'ospaye
Oglala Sioux Tribe

Alex Lunderman, Jr.
Ring Thunder Ti'ospaye
Rosebud Sioux Tribe

This article examines the broader historical context of American colonial Indian education policy, the challenges American Indian students face with successful performance in higher education today, the legacy of active resistance to culturally destructive educational policy, and the critical role of tribal colleges in preserving traditional prerogatives and values, while providing access to higher education for American Indian students living in the homelands. It examines the Council on Social Work Education's accreditation standard 6.0 and offers practical ways social work educators can collaborate with tribal colleges to further support indigenous social work education in culturally compatible and affirming ways to strengthen bicultural identity and tribal sovereignty.

My grandmother always told me that the White man never listens to anyone, but expects everyone to listen to him. So, we listen! . . . We have survived here because we know how to listen. The White people in the lower forty-eight talk. They are like the wind, they sweep over everything. (Coles, cited in Nabokov, 1991, p. 431)

Over the years the first author has spent time listening to traditional Indian people from the Great Sioux Nation, specifically what they think about professional social workers and their ideas about help and healing. One of the most eye-opening findings was the perception that some social workers were perceived as "books, not real live people, more interested in enforcing regulations than responding to [the needs of] people" (Voss, Douville, Little Soldier, &

Richard W. Voss is associate professor, Undergraduate Social Work Department, West Chester University. **Albert White Hat, Sr.,** is instructor of Lakota Studies, Sinte Gieska University. **Jim Bates** is professor emeritus, Eastern Washington University. **Margery Richard Lunderman** is an elder and **Alex Lunderman, Jr.** is a community activist, Ring Thunder Community, Rosebud Sioux Indian Reservation.
Journal of Social Work Education Vol. 41 , No. 2 (Spring/Summer 2005). © Copyright 2005 Council on Social Work Education, Inc. All rights reserved.

Note to Reader: Illustrative Reading 1.1 was written prior to the implementation of the 2008 CSWE Educational Policy and Accreditation Standards. As a result, references to specific standards and policies by number in the reading reflect the numbering used in the 2001 document. However, the questions and issues addressed in the reading remain quite relevant in the context of the 2008 document, as well.

[1]The term "homeland" which connotes a place of safety, wellbeing, and sovereignty is preferred by the *Sicangu Oyate* (Rosebud Sioux Tribe) over the term "reservation" to describe the land allocations established by treaty with the U.S. Government. This Lakota term means, "strengthening our Lakota way within oneself and in relationship with creation."

Twiss, 1999b, p. 233). The first author has also visited tribal colleges and community colleges on the homelands (reservations) and noticed that all of these institutions offer either the associate of arts degree or a bachelor of arts degree in human services, or both—rather than the baccalaureate social work degree. When asked about this, administrators have explained that this curriculum decision has been based not only on resource limitations (the lack of social work faculty available to teach on the reservation), but they also note the perception that accredited human services and counseling programs are less rigid and more accommodating to incorporating traditional pedagogy and cultural prerogatives than the social work curriculum (Personal Communication, S. L. Klein and B. Clifford, Sinte Gleska University, 2001).

These findings are corroborated by the authors' review of "Tribal College Profiles" (see the Appendix in Globalization of Tribal Colleges and Universities, 2000), which included profiles of 18 tribal colleges. The profiles included information about the respective majors offered at the tribal colleges and report on the types of majors their institutions offer. These profiles showed the following: Only two offered the associate of arts degree in social work and the Red Crow Community College in Alberta, Canada was in the process of developing a joint BSW program in concert with the University of Calgary. Most of the colleges offered other related majors which included associate of arts degrees in the following concentrations: human services, community health education, and alcohol and drug abuse studies. The associate of science degrees were also offered and include the following areas: chemical dependency counseling. social science, public and tribal administration, health information technology, and criminal justice. Sinte Gleska University offered three related bachelor of science degree programs including criminal justice, mental health, and chemical dependency. Oglala Lakota College offered the BS in human services, and Sitting Bull College offered the BS in Native American human services. The Turtle Mountain Community College offered the BS in social work in partnership with the University of North Dakota (Globalization of Tribal Colleges and Universities, 2000).

The report *Creating Role Models for Change: A Survey of Tribal College Graduates* (American Indian Higher Education Consortium, Institute for Higher Education Policy, & Sallie May Education Institute, 2000) offers additional information about courses of study at tribal colleges and includes a summary of tribal college graduates' major fields of study. Among its findings, it showed that 19% of the graduates majored in nursing and health care, 13% in computer and office technology, 11% in education/teaching, and 11% in psychology/social work/human services (p. 8). These data document interest in social work among American Indian students[2] attending tribal colleges, despite the apparent barriers to the BSW. Interestingly, all of the tribal colleges included in the tribal college profiles in Globalization of Tribal Colleges & Universities (2000) reported that they had established international partnerships and exchanges as institutional priorities, and many had developed

---

[2]The authors have decided to use the terms "American Indian," "native indigenous people or students," "Indian," or "tribal people" inter-changeably when discussing generic issues, concerns, and ideas about the subjects of this essay. The authors are well aware of the historical, social, and political complexity and controversy associated with any terms used to identify culturally distinctive groups of people and note that the term "American Indian" is the legal title of federally recognized tribes holding jurisdiction on reservation lands in the United States. The terms "native indigenous" and "tribal people" connote the originality of the people's association with creation, the land, and the Creator, and their natural, extended, familiar relationship bonds which define them. Likewise the term "homeland" is preferred over "reservation" since the later connotes a fenced in place where animals are kept; it connotes a place of containment or restriction whereas the former term better reflects the sense of kinship, a place of safety and origin, and deep-felt affection the Lakota and other traditional people feel for their ancestral homeland.

partnerships with sister universities across the United States—so there is interest in inter-institutional partnerships and collaborations here.

Similar findings about the social work curriculum, tribal concerns, and the needs of American-Indian students have been identified and discussed by Jim Bates, a Lakota/Nakota and an enrolled member of the Yankton Sioux Tribe, professor emeritus. Eastern Washington State University, social work educator, consultant to various tribes, and an American-Indian student advocate (personal communication, 1999). Professor Bates has noted how he has had to re-educate American-Indian graduates from accredited social work programs to function competently in tribal social services. Professor Bates noted that many tribes did not want to hire professional social workers for tribal services as they were not viewed as effective with Indian people, in that they were "just too complicated" for Indians to trust. Professor Bates often spoke about the need for a "shadow curriculum" for native indigenous students, a curriculum that would be grounded upon core indigenous values and traditional philosophical assumptions; a curriculum that would more appropriately prepare traditional Indians for social work in their respective tribes within the framework of their own traditional heritage (personal communication, 1999).

These observations have been further supported by Weaver's study about the experiences of American-Indian social workers in social work programs (2000). Respondents noted that, "psychodynamic theories and research methods [being] taught were sources of conflict" (p. 422); other respondents reported deep, pervasive conflicts related to broad institutional expectations. Weaver reported the following:

> Some experienced conflict between the holistic spiritual community they came from and the hierarchical, bureaucratic educational system. The emphasis on written methods to communicate knowledge was also a struggle. Some felt they must compromise their cultural identity to succeed in school. One respondent stated that, "in the small groups I try to assimilate further by being more verbal as that is important it seems and also lengthy eye contact is something I continue to work on." (p. 423)

Weaver's findings document the intensity of cultural shock and dislocation experienced by Native-American students during their transition from leaving home and attending classes in a foreign university environment, far from their homeland (reservation). Weaver (2000) quoted one respondent, who stated.

> If [I] hadn't been staying at [a nearby tribal college] the first year I went to [a social work program at a large university] I don't think I would have made it; me and my roommates would take turns crying . . . because it was so different from us, especially just coming from a boarding school . . . We only had each other for support. (p, 424)

Parallel to these discussions, a traditional Oglala medicine man[3] and other elders who live in a traditional community on the Pine Ridge Indian Reservation have discussed their concerns about and the need for social work on the reservation, the need for developing a core curriculum for tribal social workers, and the pressing needs of American-Indian people (personal communication, 2000). This medicine man asked for more discussion between traditional tribal educators and elders with mainstream educational institutions (and their respective accrediting bodies) particularly around building a curriculum that

---

[3]It is customary not to include the names of medicine men and elders in publications out of respect.

could interface with traditional knowledge keepers. He was really calling for a two-way process, one where professional social workers would collaborate with the medicine men and traditional elders, teaching basic or core helping skills, and also where the traditional knowledge-keepers would inform social work practice. He wondered why American social workers were so influenced by "English social work" when there were traditions of social work–like functions among traditional (American-Indian) people.

In the midst of these discussions, the first author found himself straddling two worlds. In the summer of the year 2000, he was adopted as a Hunka son by an Oglala elder, a descendent of Chief Red Cloud, and given the name *Ohitika Wicasa* that was translated as "Keeps His Word." It is from this relational context, with one foot in each of these worlds, that this article is written with permission from his respective elders and extended family.

The above data from traditional tribal communities suggest that the significant differences inherent in culturally diverse groups, particularly native indigenous (Indian) students are not being adequately addressed in practical, reciprocal, and developmental terms for these students in their experiences with formal social work education. The differences that come to bear are poignantly illustrated in the Red Road Approach developed by Gene Thin Elk (Red Dog, personal communication, 1999), which contrasts the "unnatural world" of the dominant culture influenced by "how one feels" versus living in the "natural world" that is not guided by "how one feels" but by responding to all life based on a spiritual understanding, by "acting responsibly and doing the right thing." The different trajectories from these epistemological stances powerfully illustrate how the values of the dominant culture have been infused into a curriculum that overly emphasizes the exploration of feelings versus the exploration of right action: "how do you feel about that?" or "reaching for feeling(s)" versus using the pedagogy of tribal values, spirituality, and traditional teaching.

The question arises, Is it possible to bring these apparently incompatible worldviews into a dialogue? Will the Council on Social Work Education's (2001) accreditation standard 6.0 offer any real avenues for dialogue and cooperation between social work educators and institutions with traditional people and their respective tribes and nations, or will it sustain the present pedagogical impasse evident in the data presented in the following discussion? When traditional people do not approve of something, the way they express their disagreement is not to show up—they will "just walk away." To illustrate this point, an elder would ask, "Do you know how the people used to vote a bad leader out of office?" He answered, "When the chief woke up one morning and all the tipis had moved away. *Then* he knew something was up. No one would tell him, 'Hey Chief, you've got a problem here.' It was understood that he should have known better and paid more attention to what was going on" (Little Soldier, personal communication, 1999). This article is a wake-up call for social work education in the homeland.

Social Work Education and Post-Colonial Resistance

The history of American-Indian education policy is problematic on many levels. The early pedagogy driven by assimilation theory attempted to extinguish what was perceived as uncivilized and untamed in Indian children and instill within them the values and work ethic seen as indispensable for productive citizenry. Many Indian children were removed from their respective reservations, separated from their families, and routinely introduced to Christianity as a civilizing methodology. They were prohibited from speaking their native languages and practicing their native spirituality. In this vacuum, they were socialized into a materialistic lifestyle in an institutional (boarding school) setting (Douville, personal communication, 1997; Little Soldier, personal communication, 1997; White Hat, personal communication, 1997; see Standing Bear, 1975, pp. 123–176).

Today few American-Indian families have not been affected by the legacy of the Indian boarding school experience. While some Indian people claim to have benefited from their boarding school experience, it is often associated with the loss of culture, loss of language, and loss of identity. In their findings from their study of historical trauma and identity, Weaver and Yellow Horse Brave Heart (1999) report that over half of the respondents rated their boarding school experiences as negative and 58% reported physical abuse by boarding school staff. Seventy-one percent reported experiencing racism from school staff; interestingly, more men reported physical and sexual abuse than women (p. 28). Currently, educators are looking at culture as a resource for students and understand that cultural identity is not a static concept, but is a dynamic and adaptive resource. We now see that exposure to diverse cultures may actually make individuals stronger and enable them to function in two or more cultural worlds, as the situation requires (McFee, 1968; Oetting & Beauvais, 1991; Weaver & Yellow Horse Brave Heart, 1999).

"Historical trauma" describes the cumulative cultural wounding across generations as well as present-day effects on one's current life circumstances (Weaver & Yellow Horse Brave Heart, 1999, p. 22) in response to systemic oppression and genocide. For American-Indian people the legacy of genocide includes imposed distortions of one's tribal identity, devalued sense of self, and suppression of tribal cultural values and traditional practices (Holler, 1995, p. 110; Lame Deer, 1992, p. 230; Voss, Douville, Little Soldier, & White Hat, Sr., 1999a; Voss et al., 1999b). While group identity continues to be strong among traditional Lakotas, it includes some features that have led to a group identity formed on the status of being persecuted and oppressed (Weaver & Yellow Horse Brave Heart, 1999, p. 23). For the Lakota, the sense of self has traditionally been associated with an intimate bond with the group (Lakota Nation) and with a profound sense of kinship with all of creation, including the natural universe and ancestral spirits articulated in the Lakota imperative *Mitakuye oyas'in!* which has been translated as "All my relations!" For the traditional Lakota self-identity does not exist apart from the spiritual world, the nation, and all creation (Weaver & Yellow Horse Brave Heart, 1999). In response to historical trauma, Lakota and other Indian people have developed various coping styles and survival strategies (trauma responses) that may appear dysfunctional when viewed outside of the historical context. Care must be taken to comprehend the level of unresolved grief, deprecated group status, and devalued self-image that continue to affect some indigenous native homelands (Weaver & Yellow Horse Brave Heart, 1999, p. 23).

Oetting and Beauvais (1991) found that an individual's identification with one culture is independent of their identification with any other culture. Therefore, increasing identification with one culture does not necessarily demand a reciprocal decrease in identification with another culture (Weaver & Yellow Horse Brave Heart, 1999, p. 21). In order to develop a strong identity with the predominant culture, an individual need not relinquish his or her identity with his or her native culture, which was the faulty assumption of the early boarding school innovators. We now know that individuals may and do identify with more than one culture for a variety of reasons, and that there are multiple sources of strength and support for overcoming even great adversity (Crozier-Hogel & Wilson, 1997).

Educational Failure as a Form of Cultural Resistance

In a survey of post-secondary school achievement of American Indians, Robert N. Wells (1997) found that the 1st-year retention rate of American-Indian students in post-secondary education was 45%, with a graduation rate of 25%. This survey found the most frequently identified factors that hindered college-level achievement for American-Indian students were the following: inadequate preparation, poor adjustment to the college environment, personal and family problems, and financial difficulties (Wells, 1997). Failure rates of American Indian students who go to college directly from reservations reportedly run nearly 70% and higher (Harriman, 2000, pp. 1–2). American Indians have the lowest level of educational attainment of any racial or ethnic group in the United States. According to the 1990 Census data, among American Indians 25 years and older, only 66% graduated from high school and only 9% had earned a bachelor's degree or higher. We also know that one out of five American Indians live on reservations where access to higher education continues to be limited (Census Bureau, 1998). In the report "Creating Role Models for Change: A Survey of Tribal College Graduates" the American Indian Higher Education Consortium (AIHEC), together with the Institute for Higher Education Policy and Sallie May Education Institute (2000), noted that

> The history of higher education for American Indians in the United States largely has been one of systemic failure. For hundreds of years, the primary goal of post-secondary education efforts for American Indians at predominantly white, mainstream institutions was cultural assimilation rather than students' educational development and progress. (p. 1)

The pedagogical dilemmas affecting American-Indian students today must be understood in the historical context of the liberal educational legacy inherited from the 1800s which embraced a "cookie cutter" or an industrial conveyer belt one-size-fits-all, or "one best system" of education built on uniformity, productivity, and compliance (Johnson & Reed, 2002). This, coupled with the legacy of the Carlisle Indian School's liberal philosophy inspired by Colonel Richard C. Pratt's notion of "kill the Indian . . . save the man" (1973), established the pedagogical template and basic philosophical foundation for American-Indian education policy in the United States for the next century. Colonel Pratt's distinction of "kill the Indian, save the man" was actually a liberal revision of the previous master text, which read "the only good Indian, is a dead Indian," and literally sought to strip the Indian youth of his or her tribal identity. This overtly racist ideology set the brutal historical context of Indian education policy, the legacy of which frames the present challenges facing contemporary social work educators interested in addressing the systemic failure in post-secondary performance measures for many American-Indian students today.

Challenging the Script of Indian Education: The Legacy of Zitkala Ša at the Carlisle Indian School

In order to better comprehend the legacy of Indian education policy one also needs to consider the legacy of resistance and the push toward intellectual sovereignty against the pedagogies that have silenced the voices of Indian children. A particularly powerful testimony of this academic resistance is found in the writings of Zitkala Ša, a turn-of-the-century Yanktoni Dakota Sioux woman (aka Gertrude Bonnin, see Fisher, 1979; Enoch, 2001), who became an Indian teacher at the Carlisle Indian School. Zitkala Ša would later construct an impassioned critique of the pedagogy of cultural and spiritual annihilation that supported and sustained the colonizing-assimilating institutions affecting Indian people. She wrote.

> For the white man's papers I had given up my faith in the Great Spirit. For these same papers I had forgotten the healing in trees and brooks. On account of my mother's simple view of life, and my lack of any, I gave her up, also. I made no friends among the race of people I loathed. Like a slender tree, I had been uprooted from my mother, nature, and God. I was shorn of my branches, which had waved in sympathy and love for home and friends. The natural coat of bark which had protected my oversensitive nature was scraped off to the very quick. (Zitkala Ša, cited in Enoch, 2001, p. 127)

By articulating her self-understanding, Zitkala Ša offers insight into the psychologically destructive pedagogy of the Indian boarding school experience that replaced the familiar self inscriptions of Indian life and culture, with the master script of the "civilized" White school masters. Zitkala Ša actively resisted full assimilation by consciously reflecting on the multiple layers inherent in the process of ideological indoctrination incorporated in Indian education, noting the following:

> As months passed over me, I slowly comprehended that the large army of white teachers in Indian schools had a larger missionary creed than I had suspected. It was one which included self-preservation quite as much as Indian education. (Zitkala Ša, cited in Enoch, 2001, p.117)

Zitkala Ša's testimony of academic survival and resistance provides insight into the power of education to subvert culture, undermine identity, and erode tribal sovereignty by a colonizing curriculum.

Core Social Work Values and Traditional Indian Wisdom: Decoding the Social Work Script

Higher education continues to be based on a modern, secular, liberal, scientific model of empiricism and interpersonal objectivity, requiring critical, detached scrutiny that assumes the investigator is separate from the subjects studied. This is not the way traditional American Indians see their world; for them the world (earth) and the above (sky) are intimate relatives, so intimate the traditional Lakota Sioux use the personal relational terms of *Maka* ("mother"), *Unci* ("grandmother"), *Ate* ("father"), and *Tunka'sila* ("grandfather") respectively. For the traditional Lakota and other traditional American Indians these are not metaphors. These are terms of endearment and reflect a way of speaking about a highly personalized environment where everything is intimately related and connected. This conflict creates an epistemological crisis for many American-Indian students whose outlook on life and the understanding of the world is holistic. Lionel Bordeaux, president of Sinte Gleska University noted, "We do have a very holistic outlook. . . . We find it difficult to separate various things within ourselves" (Harriman, 2000, p. 2).

While present-day century social work education would not consciously or overtly ascribe to Colonel Pratt's "kill the Indian, save the man" ideology, social work education is, nonetheless, situated within the broader educational institution historically embedded in the American experience. Within this broader educational context, vestiges and residues of the earlier civilizing pedagogy may be found in the profession's most fundamental values. Consider the profession's emphasis on "intervention" and ethical stance on "client self-determination" and "client confidentiality." Traditional Indian people understand their close ties to all of their relatives and ancestors who respond to their needs when they ask for help. The spirits give many options to the individual in the healing process and are always available to help the individual. The individual seeking help knows that answers are not always immediate, so he or she waits with patience and fortitude *(wo'wacini tanka)* and knows that understanding will come in the space of time. The individual knows that his or her problems will be dissolved, often in a way that is not expected. Here the spirits (relatives) really challenge one's mind or reasoning power to recognize the solution(s) as it (they) unfold in day to day life. There is great respect for the intelligence of the individual throughout this process.

What is perceived as being most real, genuine, and good (ethical) for traditional Indian people is the rhythm, interconnectivity, and cycle of creation, which is reflected in their view of all life. Here, the individual is viewed as intimately related to all of creation that includes immediate and extended family, both living and ancestors who have passed on to the spirit world, as well as the tribal family and nation. Within this cultural context the very core social work values of client "self-determination" and "confidentiality" must be nuanced carefully and may be perceived as antithetical to traditional wisdom and knowledge, and perhaps unwittingly, subvert basic traditional Indian understandings of life which revolve around shamanism and tribalism (Voss et al., 1999b). There can be cultural dissonance between these traditional Lakota prerogatives and social work practice models that overly emphasize interventions with individuals, client self-determination based on Western personality theories, and the idea of an individualistic sense of confidentiality which can place a family member at odds with his or her *Ti'Ospaye* (extended family). Such interventions may be perceived as intrusive, intimidating, and culturally subversive.

Traditional Lakota culture resonates more with social work approaches that use pragmatic, community-based, prevention-oriented, risk reduction strategies that are holistic and engage the extended family and community as the primary helping system and affirm and incorporate cultural values and tribal prerogatives in interventions (Voss et al., 1999a; White Hat, personal communication, 2004). Cognitive therapies that emphasize personal and social responsibility and incorporate a discussion about the "false self" and the "true self" more closely correspond to the traditional Indian understanding of the challenges of choosing the good over the bad and learning from both. Within this tribal context, the individual is not alone in this arduous and difficult process; he or she has powerful spiritual resources that are available in the helping process. This well illustrates the concept incorporated into the title of this article, *Wo'Lakota Unglu'su'tapi,* "Strengthening our Lakota way within oneself and in relation with creation" and provides the nuance in understanding a traditional Lakota view of personal responsibility or self-determination.

Traditionally, the extended family was responsible for dealing with the problems of living that arose in pre-reservation tribal society (Douville, personal communication, 1997; Voss et al., 1999a; White Hat, personal communication, 1997, 2004). The idea of an elder sitting down with a social worker who is not a relative, perhaps a non-Indian, a stranger really, often someone much younger and inexperienced with life; who comes into his or her home asking personal questions and discussing personal matters, often recording or writing down what is said would be viewed as a cultural violation by most traditional people (White Hat, personal communication, 2004). "Out of respect for the visitor the elder will talk to the social worker politely," but there are deep questions about why such personal information is necessary (White Hat, personal communication, 2004). If and when such information is later used in court, there is a sense of deep betrayal and mistrust. If it is known that the social worker is a relative, he or she risks being ostracized by, and even cut-off from extended family. The situation is fraught with risk and danger. American-Indian social workers providing social services in native homelands (reservations) walk a tight-rope between these two confounding worlds. The first author has often heard the advice that social workers working with Indian people in the homelands "should not live on the reservation" (Matthew Cash, personal communication, 2004) so they can avoid being overly involved with their clients "in order to be professional." This conventional advice underscores the challenges and pressures tribal social workers face as they seek to engage in more culturally compatible practices with their relatives in their homelands.

The post-modern take on "kill the Indian, save the man" comprehends the destructiveness in the modern liberal interpersonal split between the subjective (personal) self and the objective (professional) self. This philosophical stance, consistent with 19th-century missionary ideals, focuses on socializing the student in core social work values that embed the message that shamanism (spirit-calling) and tribalism (multiple kinship attachments and loyalties) as foundational to traditional Indian identity (Voss et al., 1999b) are unprofessional because they are nonempirical (superstitious), undifferentiated (primitive), and undefined (porous)—all code words for the "savage" or shadow curriculum. The jury is still out on whether there is any way to bring these different worldviews into any kind of meaningful dialogue. The Council on Social Work Education (2001) accreditation standard 6.0, however, extends such an opportunity for bicultural social work educational transformation.

Role of Tribal Colleges in Native Indigenous Homelands

In order to address the lack of access to higher education, and fueled by the American Indian self-determination movement that coalesced in the 1960s, 33 tribal colleges and universities were established in the United States and Canada to help increase access to higher education by American Indians who live on remote tribal lands (AIHEC et al., 2000, p. 1). Located on homelands (reservations) and administered by American-Indian staff, the tribal colleges and universities are a unique resource in bridging traditional American-Indian knowledge, understandings, and cultural practices to the academic disciplines (Red Bird & Mohatt, 1976). The development of these colleges was further supported by the developing "theory of Indian-controlled schools" (Clifford, 1974), which rejected the assimilation process in education and asserted the new Indian ideologies and belief systems that looked to the "internal forces in the Indian community," demanding local control of Indian education that could promote social change from within the reservation. Clifford identified five critical elements of Indian-controlled schools. First of all, there would be an immediacy of contact between young and old; second, it would promote rootedness in the local environment and encourage exploration of traditional wisdom through modern technology; third, it would provide a forum for cultural expansion and creativity; fourth, it would provide employment at the local level; and finally, it would establish control of federal monies to better leverage and promote Indian development and capital. So the shifts in traditional Indian views toward formal education have a long history of Indian intellectual resistance and tribal commitment to the preservation of cultural prerogatives. The authors argue these components are relevant to social work education, particularly in light of the Council on Social Work Education

(CSWE) (2001) accreditation standard 6.0, Nondiscrimination and Human Diversity.

As we look at the troubling failure rates discussed above we must also look at this situation in the context of developing strategies to implement the CSWE (2001) Educational Policy and Accreditation Standards (EPAS) curriculum. To what extent are our post-secondary educational settings and credentialing bodies developing culturally competent curricula and partnerships with tribal colleges as critical cultural resources? Or do they uncritically (unconsciously) apply a set of social expectations inherited from an arcane 19th-century American-Indian education policy modeled on forced assimilation which, unwittingly, creates hostile learning environments for native indigenous (American-Indian) students. Perhaps the under-representation of traditional American Indians within the profession of social work, and overall, low retention and completion rates in the academy provide evidence of active resistance to continuing cultural genocide.

Accreditation Standard 6.0, Nondiscrimination and Human Diversity

The CSWE (2001) EPAS accreditation standard 6.0 mandates that "specific, continuous efforts to provide a learning context in which understanding and respect for diversity . . ." are practiced and *"the program provides a learning context that is nondiscriminatory and reflects the profession's fundamental tenets* [italics added]". While the term "diversity" is not defined in the document, it is significant that "learning environment" is, i.e., that it should be *nondiscriminatory.* Based on the above data documenting the failure of the academy to retain and graduate native indigenous, American-Indian students living in their homelands, how does the CSWE (2001) EPAS accreditation standard 6.0 measure whether, and to what degree, accredited social work programs serving a native indigenous student population meet this standard? Again the CSWE (2001) accreditation standard 6.0 is very clear in identifying criteria to measure compliance in this area, these include *"faculty, staff, and student composition; selection of agencies and their clientele as practicum settings; composition of program advisory or field committees; resource allocation; program leadership; speakers series, seminars, and special programs; research and other initiatives* [italics added]."

To what extent do we see CSWE-accredited programs located near traditional homelands (reservations) incorporating American Indians in these areas? Alex Little Soldier, former chairman of the Rosebud Sioux Tribe viewed tribal sovereignty (see Pevar, 1992, p. 79) as a critical issue in the restoration of tribal identity for his people (Lunderman/Little Soldier, 1992). This issue was also raised by Paul Boyer in his discussion about the critical role of tribal colleges in educating both tribal leadership, native students, and the larger community about sovereignty as a reality for Indian people and not just rhetoric (Boyer, 2004). How does accreditation standard 6.0 incorporate tribal sovereignty into its diversity standard? To what extent are CSWE-accredited programs actively engaged in dialogue with tribal governments and colleges and jointly developing social work curricula that can respond to the realities of our native indigenous homelands (reservations), integrating shamanism and tribalism (Voss et al., 1999b) in substantive ways where the "diversity" standard actually supports tribal sovereignty and cultural integrity? How can accredited social work programs serving native indigenous (American-Indian) students living in their native homelands provide a "nondiscriminatory learning environment" without literally having one (programmatic) foot in the student's homeland (reservation)? Recall the respondent in Weaver's (2000) study who noted, "if [I] hadn't been staying at [a nearby tribal college] the first year I went to [a] social work program . . . I don't think I would have made it" (p. 424). Clearly, the tribal college was part of this student's survival strategy in completing the program, and by extension is a natural resource for CSWE programs seeking cultural proficiency in serving Indian people.

Integrating the "Shadow Curriculum" into the Academy

The route for the effective integration of the shadow curriculum (traditional Indian way) into the institutionalized curriculum (dominant master script) begins by building familial and community connections between the social work program (and respective host university institution) and the student's extended family and respective tribe, including both formal and informal tribal leaders that reflect the student's primary support system. In the dominant institutional model, faculty rarely interact with students' family, generally only on very special circumstances, e.g., at new student orientation, when students are either in academic jeopardy or being recognized for academic excellence, and at commencement. Otherwise faculty-student-family interaction is generally not encouraged. It is viewed as intrusive to the broader expectation that the student should be dealt with as an autonomous individual responsible for him or herself—the mark of maturity. Privacy and confidentiality laws and regulations reinforce this standard. The shadow curriculum begins with a view of the family, extended family, ancestors, and tribe as the most important and essential relational bond between the university and the student. In tribal colleges, extended family members are in positions of power as teachers, administrators, advisors, counselors, and consulted elders and spiritual advisors. Here, non-Indian faculty and staff assimilate tribal values and comprehend traditional practices and also appreciate and support effective survival strategies—there is a deep-felt sense of cultural understanding or awareness *(wo'a'blaza).*

Universities whose mission and purpose are to educate a diverse student population and are interested in the inclusion of traditional American Indians in their respective settings can implement a number of feasible measures to both integrate and infuse traditional content and traditional indigenous native (American-Indian) pedagogies that respect and support both tribal and pedagogical sovereignty as standards for practice.

First of all, social work programs serving traditional Indian homelands should examine the biases in their theoretical orientations and practice frameworks to ensure that alternative theory and value bases are included in their curricula. The incorporation of ethnography and use of narrative theory drawing on cultural oral traditions, the use of contextual and family-systems approaches to social services that emphasize prevention and use risk reduction strategies may reduce the cultural dissonance experienced by indigenous native students from homeland (reservation) communities, by providing theoretical frameworks that are much more consistent with traditional values than more individualistically-oriented intervention approaches. Schriver (2004) offers a detailed discussion of alternative models and approaches in social work practice that addresses this concern. Along with an examination of cultural bias in theoretical models, social work programs should also look at their student service policies to see if there is sufficient flexibility to accommodate cultural needs of Indian students, e.g., are there ample leave or "stop-out" policies that allow Indian students to return home for periods of time to assist family members and to participate in cultural practices (mourning periods, spiritual commitments, etc.)? This specific question was raised by Professor Bates (personal communication, 2004) and echoed by Marjane Ambler (2004) in the "Editor's Essay" in the recent edition of the *Tribal College Journal of American Indian Higher Education*.

Second, social work programs that are situated near native indigenous homelands can explore ways to work together to advance mutual goals and interests; recognized tribal elders may be invited to participate as consultants and advisors or cultural guides to assist university personnel in navigating the cultural differences and issues that will often surface in cross-cultural dialogue between the dominant and traditional communities of the academy and traditional tribal leadership groups (both formal and informal). Social work faculty from CSWE-accredited programs can arrange visits to tribes and develop relationships on a one-on-one basis with faculty at tribal colleges; faculty might also attend the annual AIHEC conference that addresses many of the issues discussed in this paper in practical terms. A directory of tribal colleges is available through AIHEC. Where there is interest and openness, faculty may coordinate student visits and exchanges to, and workshops with, the respective native homelands and tribal colleges. In such a dynamic social context faculty can encourage inter-cultural student discussions, visits with community and reservation elders and cultural keepers, thereby establishing some common ground for collaboration in creating a "nondiscriminatory learning context" effectively building their own respective "shadow curriculum." Where tribal colleges and visiting institutions identify common and compatible interests and mutual trusts, they may develop more formal agreements of cooperation and become partners where they identify ways of sharing resources, developing innovative recruitment programs that include collaboration with high schools serving a majority Indian population on reservations, providing pre-college preparatory programs that specifically address the academic vulnerabilities identified by Wells and others (1997) discussed above (e.g., Upward Bound programs, etc).

For collaborating institutions the options for ensuring cultural proficiency are endless. They can develop cross-listed courses, distance learning/tele-courses, Blackboard chats around topics of interest, as well as jointly developing opportunities for innovative practicum, faculty exchanges, collaborative studies and research projects, etc. with tribal colleges and community colleges serving native indigenous students. It is in this later stage that CSWE-accredited social work programs begin to access the "shadow curriculum" in a meaningful way and find opportunities to infuse the shadow with the institutionalized curriculum, where both can benefit from the new synthesis or even newly uncovered antitheses (e.g., ethical dilemmas, value conflicts, relational patterns, etc.), which may create or sustain impasses. Here cooperating institutions can work together to overcome such obstacles once they are identified.

Conclusion and Recommendations

This paper is an invitation for an engaged dialogue and creative exploration of common concerns and interests between tribal colleges, traditional spiritual leaders, tribal leaders, and elders with social work educators, social work practitioners, and educational policy advocates. The authors conclude with a sense of optimism and hope that CSWE (2001) accreditation standard 6.0 can serve as the catalyst to help shape a traditional shadow curriculum in true partnership between accredited social work programs and tribal colleges genuinely committed to supporting tribal sovereignty. Such partnering will challenge the colonial residue from the 19th-century American-Indian education policy in the U.S. and better reflect and assert the profession's commitment to cultural competence by inventing and designing more inclusive, fluid, responsive, and non-discriminatory educational environments for the development and delivery of social work curricula and practice with Indian people in the homelands. The CSWE (2001) accreditation standard 6.0 is really a mandate for such innovation.

Accreditation Standard 6.0: Inviting Social Work Educators to Think Out-of-the-Box: Suggestions for Transformation in American-Indian Social Work Education

The authors recognize there are countless pressures and pulls from multiple constituencies on all CSWE-accredited social work programs, and that the last thing our colleagues often need is yet another demand for accountability from yet another constituency. The purpose of this article is not to ask the impossible of our social work programs and require ever-greater expenditures with ever-decreasing resources in the ever-increasingly competitive educational environment. What the authors are asserting is that when CSWE-accredited universities partner with or otherwise collaborate with tribal colleges, a new synergy can actually be generated and valuable resources shared among both educational partners, with potential benefits to faculty, students, and administration. Such transformative activities can also have a ripple effect in the way we view the mission, scope, and very identity of the social work profession. We are suggesting that partnerships between CSWE-accredited university programs located near federally recognized American-Indian reservations present a potential cost benefit to both partners. The authors are concerned that social work education is not being incorporated in tribal colleges and that the perception that human services and other counseling degree programs are more workable for Indian students may limit tribal access to professional social work, further alienating the profession from tribal relevance (see above discussion by Klein and Clifford). Accreditation standard 6.0 provides an opportunity for re-engagement by the profession with the federally recognized tribes. It's not too late. Maybe some fresh ideas are needed to activate action.

Contemporary Chinese Social Work Education: Cross-Cultural Comparisons of Resistance and Transformation in Social Work Education

Accredited social work programs interested in partnering with federally recognized tribes could take some cues from our Chinese colleagues who are involved in broad-based educational reforms that are prompting a rigorous analysis of social work practice and education across China that promise to have ripple effects across the profession. Presently, the very core mission of the social work profession is coming under close scrutiny in the face of historical and cultural analysis by indigenous Chinese social work educators and others. This Chinese analysis is relevant to traditional American-Indian experience, particularly in that indigenous Chinese scholars have scrutinized the profession's western biases embedded in its core identity, methods, skill-sets and knowledge-bases, its historical association with Christian evangelization, and the over-emphasis on individual (casework) treatment and empiricism over communal (tribal) and cultural (shamanic) resources and strategies for intervention (Fulcher, 2003; Nimmagadda & Cowger, 1999; Ng, 2003; Tsang, 2000; Tsang & Yan, 2001; Yuen-Tsang & Wang, 2002). There is a growing chorus arguing for substantial change in the way social work is taught and practiced in China, including increasing calls for greater indigenization in social work education and pedagogy through the 21st century (Cheung, Sharon, & Liu, 2004; Jinchao, 1995; Voss, 2004; Xia & Guo 2002).

Policy Themes for American Social Work Transformation in the American Indian Homelands: Cues From the Contemporary Chinese Experience

In the wake of modernization that re-established social work as a sanctioned profession in China in 1986 after its formal abrogation in 1952 (Chamberlain, 1991), Yuen-Tsang & Wang (2002) analyzed developments in social work education in China over the past decade. They noticed some important features that could have bearing on this discussion about social work education in the homelands. A few parallels will be drawn here after summarizing the researchers' key points. They noted that Chinese social work educators rejected borrowing directly from the West and "indiscriminately transplanting those universally accepted standards and models *en bloc* to the Chinese context. Instead, they took a complementary stance whereby universal norms and standards were used as helpful guidelines and references to complement indigenous understanding and practices" (p. 382). Likewise, among tribal colleges across our native homelands, American-Indian faculty and their colleagues are critical of blindly incorporating non-Indian standards and models, and are engaged in a broad-based indigenization process across their curriculum (see AIHEC et al., 2000; White Hat, 1999). From their analysis of this developmental process, Yuen-Tsang & Wang (2002) noted three major features of Chinese social work education transformation in contemporary China, which the authors assert are also relevant to social work education in our native homelands.

First, they noticed a *commitment to community development and social integration.* In response to the China Association for Social Work Education where "it was unanimously agreed that the role of social work education was 'to develop high quality social work expertise, to enhance social development, and to improve the welfare of the people,'" they noticed that "social work education positioned itself as a catalyst for community improvement and social development" (p. 382). In many ways, this is true about social work in the native homelands. Social work should not be an abstraction or just about the administration of mandated social and child welfare programs. It must be a catalyst for social transformation and community improvement. Likewise, research or methods of social inquiry must be related to these transformation goals as well. Here, participatory action research (PAR) (Healy, 2001) is particularly fitting as it draws on core assumptions that reinforce genuine social transformation. PAR assumes that the causes of social problems and oppression lie in macro-social structures and that authentic social change can only be achieved by social transformation. Second, it argues that social forces reinforce the privileges of the "haves" over the "have-nots" and that the dynamics of society maintain this relationship. Finally, PAR seeks "to empower participants to take control of the political and economic forces that shape their lives" (Healy, 2001, p. 95). Selener (1997) noted that "participatory research assumes that returning the power of knowledge generation and use to ordinary, oppressed people will contribute to the creation of more accurate, critical reflection of social reality, the liberation of human potential, and the mobilization of human resources to solve problems" (p. 28).

Second, Yuen-Tsang and Wang (2002) also noticed the pragmatic role that developing *partnerships with government in educational and service development* played in Chinese social work programs. The fact that most social work graduates are employed by the government drew a close connection between social work education and a "heavy emphasis on knowledge and skills pertaining to working with the government bureaucracy" (p. 384). Similarly, most graduates of tribal colleges, for example, from Sinte Gleska University, the tribal college affiliated with the Rosebud Sioux Tribe are recruited for tribal service, often as tribal police, health-care providers, and in support of other tribal services, e.g., human services, drug and alcohol treatment, and tribal administration (White Hat, personal communication, 2004). So, social work education in the homelands needs to teach and relate to tribal law, customs, and procedures on a priority basis—not the other way around, i.e., learning non-Indian law, practices, and procedures and only afterward learning the indigenous bureaucracy.

Finally, Yuen-Tsang and Wang (2002, citing Wang) noted in their analysis "a commitment to the *indigenization of theory and practice in social work in the Chinese context*" (p. 384). Here, "indigenization" was defined as the need to "consider the traditional Chinese culture, the impact of the market economy on people's livelihood, as well as the impact of collectivism and welfarism on the mentality of the people." (p. 384). Curricula at tribal colleges are committed to the indigenization and integration of traditional knowledge, values, and prerogatives throughout the curriculum. Social work education needs to actively engage in this discovery process, not with a rigidly prescribed *a priori* set of standards, but with the capacity to transform its core knowledge, values, and skills within the tribal context in which it is to function. The process needs to be dynamic and interactive versus static and reactive.

It is argued here that if social work education is to be relevant to traditional American Indians living on federally recognized reservations, American social work education must enter a similar period of transformation and indigenization in our native homelands (reservations) as our Chinese colleagues are currently engaged. CSWE-accredited social work programs can support and assist in this creative developmental process. The CSWE (2001) accreditation standard 6.0 provides an impetus for such developmental work.

In closing, the authors recognize they speak from a distinct Lakota cultural and tribal vantage point, and are aware that indigenous people across the Americas and around the world have very different and varied cultural practices, styles of relating, and views about education and pedagogy. This paper is offered not as an overgeneralization about traditional indigenous people, but as an affirmation that traditional indigenous people everywhere have something very important to contribute in educating future social workers. As we reflect on the 30 years that have passed since the American-Indian Movement occupation and confrontation with the U.S. government at Wounded Knee, South Dakota, the authors challenge the social work profession to re-examine the plight of American-Indian education policies and indigenous experiences in light of CSWE (2001) accreditation standard 6.0 to ensure that this standard is not an empty document—words on paper without a commitment to real social change.

References

1. Ambler, M. (2004). The rights and responsibilities of sovereignty. *Tribal College Journal of American Indian Higher Education, 16*(1), 8–9.
2. American Indian Higher Education Consortium, Institute for Higher Education Policy, & Sallie May Education Institute. (2000, May). *Creating role models for change: A survey of tribal college graduates* [Electronic version]. Retrieved February 24, 2005, from http://new.aihec.org/research.html
3. Boyer, P. (2004). Sovereignty: The rhetoric v. the reality. *Tribal College Journal of American Indian Higher Education, 16*(1), 10–13.
4. Chamberlain, E. R. (1991). The Beijing seminar: Social work education in Asia and the Pacific. *International Social Work, 34,* 27–35.

5. Cheung, M., Sharon, B., & Liu, M. (2004). The self-concept of Chinese women and the indigenization of social work in China. *International Social Work, 47,* 109–128.

6. Clifford, G. M. (1974). *The theory of Indian controlled schools.* Washington, DC: Department of Health, Education, and Welfare—Office of Indian Education.

7. Cross, T., Bazron, B. J., Dennis, K. W, & Isaacs, M. R. (1989). *Towards a culturally competent system of care: A monograph on effective services for minority children who are severely disturbed* (vol. 1). Washington, DC: CASSP Technical Assistance Center, Georgetown University Child Development Center.

8. Crozier-Hogle, L., & Wilson, D. B. (Compilers). (1997). *Surviving in two worlds: Contemporary Native American voices.* Austin: University of Texas Press.

9. Enoch, J. (2001). Resisting the script of Indian education: Zitkala Ša and the Carlisle Indian School. *College English, 65*(November), 117–141.

10. Fisher, D. (1979). *American Indian stories.* Lincoln: University of Nebraska Press.

11. Fulcher, L. C. (2003). The working definition of social work doesn't work very well in China and Malaysia. *Research on Social Work Practice, 13,* 376–387.

12. Globalization of Tribal Colleges & Universities: Proceedings and Reference Guide [Electronic version]. (2000, August). Washington, DC: United States Agency for International Development and the United States Department of Agriculture. Retrieved February 24, 2005, from www.aihec.org/AIHEC%20Documents/PDFS/proceedings.pdf

13. Harriman, P. (2000, March). Indian Series. Brain power and the native dream: SD universities, tribal colleges partner to bridge educational gaps [Electronic version]. Retrieved February 24, 2005, from http://nl.newsbank.com/nlsearch/we/Archieves?p_action=doc&p_docid=0F6ABA5711427

14. Healy, K. (2001). Participatory action research and social work. *International Social Work, 44*(1), 93–105.

15. Holler, C. (1995). *Black Elk's religion: The Sun Dance and Lakota Catholicism.* Syracuse, NY: Syracuse University Press.

16. Jinchao, Y. (1995). The developing models of social work education in China. *International Social Work, 38,* 27–38.

17. Johnson, T. W., & Reed, R. F. (Eds.). (2002). *Historical documents in American education.* Boston: Allyn & Bacon.

18. Lame Deer, A. F., & Erdoes, R., (1992). *Gift of power: The life and teachings of a Lakota medicine man.* Santa Fe, NM: Bear & Company.

19. Lunderman, A. (aka Little Soldier). (1992). *Federal policy and social disparity on Indian reservations: Problems and solutions for the 1990s.* Unpublished manuscript. Mission, SD: Sinte Gleska University.

20. McFee, M. (1968). The 150% man, a product of Blackfeet acculturation. *American Anthropologist, 70,* 1096–1103.

21. Nabokov, P. (Ed.). (1991). *Native American testimony: A chronical of Indian-White relations from prophecy to the present.* New York: Penguin.

22. Ng, H-Y. (2003). The 'social' in social work practice: Shamans and social workers. *International Social Work, 46,* 289–301.

23. Nimmagadda, J., & Cowger, C. (1999). Cross-cultural practice: Social worker ingenuity in the indigenization of practice knowledge. *International Social Work, 42,* 261–276.

24. Oetting, E. R., & Beauvais, F. (1991). Orthogonal cultural identification theory: The cultural identification of minority adolescents. *International Journal of the Addictions, 25*(5A and 6A), 655–685.

25. Pevar, S. L. (1992). *The rights of Indians and tribes: The Basic ACLU guide to Indian and tribal rights* (2nd ed.). Carbondale: Southern Illinois University Press.

26. Pratt, R. D. (1973). Official Report of the Nineteenth Annual Conference of Charities and Corrections. In R. H. Pratt (Ed.), *The advantages of mingling Indians with Whites: Americanizing American Indians: Writings by the "friends of the Indian" 1880–1900* (pp. 260–271). Cambridge, MA: Harvard University Press. (Original work published 1892).

27. Red Bird, S., & Mohatt, G. (1976). *Identity through traditional Lakota methods, detailed report.* Rosebud, SD: Sinte Gleska University Archives.
28. Red Lake Band of Chippewa Indians [Web site]. Retrieved July 26, 2004, from http://www.kstrom.net/isk/maps/mn/redlake.htm
29. Schriver, J. M. (2004). *Human behavior and the social environment: Shifting paradigms in essential knowledge for social work practice* (4th ed.). New York: Pearson.
30. Selener, D. (1997). *Participatory action research and social change.* Ithaca, NY: Cornell University Participatory Action Research Network.
31. Standing Bear, L. (1975). *My people the Sioux.* Lincoln: University of Nebraska Press. (Original work published 1928).
32. Tsang, N. M. (2000). Dialectics in social work. *International Social Work, 43,* 421–434.
33. Tsang, A. K. T, & Yan, M-C. (2001). Chinese corpus, western application: The Chinese strategy of engagement with western social work discourse. *International Social Work, 44,* 433–454.
34. Voss, R. W., Douville, V., Little Soldier, A., & White Hat, Sr. (1999a). Wo'Lakol Kiciyapi: Traditional philosophies of helping and healing among the Lakotas: Toward a Lakota-centric practice of social work. *Journal of Multicultural Social Work, 7* (1/2), 73–93.
35. Voss, R. W., Douville, V., Little Soldier, A., & Twiss, G. (1999b). Tribal and shamanic-based social work practice: A Lakota perspective. *Social Work, 44,* 228–241.
36. Voss, R. W. (2004). Building global relations through ethnography—Indigenous traditions of help and healing: An East-West dialogue. In I. M. Corbett, G. Sankaran, & W. W. Cai (Eds.), *Connections and Collaborations in Higher Education* (pp. 69–78). West Chester, PA: West Chester University Printing Services.
37. Weaver, H. N., & Yellow Horse Brave Heart, M., (1999). Examining two facets of American Indian identity: Exposure to other cultures and the influence of historical trauma. In H. N. Weaver (Ed.), *Voices of First Nations People* (pp. 19–33). New York: Haworth Press.
38. Weaver, H. N. (1999). Indigenous people and the social work profession: Defining culturally competent services. *Social Work, 44,* 217–225.
39. Weaver, H. N. (2000). Culture and professional education: The experiences of Native American social workers. *Journal of Social Work Education, 36,* 415–428.
40. Wells, Jr., R. N. (1997). *The Native American experience in higher education: Turning around the cycle of failure II.* New York: St Lawrence University. (ERIC Document Reproduction Service No. ED414108).
41. White Hat, Sr., A. (1999). *Reading and writing the Lakota language. Lakota Iyapi un Wowapi nahan Yawapi.* Salt Lake City: University of Utah Press.
42. Xia, X., & Guo, J. (2002). Historical development and characteristics of social work in today's China. *International Social Welfare, 11,* 254–262.
43. Yuen-Tsang, A. W. K., & Wang, S. (2002). Tensions confronting the development of social work education in China: Challenges and opportunities. *International Social Work, 45,* 375–388.

2

Traditional and Alternative Paradigms

CONNECTING CORE COMPETENCIES *in this chapter*

| Professional Identity | Ethical Practice | Critical Thinking | **Diversity in Practice** | **Human Rights & Justice** | **Research Based Practice** | Human Behavior | Policy Practice | Practice Contexts | Engage Assess Intervene Evaluate |

This chapter outlines the conceptual framework we will use throughout this book. Traditional and alternative paradigms for gathering and organizing knowledge for social work practice are described, compared, and contrasted in this chapter. Five dimensions of traditional and alternative paradigms are outlined. These five dimensions offer some basic perspectives social workers can use to organize a wide range of information about human behavior and the social environment from a number of different disciplines. This framework provides the basic vehicles we will use on our journey to more comprehensive and critical understanding of human behavior and the social environment.

DIMENSIONS OF TRADITIONAL AND DOMINANT PARADIGM

Like paradigms or worldviews in general, the traditional and dominant paradigm is viewed here as a set of interrelated and interlocking dimensions through which what and how we know about the world around us is created, communicated, and controlled. These dimensions include methods (processes), attributes, perspectives, standards, and ways of relating. When these dimensions come together to form the traditional and dominant paradigm, they represent in large part what we are taught to believe in the United States to be right and true.

The traditional and dominant paradigm gains its specific identity in the following ways. It gives primacy to the use of **positivistic, scientific, objective, and quantitative methods (processes)** for creating knowledge upon which to base actions and beliefs. The dominant paradigm places primary value on and reflects **masculine attributes and patriarchal perspectives.** The dominant paradigm evaluates persons' worth and importance according to standards of **whiteness.** Relations with others are constructed with concern for maintaining high degrees of **separateness and impersonality.** Within the dominant paradigm concepts and people tend to be placed in **oppositional or competitive positions** in relation to each other. **Privileged status** is awarded according to the degree to which one displays and adheres to the methods (processes), attributes, perspectives, standards, and ways of relating to others that characterize the traditional and dominant paradigm. We will explore in more depth these dimensions of the traditional and dominant paradigm in the sections that follow.

Positivistic/Scientific/Objective/Quantitative: Ways of Knowing

An important means of understanding the traditional and dominant paradigm is the examination of methods or processes through which knowledge or information is gained and evaluated. These methods or processes are in themselves important components of the traditional and dominant paradigm at the same time that they are mechanisms for creating that worldview. They represent both "ways of knowing" and what is considered "worth knowing." They are central "processes" and essential qualities of "products" in the traditional paradigm. In other words, they are in many respects both *how* and *what* we need to know according to the traditional and dominant paradigm.

Characteristics of this dimension of the traditional and dominant paradigm are: **positivistic, scientific, objective, and quantitative.** These dual purpose characteristics are presented here as an interrelated group. These characteristics are considered together because they are so often applied almost interchangeably in references to the "ways of knowing" and to what is accorded

Research Based Practice

Social workers are expected to comprehend quantitative research and understand scientific approaches to building knowledge. How does the dimension of the traditional paradigm discussed in this section assist us in meeting this expectation?

"worth knowing" (or valid knowledge) according to the traditional paradigm. However, separate descriptions and discussions of these process/product characteristics are presented below for clarity. While we discuss each of these interrelated characteristics separately, we must keep in mind that these characteristics combine to form a single perspective or standpoint from which the world is viewed and evaluated.

Positivistic

The first of these characteristics is a positivistic approach or positivism. Positivism is also often referred to as **empiricism** (Imre 1984:41; Bottomore 1984:22–23). The words **positivism** and **empiricism** refer to *the belief that knowledge is gained through objective observations of the world around us.* Conclusions drawn about that world must be based only on those objective observations (Manheim 1977:12–14; Dawson et al. 1991:247–8, 432). The positivist or empiricist standpoint suggests that *we can know the world with certainty only if we can observe it through our senses.* This perspective carries the assumption that any capable person observing the same event, experience, or object will see, feel, taste, smell, or hear that event, experience or object in exactly the same way. "Truth" or "knowledge" is in fact verified in this way and only in this way (Manheim 1977:12, Dawson et al. 1991:19–20). While many researchers consider positivism and empiricism synonymous, other scholars differentiate the terms. They suggest that *positivism* is a more narrow concept, always based on use of the scientific method (see below) to determine what is knowledge. *Empiricism* is sometimes considered a broader or more inclusive concept that may be applied to ways of gaining knowledge other than through scientific method, such as through qualitative approaches (Heineman Pieper 1995:xxiii; Tyson 1995:9).

Scientific

The second characteristic necessary for knowing and evaluating the world according to the traditional and dominant paradigm is science or the scientific approach. Like the positivistic or empiricist standpoint, a scientific approach requires observation of experiences, events, or objects through our senses. In addition, the **scientific approach** requires "*systematic, controlled, empirical, and critical investigation of hypothetical propositions about the presumed relations among natural phenomena*" (Kerlinger 1973:11). It is through this kind of investigation of the relationship among observable phenomena that we come to know the world and its occupants according to the scientific approach. It is difficult to understate the power accorded the scientific approach to determining what we know and what is worth knowing in dominant U.S. society. In the box below is a summary of the scientific method.

The Scientific Method

"Scientific Method consists of a series of steps for conducting research and a set of prescriptions about how scientific knowledge should be created and judged."

Steps in Scientific Method
1. Choosing research topics
2. Constructing hypotheses
3. Selecting methods
4. Collecting data
5. Analyzing data
6. Interpreting findings and drawing conclusions
   (Alix 1995:41)

Objective

Central to the scientific approach is the third characteristic necessary for knowing and evaluating the world according to the traditional and dominant paradigm—objectivity. An **objective approach** *places a premium on being "unbiased, unprejudiced, detached, impersonal."* **Objectivity** is *"the characteristic of viewing things as they 'really' are"* (Manheim 1977:10). Objectivity requires that the values of the studier be kept completely separate from any event, experience, or object being studied. The person with a scientific perspective "believes...that there is some ultimate link between logical thinking and empirical facts...that objective reality not only exists, but is essentially in one piece, so that there should be no disparity between what is logical and what is empirical" (Dawson et al. 1991:20).

Quantitative

It is not surprising that a paradigm such as the traditional and dominant paradigm—with so much emphasis on gathering and validating knowledge through systematic, objective observations, using our human senses and the senses of others for verifying that knowledge—places great importance on keeping a record of the nature and number of the events, experiences, or objects observed. Thus, the fourth ingredient necessary for knowing and evaluating the world according to the traditional and dominant paradigm is quantitative. A **quantitative approach** *assumes that "all materials are potentially quantifiable"* (Kerlinger 1973:529). *This approach seeks answers to questions by making generalizations about people and things "based on precisely measured quantities"* (Dawson et al. 1991:436). Value, veracity, importance, and power are determined by how often and how much or how many of a given commodity has been observed or accumulated.

As we continue our exploration of other dimensions of the traditional and dominant paradigm, we need to keep in mind their interrelatedness with this powerful and fundamental group of interlocking characteristics. It is through struggling with the complexities of the interwoven nature of the dimensions of the traditional and dominant paradigm that we can come to appreciate the power of this paradigm in our own and others' lives. Just as these four characteristics—positivistic, scientific, objective, and quantitative—depend upon and reinforce each other throughout this "way of knowing" and this means of judging what is "worth knowing," we must recognize the interdependence of this group of processes/products with other dimensions of the traditional and dominant world view.

Masculinity/Patriarchy

The traditional and dominant paradigm places great value on, and reflects attributes that have come to be associated with, maleness or masculinity. This emphasis on valuing masculine attributes has resulted in a system or set of perspectives and institutions referred to as a patriarchy. Interestingly, we will see in our exploration of the masculinity/patriarchy dimension of the traditional and dominant paradigm that a number of the processes/products discussed above—positivistic, scientific, objective, quantitative—have come to be associated closely with maleness or masculinity. These processes/products are also important elements of patriarchal perspectives and institutions.

Patriarchy

Literally, **patriarchy** means "*the rule of the fathers.*" In the social sciences, the meaning of patriarchy is very close to this literal definition. "A **patriarchy** *is a society in which formal power over public decision and policy making is held by adult men*" (Ruth 1990:45). This is a helpful definition for us to use in our exploration of the traditional and dominant paradigm. It implies that the nature of the society and institutions in which we live, their values and priorities, are determined almost exclusively through patriarchy, which is the "embodiment of masculine ideals and practices" (Ruth 1990: 45). It is the contention in this book that the United States is a patriarchy in that public (and many private) decisions and policies are in fact made almost entirely by men. We need only think about the gender composition of such public-policy and decision-making arenas as state legislatures and the U.S. Congress and Supreme Court to verify this assertion (although challenges to exclusive patriarchy are reflected in the candidacies and election of women).

We can find evidence and examples of patriarchy and its influence in realms of our lives other than politics. Belenky et al. (1986:5–6), for example, remind us "that conceptions of knowledge and truth that are accepted and articulated today have been shaped throughout history by the male-dominated culture." They assert that men have drawn on their own perspectives and visions to construct prevailing theories, to write history, and to set values "that have become the guiding principles for men and women alike." Belenky et al. focus their analysis primarily on the patriarchal domination of our educational institutions. Educational institutions, we must remember, are fundamental shapers and socializers of the members, male and female, of society. If you are reading this book as part of a course in a school or program of social work, you are being socialized within the context of an educational institution.

Masculinity

If patriarchy is the embodiment of control over decision and policy making by men, what are some of the attributes of maleness or masculinity that are reflected in patriarchal decisions and policies? Different observers differ somewhat about the specific attributes of masculinity. Ruth provides one useful list of attributes that are representative of what she calls the "**patriarchal ideal of masculinity.**" These attributes include: "aggressiveness, courage, physical strength and health, self-control and emotional reserve, perseverance and endurance, competence and rationality, independence, self-reliance, autonomy, individuality, sexual potency" (Ruth 1990:47).

Easlea (in Ruth 1990:61) provides an illustration of how some of these masculine attributes are reflected in and influence processes and products in the natural sciences, specifically physics. He illustrates how two different dimensions of the traditional and dominant paradigm—masculinity and science—are intertwined. Easlea concurs with the anthropologist Traweek that "those most prestigious of physicists—the members of the high-energy physics 'community'—display the highly masculine behavioral traits of 'aggressive individualism, haughty self-confidence, and a sharp competitive edge' " (Easlea in Ruth 1990:61). This mirroring of masculine traits within physics should come as no surprise when one considers the extent of underrepresentation of women on the faculties of college and universities. For example, the percentage of women full professors in U.S. physics departments was as follows: 1998, 3 percent; 2002, 5 percent; and 2006, 6 percent (Ivie, 2009).

Human Rights & Justice

Social workers are expected to be competent in advancing human rights and social and economic justice. How does the Masculinity/ Patriarchy dimension of the traditional paradigm help us understand the importance of advancing human rights and social and economic justice, especially regarding women?

As long ago as 1913, Bertrand Russell offered an interesting description of the "scientific attitude of mind." His description is strikingly consistent with the attributes of masculinity, the perspectives of patriarchy, and the other characteristics (positivist, objective, scientific, quantitative) of the traditional and dominant paradigm we examined earlier. Russell suggested that "the scientific attitude of mind...involves a sweeping away of all other desires in the interests of the desire to know—it involves the suppression of hopes and fears, loves and hates, and the whole subjective emotional life, until we become subdued to the material, able to see it frankly, without preconceptions, without biases, without any wish except to see it as it is" (Easlea in Ruth 1990:63).

Women and patriarchy

If such fundamental social institutions as politics, education, and the sciences reflect overwhelmingly male attributes and patriarchal perspectives, what are the consequences for women? Westkott (1979:424) offers an observation important for us as students of human behavior about the consequences for women of a traditional and dominant worldview that is so heavily influenced and controlled by masculinity and patriarchy. She observes that "the male character structure and patriarchal culture mutually reflect and support one another through social, political, and economic institutions." The result, she believes, is that "women and other deviants must either become invisible or their estrangement from, or failure in, such a society must be explained in terms of their 'natural' inferiority.... These social contexts...are patriarchal: through the organization of social relations women are controlled by men and are culturally devalued" (Westkott 1979:424).

The powerful interlocking nature of the positivistic, scientific, objective, and quantitative dimension of the traditional/dominant paradigm, along with that of masculinity/patriarchy can hardly be understated. We will continue to explore the consequences and implications for women and for others of the traditional and dominant paradigm as we proceed through this book. Next, however, we will explore how, from the standpoint of the traditional and dominant paradigm, people are viewed and evaluated according to standards of whiteness.

Whiteness

The traditional and dominant paradigm is inordinately influenced by, and its content controlled by, white persons of European descent. What this has come to mean is that all persons, both white and nonwhite, have come to be judged or evaluated in virtually all areas of life according to standards that reflect the values, attitudes, experiences, and historical perspectives of white persons, specifically white persons of European descent. This perspective is so influential that the traditional and dominant world view is increasingly referred to as Eurocentric.

Whiteness, power, and social institutions

The dimension of whiteness, as in the cases of the masculinity/patriarchy and positivistic/scientific/objective/quantitative dimensions, permeates processes and products that make up our worlds and that shape and are shaped by the traditional and dominant worldview. For examples of the predominance of whites in positions of power in this society, one need only look again to the public decision- and policy-making arenas as we suggested in our exploration of masculinity/patriarchy. Pharr (1988) suggests that we also examine through a lens of color the leadership of other social institutions, such as finance and banking, churches and synagogues, and the military. Such an examination will reveal that not only does whiteness predominate in the leadership of social institutions, but it permeates the very nature of what is communicated through those social institutions as well. Pharr reminds us that "in our schools, the primary literature and history taught are about the exploits of white men, shown through the white man's eyes. Black history, for instance, is still relegated to one month, whereas 'American history' is taught all year round" (Pharr 1988:54).

Collins (1989:752) reminds us that when one group, white males, for example, controls fundamental social processes such as the "knowledge-validation" or education/research processes, other voices and ways of knowing are suppressed. She notes that "since the general culture shaping the taken-for-granted knowledge of the community of experts is one permeated by widespread notions of Black and female inferiority, new knowledge claims that seem to violate these fundamental assumptions are likely to be viewed as anomalies." In fact, questions about such notions are unlikely even to be raised "from within a white-male-controlled academic community" (Collins 1989:752).

Whiteness and ethnocentrism

Leigh (1989:6–7) notes that the existing dominant paradigm is highly ethnocentric in its white European bias. This bias has resulted in the oppression of other races and cultures by design. **Ethnocentrism** is the tendency to see one's own group as more important, more valuable than others. We will return to this concept later, but suffice it to say here that white Eurocentric ethnocentrism is a powerful influence in the traditional dominant paradigm. Leigh believes that the negative worldview of African Americans by a dominant white society is a barometer for how all people of color are viewed. For example, the percentage of PhDs in physics awarded to African Americans in 2006 was 2 percent of the total PhDs granted. The percentage for Hispanic Americans was 3 percent of the total. Clearly, these percentages do not reflect the percentages of members of these groups in the general population (AIP 2006). Leigh concludes that social institutions, including social work, have historically failed and continue to fail to recognize minority experiences and wrongfully use white majority experiences as the model experience (Leigh 1989:9). In other words the white bias of the traditional/dominant paradigm excludes as, lacking any significant value, the experiences of people of color.

Exploring Whiteness

To more directly explore the dimension of whiteness and to bring this exploration a little closer to home, you might ask the following questions. How many courses focusing on African Americans, Asian Americans, Latinos, or American Indians are taught in your college or university? Are they required or elective? How many courses focusing on people of color have you taken? How many white students enroll in these courses? How many courses focusing on the experiences of white, Eurocentric people must people of color take in order to meet the graduation requirements in your college or university—history, philosophy, art, music, drama, literature? How many non-Western (non-Eurocentric) civilization courses are required? What was the extent of resistance to the introduction of courses focusing on the history, experiences, and cultural expressions of people of color, if such courses exist at all? These same questions could be asked also about courses reflecting the history and experiences of women in relation to the dimension of masculinity/patriarchy. The results of your assessment will vary somewhat if you are enrolled in a nondominant group institution, for example, a historically black college or university (HBCU).

Again, we notice that fundamental elements of the traditional and dominant paradigm are interwoven. The processes for creating knowledge, masculine and patriarchal attributes and perspectives, and standards of whiteness all interconnect in the traditional and dominant worldview. These interconnecting elements create the conditions for excluding those persons who do not behave in accordance with, or reflect these fundamental dimensions of, the dominant paradigm.

Racisms and power

One way that whiteness finds negative expression in this society is through racism. Jones in Carter and Jones (1996) provides a definition of racism emphasizing the ability of a more powerful group to subordinate a less powerful group:

> Racism results from the transformation of race prejudice and/or ethnocentrism through the exercise of power against a racial group defined as inferior, by individuals and institutions with the intentional or unintentional support of the entire (race or) culture.

Based on the general definition of racism above, Jones in Carter and Jones demonstrates that it is possible to further define and identify the operation of racism at individual, institutional, and cultural levels.

Three types of racism

1. *Individual Racism*—"One considers that Black people (or people of color) as a group are inferior to Whites because of physical (genotypical and phenotypical) traits. [She or] he further believes that these physical traits are determinants of (inferior) social behavior and moral or intellectual qualities, and ultimately presumes that this inferiority is a legitimate basis for inferior social treatment of Black people (or people of color) in American society."

2. *Institutional Racism*—"those established laws, customs, and practices which systematically reflect and produce racial inequalities in American society...whether or not the individuals maintaining those practices have racist intentions" (Carter and Jones 1996). "The clearest indication of institutional racism is disparity in the circumstances of Whites and people of color, which continues from the past into the present."

3. *Cultural Racism*—"the belief in the inferiority of the implements, handicrafts, agriculture, economics, music, art, religious beliefs, traditions, language and story of African (Hispanic, Asian and Indian) peoples;... [and the belief that] Black (and other non-White) Americans *have no* distinctive implements, handicrafts, agriculture, economics, music, art, religious beliefs, traditions, languages or story apart from those of mainstream white America" (Carter and Jones 1996:2–3).

Separate/Impersonal/Competitive

The traditional and dominant paradigm places primacy in relations and relationships on separation, impersonality, and on viewing the world in oppositional or competitive ways. Often this has meant the world has been viewed in what has been referred to as binary or competing and oppositional terms such as "either/or" and "we/they" rather than in cooperative and inclusive terms such as "both/and" and "us" (Derrida in Scott 1988:7).

Separateness and impersonality

In Western philosophy this focus on separateness is seen in the traditional concern for separation of mind (thought) from body (physical). In the natural and the social sciences emphasis is placed, as we saw earlier in our discussions of the scientific approach generally and in physics specifically, on separating personal values from the empirical process of knowledge building. The scientific process, in fact, has long considered any integration of subjective and objective elements as contaminating the process of knowledge building. Science, in order to be scientific, must be conducted impersonally. The education of natural scientists continually stresses the importance of being value free, of being objective, of separating studier from studied (subject from object). The social sciences and many in social work have modeled their approaches to knowledge building on the impersonal and value-free tenets of the natural sciences.

Impersonality and separateness are also associated closely with such valued masculine attributes as independence, autonomy, and individuality. These, you will recall, are elements of the "patriarchal ideal of masculinity." The value placed on these attributes in combination with the importance placed on separateness and impersonal approaches has heavily influenced the nature and focus of research on human development and behavior. Belenky et al., for example, remind us that "the Western tradition of dividing human nature into dual...streams" has resulted in our learning "a great deal about the development of autonomy and independence...while we have not learned as much about the development of interdependence, intimacy, nurturance, and contextual thought" (Belenky et al. 1986:6–7).

We will look in some detail at issues of autonomy and interdependence in Chapters 4 and 5 when we explore traditional and alternative approaches to understanding individual behavior and development. Belenky et al. also point out that "the mental processes that are involved in considering the abstract and the impersonal have been labeled 'thinking' and are attributed primarily to men, while those that deal with the personal and interpersonal fall under the rubric of 'emotions' and are largely relegated to women" (1986:7). Again, the interweaving of the dimensions of the traditional and dominant paradigm is obvious.

Competitiveness: binaries and hierarchies

When ideas or characteristics are divided into **dichotomies or binary oppositions**—as French philosopher/linguist Jacques Derrida refers to this tendency to separate into opposite and competing forces—the opposing sides tend to be hierarchical, with one dominant or primary, the opposite subordinate and secondary (Scott 1988:7). Collins also stresses the tendency of such dichotomous thinking to carry strong implications of systemic inequality. She stresses that "dichotomous oppositional differences invariably imply relationships of superiority and inferiority, hierarchical relationships that mesh with political economies of domination and subordination" (Collins 1986:20).

The Western philosophical tradition, Derrida argues, rests on these binary oppositions or dichotomies in many other areas such as unity/diversity, identity/difference, presence/absence (Scott 1988). Collins addresses the meaning of dichotomous thinking from an African American feminist perspective in the context of human oppression. In doing so she demonstrates the interlocking and interdependent nature of the several dimensions of the traditional/dominant paradigm. "Either/or dualistic thinking, or...the construct of dichotomous oppositional difference, may be a philosophical linchpin in systems of race, class, and gender oppression," she believes. "One fundamental characteristic of this construct is the categorization of people, things, and ideas in terms of their difference [separateness] from one another." The examples of dichotomies she provides—black/white, male/female, reason/emotion, fact/opinion, and subject/object (Collins 1986:20)—speak loudly of the dichotomies implicit in the traditional and dominant paradigm.

Social work also has a history of struggling with dichotomies or dualities. Berlin points out that social work "is built on a foundation of dualities." She notes our contrasting commitments to "individual adaptation and social change" or "to humanistic values and scientific knowledge development." Social work continues to struggle over which side of these dualities to align itself with. Over our history we have moved from side to side at different points—sometimes moving toward a focus on individual change, sometimes toward social change; sometimes emphasizing our humanistic values as primary, sometimes emphasizing scientific aspects of social work. Many would argue that our alignments have more often gone with individual adaptation and science than with social change and humanistic values. That the struggle and tension continue to involve both sides of these dichotomies rather than shifting entirely to one side and remaining there can be considered a strength of the field (Berlin 1990:55).

Privilege

Human Rights & Justice

Professional social workers are expected to understand the forms and mechanisms of oppression and discrimination. How do the concepts of privilege and white privilege assist us in gaining this understanding?

The impact of the traditional and dominant paradigm in all its varied manifestations is hardly neutral or value free. The paradigmatic elements that we have explored so far all carry with them differential meanings and very different results for different people. Those who benefit are those who define, fit, and enforce the processes, attributes, perspectives, standards, and ways of relating that characterize the traditional and dominant paradigm. The set or system of benefits that accrue to these persons is referred to as **privilege.** We end our examination of the elements of the traditional and dominant paradigm with a brief exploration of privilege. The concept of privilege will be a continuing concern for us as we move on in our journey toward greater understanding of human behavior and the social environment.

Norm of rightness

Privilege is used synonymously here with what Pharr (1988:53) refers to in discussing the common elements of oppressions as a "**defined norm, a standard of rightness and often righteousness.**" This norm is used to judge all other persons. It is backed up by institutional and economic power; by institutional and individual violence. In the United States, Pharr characterizes the determiner and enforcer of this norm as "male, white, heterosexual, Christian, temporarily able-bodied, youthful with access to wealth and resources." She makes an important observation about this "defined norm" that is essential to our understanding of privilege. She urges us to remember "that an established norm does not necessarily represent a majority in terms of numbers; it represents those who have the ability to exert power and control over others" (Pharr 1988:53).

White privilege

In U.S. society, the ability to exert power and control over others is often associated with whiteness, what one might refer to as *white privilege.* However white people are often unaware or unwilling to recognize how closely whiteness is associated with privilege in the United States Helms (1994:305) suggests that the reality, existence, and persistence of white privilege is often denied by white people. This denial may even take the form of denying that an identifiable

privileged white racial group exists. She argues that "disavowal of the existence of White privilege takes the form of denying that a White *racial* group
exists that benefits from White privilege." We will further explore issues and
models related to white racial identity and identity development in Chapter 5.

Privilege is that powerful but often unspoken and taken-for-granted sense
that one fits, that one is an active and powerful participant and partner in
defining and making decisions about one's world. It is that sense that one's
worldview is in fact dominant. Privilege is the total of the benefits one accrues
as a result of that dominance. Unfortunately, such a definition of privilege is
accompanied by the reality that this privilege is gained and maintained at the
expense of others: It is exclusive.

Peggy McIntosh, a feminist scholar, offers dramatic, real-life examples of
the benefits that accrue to those of us who reflect characteristics of the "norm
of rightness" and who "fit" the dimensions of the traditional and dominant
paradigm. McIntosh specifically addresses what she refers to as "skin-color
privilege," or what we have referred to here as "whiteness." However, implications for the meaning of privilege flowing from other attributes of the "norm of
rightness" can be drawn from her examples as well. The following are some
particularly illuminating and concrete examples of what it means on a day-to-
day basis to have white privilege. These examples can help bring to a conscious level many of the "taken-for-granted" aspects of both whiteness and
other elements of privilege.

As a white person, McIntosh, points out:

- I can turn on the television or open to the front page of the paper and
  see people of my race widely and positively represented.
- I can be sure that my children will be given curricular materials that
  testify to the existence of their race.
- I can be reasonably sure that if I ask to talk to "the person in charge," I
  will be facing a person of my race.
- I can easily buy posters, postcards, picture books, greeting cards, dolls,
  toys, and children's magazines featuring people of my race.
- I can be late to a meeting without having the lateness reflect on my
  race.
- I can choose blemish cover or bandages in "flesh" color and have them
  more or less match my skin. (McIntosh 1992:73–75)

McIntosh offers many more examples illustrating the privileges that accrue
to white people by virtue of their color. (The reader is encouraged to read
McIntosh's article, "White Privilege and Male Privilege," cited at the end of
this chapter.)

DIMENSIONS OF ALTERNATIVE/POSSIBLE PARADIGMS

As is the case with paradigms in general, alternative paradigms are sets of
interrelated and interlocking dimensions through which what and how we
know about the world around us is created, communicated, and controlled.
Like all paradigms, alternative paradigms include methods (processes), attributes, perspectives, standards, and ways of relating.

Alternative paradigms incorporate **interpretive, intuitive, subjective, and
qualitative** products and processes for creating knowledge upon which to base
actions and beliefs. Alternative paradigms do not necessarily exclude the
processes and products (positivistic, scientific, objective, quantitative) of the

traditional/dominant paradigm. They do not, however, recognize those processes and products as the only or necessarily the most appropriate avenues to understanding and action. The alternative paradigms we consider value and reflect **feminine attributes and feminist perspectives.** They do not give primacy to masculine attributes or patriarchal perspectives. The alternative paradigms we explore evaluate persons' worth and importance according to standards of the inherent worth and dignity of all humans, and they especially recognize the benefits of **human diversity.** Persons are not evaluated according to standards of whiteness. The alternative paradigms we will explore structure relations with others around recognition of the **interconnected and personal** nature of our relationships with other persons and with the elements of the worlds around us. Separateness and impersonality are seen as obstacles to constructing effective relationships. The alternative paradigms with which we are concerned do not assume a competitive stance in which people or ideas are in opposition to one another. They instead focus on the **integrative and complementary** nature of differences among people and ideas. The alternative paradigms through which we will attempt to view our worlds seek recognition of **oppressions** and the elimination of conditions and relations that allow some persons and groups privilege at the expense of others. These are the critical dimensions of alternative paradigms through which we will attempt to find and create new ways to view our worlds. These interrelated dimensions are explored in more detail in the following sections.

Interpretive/Intuitive/Subjective/Qualitative: Ways of Knowing

Research Based Practice

Professional social workers comprehend qualitative research. How does the alternative paradigm dimension of "Interpretive/Intuitive/ Subjective/Qualitative: Ways of Knowing" addressed in this section reinforce the importance of comprehending qualitative research?

In our discussion of the traditional and dominant paradigm, we noted that examination of the methods and processes through which knowledge or information is gained and evaluated is essential for understanding that paradigm. The methods and processes for gaining and evaluating information and knowledge are essential components of and avenues for creating alternative worldviews as well. Our alternative paradigms are characterized by an emphasis on "ways of knowing" that are more interpretive, intuitive, subjective, and qualitative than those of the dominant paradigm we explored earlier in this chapter. These characteristics also represent alternative types of knowledge "worth knowing." Although these alternative ways of knowing and of evaluating what is worth knowing often have not been valued within the purview of the traditional and dominant paradigm, they offer essential avenues for social workers to gain a more complete understanding of humans, our behaviors, and the social environments we construct and inhabit.

The interpretive, intuitive, subjective, and qualitative dimension of alternative paradigms for understanding human behavior is discussed in some detail next. Although we discuss the characteristics—interpretive, intuitive, subjective, and qualitative—of this dimension separately, it is important to keep in mind that all these characteristics are interrelated and combine to form the process/products of the alternative worldviews we are seeking to understand.

Interpretive knowledge

The first characteristic of alternative paradigm knowledge building and validating processes we will consider is the interpretive aspect. While they are often controversial, shifts toward more interpretive approaches to understanding humans and their behaviors have been under way for some time. (In Chapter 1, you might recall, we explored in some detail the concept and consequences of "shifts" in paradigms.) Edmund Sherman (1991:69) discusses shifts occurring in the ways we think about and gather information in the social sciences. He notes that many people in these fields "are questioning just how scientific the social sciences can and should be." Rather than using the "science" dimension of the traditional/dominant paradigm as the sole methodology for understanding our worlds, some social scientists are shifting to methods more characteristic of those used in the liberal arts, specifically, the humanities.

Sherman suggests that representative of this shift are changes in the language used to describe knowledge-gathering methods or processes in the social sciences. He notes that many social scientists are using words such as " 'interpretation,' 'hermeneutics,' and 'rhetoric' in calling for a new mode of inquiry that draws as much from the humanities as from the natural sciences, if not more" (Winkler 1985 in Sherman 1991:69). These descriptors—interpretation, hermeneutics, rhetoric—are much more consistent with knowledge-gathering processes in the liberal arts and humanities than those in the natural sciences. It should come as no surprise that those of us who depend on knowledge of human behavior to do our work would look to the "humanities"—"the branches of learning having primarily a cultural character" (Webster 1983)— for help in understanding the human condition.

A term often used as a synonym for these **interpretive approaches** to gaining understanding is **hermeneutics.** According to Webster, "Hermeneutics can be most simply defined as 'the science of interpretation' " (1983:851). Perhaps a good way to expand our understanding of interpretive or hermeneutic approaches to knowledge building is to visit some of the humanities from which the concept is taken—philosophy and history. Philosopher and historian Wilhelm Dilthey used the term **hermeneutics** to denote "the discipline concerned with the investigation and interpretation of human behavior, speech, institutions, etc., as essentially intentional" (Dilthey in Sherman 1991:71). Dilthey's hermeneutic approach to understanding history "emphasized the 'reliving' or entering into the subjective, experiential worlds of those who lived and originally wrote about the historical events under study" (Sherman 1991:71). This meaning sounds a lot like what we are seeking to learn to do as we study HBSE, does it not?

This interpretive, hermeneutic approach is quite similar to what social workers mean when we talk about such basic concepts as "**empathy**" and "**beginning where the client is.**" These interpretive approaches to knowing are concerned in large part with understanding the meaning of human experiences. These attempts to understand the meaning of human experiences take us well beyond the realm of traditional scientific approaches to knowledge building. They take us out of the laboratory and into the everyday worlds in which we and the people with whom we work actually live our lives.

This search involves going from the detached observation characteristic of science to the kind of expressive involvement more often associated with the arts. Reason and Hawkins (in Reason 1988:80) suggest that understanding the meaning of experience is accomplished "when we tell stories, write and act in plays, write poems, meditate, create pictures, enter psychotherapy, etc. When we partake of life we create meaning; the purpose of life is making meaning." These diverse methods/processes for expanding our understanding of human behavior and experience hold rich and varied potential (some already in use, such as art therapy, others virtually unexplored) for use by social workers. These approaches or "ways of knowing" are unavailable through the knowledge-building processes of the traditional/dominant paradigm.

Another important benefit of a hermeneutic or interpretive approach to understanding is its emphasis on encouraging "observers to understand their own preconceptions and take into account their own values" (Dean and Fenby 1989:48). This is another important part of the practice of professional social work. As social workers we must develop **self-awareness**—an awareness of the influence of our personal worldview on our own behaviors and on our perceptions of the behavior of others.

Intuitive knowledge

A second characteristic of alternative routes to knowing and understanding is **intuition** or **intuitive knowledge.** Fritjof Capra (1983), a physicist, explains that "**intuitive knowledge** . . . is based on a direct, nonintellectual experience of reality arising in an expanded state of awareness. It tends to be synthesizing, holistic, and nonlinear." Reason (1981) offers a similar description in the profile proposed by Jung to describe persons who use intuition as a way of knowing. These persons "take in information through their imagination, and are interested in the whole, in the gestalt; they are idealists, interested in hypothetical possibilities, in what might be, in the creation of novel, innovative viewpoints" (Reason 1981:44). This kind of holistic thinking, the ability to see the "big picture," is essential to social work knowledge and practice.

The intuitive element of our alternative paradigm is often difficult to grasp, especially for those of us (and that is virtually all of us) who have been educated almost exclusively to think according to the dominant paradigm.

Abraham Maslow (1962) referred to such intuitive knowledge as "peak experience." More commonly, we talk about "the light bulb going on" in our heads when we suddenly attain new understanding, but we are not sure precisely how we attained that understanding. Esterson (in Reason and Rowan 1981:169) describes the combination of interpretation and intuition as part of the process in new paradigm research leading to the emergence of a hypothesis about or "some interpretation of the events being considered—some guess as to what's going on . . . this often appears as an intuitive flash, emerging between a period of active reflection and a period of rest."

Some scholars suggest that intuition plays a part in knowledge-building processes of all kinds, even those in the natural sciences. Polanyi (1964 in Moustakas 1981:209) suggests that "some intuitive conception of the general nature of things" is involved in "every interpretation of nature, whether scientific, non-scientific or anti-scientific." Some social workers historically have referred to this more intuitive/interpretive aspect of knowledge building as the art of social work.

Subjective understanding

A third element valued in alternative approaches to gaining knowledge and closely related to intuitive ways of knowing is **subjective understanding.** Subjective knowledge, like intuitive ways of knowing, respects personal experience as an important/valuable/valued influence on what is known and how we view the world.

Experiencing Intuition by Zukav 1980:40

The next time you are awed by something, let the feeling flow freely through you and do not try to 'understand' it. You will find that you *do* understand, but in a way that you will not be able to put into words. You are perceiving intuitively.

Subjective Understanding by James Hillman 1975 in Reason 1988:80

My soul is not the result of objective facts that require explanation; rather it reflects subjective experiences that require understanding.

Belenky et al. describe subjective knowledge as "a perspective from which truth and knowledge are conceived of as personal, private, and subjectively known or intuited" (1986:15).

Subjective knowledge calls into question the exclusive focus on objectivity as *the* most valuable path to knowing that is characteristic of the dominant paradigm. Belenky et al. remind us of the Eurocentric bias at work in thinking of objectively derived knowledge as the only real or legitimate knowledge. Such a perspective is not universal: "In many non-Western and non-technological societies, subjective knowledge and intuitive processes hold a more esteemed place in the culture" (Belenky et al. 1986:55). To accept as valuable knowledge that which comes about through personal, subjective experience is an example of respecting and learning through diverse non-Western, alternative paradigms.

A **subjective perspective** on knowledge building assumes that "realities are not objectively 'out there' but are constructed by people, often under the influence of a variety of social and cultural factors that lead to shared constructions" (Guba and Lincoln 1989). Knowledge building or the development of understanding from this perspective "involves a state of awareness which integrates our subjective experience with our critical faculties so that we can develop a perspective on our discoveries and learning" (Reason 1988:230). This kind of knowledge building begins with and values personal experiences and perspectives, but it is also influenced by and develops collective meanings through rigorous processes of exchanging criticism and sharing of personal/subjective experiences with others in the social and cultural environment. Thus, personal or subjective approaches to knowledge building require rigorous processes of validation and testing in social and environmental contexts (Reason and Rowan 1981:xii–xiv).

In a study of the ways women derive and validate knowledge, Belenky et al. identified "subjective knowers." Their description of subjective knowers suggests how neglected and unrecognized intuitive or subjective sources of understanding remain. One of the women in their study eloquently described the intuitive/subjective dimensions of these avenues to knowing about and understanding the world around her: "There's a part of me that I didn't even realize I had until recently—instinct, intuition, whatever. It helps me and protects me. It's perceptive and astute. I just listen to the inside of me and I know what to do" (Belenky et al. 1986:69). This woman articulates not only the personal and powerful nature of this way of knowing, but she also reminds us that we are often unaware of this important and personally affirming dimension of knowing. Social workers who recognize, respect, and trust this way of knowing open up important pathways to insight into human behavior at the same time that we facilitate the active, personal involvement in the knowledge-building process of those persons with whom we work.

Spirituality   An often neglected area of subjective approaches to understanding is that of spirituality. Cowley and Derezotes suggest that social workers must "begin to look at the spiritual dimension—along with other dimensions such as physical, emotional, cognitive, cultural, organizational, or socio-political—in the client systems, organizations, and communities that they serve" (1994:33).

Sermabeikian points out that "Our professional knowledge and understanding of spirituality can be enhanced by an examination of traditional and nontraditional religions and of nonreligious humanistic and existential philosophies" (1994:182).

It is also helpful to understand the major schools of thought concerning the basic nature of spirituality. Miovic (2004:106) defines three basic perspectives that define the nature of one's spiritual beliefs:

1. *Theism* is the belief in the existence of God (a supreme being or spiritual reality), an immortal soul, or any other type of deity or deities.

2. *Atheism* is the belief in the nonexistence of God (or any type of soul or deity), which in the modern world is often expressed as the materialist hypothesis that matter is the only reality.

3. *Agnosticism* is the belief that the question of whether or not God (or any type of soul or deity) exists either has not been or cannot be answered.

Cowley and Derezotes note that spirituality is considered by many to be a "universal aspect of human culture." However, they are also careful to point out (and as we differentiate below) "spirituality is not considered as equivalent with *religion, religiosity, or theology*. . . . The use of the word 'spiritual,' then is neither a statement of belief per se nor a measure of church attendance; indeed an atheist can have a profound spiritual life." They do point out clearly, however, their conclusion of the importance of spirituality as a part of our subjective understanding and experience of ourselves and the world around us. They assert that "spirituality is an essential aspect of being that is existentially subjective, transrational, nonlocal, and nontemporal" (Cowley and Derezotes 1994:33).

Sermabeikian points out the alternative paradigm thinking necessary to incorporate understanding of spirituality. She suggests that "To understand the spiritual perspective, we must be willing to reverse our usual way of thinking and looking, which is linear and externally focused. We must look beyond what is easily counted and accounted for and examine what does not fit into our categories and conceptions of the world. There can be no preconceived notions about what may be helpful. The spiritual perspective requires that we look at the meaning of life, that we look beyond the fears and limitations of the immediate problem with the goal of discovering something inspirational and meaningful rather than focusing on the past and on pathology" (1994:179). To express the fundamental nature of spirituality for humans Sermabeikian uses Siporin's description of the transcendent and multisystem nature of spirituality. Siporin suggests that "It is in terms of a spiritual dimension that a person strives for transcendental values, meaning, experience and development; for knowledge of an ultimate reality; for belonging and relatedness with the moral universe and community; and for union with the immanent, supernatural powers that guide people and the universe for good and evil" (1994:180).

As is the case with social work, in its increasing attention given to the importance of spirituality in the lives and environments of the persons, families, and communities we serve, psychology and psychiatry have also given increased attention to the significant role of spirituality in both assessment and intervention. For example, Miovic notes:

Other important contemporary developments in Western spiritual psychology include the continued growth of 12-step programs for substance abuse and other addictive disorders, as well as hospice care and psychooncology. In these two, independent clinical traditions, spirituality is taken seriously and theistic worldviews are accepted, according to patient preference and provider comfort level. Moreover, new educational initiatives have introduced curricula on religion and spirituality into the training of psychiatric residents. (Miovic, 2004:109)

Religion and spirituality   While spirituality is not the equivalent of religion or religiosity, as we noted above, the two concepts are often related in many ways. Canda (1989:39) differentiates between religion and spirituality. **Spirituality** is "the general human experience of developing a sense of meaning, purpose, and morality." **Religion,** on the other hand is the "formal institutional contexts of spiritual beliefs and practices" (Canda 1989:39).

Canda recommends a comparative approach to incorporating religious content into social work and offers a set of guidelines for approaching issues related to religion and spirituality in practice. The guidelines suggest the social worker:

1. Examines religion and spirituality as general aspects of human culture and experience
2. Compares and contrasts diverse religious behaviors and beliefs
3. Avoids both sectarian and anti-religious biases
4. Encourages dialogue that is explicit about value issues and respects value differences
5. Examines the potential benefit or harm of religious beliefs and practices
6. Emphasizes the relevance of the social worker's understanding of religion to providing effective service to clients. (1989:38–39)

Canda also presents Wilber's description of several common ways of defining religion in sociological and psychological thinking:

- An engagement of non-rational, intuitive, and symbolic mental activity
- An existential process of developing personal and collective understandings of life's meaning, purpose, and the integration of self and world
- A psychosocial attempt to defend against anxiety aroused by crisis, suffering, and the inexplicable
- A personal and collective process of developing greater depth of communion between the human and the divine or transcendent
- A fantasy produced as the result of developmental fixation or regression
- An esoteric aspect of behavior involving participation in institutions of religion and codifications of belief
- An esoteric aspect of human experience involving mystical awareness and expanded states of consciousness. (1989:39)

It is important to develop an open and critical approach to understanding spirituality and religion and the roles they play in our personal, community, and social lives. For example, Sermabeikian notes the potential of spirituality and religion to be both helpful and harmful depending on the nature of their expression. She notes specifically that

As a human need, spirituality is multidimensional, and as such it can be manifested in healthy and unhealthy ways. Bergin (1990) noted that "spiritual phenomena have equal potential for destructiveness, as in the fundamentalist hate groups" (p. 401). Religious pathology, rigid ideologies, religious fervor associated with mental illness, cult involvement, and the nonconstructive consequences of certain beliefs and practices present additional challenges to professionals. (1994:181–182)

Science and spirituality

Science and spirituality are often considered two incompatible or even opposing worldviews. For example, Miovic (2004:107) notes:

> science is often wrongly equated with atheism, whereas the scientific method is, properly speaking, agnostic. Science does not *prove* that matter is the only reality. Instead, science starts with the operational *assumption* that it can fruitfully apply the experimental method only to material events, forces, and processes that are quantifiable, repeatable, and measurable. It can say nothing about immeasurable and unique material phenomena (which may well exist) or about nonmaterial forces, beings, and events, because neither of these can be subjected to the experimental method. Therefore, science ought not to be invoked as an arbiter of truth in debates on the ultimate nature of reality, although it is an excellent tool for investigating the material universe.

Contrary to science and spirituality existing in opposition to one another, some findings in areas such as quantum physics (discussed in Chapter 3), actually question the ability to simplistically view the world only through a traditional objective scientific lens. Some of these findings, according to Miovic, "completely discredit the simplistic notions of space, time, and causality that most of us take for granted in daily life, and show matter to be far more mysterious and problematic than psychological and neurophysiological models of mind generally assume" (Miovic 2004:107).

In addition, Miovic notes the emergence of empirical evidence to support the significance of spiritual perspectives in addressing a number of specific mental health concerns. For example, he notes, "today, the Buddhist influence is seen in empirical research on both mind-body medicine and psychotherapy. Herbert Benson's pioneering work on meditation and the relaxation response...has been replicated and extended in studies of Buddhist 'mindfulness' meditation (nonjudgmental awareness of the moment), which show that this type of practice ameliorates symptoms of anxiety,...chronic pain,...and fibromyalgia" (2004:110).

Sermabekian suggests there is a spiritual component in social work: "Our professional spirituality could be defined as the collective inspiration derived from the ideal of human compassion or well-being that drives us to advance our cause" (1994:182).

Qualitative approaches

A fourth avenue to knowing valued in alternative paradigms is **qualitative information and approaches.** Capra suggests that "a true science of consciousness will deal with qualities rather than quantities, and will be based on shared experience rather than verifiable measurements. The patterns of experience constituting the data of such a science cannot be quantified into fundamental elements, and they will always be subjective to varying degrees" (Capra 1983:376). Our alternative paradigm for gathering and creating social work knowledge respects and values qualitative ways of knowing. This area of knowledge seeking and understanding is especially fitting for studying HBSE because of its consistency with social work values, practices, and goals. The qualitative characteristic is interwoven with the other characteristics—interpretive, subjective, intuitive—of this dimension of alternative-paradigm thinking we have discussed here.

Cobb and Forbes (2002:M197) refer to "qualitative research as an approach to the study of human behavior that relies on the analysis of narrative data to create an interpretation of the meaning of these behaviors from the perspective of the participants themselves, within their own social context. Put more simply, qualitative researchers go into a particular setting such as a nursing home, clinic, or community, and, over time, they watch, listen, ask questions, take notes, and try to understand as fully as possible how persons in that setting see and experience their world. Qualitative research requires the researcher to be engaged in the lives of the people studied—to hear their stories, grasp their point of view, and understand their meanings."

Cobb and Forbes (2002:M198) note that "the three most commonly used qualitative approaches are ethnography, which originated in anthropology; grounded theory, which was developed in sociology; and phenomenology, descended from philosophy and psychology." They also note that these three approaches have both similarities and differences:

- Ethnography has as its purpose the description of a culture and the meaning of human behaviors within the cultural context.
- The goal of a grounded theory study is to inductively develop a theory "grounded" in data obtained through direct observation, interviewing, and field work.
- Phenomenological studies rely primarily on in-depth interviews with a small number of people who share a common experience, often one that is difficult to measure, such as an emotion like suffering or courage. The goal is to identify and describe the essence of the experience as it is lived by those who have the experience.

Qualitative ways of knowing respect the importance of "subjective meanings of events to individuals and groups" (Epstein in Dawson et al. 1991:244). This approach also "allows the acceptance of multiple rationales, conflicting value systems, and separate realities" (Rodwell in Dawson et al. 1991:244). In this way it shares with social work an appreciation of diversity and of the importance of participation and partnership by all persons involved.

Alternative approaches to knowing: heuristic, naturalistic, and postmodern

Two interrelated alternative approaches to traditional positivistic, scientific, objective, and quantitative approaches to creating knowledge and understanding are heuristic and naturalistic research approaches or paradigms. It is important to note that rather than simply being the opposite of traditional ways of knowing (scientific, positivistic, etc.), heuristic approaches encompass many aspects of traditional scientific approaches. Heuristic researchers simply do not consider traditional scientific approaches to be the only or necessarily the best approaches to knowledge building. Note in the discussion below that heuristic research is referred to as scientific, though, the meaning of "science" is very different from traditional positivistic, quantitative, objective views of science. Many supporters of heuristic approaches suggest these approaches are especially applicable to the human-focused concerns of social workers. We will examine both heuristic and naturalistic modes of inquiry or research next. One way to begin to think about these alternative approaches is to think of them as closely related and to some extent containing each other. Heuristic approaches, however, seem to be more general ways of thinking about doing research and naturalistic approaches as described here are more specifically focused on the methods and "how-tos" of conducting research using a naturalistic paradigm.

Heuristic research Heineman Pieper, one of social work's leading proponents of this approach, defines **heuristic** very broadly to mean "any problem-solving strategy that appears likely to lead to relevant, reliable, and useful information." She adds that "a 'heuristic' is a problem-solving strategy whose goal is utility rather than certainty" (1995:207). The heuristic researcher takes the realistic view that real-life problems are too complex, interactive, and perceiver-dependent to lend themselves to comprehensive analysis and exact solutions" (Heineman Pieper 1995:209). Tyson offers perhaps the most inclusive description of heuristic research in her statement that "One of the central ideas in the heuristic approach to scientific research...is that all ways of knowing are heuristics, and that no one way of knowing is inherently superior to any other for generating scientific knowledge" (1995:xiv).

While both Tyson and Heineman Pieper refer to the heuristic paradigm as scientific, Heineman Pieper is careful to distinguish between traditional and alternative meanings of science and to argue that the heuristic approach is more appropriate for social work research, especially in the context of practice: "Unlike the logical positivist paradigm, the heuristic paradigm welcomes the complex, ill-structured, substantively important problems that have been social work's abiding focus" (1995:207). In addition, she argues that heuristic approaches can produce information more directly meaningful to both social work practitioners and the consumers of our services. "In contrast to the logical positivist assumption that the five senses give us direct reports of reality, reality is actually constructed through the interpretation of sensory experience within a preexisting framework of meanings. In other words, knowledge is to some extent perceiver dependent.... [T]he heuristic researcher selects types of data and methods of data gathering for their appropriateness both to the theory chosen to guide the research and also to the problem under study.... The heuristic paradigm suggests that practitioners' and clients' judgments should be evaluated by the same rules as any other data, namely, by whether they lead to useful knowledge and more effective service" (Heineman Pieper 1995:211–212). However, heuristic research proponents acknowledge a number of misunderstandings about this approach.

Heuristic and naturalistic research advocates hope that increasing attention to research done consistent with this alternative paradigm will be not only more meaningful for practitioners and consumers of research, but will actually re-engage practitioners in doing research, because this approach to research does not alter their practice and does respect their abilities and judgments as appropriate and important in the research process. This alternative has the potential for removing the false separation, proponents believe, that has existed between research and practice and between researchers and practitioners, because they are one and the same.

Naturalistic inquiry A more specifically delineated approach to naturalistic research has been described by Lincoln and Guba. They offer the following definition of naturalistic inquiry and then describe fourteen "interdependent characteristics" of naturalistic inquiry. **Naturalistic inquiry** is devoted to understanding

> actualities, social realities, and human perceptions that exist untainted by the obtrusiveness of formal measurement or preconceived questions. It is a process geared to the uncovering of many idiosyncratic but nonetheless important stories told by real people, about real events, in real and natural ways.... Naturalistic inquiry attempts to present 'slice-of-life' episodes documented through natural language and representing as closely as possible how people feel, what they know, and what their

concerns, beliefs, perceptions, and understanding are. (Wolf and Tymitz in Guba and Lincoln 1981:78)

The concepts, inductive and deductive reasoning, can help differentiate knowledge creation using traditional positivistic approaches and those using alternative

Fourteen Interdependent Characteristics of Naturalistic Inquiry (Research)*

1. *Natural setting*—Researcher carries out research in the natural setting or context of the entity for which study is proposed because "realities are wholes that cannot be understood in isolation from their contexts, nor can they be fragmented for separate study of the parts."

2. *Human instrument*—Researcher uses "him- or herself as well as other humans as the primary data-gathering instruments (as opposed to paper-and-pencil...instruments) because it would be virtually impossible to devise...[prior to entering the research environment] a non-human instrument with sufficient adaptability to encompass and adjust to the variety of realities that will be encountered."

3. *Utilization of tacit knowledge*—Research argues for valuing "tacit (intuitive, felt) knowledge in addition to propositional knowledge (knowledge expressible in language form) because often the nuances of the multiple realities can be appreciated only in this way."

4. *Qualitative methods*—Researcher uses "qualitative methods over quantitative (although not exclusively) because they are more adaptable to dealing with multiple [and less quantifiable]... realities."

5. *Purposive sampling*—Researcher is likely to forego "random or representative sampling in favor of purposive or theoretical sampling because he or she thereby increases the scope or range of data exposed (random or representative sampling is likely to suppress more deviant cases) as well as the likelihood that the full array of multiple realities will be uncovered."

6. *Inductive data analysis*—Researcher "prefers inductive (to deductive) [see below for definitions of inductive and deductive] data analysis because that process is more likely to identify the multiple realities to be found in those data."

7. *Grounded theory*—Researcher "prefers to have the guiding substantive theory emerge from (be grounded in) the data because *no* [pre-existing]... theory could possibly encompass the multiple realities that are likely to be encountered."

8. *Emergent design*—Researcher "elects to allow the research design to emerge (... unfold) rather than to construct it preordinately (a priori) because it is inconceivable that enough could be known ahead of time about the many multiple realities to devise the design adequately."

9. *Negotiate Outcomes*—Researcher "prefers to negotiate meanings and interpretations with the human sources from which the data have chiefly been drawn because it is their constructions of reality that the inquirer seeks to reconstruct."

10. *Case study reporting mode*—Researcher "is likely to prefer the case study reporting mode (over the scientific or technical report) because it is more adapted to a description of the multiple realities encountered at any given site."

11. *Idiographic interpretation*—Researcher "is inclined to interpret data including the drawing of conclusions **idiographically** (in terms of the particulars of the case) rather than **nomothetically** (in terms of law-like generalizations) because different interpretations are likely to be meaningful for different realties."

12. *Tentative application*—Researcher "is likely to be tentative (hesitant) about making broad application of the findings because realities are multiple and different."

13. *Focus-determined boundaries*—Researcher "is likely to set boundaries to the inquiry on the basis of the emergent focus (problem for research, evaluands, for evaluation, and policy option for policy analysis) because that permits the multiple realties to define the focus (rather than inquirer preconceptions)."

14. *Special criteria of trustworthiness*—Researcher "is likely to find the conventional trustworthiness criteria insufficient (validity, reliability, and objectivity) for naturalistic inquiry. Will probably need to define substitute criteria...in place of positivist trustworthiness criteria." (See below for alternative examples of "trustworthiness criteria.")

*Lincoln and Guba, Naturalistic Inquiry, pp. 39–43. Copyright © 1985 by Sage Publications, Inc. Reprinted with permission.

approaches such as naturalistic inquiry. **Inductive reasoning** is reasoning "from particular instances to general principles.... In induction one starts from observed data and develops a generalization which explains the relationships between the objects observed." **Deductive reasoning** is reasoning "from the general to the particular, applying a theory to a particular case...in deductive reasoning one starts from some general law and applies it to a particular instance" (Rubin and Babbie 1997:48).

Naturalistic research and rigor: trustworthiness criteria   Rigor for both traditional scientific inquiry and naturalistic inquiry involves four concerns. These concerns are listed below along with examples of mechanisms that can be used in naturalistic research contexts to test for these measures of rigor. [Note: Postivitistic scientific terms comparable to the naturalistic terms are listed in parentheses.]

1. *Truth Value/Credibility (Internal Validity)*—How do you know the findings are true? Corroborate findings with multiple audiences and groups; recontact and recheck findings consistently over time; establish standards for adequacy against which to check credibility with various audiences; use "triangulation" (use multiple measurement processes for the subject under study).

2. *Applicability/Fittingness (External Validity)*—How do you know if the findings from this research are applicable to other people and contexts? How can you answer the question of "fittingness"? Ask the potential audience to which the information may be applied if it is applicable in their situation as it was found to be in the original research context. Think of generalizations as "working hypotheses" subject to change depending on changes in situations or contexts or times. The notion of "thick description," is useful: "literal description of the entity being evaluated, the circumstances under which it is used, the characteristics of the people involved in it, the nature of the community in which it is located, etc."

3. *Consistency/Auditability (Reliability)*—How do you know if the same results would occur if research was replicated? Naturalistic inquiry, given its "context-based" nature, is rarely replicated. However, researcher must still answer questions about the consistency with which the research was carried out. Suggestions for addressing consistency include internal reliability check with different members of a research team cross-checking each other's work as it progresses; external reliability checks by bringing in outside evaluators or "judges" to "audit" the work as it progresses.

4. *Neutrality/Confirmability (Objectivity)*—How do you know the effects of your research result from the subjects and materials you are studying or from your own biases, interests, perspectives as the researcher? Data must be factual and confirmable; recognize that values of the researcher do in fact enter into the research; try for objectivity of facts over the false notion of objectivity of researcher. (Guba and Lincoln 1981:103–127)

Postmodern ways of knowing   As we saw in Chapter 1, many scholars today are beginning to think of the current period in which we live as one of paradigm shift from modernism and an almost complete allegiance to traditional ways of knowing (positivistic, scientific, objective, quantitative) to a postmodern period in which traditional ways of knowing are increasingly questioned at many levels. This shift toward postmodern thinking is increasingly influenc-ing the way many social workers approach both education and practice. Ann Hartman (1995:xix), in her introduction to Tyson's book, *New Foundations for Scientific and Behavioral Research: The Heuristic Paradigm,* conveys her sense of the rise and subsequent questioning of traditional ways of knowing that is so much a part of postmodernism. Hartman speaks of this reaction to the privileging of traditional scientific and university-based ways of knowing as

> the complex social and political processes that gradually concentrated knowledge-power in the hands of primarily university-based researchers, and how as positivist discourse about the nature of 'truth' became increas-ingly privileged, other knowledge, other ways of knowing were discredited or subjugated.... [T]he privileging of the methods of science has led to the subjugation of both previously established erudite [scholarly] knowledge and local popular or indigenous knowledge, located on the margins, 'exiled from the legitimate domains of the formal knowledge.' (White & Epson 1990, p. 26 in Hartman 1995)

Given this time of turbulence about the very bases of how and what we know as fact or truth, it is important for us to examine a bit more closely what we mean by postmodernism and concepts related to postmodernism. Lather describes her vision of the postmodern world in an interesting way that captures much of what is central to postmodern thinking. Lather's description also reflects much about the various dimensions of alternative paradigm think-ing we explore in this book. Lather quotes a statement by Riley that "we live in both/and worlds full of paradox and uncertainty where close inspection turns unities into multiplicities, clarities into ambiguities, univocal simplicities into polyvocal complexities" (Riley 1988 in Lather 1991:xvi). Van Den Bergh, a social worker, describes the postmodern perspective as one questioning the "taken for granted" or "grand" theories we take almost as givens in social work. She also sees postmodernism as indicative of the coming of significant change in the "taken for granted" assumptions we make (1995:xii–xiv). Van Den Bergh gives as examples of "grand theory" used in social work (often borrowed from other social sciences), systems and ecological theories, ego psychology, cogni-tive or behavioral theories, psychological and moral development paradigms, and political or economic models of societal relations such as Marxism. In the chapters that follow in this book we will examine many of these theories as they apply to our work as social workers. Postmodernists would suggest, however, that we critically examine these theories each time we attempt to apply them in our work, so that we do not overgeneralize and assume they apply to every person, family, group, organization, community, or nation with which we work.

Comparison of Traditional and Alternative Ways of Knowing

It may be helpful at this point to compare some of the basic differences between traditional and alternative paradigms in terms of the "ways of know-ing" or building knowledge (see Table 2.1). In comparing the paradigms along this dimension, the reader is encouraged to consider the implications of the other paradigmatic dimensions with which we are concerned in this chapter: masculinity/patriarchy; whiteness; separateness/impersonality/competitive-ness; privilege and feminisms; diversities; interrelatedness/personal/integra-tiveness; oppressions.

The interpretive/intuitive/subjective/qualitative dimension of the alterna-tive paradigm, and the related alternative "ways of knowing" described above

Table 2.1   **Contrasting Positivist and Naturalist Axioms**

Axioms About	Positivist Paradigm	Naturalist Paradigm
The nature of reality	Reality is single, tangible, and fragmentable.	Realities are multiple, constructed, and holistic.
The relationship of knower to the known	Knower and known are independent, a dualism.	Knower and known are interactive, inseparable.
The possibility of generalizations	Time- and context-free generalizations (nomothetic statements) are possible.	One time- and context-bound working hypotheses (idiographic statements) are possible.
The possibility of causal linkages	There are real causes, temporally precedent to or simultaneous with their effects.	All entities are in a state of mutual simultaneous shaping, so that it is impossible to distinguish causes from effects.
The role of values	Inquiry is value-free.	Inquiry is value-bound.

Source: Lincoln, Y. S. and Guba, E. G. *Naturalistic Inquiry,* p. 37. Copyright © 1985 by Sage Publications, Inc. Reprinted with permission.

along with the other dimensions of alternative paradigms we will explore next, offer a more holistic approach to understanding—to finding meaning. Feminism, the dimension of the alternative paradigm we will explore next, integrates the elements of the interpretive/intuitive/subjective/qualitative dimension. It moves us still closer to a holistic approach to understanding HBSE—to finding meaning.

Feminisms

Feminism offers a significant and far-reaching approach to developing alternative paradigms for understanding human behavior and the social environment. Feminism or feminist thinking is both an essential dimension of the alternative paradigm we wish to develop and explore and an alternative paradigm or worldview in itself. Feminism is multidimensional and has many meanings to different people. It is perhaps really more accurate to think in terms of feminisms than in terms of feminism. Ruth (1990:3) suggests the comprehensive, multidimensional nature of feminism. She presents feminism as "a perspective, a worldview, a political theory, a spiritual focus, or a kind of activism."

Van Den Bergh and Cooper, social workers, offer a definition of feminism that reflects the consistency between this worldview and the purposes and values of social work: "*Feminism* is a conceptual framework and mode of analysis that has analyzed the status of women (and other disempowered groups), cross-culturally and historically to explain dynamics and conditions undergirding disparities in sociocultural status and power between majority and minority populations" (1995, p. xii).

Fritjof Capra (1983:415) finds feminism consistent with and encompassing other alternative paradigms such as ecological and holistic worldviews. Ecological and holistic approaches also offer important perspectives for expanding our understanding of HBSE. He suggests, for example, that the "spiritual essence of the ecological vision seems to find its ideal expression in the feminist spirituality advocated by the women's movement." Capra reminds us that "feminist spirituality is based on awareness of the oneness of all living forms and of their cyclical rhythms of birth and death, thus reflecting an attitude toward life that is profoundly ecological."

Limitations of conventional ecological/system models

A more recent expansion of the feminist wolrdview has been that of ecofeminism. According to Berman (in Besthorn and McMillen 2002) **ecofeminism** "is a theory and movement for social change that combines ecological principles with feminist theory" (p. 173). In addition, Sandilands (in Besthorn and McMillen 2002), defines *ecofeminism* as "a theory and movement which bridges the gap between feminism and ecology, but which transforms both to create a unified praxis to end all forms of domination" (p. 90). This connection of feminism and ecological concern and advocacy is similar to the connections with feminism made by Capra in his work to provide more interconnected perspectives on biology, the natural sciences, and ecology.

Capra offers a vision of a world emerging from feminist ideals. It is a vision, important for men to realize, in which both men and women are more free to reach their full human potential. Capra offers this glimpse and prediction:

> Thus the feminist movement will continue to assert itself as one of the strongest cultural currents of our time. Its ultimate aim is nothing less than a thorough redefinition of human nature, which will have the most profound effect on the further evolution of our culture. (1983:416)

To accomplish such re-visioning of the world, feminism requires recognition of current inequality. Donadello (1980:214–215) suggests that central to the definition of feminism "is the conscious explicit awareness that women in our culture and in society are systematically denied equal rights, opportunities, and access to the services and goods available in the society." Out of the recognition of current inequalities can come change. Such change must include exchanging "a patriarchal system for a healthier commitment to an equalitarian system providing the potential and opportunity for self-actualization for everyone." This humanistic worldview will emphasize the value of "every individual and offer each a maximum of human freedom and dignity." This perspective not only unites the core concerns of social work with feminism, but it clearly distinguishes feminist perspectives from a traditional/dominant perspective.

Bricker-Jenkins and Hooyman (1986:8) further unite social work and feminism in their description of feminism from a social work perspective. They assert that "feminism insists on removing any sanction from choices that are judged to be inimical to human development, freedom, and health....[A]n underlying consensus exists: that barriers to the realization of the full and unique human potential of women can and must be challenged and changed."

These descriptions of the goals and ideology of feminism are not only consistent with the values and philosophy of social work but are also consistent with the alternative worldview we seek to articulate here.

Feminism, social work and postmodernism

There are many commonalties between feminist and postmodern perspectives which in turn share commonalties with a social work worldview. However, there have also been some significant difficulties reconciling purist postmodernism and social work and feminist perspectives. Postmodernism in its purist form claims to be apolitical and everything is subject to deconstruction. Feminism and social work are clearly "political." Postmodernism also is suspicious of categories and general versus local knowledge, while social work focuses on such "categories" as gender, race, class, and sexual orientation as central to its very purposes as a profession (Van Den Bergh 1995:xxv–xxvi).

Feminist standpoint theory

One attempt at reconciling this tension is suggested by Van Den Bergh, using Swigonski's and other writers' perspectives on standpoint theory. She suggests that (1995:xxvii) "**Standpoints** are truths or knowledge created through awareness of reality gleaned from particular social locations. The concept of standpoint assumes that all people see the world from the place in which they are situated socioculturally. What is considered to be real depends on one's standpoint and is grounded in experiences related to one's position within the sociocultural topography."

Van Den Bergh points out, "Where this perspective differs from earlier feminist analysis is in the standpoint emphasis on multiplicity and diversity within women's experiences. As opposed to proposing a unilateral feminist standpoint, there are multiplicities (that is, African American women's standpoints, lesbian standpoints, Latina standpoints, and older women's standpoints" (1995:xxvii). This allows a degree of respect for the particular or local experience of specific women within the larger universe of "women." It also reflects the need to think about feminist perspectives and feminisms as plural rather than singular. Collins (1997) argues further that standpoint can only be fully understood by appreciating that social location is determined externally by hierarchical power relations. This, rather than the member of groups themselves, determines actual social location and standpoint.

African American Feminism, Standpoint Theory, and Global Feminism

Within the context of standpoint determined by hierarchical power relations, Patricia Hill Collins, a leading African American feminist scholar, suggests that standpoint theory and feminism have different interpretations and implications for understanding the lives and experiences of African American women and other women. In addition, she suggests these different interpretations can also assist in defining and understanding a more global approach to feminist analyses. She notes significant developments in these analyses from the perspectives of women of color over the past 20 years:

> African American women in the 1980s and 1990s developed a "voice," a self-defined, collective black women's standpoint about black womanhood (Collins 1990). Moreover, black women used this standpoint to "talk back" concerning black women's representation in dominant discourses (hooks 1989). As a result of this struggle, African American women's ideas and experiences have achieved a visibility unthinkable in the past (Collins 1996:9).

These developments, according to Collins, have allowed deeper understanding among African American women of the interplay of multiple standpoints within what had been considered a monolithic group. In other words, it has allowed a fuller recognition of the diversity within diversity (see the following section, "Diversities," for a detailed discussion of "diversity within diversity"). She points out that, specifically, "the new public safe space provided by black women's success allowed longstanding differences among black women structured along axes of sexuality, social class, nationality, religion, and region to emerge." As a result of this heterogeneity, "ensuring group unity while recognizing the tremendous heterogeneity that operates within the boundaries of the term 'black women' comprises one fundamental challenge now confronting African American women." Given this heterogeneity, she suggests that commitments to social justice and participatory democracy provide key ground rules for individuals within the larger group to relate to each other across differences (Collins 1996).

Collins uses this expanded and more diverse perspective to outline some of the elements of a global feminist agenda. She suggests that this agenda includes four major areas for attention. First is the *economic status* of women, that of global poverty reflected in the areas of "educational opportunities, industrial development, environmental racism, employment policies, prostitution, and inheritance laws concerning property." Second is *political rights* for women. Specific areas of concern are "gaining the vote, rights of assembly, traveling in public, officeholding, the rights of political prisoners, and basic human rights violations against women such as rape and torture." Third is *marital and family issues* "such as marriage and divorce laws, child custody policies, and domestic labor." Fourth is *women's health and survival issues.* These issues include "reproductive rights, pregnancy, sexuality, and AIDS" (Collins 1996).

Diversities

A key to conceptualizing an alternative paradigm for understanding human behavior and the social environment is recognition of the centrality of **diversity and difference.** The importance of human diversity is interwoven with all the other dimensions of our alternative paradigm. Diversity is central to alternative routes to knowledge building, to feminism, to interrelatedness, and to understanding and eliminating oppressions. Our alternative paradigm recognizes human diversity as a source of strength, creativity, wonder, and health. This alternative paradigm is one in which processes of discovery are central. It is one in which there is not one answer but many answers; not one question but many questions. Only by recognizing both our differences and our similarities as humans can we proceed toward reaching our full potential. The search for an alternative paradigm is at its core a search for diversity. It is a search for new ways to answer age-old questions. It is a process of attempting to allow voices, long silenced, to be heard. Our alternative paradigm is one in which the complex questions of human behavior welcome and respect multiple answers suited to the multiple needs and views of the humans with whom social workers interact.

The human diversities with which we are concerned include those resulting from gender, color, sexual orientation, religion, age, disabling condition, culture, income, and class. Acquainting ourselves with the voices and visions of these different individuals and groups will provide us with important, useful, and creative alternative ways of thinking about such basic concerns of social work and HBSE as individuals, families, groups, organizations, communities, and nations. Next, we will explore some examples of how the worldviews of diverse people and groups can provide social workers with new ways to think about HBSE.

Diversities and worldviews: what can we learn from others?

One example of diverse avenues to understanding human experience more completely can be found in elements of a worldview based on the experiences and history of many persons of African descent. These experiences and shared history translate into values and perspectives that shape a worldview quite different from that reflected in the dominant paradigms. According to Graham (1999) in (Bent-Goodley 2005):

> The African-centered worldview goes beyond the issues of historical oppression and draws on historical sources to revise a *collective text— the best of Africa*—to develop social work approaches and patterns which support the philosophical, cultural, and historical heritage of African people throughout the world. (emphasis added)

Bent-Goodley (2005:199–200) summarizes a number of interrelated principles that reflect an "African-centered paradigm" and that can inform social work practice with African Americans. These include the principles of *fundamental goodness, self-knowledge, communalism, spirituality, self-reliance, language and oral tradition,* and *thought and practice* (emphasizes combining knowledge with social action). These principles will be explored further in Chapter 5. Respect for and understanding of this complex set of values is essential to expanding our understanding of HBSE.

The experiences and perspectives of lesbians and gay men also have rich potential for providing new insight into questions of human behavior. These experiences and perspectives have much to offer, not only in terms of understanding the complexities of sexual orientation—lesbian, gay, bisexual, transgendered, and heterosexual—but also in providing new perspectives on such wide-ranging but essential concerns as human diversity itself, innovative alternative structures for family, and strengths-based perspectives on help seeking.

Diversity in Practice

Recognizing and communicating an understanding of the importance of difference in shaping life experiences is an expectation of professional social work. How does the alternative paradigm dimension of "Diversities" discussed in the section help us understand the complex nature of meeting this expectation?

We can learn about what it means to be bicultural through the experiences of lesbians and gay men who must function simultaneously in both the heterosexual and gay/lesbian worlds. We will discuss **biculturality** or the ability to function in two cultures simultaneously in more detail in later chapters. At this point we simply need to be aware that members of diverse groups such as lesbians and gay men and people of color are expected to be able to function effectively according to the expectations of both the dominant paradigm and their own alternative worldviews. This ability to be bicultural, however, is usually not expected of members of the dominant group. Models for becoming bicultural are important for us as social workers, since we will frequently be called upon to work with persons from many different cultural backgrounds.

Alternative perspectives of some American Indian cultures offer helpful models for seeing strength in diversity. These cultures offer models not of merely accepting such differences as those between gay and nongay persons, but of finding respected roles and responsibilities for these special members of the community. Evans-Campbell and colleagues note, "many indigenous societies in North America have historically acknowledged and incorporated the existence of diverse gender and sexual identities among community members.... Although there were exceptions, these community member tended to be well integrated within Native communities and often occupied highly respected social and ceremonial roles." For example, they point out, "Native LGBTQT-S (lesbian, gay, bisexual, transgender, queer or two-spirit)" people often have cultural roles and responsibilities focused on caregiving (Evans-Campbell, Fredriksen-Goldsen, Walters, & Stately 2007:78). These cultures perceive of their gay and lesbian members as transcending limits imposed by roles traditionally assigned to people based on gender.

Many other similarly significant alternatives to traditional paradigm thinking can be found by exploring diversity. Belief systems about the appropriate relationship of humans to the natural environment of many American Indian, Asian American, Muslim American, and African American people also offer much that might well be essential to our very survival on this planet. These diverse groups have shared a historic sense that humans must exist in harmony with all the elements of the natural world—human, animal, or inanimate. Such belief systems result in a deep respect and concern for preserving the natural world. This sense of interconnectedness and mutual responsibility is quite consistent with core concerns of social work as well as alternative paradigm dimensions. This perspective is quite different from dominant perspectives based on the belief that the natural world is to be controlled and harnessed in service to humans. The dominant perspective has resulted too often in the abuse and destruction of the natural environment in order to control and exploit it for the immediate benefit of some humans.

Learning about diversity can expand our understanding of still another area of concern to social workers. We can find helpful alternative perspectives on the roles of elders and their contributions to the common good. Many American Indian, African American, Asian American, and Hispanic families and communities reserve positions of great respect and importance for their elder members. Many families and communities of African heritage, for example, see elders as holding the wisdom of the culture, and they entrust them to impart their wisdom and the history of the people to younger members through oral tradition. Other meaningful roles for elders, especially for grandparents, are found in actively participating in child rearing and in assuming foster and adoptive parent roles for the family's children when necessary. In many African American families and communities, responsibilities for child rearing may be shared among parents and grandparents as well as other adult and elderly members of the community who function as grandparents and care givers outside the traditional blood-related or legally sanctioned family network. Such inclusiveness not only creates more opportunities for meaningful roles for elders, it also affords a larger system of care givers for the community's children. Through such extended systems as these there is the opportunity for mutual benefits and obligations across generations and traditional family boundaries (Beaver 1990:224; Turner in Everett et al. 1991:50–51).

Diversity within diversity: beyond binaries

The traditional paradigm tendency to view the world in binary terms of either/or greatly oversimplifies the richness and multiple realities of many persons. The historic tendency of the dominant group (whites) literally to see the world in "black and white" reflects this binary tendency.

Historically, "U.S. society was widely spoken of as consisting of two races, one white and one black. The white-Caucasian-European race was deemed biologically pure. People with any known African ancestry ('one drop of black blood') [This was the so-called: "one-drop" rule or "the rule of hypodescent" (Daniel 1992:336)] were put in the black-Negro-African American category. Other people—those who were neither white nor black—were seldom noted or were placed on the margins" (Spickard et al. 1996:14).

The Census   This binary tendency to deny multiple racial realities was perhaps most clearly reflected in traditional U.S. Census Bureau policy. However, this is changing. According to the AmeriStat Population Reference Bureau and Social Science Data Analysis Network, "the shifting labels and definitions used in the U.S. census reflect the growing diversity of the population and changing political and social climate." According to AmeriStat:

> The first population census in 1790 asked enumerators to classify free residents as white or "other." Slaves were counted separately. By 1860, the census requested that residents be classified as white, black, or mulatto [see Table 2.2]. American Indian and Chinese were added as separate categories in 1870. In the 1890 census, census-takers were instructed to distinguish the color of household members as white, black, octoroon (one-eighth black), quadroon (one-quarter black), mulatto (one-half black), or as Chinese, Japanese, or American Indian. (AmeriStat 2000)

Fortunately, over time racial categories have dramatically increased, as is indicated in Table 2.2, until in the 1980 and 1990 censuses "there were 43 racial categories and subcategories on the 1990 census forms, including white, black; American Indian, Eskimo, or Aleut; Asian or Pacific Islander, with 11 Asian subcategories and four Pacific Islander subcategories; other race; and Hispanic origin grid with 15 subcategories that included Mexican, Puerto Rican, Cuban, and other Hispanic (U.S. Bureau of the Census 1992)" (Spickard et al. 1996:15).

For the first time, the year 2000 census allowed respondents to mark multiple categories. With this change as many as 63 racial combinations were possible. The

Table 2.2   Race/Ethnicity Categories in the Census 1860–2000 Census

Census	1860	1890[1]	1900	1970	2000[2]
Race	White Black Mulatto	White Black Mulatto	White Black (of Negro descent)	White Negro or Black	White Black, African American, or Negro
		Chinese Indian Quadroon Octoroon	Chinese Indian	Chinese Indian (Amer.)	Chinese American Indian or Alaska Native
		Japanese	Japanese	Japanese Filipino	Japanese Filipino Asian Indian
				Korean	Korean
				Hawaiian	Native Hawaiian Vietnamese
					Guamanian or Chamorro Samoan Other Asian Other Pacific Islander
				Other	Some other race
Hispanic ethnicity				Mexican	Mexican, Mexican American, Chicano
				Puerto Rican Central/So. American	
				Cuban	Cuban
				Other Spanish	Other Spanish/ Hispanic/Latino
				(None of these)	Not Spanish/ Hispanic Latino

Source: 200 Years of U.S. Census Taking: Population and Housing Questions 1790–1990. U.S. Department of Commerce. U.S. Bureau of the Census. Available: http://www.ameristat.org/racethnic/census.htm. Reprinted with permission. Population Reference Bureau, www.ameristat.org

[1]In 1890, mulatto was defined as a person who was three-eights to five-eights black. A quadroon was one-quarter black and an octoroon one-eighth black.

[2]Categories printed in the 2000 Census Dress Rehearsal questionnaire.

Note: Prior to the 1970 census, enumerators wrote in the race of individuals using the designated categories. In subsequent censuses, respondents or enumerators filled in circles next to the categories with which the respondent identified. Also beginning with the 1970 census, persons choosing American Indian, other Asian, other race, or (for the Hispanic question) other Hispanic categories, were asked to write in a specific tribe or group. Hispanic ethnicity was asked of a sample of Americans in 1970 and of all Americans beginning with the 1980 census.

year 2000 census was also more responsive to persons of Hispanic heritage. The Census Bureau coding (including the option of writing in specific group of origin, such as Salvadoran, Nicaraguan, Argentinean, etc.) allowed over 30 Hispanic or Latino(a) groups to be specified. This is a significant change, allowing multiracial people to more accurately report their multiracial identities (Armas 2000; Bureau of the Census 2000). The data in Table 2.3, from the 2000 Census, dramatically reflect the growing multiple diversities in the U.S. population.

Table 2.3   Census 2000 Summary File 1

Subject	Number	Percent
RACE		
Total population	**281,421,906**	**100.0**
One race	274,595,678	97.6
White	211,460,626	75.1
Black or African American	34,658,190	12.3
American Indian and Alaska Native	2,475,956	0.9
American Indian	1,865,118	0.7
Alaska Native	97,876	0.0
Both American Indian and Alaska Native	1,002	0.0
American Indian or Alaska Native, not specified	511,960	0.2
Asian	10,242,998	3.6
Asian Indian	1,678,765	0.6
Chinese	2,432,585	0.9
Filipino	1,850,314	0.7
Japanese	796,700	0.3
Korean	1,076,872	0.4
Vietnamese	1,122,528	0.4
Other Asian category	1,061,646	0.4
Two or more Asian categories	223,588	0.1
Native Hawaiian and Other Pacific Islander	398,835	0.1
Native Hawaiian	140,652	0.0
Samoan	91,029	0.0
Guamanian or Chamorro	58,240	0.0
Other Pacific Islander category	99,996	0.0
Two or more Native Hawaiian or Other Pacific Islander categories	8,918	0.0
Some other race	15,359,073	5.5
Two or more races	6,826,228	2.4
Two races including Some other race	3,001,558	1.1
Two races excluding Some other race, and three or more races	3,824,670	1.4
Two races excluding Some other race	3,366,517	1.2
Three or more races	458,153	0.2
HISPANIC OR LATINO		
Total population	**281,421,906**	**100.0**
Hispanic or Latino (of any race)	35,305,818	12.5
Mexican	20,640,711	7.3
Puerto Rican	3,406,178	1.2

continued

Table 2.3   Continued

Subject	Number	Percent
Cuban	1,241,685	0.4
Other Hispanic or Latino	10,017,244	3.6
Not Hispanic or Latino	246,116,088	87.5
RACE AND HISPANIC OR LATINO		
Total population	**281,421,906**	**100.0**
One race	274,595,678	97.6
Hispanic or Latino	33,081,736	11.8
Not Hispanic or Latino	241,513,942	85.8
Two or more races	6,826,228	2.4
Hispanic or Latino	2,224,082	0.8
Not Hispanic or Latino	4,602,146	1.6

(X) Not applicable.

Source: U.S. Census Bureau, Census 2000 Summary File 1, Matrices P3, P4, PCT4, PCT5, PCT8, and PCT11.

Multiple diversities   In addition to multiple diversity in terms of race, culture, and ethnicity, there is growing recognition that individuals may identify with other multiple diversities. It is extremely important to recognize that diversity is not a unitary status, though it is often considered to be so. There is considerable variability among the members of any one diverse group. In addition, individuals may simultaneously have membership in multiple diverse groups. For example, an individual may identify as a gay male, person of color, with a physical disability. All of these identifications have significance for how people see themselves and how others view them. These multiple identities interact in complex ways as a person grows and develops and interacts in different social environments. Spickard points out, "Genetic variability within populations is greater than the variability between them" (1992:16). This variability is true in terms of gendered categories as well. Demo and Allen, in their discussion of gender and sexual orientation, note that "It is important to recognize that there is greater variability within gendered categories than between males and females as gender groups" (1996:418).

Fong et al. stress, "Social workers have a responsibility to consciously reverse the historic binary system, enforced more strongly against African Americans than people of any other race or ethnicity, by seeking to understand the full background of clients and clients' perceptions of their identities, rather than allocating them into preconceived categories" (1996:21). Parks et al. expressed similar concerns about the counseling and development field in their statement that "Another weakness in many recent theories and treatment approaches is that they assume that racial and gender groups are essentially monolithic. Little attention is paid to the question of the various types of identification an individual might have with his or her race and gender and, in turn, the effect that these attitudes might have on functioning. Many theorists instead present a psychology of women or a Black psychology that is meant to apply to all women or to all Blacks" (1996:624). Root stresses that "The recent consideration of multidimensional models has allowed the possibility that an individual can have simultaneous membership and multiple, fluid identities with different groups.... These models abolish either/or classifications systems that create marginality" (1992:6). When we explore identity development more completely in Chapters 4 and 5 we will return to issues of multiple diversity.

The above examples demonstrate that, like feminism, diversity is much more than a single dimension of an alternative paradigm for thinking about HBSE. The notion of diversity opens doors to a multitude of alternative paradigms. Through the door of diversity we can enter worlds offering vastly differing and rich ways of thinking about the world and the individuals, families, groups, organizations, communities and nations that make it up. Diversity, then, is not a single dimension of a single alternative paradigm; it offers both a cornerstone and an organizing framework for our attempts to think more broadly, more progressively, more creatively, more humanely about HBSE in every chapter at every point throughout this book.

Interrelatedness/Personal/Integrative

The alternative paradigms with which we are concerned are characterized by a recognition of the **interrelatedness and interconnectedness** of all humans. Many alternative paradigm thinkers go beyond recognition of the interrelatedness of all humans with each other to suggest "the intrinsic and ineluctable interconnectedness of all phenomena, human or otherwise" (Guba and Lincoln 1989:66). Many Afrocentric, American Indian, and Asian influenced worldviews share this sense of the interrelatedness of humans with all elements of the environment in which we exist. Such a holistic perspective is useful and appropriate for social work with its concern for human behavior in the context of the larger environment. Alternative paradigm thinking challenges us to take the broadest most inclusive approach possible to what constitutes context or environment including both the built and natural environments.

Capra suggests that from new perspectives in physics emerges a picture of the physical world characterized by an extremely high degree of interrelatedness. He suggests that the new perspectives in physics have significant implications for and connections with the "human sciences." The new perspectives in physics are based on "the harmonious interrelatedness" of all components of the natural world. Capra finds this view of the world inconsistent with dominant paradigm perspectives that see society made up of unconnected and competing forces. To bring social and economic theory in line with newer perspectives in the natural sciences, Capra believes that "a radically different social and economic structure will be needed: a cultural revolution in the true sense of the word" (1983:17–18). Such a statement from the perspective of a physicist about social change has striking and interesting links to core social work values and philosophy.

Ann Weick, a social worker, also suggests that we look to emerging alternatives to the traditional paradigm in the natural sciences to inform our thinking about society. She, like Capra, suggests that new perspectives in physics (quantum theory) illustrate the centrality of interrelatedness. Using the findings in physics as a metaphor, she believes, we can recognize "that human behavior is set within a web of relationships where dynamic interaction is a key feature. It is not possible to isolate one element in the web without disrupting the pattern or patterns in which it exists" (Weick 1991:21).

Jean Baker Miller, a researcher who has extensively studied and developed alternative perspectives on women's development, finds the importance of connection and inter-relatedness with others central to the individual development of women. Miller stresses, "women stay with, build on, and develop in a context of connections with others. Indeed, women's sense of self becomes very much organized around being able to make and then to maintain affiliations and relationships." Miller's findings are quite contrary to dominant paradigm perspectives on individual development that stress the importance of separation, individuation, and autonomy in the development of both men and women. Miller posits "that for everyone—men as well as women—individual development proceeds *only* by means of connection. At the present time, men are not as prepared to *know* this" (1986:83). We will return to the importance of connection and relationship in human development in Chapter 5.

An important aspect of interrelatedness especially significant to social workers is that of mutuality or partnership between the actors involved in human interactions. This mutuality is central to the approaches we take to understanding HBSE in this book. We learn about ourselves through our attempts to understand the behaviors of others and we learn about others through our attempts to understand our own behaviors. Such a perspective emphasizes that as social workers we are not separate from the persons with whom we interact and work. We are, instead, partners in a mutual process of seeking meaning and understanding. Out of this mutual meaning and understanding can come action to help ourselves and the people with whom we work to reach our fullest potential as humans. One form of this relationship-based action to accomplish personal and collective goals is referred to as **social capital.** We will examine this concept in more detail in later chapters.

Alternative paradigms of concern to us also recognize the importance and power of personal experience and action to understand and transform the elements of our worlds. This standpoint emphasizes that our personal day-to-day experiences, challenges, accomplishments, and struggles have meaning and importance. For it is through our personal day-to-day experiences that we come to know our worlds. It is through sharing our personal experiences with those around us that we recognize similarities and differences between our experiences of the world and those of others.

The process of sharing personal experiences and analyses of those experiences results not only in more fully understanding the world around us, but it can result in joining with others around us to transform that world to allow ourselves and others more opportunity to reach our human potential. This process is perhaps most effectively and completely developed in the women's movement and in liberation movements in some developing countries through what is known as consciousness-raising or CR. This approach assumes not only that the personal is important, but that it is political. Joining together to share personal experiences not only validates those experiences, but it can also empower us to take action. As Longres and McLeod point out in their discussion of the place of consciousness-raising in social work practice, CR "enables people to become involved in overcoming ways by which societal conditions negatively affect their lives.... [It can] enable people to make connections between adverse conditions in the fabric of society and the problems experienced by them in everyday life, and, through action, to overcome those conditions" (1980:268).

The personal characteristic of an alternative paradigm requires a rethinking of traditional approaches in many areas. Alternative approaches, unlike traditional approaches to the study of history, for example, see history not simply as a story of "great" people and "great" events, it is the stories of all of us and of *all* of the events that shape *all* our lives. Respecting and valuing our personal experiences and perspectives can be an important source of empowerment, especially for persons whose experiences and lives are not reflected in histories and institutions that emerge from the dominant/traditional paradigm. Collins (1986:16) suggests that recognizing and valuing the importance of our own personal experiences in the face of oppressive forces that seek to devalue those personal experiences are important in overcoming oppression.

Oppressions

Human Rights & Justice

In order to advance human rights and social and economic justice, social workers must understand the forms and mechanisms of oppression and discrimination. How does the alternative paradigm dimension of "Oppressions" help us recognize the complex and interlocking nature of multiple or intersecting oppressions?

Collins (1990) finds oppositional or binary thinking that places differences (among people, beliefs, etc.) in direct opposition to or competition with one another to be an important part of dominant paradigm approaches for ordering and valuing people and information. In this respect, she finds binary thinking a major component linking oppressions. If this is the case, then more integrative and cooperative processes are likely to offer means for reducing interlocking oppressions. Integrative approaches call for us to think in terms of both/and rather than in dichotomous either/or terms. Such an integrative perspective also allows us to take seriously such diverse approaches as Eastern philosophical notions of balance, and quantum notions of interrelatedness of observer and observed.

Interlocking oppressions

In our explorations we will seek recognition and awareness of what Collins (1990: 222ff.) refers to as "**interlocking systems of oppression.**" We will focus our concern on oppressions as they manifest themselves throughout the institutions and systems that constitute U.S. society and increasingly in global society. This alternative approach recognizes the interrelatedness of oppressions and the interconnections between oppressions and the other dimensions of both traditional/dominant and alternate paradigms. We will recognize that oppression in any institution directed toward any individual or group is connected with and results in oppression in other institutions and of many other individuals and groups. This interrelated or interlocking quality gives oppression its systemic nature.

Such a multifaceted and interconnected conceptualization of oppression requires a significant change in thinking for many of us. Collins suggests that we must move away from simple additive approaches that may recognize oppression in multiple institutions or directed toward multiple persons or groups, but do not recognize the interplay of these oppressions among different systems. Collins illustrates the interlocking nature of oppressions from the perspective of the multiple and interlocking oppressions experienced by African American women. She suggests that black feminist thought offers an alternative paradigm for understanding oppressions by calling for "a fundamental paradigmatic shift that rejects additive approaches to oppression. Instead of starting with gender and then adding in other variables such as age, sexual orientation, race, social class, and religion, Black feminist thought sees these distinctive systems of oppression as being part of one overarching structure of domination" (Collins 1990:222). This perspective assumes "that each system needs the others in order to function" (Collins 1990:222).

"Attention to the interlocking nature of race, gender, and class oppression is a...recurring theme in the works of Black feminists" (Collins 1986:19) and recognition of these complex and mutually reinforcing dynamics is essential for social workers. The implications of this alternative perspective on oppression are multiple for social workers. As Collins points out, "this viewpoint shifts the entire focus of investigation from one aimed at explicating elements of race or gender or class oppression to one whose goal is to determine what the links are among these systems" rather than prioritizing one form of oppression as being primary (Collins 1986:20).

Intersectionality

One recent approach to understanding the complexity and interwoven nature of human behavior and the social environment is intersectionality. This approach prevents us from taking an either/or approach to such issues as race, class, gender, and sexuality and, instead, suggests that any one of these dimensions can be more fully understood by appreciating the simultaneous interplay of each of these dimensions at any point in time. It, in effect, calls for a paradigm shift in social work at many levels. As Murphy, Hunt, Zajicek, Norris, & Hamilton (2009:2) point out, "a paradigm shift that embraces intersectionality in the most comprehensive manner is both appropriate and necessary to capturing the depth and breadth of human experiences within the complex social contexts that social workers encounter while working in increasingly diverse and global communities." They also stress:

> the intersectional perspective acknowledges the breadth of human experiences, instead of conceptualizing social relations and identities separately in terms of either race *or* class *or* gender *or* age *or* sexual orientation. An intersectional approach builds on theoretical contributions made by women of color to address their *interactive* effects. Additionally, an intersectional approach recognizes the power and complexity of socially constructed divisions. (2009:2)

An intersectional approach allows a more holistic understanding of both individual and group experiences by considering multiple characteristics and identities while also accounting for their social and political locations within dominant power structures and hierarchies. Cole and Omari note, "Ortner (1998), an anthropologist, has observed, because every individual occupies multiple social locations, all identities are fundamentally intersectional" (Cole & Omari, 2003:786).

According to Stewart and McDermott, there are three central tenets of **intersectionality** (2004:531-2):

(a) no social group is homogenous,

(b) people must be located in terms of social structures that capture the power relations implied by those structures, and

(c) there are unique, nonadditive effects of identifying with more than one social group.

Pastrana points out that consistent with the premises of intersectionality, "the notion of simultaneity, of being multiple things at the same time has also been quite visible in non-White feminist...and bisexual...investigations" (2004:81). Fernandes (2003:309) notes that the focus of legal academics in developing an intersectionality perspective "was how race, gender and class interact for black women within a system of white male patriarchy and racist oppression. Intersectional analysis names and describes these hidden acts of multiple discrimination and how they obfuscate damaging power relations."

Crenshaw...distinguished between "*structural intersectionality*", which identifies the political, economic, representational and institutional forms of oppression and domination within a society, and the resulting systems and structures, which perpetuate the privilege for some groups while restricting others, and "*political intersectionality*", which stresses how legal directives and government policies are produced from the dominant cultural perspective, with its uni-dimensional and static definitions of race, gender, class, ethnicity, age and sexual orientation. (emphasis added; Fernandes, 2003:310).

As students of social work and of HBSE, we must critically examine each theory, perspective, or paradigm that we explore, whether traditional or alternative, for its implications for recognizing and challenging existing interlocking systems of oppression. In the next chapter we will address some of the implications for social work practice of the emerging intersectionality perspective.

Oppressions and oppressors

Paulo Freire (1992) looked at the mutual impact of oppression on both the oppressed and the oppressor: "Once a situation of violence and oppression has been established, it engenders an entire way of life and behavior for those caught up in it—oppressors and oppressed alike. Both are submerged in this situation, and both bear the marks of oppression" (Freire in Myers and Speight 1994:108). Freire refers to this as dehumanization and emphasizes that "those whose humanity was stolen and those who stole it are both dehumanized." An oppressor's belief system, according to Freire, perceives everything as an object of domination, resulting in a materialistic concept of existence. The oppressed often cannot perceive the oppressive system and instead end up identifying with their oppressor. They may internalize the opinion the oppressor holds of them" (Myers and Speight 1994:108). "Devaluation of self results from a self-negation fostered by the internalization of experiences of discrepancy, ambiguity, and rejection—what has come to be called 'internalization of racism' and 'internalized oppression'" (Kich 1992:307–308).

Oppressions and social and economic justice

For social workers, awareness of the multiple dynamics and impacts of oppressions is only the first step. Awareness must lead to action which in turn can lead to change resulting in social and economic justice. Watts provides a helpful sketch showing how awareness of oppression and injustice can evolve into action to end oppression and injustice. This sketch demonstrates the important relationship of theory to practice and the interrelatedness of personal and political perspectives. It also reflects the need for multisystem analysis and action (individual, group, organizational, community, society— (1994:67–68).

SUMMARY/TRANSITION

In this chapter we have outlined a conceptual framework for approaching human behavior and the social environment content. The conceptual framework is built around the notions of traditional and alternative paradigms. A traditional paradigm was explored through five interrelated dimensions: (1) positivistic/scientific/objective/quantitative; (2) masculinity/patriarchy; (3) whiteness; (4) separateness/impersonalness/competitiveness; and

(5) privilege. An alternative paradigm was explored also through five interrelated dimensions: (1) interpretive/intuitive/subjective/qualitative; (2) feminism; (3) diversity; (4) interrelatedness/personal/integrative; and (5) oppressions.

In Chapter 3 we will explore ways of using our new understandings of dominant and alternative paradigms for gathering knowledge for use in social work practice. We will also explore some of the tools available to social workers to do our work.

Succeed with **PEARSON mysocialworklab**

Human Rights & Justice **Diversity in Practice** **Research Based Practice**

Log onto **www.mysocialworklab.com** to watch videos on the skills and competencies discussed in this chapter. (If you did not receive an access code to **MySocialWorkLab** with this text and wish to purchase access online, please visit www.mysocialworklab.com.)

PRACTICE TEST

1. An important means of understanding any paradigm is the examination of "ways of knowing" and what is considered "worth knowing" according to that paradigm. In other words, we attempt to understand how knowledge is _____.
   a. discussed and appreciated
   b. built and valued
   c. lost and retrieved
   d. replicated and documented

Human Rights & Justice

2. Established laws, customs and practices which systematically reflect and produce racial inequalities in American society whether or not the individuals maintaining those practices have racist intentions is _____.
   a. institutional racism
   b. unintentional racism
   c. cultural racism
   d. impersonal racism

3. The concept of_____ often utilized by social workers is similar to the interpretive, hermeneutic approach.
   a. diversity
   b. empathy
   c. paradigm
   d. bi-culturality

4. Family members who are not biologically or legally related to other family members but who actually carry family responsibilities and rights are known as _____.
   a. extended family
   b. fictive kin
   c. domestic partners
   d. nuclear family

5. Which of the following is NOT characteristic of the traditional or dominant paradigm _____?
   a. interpretive and subjective processes
   b. objective, positivistic, and quantitative
   c. masculine attributes
   d. patriarchal perspectives

Research Based Practice

6. A social worker who studied a community by listening, asking questions, taking notes and trying to understand how persons in that community see and experience their world would be engaging in what type of research?
   a. personal research
   b. quantitative research
   c. positive attribute research
   d. qualitative research

7. Which of the following is NOT considered a qualitative research approach?
   a. phenomenology
   b. ethnography
   c. norm of rightness
   d. grounded theory

8. In general, the type of thinking that does not emphasize universal laws and theories and emphasizes diversity, multiplicity, and pluralism is described as _____.
   a. empirical   c. dichotomies
   b. postmodern   d. objective

9. This concept assumes that all people see the world from the place they are situated socioculturally; what is considered to be real is grounded in experiences related to one's position within the sociocultural topography.
   a. grounded theory
   b. interpretive knowing
   c. heuristic research
   d. standpoint theory

10. The concepts that no social group is homogenous, that people must be located in terms of social structures that capture the power relations implied by those structures, and that there are unique, nonadditive effects of identifying with more than one social group are central tenets of _____.
   a. social systems models
   b. interpretive knowlodge
   c. intersectionality
   d. diversity theory

Log onto **MySocialWorkLab** once you have completed the Practice Test above to take your Chapter Exam and demonstrate your knowledge of this material.

Answers

1) b 2) a 3) b 4) b 5) a 6) d 7) c 8) b 9) d 10) c

The Myth of Cross-Cultural Competence

Culture and Practice

Ruth G. Dean

Abstract

Cross-cultural competence has become a byword in social work. In a postmodern world in which culture is seen as individually and socially constructed, evolving, emergent, and occurring in language (Laird, 1998), becoming "culturally competent" is a challenging prospect. How do we become competent at something that is continually changing and how do we develop a focus that includes ourselves as having differences, beliefs, and biases that are inevitably active. After considering this and several other contemporary perspectives on cultural competence, the author questions the notion that one can become competent at the culture of another. The author proposes instead a model based on acceptance of one's lack of competence in cross-cultural matters.

A Clinical Vignette

Two children in an african american family, Kareem (age 13) and Malik (age 10), were brought to the child unit of a community mental health clinic by their 62-year-old, great aunt and legal guardian, Mrs. W. She was seeking help because the children were "acting up" at school and in church, and she had been advised to get psychological testing for the oldest boy. Mrs. W took custody of these boys, their older sister, Jade (14), and younger brother, Ken (7), and brought them to live with her 4 years ago when the Department of Social Services (DSS) removed them from their grandmother's home where they had been severely neglected. According to Mrs. W, the children were "wild" when they first came to live with her and she spoke with pleasure of the ways she had introduced them to disciplined living and to religion through her church, where they were now enthusiastic members of the band. Although she made it clear that raising four young children was not what she wanted to be doing at age 62, having raised her own children to be responsible adults, Mrs. W was clearly proud of what she had been able to accomplish. The children's mother, her sister's daughter, a woman who chronically suffered from substance abuse, had given up each child at birth and never saw them again. Kareem was born with an addiction to cocaine.

At the intake meeting Mrs. W focused on Kareem who, she explained, was lying and stealing. He had recently solicited money from one of her friends at church and then lied about it; he also stole money from her and denied it when confronted. Touched by Mrs. W's efforts to raise this second family, I volunteered to be the member of our intake team who would work with them. At the time, I was on sabbatical from my job as a professor of clinical social work and I was volunteering at the clinic to learn more about practice in the inner city.

Ruth G. Dean is professor, Simmons College School of Social Work. 51 Commonwealth Avenue, Boston. MA 02116; e-mail: rdean@simmons.edu.

Dean, R. (2001) "The Myth of Cross-Cultural Competence," *Families in Society*, v. 82 (6), pp. 623.

Reprinted with permission from Families in Society (www.FamiliesInSociety.org), published by the Alliance for Children and Families.

I am a White, Jewish woman, the same age as Mrs. W, and have over 35 years of experience in direct practice including some work with families living in economically disadvantaged communities.

Within a few weeks of beginning my work with Kareem, and after he charged some pornographic videos to her account, Mrs. W decided to ask DSS to arrange a voluntary foster home placement for him. I was concerned about the disruption this would create in Kareem's life and wanted more time to work with the family but she was determined to proceed. We agreed on the need for the family to maintain close contact with Kareem after his placement and for my work with him to continue, but this was not possible. The DSS worker could not provide Mrs. W or myself with a phone number for Kareem due to a requirement that protected the foster mother's privacy. Initially, no other plan for maintaining contact was provided and the DSS worker and her supervisor perceived as rude my insistent efforts to reinstate communication for this family and to resume my work with Kareem. When the DSS worker told this to Mrs. W, she disagreed and protested that I was helping the family. After 6 weeks, Kareem began regular weekend visits to his aunt's home.

Following his brother's placement, Malik's disruptive behavior in school increased. I began to see him and Mrs. W on a weekly basis—both separately and together. Malik told me that he was sad at night when he looked across the room and saw his brother's empty bed. Malik's teacher was sending home frequent notes indicating that he was leaving his seat, disrupting the class, and had become a serious behavior problem in the classroom. Mrs. W became more and more concerned over his behavior and indicated that she was now thinking of placing him in a "disciplinary" setting where he would learn to behave. Malik looked very upset each time she spoke of this, and again I tried to persuade her to give us time to work together. With Mrs. W's permission. I arranged for a psychiatric consultation to see if medication might help Malik stay more focused in school. When the psychiatrist recommended a trial of medication based on a tentative diagnosis of attention deficit disorder, Mrs. W rejected this idea. She was concerned that Malik would have the same problem when he stopped using the medication and worried about the family history of addiction. She said she would try to monitor his school behavior more closely and I agreed to help with this.

I visited Malik's school and talked with his very experienced and strict, African American teacher. I arranged for the social worker regularly assigned to Malik's school, who was a member of our intake team, to consult with the teacher regarding Malik's behavior to see if he could help mediate this situation. Mrs. W pursued the idea of placement for Malik, but also made arrangements for Kareem to return to her home because she was troubled by his reports of discriminatory treatment in the foster home.

I approached this case with the idea that maintaining continuity of care for these boys whose lives had already been disrupted was paramount. When I tried to discuss this with Mrs. W, she told me that Malik was "conning" me. She assumed that he could control himself when he wanted to. She asked why it was that he could sit still for 5 hours in church every Sunday but not sit still in school. We seemed to be at an impasse with her believing that the only way to cure Malik of his bad behavior was to scare him by placing him out of the home. I thought this would be very hard on Malik. Mrs. W could now point to a "reformed," well-behaved Kareem, who had just returned to her home, as evidence that her method worked. I wondered if our positions represented cultural differences.

"Competence" and Cross-Cultural Work

The purpose of this article is to show that the concept of multicultural competence is flawed. I believe it to be a myth that is typically American and located in the metaphor of American "know-how." It is consistent with the belief that knowledge brings control and effectiveness, and that this is an ideal to be achieved above all else. I question the notion that one could become "competent" at the culture of another (Goldberg, 2000). I would instead propose a model in which maintaining an awareness of one's lack of competence is the goal rather than the establishment of competence. With "lack of competence" as the focus, a different view of practicing across cultures emerges. The client is the "expert" and the clinician is in a position of seeking knowledge and trying to understand what life is like for the client. There is no thought of competence—instead one thinks of gaining understanding (always partial) of a phenomenon that is evolving and changing.

Much has been written about multicultural practice in social work and the need for competence in working with people from whom one is different. This seems to be an important goal. We live in a multiethnic, multiracial, multiclass society. We work with people who represent every subgroup or identity imaginable. In our schools of social work, we attempt to prepare students for practice in a culturally diverse world. We want them to be competent to practice with members of many groups (Goldberg, 2000). This is currently referred to as being "culturally competent" or "multiculturally competent."

In order to discuss the concept of "cultural competence," it is necessary to first define "culture." In *Webster's New World Dictionary*, culture refers to "ideas, customs, skills, arts, etc of a people or group, that are transferred, communicated, or passed along...to succeeding generations" (1988, p. 337). In a slightly different approach, Becker states that culture is "concerted activity" based on shared ideas and understanding (1986, p. 12). Membership in cultural categories can be assigned according to particular aspects of identity such as race, ethnicity, class, age, gender, sexual orientation, or able-bodiedness.

In these early definitions, cultural categories or groups are treated as if they are static and monolithic with defining characteristics that endure over time and in different contexts. Within this definition of culture, "cultural competence" involves learning about the history and shared characteristics of different groups and using this knowledge to create bridges and increase understanding with individual clients and families.

In more contemporary views, culture is believed to be individually and socially constructed. "It is always contextual, emergent, improvisational, transformational, and political; above all, it is a matter of linguistics or of languaging, of discourse (Laird, 1998, p. 28–29). If we start with this view of culture, then the prospect of becoming "culturally competent" takes on a different meaning. How do we become competent at something that we see as continually changing? How do we move beyond "the limited number of ways" our culture provides for portraying subgroups (Harris, 1998) and the tendency to think in terms of common and fixed characteristics? How do we shift the center in our discussions of culture to keep the focus on ourselves as having the difference that must be encountered in some way (Laird, 1998)?

These different ways of defining "culture" represent two perspectives that are prominent in the current discourse on cross-cultural practice—modernist and postmodern. In the material that follows, each will be discussed briefly along with two other important viewpoints: psychoanalytic intersubjectivist and sociopolitical. I will consider my work with Mrs. W and the boys in light of each of these perspectives and then discuss what I believe to be the important elements in cross-cultural work.

Some Current Perspectives

A modernist view. In the 70s and early 80s, a small number of studies of African American families and other ethnic and racial groups began to emerge and become integrated with clinical literature (Atkinson, Morten, & Sue, 1979; Staples, 1971; Sue, 1981). McGoldrick, Giordano and Pearce's *Ethnicity and Family Therapy*, first published in 1982, is one example of early clinical writing on culture and ethnicity. These books tended to contain chapters about the particular beliefs, practices, and characteristics of different ethnic groups.

These initial writings, rooted in ethnological and anthropological studies, are based on more static or modernist views of ethnicity and culture. Members of a group are seen as sharing some essential characteristics that define them. If a group can be seen as a stable entity that can be characterized in certain ways, then it is possible for clinicians to develop schema that allow them to interact "more competently" with members of the group. There continues to be support in the clinical community for this position.

A postmodern view of cross-cultural practice. By highlighting the continually changing and evolving nature of cultural identities, Laird (1998, p. 23) and others who write from this perspective, encourage us to engage in an ongoing process of learning about others and to operate, as much as possible from a "not-knowing" position (Anderson & Goolishian, 1992). But with some deliberate contradiction, Laird states that we must be "informed not-knowers" (1999, p. 30). She asks us to become aware of our own cultural baggage and separate ourselves from it in so far as is possible so that it will not interfere with our efforts to get to know another. I would agree but emphasize that it is very difficult to separate ourselves from our own "cultural baggage." Becoming aware of it and keeping this awareness in the forefront of consciousness, makes it more likely that we will limit its impact on our work. Our task as clinicians is to sift through and sort our different impressions, layers of meaning and awareness as we concurrently learn about others and ourselves. Laird's important contribution here is to emphasize what we do not know. What if we shift the focus so that we are as concerned with increasing self-knowledge as with increased understanding of the other?

A psychoanalytic intersubjectivist position. Foster (1999), a self-defined psychoanalytic intersubjectivist, takes a psychological perspective on cross-cultural clinical work that focuses attention on the clinician's self-knowledge. In the intersubjective view, therapists are seen as bringing a mixture of knowledge and feelings to work with clients at conscious and unconscious levels and this participation forms an "ineradicable" part of the therapeutic exchange (Gerhardt, Sweetnam, and Borton, 2000, p. 8). This, together with clients' thoughts and feelings becomes a field of interaction operating on multiple levels, within which client and clinician work to construct meaning together.

Foster's contribution to the intersubjective paradigm has been to focus on those aspects of the interactional field that operate in cross-cultural clinical situations. She speaks of "the clinician's cultural countertransference"—defined as cognitive and affect-laden experiences and beliefs that exist at different levels of the therapist's consciousness. They include the therapist's values, academic theories, practice orientations, personally driven idealizations and prejudices toward ethnic groups, and personally driven biases about one's ethnicity (1999, p. 276). In a similar approach, Comas-Diaz and Jacobsen state that ethnicity, culture, and race activate deep unconscious feelings and "become matters for projection by both patient and therapist, usually in the form of transference and countertransference" (1991, p. 401).

It is important that clinicians explore the beliefs and affects that inform their views of themselves and their clients as cultural entities. The way these phenomenon operate in the treatment can be investigated introspectively, and then discussed with clients so as to avoid their enactment in ways that distort, limit, or prematurely end the clinical work. But the timing of these discussions is critical. They need to unfold within the natural flow of the clinical work. While they help us build relationships with clients, they require exquisite sensitivity and are easier to conduct in the context of already strong and trusting relationships. While recommending an introspective process, these writers do not indicate how we get beyond rationalization to a kind of reflection that opens new possibilities.

Thus far, we have considered three views that inform cross-cultural work: an anthropological approach to culture, a postmodern view of cultural identity and a psychoanalytic intersubjectivist perspective. Each directs the clinician's attention to the micro level, the client–worker dyad, albeit in different ways. We have shifted from an emphasis on "competence" to an emphasis on lack of cultural competence and the need for therapists to learn about their own biases and values. But in order to see values clearly, it is necessary to see them in relation to the larger system in which they are embedded. The fourth perspective to be considered shifts the conversation about culture to a macro, sociopolitical level of analysis that challenges some of the basic assumptions of the society.

A sociopolitical perspective on oppression and social justice. Green asserts that issues of "minority group oppression" are at times confused with "minority group differentness" (1998, p. 99). He states that it is not just the traditions, norms, and patterns of behavior that influence the functioning of a member of a cultural group but also the way that group is treated within the larger culture. This treatment is based on various racial ideologies operating in the larger society that attribute particular cultural traits to certain groups (Wilson, 1987). "Cultural, racial, and sexual orientation differences are *not* problems in and of themselves. Prejudice, discrimination, and other forms of aggressive intercultural conflict based on these differences *are* problems" (Green, p. 100). Furthermore, the "dynamic interplay" between the lack of economic opportunities and characteristics that are observed in individuals and families who are systematically oppressed is often overlooked as these characteristics become defined as cultural differences.

If we start with this sociopolitical analysis, we are likely to inquire as to the ways that various forms of oppression have resulted in racial and economic stratification and limited opportunities for our clients and ourselves. This perspective brings in issues of power and the ways that some cultural groups are positioned to control other groups in society. Limiting our focus to studying the beliefs, customs, and historical traditions of individual groups can obscure the oppressive relations between groups.

Discussion

Using the four perspectives briefly outlined above—what I have called modernist, postmodern, intersubjective, and sociopolitical—let us now return to the case introduced at the beginning. How would each of these approaches have affected work with this family?

The modernist perspective instructs me to read about African American families and become better informed about their cultural traditions and customs. I would need to find out more about Mrs. W's history such as when and how her family came to this country, whether or not they lived in the South and their possible experience of slavery to fully appreciate the aspects of African American culture that pertained.

In doing so, I might come to understand the importance of kinship bonds and role flexibility in African American families and this would help me understand Ms. W's commitment to her cousins (Boyd-Franklin, 1989). I would also see Mrs. W's concern with school performance as part of a "strong achievement orientation" that is common in African American families (Boyd-Franklin, p. 17). Her strict discipline and use of a temporary placement as a way of demonstrating her seriousness could be understood as an effort to protect these children from the potentially serious consequences of acting out behavior in a community where violent responses from police or peers are common. Studying about African American families would also allow me to appreciate the centrality of a spiritual orientation and of the church in the Black community. All of this information would serve as an important backdrop to understanding Mrs. W's life and belief system.

"Knowing" about these issues might have prepared me for Mrs. W's emphasis on discipline and her efforts to achieve it through expelling Kareem and Malik for brief periods when they misbehaved. Perhaps this knowledge would have enabled me to understand and integrate her emphasis on discipline with my emphasis on continuity of care. But I'm not sure that this understanding would have resolved our strongly felt differences. And if having this limited information had caused me to *act* as if I *knew* what Mrs. W was going through, it might also have alienated her from me. Without further exploration of her ideas and beliefs, I could not have understood her struggles.

My ideas, based on what I had read would only lead to tentative hypotheses until I had inquired about and understood Mrs. W's specific concerns. But this knowledge might have guided my efforts at understanding in certain directions—for example toward asking about the need for discipline and ways Mrs. W had achieved this with her own children or asking about her church and the support it provided. My reading would have led me to ask more focused and informed questions. As it happened, at the time of Kareem's placement, my efforts at understanding Mrs. W's decision were limited by the force of my own, very different ideas. It was a challenge to contain my own belief in stability for the children and continuity of care while trying to understand her beliefs and how they came to be and still maintain a new and fragile relationship.

The postmodern perspective offered by Laird encourages me to consider the "cultural baggage" I brought to this family situation. This included a theoretical orientation toward a gradual unfolding of the separation/individuation process that avoided premature separation and loss. While I could understand Mrs. W's emphasis on teaching values and discipline to Kareem and his brother Malik, I was put off by what I experienced as an unneccssarily harsh approach. The rapidity with which the placement of Kareem occurred left little time for me to examine the differences in our perspective and I was not particularly in touch with my own biases.

Foster recommends that clinicians work actively with such feelings that she labels the "cultural counter-transference." She would encourage me to dig deeper into the forms that my so-called "American values" take and to consider any particular idealizations, biases, and prejudices that might be operating in regard to African American families, fundamentalist religions, and ideas about disciplining children. Finally, she would have me consider the ways that my own identity as a White, Jewish, middle-class woman might be entering the intersubjective matrix. If I was not consciously aware of the impact of my identity and beliefs she would look for signs of unconscious ideas that were being enacted and possibly distancing Mrs. W.

This analysis causes me to reconsider my response to learning of the misbehavior of first Kareem and then, Malik. While their aunt was alarmed, I saw their behavior as problematic but still within the normal range. While I agreed that it was clearly wrong of Kareem to order and charge pornographic films to his aunt's account, I, with a more liberal orientation, saw his interest in the pornography as part of normal adolescent development. It came on the heels of a letter he had written to a girl in church that had been intercepted by Mrs. W that contained some sexually explicit invitations. While Mrs. W was horrified by the letter and the pornography, I was more amused and sanguine. I tried to encourage Mrs. W to get a male leader at the after-school program to talk to Kareem about his sexual development but she was not interested in encouraging this discussion. She wanted him to stop acting and thinking and feeling this way. I made little effort to bridge the gap between our different approaches—assuming a rightness about my position without exploring her concerns and understanding them in the context of her own history, her belief system, and her current situation with her second family. I wonder if showing an interest in her ideas and how they came to be would have allowed me to understand and accept her more fully. Then, perhaps I might have shared my views with her about Kareem's behavior and we might have had a true exchange of ideas and an awareness of our differences and similarities.

Finally, if I had been operating out of a sociopolitical perspective on oppression and social justice, I might have spent more time asking about and trying to understand the social context for Mrs. W's fears for her charges. We would have discussed the problems she experienced living in a neighborhood with high levels of poverty, unemployment, violence, drugs, and other forms of crime. Her approach to discipline would have made more sense to me if our discussions had included the context in which it occurred. We could have considered how her need to continue to work at age 62, and place the children in afterschool programs affected her ability to raise them in the way she thought was best. Perhaps Mrs. W's sense of frustration and fatigue could have been linked to her concern for the limited opportunities for her family due to racism and oppression. I needed to appreciate her relationship to the staff of the neighborhood schools and other institutions serving her family, including her difficulty in getting attention and services for them. These concerns, if articulated, would have provided a broader context for our discussions and might have led Mrs. W to see that I more fully understood and sympathized with the family's situation.

In summary, each of these perspectives directs my attention to an important area for study and questioning. The modernist orientation encourages reading about the culture; the postmodern perspective turns my attention to my own cultural baggage; the intersubjective focus suggests digging deeper into understanding the kinds of countertransferential feelings operating at conscious and unconscious levels that are at risk of being enacted. Finally, the sociopolitcal analysis directs my attention to intersecting forms of oppression as they impact on the client's life. Together these four perspectives help clinicians to become, in Laird's words, "more informed not-knowers" (1998, p. 30).

The paradoxical combination of these two ideas—being "informed" and "not knowing" simultaneously—captures the orientation to one's "lack of competence" that I am suggesting is needed in cross-cultural work. I believe that while the information I would have obtained if I had pursued the lines of questioning suggested above would have been helpful, it is not the information per se that would have made a difference with the W family. It is the act of respectful, nonjudgmental, and deeply interested questioning and the exchange of beliefs that would have strengthened the trust and understanding between Mrs. W and myself. If I see my limitations as the problem, then I see Mrs. W as someone who can, in telling me about her life, provide opportunities for me to do the work involved in better understanding myself and my cultural attitudes. This approach could lead to a truer exchange of ideas between us.

Working from an Appreciation of One's Lack of Competence

Using the example of my cross-cultural experiences with the W family, I would propose that it is not so much "knowledge" but rather "understanding" that is basic to successful clinical work across cultural divides. When we work toward understanding, we are engaging in building a relationship. These two ongoing processes of understanding and relationship building are mutual and intertwined and at the heart of successful cross-cultural clinical work.

We enter cross-cultural work with limited understanding and many biases. This is inevitable because we are all embedded in cultural discourses that are based on stereotypes. And it is the clinician's cultural surround, including all the prejudices (prejudgments) that it entails, that are the problem—not the client's so-called cultural differences. If we believe that culture is a moveable feast and ever evolving, then understanding and self-understanding are, in Gadamer's terms, "always on the way" (1989, p. 102). In that sense, our knowledge is always partial and we are always operating from a position of incompletion or lack of competence. Our goal is not so much to achieve competence but to participate in the ongoing processes of seeking understanding and building relationships. This understanding needs to be directed toward ourselves and not just our clients. As we question ourselves we gradually wear away our own resistance and bias. It is not that we need to agree with our clients' practices and beliefs; we need to understand them and understand the contexts and history in which they develop.

In building this process of self- and other-understanding we rely on overarching clinical skills and attitudes that are fundamental to all good clinical work—introspection, self-awareness, respectful questioning, attentive listening, curiosity, interest, and caring. These are the elements of relationship building that lead to mutual respect and help us find our similarities as well as our differences.

This is not to say that becoming informed about the history and central issues of a particular cultural group at different periods in time is not an important aspect of clinical work. Nor do I intend to denigrate learning about culture from books, newspapers, and other forms of discourse. These sources of information can provide a beginning step in the process I am describing as long as they don't lead to a presumption of knowledge or competence. Once we presume to "know" about another we have appropriated that person's culture and reinforced our own dominant, egocentric position. I am proposing that we distrust the experience of "competence" and replace it with a state of mind in which we are interested, and open but always tentative about what we understand.

We need to keep in mind that the narratives that come to dominate the ways we interpret people and culture in our writings, at any given time, are social constructions. We only become aware of the limitations of past narratives and understandings when new and different ones take their place (Bruner, 1986). Consider, for example, the "melting pot" theory and ideas of assimilation that once dominated our thinking about ethnic differences. As Crawford states in advising "Whitefellas" about work with aboriginal people in Australia,

> Be tactful and discreet and quietly compare any book learning against the actual situation. Use book learning as an aid to understanding, NOT as a template into which the actual will be fitted. (1989. p. 56)

Learning about the "actual situation" requires humility and respect for the time and work required to achieve understanding and develop a common set of goals and purposes. If I had begun my work with the W family with a greater appreciation of my lack of understanding, I might have been less sure of what was needed for Kareem and Malik and more willing to listen and explore Mrs. W's ideas. I would have recognized that I did not necessarily "know" what was best in this situation. I would have worked toward establishing a common language with Mrs. W that took into account our differences and similarities.

Our differences only have meaning in the context of an appreciation of our sameness and at the same time, our similarities must not allow us to miss important differences. Clinicians need to contain both experiences of sameness and differences simultaneously and tolerate the tension inherent in doing so. If we are guided by principles of social justice and a belief in a common fate—that there but for the grace of God go I—and if we see our lack of competence as the problem and not the client's culture, then there is more of a chance of coming together from our separate centers. Finally, we need to study our society to reveal the ways that forms of oppression create problems out of difference. This form of questioning would allow us to build better communities with more trustworthy services and institutions, as well as better relationships and understanding with our clients.

Epilogue

My work with Mrs. W and her boys has continued. I have observed Malik's class at school and seen how Malik and his classmates are continually scolded and told to sit still and be quiet by a teacher who is herself overwhelmed by a large class containing many kids with problems. I saw how quickly education becomes a tense, unpleasant experience. I found it hard to sit still in such a setting. I have visited their church and seen how children are treasured and that Mrs. W is a highly esteemed leader in this rich, spiritual community. I now understand why it is that Malik can sit still in church and not in school.

Both boys continue to have intermittent and fairly frequent episodes of misbehavior and Mrs. W, who is concerned about her health, is again speaking of placing them out of her home. I am trying to create as many sources of support for this family as possible, with after-school tutoring, camp and recreation programs, and programs that build esteem in becoming a young African American man. But it takes time to put these programs in place and money that Mrs. W does not have and so it is a slow process. Mrs. W and I go to meetings at the school together and try to obtain testing and services none of which have been forthcoming. Other workers come and go, with recommendations and brief interventions but little time to do the actual day-by-day work with the family and the boys. I am committed to do what I can. I understand Mrs. W much better now and there is a bond between us. She knows that I am there to help but we both know that what I can do is limited and may not be enough.

Most recently Kareem came to my office for a meeting. After telling me how scared he was to cross big streets (he had to walk home alone) and how frightened he was of heights, (as we looked out of my third-floor window) he told of the many times he was beaten up by kids on the streets when he was living with his grandmother. After hearing and commiserating with him about his fears and frightening experiences, I told him about a program I had discovered where he can learn how to repair a bike and then get to keep it. He and I will visit the program together in 2 weeks. He is excited about it. He knows that he has to keep himself from stealing and lying in the next months or he will be forced to leave Mrs. W's home and we will not be able to work together. He says he can do it. I'm not sure. In the meantime, our work continues.

References

1. Anderson, H., & Goolishian, H. (1992). The client is the expert: A not-knowing approach to therapy. In S. McNamee & K. Gergen (Eds.), *Therapy as social construction* (pp. 25–39). Newbury Park, CA: Sage.
2. Atkinson, D. R., Morten, G., & Sue, D. W. (1989). *Counseling American minorities: A cross cultural perspective* (3rd ed.). Dubuque, IA: Wm. C. Brown Publishers.
3. Becker, H. S. (1986). *Doing things together: Selected papers.* Evanston, IL: Northwestern University Press.
4. Boyd-Franklin, N. (1989). *Black families in therapy.* New York: The Guilford Press.
5. Bruner, E. (1986). Ethnography as narrative. In V. W. Turner & E. M. Bruner (Eds.) *The anthropology of experience* (pp. 139–155). Urbana, IL: University of Illinois Press.
6. Comas-Diaz, L., & Jacobsen, F. M. (1991). Ethnocultural transference and countertransference in the therapeutic dyad. *American Journal of Orthopsychiatry*, 61, 392–402.
7. Crawford, F. (1989). *Jalinardi ways: Whitefellas working in Aboriginal communities.* Western Australia: Curtin University of Technology.
8. Foster, R. (1999). An intersubjective approach to cross-cultural clinical work. *Smith College Studies in Social Work.* 69(2), 269–292.
9. Gadamer, H. (1989). *Reason in the age of science.* Cambridge, MA: MIT Press.
10. Gerhardt, J., Sweetnam, A., & Borton, L. (2000). *Psychoanalytic Dialogues* 10(1), 5–42.
11. Goldberg, M. (2000). Conflicting principles in multicultural social work. *Families in Society,* 81, 12–21.
12. Green, R. J. (1998). Race and the field of family therapy, In M. McGoldrick, (Ed.), *Re-visioning family therapy.* (pp. 93–110). New York: Guilford Press.
13. Harris, S. K. (1998). Introduction to *The minister's wooing*, by H. B. Stowe, New York: Penguin.
14. Laird, J. (1998). Theorizing culture: Narrative ideas and practice principles, in M. McGoldrick, (Ed.), *Re-visioning family therapy,* (20–36). New York: Guilford.
15. McGoldrick, M., Giordano, J., & Pearce, J. K. (Eds.) (1996). *Ethnicity and family therapy,* (2nd ed.). New York: Guilford.
16. Staples, R. (1978). *The Black family: Essays and studies* (2nd ed.). Belmont, CA: Wadsworth.
17. Sue, D. W. (1981). *Counseling the culturally different: Theory and practice.* New York: John Wiley & Sons.
18. Webster's New World Dictionary of American English (3rd college ed.). (1988). V. Neufeldt (Ed.) & D. B. Guralnik (Ed. In Chief Emeritus). New York: Simon & Schuster.
19. Wilson, W. J. (1987). *The truly disadvantaged: The inner city, the underclass and public policy.* Chicago: University of Chicago Press.

3

Paradigm Thinking and Social Work Knowledge for Practice

CONNECTING CORE COMPETENCIES *in this chapter*

| Professional Identity | **Ethical Practice** | Critical Thinking | Diversity in Practice | Human Rights & Justice | Research Based Practice | **Human Behavior** | Policy Practice | Practice Contexts | Engage Assess Intervene Evaluate |

This chapter presents content about tools we can use to understand traditional and alternative views of human behavior and the social environment. These tools include frameworks, concepts, models, and theories. We will use these tools as we would use maps or directions when trying to find our way to a destination we have not visited before. These maps and directions can help guide us on our journey through traditional and alternative paradigms in our search for more complete understandings of human behavior and the social environment.

In addition to frameworks, concepts, models, and theories, we will use a number of other tools to help us "think about thinking" including: metaphor, appreciation for ambiguity, the intersection of personal and political issues (or individual and social change), the importance of language and words, and social work assessment.

We will use all these different forms of guidance to help us make connections between traditional and alternative paradigms and issues important to us as social workers. The tools, directions and maps we explore in this chapter are intended to be of assistance to us on the journey we shall take in this book. They can help us gain a more complete understanding of humans' individual, family, group, organizational, community, and international behaviors and of the social environments that influence and form the contexts in which human behavior takes place. Equally important, these tools can help us do our work as social workers.

TOOLS AND TERMS FOR THINKING ABOUT THINKING

Before we explore some specific tools for practice, we will explore some tools for thinking about thinking. These tools are intended to help us understand the processes involved in creating and organizing knowledge.

We previously defined paradigm as the "entire constellation of beliefs, values, techniques, and so on shared by the members of a given community." Others (Dawson et al. 1991:16; Brown 1981:36) add that research paradigms incorporate theories, models, concepts, categories, assumptions, and approaches to help clarify and formulate research. All these notions are central to the approach taken in this book, but what do we really mean when we use such terms? There is a good deal of overlap among and ambiguity about the meanings of these terms. However, they also have some commonly accepted meanings that we might agree upon for use in this book.

Ontology and Epistemology

Two important terms for helping understand the creation and organization of knowledge are *ontology* and *epistemology*. Stanley and Wise (in Van Den Berg 1995) suggest that **ontology** is a "theory about what is real." (We address the meaning of "theory" later in this section.) Van Den Bergh suggests on a larger scale that social work's **ontological** perspective about clients and their problems (we might add their strengths as well) "is that they are contextually based in the client's history or 'life space'" [or environment]. **Epistemology** can be defined as "the study of knowledge and knowledge-generating processes" (1995:xii). An **epistemology** is a "theory about how to know" what is reality (Tyson 1995:10). It is the study of how knowledge is created. Harding defines epistemology as "a theory of knowledge, which includes such questions as 'Who can be a knower?' and 'what test must beliefs pass in order to be legitimated as knowledge?'" (in Trickett et al. 1994:16). The discussions in Chapter 2 about how knowledge is created according to traditional and alternative paradigms, then, can be referred to as discussions and comparisons of two very different approaches to the study of knowledge and knowledge-creation processes (epistemologies) and two approaches to determining the nature of reality (ontology).

Concepts are "general words, terms, or phrases that represent a class of events or phenomena in the observable world. . . . Concepts direct our attention, shape our perceptions, and help us make sense of experience" (Martin and O'Connor 1989:39). We will consider many different concepts as we proceed on our journey. "A **conceptual framework** (also known as a school of thought, a substantive theory, or a conceptual scheme) is defined as a set of interrelated concepts that attempt to account for some topic or process. Conceptual frameworks are less developed than theories but are called theory anyway" (Martin and O'Connor 1989:39). The meaning we give to **conceptual framework** in this book is that of a conceptual scheme consisting of a set of interrelated concepts that can help explain human behavior in the context of environment. Our "conceptual scheme" consists of the two kinds of paradigms—traditional and alternative—that we outlined in the previous chapter. Each of these paradigms was divided into five dimensions. The dimensions include theories, feminist theory for example, and concepts such as diversity or oppression.

Mullen (in Grinnell 1981:606) uses Siporin's definition of a **model** as "a symbolic, pictorial structure of concepts, in terms of metaphors and propositions concerning a specific problem, or a piece of reality, and of how it works . . . a problem-solving device." We will discuss several models for helping us expand our understanding of human behavior and the social environment later in this chapter. The models we will explore include social systems, life span, and ecological models. We will also describe a strengths-based model for selecting knowledge upon which to base our social work practice along with other models.

Dawson et al. (1991:438) describe **theory** as "a reasoned set of propositions, derived from and supported by established evidence, which serves to explain a group of phenomena." Martin and O'Connor (1989:39) suggest that theory "most often indicates a conceptual framework that accounts for a topic or process in the observable world." Shafritz and Ott (1987:1) say that "by **theory** we mean a proposition or set of propositions that seeks to explain or predict something." These definitions of theory are helpful because they suggest that theories function to give us directions or they act as guides that suggest some explanation about why something happens as it does. It is important to recognize that theories are only guesses based on observations about how and why things happen as they do. Theories do not offer absolute answers.

The theories with which we are concerned in this book are those that seek to explain a variety of aspects of human behavior. We are concerned with the traditional theories we have relied most heavily on for explaining our behaviors, their environmental contexts, and the possible interplay of person and environment. We are also interested in alternative theories that offer other possible explanations in addition to traditional and dominant theories of human behaviors, their environmental contexts, and the interaction of person and environment.

What do we mean when we refer to environment? When we refer to **environment** we mean the social and physical context of the surroundings in which human behavior occurs. In addition to the social and physical context, we concur with Germain (1986:623) that environment also includes such elements as time and space. These unseen but influential aspects of environment are especially important to social workers when working across cultures.

Different cultures emphasize very different perspectives on such unseen elements as time and space. For example, members of one culture may arrange their activities and environments according to very precise time schedules (as is the case with most members of urban, dominant, white society in the United States). Members of other cultures may arrange their activities in an environment organized by much more natural and less specific divisions of time such as morning, afternoon, and evening or according to seasonal changes (as is the case with many American Indian cultures and with many traditional rural and agrarian people). If we are not aware of alternative perspectives on these unseen but critical environmental characteristics, we risk insult and misunderstanding in our interactions with others.

The Meaning of Metaphor

Another tool for helping us understand HBSE is metaphor. Much thinking in social work directed toward understanding HBSE is done with the assistance of metaphors. Social work is not alone in this respect, for much social science thinking is carried out with the assistance of metaphors. Certainly metaphors are used often to communicate ideas about ourselves and the world around us. An example of a metaphor is "education is the key to success." The word "key" might suggest the importance of education to your future well-being. The word "key" might also suggest education's potential to "open doors" that can lead to your future success. Aristotle defined **metaphor** as "giving a thing a name that belongs to something else" (Aristotle quoted in Szasz 1987:137). Much of our ability to understand the world and the behaviors of humans comes from our ability to use metaphors. We attempt to explain something we do not yet understand by comparing it to or describing it in terms of something we do understand.

In the introduction to this chapter, we employed metaphors to describe the things we are going to try to achieve in this chapter. We used the concepts of tools, maps, and the process of receiving directions to a new destination as metaphors for what we are attempting to do in this chapter. The comparison of our efforts in this book to develop understanding of HBSE to the processes and tasks involved in traveling on a journey is also a metaphor. We must recognize the limits of metaphors at the same time that we appreciate their helpfulness. When we say something is comparable or similar to something else, we are not saying the two things are exactly the same. Social systems thinking is similar to a map, for example, but it is not in fact a map as maps are traditionally defined. As with all tools for improving our understanding of HBSE, we must use metaphors critically. We must appreciate what they are as well as what they are not. These cautions about the use of metaphors to help us understand and explain phenomena suggest a need to be conscious of ambiguity.

The Necessity of Appreciating Ambiguity

To be ambiguous or to exhibit ambiguity is often considered a negative attribute. This is especially true when our thinking is confined to traditional "either/or" approaches to understanding the world around us. Such approaches leave no room for the vagaries or subtleties that alternative approaches incorporate as essential elements for understanding the complexity and richness of human experience and behavior.

In our travels we will try to make room for and appreciate the usefulness of ambiguity. We will try to suspend our dependence on the need for certainty.

Ethical Practice

Professional social workers tolerate ambiguity in resolving ethical conflicts. Why do you think understanding ambiguity is an important part of the process of resolving ethical conflicts?

We will attempt to recognize that appreciating ambiguity can lead to more complete understanding. **Ambiguity** is a healthy sense of "maybe" or "could sometimes be" rather than a need to always be able to answer a question "definitely" or "must always be." Let's explore the implications for social workers of the concept of ambiguity.

Ann Weick (1991:19) aptly describes the need to incorporate ambiguity into social workers' thinking and theorizing about human behavior and the social environment. She suggests appreciating ambiguity as one way to correct for the limits of metaphorical thinking. She reminds us that "the basic problem with any theory or map is that it becomes reified [considered real in some absolute sense]; by using the map, we come to believe that it presents the world the way it really is." She suggests that "it takes discipline and confidence to treat theory the way it must be treated: as a provisional, imperfect and occasionally useful way to package and repackage the continual blur of images and ideas that bombard us." Her words paint a helpful picture of the benefits and limits of incorporating ambiguity into our thinking processes.

Weick (1991:23) suggests the importance of appreciating ambiguity for social workers by using as a metaphor the appreciation of uncertainty and unpredictability within quantum theory in the natural sciences. Quantum theorists posit that uncertainty and unpredictability are as characteristic of behavior in the physical world as traditional Newtonian assertions that certainty and predictability characterize reality in the physical world. If we think for a moment about human behavior from the perspective of quantum theorists, Weick suggests, we will find ourselves including ambiguity as a necessary element for achieving understanding. This alternative way of thinking, however, requires us to shift from the traditional natural science paradigm that suggests that certainty and predictability are the keys to understanding to alternative paradigms flexible enough to allow room for ambiguity. Such alternative perspectives recognize that humans are at least as likely to behave unpredictably as they are to behave in completely predictable ways. We will explore some extensions of other theories from the natural sciences that might help us appreciate ambiguity later in this chapter (see discussion of chaos and complexity).

Using this metaphor can help us recognize that "the nature of [human] relationships is not governed by determinism. Human behavior is acausal, in the sense that human action, except in the most narrow sense, cannot be predicted from prior behavior" (Weick 1991:21). Prediction is really only possible when based on the aggregate behavior of large groups. One cannot accurately or consistently predict the behavior of any single individual within the group. As social workers we need to recognize this as an important limitation of statistics that present aggregate data. Such data are helpful in pointing out patterns or trends, but they are much less useful as tools for predicting the behavior of any one individual. For example, aggregate data may help us recognize a dramatic increase in the number of teenage pregnancies over time. However, these data do not tell us with any certainty about the specific factors leading to the pregnancy of the teenage client sitting at our desk.

The Personal as Political: Individual and Social Change

Feminist theory incorporates not only the fundamental spirit of social work but many of the dimensions of alternative paradigm thinking we have been exploring in this book. It incorporates the power of people's personal stories and experiences as avenues to understanding human behavior and for bringing about social change. It, in essence, unites the personal and the political through its focus on "consciousness raising that occurs when people explore their own stories or the stories of others in troubling circumstances" (Goldstein 1990:40–41).

Bricker-Jenkins et al. (1991:279), in their overview of dimensions of feminist social work practice, provides an important summary of the meaning and implications of seeing individual and social change as closely interconnected—of the unity of the personal and the political. She asserts that "individual and collective pain and problems of living always have a political and/or cultural dimension." Bricker-Jenkins and Hooyman (1986:14) remind us that "our feelings about ourselves and our conditions—our consciousness—are shaped by political forces." They also remind us that the "sum of our individual actions create the social order, [and] we are thereby responsible to each other for our actions" (1986:14). These assertions about feminism and feminist social work practice both inform and reinforce the importance of recognizing that what we do (or do not do) as individuals influences the social and political environment as well. Likewise, what happens at the sociopolitical level has an impact on our individual lives. Bricker-Jenkins and Hooyman explain this interdependent dynamic in terms of social work practice: "In the process of taking collective action to change the historical, material and cultural conditions reflected in clients' shattered images and personalized in their psychic pains, we expect to change our *selves* as much as anything else" (1986:14).

Human Behavior and the Social Environment (HBSE) and the Social Environment and Human Behavior (SEHB)

We raised the question in Chapter 1 about the implications of the name "human behavior and the social environment," and questioned how our focus might shift if we referred instead to "social environment and human behavior." Some social work scholars suggest a similar consideration in discussing traditional perspectives on the relationship of the individual and social change missions of social work.

Traditional perspectives on social work have often included debates about whether social workers should focus their energies and attention on the individual or on the social aspects of our worlds. The perspective suggested here is that we can and must focus our energies and attention on both the individual and the social simultaneously. As in the feminist perspective described above, it is not a question of either/or, but both/and. As Bricker-Jenkins and Hooyman (1986:13) put it, "we change our world by changing ourselves as we change our world." Put another way, one might say that in order for me to be better off, you must be better off—we must be better off.

Our discussion of HBSE versus SEHB reminds us that the way we arrange words can carry a suggestion of the priority or importance given to those words. Next we discuss the significance of words themselves as carriers of meaning and power.

The Substantive Nature of Language and Words

It is vitally important that social workers recognize and continually reflect on the content and messages conveyed by the language and words we and others use. Language and words are primary means through which we communicate the nature of the paradigms we use to understand human behavior and the social environment. Language and words also play an important part in shaping our own and others' views of the world. The implications of language and words for us as social workers include but go well beyond the narrow and traditional meanings of these words. They are themselves important vehicles for assisting us in our journey toward fuller understanding of HBSE.

Language, texts, and discourse

Joan Scott (1988:34) describes an expanded view of language that reflects its substantive nature as a vehicle for increasing our understanding of our worlds. Scott's description offers us a means to better appreciate the central place of language and words in understanding HBSE. She describes **language** as "not simply words or even a vocabulary and set of grammatical rules but, rather, a meaning-constituting system: that is, any system—strictly verbal or other—through which meaning is constructed and cultural practices organized and by which, accordingly, people represent and understand their world, including who they are and how they relate to others."

Scott (1988) suggests that we be carefully analytical of the language of the specific "texts" we use to construct, describe, and understand our worlds. "**Texts,**" she says, are not only books and documents (like this book, for example) but also "utterances of any kind and in any medium, including cultural practices" (institutionalized cultural rituals, such as those surrounding marriage in many cultures, for example). In addition to these expanded notions of language and text, Scott offers the helpful concept of discourse. She uses Michel Foucault's conceptualization of **discourse** as neither a language nor a text "but a historically, socially, and institutionally specific structure of statements, terms, categories, and beliefs" through which meaning is constructed, conveyed, and enforced. This notion of discourse certainly includes the languages and texts we create and use to describe and define our worlds, but it goes beyond this to include organizations and institutions that make up our worlds. This notion of discourse also incorporates the important concepts of conflict and power through which meanings are contested, controlled, or changed.

This expanded vision of language and discourse offers a helpful way for social workers to build and practice our analytical skills as we seek to examine alternative and traditional paradigms for their consistency with the core concerns of social work. In fact such a vision allows us to incorporate in our analyses such elements of core concerns as power, empowerment, and conflict.

As social workers, we need to continually "read" or "deconstruct" the world around us for the meanings it conveys about the core concerns of social work. This is especially important for us to do as we examine theories and models for understanding HBSE, for it is through these theories and models that we construct our social work practice. This perspective on language and words also underscores the importance of such basic social work skills as listening, clarifying, and restating. (If you have not already explored and/or practiced these skills, you will in all likelihood get the opportunity to do so before you complete your social work education.)

This notion of our worlds as made up of fields of discourse through which meanings are created and conveyed suggests that the meanings created can and do change over time according to the historical, political, and social contexts of the times. These meanings, created by humans, can therefore be changed by human efforts. The process of changing meanings and the organizations and institutions through which those meanings are constructed and communicated reflects the essence of the process of social change or social transformation.

Language: Exclusiveness versus Inclusiveness

Several of the perspectives we have discussed come together around issues of inclusiveness versus exclusiveness in our efforts to understand HBSE and to practice social work. Concern for the emergent and process nature of knowledge and knowledge building, concern for the unity of personal and political dimensions, and concerns about the power of words and language all can be thought of in relation to the issue of inclusiveness or exclusiveness.

An important example of the complex interplay of the personal and political implications of language and words as we construct knowledge about others is reflected in the words used to name the diverse peoples of the United States. The process of naming or labeling has important implications for social work and for thinking about issues of inclusiveness and exclusiveness.

Language: labels and people of color

Asamoah et al. point out that the **labels** applied to racial/ethnic groups are of major significance. They are "structural perceptions with implications for access to power, distribution of resources, and for social policy and practice." In addition, labels "can be inclusive or exclusive, can promote unity or divisiveness, can blur or highlight the distinctions between cultural, political and national identity, and can positively or negatively affect daily social interaction among and between groups" (1991:9).

Central to both the personal identity implications and the political meanings of labels of diverse peoples is the issue of who controls the naming or labeling. In reference to African Americans, Harding (in Asamoah et al. 1991:10) "suggested that self-identification is the foundation on which a sense of peoplehood develops and provides the rootage necessary to effectively meet mainstream challenges." So, in accordance with this suggestion and with social workers' concern for self-determination, we should find out from and respect the names preferred by the persons with whom we work rather than assume that the name with which we may be most familiar and comfortable is appropriate. This is especially the case with persons who have historically been oppressed and denied access to power. It is also important to recognize that even self-determined labels can change over time in accordance with the changing perspectives and experiences of individuals and groups. It is the responsibility of the social worker to remain current with the descriptive labels preferred by the range of diverse persons with whom we work.

The meanings of "minority"

Another issue related to specific labels for diverse peoples is the more general word minority. Asamoah et al. suggest that the term **minority** "obliterates the uniqueness of groups and implies that those subsumed under the term share certain characteristics, which may not be the case" (1991:10). This kind of overgeneralization robs persons of their individuality and uniqueness. This certainly is an important consideration given our earlier discussion of Diversity within Diversity (see Chapter 2). The National Association of Black Social Workers has campaigned to abolish the term minority because of its negative political connotations. "Once the impression is formed that an individual belongs to a devalued group . . . then every event and every encounter gets processed through this lens" (Asamoah et al. 1991:20).

The term **minority** is also inaccurate in reference to many groups, such as women, who are a numerical majority. It is also inaccurate in this sense for many persons of color who are part of numerical majority groups in many cities and regions of the United States. Certainly, this is the case globally. It is important to recognize, though, that there is not universal agreement on whether the term "people of color" is always more descriptive or appropriate than the term "minority." Some people argue that "minority" is an appropriate term when referring to oppressed people if we are referring to the rights, resources, and opportunities available to or held by members of different groups. For example, black South African people, a vast numerical majority, were in fact a minority when comparing their access to rights, power, and resources with that held by whites who were clearly a numerical minority. The recent advances in dismantling apartheid in the struggles of black South Africans for rights, power, and resources more in keeping with their numerical majority signifies that minority status defined in terms of rights, power, and resources can in fact change over time as a result of demands and actions on the part of the oppressed "minority" population.

A key to the personal and political implications of labeling is the issue of whether the label is determined by members inside the group or by persons external to the group. Whenever the label is imposed externally by persons other than members of the group being named, the members of the group end up being evaluated "in terms of how or whether they measure up to some external standard, the parameters of which may not even be totally known to them" (Asamoah et al. 1991:20). A large body of sociological theory referred to as labeling theory focuses on this aspect of labeling. **Labeling theory** "describes the ability of some groups to impose a label of 'deviant' on certain other members of society" (Persell 1987:163).

A consequence, then, for members of oppressed groups of naming themselves is empowerment. As Asamoah et al. (1991:20) remind us, "Once we define ourselves, it no longer matters what 'they' call us. What matters is what 'we' answer." Clearly, again, the interplay of the various vehicles for achieving understanding of HBSE is apparent when we think about the importance of words and naming for their ability to determine who is included and who is excluded in the worldviews we create.

Language: Inclusiveness and persons with disabilities

Patterson et al. stress that it is important to remember that a "disability represents only one facet of any person" (1995:76). They also note that in 1990 there were 43 million people with disabilities in the United States and that people with disabilities constitute the largest "minority" in the United States. Language is a significant element of both defining and reflecting a paradigm that is inclusive and respectful of persons with disabilities. Patterson et al. suggest that **inappropriate language is language that:**

1. reinforces myths [and] stereotypes about people with disabilities:
   - 'wheelchair bound,' 'confined to a wheelchair,' 'afflicted,' 'suffers from' vs. 'uses a wheelchair'
   - 'you do that just like a normal person' implies the person with a disability is abnormal versus 'able-bodied'
   - disability, sickness and disease are not synonyms

2. equates the person with the disability by using the disability as a noun
   - 'the disabled', 'the handicapped,' 'the blind': "they equate people with their disability . . . the disability is . . . only one characteristic of a unique and complex person."

   3. uses demeaning and outdated words and phrases when referring to people with disabilities.
      • terms that no longer have scientific meaning: 'crippled,' 'idiot,' 'handicapped.' (1995:77–78)

Patterson et al. stress that **disability** is the preferred term, and refers to "a physical, mental, emotional or sensory condition that limits a person in any major life area, such as self-care, transportation, communication, mobility, activities of daily living, and work" (1995:78). For a more detailed discussion of the impact of language, especially in the media, on members of the disability community, see chapter 9, Illustrative Reading 9.1.

Language and sexual orientation: No words

In addition to inappropriate language or labels for members of diverse groups, an important issue for lesbian and gay family members is the lack of words, labels, guidelines, and norms for the relationships in which gay and lesbian family members are involved. For example, Demo and Allen raise a number of questions/issues about the lack of language or words to convey relationships, roles and meanings for lesbian and gay persons and their families:

   1. How does an adolescent refer to her biological mother's lifelong partner?

   2. How should family members and others refer to the abiding family friend whose frequent and nurturing involvement with the family resembles a loving uncle or brother?

   3. What if he is also the daughter's biological father through donor inseminations?

   4. What terms and norms govern how lesbian or gay partners refer to and interact with their affinal kin, such as their partner's parents or siblings? (1996:426)

Technology

As we noted in Chapter 1 new technologies are increasingly providing new tools for social work education and practice. Distance learning technologies such as Web-based supplements to traditional courses as well as complete courses offered on line in addition to such technologies as video conferencing are expanding the tools available for social work education. These new tools offer exciting possibilities for improving the access to social work education and for providing more individualized education for many students. Gardner describes the changes that technology can bring to education:

> In the future, however, education will be organized largely around the computer. Computers will permit a degree of individualization—personalized coaching or tutoring—which in the past was available only to the rich. All students may receive a curriculum tailored to their needs, learning style, pace, and profile of mastery, and record of success with earlier materials and lessons. Indeed, computer technology permits us to realize, for the first time, progressive educational ideas of "personalization" and "active, hands-on learning" for students all over the world. (Gardner 2000)

Practice Contexts

Professional social workers continuously discover, appraise, and attend to contextual change, including technological change. How do you think the rapid and continuous changes in the development of new technologies will influence your future as a social worker?

However, new technological tools are also sometimes criticized for their lack of personal face-to-face exchanges among students and teachers. It is important to recognize these new technologies as tools for enhancing opportunities for education, rather than as mechanisms for replacing traditional approaches to education. It is also important to recognize the lack of equal access to these new tools for many individuals and agencies.

It is also important to recognize that new skills are necessary to both teach and learn using these technologies. A most basic skill set necessary is referred to as digital literacy. According to Gilster, "Digital literacy is the ability to understand information and—more important—to evaluate and integrate information in multiple formats that the computer can deliver. Being able to evaluate and interpret information is critical." **Digital literacy** also requires the use of critical thinking skills. Gilster emphases that "you can't understand information you find on the Internet without evaluating its sources and placing it in context" (in Pool 1997).

Technology is also providing a range of new tools for assisting social workers in practice with individuals, groups, organizations, and communities. In addition to e-mail, listserves, social networking sites (for example, Facebook), and conferencing technologies that allow professionals new ways of communicating with each other and with consumers of their services, there are also new technologies emerging for use at the community, international, and policy levels. Among these are geographic information systems (GIS). GIS are "computer systems for capturing, storing, manipulating, analyzing, displaying, and integrating spatial (that is, geographical or locational) and nonspatial (that is, statistical or attribution) information" (Queralt and Witte 1998). GIS technology combines satellite global positioning and mapping systems with data such as census data and agency data on client demographics to generate reports and maps that can show both patterns and trends of service use and service needs. According to Queralt and Witte, some of the uses of GIS technology include:

- To assess the sociodemographic characteristics of the neighborhoods served by the agency
- To assess whether the supply of services in a given community is adequate and appropriate for the target population in order to determine which areas may be in special need of outreach initiatives, such as activities to encourage the development of services in neighborhoods where the supply appears deficient
- To help determine the locations of new branch offices, client groups to be targeted, and services to be offered
- To delineate catchment areas for various facilities (for example, special schools, transitional aid offices, specialized health services, outpatient psychiatric services), taking into consideration maximum distances and travel times appropriate to the life situations of potential clients
- To map the flow of clients to and from various community services; for example, to compute travel times and distance from areas with large concentrations of elderly people to the closest geriatric hospital or from home to work for those transitioning from welfare to work
- To plan routes; for example, in community policing, to develop daily police patrol routes that cover the areas where crimes are most frequently reported (1998).

GIS is just one example of new technologies that can be important tools in understanding human behavior and the social environment.

Social Work and Assessment

Engage Assess
Intervene Evaluate

Using conceptual frameworks to guide assessment processes and doing assessments as part of social work practice are important expectations of social workers. How can the information on assessment in this section and the range of assessment tools presented in Chapter 4 help us understand and actually do assessments in our future social work practice?

Much of HBSE is about gaining information and perspectives to effectively assess the social contexts and the people with whom you are working to determine how to appropriately interact with people for effective practice. Norman and Wheeler suggest a three-dimensional model of social work assessment. They assert that "practitioners must keep in mind that each individual is unique, with unique experiences, perceptions, feelings, and behaviors, and yet has much in common with other human beings." They offer a model that recognizes that any individual is:

1. like no other human being: "The fact that a client is a woman does not mean that she shares the views and experiences of other women."

2. like some others (other females or other males): "all humans are identified as belonging to subgroups or categories. Gender is one of those categories and should be considered in assessments or interventions."

3. like all others in the human community (female and male): "humans share common needs." Jung (1964) "proposed a 'collective unconscious,' a storehouse of latent memory traces inherited from humanity's ancestral past." "To fully understand a single human being, we must first comprehend all human beings, that is, the commonalties that connect us all." (1996:208–210)

While references in this model are to individuals, the authors suggest such a schema can assist in assessment with clients systems of varying sizes. Try substituting family, group, organization, community, or an entire culture in each of the three dimensions above. At each system level we must recognize uniqueness, similarities with others in similar categories, and universal human commonalties.

Social work assessment and other disciplines

Bergen (1994) offers a helpful continuum of assessment processes carried out with differing degrees of interaction with and across disciplines. Much of your work as a social worker will be carried out through interaction with other helping professionals from a variety of disciplines. Bergen's continuum suggests that there are a variety of degrees of cross-disciplinary interaction possible depending to a great extent on the context in which assessment occurs. Bergen uses the example of assessment of young children to describe three quite different approaches to cross-disciplinary work. Her model is described below:

Defining a transdisciplinary perspective

1. *Multidisciplinary Assessment:* involves having each professional conduct a separate evaluation, using the major instruments or procedures common in that discipline. The results are then reported in writing to an individual who is central to the process (e.g., a director of a medical or clinical team). In this model, the professionals who do the assessment are often not involved in developing the intervention plan. . . . Parents are involved primarily in making sure their children get to the various professional offices where the assessments will be made and in hearing the results of the assessment from each professional's perspective.

2. *Interdisciplinary Assessment:* the assessments are still conducted independently by the professionals, using their discipline-specific instruments. However, there are usually communication and results-sharing

among the assessors, often through a meeting with the parent and at least some of the team members. Typically, at the group meeting each professional takes a turn in telling the parent the results and giving recommendations for intervention . . . and although the parent is asked to question or comment, the assessment profile and the decisions regarding appropriate intervention are usually made by each professional prior to the meeting and are not often changed as a result of the team meeting.

3. *Transdisciplinary Assessment:* differs both in the procedures for assessment and in the determination of actions based on the assessment. At least in its ideal form, parents are involved even before the actual assessment procedures begin; they are asked to give their own assessment of the child and to identify areas of concern that the parents feel are particularly important to assess and remediate. The parents also have the opportunity to identify needs of the family that relate to their child, and to affirm the strengths they can bring to that child's care and education. Then the team as a whole decides on the appropriate methods for assessing each child and conducts an integrated assessment, using the methods from all disciplines that appear to be appropriate. (Bergen 1994:6)

Bergen's cross-disciplinary approach to assessment seems especially well-suited to more holistic approaches consistent with alternative paradigm thinking. A combination of Norman and Wheeler's social work assessment model and Bergen's model, particularly transdisciplinary assessment, may be an especially beneficial approach to thinking about assessment in your work. We explore some specific traditional assessment tools in Chapter 4, and we explore strengths-based approaches to assessment later in this chapter.

TOOLS FOR SOCIAL WORKERS: THEORIES FOR PRACTICE

Traditional Theoretical Approaches

There are a number of traditional theories about humans' behavior and their interactions in the social environment that originate in the social and behavioral sciences. For example, if you have completed introductory level psychology, sociology, anthropology, or political sciences courses prior to taking this HBSE course, a number of the theories described in the following sections may be familiar to you. As we proceed through the other chapters in this book it may be helpful to refer back to the theories described here to help you connect the social work emphases on individuals, families, groups, organizations, communities, and global issues to these traditional approaches to understanding human behavior in a variety of contexts.

It is important to note that there are differing opinions in the profession about whether or not these traditional theories are supported by sufficient empirical evidence to warrant them as direct underpinnings of practice (Thyer 2001).

Functional theory

According to Alix, "The functionalist perspective favors a consensus view of social order. It sees human beings as naturally caring and cooperative but also as rather undisciplined. They need some regulation to keep them from pursuing goals that are beyond their means. This control is exercised through consensus—agreement among most of a society's members" (1995:27). Henslin describes the central idea of **functional theory** as the belief "that society is a whole unit, made of interrelated parts that work together" (1996:11). Alix notes, however, that "critics . . . claim that the perspective's view that everything in society (including such negative arrangements as racial/ethnic and gender discrimination) somehow contributes to the functioning of society as a whole renders the perspective inherently conservative" (1995:29).

Conflict theory

Conflict theory offers a dramatic contrast to functional theory. "Unlike the functionalist who views society as a harmonious whole, with its parts working together, **conflict theorists** see society as composed of groups fiercely competing for scarce resources. Although alliances or cooperation may prevail on the surface, beneath that surface is a struggle for power" (Henslin 1996:13). Karl Marx, the founder of conflict theory, believed "the key to all human history is class struggle. In each society, some small group controls the means of production and exploits those who do not" (Henslin 1996:13). Basically, "**the conflict perspective** favors a coercion view of the social order." In this view, human beings are self-interested and competitive, but not necessarily as the result of human nature. . . . We are forced into conflict with one another over such scarce resources as wealth and power. The **conflict perspective** sees as the basis of social order the coercion of less powerful groups and classes by more powerful groups and classes" (Alix 1995:29).

Interactionist theory

This area of theory differs from either conflict or functional theory and focuses on the nature and meaning of the interactions between and among humans. There are several theoretical variations of interactionist theory. Interactionist theory takes a more micro (individuals or small groups) than macro (societal) approach to attempting to explain human behavior. It is also a bit less traditional in that it focuses on subjective meanings of behavior. From the **interactionist perspective** behavior is "much less scripted. Instead, it appears more fluid, more tentative, even negotiable. In other words, although people may have been given parts to play in society, they have a good deal of freedom in how they are going to play the parts—for example, with or without enthusiasm" (Alix 1995:31). Alix describes three variations on interactionist theory:

> **Exchange Theory:** proposes that human interaction involves rational calculations. People calculate how much pleasure and pain they are likely to experience in current social situations based on their experience in past situations. . . . They seek to repeat pleasurable situations and to avoid painful ones. (1995:33)
>
> **Symbolic Interaction Theory:** proposes that, in addition to any objective assessment of the costs and benefits of interacting with other people, you also are involved in a subjective, symbolic process . . . symbolic interaction theory proposes that, before interacting, human beings size up one another in terms of these symbolic meanings. Ex. woman, instructor, student. . . . (1995:33–34)
>
> **Dramaturgical Theory:** Goffman's (1922–1882 [sic]) more theatrical (and more cynical) view of human society . . . portrays people as actors in the literal sense. We act out our everyday lives on a succession of stages (social situations). We script scenes (interaction episodes) to serve our interests. We dress ourselves in the costumes of the characters we play. (1995:35)

Role theory

Role theory is another influential theory about human behavior. **Role theory** seeks to explain behavior as action taken in accordance with agreed-upon rules of behavior for persons occupying given positions. For example, we might behave in accordance with our roles as parent, sibling, worker, student, teacher, and so forth. We will explore roles people play as members of groups, in Chapter 7, and we will explore gender roles in the context of family in Chapter 6.

Psychoanalytic theory

Psychoanalytic theory is one of the most influential theories for explaining human behavior. We will explore psychoanalytic theory, in Chapter 4, as a traditional theory of individual development focusing on internal and often unconscious origins of human behavior.

Behavioral/Learning theory

Behavioral theory or **learning theory,** in contrast to psychoanalytic theory, sees human behavior as almost entirely determined through learning that takes place as a result of reinforcement of our behaviors by others or as a result of our observation of behaviors modeled by others. The reinforcement or modeling necessary for learning behaviors comes almost exclusively from the environment. In Chapter 5 we will explore alternative theories of individual development, such as theories of women's development, the development of ethnic identity, and gay and lesbian identity development. Many of these alternative theories see human development as a result of the interactions of multiple factors, some of which come from within us and some of which come from the social environment.

Mid-Range Theoretical Approaches

There are several theoretical approaches that we can consider mid-range theories to help us understand HBSE. These are theories that go beyond traditional theories and emphasize the importance of the social environment as a critical factor in human behavior. These middle-range theories also incorporate notions of change over time more than the traditional theories we explored above. However, these theories nevertheless flow from traditional paradigm thinking and tend not to emphasize dimensions of alternative paradigm thinking such as interpretive and intuitive ways of knowing, feminist approaches, diverse worldviews, and issues of power and oppression. The middle-range theories or perspectives we will consider here are human development, life span, life course, and social systems or ecological frameworks.

Human development

Theories of human development have been extremely important in social work approaches to understanding and assessing human behavior and the social environment. Bergen defines **human development** as

1. Changes in the structure, function, or behavior of the human organism
2. that occur over some period of time (which may be of long or brief duration)
3. and are due to an interactive combination of maturation and learning (heredity/environment interaction). (1994:13)

Life span perspective

Another common framework used by social workers for organizing knowledge about human behavior is referred to as the life span perspective. This perspective is most often used in discussing human behavior at the individual level. However, life span perspectives can be applied also to families, groups, organizations, and even communities.

A life span perspective is sometimes used almost interchangeably with life cycle or stage theories about human behavior. The perspective on life span taken here is one that is broader and less linear than traditional life-cycle or stage-based theories. Newman and Newman (1991) outline a set of underlying assumptions about a life span perspective on individual development that is compatible with the broader, less linear approach taken here.

The Newmans' approach to life span development of the individual is organized around four major assumptions. While they make these assumptions specifically about individual life span, with some adaptation these assumptions can provide helpful guidance to us as we explore human behavior at a variety of levels in a variety of contexts. Their assumptions follow:

1. Growth occurs at every period of life, from conception through old age.

2. Individual lives show continuity and change as they progress through time. An awareness of processes that contribute to both continuity and change is central to an understanding of human development.

3. We need to understand the whole person, because we function in an integrated manner on a day-to-day basis. To achieve such an understanding we need to study the major internal developments that involve physical, social, emotional, and thinking capacities and their interrelationship.

4. Every person's behavior must be analyzed in the context of relevant settings and personal relationships. Human beings are highly skilled at adapting to their environment. The meaning of a given behavior pattern or change must be interpreted in light of the significant physical and social environments in which it occurs. (Newman and Newman 1991:4)

These assumptions allow somewhat more emergent, holistic, and contextual alternatives to traditional ways of thinking about how individuals (and other social system levels) develop and change over time.

Social systems/Ecological perspectives

Social systems perspectives (Anderson and Carter 1990; Martin and O'Connor 1989) and ecological perspectives (Germain 1991) have for some time been important frameworks for organizing social work knowledge and for conceptualizing approaches to using that knowledge in practice. There is some disagreement about the similarities and differences between social systems and ecological approaches. It is clear that general systems theory, because its application includes the entire physical world as well as the human world, differs from both social systems and ecological perspectives that concern themselves primarily with humans and their interactions with each other and the world around them. The ecological perspective, however, explicitly defines the environment as including physical (nonhuman) elements. Social systems perspectives are less explicit about the place and role of nonhuman elements in the environment. Some would also argue that social systems and ecological approaches differ in their conceptualizations of boundaries and exchange across boundaries that occur in human interactions. Recognizing these areas of disagreement, we will consider these two perspectives similar enough to be treated together here.

Social systems or ecological perspectives can help us bridge the gap between traditional and alternative paradigms. Central to these approaches, for example, are notions of the interrelatedness or interconnectedness of the various components constituting individual behavior and the parts of the social environments in which individuals interact with each other. These approaches also tend to recognize that we must grasp both process and change if we are to understand HBSE. These notions are consistent with some of the dimensions of alternative paradigms we have explored.

While they recognize their importance for social workers, social systems and ecological perspectives, however, tend to be less focused on and offer less direction regarding fundamental social transformation or social change and the unity of personal and political issues than is the emphasis in much alternative paradigm thinking, such as that found in feminist or empowerment perspectives. Social systems perspectives recognize that systems are constantly changing or "in process," but they tend to emphasize these change processes as functional and self-righting much more than they emphasize the possibility of these processes to reinforce existing exclusion and oppression within systems. (See Social Systems critiques below.)

Both social systems and ecological perspectives do recognize that adaptation sometimes involves altering the environment. Anderson and Carter (1990:39), for example, "reject the view that the adjustment must be made only by the system and not by the suprasystem or environment." Germain (1979:8), in her discussion of the ecological perspective, stresses that "living organisms adapt to their environments by actively changing their environment so that it meets their needs." She uses the examples of nest building by birds and tilling the land by humans. It is important to recognize that the level and intensity of alteration of the environment suggested by both social systems and ecological theorists is more incremental (adaptive) than the more fundamental structural or institutional changes called for by some alternative paradigm theorists. For example, feminists call for fundamental changes in the distribution of personal and political power and in the ways people relate to each other in the environment in order to bring an end to oppression of women and other groups denied equal power by the dominant group. Social systems and ecological perspectives nevertheless are helpful vehicles to use in our journey.

Capra (1983) finds a place for ecological and social systems approaches in his alternative views emerging from new thinking in the natural sciences. He suggests that these approaches to understanding the social world are closely connected to alternative ways of viewing the physical world. He suggests, for example:

> Deep ecology is supported by modern science . . . but is rooted in a perception of reality that goes beyond the scientific framework to an intuitive awareness of the oneness of all life, the interdependence of its multiple manifestations and its cycles of change and transformation. When the concept of the human spirit is understood in this sense, as the mode of consciousness in which the individual feels connected to the cosmos as a whole, it becomes clear that ecological awareness is truly spiritual. (Capra 1983:412)

Capra also connects systems and ecological thinking to feminist and spiritual perspectives, other important elements of our alternative paradigm framework. He asserts that "the spiritual essence of the ecological vision seems to find its ideal expression in the feminist spirituality advocated by the women's movement, as would be expected from the natural kinship between feminism and ecology, rooted in the age-old identification of woman and nature" (1983:415). "Feminist spirituality is based on awareness of the oneness of all living forms and of their cyclical rhythms of birth and death, thus reflecting an attitude toward life that is profoundly ecological" (Capra 1983:415). Again we find the various directions and maps for pursuing alternative views of HBSE, in this case social systems and ecological perspectives, intersecting and interconnecting with other dimensions of new paradigm thinking such as feminist perspectives, although as we noted earlier, they also represent very different approaches.

More recently the concepts of deep ecology and feminism have been synthesized from a social work perspective. Besthorn and McMillen (2002) offer an interesting analysis of ecological and feminist perspectives and their potential for improving social work practice. They suggest that "an important, contemporary environmental philosophy known as ecological feminism or ecofeminism offers social work important conceptual assistance as it searches for language and descriptions to help it better depict and explain the relationship between person and the natural realm" (Besthorn and McMillen 2002:221). Berman (in Besthorn and McMillen 2002:224) argues that ecofeminism "is a theory and movement for social change that combines ecological principles with feminist theory." Ecofeminism seeks to reweave "the inherent interconnectedness in all of the universe through a revitalization of each person's direct, lived, and sensual experience with the complex whole of nature" (Besthorn and McMillen 2002:226).

Ecofeminism posits that "nature is one with and beneficial for humanity. A second premise derived from ecofeminism is that in large measure social, political, economic and environmental issues are interrelated and fundamentally associated with humanity's philosophical understanding of its relationship with nature and the practices that stem from it" (Besthorn and McMillen 2002:227). They suggest, in summary:

> [an] expanded ecological social work model . . . emphasizes interactions and actions based on caring and compassion rather than the dominance, competition, and exploitation inherent in our current competition-based social systems. This model presents social work with the opportunity to take a philosophically grounded position that publicly and openly acknowledges an awareness of the interrelatedness of social, political, economic, and environmental issues. (2002:229)

Clearly, this approach is consistent with a number of dimensions of the alternative paradigm—feminisms, interrelatedness, and oppressions.

Systems models have been applied at many levels of human behavior. As we continue our journey in this book, we will find systems perspectives among vehicles often used in social work to organize and guide thinking about human behavior of individuals, families, groups, organizations, communities, and globally. Sometimes systems models reflect traditional paradigms and sometimes they represent alternative paradigms.

Social systems terms

The themes or assumptions of the various systems perspectives are often quite similar. However, there is considerable variation in the specific terms used to describe social systems' structures and dynamics. Anderson and Carter's (1990) and, more recently, Anderson, Carter and Lowe's (1999) treatment of social systems, perhaps the most widely used set of terminology for discussing social systems in HBSE courses in the United States, is summarized here to provide us a social systems map for HBSE. There are others, such as the "open systems applications" model of Martin and O'Connor (1989), that offer rather comprehensive social systems frameworks as well. The approach taken by Anderson and Carter is for the most part compatible with the systems perspectives you will find in the chapters that follow, although the specific terms used may vary.

Anderson and Carter (1990:266–267) define a **system** as "an organized whole made up of components that interact in a way distinct from their interaction with other entities and which endures over some period of time." They offer a number of basic systems concepts that communicate the ideas essential to a social systems perspective. They suggest that all social systems, large or small, are simultaneously part of other systems and a whole in themselves. This they refer to as **holon.** They suggest it is essential, in order to use social systems thinking, that we set a perspective that allows us to focus by declaring a **focal system,** the system of primary concern. Only after a focal system has been declared can we begin to distinguish the parts or **subsystems** of which the focal system is composed from the parts and other entire social systems constituting the environment or **suprasystem** surrounding and influencing the focal system.

In addition to these basic perspective-setting concepts, Anderson and Carter suggest other fundamental aspects of social systems. Among these are the concept of **energy,** or the "capacity for action," "action," or the "power to effect change" (1990:11). Energy is a rather inclusive aspect of systems and suggests their dynamic or "process" nature. Energy is what allows systems to move, regardless of the direction in which they move. Energy is necessary for a social system to remain alive, it is the "stuff" that makes a system go. A healthy system can be characterized by **synergy** or the ability to use energy to create new energy. A system that is losing energy faster than it is creating or importing it is characterized by **entropy.** It is "running down"; it is in a state of decline (1990:13). Another fundamental aspect of social systems, according to Anderson and Carter, is organization. **Organization** is the "grouping and arranging of parts to form a whole, to put a system into working order" (1990:20). Organization provides structure for a system, just as energy provides movement and the ability to change. These concepts suggest that the system must be able to sufficiently organize or arrange its components to accomplish its goals or get its work done. Important concepts related to structure or organization of social systems include **boundary,** the means by which the parts of a system can be differentiated from the environment in which the system exists. Anderson and Carter offer an interactional definition of boundary as the location "where the intensity of energy interchange is greater on one side of a certain point than it is on the other, or greater among certain units than among others." They stress that boundary does not mean barrier, because systems must exchange energy with other systems across their boundaries in order to survive and thrive. This process of energy exchange is accomplished through **linkage.** A social system can be relatively **open** or relatively **closed** to energy exchange across its boundaries (Anderson and Carter 1990:29–31).

Additional systems characteristics discussed by Anderson and Carter (and others) include **hierarchy,** the particular order in which system parts are arranged; **differentiation,** a division of labor among system parts, and **specialization,** a division of labor in which only certain parts can perform certain functions; **socialization,** imparting to system parts the rules for behavior, and **social control,** the pressure (persuasive or coercive) put on deviant system parts to return to behavior in accord with the rules of the system; **communication,** the transfer of energy to accomplish system goals, and **feedback,** the information received by systems about the progress toward goals and the system's response to that information (1990:31–38).

Together these basic concepts create a "language" of social systems that we will find useful at various points along our journey to understand HBSE. These concepts are often used in discussions of both traditional and alternative perspectives on HBSE. In this respect they tend to seem fairly neutral. Their real power flows from the context in which they are used and the purposes for which they are used. These basic concepts can be used to defend and maintain the status quo or they can be used to indicate the need for change. The perspective of the user of these concepts is essential to their meaning in any particular context.

Social systems critiques.   Given the potential for social systems thinking to be both a mechanism for maintaining the status quo and for indicating the need for change, we will explore some recent critiques of social systems thinking. In addition, we explore some more alternative views on systems thinking. These more recent alternatives will include chaos and complexity theory as well as the Gaia hypothesis. We should note that Berman's (1996) critique of system thinking includes traditional social systems notions as well as the more recent alternatives of chaos/complexity and the Gaia hypothesis.

A number of the criticisms are summarized below. As you read this criticism, consider whether you find the criticisms justified, whether some are justified and some are not, and what you might do as a social worker to minimize the weaknesses suggested by this criticism. Finally, ask yourself whether systems thinking is, in fact, an appropriate approach to organizing social work knowledge for practice.

In addition to the general criticism of systems thinking above, feminist scholars have criticized social systems approaches for their neglect of biases against women built into social systems. This has been especially true of criticisms directed to social systems approaches in family therapy. For example, feminist scholars point out that resources and power in society are "so unequally distributed to favor men over women and children" that it is impossible to be unbiased or rational in application of systems theories. Critics also point out that systems thinking suggests "that all parts of the system contribute *equally* to dysfunction" and as a result such interpersonal problems as violence and incest are minimized (Whitechurch and Constantine 1993:325). Illustrative Reading 3.1 offers additional criticisms of social systems perspectives.

Alternative Theoretical Approaches

Some emerging alternative theoretical approaches for understanding human behavior and the social environment call into question many of the taken-for-granted assumptions of traditional paradigm thinking. These theories provide social workers with alternative tools to use for understanding HBSE and for using that understanding in practice. These alternative approaches emphasize such dimensions of the alternative paradigm as subjective, interpretive, intuitive, qualitative thinking, interrelatedness, positive elements of human diversity, feminist thinking, and commitment to action to end oppression. The alternative approaches we explore next include: strengths-based, wellness,

Criticisms of Systems Theory

1. *Systems thinking consists of confusing generality and ambiguity* which make it difficult to operationalize through empirical research. *It helps conceptualize/organize phenomena, but it does not explain anything* (Whitechurch and Constantine 1993:346).

2. *Every part of the system has equal weight,* thus elements of little importance have the same weight as elements with major importance (Whitechurch and Constantine 1993:346).

3. *It is potentially coercive in nature.* Potential for megamachine version of "holistic" society, totalitarian in nature, managed by social engineers (Berman 1996:39).

4. *View of reality as a system of information exchange omits the social contexts.* It omits power differences and assumes equality. "It presupposes a society of equals in which all conflicts can be resolved by means of improved communication." However, "the truth is that the relationship of oppressor to oppressed is not one of semantics, and this sort of misguided emphasis can serve to reinforce political inequality by assuming it does not exist" (Berman 1996:39).

5. *Question of whether the cybernetic model is really very different from mechanistic thinking.* Is a computer not simply a very sophisticated clock? If everything is a functional system of interconnected feedback loops it can easily be argued "that victims (e.g., battered wives) are co-creating the violence being done to them." Rather than regarding power

as an "epistemological error", in "reality it is fundamental to human relations" (Berman 1996: 39–41).

6. *It is anti-individual:* The systems "emphasis on wholes, as opposed to parts" suggests that systems thinking "tends not to allow a place for individual differences or for individuals apart from the whole" (Berman 1996:41).

7. *The metaphors from science to human behavior stretch too far.* "the gap that exists between the laboratory research and the philosophical extensions that the authors wish to draw from this" (Berman 1996:42).

8. *Argument that worldviews are shaped by vested interests: systems approach serves very well the current global economic sector.* "It did not arise in a socioeconomic vacuum. Its concepts and conclusions are conditioned by the social and economic processes of the late 20th century." "I know of no way that one could prove, for example, that the earth is dead *or* alive. All one can say is that it displays both mechanical and organic aspects, and probably a few others as well" (Berman 1996:44).

9. *Social systems is very conservative.* Notion that overall, everything is in harmony. "The evolutionary-systemic vision comes down on the side of the status quo" or a "tyranny of harmony"; "much of the systems orientation is consistent with the propositions of structural-functionalism with its notorious justification of inequality and caste in complex society" (Berman 1996:39–45).

empowerment, cultural competence, assets, standpoint, and transpersonal spiritual. We will also explore alternative extensions of social systems thinking including chaos, complexity, and Gaia theories.

Life Course Theory

Life course theory

Is a contextual, process-oriented, and dynamic approach. It also addresses multiple system levels along the continuum of micro or small systems to macro or large systems by attending to individual, family, and community intersections during the life course (Bengston and Allen 1993:469–499). George notes, "for more than two decades, the work of Glen Elder and his colleagues . . . has consistently demonstrated that life-course experiences, such as living through the Great Depression and military participation during World War II, have demonstrable effects on subjective outcomes (e.g., sense of self, levels of psychological distress, attitudes toward work and family life)" (George 1996:248). She describes some of the basic elements of life-course theory, "first, at the broadest level, life-course research focuses on the intersection of social and historical factors with personal biography" (George 1996:248ff). In addition:

> the concepts of transitions and trajectories have become key themes in life-course research. . . . *Transitions* refer to changes in status (most often role transitions) that are discrete and relatively bounded in duration, although their consequences may be observed over long time periods. *Trajectories* refer to long-term patterns of stability and change that can be reliably differentiated from alternate patterns. (emphasis added).

George points out the interrelatedness and overlapping of trajectories and transitions. For example, "trajectories often include multiple transitions . . . [and] transitions are always embedded in trajectories that give them distinctive form and meaning" (George 1996:248ff). We will address life-course theory in more detail in Chapter 6 as it relates to families.

Strengths-based perspective

De Jong and Miller (1995) and Saleebey (1992, 1996) remind us that adopting a strengths perspective as individuals and as a profession requires a significant paradigm shift away from traditional approaches to practice. De Jong and Miller find that strengths "assumptions are grounded in the poststructural notion that social workers must increasingly respect and engage clients' ways of viewing themselves and their worlds in the helping process. Or, to put it differently, the strengths perspective asserts that the client's 'meaning' must count for more in the helping process, and scientific labels and theories must count for less" (1995:729).

Strengths: Related concepts and sources.   There are a number of important concepts related to a strengths-based approach including resilience, membership, dialogue, collaboration, and suspension of disbelief. An important concept related to a strengths perspective is resilience. **Resilience:** "means the skills, abilities, knowledge, and insight that accumulate over time as people struggle to surmount adversity and meet challenges" (Saleebey 1996:298). Scannapieco and Jackson expand the concept of resilience to go well beyond traditional notions of individual resilience. They suggest that while resilience "has been most often defined as an individual's ability to overcome adversities and adapt successfully to varying situations. . . . Recently, the concept of resilience has been used to describe families and schools and communities" (1996:190). Another key concept for understanding the strengths perspective is membership. According to Saleebey **membership** "means that people need to

---

How a Strengths Perspective Requires us to Think Differently by Saleebey 1996:297–298

The strengths perspective demands a different way of looking at individuals, families, and communities. All must be seen in the light of their capacities, talents, competencies, possibilities, visions, values, and hopes, however dashed and distorted these may have become through circumstance, oppression, and trauma. The strengths approach requires an accounting of what people know and what they can do. . . .

It requires composing a roster of resources existing within and around the individual, family, or community. . . . Pursuing a practice based on the ideas of resilience, rebound, possibility, and transformation is difficult because, oddly enough, it is not natural to the world of helping and service. . . . Such a 're-vision' demands that [social workers] suspend initial disbelief in clients.

be citizens—responsible and valued members in a viable group or community. To be without membership is to be alienated, and to be at risk of marginalization and oppression" (1996:298–299). Membership suggests that "as people begin to realize and use their assets and abilities, collectively and individually, as they begin to discover the pride in having survived and overcome their difficulties, more and more of their capacities come into the work and play of daily life" (Saleebey 1996:299).

Saleebey illustrates that a "strengths based approach is an alternative to traditional pathology based approaches which underly much of social work knowledge and practice theory" (1996:298). Saleebey's comparison of the two approaches is provided in the box, "Comparison of Pathology and Strengths."

Strengths-based assessment.   Earlier in this chapter we explored the importance of assessment as an essential part of understanding HBSE and applying that understanding in practice. Assessment is central to the strengths perspective. Cowger reminds us that "If assessment focuses on deficits, it is likely that deficits will remain the focus of both the worker and the client during remaining contacts [and that]. . . . Assessment is a process as well as

Comparison of Pathology and Strengths

Pathology	Strengths
Person is defined as a 'case'; symptoms add up to a diagnosis.	Person is defined as unique; traits, talents, resources add up to strengths.
Therapy is problem focused.	Therapy is possibility focused.
Personal accounts aid in the evocation of a diagnosis through reinterpretation by an expert.	Personal accounts are the essential route to knowing and appreciating the person.
Practitioner is skeptical of personal stories, rationalizations.	Practitioner knows the person from the inside out.
Childhood trauma is the precursor or predictor of adult pathology.	Childhood trauma is not predictive; it may weaken or strengthen the individual.
Centerpiece of the therapeutic work is the treatment plan devised by practitioner.	Centerpiece of work is the aspirations of family, individual or community.
Practitioner is the expert on clients' lives.	Individuals, family, or community are the experts.
Possibilities for choice, control, commitment, and personal development are limited by pathology.	Possibilities for choice, control, commitment, and personal development are open.
Resources for work are the knowledge and skills of the professional.	Resources for work are the strengths, capacities, and adaptive skills of the individual, family, or community.
Help is centered on reducing the effects of symptoms and the negative personal and social consequences of actions, emotions, thoughts, or relationships.	Help is centered on getting on with one's life, affirming and developing values and commitments, and making and finding membership in or as a community.

From Saleebey (1996:298). Copyright 1996, National Association of Social Workers, Inc., *Social Work*. Reprinted with permission.

a product" (1994:264–265). In the box, "Guidelines for Strengths Assessment," Cowger (1994) provides some helpful guidelines for conducting strengths-based assessments that appreciate that different persons' views of reality regarding any situation (including those held by workers and clients about the same situation) vary widely and "are interactive, multicausal, and ever-changing."

A strengths-based approach requires **dialogue and collaboration** with the people with whom we work. This requires the formation of a genuine relationship between the social worker and the person with whom she or he is working marked by empathy, inclusiveness, and equality. Perhaps most important, it requires the social worker to listen, really listen, to what the other person has to say and to value the client's voice as essential to understanding and action. Collaboration requires the social worker to exchange the expert role for a role as partner with the client in completing a "mutually crafted" product. Finally, Saleebey calls for the strengths-based worker to **suspend disbelief**— in other words, we must not only listen to and really hear what the client has

Guidelines for Strengths Assessment

1. *Give preeminence to the client's understanding of the facts.* "The client's view of the situation, the meaning the client ascribes to the situation, and the client's feelings or emotions related to that situation are the central focus for assessment."

2. *Believe the client.* "Central to a strengths perspective is a deeply held belief that clients ultimately are trustworthy . . . clients' understandings of reality are no less real than the social constructions of reality of the professionals assisting them."

3. *Discover what the client wants.* "What does the client want and expect from service? . . . What does the client want to happen in relation to his or her current situation?"

4. *Move the assessment toward personal and environmental strengths.* Must recognize there are obstacles, but "if one believes that solutions to difficult situations lie in strengths, dwelling on obstacles ultimately has little payoff."

5. *Make assessment of strengths multidimensional.* Strengths and resources are both internal and external (environmental), "the client's interpersonal skills, motivation, emotional strengths, and ability to think clearly." The client's "family network, significant others, voluntary organizations, community groups, and public institutions." Multidimensional assessment "also includes an examination of power and power relationships in transactions between the client and the environment."

6. *Use the assessment to discover uniqueness.* "Assessment that focuses on client strengths must be individualized to understand the unique situation the client is experiencing."

7. *Use language the client can understand.* Professional jargon does not help establish "mutual participation of the worker and the client." Assessment products "should be written in simple English and in such a way as to be self-explanatory."

8. *Make assessment a joint activity between worker and client.* This can help minimize the power imbalance between worker and client. "The client must feel ownership of the process and the product and can do so only if assessment is open and shared."

9. *Reach a mutual agreement on the assessment.* There should be no secret assessments. "All assessments in written form should be shared with clients."

10. *Avoid blame and blaming.* "Blame is the first cousin of deficit models of practice."

11. *Avoid cause-and-effect thinking.* "Causal thinking represents only one of many possible perspectives of the problem situation and can lead to blaming. Client problem situations are usually multidimensional, have energy, represent multidirectional actions, and reflect dynamics that are not well-suited to simple causal explanations."

12. *Assess; do not diagnose.* "Diagnosis is understood in the context of pathology, deviance, and deficits . . . diagnosis is associated with a medical model of labeling that assumes unpopular and unacceptable behavior as a symptom of an underlying pathological condition." (Cowger 1994:265–267)

Human Behavior

Professional social workers critique and apply knowledge to understand person and environment. What are some examples from social systems perspectives, strengths based approaches, and life course theory of knowledge that can help us understand person and environment in individual, family, group, organizational, community, or global contexts?

to say, the worker must believe the client and not assume the client has "faulty recall, distorted perceptions, and limited self-awareness" that render what the client says as somehow suspect or only partially true (Saleebey 1997:10–11).

Criticisms of strengths perspective. Many social workers are finding the strengths perspective to be a useful alternative to more traditional approaches to practice. However, the perspective has been questioned by some social workers in terms of whether it really is an alternative and whether it is a helpful alternative perspective. Saleebey outlines some of these criticisms and offers a response from his perspective as an advocate for the strengths approach:

1. It's just "positive thinking" in disguise: **Response:** Strengths is more than uplifting words and sayings about everything being ok. For people to reach the point of really seeing themselves as strong, worthy, competent is extremely hard work both for the social worker and the person or communities involved.

2. Reframing misery: Notion that strengths approach simply reframes reality in such a way that conditions don't change and transformation does not take place, but instead clients are taught to "reconceptualize their difficulties so that they are sanitized and less threatening to self and others." **Response:** "The strengths perspective does not deny reality; it demands some reframing, however, to develop an attitude and language about the nature of possibility and opportunity and the nature of the individual beneath the diagnostic label."

3. Pollyannaism: Strengths perspective "ignores how manipulative and dangerous or destructive clients and client groups can be. The argument is, apparently, that some people are simply beyond redemption." **Response:** Strengths approach does not deny that some people engage in behavior and hurtfulness to themselves and others beyond our ability to understand. However, strengths approach demands that we "ask what useful qualities and skills or even motivation and aspirations these clients have. . . . Social workers cannot automatically discount people. There may be genuinely evil people, beyond grace or hope, but it is best not to make that assumption first."

4. Ignoring reality: Downplays real problems. **Response:** "does not discount the problems of clients. . . . All helpers should assess and evaluate the sources and remnants of client troubles, difficulties, pains, and disorders." However, they must also "calculate how clients have managed to survive thus far and what they have drawn on in the face of misfortune." (Saleebey 1996:302–303)

Wellness

Closely associated with the strengths perspective is wellness theory. Jones and Kilpatrick assert the premise of wellness theory to be that "the thoughts and feelings we experience directly affect our physical functioning and well-being, just as our physical functioning directly affects our emotional states and thought processes" (1996:262). The **wellness** perspective recognizes the extremely strong and important relationship between "body, mind and environment and health and wellness" (Saleebey 1996:300) and that "the unit of attention is the physical, mental, spiritual, and social well-being of the individual, family, and/or specific population involved in the intervention process" (Jones and Kilpatric 1996:263). The complex interplay of these areas has significant influence in "keeping people well, assisting individuals in regenerating after trauma, and helping individuals and communities survive the impact and aftermath of calamity and ordeal" (Saleebey 1996:300). "Wellness theory recognizes that the development of the wellness state is an ongoing, life-long process. Quality of life, rather than length of life, is of primary concern" (Jones and Kilpatrick 1996:264).

Jones and Kilpatrick define **wellness** as "a state of harmony, energy, positive productivity, and well-being in an individual's mind, body, emotions, and spirit. The state of wellness also extends to the relationships between the individual and his or her family and other interpersonal connections as well as the relationships between, the person and his or her physical environment, community, and larger society" (1996:259).

Philosophical, biological and social components of wellness.   Illustrations of philosophical, biological, and social theories that inform wellness theory and emphasize the interplay of multiple aspects of our lives in the creation and maintenance of wellness include constructivism, psychoneuroimmunology, and social development theory. **Constructivism** is the theory that "for any single event or situation" there are multiple perceptions of reality all of which have validity. People in the helping relationship work to respect and understand the narratives that constitute reality for the persons involved. "In wellness theory the client's role is as important as the practitioner's role" (Jones and Kilpatrick 1996:263). Practitioners must be honest about what they do not know and respect that the client is the expert on his/her situation (Jones and Kilpatrick 1996:260, 264–265). Practitioners must be as informed as possible about what helps people stay well. **Psychoneuroimmunology** is a biological perspective that informs wellness theory and focuses on "the reciprocal relationship between mind and body" (Jones and Kilpatrick 1996:261). It assumes "the mind and body are inseparable and that continuous reciprocal communication occurs between the mind and the various organ systems of the body via the brain's chemistry" (Jones and Kilpatrick 1996:261). Social development theory is a social or macro perspective on how the larger society either helps or hinders in the creation and maintenance of wellness. **Social development theory** "recognizes the societal and political aspects of human functioning and attempts to address inequities caused by oppression or discrimination targeted toward certain subgroups of society" (Jones and Kilpatrick 1996:261). We explore social development theory in more detail in Chapter 9 in our discussion of communities.

Wellness and social change.   It is important to realize and reinforce that wellness theory is a theory for both individual and social change. Jones and Kilpatrick remind us that *"Wellness theory can be used to empower oppressed groups such as the aging poor, the homeless, and people with disabilities, targeting enhanced quality of life as its primary goal"* (1996:260).

Empowerment

We explored the basic concept of empowerment in Chapter 1. Now we will explore empowerment as a combination of theory and practice and as a process of change as well.

Gutierrez et al. suggest that "empowerment practice in social work emerged from efforts to develop more effective and responsive services for women and people of color" (1995:534). **Empowerment** "focuses on changing the distribution of power" and it "depicts power as originating from various

Wellness and Disabilities: Illustrations of the Application of Wellness Theory

An interesting application of wellness theory to working with persons with disabilities is offered by Jones and Kilpatrick. They stress that *"Wellness does not preclude having a disability or experiencing positive stress"* (1996:259).

1. A wellness perspective applied to working with persons with disabilities first and foremost requires that everyone "involved in the goal-identification and problem-solving process [must] separate the individual from the disability because these two entities are not interchangeable" (Jones and Kilpatrick, 1996:264).

2. "If society, the helping professions, and the general public were to truly embrace the idea that it is acceptable to be disabled, then people might concentrate on reducing the barriers to life with disability" (Asch and Mudrick in Jones and Kilpatrick 1996:261). For example: "In Martha's Vineyard during the nineteenth century, the majority of the families inhabiting that area had relatives who were deaf. To facilitate communication in the community, virtually everyone learned American Sign Language. Within a brief period, signing became so common that hearing people often used it to communicate among themselves. Individuals signed to one another across the water while fishing when voicing was not effective. For a time, language barriers dissolved and deafness did not imply disability" (Shapiro in Jones and Kilpatrick 1996:261).

3. "In macro social work practice, disability activists have reauthored their stories in an effort to change society's perceptions and attitudes toward disability and people who have disabilities. . . . They have redefined disability as a challenge that can be met through assistive technology and personal-care assistance that allow the person with a disability to work and live independently at the same level as people without disabilities" (Jones and Kilpatrick 1996:263). We explore the independent living movement in more detail in Chapter 9.

From Jones and Kilpatrick (1996). Wellness theory: A discussion and application to clients with disabilities, *Families in Society.* Reprinted with permission from *Families in Society* (www.familiesinsociety.org), published by the Alliance for Children and Families.

sources and as infinite because it can be generated in the process of social interaction" (Gutierrez et al. 1995:535). For Gutierrez et al., empowerment has multiple characteristics and can occur at multiple levels including individual, group and community. Empowerment is:

1. Both a *theory and practice* that deal with issues of power, powerlessness, and oppression and how they contribute to individual, family, or community problems and affect helping relationships.

2. A perspective whose *goal* is to increase personal, interpersonal, or political power so that individuals, families, or communities can take action to improve their situations.

3. A *process* that can take place on the individual, interpersonal, and community levels of intervention. It consists of the following subprocesses:
   • development of group consciousness
   • reduction of self-blame
   • assumption of personal responsibility for change
   • enhancement of self-efficacy (1995:535).

According to Gutierrez et al., empowerment occurs through *intervention methods* that include:

▶ Basing the helping relationship on collaboration, trust, and shared power
▶ Utilizing small groups
▶ Accepting the client's definition of the problem
▶ Identifying and building upon the client's strengths
▶ Raising the client's consciousness of issues of class and power
▶ Actively involving the client in the change process
▶ Teaching specific skills
▶ Using mutual-aid, self-help and support groups

Might the people in this photo and their activity reflect the concepts of culture, ethnicity, and race? How might the meaning differ depending on whether the people in the photo or others (you, for example) provide the definitions?

▶ Experiencing a sense of personal power within the helping relationship
▶ Mobilizing resources or advocating for clients (1995:535).

Gutierrez contrasts empowerment and traditional coping approaches. She notes that "the coping perspective has most typically looked at how the person/environmental fit can be improved upon by making changes on the individual or psychological level . . . [while] the empowerment perspective focuses almost exclusively on how environments can be modified to improve the person/environment fit" (1995:208–209).

Cultural competence

A **cultural competence** approach to thinking about and doing social work is emerging as one of the most essential perspectives for social work as it struggles to maintain its effectiveness and relevance in a twenty-first century marked by an increasingly diverse U.S. population. In addition, global economic, political, and technological realities make interacting with persons different from ourselves an almost daily occurrence. This trend toward more diversity and globalization can be expected to increasingly influence not only our personal life experiences but our professional work as social workers as well. A number of scholars have worked to define what we mean by culturally competent social work practice (Green 1999; Leigh 1998; Lum 1999; Weaver 1999; Williams 2006). Although a good deal of progress has been made toward a definition, we will likely continue to see the concept evolve in the future. Cultural competence is often described as a continual process of striving and learning rather than a clear end product. Diller, for example, describes cultural competence as "a developmental process that depends on the continual acquisition of knowledge, the development of new and more advanced skills, and an ongoing self-evaluation of progress" (Diller 1999:10). Lum defines **cultural competency** as "the experiential awareness of the worker about culture, ethnicity, and racism; knowledge about historical oppression and related multicultural concepts; development of skills to deal effectively with the needs of the culturally diverse clients;" and the process of continuous learning to incorporate new multicultural knowledge (1999:174).

Williams (2006:110) suggests that, though social work has given considerable attention to defining and operationalizing what we mean by cultural competence, we continue to lack the necessary theoretical foundation upon which to base our understanding of cultural competence and to evaluate our effectiveness as practitioners in this arena. In response to this need she provides a helpful presentation of central issues related to cultural competence and organizes these issues around several traditional and alternative paradigms. She addresses cultural competence through the multiple epistemological lenses (approaches to studying the nature of knowledge; see Chapter 2) of postpositivism, constructivism, critical theory, and postmodernism. Briefly, these paradigms can be summarized as follows: *postpositivism* is somewhat similar to our earlier discussions of the traditional paradigm dimension of positivism and of the modernist historical period in its assumption that "reality is something that we can understand and capture probabilistically using the right tools." Postpositivism is differentiated from positivism and modernism by its acknowledgement that "research is influenced by the theories and biases of researchers." However, similar to positivism, researchers using this lens assume we "can pursue knowledge that is uncontaminated and reasonably stable" (2006:211). A *constructivist* paradigm suggests, "reality is constructed through social interaction and dialogue. What we come to understand as knowledge is based on the shared experiences of groups and is inextricably connected to the participants who are involved in knowledge production" (2006:212). The *critical theory* paradigm suggests that reality is produced through historically based social and political processes" that serve "the purposes of the powerful" (2006:213). *Postmodernism*, as we learned in Chapter 1, "suggests that reality is a moving target that cannot be reduced to reassuring regularities" (2006:214). Table 3.1 is helpful in organizing concepts and practices related to cultural competence.

Weaver summarizes three major principles of **cultural competence:**

▸ The human services provider must be knowledgeable about the group in question;
▸ The human services provider must be able to be self-reflective and to recognize biases in himself or herself and within the profession;
▸ The human services provider must be able to integrate this knowledge and reflection with practice skills. (Weaver 1998:204)

These definitions and principles reflect the critical need for a culturally competent social worker to have knowledge about the members of the different cultures with which we work; self-awareness of our own culture, biases, and racism; a willingness to continually learn both about others and ourselves as cultural beings; and a willingness to incorporate our knowledge into practice skills. It is important to recognize that culturally competent practice is essential, whether working with individuals, families, groups, organizations, communities, and especially globally. (See also Chapter 2, Illustrative Reading 2.1.)

Solution-Focused Brief Therapy (SFBT)

Another tool now commonly used in social work practice in a variety of settings is Solution-Focused Brief Therapy (SFBT). This approach has been used

Table 3.1   Paradigms for Culturally Competent Social Work

Variable	Postpositivism	Constructivism	Critical Theory	Postmodernism
Nature of culture	Relatively stable, verifiable	Constructed in local and specific relationships	Historically derived from social, political, economic arrangements	Unfixed, constantly evolving
Practitioner role	Expert, anthropologist	Insider, cultural promoter	Advocate, mentor	Explorer, facilitator
Methods of practice	Learning cultural knowledge, including it in formulations	Immersion in cultural experience, using insider frame of reference	Consciousness raising, activism, collective participatory action	Not knowing, eliciting, reframing, reauthoring
Limitations	Stereotyping, overgeneralization	Cultural chauvinism, mainstream appropriation	Ideological barriers to implementation, neglecting individual problems	Not knowing is not feasible for practice
Goals, outcomes	Technically proficient practice across populations	Group affirmation and well being	Empowerment and social change	Self-definition, multiple identities
Compatible social work models	Generic, etic	Culture-specific service provision	Anti-oppressive, feminist, antiracist	Narrative, intersubjective

Source: Adapted from Williams, C. (2006). The Epistemology of Cultural Competence. *Families in Society, 87*(2).

in medical settings, group settings, prisons, cross-cultural settings, and many others. The approach has also been evaluated in a number of studies to determine if there is empirical evidence to support its continued use (Gingerich 2000). According to Lee (2003:387), the basis of SFBT is found in its efforts to find "what works in therapy."

According to Gingerich (2000:478), "SFBT evolved out of the clinical practice of Steve de Shazer, Insoo Kim Berg, and colleagues at the Brief Family Therapy Center in Milwaukee, Wisconsin, in the early 1980s. . . . As the name suggests, SFBT is defined by its emphasis on constructing solutions rather than resolving problems." Gingerich also provides a summary of the main elements of SFBT:

> The main therapeutic task is helping the client to imagine how he or she would like things to be different and what it will take to make that happen. Little attention is paid to diagnosis, history taking, or exploration of the problem. Solution-focused therapists assume clients want to change, have the capacity to envision change, and are doing their best to make change happen. Further, solution-focused therapists assume that the solution, or at least part of it, is probably already happening. . . . Treatment is brief, usually lasting less than six sessions. (2000:478)

In addition, Lee notes the connection to and consistency with SFBT and other tools and concepts we have addressed in earlier sections, including social constructivism, empowerment, strengths perspective, and cultural competence (2003:389).

Lee suggests, "the purpose of solution-focused intervention is to engage the client in a therapeutic conversation that is conducive to a solution-building process" (2003:390) focused on pragmatic goal setting with the client. Since its beginning in the 1980s a number of specific techniques have been developed to operationalize and implement SFBT. For example, emphasis is placed on several questions used by the practitioner with the client to create a dialog or conversation "to fully utilize the resources and potential of clients" in finding solutions (2003:390). These questions include:

- *Exception questions* ask client to recall times when the problem is either absent, less intense, or dealt with in a manner that was acceptable to the client. . . . Examples: When don't you have this problem? When is the problem less bad? What is different about these times? (Lee 2003: 390)
- *Outcome questions* help clients to envision life without the presenting complaint or with acceptable improvements in the problem. A widely used format is the miracle question. (Lee 2003:390)
- *Miracle question*: "Suppose that tonight, while you were asleep, there is a miracle and the problem that brought you here today has been solved. However, because you were asleep you were unaware that this miracle happened. Could you tell me, what would be different in the morning that would tell you a miracle has taken place? (Newsome and Kelly 2004:70)
- *Coping questions* help clients to notice times when they are coping with their problems and what they are doing when they are successfully coping. . . . Examples: How have you been able to keep going despite all the difficulties you've encountered? How are you able to get around despite language barriers? (Lee 2003)
- *Scaling questions* ask clients to rank their situation and/or goal on a scale of 1 to 10. . . . Usually, one represents the worst possible scenario and 10 is the most desirable outcome. . . . A scaling question may be phrased as "On a one to 10 scale, with one being the worst possible outcome and ten the most desirable outcome, how would you rank your situation?" (Lee 2003:390)
- *Relationship questions* ask clients to imagine how significant others in their environment might react to their problem/situation and to the changes that the client might make. . . . Examples: What would your mother (or spouse, sister, etc.) notice that is different about you if you are more comfortable with the new environment? On a scale of 1 to 10, how would your wife (or other significant others) rank your motivation to change? (Lee 2003:390–391)

In addition, SFBT also includes the assignment of tasks or "homework" to help clients notice solutions in their day-to-day environment. "If clients are able to identify exception behaviors to the problem, clients are asked to 'do more of what works.'" (Lee 2003:391)

SFBT in a ranges of settings has been subjected to empirical study and analysis to determine its effectiveness. After completing a systematic review of literature and studies related to SFBT effectiveness, Gingerich concluded:

Although the current studies [reviewed] fall short of what is needed to establish the efficacy of SFBT, they do provide preliminary support for the idea that SFBT may be beneficial to clients. The wide variety of settings and populations studied and the multiplicity of modalities used suggest that SFBT may be useful in a broad range of applications, however, this tentative conclusion awaits more careful study. All five of the well-controlled studies [analyzed] reported significant benefit from SFBT—four . . . found SFBT to be significantly better than no treatment or standard institutional services. (2000:496)

Tools for social workers from an SEHB perspective—poverty reduction and assets development

Theoretical tools are also needed to address the fundamental concern for poverty reduction. Some exciting approaches and tools are emerging in social work and other fields to address this issue. Many of these tools and approaches share a focus on strengths-based thinking, but differ in their concern for addressing poverty in more comprehensive ways at the macro or community level. These tools include assets-development approaches that shift the focus of poverty policies and programs from an income support (or traditional welfare check to meet subsistence requirements) to an assets approach to allow people and communities to move permanently out of poverty. Rather than simply supporting persons' and communities' continuing subsistence at poverty or below-poverty levels, these approaches foster the development of individual and collective reserves of resources to invest in home ownership, education, or business enterprises that can result in moving out of poverty. These newer, more comprehensive, community-based approaches focus on developing reserves of individual, family, and community human, financial, and social capital rather than simply supporting existence within an environment of permanent poverty. These tools include community-building initiatives, community renewal, assets development, and social capital. We will examine these tools and concepts related to poverty reduction in more detail in Chapter 9.

Standpoint theory

In Chapter 2, standpoint theory was described as an approach to research and practice perspectives that combined a postmodern concern for recognizing political, personal, and social contexts as an integral part of the research and practice environment with the historical concerns of feminism for political action to end oppression. Swigonski defines a **standpoint** as

> a social position from which certain features of reality come into prominence and other aspects of reality are obscured. From a particular social standpoint, one can see some things more clearly than others. Standpoints involve a level of conscious awareness about two things: A person's location in the social structure and that location's relationship to the person's lived experience (Hartsock 1987). One's standpoint emerges from one's social position with regard to gender, culture, color, ethnicity, class, and sexual orientation and how these factors interact and affect one's everyday world. (1993:172)

Standpoint theory emphasizes the strengths and potential contributions of marginalized groups because of their lived experiences. Swigonski calls upon researchers to identify areas of study out of the life experiences of marginalized groups and "to take these groups . . . out of the margins and place their day-to-day reality in the center of research" (1993:173). According to Swigonski, "Standpoint theory builds on the assertion that the less powerful members of society experience a different reality as a consequence of their oppression." As a result of this different reality, "to survive, they must have knowledge, awareness, and sensitivity of both the dominant group's view of society and their own—the potential for 'double vision' or consciousness—and thus the potential for a more complete view of social reality" (Swigonski 1993:173).

Transpersonal/Spiritual approaches

As we noted in the discussion of spirituality in Chapter 2, this is an area many social work educators and practitioners believe has been neglected in both the contexts of social work education and of practice. We explore some current thinking here about transpersonal and humanistic psychology and their potential adaptability to social work education and practice. Clearly the areas of transpersonal and humanistic psychology and their applications to social work are currently considered alternative approaches.

Cowley and Derezotes call for a paradigm shift toward "incorporating the phenomenological aspects of transpersonal theory that come from Eastern contemplative practice"—to help incorporate spiritual aspects of being into social work education and practice (1994:32). They suggest that "transpersonal means going beyond the personal level . . . to include the spiritual or higher states of consciousness" (1994:33). They place transpersonal psychology among the basic theoretical paradigms of the discipline. They note that transpersonal psychology was referred to by Maslow as the Fourth Force in psychology:

- First Force: Dynamic (psychoanalytic)
- Second Force: Behavioral
- Third Force: Experiential, humanistic, existential
- Fourth Force: Transpersonal (Cowley and Derezotes 1994:34)

Transpersonal psychology was an alternative theory that challenged the notion of such psychologists as Maslow that self-actualization was the highest level of human development. You might recall our discussion of Maslow's notion of peak or "aha" experience as an example of intuitive understanding in Chapter 2. Transpersonal psychology is a synthesis of Eastern and Western psychologies that "offers an expanded notion of human possibilities that goes beyond self-actualization and beyond ego . . . and beyond the limitations of time and/or space" (Cowley and Derezotes 1994:33).

Miovic discusses two Eastern spiritual belief systems that have influenced Western understanding of transpersonal/spiritual approaches—Buddhism and Hinduism. Buddhism is an agnostic belief system and Hinduism is theistic (see our discussion of agnostic and theistic spiritual belief systems in Chapter 2). Miovic points out:

> The two largest religious/spiritual traditions in Asia are Buddhism and Hinduism, both of which have developed sophisticated systems of spiritual psychology in which philosophy and religion are not divorced from psychology as they typically are in the West. Of these two major traditions . . . Buddhism has made a larger impact on Western psychology thus far. One important reason for this differential impact is that many schools of Buddhism are non-theistic, as the historical Buddha chose to remain silent about the ultimate nature of reality. . . . [T]he Buddha's non-theism is closer to the world view of Western science than is the . . . monotheism of Hindu thought.
>
> The essence of agnostic Buddhist psychology . . . lies in using mindfulness (open awareness of the moment) and *vipassana* meditation (focused concentration) to reveal the "self" as a fluid construct that has no permanent, objective identity. (2004:109–110)

Social workers operating from transpersonal theory "would consider human potential as inherently able to evolve beyond self-actualization toward states of exceptional well-being and self-transcendence" (Cowley and Deregotes 1994:34). Such social workers believe "the needs for meaning, for higher values, for a spiritual life, are as real as biological or social need" (Keen in Cowley and Derezotes 1994:34).

Sermabeikian (1994:179) points out that the psychologist, Carl Jung, "sought to prove that the spiritual dimension is the essence of human nature." Two important concepts for Jung were the notions of "**collective unconscious** and the **archetypes of the psyche,** thought to contain the inherited and accumulated experiences of the human and prehuman species evidenced by the symbols, myths, rituals, and cultures of all times" (emphasis added). Walsh and Vaughan (1994:10) stress a similar conceptualization, by Ken Wilber a leading transpersonal psychologist, but one differentiated by levels of consciousness. Wilber hypothesizes two distinct lines of evolution:

1. The average or collective consciousness.
2. The pioneers who preceed and inspire the collective (shaman, yogi, saint, sage) (Walsh and Vaughn 1994:10).

Wilber argues that we need to use multiple paradigm approaches to help us understand the complexity of human behavior and the social environment. He suggests that there are three epistemological modes or ways of knowing:

1. The sensory: scientific approaches to knowing.
2. The intellectual or symbolic: hermeneutic or interpretive approaches.
3. The contemplative: intersubjective testing by masters/teachers in this realm (Walsh and Vaughn 1994:11–14).

Wilber argues that "reality is multilayered and that the levels of existence form an ontological hierarchy, or *holoarchy* as he prefers to call it, that includes matter, body, mind, and spirit" (Walsh and Vaughn 1994:16–17). Wilber suggests that "we first identify with the body, then with the ego-mind, and perhaps thereafter, as a result of contemplative practices, with more subtle mental realms and eventually pure consciousness itself"(Walsh and Vaughn 1994:17). Wilber also notes that the concept of ontological hierarchy has historically been used to dominate and devalue the lower end of the spectrum, e.g., the body, emotions, sexuality, and the earth" (Walsh and Vaughn 1994:17).

While perhaps controversial, these notions of transpersonal realities that transcend those we experience through our senses everyday, may be valuable to us as we attempt to more fully understand the behaviors and worldviews of ourselves and those with whom we work.

Alternative extensions of systems approaches

Since social systems thinking has been and continues to be such an important force in conceptualizing and organizing the way social workers think about humans and their interactions with the social environment, we will now return to systems approaches and explore some more recent extensions of this approach. Recently systems thinking has been extended beyond using it to understand the basic order of systems to include disorder or chaos and other types of complexity within both human and other physical systems. Another interesting extension of systems thinking is the Gaia hypotheses which has called into question some of our basic thinking about human evolution and about the relationship of humans to the inanimate world.

Chaos/Complexity

Krippner provides a definition of chaos theory that comes from the dynamical systems theory of mathematics. He explains that "**chaos theory** *is the branch of mathematics for the study of processes that seem so complex that at first* *they do not appear to be governed by any known laws or principles, but which actually have an underlying order. . . .* Examples of chaotic processes include a stream of rising smoke that breaks down and becomes turbulent, water flowing in a stream or crashing at the bottom of a waterfall, electroencephalographic activity of the brain, changes in animal populations, fluctuation on the stock exchange, and the weather. All of these phenomena involve the interaction of several elements and the pattern of their changes over time as they interact . . ." (emphasis added). Krippner explains that "Chaos theorists . . . look for patterns in nature that, while very complex, nonetheless contain a great degree of eloquent and beautiful order, and chaos theory attempts to direct investigators to a cosmic principle that can both simplify and deepen their understanding of nature" (1994:49).

James Gleick, in one of the first books about chaos theory published for readers outside of mathematics and the natural sciences, described the intense paradigm shift within the natural sciences that this theory was causing:

> Where chaos begins, classical science stops. For as long as the world has had physicists inquiring into the laws of nature, it has suffered a special ignorance about disorder in the atmosphere, in the turbulent sea, in the fluctuations of wildlife populations, in the oscillations of the heart and the brain. The irregular side of nature, the discontinuous and erratic side—these have been puzzles to science, or worse, monstrosities. (Gleick 1987:3)

Gleick believes that chaos cuts across the many different scientific disciplines and "poses problems that defy accepted ways of working in science. It makes strong claims about the universal behavior of complexity" (1987:5). Gleick believes this shift will help return the natural sciences to considering questions of more direct and immediate meaning to humans.

Gleick stresses that chaos and complexity theorists believe they have discovered that contrary to traditional scientific thinking "tiny differences in input could quickly become overwhelming differences in output—a phenomenon given the name '**sensitive dependence on initial conditions.**' In weather, for example, this translates into what is only half-jokingly known as the **Butterfly Effect**—the notion that a butterfly stirring the air today in Peking [sic] can transform storm systems next month in New York" (1987:18).

Order in disorder. According to Gleick: "Those studying chaotic dynamics discovered that the disorderly behavior of simple systems acted as a *creative* process. It generated **complexity:** richly organized patterns, sometimes stable and sometimes unstable, sometimes finite and sometimes infinite, but always with the fascination of living things" (1987:43). A related concept for describing this notion of order within disorder is that of fractal. **Fractals** are "geometric patterns with repetitive self-similar features have been called 'fractal' . . .

Chaos and Order by Gleick 1987:6–8

Physicists are beginning to return to serious consideration of phenomena on a human scale as opposed to either the cosmos or the tiniest of particles. And in this turn they are finding equal wonder at the complexity and unpredictability of these everyday phenomena. . . . They study not just galaxies but clouds. . . . The simplest systems are now seen to create extraordinarily difficult problems of predictability. Yet order arises spontaneously in those systems—chaos and order together.

because of their fractional dimensions." Mandelbrot, a scientist who studied "irregular patterns in natural processes" found "a quality of self-similarity. . . . **Self-similarity** is symmetry across scale. It implies recursion, pattern inside of pattern. . . . Self-similarity is an easily recognizable quality. Its images are everywhere in the culture: in the infinitely deep reflection of a person standing between two mirrors, or in the cartoon notion of a fish eating a smaller fish eating a smaller fish eating a smaller fish" (Gleick 1987:103).

Gleick and others suggest that chaos and complexity theory reflect a paradigm shift of major proportions within science. Think about our discussion in Chapter 1 of history and how what were once alternative paradigms, became traditional and dominant wordviews held universally by large groups of people. If traditional approaches to science are replaced by or even begin to substantively include notions of chaos and complexity, how might our definitions of both physical and social realities change? To many people today, this is not a question to consider in the future, it is a part of present discourse about the nature and behavior of reality.

While chaos theory has typically been considered within the realm of mathematics and the natural sciences, interest in this phenomenon is rapidly spreading to the social sciences and to other areas of the natural sciences such as health care and medicine.

Chaos, biology, and health. Krippner points out that, for example:

> Chaos theory has also been used to construct models of illness and health that take exception to certain aspects of medical models. For example, the standard medical model holds that a healthy body has rather simple rhythms. . . . An unhealthy body, therefore, would have a more complex, less controlled tempo. Contrary to this notion

> 1. In leukemia, the number of white blood cells changes dramatically from week to week but is more predictable than that of healthy people who have chaotic fluctuations in their levels of white blood cells.
>
> 2. Congestive heart failure is typically preceded by a stable, periodic quickening and slowing of respiration.
>
> 3. The brain "has to be highly irregular; if not you have epilepsy."
>
> 4. Brains of schizophrenics . . . suggest that "the schizophrenia victim is suffering from too much order—trapped order." (Briggs and Peat 1989 in Krippner 1994:54–55).

Chaos and creativity. Others have applied the notions of complexity and chaos to psychology and creativity. Rossi suggests that "human creativity may have an underlying chaotic process that selectively amplifies small fluctuations and molds them into coherent mental states experienced as thought and imagination" (in Richards 1996:53–54). Richards also argues that "chaotic models seem particularly appropriate for humanistic psychology—they are open, complex, evolving, and unpredictable—by contrast with the linear, bounded, cause-and-effect models of a more constrained science of human behavior. They also, to reemphasize, seem to provide the ultimate in uniqueness along with the ultimate in interconnectedness" (1996:57).

Gaia

Perhaps the most controversial alternative extension of systems thinking flowing from chaos and complexity theory is known as the **Gaia Hypothesis.** This is a perspective on systems thinking that goes well beyond the traditional notions of thinking in terms of specific systems, for example, social systems or human systems, to viewing the entire earth as a whole system. James Lovelock and Lynn Margulis are usually credited with formulating and putting forward the Gaia hypothesis. Lovelock and Margulis's **Gaia hypothesis** includes two fundamental components:

1. The planet is . . . a "super organismic system."
2. Evolution is the result of cooperative not competitive processes. (Stanley 1996:www)

Lovelock describes the "Earth as living organism" component of the Gaia hypothesis in the following excerpts:

> The entire range of living matter on Earth from whales to viruses and from oaks to algae could be regarded as constituting a single living entity capable of maintaining the Earth's atmosphere to suit its overall needs and endowed with faculties and powers far beyond those of its constituent parts . . . [*Gaia* can be defined] as a complex entity involving the Earth's biosphere, atmosphere, oceans, and soil; the totality constituting a feedback of cybernetic systems which seeks an optimal physical and chemical environment for life on this planet. (Stanley:www)

Stanley (1996:www) describes the Gaia hypothesis as follows

> Just as human physiology can be viewed as a system of interacting components (nervous, pulmonary, circulatory, endocrine systems, etc.), so too can the Earth be understood as a system of four principal components (atmosphere, biosphere, geosphere, and hydrosphere).

The Gaia Hypothesis calls into question some of the basic Darwinian notions about survival of the fittest as the central component of evolution.

Margulis has said Darwin's theory was not incorrect, but merely incomplete. She contended that her research on the evolution of certain organisms (referred to as endosymbiosis) revealed that a symbiotic, or mutually beneficial, relationship was central to their ongoing evolution. She contended that "symbiosis, not chance mutation (as Darwin had theorized), was the driving force behind evolution and that the cooperation between organisms and the environment are the chief agents of natural selection—not competition among individuals" (Stanley 1996:www).

Lovelock argued for this extended notion of symbiotic and system-like functioning as an enlargement of ecological theory:

> By taking the species and their physical environment together as a single system, we can, for the first time, build ecological models that are mathematically stable and yet include large numbers of competing species. In these models increased diversity among the species leads to better regulation. (Stanley 1996:www)

Gaia: Was Darwin Wrong? by Stanley 1996:www

In classical science nature was seen as a mechanical system composed of basic building blocks. In accordance with this view, Darwin proposed a theory of evolution in which the unit of survival was the species, the subspecies, or some other building block of the biological world. But a century later it has become quite clear that the unit of survival is not any of these entities. What survives is the organism-in-its-environment.

An organism that thinks only in terms of its own survival will invariably destroy its environment and, as we are learning from bitter experience, will thus destroy itself.

From the system point of view the unit of survival is not [an] entity at all, but rather a pattern of organization adopted by an organism in its interactions with its environment.

When the activity of an organism favors the environment as well as the organism itself, then its spread will be assisted; eventually the organism and the environmental change associated with it will become global in extent. The reverse is also true, and any species that adversely affects the environment is doomed; but life goes on (Stanley 1996:www).

SUMMARY/TRANSITION

In this chapter we have explored some additional tools that can help organize and guide our thinking as we proceed to examine alternative and traditional perspectives on human behavior at a variety of levels—individual, family, group, organization, and community. We have explored the use of metaphors, the need to appreciate ambiguity, the unity of personal or individual and political or social change, the power of language and words, and the need to consider inclusiveness and exclusiveness as we continue our journey. We summarized a number of traditional, middle-range, and alternative theories used by social workers to think about HBSE. Along with our knowledge of the dimensions of traditional and alternative paradigm thinking, we will now use this collection of tools to continue our journey toward more complete understanding of human behavior and the social environment.

Succeed with PEARSON mysocialworklab

Log onto **www.mysocialworklab.com** to watch videos on the skills and competencies discussed in this chapter. (*If you did not receive an access code to **MySocialWorkLab** with this text and wish to purchase access online, please visit* www.mysocialworklab.com.)

Ethical Practice Human Behavior Engage Assess Intervene Evaluate Practice Contexts

---

PRACTICE TEST

1. A social worker who practices according to the concept of "personal as political" would most likely _____
   a. be involved in individual and social change activities.
   b. urge clients to run for political office.
   c. work only with community systems.
   d. insist that his/her agency focus on group work.

Human Behavior

2. Which of the following statements is consistent with a strengths perspective?
   a. The strength of the helping relationship comes from the social workers' role as a professional.
   b. In many situations the client is the victim of a harsh environment.
   c. The social worker works as a collaborator with the client.
   d. Strengths must come from the environment since the client lacks sufficient strengths.

3. A symbolic, pictorial structure of concepts, in terms of metaphors and propositions, concerning a specific problem, or a piece of reality and of how it works is a _____.
   a. theory
   b. model
   c. conceptual framework
   d. epistemological outline

4. _____ refers to not only books and documents but also utterances of any kind and in any medium, including cultural practices.
   a. texts
   b. language
   c. discourse
   d. metaphor

Engage Assess Intervene Evaluate

5. A model of assessment that involves the client providing their assessment of needs and strengths and working with the team as a whole to decide on appropriate methods for assessment and using methods from disciplines that appear appropriate is
   a. wholistic assessment
   b. multidisciplinary assessment
   c. transdisciplinary assessment
   d. client-centered assessment

6. A social worker that looks at change in individual lives and in family units over time by tracing individual developmental trajectories or paths in the context of development of family units would be utilizing _____.
   a. life course theory
   b. life span theory
   c. family role theory
   d. human development theory

7. Which of the following statements is NOT representative of empowerment?
   a. Intervention occurs after the social worker determines what the client's strengths are.
   b. It is a theory and practice that deal with issues of power, powerlessness and oppression.
   c. It is a process that can take place on the individual, interpersonal, and community level.
   d. It teaches specific skills.

8. The _____ assumes that all people see the world from the place in which they are situated socioculturally.
   a. Afrocentric epistemological theory
   b. multiple diversities theory
   c. feminist standpoint theory
   d. Eurocentric patriarchal feminist theory

9. A social worker who spends little time on diagnosis and history taking, and feels the main therapeutic task is helping the client imagine how he/she would like things to be different and what it will take to make that happen is employing _____.
   a. an ecological perspective
   b. a transdisciplinary perspective
   c. systems theory
   d. solution-focused brief therapy

10. Which of the following is an approach that a social worker could use that shifts the focus of poverty policies from income support to an assets approach to help individuals and communities move out of poverty?
    a. social capital
    b. community building initiatives
    c. assets development
    d. all of the above

Answers

1) a 2) c 3) b 4) a 5) c 6) b 7) a 8) c 9) d 10) d

Using Solution-Oriented Interventions in an Ecological Frame: A Case Illustration

Bruce Teall

The ecological conceptualization of the person-in-environment has long been the basis of social work practice. The ecological perspective presents an easily understood metaphor for seeing the client as coexisting with his or her environment, not as existing separately from the environment. Germain (1973) first presented ecological interactions as a model for social work practice. By acknowledging that the client functions reciprocally with the environment, interventions can occur through any system with which the client interacts. The metaphor has been extended to create the life model of social work practice, which focuses on people's strengths and growth toward health, modification of the environment, and raising the level of person–environment fit (Germain and Gitterman 1996). The life model does not stipulate specific techniques, however. It is an open structure in which various treatment modalities, in this case a solution-focused model, can be used to assist clients in attaining their goals (Germain and Gitterman 1980).

There are many excellent descriptions of solution-oriented treatment techniques for both general use (see de Shazer 1985, 1988, 1991; de Shazer et al. 1986; O'Hanlon and Weiner-Davis 1989; Walter and Peller 1992) and specialized uses such as family preservation (Berg 1994), chemical dependency treatment (Berg and Miller 1992), and school counseling (Metcalf 1995; Murphy 1996). In brief, however, solution-focused models are oriented toward the elements of a client's experience that are positive and growth promoting, not toward elements that are problematic and stagnant (Cade and O'Hanlon 1993; Molnar and de Shazer 1987).

After time spent joining with the client and eliciting a description of the problem, the counselor begins to look for exceptions (see Figure 1 [missing in original]). Within solution-oriented approaches, an exception is defined as any time the problem does not occur or is less problematic (de Shazer 1991). If an exception is found, then the counselor asks questions to help the counselor and the client more fully understand the structure of the exception. If no exception can be found, the counselor begins to look for a hypothetical solution through devices such as the Miracle Question (de Shazer 1988) or Fast Forward Questions (O'Hanlon and Weiner-Davis 1989). Both of these devices use language to help the client imagine a future when he or she has achieved the treatment goal. Whether the solution is based on an exception from the client's past or an imagined event in the client's future, the distinctions made by the client become the basis of a task to assign (Walter and Peller 1992). After a break, the counselor returns to deliver the intervention and task to the client (Berg and Miller 1992).

This article presents a case illustration of a solution-focused model used in an ecological practice perspective, as well as data analysis using a

---

Teall, B. (2000, January). "Using Solution-Oriented Interventions in an Ecological Frame: A Case Illustration." *Social Work in Education,* 22(1), 54–61. Retrieved March 16, 2009, from Academic Search Premier database.

single-subject design to evaluate the treatment outcome. The case shows how a solution-focused model can be used not only with the client, but also with the client's environment. No search for hypothetical solutions is necessary because exceptions are identified at each level: the individual, the family, and the school. These exceptions are then used by the client, the client's mother, and the client's teaching team to cooperate with the student in improving his performance at school.

Case Example

Simon was an 11-year-old white boy attending the 6th grade when he was referred by his guidance counselor for additional counseling at an out-of-school agency. Simon had not satisfactorily completed his homework or classroom assignments in over four years. He was being considered for retention despite above-average standardized test scores. Simon was residing with his mother and older brother; his father had died of an AIDS-related illness two years earlier. Treatment was conducted in nine sessions over four weeks.

During the first session, Simon was asked what he would like to achieve through treatment. Cooperation with the client by honoring his or her choice of treatment goals is a vital component of the solution-focused models (Berg & Miller, 1992). Simon stated that he wanted to get good grades in school. This was operationalized as no grades lower than a C– in the next marking period. In addition, Simon stated that although he did well on tests, he needed to complete his assignments to raise his grades. It had become clear to Simon that he needed to do his homework.

Having decided on an immediate treatment goal of increasing his number of assignments completed, the task became to uncover two of eight and organize the resources Simon already had at his disposal. One way to begin this process is by searching for exceptions to the problem. When Simon was asked to remember a time when he had completed his homework, Simon was able to give an example. Simon and the counselor then explored how it was that Simon managed to do his homework. As unsatisfying as it may seem, the only difference Simon identified when comparing times when he did his work with times when he did not was when "My mom asked me to do it."

It could be said that Simon was abdicating his own responsibility for completing his assignments by relying on his mother to prompt him. However, in the solution-focused model, what is important is the isolation of a previously successful behavior. One of the central tenets of solution-oriented treatment is that if you find something that works, do more of it (Berg and Miller 1992; Molnar and de Shazer 1987; Walter and Peller 1992). But, to capitalize on this information with Simon, the counselor must be able to use a multisystems perspective. In ecological terminology, the solution resides at the point of interaction between the client system and the family system (Kirst-Ashman and Hull 1993): in this case, Simon's mother telling him to do his homework.

Session three was scheduled with Simon and his mother to join with the family and begin goal setting. In session four, Simon and the counselor met at school and explored the possibility of additional exceptions as well as continuing to refine Simon's goal of increasing his grades. During session five, the counselor met with Simon and his mother and reviewed the treatment goal and the uncovered exception. Simon's mother indicated that she shared an interest in Simon's goal and that she was willing participate in the process.

When asked what she needed to help Simon, she stated that their family was currently quite chaotic. A search for exceptions with her revealed an early morning ritual that she no longer used. She reported that this ritual had been helpful for maintaining family structure in the past. Specifically, she would wake up 30 minutes before her sons and have a cup of coffee while making a daily list of things to do. In addition, she and Simon decided that setting a daily homework time would be helpful. The task assigned at the end of the fifth session was for the mother to resume her morning ritual.

In the sixth session, Simon's mother reported that she had been rising early to do her list and have a cup of coffee. She also stated that Simon had been doing his homework. They had set and observed a homework time, and Simon proudly reported that he had already completed five of seven missing assignments. He expected to be completely caught up by the end of the week. At this point his mother related concerns about being able to maintain changes and asked the counselor to attend a meeting with Simon's teaching team. The therapeutic task given to Simon and his mother was to do more of what was working (Molnar and de Shazer 1987; Walter and Peller 1992).

When engaging the next system, Simon's teaching team, the same strategy was used—during a school meeting the team was asked to recount times when they had found solutions in the past. They related examples of using an assignment book coupled with parent and teacher signatures. The teachers and Simon's mother expressed a willingness to use the same strategy in Simon's case.

In the ninth and final session, Simon and his mother related that he was current with all his assignments. Simon sat up straight in his chair, smiled broadly, and said that he was extremely proud of himself. His mother reported that "he was like a new kid," and that he was much more cooperative around the house. She also felt he seemed more energetic and happier. Simon agreed with his mother's assessment. The remainder of the session was spent reviewing what had worked for them, what problems might potentially appear in the future, and how they could manage the problems with the skills they had developed.

As well as collecting data from teachers regarding the follow-up period, Simon and his mother were contacted by telephone at two, four, and six weeks. Both Simon and his mother reported that they were still on track. The mother stated that Simon's behavior and mood continued to improve. Simon related that he continued to do his homework and that he felt really good about it.

Single-Subject Design

The setting and goals of Simon's case allowed for an analysis of whether the treatment was effective by use of a single-subject design. Simon's teachers provided data six weeks after Simon's treatment was completed. These grades were used to examine the fit between the case and the use of a solution-oriented model in an ecological frame. It was expected that if solution-oriented interventions were used in multiple systems, then the client's school performance would improve despite the short duration of the treatment. Performance was operationalized as a ratio of completed work:

assignment completion ratio = assignments handed in to instructor/assignment given by the instructor to date

Improvement was defined as an increase in the assignment completion ratio.

Method

After the school's initial referral, the counselor met with the teaching team. At that time the instructors were asked if they were willing to cooperate with a study of solution-focused treatment methods by sharing the data they routinely collected for purposes of grading. The team agreed, and it was arranged that the teachers would follow their usual procedures of recording grades and assignments completed in their grade books. Six weeks after termination with the client, a meeting between the counselor and the treatment team was scheduled.

Each instructor supplied data relating to assignments on a weekly basis. For each week the total number of assignments given to date and the total number of assignments handed in by the client were provided. Data were collected for each of the four weeks before the start of treatment (baseline period), each of the four weeks while the counselor conducted nine sessions (treatment period), and each of the six weeks following treatment (follow-up period). For each week the total number of assignments completed was divided by the total number of assignments due, thus supplying the assignment completion ratio for that week.

One problem in data collection occurred. During week three of the treatment period, one of Simon's instructors was replaced with a long-term substitute teacher. Unfortunately the original teacher's data were not available. Although inclusion of the replacement instructor's data in follow-up results show an even higher assignment completion ratio, these figures were dropped from the analysis for the sake of consistency.

Results

The data collected show a distinct improvement in the assignment completion ratio (Table 1) Bloom, Fischer, and Orme (1995) suggested a measure of significance for a single-system design. They related that the occurrence of at least two consecutive observations, each of which is more than two standard deviations in the desirable direction from the baseline mean, is significant at an alpha level of .05 (Bloom, Fischer, and Orme; Gottman and Leiblum 1974). As can be seen in Figure 2 [missing in original], the assignment completion ratios for treatment weeks 6, 7 and 8, as well as the ratios for follow-up weeks 9 through 14, are all significant (p < .05).

Discussion

The results support the hypothesis that a solution-oriented model used within multiple client systems concurrently would result in an increase in the assignment completion ratio. This article offers an example of the practical application of a combined model and support for its effectiveness rather than expand the knowledge base within the field of school social work.

Although a single-subject design has very limited external validity, it could be inferred that a multisystemic approach can be helpful when many sessions

| Table 1 | **Assignment Completion Ratios for Each Phase** | | | |

Legend for Chart:
A - Phase
B - M
C - SD
D - Min
E - Max

A	B	C	D	E
Baseline	.39	.06	.30	.44
Treatment	.84	.31	.38	1.00
Follow-up	.96	.01	.94	.97

can be used within a short period of time it. In addition, the solution-focused method was shown to be effective with an individual, a family, and a teaching team. The combined model also was shown to be useful in creating cooperative interventions across systems (that is, parent and child set up a homework time, and parent and school worked together with the assignment book).

Unfortunately, the use of a single-system design precludes generalizing about a larger population. Also, there has been no comparison to other modes of treatment, and a single-subject design does not incorporate a control group. Finally, this study does not account for factors such as artificial motivation created by a fear of being kept back a grade, the power of a positive relationship with the counselor, or nonsolution-oriented techniques used during sessions. Nonetheless, this article has implications for school social workers relating to both solution-focused techniques and practice evaluation using single-subject designs.

Schools offer many occasions for social workers to use single-subject designs. The main limitations of single subject-designs are poor external validity, defining problem targets in operational terms, and challenges in data collection (Rubin and Babbie 1993). Defining operational terms and collecting data are simplified because of the many measures routinely used in school settings. Standardized test scores, attendance records, and grades can be used as problem targets that are quantifiable, and data can be collected unobtrusively, objectively, and consistently. Perhaps most important, however, is the opportunity for replicating and aggregating the results of consistent designs with different clients. This is the most effective way to establish external validity for single-subject designs (Rubin and Babbie).

A combined model of solution-oriented techniques in an ecological frame also has important implications for school social workers. As schools continue take on more social functions, school social workers find themselves acting as the interface among students, families, teachers, administrators, and communities, as well as local, state, and federal governments. Although this can be overwhelming, it can also be an opportunity. As shown in this case, the ability to shift from one system to another can make the difference between a student being stuck and a student reaching their goal. With this in mind, each system involved in a case becomes a new place to intervene. Also, each system offers its own expert knowledge and resources. Solution-oriented models combined with an ecological perspective allow school social workers to efficiently use a wide range of resources and co-create solutions to a student's problem.

[Diagram (Figure 1) and Graph (Figure 2) missing in original html version.]

References

1. Berg, I. K. (1994). *Family-based services*. New York: W. W. Norton.
2. Berg, I. K., and Miller, S. D. (1992). *Working with the problem drinker: A solution-focused approach*. New York: W. W. Norton.
3. Bloom, M., Fischer, J., and Orme, J. G. (1995). *Evaluating practice* (2nd ed.). Boston: Allyn and Bacon.
4. Cade, B., and O'Hanlon, W. H. (1993). *A brief guide to brief therapy*. New York: W. W. Norton.
5. de Shazer, S. (1985). *Keys to solutions in brief therapy*. New York: W. W. Norton.
6. de Shazer, S. (1988). *Clues: Investigating solutions in brief therapy*. New York: W. W. Norton.
7. de Shazer, S. (1991). *Putting differences to work*. New York: W. W. Norton.
8. de Shazer, S., Berg, I. K., Lipchik, E., Nunnally, E., Molnar, A., Gingerich, W., and Weiner-Davis, M. (1986). Brief therapy: Focused solution development. *Family Process*, 25(6), 207–222.

9. Germain, C. B. (1973). An ecological perspective in casework practice. *Social Casework*, 54, 323–330.
10. Germain, C. B., and Gitterman, A. (1980). *The life model of social work practice* (rev. ed.). New York: Columbia University Press.
11. Germain, C. B., and Gitterman, A. (1996). *The life model of social work practice.* New York: Columbia University Press.
12. Gottman, J. M., and Leiblum, S. R. (1974). *How to do psychotherapy and how to evaluate it.* New York: Holt, Rinehart and Winston.
13. Kirst-Ashman, K. K., and Hull, G. H. (1993). *Understanding generalist practice.* Chicago: Nelson-Hall.
14. LeCroy, C. W. (Ed.). (1992). *Case studies in social work practice.* Belmont, CA: Wadsworth.
15. Metcalf, L. (1995). *Counseling toward solutions.* West Nyack, NY: Center for Applied Research in Education.
16. Molnar, A., and de Shazer, S. (1987). Solution-focused therapy: Toward the identification of therapeutic tasks. *Journal of Marital and Family Therapy*, 13, 349–358.
17. Murphy, J. J. (1996). Solution-focused brief therapy in the school. In S. D. Miller, M. A. Hubble, and B. L. Duncan (Eds.), *Handbook of solution-focused brief therapy* (pp. 184–204). San Francisco: Jossey-Bass.
18. O'Hanlon, W. H., and Weiner-Davis, M. (1989). *In search of solutions.* New York: W. W. Norton.
19. Rubin, A., and Babbie, E. (1993). *Research methods for social work* (2nd ed.). Pacific Grove, CA: Brooks/Cole.
20. Walter, J. L., and Peller, J. E. (1992). *Becoming solution-focused in brief therapy.* New York: Brunner/Mazel.

4

Traditional/Dominant Perspectives on Individuals

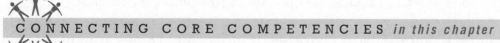

CONNECTING CORE COMPETENCIES *in this chapter*

| Professional Identity | Ethical Practice | **Critical Thinking** | **Diversity in Practice** | Human Rights & Justice | Research Based Practice | Human Behavior | Policy Practice | Practice Contexts | **Engage Assess Intervene Evaluate** |

As we proceed we need to continually weigh what we discover about any of the paradigms and perspectives we explore against the purpose of the social work profession—"to promote human and community well-being" and be guided by its principles and constructs, including:

> a person and environment construct, a global perspective, respect for human diversity, knowledge based on scientific inquiry . . . [a] quest for social and economic justice, the prevention of conditions that limit human rights, the elimination of poverty, and the enhancement of the quality of life for all persons (CSWE, 2008:1).

As we consider different perspectives (traditional in this chapter and alternative in the following chapter) on individuals, we need to keep in mind their potential roles in facilitating or hindering social change/transformation.

The tasks we set for ourselves as we continue our journey toward more complete understanding of HBSE are certainly challenging ones. However, like the assumptions of interconnectedness and interdependence we made in Chapter 1 about social work, ourselves, and the people with whom we work, all the chapters of this book are interconnected and interdependent. For example, in this chapter and the next one we focus on individuals, but we will not leave the things we learn and the questions we raise about individual development and behavior when we reach the end of the next two chapters. After we complete our exploration of traditional and alternative perspectives on the individual, in this chapter and the next one, the chapters that follow these—on familiness, groups, organizations, community(ies), and the global context—will continue to be heavily concerned with individual development. Families, groups, organizations, communities, and international issues are, in fact, fundamental contexts within which our own and others' individual development takes place. These contexts affect our development as, simultaneously, we affect the nature of these contexts.

A CRITICAL PERSPECTIVE ON DEVELOPMENTAL JOURNEYS: LADDERS TO CLIMB?

Perhaps the most traditional and widely used models of individual behavior and development are linear approaches focusing on a chronological series of age-related developmental stages and tasks. These models or frameworks present the tasks and expectations of human development as though we each must "climb a developmental ladder." We step onto the first rung at conception or birth (depending on the particular model or theorist) and we step off the last rung at death.

These linear approaches are attractive because they offer an optimistic view of development as continuous growth and progress. They also lend simplicity, predictability, and order to the apparent chaos of human change (Steenbarger 1991:288). However, these approaches tend to leave us with the impression that the "developmental ladder" is virtually the same for everyone and that the ladder is equally accessible to everyone. They oversimplify the complexities, diversities, and ambiguities that characterize human development.

Critiques of Traditional Stage-Based Theories of Individual Development

A number of scholars have described a variety of criticisms of traditional theories of human development, especially strict adherence to linear stage theories of development. In order to maintain a critical approach to using

Social workers apply critical thinking to inform professional judgments and, as part of professional practice, they critique knowledge to understand person and environment. Using your critical thinking skills as you read this section, what conclusions do you reach regarding the value of traditional stage-based theories of individual development? You need not agree with the content of this section in reaching your conclusions. However, you do need to use your knowledge of principles of logic, scientific inquiry, and reasoned discernment.

traditional theories of development in our work as social workers, we should be aware of these critiques. The critiques below center around overemphasis on individual or internal influences and minimizing the impact of environmental influences on development; the inadequacy of chronological age as the determiner of transition from one stage to the next; overemphasis on development as achievement rather than simply change; and inadequacy for explaining or incorporating human diversity.

The social environment and traditional theories of individual development: Too little "SE" and too much "HB"

This critique of traditional theories of individual development is consistent with our concern for considering HBSE from an SEHB perspective. What are some of the consequences, if traditional theories of individual development have their primary emphases on internal processes of development to the exclusion of social environmental influences? One critical consequence of the omission of concern for social environmental processes is failure to consider the impact of poverty and oppressions on development. Traditional perspectives often fail to question how individual developmental experiences and outcomes might be very different for persons living in poverty and/or faced with oppression from the larger environment because of gender, race/ethnicity, sexual orientation, or disability, than for financially well-off persons not faced with oppression.

Global perspective and traditional theories of individual development

Another area related to concern about the underemphasis on social environmental issues in traditional thinking about individual development is that of a global or international perspective. Chatterjee and Hokenstad argue that

> Full appreciation and understanding of human behavior in the context of the social environment requires inclusion of an international and comparative dimension. . . . The globalization of contemporary society influences all aspects of human life. A world economy increasingly impacts on the social and psychological well-being of individuals in every country. Worldwide problems such as environmental pollution and global warming affect everyone's biological well-being. Mass migration of people coupled with increasingly unequal distribution of wealth among nations have a direct impact on the quality of life for most if not all Americans. (Chatterjee and Hokenstad 1997:186)

In addition, the lack of international perspectives in traditional theories of individual human behavior causes omission of a comparative approach and risks assumptions that human behavior can be measured everywhere with the same "yardstick." Chatterjee and Hokenstad argue that "only a comparative mode of analysis can provide full understanding of how people function in different social environments" (1997:186). For example, "cross-national . . . research helps students identify culturally specific behaviors" such as "what certain groups take to be the 'right' way for performing basic human tasks such as disciplining children or toilet training. . . . or how different cultures construct their views of the sacred" (Chatterjee and Hokenstad 1997:186–7).

Environmental, internal, chronological issues

Criticisms of stage-based theories include **failure to consider environmental influences sufficiently**. Miller notes that "Bronfenbrenner (1977) describes the greatest limitation of the study of human development as the failure to go beyond the focus on the individual; he suggests that a full understanding of individual development requires an examination of the larger social ecology" (1992:34). Another criticism of stage theories is their **overemphasis on internal processes.** D'Augelli "suggests that many current models of lesbian and gay male identity formation suffer from an excessive emphasis on the internal processes of personal development, usually conceived of in stage-model terms" (1994:324–328). A third criticism of stage theories stresses the **limits of chronological age.** Jendrek and other critics of age-stage based approaches suggest that connections between chronological age and life periods (traditional role sets such as grandparenthood) have become blurred. They suggest instead the notion of "fluid-cycle" patterns. "This model also contains patterns and expectations, but they are *less* likely to be geared to age" (1994:207).

These increasing variations lead "proponents of the fluid-cycle model [to] argue, therefore, that it becomes difficult to distinguish major life events in terms of age. Despite the theme of orderliness in the life-course literature, research suggests "that 'disorder' may be more 'normal' than 'order'" (Jendrek 1994:207). This is consistent with notions of chaos and complexity and with other alternative paradigm approaches that question both "grand narratives or theories" such as 'life course' and orderly stage-based approaches to human development.

Developmental change as achievement

Bergen reminds us that the achievement orientation prevalent in dominant U.S. society has resulted in seeing "'development as achievement.' Thus, American parents and teachers see young children's developmental changes as the attainment of milestones or stages that mark progress." Bergen (quoting Feinman and Bruner) "questions our view that development is progress rather than just change" and urges us to remember that "human beings, whatever their age, are completed forms of what they are" (1994:13). This definition of "development as achievement" leads to such concepts as "'developmental delay,' which implies that, for some young children, developmental achievements have not occurred in a timely, sequential fashion." Bergen reminds us that "the sequences, milestones, and stages outlined by numerous researchers and theorists describe normative developmental features, usually called *universals* of development. However, these professionals, like most parents, have also found that wide *individual variations* occur within the universal developmental patterns. The individual variations form a range within typical development that has been called the 'range of normality.' Extreme variations that go beyond the borders of these ranges have traditionally been categorized as atypical developmental patterns or disabilities" (1994:13).

Summary of critiques

Steenbarger (1991:288–289) summarizes "three particularly troublesome shortcomings" for which these models have been criticized.

1. "In their emphasis on linearity, stage-based models cannot account for the complexity of human development."

2. "In their emphasis on invariant sequences of structural unfolding, stage-based models cannot account for important situational influences in the developmental process."

3. "In an attempt to reduce development to uniform sequences, stage-based theories embody troublesome value premises."

By emphasizing uniformity these theories "implicitly negate the values of pluralism and diversity."

Stage theories and diversity

To explore these criticisms further, let us return to our "developmental ladder" analogy. Not only do traditional linear developmental approaches assume that for everyone the ladder is the same type or design, but they also assume that everyone's ladder has the same number of rungs (steps), the same distance between rungs (steps), the same total height, and the same width between the sides. Traditional developmental theories also too often assume that the context or environment in which the developmental ladder exists is virtually identical or at least equally benign for everyone. This assumption leads us to believe that for everyone the ladder is leaning at the same incline, against the same surface, and that each person climbing the ladder steps onto the first rung from the same surface at the bottom and steps off the last rung onto the same surface at the ladder's top.

We know, though, that the characteristics of ladders and the conditions or contexts in which they are used vary tremendously. (See Figure 4.1.) If all ladders were the same regardless of environmental conditions, they would be of extremely limited use. How can one use a five-foot stepladder to change the light bulb in a twenty-foot-high street light? A ladder's effectiveness depends a great deal on the task to be accomplished, the type of ladder available, the conditions in which it is used, and, perhaps most important, its effectiveness is determined by the skill and ability of the person using it. Effective approaches to human development must incorporate similarly diverse characteristics and conditions as well. Effective approaches to understanding human development must recognize that developmental ladders vary tremendously according to the needs, resources, and environments of individuals.

In addition to the tremendous variation in the characteristics of ladders and the conditions in which they are used, we also recognize that sometimes a

Figure 4.1
In the first illustration the person is unable to change the bulb in the streetlight because the ladder is not tall enough. In the second illustration the ladder is tall enough to reach the bulb but is inaccessible to the person in the wheelchair.

ladder of any type is not the most appropriate or useful tool to get from one place to another. (And even if it is, we may not have a ladder available to us.) A ladder is of limited use, for example, if we need to get from Arkansas to Washington.

Sometimes a level sidewalk, a bridge, an inclined plane, a circular stair, an elevator, an automobile, a jet, a space shuttle, or even a "transporter" from the fictional *USS Enterprise* of Star Trek might be more appropriate and useful in moving us along. Lacking any of these alternatives, sometimes we might be forced simply to try to jump from one point to the next. Sometimes, depending on needs, conditions, final destinations, or available resources, a combination of or even *all* these tools for getting from one place to another might be useful. Ladders are but one tool for getting us from one place to another. Linear developmental ladder or stage models of human development are but one tool for understanding our developmental journeys.

Developmental Perspectives: Commonality and Diversity

Recognizing, incorporating, and respecting developmental diversity does not require that we deny the many developmental tasks and needs shared by all humans. Certainly we have many developmental tasks and needs in common. These commonalities are a vital source of the bonds that serve to unify all people. These commonalities remind us that we are all linked in basic ways that define our common humanity and reflect common rights and responsibilities. However, it is the contention here that these commonalities should not overshadow or be valued any more than our rich diversities.

There are many common developmental tasks and needs, but all people do not develop at the same pace, in the same environments/conditions, or with the same resources or hindrances (obstacles). Unidimensional or linear approaches to individual behavior and development might result in ineffective social work practice and may be contrary to social work values. Such approaches deny the uniqueness of individuals and deprive many persons of the opportunity to celebrate their developmental uniqueness.

For example, a traditional developmental perspective is to assume that the task of walking unaided is a universal developmental task. However, development of the ability to walk unaided by other persons or devices is not a developmental task shared by all persons (or even by most persons). Consider, for a moment, realities such as developmental differences at birth, accidents, and physical changes as a result of aging or disease. Expanding the task of walking unaided to that of achieving sufficient mobility to negotiate one's environment and to allow one to maximize her/his human potential is inclusive of many more of us, at many more points in the life course.

To illustrate both commonality and diversity in development we will examine next the developmental universal, play, and then we will explore developmental risks and conditions that result in very different developmental experiences and results for different persons. We will also explore some common assessment tools used to assess developmental commonality and diversity.

Play: A universal of human development

Play is an example of a developmental universal, shared by all developing humans, but unique to each developing human in the specific activities and contexts in which it takes place. Play is also a significant assessment context for social workers to understand individual and group human behavior and development. What follows is an examination of this developmental universal in terms of definition, learning, characteristics, and functions of play.

Definition of Play

1. Play is the way children learn what no one can teach them. It is the way they explore and orient themselves to the actual world of space and time, of things, animals, structures, and people.
2. To move and function freely within prescribed limits.
3. Play is children's work.

What Children Learn through Play

1. They are helped to develop social relationships and skills.
2. They learn to use play materials and equipment with others.
3. They learn to take turns.
4. They learn how to ask for what they want or need.
5. They understand the role of others (mother, baby, father, doctor, etc.).
6. They master skills.

Characteristics of Play

1. Play is pleasurable (even when there are no signs of enjoyment, it is still gratifying to the players).
2. Play serves no particular purpose (it does not mean that play is unproductive).
3. Play is spontaneous and voluntary rather than obligatory.
4. Play actively involves the player.

Functions of Play

1. Play may serve as a means of helping the child solve a problem.
2. Play serves as a means of self-assertion through which a child can declare his or her needs.
3. In play, contact with other children and the need to communicate with them help stimulate language growth.

Learning is a continuous process. In play, young children are learning to manage impulsive behavior, to gain skill in living, and to work with others (adapted from University of Arkansas Nursery School 1996).

Developmental risk assessment

Bergen (1994) provides a helpful approach to thinking about several types of vulnerabilities or developmental risks that may challenge the developmental processes of humans and result in diverse developmental experiences and outcomes. These vulnerabilities are often considered in assessment approaches and tools used by a variety of disciplines. We will examine several of these assessment tools in the following section. When you examine the assessment tools, see if you can connect the tool to the three arenas of risk—established, biological, and environmental—Bergen describes.

    1. *Established Risk:* These "conditions include neurological, genetic, orthopedic, cognitive, or sensory impairments or other physical or medical syndromes that have been strongly linked to developmental problems. . . . Established risks are often called disabilities. They include diagnoses such as Down's

Engage Assess Intervene Evaluate

Professional social workers use conceptual frameworks to guide assessment processes and assessment is a critical component of social work practice. As you read the following sections and review the various risk assessment mechanisms described in the figures and tables, which do or should involve professional social workers in the assessment processes?

syndrome, spina bifida, cerebral palsy, blindness, limb loss or deformity, and other such genetic, motor, sensory, and cognitive impairments."

2. *Biological Risk:* "conditions are physical or medical trauma experiences that occur in the prenatal period, during the birth process, or in the neonatal period that have a high probability of resulting in developmental delay but that do not always cause delay. . . . For example, extremely low birth weight is often related to developmental delay; however, some children who are of low birth weight are able to overcome this condition and do not experience permanent delays in development."

3. *Environmental Risk:* "conditions are those factors in the physical setting (e.g., substandard housing, exposure to lead paint) or in the family or other social institutions (e.g., parent caregiving capabilities, low socioeconomic level, cultural values that preclude medical care) that have the potential to influence negatively young children's developmental progress. Negative environmental conditions internal to the family (e.g., family violence, parental drug abuse) and external to the family (e.g., unemployment, lack of access to health care) have an impact both on the development of all family members and on the capacity of these families to provide appropriate environments for their young at-risk children" (Bergen 1994:4–5).

Traditional developmental assessment tools   We outlined some different types of cross-disciplinary approaches in Chapter 3. We also mentioned that social workers are often members of multidisciplinary assessment teams. One of the clearest ways to gain an understanding of traditional perspectives on determining individual developmental vulnerabilities is to examine the assessment principles, language, and tools used by various professions. Table 4.1 provides an overview of traditional developmental principles, typical examples of developmental principles, and relation to risk conditions for each developmental principle.

Kalmanson notes that in assessing developmental vulnerabilities "patterns of behavior are more important to identify because they may be likely to indicate intervention is needed, while 'singular behaviors are likely to indicate individual differences within the normal range of development'" (in Bergen 1994:36). Table 4.2 presents an overview Kalmanson's indicators of developmental vulnerabilities in infants and toddlers.

For newborns and very young infants the Apgar and Brazelton Neonatal Assessment scales are commonly used. The Apgar Score (Table 4.3) is used at one and five minute intervals after birth to assess five characteristics of newborns indicative of overall health. An overall Apgar score of 10 indicates the best condition possible. The Brazelton Scale (Table 4.4) assesses behavioral and neural functioning and is considered a "better predictor of later developmental outcomes than the Apgar Score" (Bergen 1994:42).

Table 4.5 provides a summary of common medical diagnostic tests and procedures. Any one or combination of these tests and procedures may be used depending on concerns of medical staff. Table 4.6 provides an overview of the elements of a physician's psychosocial assessment form.

Table 4.7 provides a helpful overview of assessment terms commonly used by psychologists. These terms reflect a number of elements of traditional paradigm approaches to measuring and understanding human behavior.

Table 4.8, 4.9 and 4.10 provide examples of assessment concepts and terms used by speech and hearing professionals. The information in these figures helps give a sense of degrees of hearing loss as well as comparative sound levels and definitions of basic speech concepts. *(Text resumes on page 157.)*

Table 4.1	**Developmental Principles, Typical Examples, and Relation to Risk Conditions**	
Principles	**Typical Examples**	**Risk Conditions**
1. Human beings are active in the process of their own development.	Infants actively seek stimulation by visual search and by grasping or moving toward novel phenomena.	Children who are at risk actively select and attend to environmental stimuli and attempt to act on these stimuli; if disabilities hamper self-efficacy, adaptive devices and social stimulation must be enablers of action.
2. Development change can occur at any point in the life span.	Adolescent parents and middle adult parents experience developmental change when they have a child.	Those at risk may not reach some developmental milestones until they are older, but they will continue to make progress; education continues to make a difference throughout the life span.
3. The process is not a smooth, additive one; it involves transitions and cycles, which include chaotic and disorganized as well as integrated and coordinated periods.	In the "terrible twos" the child strives for autonomy while still being dependent and so behavior fluctuates between seeking nurturing and gaining control of self and others.	Those at risk also experience setbacks, plateaux, disorganized periods, and new beginnings; these cycles may not be evidence of pathology but of developmental transition periods similar to those of typical children.
4. Biological maturation and hereditary factors provide the parameters within which development occurs.	A child's physique (e.g., wiry or solidly built) may affect timing of walking.	Biological and hereditary factors affect the levels of progress and the end points of development in areas of risk.
5. Environments can limit or expand developmental possibilities.	A child with poor nutrition or who is confined to a crib may walk later than is typical.	Certain types of delay (e.g., language, social) are very much influenced by home, school, and community environments.
6. There are both continuity and discontinuity (i.e., gradual, stable growth, and abrupt changes) in development.	The temperament of a child (e.g., slow-to-warm-up) may be evident throughout life; thinking patterns will differ qualitatively from infancy to adolescence.	Continuity of development may be less easily recognized and discontinuities may be more noticeable or attributed to nondevelopmental causes in those at risk.
7. Many developmental patterns and processes are universal (i.e., they follow similar time intervals, durations, and sequences of change in most individuals, no matter what their cultural group).	Children in all cultures use a type of "baby" grammar when they first learn to talk.	Children at risk will also show these patterns, although they may be distorted or delayed due to disabilities.
8. There are unique individual biological characteristics as well as culturally and environmentally contingent qualities that influence timing, duration, sequence, and specificity of developmental change.	Most girls talk earlier than boys, but in cultures where mothers talk more to boys, they talk early; girls in some cultures are permitted to be active and in those cultures they show higher activity levels.	Children at risk are more likely to have unique characteristics and experiences that influence how universals of development are manifested.

continued

Table 4.1	**Continued**	
Principles	Typical Examples	Risk Conditions
9. Developmental changes may be positive or negative, as they are affected by health and other factors.	A chronic illness may affect a child's progress and cause some regression to "baby" behavior.	Children with severe or progressive syndromes may show deteriorating development; a balance between maintenance of positive developmental signs and control of negative indicators may be required.
10. Developmental change intervals tend to be of shorter time spans for younger than older individuals.	Infants' motor skills are very different at 6 months and at 1 year, but there is not much change in motor skills between ages 15 and 17.	Time intervals of change are often long with children with disabilities, but developmental progress will usually occur more quickly at younger rather than older ages, making early intervention important.

Table 4.2	**Developmental Vulnerabilities in Infants and Toddlers**	
	Infancy	Toddlerhood
Self-Organization	Difficulty with regulation of states, irritability, crying, trouble falling asleep Attention seems random, not focused or responsive to adult interaction	Little organized attention to people or objects Difficulty falling asleep, wakes up irritable Irregular food intake
Social-Emotional	Unresponsive Lack of reciprocal gaze Absence of anticipatory response to being held Seems to prefer being alone Fails to form strong personal attachments	Little or no reciprocal interaction/play Little attachment to primary caregivers Indifference or extreme prolonged distress at comings or goings of primary caregivers Absence of imitative play
Motor	Lack of motor response to voice Arches back when held Doesn't mold to parent's body, limp	Disorganized, random movement Impulsive racing and falling Apathetic, little interest in movement
Sensory Integration	Easily upset by extraneous sounds/ sights, startles easily Trouble coordinating input from parents (can't look at mother while being held and talked to)	Easily startled Doesn't localize sound Overwhelmed by moderate stimulation and withdraws Engages in self-stimulation
Language	Absence of cooing in response to parents' vocalizations Lack of attention to parent's voice	Absence of communication/gestures Little imitation of words No words for important people/objects Lack of intentionality in communication

Table 4.3   Immediate Evaluation of the Newborn: The Apgar Score

Sign	0	1	2
1. Heart rate	Absent	Below 100	Over 100
2. Respiratory effort	Absent	Slow, irregular	Good, crying
3. Muscle tone	Limp	Some flexion of extremities	Active, motion
4. Response to catheter in nostril (tested after oropharynx is clear)	No response	Grimace	Cough or sneeze
5. Color	Blue, pale	Body pink, extremities blue	Completely pink

Source: Reprinted with permission from Apgar (1953). "A proposal for a new method of evaluation of a newborn infant, Anesthesia and Analgesia." Reprinted by permission of Lippincott Williams & Wilkins. From: Bergen, D. (1994). *Assessment Methods for Infants and Toddlers*. New York: Teachers' College Press, Columbia University. All rights reserved.

Table 4.4   Infant Neurodevelopmental Assessment: Brazelton Neonatal Behavioral Assessment Scale (BNBAS)

A 7 cluster scoring scheme summarizes the Brazelton Scale Scores:

1. Habituation:
   Habituation to a bright light, a rattle, a bell, a pinprick

2. Orientation:
   Attention to visual and auditory stimuli

3. Motor processes:
   Quality of movement and tone

4. Range of state:
   Peak of excitement
   Rapidity of buildup
   Irritability
   Lability of state

5. Regulation of state:
   Cuddliness
   Consolability
   Self-quieting
   Hand-to-mouth activity

6. Autonomic stability:
   Tremors
   Startles
   Reactive skin color changes

7. Reflexes:
   Number of abnormal reflexes

Source: Information from Brazelton, Nugent, & Lester, 1987. Reprinted by permission of John Wiley & Sons, Inc. Reprinted by permission of the publisher. From: Bergen, D. (1994). *Assessment Methods for Infants and Toddlers*. New York: Teachers' College Press, Columbia University. All rights reserved.

154Chapter 4

Table 4.5 — Common Diagnostic Tests and Procedures

Test/Procedure	Description
Ultrasound scan	Uses sound waves to look inside different parts of the body. The image on the screen is transferred to a regular X-ray film for the doctor to interpret.
Electrocardiogram (EKG)	A recording of the child's heartbeats. The EKG detects changes or alterations in heart rate and rhythm, in heart ventricular size and heart strain (e.g., coronary artery occlusion).
Computer tomography (CT)	A type of X-ray that takes pictures of the child's brain and abdomen. At certain times medication is given intravenously. This medicine circulates in the blood and causes parts of the brain or abdomen to show up more clearly on the pictures.
Spinal tap	Measures the amount of pressure in the spinal canal; removes a small amount of fluid for examination. After the lower part of the spine has been anesthetized, a needle is inserted in the spinal canal and fluid is withdrawn.
Electroencephalogram (EEG)	A recording of the electrical activity generated by the brain that represents the summed results of excitatory and inhibitory postsynaptic potentials.
Magnetic resonance (MRI)	A noninvasive imaging method of examining the brain and other internal organs of the body. This test uses magnetic fields instead of X-ray to produce images on film by computer analysis. The MRI provides excellent detail of anatomic structures.
Event related potential (ERP)	Assesses a transient electrical signal following stimulation of a peripheral sensory modality (e.g., ear-brainstem evoked response; eye-visual evoked response; peripheral nerve-somatosensory evoked response). The signal is recorded over the appropriate area of the scalp with EEG electrodes. The small signal needs to be averaged to be detectable and differentiated from ongoing EEG activity.
Extracorporeal membrane oxygenation (ECMO)	Machine acts as an artificial heart and lung membrane adding oxygen for a baby whose own heart or lungs cannot get enough oxygen into the blood to circulate through the body. The goal of ECMO is to let the heart and lungs recover while the baby is supported by the ECMO.
Ventricular shunt	A small tube that has been placed in the child's head to reduce hydrocephalus. The shunt carries extra fluid from the head to the blood stream (ventriculo-jugular [VJ] shunt) or to the abdomen (ventriculoperitoneal [VP] shunt) where it is absorbed.
Shunt-o-gram	Used to determine why a child's ventricular shunt is not working properly. A small needle is put into the valve of the shunt. Fluid is drawn out of the valve and sent to the laboratory for testing. A dye that shows up on X-rays is put into the valve and X-rays are taken. After pumping the shunt, X-rays are again taken to watch the dye pass through the shunt tube.

Source: Reprinted by permission of the publisher. From: Bergen, D. (1994). *Assessment Methods for Infants and Toddlers*. New York: Teachers' College Press, Columbia University. All rights reserved.

Table 4.6   Contents of the Physician Psychosocial Assessment Form

Category	Specific Problems
Physical growth	Slow weight gain, non-organic failure and development to thrive, obesity
Sleep	Trouble sleeping, sleepwalking, night terrors
Motor	Hyperactivity, overactivity; gross motor delay, fine motor delay
Cognitive—language	Mental retardation, learning disabilities, language delay, attention problems, speech problems
School	School failure, school refusal, absenteeism or truancy
Behavior	Enuresis, temper tantrums, fire setting, stealing, tics, encopresis, excessive masturbation
Psycho-physiological	Recurring stomach pain, headaches, recurring knee or leg pain
Feelings	Anxiety or nervousness, feelings of depression, low self-esteem, excessive anger or irritability
Thought	Delusions, hallucinations, incoherence
Peer activity	No confidence, social isolation, fighting and bullying
Parent-child	Problems separating, physical abuse, psychological abuse, sexual abuse, physical neglect
Social	Lack of housing, frequent moves, financial problems, sexual abuse (other than parent)
Family	Divorce or separation, physical or mental illness of parent, drug or alcohol abusing parent, parental discord, spouse abuse, few social ties, problems with siblings, death of parent

Table 4.7   Assessment Terms Used by Psychologists

Achievement	The amount of success children exhibit at a given task
Average	The most representative measurement or score (expressed as mean, median, or mode)
Developmental norm	Age at which 50% of tested group successfully completes the task
Normative	Measurement results within the average or typical range
Norms	Typical scores on standardized measures representative of certain groups (e.g., age, ethnic, or local)
Psychometrics	Measurement of human cognitive, motor, or affective behavior using a standard of performance

continued

Table 4.7   Continued

Reliability	The extent to which a test or observation shows consistent results
Standard scores	Scores that are mathematically transformed so that results from different tests can be compared
Standardized tests	Testing processes that use consistent methods, materials, and scoring procedures
Validity	The extent to which a test or observation measures what it is intended to measure

Table 4.8   Categories of Sound Loss and Effects on Language and Cognition

Mild Hearing Loss (15–30 dB HTL)

- Vowel sounds are clear, except for voiceless consonants such as "s" (*lost* may be heard as *loss*).

- Hearing of short unstressed words and less intense speech sounds are inconsistently perceived.

Moderate Hearing Loss (30–50 dB HTL)

- Most speech sounds at conversational levels are lost, but with amplification can be heard.

- Sounds of low energy and high frequency, such as fricatives (see Figure 4.10), may be distorted or missing (*stroke* may be heard as *soak*).

- Short unstressed words are not heard.

- Difficulty learning abstract concepts, multiple word meanings, and development of object classes.

Severe Hearing Loss (55–70 dB HTL)

- Only loud environmental sounds and intense speech at close range can be heard.

- Language does not develop without amplification.

- Vowel sounds and consonant group differences can be heard with amplification.

- Development of grammar rules and abstract meanings is delayed or missing.

Profound Hearing Loss (75–90 dB HTL)

- Not even intense speech sound can be heard without amplification.

- Hearing does not have a major role in language acquisition, without amplification.

Note: dB = decibel; HTL = hearing threshold level

Table 4.9	Examples of Different Sound Pressure Levels
Decibel	Stimulus
20	Forest
30	Whisper
60	Conversation
80	Average street traffic

Source: Reprinted by permission of the publisher. From: Bergen, D. (1994). *Assessment Methods for Infants and Toddlers.* New York: Teachers' College Press, Columbia University. All rights reserved.

Table 4.10	Definitions of Speech Elements
Voiced sounds	Produced by flow of air from the lungs causing the vocal chords to vibrate ("u" as in cup). All vowels are voiced sounds.
Voiceless sounds	Produced by flow of air without vibration of the vocal chords ("p" as in pit; "f" as in fun).
Fricatives	Consonants produced by rapid changes in pressure constricted through air passage cavities. They come in voiced or unvoiced pairs ("z," "s").
Plosives	Consonants produced by brief obstructing of vocal track so sound comes in quick bursts. They are also paired ("p," "b").
Nasals	Voiced consonants in which sound passes through the nose (*man*).

Source: Reprinted by permission of the publisher. From: Bergen, D. (1994). *Assessment Methods for Infants and Toddlers.* New York: Teachers' College Press, Columbia University. All rights reserved.

Normal and abnormal: Traditional and alternative perspectives

If we are concerned with traditional and alternative perspectives on individual behavior and development, we must question the very concepts of normal and abnormal as they are traditionally presented to us. To discuss human behavior in narrow terms of aggregates or so-called norms or average behaviors is consistent with dominant/traditional paradigm thinking. Others have gone even further to suggest "that a statistical concept of 'normal' can be pathological since it reflects only false consciousness. . . . [A] false consciousness of ideologies and norms imposed from outside the individual and resulting in social and organizational behaviors that are characteristically pathological and neurotic" (Fromm in Gemmill and Oakley 1992:116).

When we recognize that social workers work with persons, groups, families, organizations, and communities with endless combinations of individual needs, histories, cultures, experiences, and orientations, the concept of "normal" must be questioned. We must seek some more holistic alternative for achieving understanding. Normal for whom?; in whose eyes?; according to whose values?; during what time period?; in what context?; under what conditions? we must ask.

We will try here to learn to think about multiple ranges and ways of ordering and understanding what is "normal" human behavior and development. In the next chapter, we will explore more holistic approaches in recognition of the diverse characteristics, needs, histories, and environments of the persons with whom we interact. We can best accomplish this by seeking out developmental approaches/perspectives/models that emerge from the persons who live and represent those experiences, conditions, and histories.

Traditional perspectives on what is "normal" human behavior leave much unanswered and much to be desired if we are searching for ways to make maximum use of the strengths of people and if we are attempting to respect people's differences as sources of strengths. Weick (1991:22) reminds us that traditional notions of "normal" flow from efforts to view human behavior only from a scientific or positivistic perspective. Such a perspective "searches for law-like occurrences in the natural world" or "norms." Weick argues for different approaches that help us build less rigid or limiting theories of human growth and development; that are "unhinged from the lockstep view of what is considered 'normal' development" (Weick 1991:23). These alternative approaches should be "fluid models built on assumptions that recognize the creative and powerful energy underlying all human growth" (Weick 1991:23).

"Normal" is assumed here to be extremely relative—to individual, environment, culture, gender, history, race, class, age, ability, and sexual orientation—and to the complex interplay of these diversities. To be "abnormal" is, in fact, "normal" for most of us, if we focus on our rich diversity. This contradictory-sounding assertion requires us to recognize that by "abnormal" we mean a wide range of differences, some of which fit traditional definitions of pathology such as schizophrenia or criminality, but most of which simply mean different from or alternative to the norms established according to traditional/dominant paradigms, theories, and assumptions about human behavior and development.

Our wide-ranging differences result in wide ranges of what can be considered normal. However, all of us as humans also share developmental "milestones" or expectations in the sense that if the milestone is not reached, or is not reached within some appropriate range of time, some adjustment will be required by the person or by others in the environment to allow the individual to continue on his/her developmental journey toward reaching her/his fullest human potential.

To accommodate both the realities of diversity and the commonalities in human behavior, development approaches to gathering knowledge for practice that equally respect common developmental milestones and differences are required. Understanding both traditional and alternative approaches to individual development will help us achieve this balance.

Richards points out the costs of confusing diversity with abnormality and notes "How tragic if we mindlessly equate the abnormal with the pathological and demean the very diversity that can be enhancing and life-giving. To function fully as human beings, we need to broaden and redefine our acceptable 'limits of normality'" (1996:50).

Traditional Notions of Intelligence: IQ

An example of one of the most influential traditional mechanisms for determining what is normal is that of traditional **Intelligence Quotient** or **IQ**. Traditional views of intelligence refer to a general level of intelligence that is most often referred to as "g" or general intelligence. **General intelligence** is defined "operationally as the ability to answer items on tests of intelligence." The test scores then infer underlying intelligence, called **IQ** or an **intelligence quotient** through the use of "statistical techniques that compare responses of subjects at different ages." The fact that these scores are correlated "across ages and across different tests" is used to support the notion that intelligence does not change much with age or training or experience (Gardner 1993:15).

The cultural bias of IQ tests has been a controversial issue in the use of IQ tests to determine access to and positions within various social institutions like schools, the military and the workplace. **Cultural bias** refers to the perceived advantage gained by persons taking intelligence tests who are members of the same dominant culture as the persons creating the test. In addition, this bias works to the disadvantage of persons not from the dominant culture who take the test. For example, Stephen Jay Gould in his book, *The Mismeasure of Man,* argued that IQ tests served to continue and to exacerbate the historic exclusion of many lower SES [Social-Economic Status] persons, especially many African Americans (in Herrnstein and Murray 1994:11–12).

A controversial traditional approach to IQ is that put forth by Herrnstein and Murray in the book *The Bell Curve.* They support the notion of "g" or general intelligence. In addition they argue that IQ tests do not necessarily reflect cultural bias. They argue that when "properly administered, IQ tests are not demonstrably biased against social, economic, ethnic, or racial subgroups" (1994:23). In Chapter 5 we will further explore the notion of intelligence as a factor in individual development and we will examine an alternative perspective on intelligence offered by Gardner and referred to as multiple intelligence that challenges the traditional notion of IQ.

Developmental Paradigms and Social Work

Like the need for variety in models for moving from one place to another, knowledge of a wide range of different developmental theories and perspectives is essential for effective social work practice. Knowledge of diverse theories can provide us with multiple tools for multiple applications. This is especially true given the rich and varied range of people and experiences with which social workers deal. The worldviews or paradigms from which our perspectives on human behavior and development emerge must adequately recognize the dramatic developmental variations among individuals. These variations may include the very nature of the specific tasks to be accomplished, the timing of those tasks, the means used to accomplish tasks, and the historical and current patterns of resource availability or lack of availability for use in accomplishing tasks. In other words, we must recognize that such differences as race, class, sexual orientation, and gender have significant impact on the nature of our developmental experiences.

If these variations are not recognized or if differences are only narrowly recognized, the theories and approaches we use to guide our social work practice will offer helpful guidance for only some persons and will be confusing, frustrating, and even damaging to others. Theories or perspectives that neglect to take into account variations in individuals' characteristics, histories, and environments render those individuals at variance as developmentally inadequate (abnormal) or entirely invisible. If traditional developmental theories or perspectives reflect only the developmental experiences of white, middle-class, heterosexual, males, for example, it is extremely likely that people of color, low-income persons, gay men or lesbians, and women will either be ignored completely by the theories or they will be found to be inadequate or abnormal according to the criteria of the traditional theories.

The Traditional and the Possible (Alternatives)

Chapter 5 will focus on exploration of alternative approaches to understanding human behavior and development. However, in order to understand these alternative approaches, we need to be cognizant of the more traditional theories about human behavior and development. Traditional theories are incomplete, they exclude many people, and they reflect biases due to the value assumptions and historical periods out of which they emerged. However, these inadequacies do not decrease the powerful influences these traditional theories have had in the past, currently have, and will continue to have on the construction and application of knowledge about human behavior and development. Traditional approaches also provide a departure point from which we may embark on our journey, in Chapter 5, toward more complete, more inclusive, and less biased visions (or visions in which bias is recognized and used to facilitate inclusiveness) of development to improve all our efforts to reach our fullest potential. Many of the alternative models of development we will explore began as extensions or reconceptualizations of traditional theories.

There is another very practical reason for learning about traditional theories of human behavior and development. The practice world that social workers inhabit and that you will soon enter (and we hope transform) is a world constructed largely on traditional views of human behavior and development. To survive in that world long enough to change it we must be conversant in the discourse of that world. We must have sufficient knowledge of traditional and dominant paradigms of human behavior and development to make decisions about what in those worldviews we wish to retain because of its usefulness in attaining the goal of maximizing human potential, and what we must discard or alter to better serve that same core concern of social work.

Reductionism and Determinism

In order to make appropriate decisions about the traditional approaches we explore we must recognize their limits. The developmental models we have historically used are not representative of even most people when we compare the race, gender, and class diversity of the people with whom social workers work and the race, class, and gender reflected in traditional models. This is to say nothing of differences in sexual orientation, age, and disabling conditions completely ignored or specified as abnormal in many traditional models. Traditional developmental models emphasize almost exclusively the experiences of white, young, middle-class, heterosexual men who have no disabling conditions.

Many traditional theories of human development are also limited because they present people as if they can be reduced simply to the specific elements focused on by the theory. This reductionism, for example, is evident in Erikson's much-used theory of the life cycle. Erikson's theory of development is often presented as if the human is composed entirely of, and behaves and develops solely as a result of, ego dynamics put into place or determined as a result of life experiences occurring during infancy and very early childhood. The same reductionist and deterministic tendencies can be found in the focus on infantile sexuality of Freudian developmental theory, on cognition and young children in Piaget's theory, and on the development of moral judgment in the theory of Kohlberg.

Erikson was aware of these tendencies in his own and in Freud's approaches and cautioned against them: "When men concentrate on an uncharted area of human existence, they aggrandize this area to become the universe, and they reify its center as the prime reality" (Erikson 1963:414–15). When we do this we are left with tremendous voids in our knowledge about human development upon which to base our practice. We will attempt to be aware of this tendency as we explore traditional and dominant perspectives in this chapter. We will also try to guard against this tendency as we explore alternative perspectives in the next chapter.

The reader should be alert to the exclusive use of male pronouns and exclusive references to males in direct quotations of traditional developmental theorists used in this book. This reflects the writing style of the time when the work was done. References to males were considered universal and inclusive of females. An exclusive reference to males also reflects actual populations on which many traditional models were based. These models were in fact much more about men's developmental experiences than they were about those of women. They, in effect, rendered women invisible both figuratively and literally.

TRADITIONAL AND DOMINANT DEVELOPMENTAL THEORIES

Diversity in Practice

As you read the section, "Traditional and Dominant Developmental Theories," how inclusive are the theories of the developmental experiences of persons who are diverse in terms of age, class, color, culture, disability, ethnicity, gender, gender identity and expression, immigration status, political ideology, race, religion, sex, and sexual orientation?

The following sections offer summaries of several of the most prominent and influential traditional/dominant theories or models for understanding or explaining individual human behavior and development. The approaches presented have been chosen for several reasons. These models represent not the totality of traditional approaches to understanding individual behavior and development, but they are models that have had powerful influences on social work education and practice related to individuals. They have been extremely influential determiners and reflectors of traditional and dominant paradigm thinking in social work and in many other disciplines. Considered together they offer perspectives that address human behavior through the life span. In sum, they also articulate many of the most basic, almost universally used concepts for attempting to understand individual behavior and development. Finally, they are presented here because they have been influential departure points for a number of the alternative approaches to understanding individual behavior and development that we will explore in the next chapter.

The traditional models we will explore are those put forward by Freud, Erikson, Piaget, Kohlberg, and Levinson. While certainly not the only traditional perspectives on individual development, these theories represent some of the most influential thinking about individual human behavior and development during the twentieth century. As we review the fundamentals of these traditional approaches, we will continually evaluate them in terms of their consistency with the dimensions of the traditional and dominant paradigm.

Freud

Historical perspective

Freud was born in Moravia (a part of what was, prior to the redivision of the Soviet Union and Eastern Europe, Czechoslovakia) in 1856. He attended medical school in Vienna, a place of prominence in medical science at the time. He was trained according to the traditional/dominant paradigm as a medical scientist. His initial scientific research was focused on the physiology and neurology of fish.

Freud maintained a scientific perspective in his research later on. His research approach focused on observation rather than experimentation and was reflected later in his development and practice of psychoanalysis. Freud was also influenced by what in his time was called psychic healing, a much more intuitive, less traditional approach to understanding and intervening in human behavior, from which emerged hypnotism (Green 1989:33–35; Loevinger 1987:14–19). Freud's research and practice in psychoanalysis led him to conclude that the causes of his patients' symptoms could always be found in early childhood traumas and parental relationships (Green 1989: 36–37; Loevinger 1987:15–16).

Freud developed techniques of free association and dream interpretation to trace and intervene in the early traumas and parental relationships that he believed were the source of his patients' distress. Free association is a process in which the patient is encouraged to relax and report any ideas that come to mind. The notion is that all ideas are important and if sufficiently studied and pursued can be connected back to the unconscious and early sources of their symptoms. Dream interpretation consists of studying the content of patients' dreams in order to detect symbolic and hidden meanings that are then used to interpret and help the patient to work through the troubling early experiences in order to resolve their presenting symptoms. (Green 1989; Loevinger 1987).

The model

Freud's conclusions about often unconscious (unremembered) early experiences as a primary cause of later life troubles and his pursuit of psychoanalysis as a means of intervention in those troubles led him to construct a system through which he explained individual human behavior and development. In 1930 Healy, Bronner, and Bowers presented a summary of many of the basic concepts, processes, and structures that constituted Freud's system. Their work is helpful from a historical perspective because it was written contemporary with much of Freud's actual work and writing. Their approach is also helpful because rather than interpret Freud's work from their own perspectives, they relied heavily on Freud's words and works. This is important because so many different people have interpreted and reinterpreted Freud's work over time, it is often difficult to discern what is really Freud's perspective and what is the adaptation of his ideas by others. Such varied interpretations are understandable given the influence and revolutionary nature of his paradigm at the time, but it is important to have some sense of his original constructs and ideas. Freud's work is also an example of how a paradigm now considered traditional and limited in many ways was at the time of its development and introduction considered quite alternative, even radical.

Healy, Bronner, and Bowers presented Freud's psychoanalysis as a structure that was a synthesis of psychology and biology. They referred to it as a "structure erected within the field of psychobiologic science" (1930:xviii). They summarized this synthesis of biology and psychology:

a. Biological and psychological development are inseparably interrelated.
b. The essential nature of the individual consists in strivings and urges, innate or unlearned, which originally are quite independent of environment.
c. Whatever the individual is or does at any given moment is very largely predetermined by his earlier experiences and his reactions to them.
d. The earliest years of life represent the period when biological and mental experiences most profoundly influence the individual because he is then less pre-formed or conditioned.

    e. Existing actively in the mental life of the individual there is a vast
    amount of which he is unaware.

    f. The biological and consequently the psychological constitution varies
    in different individuals. (1930:xx)

Healy, Bronner, and Bowers suggest that to understand Freud's psychoanalytic paradigm we must first understand what they referred to as the "cardinal formulations" upon which it is based. Their cardinal formulations serve as a useful summary of the basic concepts of this paradigm. **Libido** is "that force by which the sexual instinct is represented in the mind." Libido or eros is "the energy . . . of those instincts which have to do with all that may be comprised under the word 'love.'" The suggestion here is that the concept of libido has a much wider meaning than simply "sex drive." It also incorporates love of self, of others, friendships, and love for humanity in general (1930:2–4).

Green provides a more recent but similar interpretation of this cornerstone of psychoanalytic thought, calling it instinctual or psychic energy (also referred to as nervous energy, drive energy, libido, or tension). Each person is born with a fixed amount of instinctual energy of two types. Eros, the "positive energy of life, activity, hope, and sexual desire," and thanatos, the "negative energy of death, destruction, despair, and aggression" (1989:36, 38–39).

Cathexis "is the accumulation or concentration of psychic energy in a particular place or channel, libidinal or non-libidinal" (Healy et al. 1930:8). This notion of cathexis is somewhat similar to the notion of energy we explored earlier in our discussion of social systems thinking (see Chapter 3). **Polarities** represent aspects of mental life that operate in opposition to one another. This principle of opposites emphasized the polarities of activity-passivity, self-outer world (subject-object), pleasure-pain, life-death, love-hate, and masculine-feminine (Healy et al. 1930:18). Thinking in terms of such polarities as these has much in common with our earlier discussion of the binary or competitive nature of much dominant or traditional paradigm thinking from Chapter 2. **Ambivalence** is the "contradictory emotional attitudes toward the same object" (Healy et al. 1930:20). *Ambivalence* represents an unhealthy or problematic tendency, according to Freudian theory. However, it has some similarity with the concept of ambiguity we discussed in Chapter 3 as a reality of human behavior that social workers must appreciate. *Ambivalence* suggests a negative condition; *ambiguity* suggests an alternative real and necessary aspect of human behavior.

Among the most important cardinal formulations of psychoanalysis is what Healy, Bronner, and Bowers (1930:22) refer to as the "divisional constitution of mental life." Mental life is made up of the conscious, the preconscious, and the unconscious. These notions are indeed essential to understanding Freud's approach. The **unconscious** element of our mental lives is much more powerful than the conscious as an influence on our behavior, according to psychoanalytic thinking. This is a very active part of our being and has much influence on our conscious thought and behavior. The unconscious may either have never been at a conscious level or it may contain once-conscious thought that has become repressed or submerged in the unconscious (Healy et al. 1930:24–28). The **preconscious** "is that part of mental life which in appropriate circumstances, either through an effort of the will or stimulated by an associated idea, can be brought up into consciousness." The preconscious has more in common with the conscious part of our mental selves but can at times function to bring memories from the unconscious to a conscious level. The **conscious** level is the smallest of the three levels and contains thought and ideas of which we are "aware at any given time." The content of the conscious mind is extremely transitory and is constantly changing (Healy et al. 1930:30–32).

Freud found the division of our mental life into *conscious, preconscious,* and *unconscious* helpful but insufficient for explaining human behavior. To more fully explain human behavior he later developed another three-part construct for conceptualizing our mental selves. This construct consisted of id, ego, and superego. He believed that this structure complemented his earlier construct of conscious, preconscious, and unconscious, rather than replacing it (Healy et al. 1930:34). The **id** is the source of instinctive energy. It contains libido drives and is unconscious. It seeks to maximize pleasure, is amoral, and has no unity of purpose (Healy et al. 1930:36). The **ego** represents that part of our mental life that results when id impulses are modified by the expectations and requirements of the external world. Ego emerges out of the id and represents what is commonly thought of as "reason and sanity." Ego strives to be moral and represses tendencies that might give free reign to our unmoral id impulses. The ego is in constant struggle with three influences upon it: "the external world, the libido of the id, and the severity of the super-ego" (Healy et al. 1930:38). The **superego** grows out of the ego and has the capacity to rule it. It is mostly unconscious and represents what we commonly think of as conscience. It is heavily influenced by our parents. It can evoke guilt and "exercise the censorship of morals" (Healy et al. 1930:44–46).

Green's (1989) summary of Freud's conceptualization of psychosexual stages through which humans develop is somewhat consistent with the historical summary of Healy, Bronner, and Bower (1930:80ff). Green suggests five discrete stages, however, while Healy et al. refer to three basic stages, of which the first, infancy, contains three substages (oral, anal, and genital). For clarity here we use Green's model. However, it is helpful to understand that Healy et al. reflect the dominant emphasis in traditional Freudian thinking placed on infancy and infantile sexuality by subsuming several substages under infancy.

Freud's developmental stages focus on critical developmental periods and on the role of sexuality in development from infancy on. Much traditional developmental thinking has its source in this linear, deterministic, and reductionist stage-based model. The first stage is the **oral stage** (birth to about age one). Its focus is on the mouth as a conflicting source of both pleasure (as in taking in nourishment) and pain (denial of nourishment on demand) and on parents as pivotal actors in gratification or denial of oral needs. The second stage is the **anal stage** (about age one to three). The focus of psychic energy shifts at this stage from the mouth to the anus and to control of the elimination of waste and is associated with sexual pleasure, personal power, and control. Conflict over the child's struggle for power and control during the anal stage is most often depicted in toilet training conflicts. These conflicts center on issues of independence and self-control, Freud believed. The third stage, the **phallic stage** (about three to six), is critical in development of sexual identity and sex roles. Instinctual energy is focused on the genitals in this stage and its conflict is around love/hate relationships with parents. Young boys compete for the affection of their mothers with their fathers in the **oedipal complex** that moves the boy through fear of castration by the father in retribution for the boy's desire for the mother, to a compromise in which the boy identifies with the more powerful father and accepts his values, attitudes, behaviors, and habits, resulting in the birth of the superego.

Freud describes a similar, though much less clearly articulated, process for girls that has come to be referred to as the **Electra complex** that takes the girl through penis envy symbolic of the power of the father and males, blaming the mother for depriving her of a penis, to recognition of the impossibility of attaining a penis and a resulting identification with the mother. According to Freud, out of this identification emerges a girl socialized to female sex roles. At this point she has a superego, albeit a weaker superego than that of males, because her lack of a penis prevents castration anxiety and the concomitant psychic strength (superego) that comes from the more intense repression struggles on the part of boys. Regarding women and the development of the superego or conscience, "their Super-ego is never so inexorable, so impersonal, so independent of its emotional origins, as we require it to be in men" (Freud in Healy et al. 1930:51). Healy et al. (1930:51) note that other psychoanalysts of Freud's day agreed "on the more infantile character of the Super-ego in the woman."

Agreement was not universal, however. Healy et al. reported, in their 1930 work on Freud, the important contention of Karen Horney (a female psychoanalyst, we might emphasize) "that the belief in 'penis envy' has evolved as the result of a too exclusively masculine orientation." Horney countered that "the girl has in the capacity for motherhood 'a quite indisputable and by no means negligible physiological superiority.'" She further claimed that there was sufficient data "for believing that 'the unconscious of the male psyche clearly reflects intense envy of motherhood, pregnancy, childhood'" (1930:161). According to Horney, "the whole matter has been approached too much from the male point of view" (1930:163). We shall see in the following chapter that many alternative-paradigm thinkers have taken these observations seriously and seek to redefine human behavior and development in ways that more appropriately and adequately incorporate the realities of girls' and women's developmental experiences.

The fourth stage is **latency** (about five or six to puberty). This stage includes the child's movement out of the family to influences of the larger society, primarily in the company of same-sex peers. Sexual instincts and energy are channeled to sports, school, and social play. Freud gave little attention to this stage because of lack of intense sexual conflict characteristic of the previous and following stages. The fifth stage is the **genital stage** (puberty to adulthood). The focal conflict of this stage is the establishment of mature heterosexual behavior patterns through which to obtain sexual pleasure and love (Green 1989:42–49).

Another influential component in traditional Freudian developmental thinking was that of defense mechanisms. **Defense mechanisms** are automatic patterns of thinking aimed at reducing anxiety (Green 1989:49). Healy et al. (1930:198) refer to defense mechanisms as "dynamisms" that are "very specific processes by which the unconscious Ego attempts to take care of, or to defend itself against, Id urges, desires, wishes." Thinking of these mechanisms as dynamisms or dynamic forces helps communicate their process or active nature. Some major defense mechanisms include **repression,** the submergence of memories and thoughts that produce anxiety; **regression,** reversion to an earlier, less anxiety-provoking stage of development; **projection,** attributing one's anxiety-provoking thoughts or feelings to someone else; **reaction formation,** behaving in a way that is the extreme opposite of the anxiety-producing behavior; **displacement,** unconsciously shifting anxiety-producing feelings away from threatening objects or persons (Green 1989:49–51).

Conclusion

The picture of individual development that emerges from Freud's influential model is one consistent in many ways with traditional paradigm thinking. It is linear and stage-based. Although it has been applied and interpreted very broadly, its focus is relatively narrow in its predominant concern for intrapsychic structures and processes. It is constructed on a scientific, positivistic foundation. It is based on masculinist and patriarchal perspectives that assume male experience as central. Gilligan provides evidence that the tendency to use male life as the norm for human development has a long history that goes at least back to Freud (Gilligan 1982:6). Female developmental experiences are described only in terms of their difference from normal or modal male experience. The standards of white Eurocentric culture from which the model emerged are considered universal. It reflects the white European experiences of its founder and of the patients upon which Freud's findings were based. The model reflects an individualistic bias that places primacy on separateness and autonomy as necessary end points for mature development. It is binary, with its emphasis on polarities. Implicit also in the model is the dimension of privilege. This dimension incorporates some of the other dimensions of the traditional/dominant paradigm, and from this synthesis emerges the profile of privilege that characterizes a person who is young, white, heterosexual, Judeo-Christian, male, able-bodied, with sufficient resources and power (Pharr 1988).

SEHB and Freud: A paradigm shift from the social environment to individual behavior

Freud's model has had, as noted earlier, significant influences on social work. Ann Weick (1981:140) refers to psychoanalytic theory, for example, as perhaps "the most important development in shaping the evolution of social work." A fundamental element in this evolution was the shifting of focus in social work's approach to addressing problems toward individual functioning and internal or "intrapsychic phenomena . . . as the critical variables." Such a fundamental shift toward the individual was accompanied by a shift away from environmental concerns as foremost in understanding and addressing issues of well-being. A result of this shift was a medical or pathology (illness) perspective on people's problems rather than a social change or strengths perspective.

A medical or pathology perspective also was historically significant in that it redefined human behavior as predictable according to determinable laws consistent with traditional paradigm thinking, rather than as unpredictable and contextually emergent, which would have been more consistent with alternative paradigm perspectives. Thomas Szasz, in his book *The Myth of Mental Illness,* argues that this trend in psychiatry had significant political meaning. It attempted to obscure the relationship between personal troubles and political issues. It suggested that an individual's problems were solely a result of "genetic-psychological" factors (Szasz 1961:5). On the other hand, Szasz argues, more consistent with alternative paradigm thinking (and more consistent with core concerns of social work), that "psychological laws are relativistic with respect to social conditions. In other words, *the laws of psychology cannot be formulated independently of the laws of sociology"* (1961:7). We cannot understand human behavior unless we simultaneously attend to and seek understanding of the social environment.

To suggest that we consider, in our choices about perspectives for understanding HBSE, these criticisms of Freud's model of individual development and behavior is not to suggest that we discard it wholesale. Much about Freud's approach offered new insight into the complexities of human behavior. Its suggestion that our later mental lives are influenced by the experiences of our earlier lives alone was extremely important, even revolutionary. We must, however, recognize the contradictions between Freud's approach and our attempt to develop holistic, inclusive perspectives consistent with the core concerns of social work. Thus, the recommendation here, as with all models whether traditional or alternative, is to approach this model critically, cautiously, and analytically. It is also important to note that traditional psychoanalytic theory is being questioned and revised in light of concerns about its exclusion of the experiences of many people, especially those of women. Miller (1986:28) notes, for example, that the emphasis of traditional psychoanalytic theory on autonomy and independence as central to healthy growth and development is being challenged by some theorists who say that the ability to form and maintain interdependent relationship with others is of equal importance in healthy growth and development. Miller suggests that the new call to place equal emphasis on relationship and interdependence is emerging from efforts to look at human development from the perspective of women rather than solely from the perspective of men (1986). We will explore this new emphasis more in Chapter 5.

Piaget

Historical perspective

Piaget, like Freud, began his study and research from a traditional scientific approach. Piaget focused on biology before turning to psychology and human behavior. He became interested in the study of snails and at age twelve he published his first of some twenty papers on snails. Piaget's first work in psychology was in the laboratory begun by Binet, originator of the intelligence test (IQ test) for quantitatively measuring intelligence. Piaget's interest was, however, qualitative rather than quantitative in that he was interested in why the children gave the answers they did to questions rather than in the quantity of their correct answers. His studies were carried out using complex qualitative interviews with young children, including his own three children. His research resulted in a hierarchical stage model of the development of thinking in children that has, like Freud, had a far-reaching impact on traditional thinking about how humans develop (Loevinger 1987:177–182).

The model

Piaget's developmental model includes four major developmental periods of thinking—sensorimotor, preoperational, concrete operational, and formal operational thought. The **sensorimotor period** is made up of six different stages that constitute "the precursors and first rudimentary stage of intelligence." First, are *impulsive and reflex actions* unconnected with "each other and for their own sake" (sucking). Second, *circular or repetitive actions* (kicking, grasping a blanket) that are gradually combined into two or more schemes (grasping and looking at a blanket simultaneously). To Piaget, a **scheme** (the term scheme is often translated as *schema*) is a pattern of stimuli and movements that together form a unity and result in sensorimotor coordination. Third, *practicing circular or repetitive actions for their consequences* (kicking to shake the crib). The beginning of concentration. Fourth, the baby *"coordinates schemes and applies them to new situations."* This represents the beginning of intentionality or experimentation in using one scheme to accomplish another (pulling a handkerchief to reach a toy underneath). This stage occurs near the end of the first year. The fifth stage *continues experimentation but with more novelty and variation of patterns.* The sixth sensorimotor stage *allows the baby to invent new means of doing things by thinking* rather than only by groping. At this point the baby also learns **object permanence,** which refers to understanding that when an object is out of sight it does not cease to exist (Loevinger 1987:182–183).

The next three periods involve the development of **operational thought (preoperational, concrete operations, formal operations).** In **preoperational thought** the child learns to use signs and symbols to think about and do things with objects and events that are absent. This period begins with the acquisition of language at about 18 months to two years and continues to ages six or seven. Preoperational thought is focused on concrete, external features of an object or situation and centers on the child (is egocentric) (Loevinger 1987:183).

The next period is **concrete operational thought** (about seven to fourteen, but may last through adulthood (Green 1989:178). The child reasons correctly about concrete things and events and can do so within "a coherent and integrated cognitive system" for organizing and manipulating the world (Falvell in Loevinger 1987:183). The child also begins the development of the ability to perceive what Piaget called conservation. **Conservation** refers to the ability to understand that objects can change in some respect but remain the same object. Conservation of volume refers to the ability to understand that the quantity of liquid remains the same even when it is poured from one container of a given shape into a container of a different shape. For example, pouring a cup of water from a tall slender glass into a short wide glass. The sophistication of the child's understanding of conservation to this point occurs late in this period. The final period is that of **formal operations** (fourteen through adulthood). During this stage the person reasons relatively correctly about hypothetical situations. Important for Piaget was the realization that as the child develops, thinking is not simply a collection of unconnected pieces of information, it is a system of construction. New learning is fitted into what is already known. Piaget referred to this ability as equilibration.

Conclusion

Piaget's model is less traditional in its more qualitative emphasis, but it reflects a developmental world very consistent with traditional paradigm thinking. It is positivistic or empiricist in its focus on knowledge based on direct observation as "real" knowledge. It is linear in its accent on specific progression of stages. It does not recognize differences in developmental experiences emerging from differing experiences resulting from gender. Piaget's model reflects no differentiation in developmental experiences based on race and class. It generally gives no recognition to social or environmental conditions that may impinge on individual development. Thus, it offers little guidance for connecting the personal and the political or on the interrelationships between individual and social change.

As with Freud's model, it is important to recognize that a critical approach such as that taken here is not a suggestion that we completely discard this model. It is to suggest, however, that we examine the model with a critical eye for its consistency with social work concerns. Piaget's work has been extremely influential and helpful in increasing our understanding of how some children learn to think and to think about their experiences of their worlds. His focus on understanding *how* children learn what they learn offers an important alternative to emphasizing only *how much* they learn based on quantifying *how many* correct answers they get on objective tests. To recognize these strengths we need not deny the limitations of this model and of the research upon which it is based.

Kohlberg

Introduction

Kohlberg's research focuses on the development of moral judgment and is in part an outgrowth of Piaget's work. Kohlberg's method involved presenting subjects with a series of moral dilemmas to which they were asked to respond.

Piaget's study of moral judgment included only children under twelve or thirteen years of age. Kohlberg extended the ages of his subjects beyond those studied by Piaget by interviewing a large number of adolescent boys (Loevinger 1987:193ff).

The model

Based on his research, Kohlberg found moral judgment to exist on "**three general levels—preconventional,** characterized by a concrete individual perspective; the **conventional,** characterized by a member-of-society perspective; and the **postconventional,** or principled, characterized by a prior-to society perspective" (Kohlberg in Loevinger 1987:194). Within each of the three general levels are two stages. Thus, Kohlberg's model consists of six distinct stages distributed across three more general levels of judgment.

"Stage 1 is characterized by a punishment-and-obedience orientation." Stage 2 is characterized by hedonism. Stage 3 is focused on "maintaining good relations and the approval of others." Stage 4 is focused on conformity to social norms. Stage 5 is characterized by "a sense of shared rights and duties as grounded in an implied social contract." At stage 6 "what is morally right is defined by self-chosen principles of conscience." (Loevinger 1987:194–195)

Conclusion

Kohlberg's model reflects consistency with the dimensions of the traditional/dominant paradigm. It is based on scientific, positivistic, objectivistic assumptions. The research upon which the model was based included exclusively male subjects. It reflects no recognition for differing developmental experiences based on color or class. It places a premium on development of autonomy, separateness, or individuality. It, like the other models we have explored thus far, portrays development from the perspective of privilege—the assumption of sufficient resources and power to fulfill developmental imperatives.

Analysis/Criticism: "Women's place" in Freud, Piaget, Kohlberg

Carol Gilligan (1982) examined the developmental theories of both Jean Piaget and Lawrence Kohlberg for their inclusion and treatment of the developmental experiences of women. These theories have much to say, you may recall from the summaries given earlier in this chapter, about the development of moral judgment and a sense of justice. Gilligan also discussed the treatment women received in Freud's theories in relation to these two fundamental developmental tasks. She noted that Freud found women's sense of justice "compromised in its refusal of blind impartiality" (1982:18).

According to Gilligan, in "Piaget's account (1932) of the moral judgment of the child, girls are an aside, a curiosity to whom he devotes four brief entries in an index that omits 'boys' altogether because 'the child' is assumed to be male." Kohlberg's research does not include females at all. His six stages "are based empirically on a study of eighty-four boys whose development Kohlberg followed for over twenty years." Kohlberg claimed that his model fit humans universally, but Gilligan pointed out, "those groups not included in his original sample rarely reach his higher stages." Women's judgment, for example, rarely goes beyond stage 3 on this six-stage scale. At stage 3 morality is seen in interpersonal terms; goodness is equivalent to helping and pleasing others. Kohlberg implied that only by entering the typically male arenas will women develop to higher stages where relationships are subordinated to rules (stage 4) and rules to universal principles of justice (stages 5 and 6). The paradox presented in Kohlberg's model is that characteristics that traditionally define "goodness" in women—care for and sensitivity to others—are also those that mark them as deficient in moral development. The problem in this paradox of positive qualities perceived as developmental deficiencies, Gilligan suggested, is that the model emerged from the study of men's lives (Gilligan 1982:18). Karen Horney made a very similar assessment many years ago, we might recall from our earlier discussion of Freudian theory and Horney's criticism of its treatment of women.

Erikson

Introduction

The stage-based model derived by Erik Erikson may be the model most often used to teach individual development in HBSE courses in social work curricula and in developmental psychology courses. It is difficult to understate the influence that Erikson's eight-stage model has had on the way individual development through the life span is perceived in this society.

Concepts associated with Erikson's model are used almost universally in the language of traditional human development approaches. Erikson's model is also often the departure point or base from which alternative models and theories of development emerge. Such basic concepts as developmental stage, psychosocial or developmental crisis, and the epigenetic principle all emerge from, and are central in Erikson's approach to individual development. These concepts are often used to describe central developmental processes from alternative paradigm perspectives as well. These concepts have become so central to developmental thinking that we will briefly describe them here. However, as you read the excerpts from Erikson later in this chapter, you are encouraged to take note of his discussion and use of these central developmental concepts as he summarizes his eight-stage model.

For Erikson, human development takes place according to a series of predetermined steps through which the person proceeds as he or she becomes psychologically, biologically, and socially ready. The unfolding of these steps allows the individual to participate in social life in increasingly wide-ranging and sophisticated ways. The model assumes that the environment in which development takes place provides the necessary resources and presents the necessary challenges at the proper times for the individual to move through each step. This process of orderly development through a series of steps is guided by what Erikson refers to as the epigenetic principle. The **epigenetic principle** holds that each step takes place as part of an overall plan made up of all the necessary steps or parts. Each particular developmental step emerges out of the context of the overall plan and each step comes about when the internal and external conditions exist to make the individual especially ready to do what is necessary to take the step. This time of readiness is referred to by Erikson as **ascendancy** (Erikson 1968:92–93). The necessary steps are referred to as developmental stages. A **developmental stage** is a critical period during which an individual struggles to address and resolve a developmental crisis. Resolution of each crisis enables the individual to proceed to the next stage. This process continues until the individual has progressed through all eight developmental stages. For Erikson, **developmental crisis** did not mean an impending catastrophe as much as it meant "a turning point, a crucial period of increased vulnerability and heightened potential" (Erikson 1968 in Bloom 1985:36). See Table 4.11 for an overview of Erikson's eight developmental stages and related ego strengths, crises, and explanations.

Traditional/Dominant Perspectives on Individuals

444444444444444444444444444444444444444444444444444444444444444444444444444444

Erikson's model: In his own words

Erikson's model is so fundamental to traditional paradigm thinking about individual development that it seems appropriate to include in his own words a summary of the model and descriptions of its basic concepts. This selection, "Eight Ages of Man," published by Erikson in 1950, is excerpted from a chapter in the first edition of his widely read and highly influential book, *Childhood and Society*. It provides a summary of his eight stages of the life cycle as he described them at this point in his career. In addition to giving an overview and a "flavor" for Erikson's thinking and writing, this selection reflects the significant influence of Freud and psychoanalytic thought on that of Erikson. The reader is also encouraged to consider critically, gender- and sexual orientation-related references, examples, and assumptions in this excerpt.

Eight Stages of Man by Erik Erikson

1. Trust vs. Basic Mistrust

The first demonstration of social trust in the baby is the ease of his feeding, the depth of his sleep, the relaxation of his bowels. The experience of a mutual regulation of his increasingly receptive capacities with the maternal techniques of provision gradually helps him to balance the discomfort caused by the immaturity . . . with which he was born. . . . The infant's first social achievement, then, is his willingness to let the mother out of sight without undue anxiety or rage, because she has become an inner certainty as well as an outer predictability.

. . . If I prefer the word "trust," it is because there is more naivete and more mutuality in it: an infant can be said to be trusting where it would go too far to say that he has confidence. The general state of trust, furthermore, implies not only that one has learned to rely on the sameness and continuity of the outer providers, but also that one may trust oneself and the capacity of one's own organs to cope with urges; and that one is able to consider oneself trustworthy enough so that the providers will not need to be on guard lest they be nipped.

The firm establishment of enduring patterns for the solutions of the nuclear conflict of basic trust versus basic mistrust in mere existence is the first task of the ego, and thus first of all a task for maternal care. But let it be said here that the amount of trust derived from earliest infantile experience does not seem to depend on absolute quantities of food or demonstrations of love, but rather on the quality of the maternal relationship.

2. Autonomy vs. Shame and Doubt

Anal-muscular maturation sets the stage for experimentation with two simultaneous sets of social modalities: holding on and letting go. . . . Outer control at this stage, therefore, must be firmly reassuring. The infant must come to feel that the basic faith in existence, which is the lasting treasure saved from the rages of the oral stage, will not be jeopardized by this about-face of his, this sudden violent wish to have a choice, to appropriate demandingly, and to eliminate stubbornly. Firmness must protect him against the potential anarchy of his as yet untrained sense of discrimination, his inability to hold on and to let go with discretion. As his environment encourages him to "stand on his own feet," it must protect him against meaningless and arbitrary experiences of shame and of early doubt. . . . Shame supposes that one is completely exposed and conscious of being looked at: in one word, self-conscious. One is visible and not ready to be visible; . . . Shame is early expressed in an impulse to bury one's face, or to sink, right then and there, into the ground. . . .

Doubt is the brother of shame. Where shame is dependent on the consciousness of being upright and exposed, doubt, so clinical observation leads me to believe, has much to do with a consciousness of having a front and a back—and especially a "behind." . . .

3. Initiative vs. Guilt

The ambulatory stage and that of infantile genitality add to the inventory of basic social modalities that of "making," first in the sense of "being on the make." There is no simpler, stronger word to match the social modalities previously enumerated. The word suggests pleasure in attack and conquest. In the boy, the emphasis remains on phallic-intrusive modes; in the girl it turns to modes of "catching" in more aggressive forms of snatching and "bitchy" possessiveness, or in the milder form of making oneself attractive and endearing. . . .

Infantile sexuality and incest taboo, castration complex and superego all unite here to bring about that specifically human crisis during which the child must turn from an exclusive, pregenital attachment to his parents to the slow process of becoming a parent, a carrier of tradition. . . .

The problem, again, is one of mutual regulation. Where the child, now so ready to overmanipulate himself, can gradually develop a sense of paternal responsibility, where he can gain some insight into the institutions, functions, and roles which will permit his responsible participation, he will find pleasurable accomplishment in wielding tools and weapons, in manipulating meaningful toys—and in caring for younger children. . . .

4. Industry vs. Inferiority
Before the child, psychologically already a rudimentary parent, can become a biological parent, he must begin to be a worker and potential provider. With the oncoming latency period, the normally advanced child forgets, or rather sublimates, the necessity to "make" people by direct attack or to become papa and mama in a hurry: he now learns to win recognition by producing things. He has mastered the ambulatory field and the organ modes. He has experienced a sense of finality regarding the fact that there is no workable future within the womb of his family, and thus becomes ready to apply himself to given skills and tasks, which go far beyond the mere playful expression of his organ modes or the pleasure in the function of his limbs. He develops industry—i.e., he adjusts himself to the inorganic laws of the tool world. He can become an eager and absorbed unit of a productive situation. To bring a productive situation to completion is an aim which gradually supersedes the whims and wishes of his autonomous organism. His ego boundaries include his tools and skills: the work principle . . . teaches him the pleasure of work completion by steady attention and persevering diligence. . . .

5. Identity vs. Role Diffusion
With the establishment of a good relationship to the world of skills and tools, and with the advent of sexual maturity, childhood proper comes to an end. Youth begins. But in puberty and adolescence all samenesses and continuities relied on earlier are questioned again, because of a rapidity of body growth which equals that of early childhood and because of the entirely new addition of physical genital maturity. The growing and developing youths, faced with this physiological revolution within them are now primarily concerned with what they appear to be in the eyes of

others as compared with what they feel they are, and with the question of how to connect the roles and skills cultivated earlier with the occupational prototypes of the day. In their search for a new sense of continuity and sameness, adolescents have to refight many of the battles of earlier years, even though to do so they must artificially appoint perfectly well-meaning people to play the roles of enemies; and they are ever ready to install lasting idols and ideals as guardians of a final identity: here puberty rites "confirm" the inner design for life.

The integration now taking place in the form of ego identity is more than the sum of the childhood identifications. It is the accrued experience of the ego's ability to integrate these identifications with the vicissitudes of the libido, with the aptitudes developed out of endowment, and with the opportunities offered in social roles. The sense of ego identity, then, is the accrued confidence that the inner sameness and continuity are matched by the sameness and continuity of one's meaning for others, as evidenced in the tangible promise of a "career." . . .

6. Intimacy vs. Isolation
It is only as young people emerge from their identity struggles that their egos can master the sixth stage, that of intimacy. What we have said about genitality now gradually comes into play. Body and ego must now be masters of the organ modes and of the nuclear conflicts, in order to be able to face the fear of ego loss in situations which call for self-abandon: in orgasms and sexual unions, in close friendships and in physical combat, in experiences of inspiration by teachers and of intuition from the recesses of the self. The avoidance of such experiences because of a fear of ego loss may lead to a deep sense of isolation and consequent self-absorption. . . .

While psychoanalysis has on occasion gone too far in its emphasis on genitality as a universal cure for society and has thus provided a new addiction and a new commodity for many who wished to so interpret its teachings, it has not always indicated all the goals that genitality actually should and must imply. In order to be of lasting social significance, the utopia of genitality should include:

1. mutuality of orgasm
2. with a loved partner
3. of the other sex
4. with whom one is able and willing to share a mutual trust

continued

Eight Stages of Man by Erik Erikson (Continued)

5. and with whom one is able and willing to regulate the cycles of

   a. work
   b. procreation
   c. recreation

6. so as to secure to the offspring, too, a satisfactory development.

It is apparent that such utopian accomplishment on a large scale cannot be an individual or, indeed, a therapeutic task. Nor is it a purely sexual matter by any means.

7. Generativity vs. Stagnation

. . . Generativity is primarily the interest in establishing and guiding the next generation or whatever in a given case may become the absorbing object of a parental kind of responsibility. Where this enrichment fails, a regression from generativity to an obsessive need for pseudo intimacy, punctuated by moments of mutual repulsion, takes place, often with a pervading sense (and objective evidence) of individual stagnation and interpersonal impoverishment.

8. Ego Integrity vs. Despair

Only he who in some way has taken care of things and people and has adapted himself to the triumphs and disappointments adherent to being, by necessity, the originator of others and the generator of things and ideas—only he may gradually grow the fruit of these seven stages. I know no better word for it than ego integrity. . . . It is the acceptance of one's one and only life cycle as something that had to be and that, by necessity, permitted of no substitutions: it thus means a new, a different love of one's parents. It is a comradeship with the ordering ways of distant times and different pursuits, as expressed in the simple products and sayings of such times and pursuits. . . . For he knows that an individual life is the accidental coincidence of but one life cycle with but one segment of history; and that for him all human integrity stands or falls with the one style of integrity of which he partakes. The style of integrity developed by his culture or civilization thus becomes the "patrimony of his soul," the seal of his moral paternity of himself. . . . Before this final solution, death loses its sting.

The lack or loss of this accrued ego integration is signified by fear of death: the one and only life cycle is not accepted as the ultimate of life. Despair expresses the feeling that the time is short, too short for the attempt to start another life and to try out alternate roads to integrity. Disgust hides despair. . . .

Trust (the first of our ego values) is here defined as "the assured reliance on another's integrity," the last of our values. . . . And it seems possible to further paraphrase the relation of adult integrity and infantile trust by saying that healthy children will not fear life if their parents have integrity enough not to fear death. . . .

Analysis/Criticism: "Women's place" in Erikson

Erik Erikson's influential theory of eight developmental stages portrays male development and experience as the norm. Gilligan and others (Berzoff 1989; Miller 1991) analyze and provide critiques of Erikson's theory specifically in terms of the developmental theme of relationship and connectedness and generally in terms of its treatment or representation of women.

Gilligan finds Erikson, when outlining the developmental journey from child to adult, to be talking about the male child. Much of Erikson's model focuses on the development of identity, a sense of who we are. For Erikson the normal steps to development of identity are steps requiring specifically an identity marked by primacy of separateness and autonomy. Gilligan points out, for example, that after the initial stage of establishment of a sense of trust which requires the establishment of a bond, a relationship initially with the infant's care giver (usually mother), the focus of development shifts to individuation.

The stages of autonomy versus shame and doubt, initiative versus guilt, industry versus inferiority, and identity versus identity diffusion all call for resolutions weighted toward separateness, individual drive and competence, and identity as a separate self in adolescence. The individual, then, in Erikson's male model, arrives at the adulthood crisis of intimacy versus isolation having spent all the previous years, with the exception of the establishment of trust in infancy, honing developmental skills that place a premium on separateness. But what is not indicated is that such a model is most likely to result in men who are poorly prepared for incorporating and appreciating the intimacy required of adults.

Erikson does recognize differences in the developmental experiences of women to some extent, but he describes these differences in his work virtually as afterthoughts or asides from the normal male model he presents. In his book *Identity: Youth and Crisis* (1968), for example, he addresses women's different developmental issues and experiences in the second-to-last chapter, "Womanhood and the Inner Space." The last chapter addresses, interestingly, "Race and Wider Identity." Neither of these chapters, based on lectures and papers written in 1964 and 1966 long after his original outline of the eight stages in 1950, resulted in changes or revision in the model. In his 1950 work, *Childhood and Society*, he mentions that, in the initiative versus guilt stage, boys' forms of initiative development activities focus on "phallic-intrusive modes" while girls focus on "modes of 'catching' in more aggressive forms of snatching or in the milder form of making oneself attractive and endearing" (Erikson 1950). In his 1968 work, Gilligan notes, Erikson finds identity development in adolescence for girls different from that in boys. However, these differences did not result in changes in his original outline of life cycle stages (Gilligan 1982:12).

Levinson: Adult Development

Introduction

Daniel Levinson recognized that most developmental research began with and focused on the developmental experiences and tasks of very early life. Most traditional models would then apply the concepts and patterns observed or emerging from studies of children to later points in the life cycle. The target of his research, unlike that of the others we have explored thus far, was the developmental experiences and stages of adulthood, primarily what he defined as middle adulthood. Like the other traditional models we have explored, Levinson's model, described in his book, *The Seasons of a Man's Life* (1978), talks about development only in terms of the experiences of men.

The model

Levinson and his colleagues (1978:18) concluded that generally the life cycle moves through a series of four partially overlapping eras, each of which lasts approximately twenty-two years. Their research also concluded that the cycle can be further broken down into developmental periods that "give a finer picture of the dramatic events and the details of living" (1978:19). Levinson claims a fairly high degree of specificity regarding the ages at which each era begins and ends. The range of variation is, he believes, "probably not more than five or six years." A central concept in Levinson's model is that of transition between eras. Transitions between eras last four or five years and require "a basic change in the fabric of one's life" (1978:19). The eras and transition periods are listed below:

> **Era 1.**   *[Preadulthood] Childhood and Adolescence: 0–22 years*
> *Early Childhood Transition: 0–3*
> *Early Adult Transition: 17–22*
>
> **Era 2.**   *Early Adulthood: 17–45*
> *Early Adult Transition: 17–22*
> *Mid-life Transition: 40–45*
>
> **Era 3.**   *Middle Adulthood: 40–65*
> *Mid-life Transition: 40–45*
> *Late Adult Transition: 60–65*
>
> **Era 4.**   *Late Adulthood: 60–?*
> *Late Adult Transition: 60–65*   (Levinson 1978:20)

In Preadulthood (Era 1) the social environment includes family, school, peer group, and neighborhood. Developmental tasks include becoming disciplined, industrious, and skilled. Puberty occurs at approximately twelve or thirteen and acts as a transition to adolescence, "the culmination of the pre-adult era." The Early Adult Transition (approximately age seventeen to twenty-two) acts as a bridge from adolescence to early adulthood. Levinson says, "during this period the growing male is a boy-man" and experiences extraordinary growth but remains immature and vulnerable as he enters the adult world (1978:21).

Early Adulthood (Era 2) "may be the most dramatic of all eras" with mental and biological characteristics reaching their peaks. This era includes formation of preliminary adult identity and first choices "such as marriage, occupation, residence and style of living." The man during this era typically begets and raises children, contributes his labor to the economy, and moves from a "novice adult" to a "senior position in work, family and community" (1978:22). This is a demanding and rewarding time filled with stress, challenges, and accomplishments according to Levinson.

Middle Adulthood (Era 3), with its Mid-life Transition from about forty to forty-five, Levinson refers to as "among the most controversial of our work" (1978:23). The controversy around discovery of this transition involves its lack of any clear cut universal event such as puberty in marking the transition from childhood to adolescence and early adulthood. This transition period includes more subtle, evolutionary, and thematic changes in biological and psychological functioning, the sequence of generations, and the evolution of careers and enterprises (1978:24).

This era is marked by some decline in "instinctual energies" and biological functions such as sexual capacity. Levinson describes this not necessarily as a deficit, since "the quality of his love relationships may well improve as he develops a greater capacity for intimacy and integrates more fully the tender, 'feminine' aspects of his self. He has the possibility of becoming a more responsive friend to men as well as women" (1978:25). Levinson notes differences in intensity of changes and in individual men's responses to them during this time. "The Mid-life Transition may be rather mild. When it involves considerable turmoil and disruption, we speak of a mid-life crisis." This transition involves a recognition of one's mortality and loss of youth for most men that is not completed here but continues for the remainder of life (Levinson 1978:26).

A key concept in Levinson's model is that of generation. He describes a generation in this way: "Members of a given generation are at the same age level in contrast to younger and older generations. With the passing years, a young adult has the sense of moving from one generation to the next and of forming new relationships with the other generation in his world." A generation "covers a span of some 12–15 years" (1978:27). Levinson uses Jose Ortega Y Gasset's conception of generations as a guide:

1. Childhood: 0–15;
2. Youth: 15–30;
3. Initiation: 30–45;
4. Dominance: 45–60;
5. Old age: 60+. (1978:28)

Levinson's notion of evolving career and enterprises calls on "every man in the early forties . . . to sort things out, come to terms with the limitations and consider the next step in the journey." Men around forty often experience some culminating event representing a significant success or failure in terms of movement along the life path. Levinson also describes this time of life as a period of "individuation," "a developmental process through which a person becomes more uniquely individual. Acquiring a clearer and fuller identity of his own, he becomes better able to utilize his inner resources and pursue his own aims. He generates new levels of awareness, meaning and understanding" (1978:31–33).

Late Adulthood (Era 4) is not the focus of Levinson's work, but he does give some attention to describing its tasks. He believes this era lasts from sixty to eighty-five. The developmental tasks include balancing the "splitting of youth and age" in order to sustain his youthfulness in a new form appropriate to late adulthood, terminating and modifying earlier life structure, moving off "center stage of his world," finding "a new balance of involvement with society and with the self," to gain a sense of integrity of his life, finding meaning in his life in order to come to terms with death, and making peace with enemies inside the self and in the world—not to stop fighting for his convictions but "to fight with less rancor, with fewer illusions and with broader perspective" (1978:36–38).

Levinson very briefly describes an additional era of Late Adulthood beginning at around eighty. Development at this point in life, while virtually unexplored (in 1978 when Levinson's work was first published), involved, he believed, such fundamental developmental tasks as "coming to terms with the process of dying and preparing for his own death," preparing himself for afterlife if he believes in immortality of the soul or, if not, concern for the fate of humanity and his own part in human evolution, and gaining meaning from life and death generally and his own specifically. "He must come finally to terms with the self—knowing it and loving it reasonably well, and being ready to give it up" (1978:38–39).

After publication of *The Season's of a Man's Life,* Levinson continued to explore adult development. In some of his later work, he stressed the need to develop models that appreciate and incorporate multiple and complex influences on the lives of humans. He emphasized the need to maintain an emphasis on the mutual influences of the individual and the social environment as development unfolds (Levinson 1986). Levinson also extended his theoretical position to include the developmental experiences of women. This extension to include women was based on a study of adult women and development he conducted subsequent to the original work that focused solely on the adult development of men. He concluded that the original model, with very little adaptation, fits equally the experiences of men and women. According to Levinson, "women and men go through the same sequence of periods in adult life structure development, and at the same ages" (Levinson and Levinson 1996:413). However, Levinson found that women's experiences, as they go through the same sequences of periods in adult development, differ from those of men. The major concept used to describe these differential experiences was that of gender splitting. **Gender splitting** is "a rigid division between female and male, feminine and masculine, in all aspects of life" (Levinson and Levinson 1996:414). Levinson found gender splitting to be especially apparent in the male and female experiences of public occupational and domestic spheres of life—"women's work and men's work, feminine and masculine within the self." Levinson posited that gender splitting "is encouraged by the existence of a patriarchal society in which women are generally subordinate to men, and the splitting helps maintain that society" (Levinson and Levinson 1996:414). However, as women increasingly enter the public sphere of work outside the home, Levinson concluded the "lives and personalities of women and men are becoming more similar" (Levinson and Levinson 1996:414). Levinson's perspective on the inclusion of the developmental experiences of both males and females in his model is quite different from that offered by Gilligan (1982) in her critique of Levinson's theory. Berzoff (1989) also questioned the ability to make generalizations about the patterns of adult development for men and women. (See "Analysis/Criticism" sections below.)

Disengagement Theory of Aging

Another traditional approach to understanding adult development, especially later adulthood, is **disengagement theory.** Achenbaum and Bengtson claim that "disengagement theory . . . represents the first truly explicit, truly multidisciplinary, and truly influential theory advanced by social science researchers in gerontology" (1994:756). The "disengagement theory of aging" was originally conceptualized by Cumming and Henry (1961) in their book, *Growing Old.* The central argument of the theory was that "**Disengagement** is an inevitable process of aging whereby many relationships between the individual and society are altered and eventually severed. . . . [It] could be seen in both psychological (ego mechanism) and sociological (role and normative) changes. It was also manifest in loss of morale" (Achenbaum and Bengston 1994:758).

Challenges to disengagement

Disengagement theory was challenged by researchers who suggested very different and much more varied views of the experiences of persons as they aged. According to Achenbaum and Bengston, Havighurst, in 1957, in putting forth his theory of "the social competence of middle-aged people . . . emphasized that most people ably adjusted their social roles well into their late sixties. Furthermore, he suggested that life satisfaction depended, indirectly at least, on social activity" (1994:759). They also note that in 1968 Smith "challenged both the universality and the functionality in assumptions about 'disengagement' by failing to confirm their propositions in surveys of African Americans, the chronically ill, and poor people." Tallmer and Kutner in 1969 suggested "it is not age which produces disengagement . . . but the impact of physical and social stress which may be expected to increase with age" (in Achenbaum and Bengston 1994:760). Bengtson reported in 1969 that there appeared to be "more *variation* than *uniformity* in retirement roles and activities across occupational and national groups. . . . there was little evidence for the 'universality' of disengagement" (Achenbaum and Bengston 1994:760). In a similar manner in 1968 and 1969 Neugarten "stressed *diversity* in patterns of aging, and the *variations* in the aged's personalities" (Achenbaum and Bengtson 1994:759). More recently, Tornstam (1999/2000) has reexamined this theory. As a result of his research, he has put forth an alternative theory of "gerotranscendence." See Chapter 5 for more on Tornstam's theory and other alternative theories of aging.

Analysis/Criticism: "Women's place" in adult development

Neugarten, in her research on the process of aging, argued for looking at adult development and aging from multiple perspectives in order to appreciate the diversity in the experience of aging for different people. For example, she noted that in her research she found that individuals' experiences of that aging process varied considerably according to both gender and social class. Neugarten was basically arguing against the notion of "biology as destiny" that had been put forth by traditional researchers in the area of adulthood and aging (Achenbaum and Bengtson 1994:759–60).

Does this photo communicate an image consistent with or inconsistent with Disengagement Theory of Aging? In what ways is the image consistent or inconsistent with this theory?

Achenbaum and Bengtson (1994:759) note, "Neugarten established her eminence in several domains of aging research. First, she stressed the importance of sex- and gender-based differences in biological and social time clocks." Second, she urged that researchers "look at the entire life course in addressing processes of aging, she never assumed invariant continuities in behavioral patterns." Bernice Neugarten laid the foundation for much on the later feminist and alternative approaches to considering diversity, gender, and class in research on adulthood rather than assuming only biological determinants of the aging process.

Carol Gilligan's (1982) research on women also informs adult developmental perspectives. She addresses specifically the exclusively male-based adult developmental model depicted by Levinson and the stages of adult development outlined in Erikson's male-focused model. Gilligan finds that the exclusion of the developmental experiences of women from these models results in incomplete portrayals of human development. The portrayals of the men emerging from these models lack what she considers to be some essential capacities. In existing traditional models of adult development, Gilligan finds "that among those men whose lives have served as the model for adult development, the capacity for relationships is in some sense diminished and the men are constricted in their emotional expression" (1982:154). Existing models display "a failure to describe the progression of relationships toward a maturity of interdependence [and] . . . the reality of continuing connection is lost or relegated to the background where the figures of women appear" (Gilligan 1982:155).

In adolescence and young adulthood, male and female voices reflect quite different central developmental experiences. For men "the role of separation as it defines and empowers the self" seems central. For women, "the ongoing process of attachment that creates and sustains the human community" is focal (Gilligan 1982:156). Gilligan notes that by listening to the previously unheard voices of women in thinking about adult development, one is pressed to reenvision notions of adult development. This new or extended vision is in line with Miller's description of "a psychology of adulthood which recognizes that development does not displace the values of ongoing attachment and the continuing importance of care in relationships" (Gilligan 1982:170). "By changing the lens of developmental observation from individual achievement to relationships of care, women depict ongoing attachment as the path that leads to maturity" (Gilligan 1982: 170).

Gilligan's and others' (Miller 1991 and Berzoff 1989) criticism of the traditional and dominant models of individual development for their male-focused treatment, if not their complete neglect of women, is but one example of limits of traditional developmental thinking. Perhaps as important as the implications of the treatment or neglect of women in traditional developmental thinking that Gilligan speaks of is the need for adult developmental perspectives that allow women to speak and to be heard in order to begin to develop true models of *human development.* As Gilligan points out, "Among the most pressing items on the agenda for research on adult development is the need to delineate *in women's own terms* the experience of their adult life." To listen to and learn from the developmental experiences of women is to include over one half of humanity in models of human development that has traditionally been neglected. It is also essential to realize, as Gilligan suggests above, that to listen to the voices of women is to learn a great deal about what is necessary for more completely understanding the meaning of individual development for both women and men.

Perhaps one of the most dramatic and under-examined examples of the damage that can occur as a result of uncritical traditional paradigm thinking regarding women and men and the privileging of men's power regarding women and girls at any stage of development is that of rape as a tactic of war. Illustrative Reading 4.1, "Rape as a Tactic of War," addresses such issues as cultural norms regarding gender and sexuality, gender-based issues of male power and dominance, and "a soldier's social identity as a man" (Milillo 2006:196)

Analysis/Criticism: "Lesbians' place" in adult development

According to Furst (in Wheeler-Scruggs 2008:45), "Levinson's universal developmental age-linked model of adult development disregarded culture, historical, and gender differences." Wheeler-Scruggs (2008) conducted research to assess the "goodness of fit" of lesbian adult development with Levinson's model. In her research she found, "there did seem to be the same basic ordering of structure-building and structure-changing periods" for the lesbians in her research study. She notes also, though, "how tasks are accomplished should be addressed differently for lesbians" (Wheeler-Scruggs 2008:45) She suggests, for example:

> a model of adult development for lesbians, transitional figures for separation from family, such as husbands or partners, may need to be replaced by feelings of independence, differentiation from parents, and solitary decision-making needs. Additionally, components that relate directly to being lesbian need to be considered as foundational in lesbian life structures. For example, coming out must be reflected in any adult development theory concerning lesbians. The family component also takes on different dimensions for this population. Although society does

not generally recognize the monogamous relationship between two lesbians as a family unit, lesbian couples themselves do. Friends also play
an important role in the sense of family that lesbians construct. The societal nonrecognition [*sic*] of being a family unit and the role friends play
in the makeup of that family unit will need to be considered in adult
development theories for lesbians (Wheeler-Scruggs 2008:45).

Analysis/Criticism: Traditional Developmental Approaches and People of Color

Race in developmental research/Erikson

According to Erikson successful human development depends on resolution of
intrapsychic conflict about membership in the following groups:

1. gender
2. religion
3. age
4. occupation
5. political ideology
6. sexual orientation (Helms 1992:287)

Consideration of race or ethnicity is conspicuously absent from the list
above. Helms notes that Erikson saw "racial-group membership as a significant
aspect of negative identity development in African Americans, he had no
notion of racial-group membership as a significant aspect of White people's
identities. Nor did he have a postulate by which identification with one's racial
group could have positive implications for personality adjustment for members of any racial group. . . . Yet in the United States, of the many collective
identity groups to which a person might belong, race is the most salient, enduring, recognizable, and inflammatory" (1994:287).

Parks et al. point out the neglect of diversity and the resulting image of
diversity as abnormal in much of the individual development literature. They
note that "until fairly recently, the literature was essentially comparative and
was critical of those who differed from the White male 'norm.' Theories of normal psychological functioning and development in a wide range of areas were
developed by studying groups of White men . . . and women and Blacks were
seen as deficient when differences between their experiences and those of
White men emerged . . . the general image of psychological health was developed from an essentially racist, sexist, and heterosexist frame of reference"
(1996:624).

Traditional developmental theories and multiracial people

Traditional theories of human development also do not reflect the complexities of
multiracial/ethnic developmental experiences. Miller asserts that "Largely ahis-
torical and acontextual, developmental models minimize the social-ecological
aspect of racial and ethnic classification" (1992:33). Miller describes several limitations of traditional developmental theory related to its neglect of diversities.
Compare Miller's limitations described below with the critiques of traditional
stage-based developmental theories examined earlier in this chapter.

Universality: "Eriksonian-based models of ethnic identity development
assume that the developmental process is universal (i.e., that the content
of identity development is immaterial for understanding the psychological process of coming to feel that one is a member of a social group). Similarly, social psychological theories of group affiliation assume that the

process itself is always the same, regardless of the specific self-to-other comparisons one makes." **Linearity:** "Particularly for the multiracial individual, the identification process may be far from linear. . . . The multiracial person may select behavior, labels, and perspective based on their immediate utility in a given context. The identity process is linear only to the extent that multiculturalism itself is an end state. . . . the multiracial person may shift in self-perception in appropriate contexts." **Ascription and Duality:** "Eriksonian and social theories assume that the ascribed racial or ethnic identity and heritage of an individual match. . . . These assumptions also often lead to the belief that multiracially identified people are 'mixed up' or maladjusted. . . . Eriksonian and social identity theories suggest that an individual cannot view him- or herself concurrently as a member of two groups." (Miller 1992:33–34)

These limitations reflect the binary or "either/or" nature of traditional paradigm thinking. Clearly this type of thinking does not allow room for inclusion of the richness and complexity of the experiences of persons of color and especially of bi- and multiracial people.

Themes Regarding People of Color in Traditional Developmental Approaches

Spencer (1990:267–269) summarizes some of the themes in traditional approaches to the study of development and people of color. She outlines several characteristics of traditional or dominant approaches that have resulted in inadequate and inaccurate portrayals of the developmental experiences of people of color. She argues that these portrayals have been detrimental to the African American, Asian American, Hispanic American, and American Indian people they exclude or inaccurately and incompletely depict. These traditional themes include the following:

1. Traditional-paradigm researchers have often been trained to view race and socioeconomic status as "nuisance" variables to be controlled for.

2. Study of minorities has too often been conducted from the approach of considering minorities as "deviant" from majority-based norms. The "deviance" approach neglected the often creative adaptation of people of color to the developmental barriers placed before them by hostile environments.

3. "Normative" development has too often been defined according to Eurocentric standards, excluding from the norm all but the most assimilated minorities. Cultural differences and structural explanations that recognize inequality and discrimination have often been largely ignored.

4. "The color-blind view of 'people as people' runs counter to unique cultural values, hypothesized cultural learning styles, and associated untoward social experiences. For example, the Western values of individualism and competition are in direct conflict with cooperation and collaboration, values of some minority cultures, notably American Indians, Asian Americans, and African Americans."

5. Treatment of minority group members as if they are invisible, portraying them only in a negative light (e.g., crime suspects) or providing only stereotyped, narrow portrayals (e.g., sports figures) result in a very limited and very limiting set of role models for minority children.

6. Many traditional portrayals reflect a "melting pot" perspective that was suggested over 20 years ago and that did not exist then, does not exist now, will not likely come about in the future, and is not desirable.

7. Such exclusionary and inaccurate portrayals are disadvantageous to the broader culture. Their neglect of minority experiences and problem-solving patterns deny the broader culture the opportunity to "be enriched by the talents, creativity, and intelligence of minority youngsters who have been provided an opportunity to reach their potentials" (1990:267–269).

These themes reflect many of the dimensions of traditional and dominant paradigm thinking. They clearly reflect the need for the creation and application of perspectives on the development of people of color based on the dimensions of alternative paradigms. As is the case with understanding traditional paradigm thinking generally, recognizing the weaknesses of traditional approaches to the study of the development of people of color is important for us as social workers if we are going to be advocates for more inclusive, strengths-based perspectives. The alternative perspectives on development and people of color described in the following chapter offer a number of other perspectives to help increase our understanding of HBSE and upon which to base our practice.

SUMMARY/TRANSITION

This chapter introduced a critical perspective from which to view traditional thinking about individual human development. It described the importance for social workers of applying this critical perspective to traditional thinking about individual development in order to recognize its limitations. It also explored the necessity of appreciating the importance, power, and usefulness of traditional paradigm thinking about individual development for effective social work practice.

This chapter then presented several of the most prominent traditional models of individual development. The models explored included the psychoanalytic approach of Freud; the cognitive developmental approach of Piaget; Kohlberg's extension of Piaget's work to the development of moral judgment; the developmental stage-based model of Erikson so often used to guide social workers; the adult development model of Levinson; and the disengagement theory of aging. Each of these models was subjected to analysis and criticism from the perspective of women's developmental experiences to illustrate their neglect and misrepresentation of women. In addition, a number of limitations of the approaches of traditional paradigms to the treatment of people of color were presented.

In the next chapter we continue our analytic/critical approach to thinking about individual development. In addition, we explore a number of alternative perspectives, some of which emerge as extensions of the traditional models explored in this chapter. These alternative perspectives allow us to think about the developmental experiences of the many individuals (women, people of color, persons with disabilities, gay men and lesbians) neglected or omitted entirely from traditional paradigmatic thinking about individual human development. While the models we explored in this chapter are likely to have been familiar to many of us from other courses, our travels in the next chapter are likely to take many of us to destinations quite new to us.

Succeed with PEARSON **mysocialworklab**

Critical Thinking   **Diversity in Practice**   **Engage Assess Intervene Evaluate**

Log onto **www.mysocialworklab.com** to watch videos on the skills and competencies discussed in this chapter. (*If you did not receive an access code to* **MySocialWorkLab** *with this text and wish to purchase access online, please visit* www.mysocialworklab.com.)

PRACTICE TEST

1. Erikson's theory of development which is often presented as if humans behave and develop solely as a result of experiences in infancy and early childhood is an example of _____.
   a. reductionism
   b. determinism
   c. normal development
   d. preconscious development

2. The concept of cathexis in psychoanalytic theory is somewhat similar to the concept of _____ in social systems theory.
   a. boundary
   b. hierarchy
   c. energy
   d. holon

3. Jendrek and others have suggested that it becomes difficult to distinguish major life events in terms of age and that connections between chronological age and life periods have become blurred. This model is known as_____.
   a. alternative stage model
   b. task-age relativity model
   c. fluid-cycle model
   d. age recycling model

 Human Behavior

4. According to Piaget, as a child develops, thinking is not just a collection of unconnected pieces of information. New learning is fitted into what is already known. This ability is known as _____.
   a. constructivism
   b. conservation
   c. formal operations
   d. equilibration

5. In Erikson's model of development, the developmental crisis focused on the ability to lose oneself in a committed relationship is found in the stage:
   a. identity vs. role confusion
   b. intimacy vs. isolation
   c. trust vs. mistrust
   d. autonomy vs. shame

6. Levinson's Middle Adulthood Era most closely corresponds with Erickson's stage of _____.
   a. generativity vs. stagnation
   b. intimacy vs. isolation

c. ego integrity vs. despair
   d. industry vs. inferiority

7. The view that sees development as progress rather than just change and has come to define development as achievement has led to the concept of_____.
   a. developmental risk
   b. progressive-achievement model
   c. headstart
   d. developmental delay

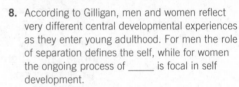 **Diversity in Practice**

8. According to Gilligan, men and women reflect very different central developmental experiences as they enter young adulthood. For men the role of separation defines the self, while for women the ongoing process of _____ is focal in self development.
   a. education
   b. attachment
   c. independence
   d. introspection

9. Historically, Freud's psychoanalytic theory was a significant influence in the development of social work. It influenced the profession by _____.
   a. causing a shift toward a medical or pathology perspective on people's problems rather than a social change or strengths perspective
   b. shifting the focus to addressing problems to internal or intrapsychic phenomena
   c. redefining human behavior as predictable according to determinable laws that are consistent with traditional paradigm thinking
   d. all of the above

Critical Thinking

10. Which of the following would NOT be considered a criticism of stage-based theories of development?
    a. provide a predictable understanding of development
    b. over emphasis on internal processes
    c. emphasis on uniformity negates the values of pluralism and diversity
    d. failure to consider environmental influences sufficiently

Log onto **MySocialWorkLab** once you have completed the Practice Test above to take your Chapter Exam and demonstrate your knowledge of this material.

Answers

1) a 2) c 3) c 4) d 5) b 6) a 7) b 8) b 9) d 10) a

Rape as a Tactic of War: Social and Psychological Perspectives

Diana Milillo
University of Connecticut, Storrs

For centuries, the rape of women has been used as a tactic of war to advance one group's political, economic, social, or religious position over another. Systematic mass rape devastates individual women and destroys the fabric of families and communities. This article argues that the systematic nature of rape as a tactic of war exists against a backdrop of rigid cultural norms of gender and women's sexuality, social dominance and power within group conflict, and a soldier's social identity as a man and a member of a particular military.

Keywords: dominance; power; rape; war

Violence against women has been part of every documented war in history (Brownmiller, 1975). Violence—specifically, rape—has been systematically used as a tactic of war by the military and governments to advance one group's political, economic, religious, or social position over another (Farwell, 2004). In some contexts, rape and torture are weapons of one tribe, nation, or region against women of another. In other cases, government-sanctioned violence is perpetrated within the same country, as in the civil wars of Rwanda and Sudan (Amnesty International, 2005). In each case, women's bodies become the receptacles of the intergroup hatred. Given the widespread history of rape used as a weapon of war, this article addresses two main questions: What functions does rape serve as a tactic of war? How do these atrocities continue to be justified? Specifically, I consider three sociocultural rationales to explain how mass victimization continues to occur: (a) cultural norms about gender and sexuality, (b) social identity, and (c) social dominance and power. Taken together, these forces oppress individual women as well as their families, communities, and larger social groups.

Rape in Times of War

In her groundbreaking analysis, Brownmiller (1975) highlighted the long history of sexually victimizing atrocities, from those perpetrated during the battles of Babylonia to the subjugation of Jewish women in World War II. More recently, mass rape and torture have been used during conflicts in Bosnia and Rwanda and in present-day Iraq, Columbia, and Sudan, among others (Human Rights Watch [HRW], 2004). The first documented mass rapes occurred in Nazi Germany during the riots of Kristallnacht in 1938. Later reports of women who were abducted followed, such as the following:

> Forty Jewish girls were dragged into the house which was occupied by German officers. There, after being forced to drink, the girls were ordered to undress and to dance for the amusement of their tormentors. Beaten, abused, and raped, the girls were not released till 3 a.m. (Brownmiller, 1975, p. 52)

At the same time, the Japanese earned notoriety for the "rape of Nanking" in 1937–1938 by executing horrific mass rapes and abuse of Chinese women

---

Diana Milillo, MA, is a PhD candidate in social psychology in the Department of Psychology, University of Connecticut, 406 Babbidge Road, U-1010, Storrs, CT 06269-1020; e-mail: diana.milillo@uconn.edu.

Affilia: *Journal of Women and Social Work* Volume 21 Number 2 Summer 2006 196–205 © 2006 Sage Publications 10.1177/ 0886109905285822 http://aff.sagepub.com hosted at http://online .sagepub.com and subsequently forcing the women into sexual slavery (Chang, 1997; Tanaka, 1998). As Brownmiller (1975) noted, "Approximately 20,000 cases of rape occurred within the city during the first month of [Japanese] occupation" (p. 61). Rape has also been a part of lesser-known interethnic conflict, such as militarized "national security rape" at the borders of nations or regions (e.g., the Mexico–U.S. border; Falcon, 2001). It is important to note, however, that even for women who live in regions in which violence is the norm, many identify with the sentiment of one victim, who recalled, "I wasn't afraid of the killing. I was afraid of the raping" (quoted in HRW, 2000, p. 2). Narratives from women all over the world have depicted the horror and devastation of victimization. One victim from Kosovo reported how her house was ambushed, as follows:

> They were wearing military clothes and had black scarves on their heads. They took my sister-in-law into the front room, and they were hitting her and telling her to shut up. The children were screaming, and they also screamed at the children. She was with the paramilitary for one half hour. She was resisting, and they beat her, and the children could hear her screaming. I could only hear what was going on. I heard them slapping her. The children did not understand that they were raping her. After they raped my sister-in-law, they put her in line with us and shot her. (HRW, 2000, p. 5)

Although not all acts of rape are committed in the same way, there are several themes that make it a systematic tactic in war. First, rape is often committed if a member of a woman's family is suspected of political activity that is incongruent with that of the state or the opposing group. Rape and torture are ways of "punishing actual or alleged deeds attributed to women or members of their family" (International Committee of the Red Cross [ICRC], 2001). For example, HRW (2000, p. 2) documented a number of rapes during 1998 that were committed by members of the Serbian police and military to punish Bosnian women whose family members were supporters of the Kosovo Liberation Army. At other times, violence is directed at women who explicitly threaten or challenge the goals of the regime in power.

Second, interviews with women who survived their attacks have revealed that the women were raped either in transition from one place to another or after they were captured and brought to a specific "rape camp" by the military. Women who fled Kosovo have spoken of the violence they encountered while leaving their homes, in which many were detained and tortured by the military and police. In these cases, groups of women would often be captured and abused, one at a time. In many other cases, soldiers pillaged villages, and women were raped in their own homes, often in front of their family members, including their fathers, husbands, and sons. One woman recounted,

> Then they took me. I was pregnant. I was holding my son. They took him away from me and gave him to my mother. They told me to get up and follow them. I was crying and screaming, "Take me back to my child!" They took me to another room. It was so bad I almost fainted. I can't say the words they said. They tortured me. (HRW, 2000, p. 8)

Similarities exist in the severity of the acts themselves. Typically, rapes reported during wartime are more violent and aggressive than are everyday accounts of interpersonal rape. Although some women are raped once, others are raped continually during a period of hours or days and sustain substantial physical injuries. Some are raped by more than one soldier. Many are also threatened with weapons, such as guns or a knives, or other materials, such as glass shards or burning charcoal (HRW, 2000). Such a situation was described by one victim from Iraq.

> They were armed, they put guns to my head and said come with us. I screamed and said take the pistol away. My daughter started to scream. They pulled my hair and pushed me in the car and they started shooting at the house, more than fifty shots. My daughter was screaming the whole time. Many neighbors started to shoot too, but they couldn't catch them. (Amnesty International, 2005, p. 20)

Narratives such as these are useful in that they put personal testimony into often-depersonalized theories of violence and aggression. Victims' narratives illustrate the range of women's lived experiences and highlight similar themes of shock and devastation.

Explaining Rape as a Function of War

Several early feminist critiques explained gender violence as a biological phenomenon that is rooted in societal structure. In *Against Our Will*, Brownmiller (1975) presumed that on realizing that their genitalia could serve as a weapon of force, all men become potential threats to all women. Men's discovery of their inherent power allows them to inflict fear or threat should they need or want to. Brownmiller's argument has a sociobiological basis in suggesting that every man has an innate drive to use his sexual power over women. Yet one long-standing criticism of sociobiological theory is that all men do *not* rape women, and, in fact, *most* men do not (Unger & Crawford, 2000). Subsequent feminist theories of rape have challenged prior notions that rape is an act of sexual aggression and have asserted instead that there is no sexual basis of rape but, rather, that it is the desire to prove and maintain one's power and control. Rape that is committed in times of war does expressly this. In critically analyzing the structural aspects of violence against women, especially during war, feminist analyses have explained interpersonal violence within a larger framework of domination and subordination between groups. It is primarily this perspective that I use here to analyze the sociocultural context of rape as a tactic of war. Next, I address several social and psychological theories to help explain the ideological and cultural backdrop against which violence against women is played out in war.

Cultural Norms About Gender and Sexuality

Almost all societies hold structural and social assumptions of the patriarchal and heteronormative power of men over women (Pratto, 1996). Ideologies of male dominance are largely institutionalized so that a woman's relationship to the men in her life (e.g., her father and husband) makes her dependent on the "capitalist mode of production" for economic support (Schwendinger & Schwendinger, 1983, p. 191). Early social and economic laws of women as the property of men reflected patterns of mating that are still seen in many societies today (Wilson, 1997). Historically, once a man claimed a woman, he was her sole protector, both domestically (e.g., providing food and shelter) and against the threat of harm from other men or groups. In return, the woman was obligated to carry out her own responsibilities, mainly reproduction and caregiving. Today, women in some cultures, even in industrialized nations such as the United States, still marry for economic and protective necessity. The pattern of "marrying up" reflects that women often choose mates who are older, physically bigger, and wealthier and who hold more prestigious jobs than they do (Bernard, 1972).

Not only do cultural norms about gender ubiquitously place women as the property of men, but ideas about women's sexuality provide ideological justification for gender violence. Stereotypes and ideals surrounding women's sexuality, fertility, and virginity are a basis for analyzing why the victimization of women in times of war not only hurts women but destroys women's ties to their families and communities of origin. Foremost, although cultural and religious prescriptions vary from place to place, many subscribe to the belief that women must be pure and untouched before marriage. For instance, Mexican women are expected to model saintly religious figures who are prized for their virginity, such as the Madonna or the Virgin of Guadalupe (Espin, 1987). Deviating from this ideal, whether it is their fault or not, has social consequences for women. First, sexual activity frequently brings a woman's family shame and dishonor. Second, the family of a woman who has been raped often disowns her, which leaves her without substantial social and economic support. Deviation from the obligation to remain a virgin until marriage inhibits or destroys a woman's potential to find a mate and thus reduces the chances that the woman will have an economically secure future. Furthermore, rape is often not excused; it is thought to be as much the woman's fault as her perpetrator's and brings no less shame or dishonor to her family name. As Tesanovic (2002) reported,

> She was a 19-year-old girl who lived in Bosnia with her family. When the war began her brothers fought on the Serbian side, while she huddled in cellars in the part of the city occupied by the army. She was raped by soldiers and became pregnant. When her father discovered that she was pregnant and by whom, he decided that she could not go on living with them. So she ran away to another city. (p. 3)

Married women who are raped bear the same strong burden. As long ago as the ancient Babylonian Code of Hammurabi, a married woman who was raped was equally stigmatized as having committed adultery, for which stoning or exile could be inflicted (Brownmiller, 1975, p. 19). Thus, intentionally inflicting shame and guilt by raping women is a major goal of those who are at war. In many cases, women are raped and abused in front of their families. As one woman remarked, "When your sexuality is destroyed, so is your motherhood and your dignity" (Tesanovic, 2002, p. 3).

Yet bringing stigma to a woman and her family is not the only goal of violence. Often, the motive for halting women's family security is part of the larger goal of "ethnic cleansing." Ethnic cleansing plays on the reproductive roles of women as the carriers of culture. By harming or shaming women out of marriage and motherhood, a conquering group may believe that they are working toward the eventual elimination of that social group while impregnating them with more "desirable" genetic material (Renzetti & Curran, 1999). On an individual level, a woman is displaced from her family, robbed of the power she once held in her reproductive capacities, or else left too psychologically damaged to be an effective caretaker of those around her. On a broader social level, mass and systematic rapes are "instrumental" to a more distal group goal for power (Jackman, 2001, p. 448).

Social Dominance and Power

Because in almost all cultures there is a hierarchy of power that is based on gender (and age and other cultural modifiers), this structure must be embedded ideologically in a culture for it to persist as just and functional. Social dominance theory (Sidanius & Pratto, 1999) asserts that members of the dominant group often believe in and ascribe to ideologies and behaviors that allow them to support group-based inequality; that is, they believe in and act in ways that support the status quo. The dominants (men) ascribe to ideologies that legitimate their power, using explanations that justify the out-group's lower status (in this case, women), such as "they are born for child care" or "their bodies are not made for this kind of work." Men have historically legitimated the exclusion of women from the military and the police force on the basis of these justifications.

Overwhelmingly, violence has been used by the conquering or dominant group in international or civil wars. One military official asserted, "Rape in warfare has a military effect as well as an impulse. And the effect is indubitably one of intimidation and demoralization for the victims' side" (quoted in Brownmiller, 1975, p. 37). However, using violence alone is not enough to assert one's male power, authority, and dominance. Rather, stereotypes help maintain the uneven distribution of power. Often, dominant group members use consensually shared ideas about fundamental or biological differences between groups (e.g., women's bodies are soft, and men's bodies are strong) to normalize power differentials (Jackman, 1994; Sidanius & Pratto, 1999). In war, there are typically group status differences between cultures or ethnicities (e.g., Japanese-Chinese and Germans-Jews, both during World War II).

Stereotypes are weapons that are used in intergroup conflict as well, such that the more dominant group ideologically justifies their position in battle as legitimate and just because of a moral, psychological, or social deficiency of the out-group. Stereotypes of the out-group are capitalized on to reinforce degradation of the out-group and are coupled with gender stereotypes in an interactive way. Women in the subordinate or opposing group are cast as immoral, dirty, cheap, or loose; for example, one woman who witnessed the rape of a Jewish woman in Nazi Germany overheard her called a "dirty Jew" (Brownmiller, 1975, p. 51). Stereotypes of women's lower status have often been used in the context of violence. For example, human rights activists asserted that when Serbian authorities told their victims to "make them coffee," they meant this term as a euphemism for sexual assault (HRW, 2000, p. 4).

Social Identity

It has been argued that violence is "an expression of the fragility of masculinity" (Kaufman, 1997, p. 40). According to Kaufman, rape and sexual assault are the outcomes of omnipresent masculine and feminine and active and passive dichotomies in social life, on which male identity and power are equated with the active assertion of masculinity. From an early age, men are socialized into a gendered role and learn from observing their environment and those who are in it that aggressiveness is reinforced (Bandura, 1977). Some research on domestic abuse or other interpersonal violence has contended that violence functions as a masculine-deficiency purpose. That is, "rape and sexual harassment can be viewed as expressions of defense of the masculine gender role" because men perceive inadequacy in some other arena in their lives (Koss et al., 1994, p. 14). For example, the loss of control or responsibility at work threatens the male ideal of being successful and powerful, so men displace this frustration on the women around them.

Yet rape in war may be a motive to bolster one's personal and group identity, rather than to fill a deficiency. Felson (1993) presented a model for understanding the means and the proximate and distal goals of rape and sexual aggression, which proves useful in analyzing the circumstances of gender violence in war as well as in instances of societies that are not under stress. His model suggests that there may be intentioned goals of rape and assault and illustrates several outcomes or goals of violence—namely, "retributive justice" and "desired social identity." First, retributive justice in war can be the collective desired outcome of one's group conquering another. Second, from a social psychological perspective, "desired social identity" could mean either the desire to express one's personal identity or group identity, which are sometimes conflated as the same identity. The desire to express a cohesive identity is encouraged and reinforced through the circumstances of war (e.g., fighting together and living together), which affirm both a personal and group identity. However, narratives that speak to the ways in which wartime violence is done suggests that there is a compelling need to affirm one's *group* or collective identity (i.e., as men and as members of a national group), which is the hallmark of social identity theory (Tajfel & Turner, 1986).

Social identity theory posits that individuals desire a positive social group identity and will engage in beliefs and behaviors that enhance the in-group's status and discriminate against the out-group (Tajfel & Turner, 1986). It suggests that even in socially neutral, laboratory-fabricated situations, in-group favoritism (e.g., the allocation of resources) persists (Brewer, 1979; Tajfel, 1978). War, however, is loaded with social meaning and vested interests. Social identity theory grew out of realistic group conflict theory, which returns to the general idea that "the perception of one's group's gains as another's loss translates into perceptions of group threat, which in turn causes prejudice against the out-group, negative stereotypes, in-group solidarity, awareness of in-group identity, and internal cohesion" (Sidanius & Pratto, 1999, p. 17; see also Campbell, 1965). Taken together, soldiers and paramilitary fighters may use gender violence as a cohesive in-group norm to support a national or group identity. Meanwhile, derogating female members of the out-group through rape and assault serves to keep their male identity intact by suppressing the power of the out-group's women.

Certain themes in the narratives of women victims of gender violence in war suggest that indeed a perpetrator's group identity, rather than a personal identity, is sought in violence. First, many narratives of rape have indicated that episodes of violence are committed by groups of men, rather than by men in solitude. Often, gang rapes occur as a function of fraternizing, such as "sharing" enemy women among the group. Many rapes of women in South Vietnam by American soldiers occurred in gangs "because Americans were trained in the buddy system" (Brownmiller, 1975, p. 98). In addition, the acceptance of group rape was sometimes institutionalized and encouraged, as in Japan's supply of prostitutes to its Imperial Army. "Comfort women," usually Korean women and girls, were there to excite soldiers and intentionally bonded them to each other and to their cause (McWilliams, 1998).

Second, the vast majority of those who commit rapes wear uniforms of national or ethnic significance. Furthermore, many men are often disguised in facial masks or scarves. As HRW (2000) noted, in the former Yugoslavia,

> the identities of perpetrators were frequently difficult to discern.... Victims described perpetrators of rape as dressed in camouflage outfits and sporting black masks or scarves. Yugoslav Army soldiers generally wore uniforms, typically green camouflage; special police units generally wore blue camouflage uniforms. (p. 3)

Dissociation from a personal identity and identification with the group induces many to behave without concern for others' harm. Deindividuation is the social psychological concept that when one is depersonalized and one with the group, he or she is "freed from restraints" and may behave are counter to social norms and values (Diener, 1979, p. 116 1969). Deindividuating conditions have been found to decrease se increase disinhibition, and increase aggressive behavior, especia group (Diener, 1979; Kugihara, 2001). Reicher, Spears, and Pos social identity model of deindividuation suggests that immersion, anonymity, and the clear salience of different social group identities will increase the likelihood of uncontrolled deindividuated behavior (see also Reicher & Levine, 1994). Under these conditions, "adherence to in-group norms will increase" (Reicher, Levine, & Gordijn, 1998, p. 17).

Psychological Consequences of Rape in War

A major consequence of rape is the social control of women by men. This article has thus far delineated the dimensions of the cultural and situational determinants on which violence against women is enacted. Particularly, it is the interaction of gender and culture that results in women bearing the horror of rape and assault. Foucault (1982) theorized on the impact of disciplinary power as an ideology of social control. It is the threat and fear of violence that creates an internalized, self-policing norm among those without power. Women in conflict-ridden societies who have not been personally victimized quickly learn the threat and magnitude of an attack. They are forced to regulate and monitor their behavior in ways that they believe will lessen the potential of an attack; thus, they apply self-protective strategies to navigate their way through everyday life (Crocker & Major, 1989; Jackman, 1994).

The social control of women largely functions in the mass silencing of women collectively or interpersonally (Lykes, Brabeck, Ferns, & Radan, 1993). The fear or threat of terror induces most women to live a life of silence. Women often remain quiet about their own victimization. Many are also reluctant to help other women, mainly because of their fear of future revictimization and the shame involved in dealing with the attacks. Women become a stigmatized majority, always vigilant and alert to what could happen.

Psychological losses of self and motivation, learned helplessness, or even suicidal wishes ensue from the past trauma. Because many women feel that they are the "psychological bearers of the collective community," a sense of guilt or depression looms for not doing more to help or to stop the violence or for not protecting their men (Tesanovic, 2002, p. 4).

Implications for Social Work

The International Federation of Social Workers (1999) explicitly stated that "social workers must commit themselves to enhancing the well being of women and girls as an essential aspect of the profession's ethical and practice commitment to human rights." One of the association's critical concerns for women is violence, including the mass rape of women. Given the expanding global nature of everyday social life and politics, social workers are impelled to create awareness and understanding of this crucial issue.

In areas that are afflicted with a high rate of intergroup violence, many rape victims continue to live in refugee camps where there is no system in place to challenge gender-based violence; thus, many women are prevented from reporting these crimes or dealing with the aftermath. However, the United Nations high commissioner for refugees (UNHCR, 2005) has supported the advancement of more services for survivors. In collaboration with nonprofit governmental organizations (NGOs), social workers are needed to help develop service programs, specifically in the areas of psychosocial support, medical assistance, and vocational training. Refugees International (2005), an aid organization, also noted the need to train staff in health and community services. Furthermore, evaluation programs would be useful to highlight specific risk factors for women. For example, in Chad, aid workers have found that women are at an increased risk of rape and assault when they travel to collect firewood (Refugees International, 2005). Social workers may work with NGOs to develop violence-prevention strategies and skill building.

It is important to note that these issues do not just affect those outside the United States. According to a report by the UNHCR (2005), the United States received the largest number of asylum-seeker applications from 2001 to 2004. Women who are able to leave their native countries and flee to the United States deal with complex emotions of coping with trauma and grief about leaving as well as practical problems that go along with living in a new culture, such as learning a new language and gaining access to health and mental health care.

Violence against women is often a complex dynamic to understand and, in large part, is usually conceptualized as an interpersonal crime, either within families or between strangers. Given the institutionalized norm of rape and assault in war and the costs of women's silence, research to help understand the prevalence and consequences of rape globally is extremely difficult (Koss, Heise, & Russo, 1997). Education must be strengthened within and among fields that are concerned with human rights violations, especially those against women. Social workers can promote change by shedding light on the relative invisibility of women's experiences as victims of violence in war and work with community and governmental leaders to create awareness of rape in war as a sociopolitically based problem.

References

1. Amnesty International. (2005). *The impact of guns on women's lives.* Retrieved from http://web.amnesty.org/library/Index/ENGACT300012005?open&of=ENG-390
2. Bandura, A. (1977). *Social learning theory.* Englewood Cliffs, NJ: Prentice Hall.
3. Bernard, J. (1972). *The future of marriage.* New York: World.
4. Brewer, M. B. (1979). In-group bias in the minimal intergroup situation: A cognitive-motivational analysis. *Psychological Bulletin, 86,* 307–324.
5. Brownmiller, S. (1975). *Against our will: Men, women, and rape.* New York: Simon & Schuster.
6. Campbell, D. T. (1965). Ethnocentric and other altruistic motives. In D. Levine (Ed.), *Nebraska symposium on motivation* (pp. 283–311). Lincoln: University of Nebraska Press.
7. Chang, I. (1997). *Rape of Nanking: The forgotten Holocaust of World War II.* New York: Basic Books.
8. Crocker, J., & Major, B. (1989). Social stigma and self-esteem: The self-protective properties of stigma. *Psychological Review, 96,* 608–630.
9. Diener, E. (1979). Deindividuation, self awareness, and disinhibition. *Journal of Personality and Social Psychology, 37,* 1160–1171.
10. Espin, O. M. (1987). Psychological impact of migration on Latinas: Implications of psychotherapeutic practice. *Psychology of Women Quarterly, 11,* 489–503.
11. Falcon, S. (2001). Rape as a weapon of war: Advancing human rights for women at the U.S.–Mexico border. *Social Justice, 28*(2), 31–50.
12. Farwell, N. (2004). War rape: New conceptualizations and responses. *Affilia, 19,* 389–403.
13. Felson, R. B. (1993). Motives for sexual coercion. In R. B. Felson & J. T. Tedeschi (Eds.), *Aggression and violence: Social interactionist perspectives* (pp. 233–253). Washington, DC: American Psychological Association.
14. Foucault, M. (1982). The subject and power. *Critical Inquiry, 8,* 777–795.

15. Human Rights Watch. (2000). *Gender-based violence against Kosovar Albanian women*. Retrieved from http://www.hrw.org/reports/2000/fry/kosovo03-02.htm

16. Human Rights Watch. (2004). *Women's rights*. Retrieved from http://www.hrw .org/women

17. International Committee of the Red Cross. (2001, October). *Women and war: Sexual violence*. Retrieved from http://www.icrc.org/Web/Eng/siteeng0.nsf/htmlall/women?OpenDocument

18. International Federation of Social Workers. (1999). *International policy on women*. Retrieved from http://www.ifsw.org/en/p38000218.htm

19. Jackman, M. R. (1994). *The velvet glove: Paternalism and conflict in gender, class, and race relations*. Berkeley: University of California Press.

20. Jackman, M. R. (2001). License to kill: Violence and legitimacy in expropriative social relations. In J. T. Jost & B. Major (Eds.), *The psychology of legitimacy: Emerging perspectives on ideology, justice, and intergroup relations* (pp. 437–467). New York: Cambridge University Press.

21. Kaufman, M. (1997). The construction of masculinity and the triad of men's violence. In L. L. O'Toole & J. R. Schiffman (Eds.), *Gender violence: Interdisciplinary perspectives* (pp. 30–51). New York: New York University Press.

22. Koss, M. P., Goodman, L. A., Browne, A., Fitzgerald, L. F., Keita, G. P., & Russo, N. F. (1994). *No safe haven: Male violence against women at home, work, and in the community*. Washington, DC: American Psychological Association.

23. Koss, M. P., Heise, L., & Russo, N. F. (1997). The global health burden of rape. In L. L. O'Toole & J. R. Schiffman (Eds.), *Gender violence: Interdisciplinary perspectives* (pp. 223–241). New York: New York University Press.

24. Kugihara, N. (2001). Effects of aggressive behaviour and group size on collective escape in an emergency: A test between a social identity model and deindividuation theory. *Journal of Social Psychology, 40*, 575–598.

25. Lykes, M. B., Brabeck, M. M., Ferns, T., & Radan, A. (1993). Human rights and mental health among Latin American women in situations of state-sponsored violence. *Psychology of Women Quarterly, 17*, 525–544.

26. McWilliams, M. (1998). Violence against women in societies under stress. In R. E. Dobash & R. P. Dobash (Eds.), *Rethinking violence against women* (pp. 111–140). London: Sage.

27. Pratto, F. (1996). Sexual politics: The gender gap in the bedroom, the cupboard and the cabinet. In D. M. Buss & N. M. Malamuth (Eds.), *Sex, power and conflict: Evolutionary and feminist perspectives* (pp. 179–230). New York: Oxford University Press.

28. Refugees International. (2005, September). *Chad: Strengthen the response to gender-based violence*. Retrieved from http://www.refugeesinternational.org/content/article/detail/5654

29. Reicher, S., & Levine, M. (1994). Deindividuation, power relations between groups and the expression of social identity: The effects of visibility to the out-group. *Journal of Social Psychology, 33*, 145–163.

30. Reicher, S. D., Spears, R., & Postmes, T. (1995). A social identity model of deindividuation phenomena. *European Review of Social Psychology, 6*, 161–198.

31. Reicher, S. D., Levine, R. M., & Gordijn, E. (1998). More on deindividuation, power relations between groups and the expression of social identity: Three studies on the effects of visibility to the in-group. *British Journal of Social Psychology, 37*, 15–40.

32. Renzetti, C. M., & Curran, D. J. (1999). *Women, men, and society* (4th ed.). Boston: Allyn & Bacon.

33. Schwendinger, J. R., & Schwendinger, H. (1983). *Rape and inequality*. Beverly Hills, CA: Sage.

34. Sidanius, J., & Pratto, F. (1999). *Social dominance: An intergroup theory of social hierarchy and oppression*. New York: Cambridge University Press.

35. Tajfel, H. (1978). Social categorization, social identity, and social comparison. In H. Tajfel (Ed.), *Differentiation between social groups* (pp. 61–76). London: Academic Press.

36. Tajfel, H., & Turner, J. C. (1986). The social identity theory of intergroup behavior. In S. Worchel & W. G. Austin (Eds.), *Psychology of intergroup relations* (pp. 7–24). Chicago: Nelson-Hall.

37. Tanaka, Y. (1998). *Hidden horrors: Japanese war crimes in World War II.* Boulder, CO: Westview.

38. Tesanovic, J. (2002). *Women and war: A Serbian perspective.* Retrieved from http://geocities.com/Wellesley/3321/win23a.html

39. Unger, R. K., & Crawford, M. (2000). *Women and gender: A feminist psychology* (3rd ed.). New York: McGraw-Hill.

40. United Nations High Commissioner for Refugees. (2005). *Asylum levels and trends in industrialized countries, 2004.* Retrieved from http://www.unhcr.org/texis/vtx/doclist?page=statistics/opendoc.pdf?tbl=STATISTICS&id=422439144

41. Wilson, K. J. (1997). *When violence begins at home: A comprehensive guide to understanding and ending domestic violence.* Alameda, CA: Hunter House.

42. Zimbardo, P. G. (1969). The human choice: Individuation, reason, and order vs. deindividuation, impulse, and chaos. In W. J. Arnold & D. Levine (Eds.), *Nebraska symposium on motivation* (Vol. 17, pp. 237–307). Lincoln: University of Nebraska Press.

5

Alternative and Possible Perspectives on Individuals

CONNECTING CORE COMPETENCIES *in this chapter*

| Professional Identity | Ethical Practice | Critical Thinking | Diversity in Practice | **Human Rights & Justice** | Research Based Practice | **Human Behavior** | **Policy Practice** | **Practice Contexts** | Engage Assess Intervene Evaluate |

In this chapter we focus on extending and deepening our understanding of individuals' developmental experiences and the social environments in which these experiences take place. We want to learn to integrate the strengths inherent, but often unrecognized, in the diverse developmental realities, experiences, and strategies of different individuals so we can do better social work.

Destinations

The destination of our journey in this chapter is not some static and final point at which we arrive upon a complete or absolute understanding of "proper individual behavior and development." In fact, our goal in this chapter is not any one destination at all. Our paramount concern is that during the journey we learn about multiple models to use as resources—tools, information, awarenesses, ways of thinking about developmental issues—to help us recognize the developmental commonalities shared by us all as humans and to recognize and respect how different humans develop differently. In addition, the information provided in this chapter is intended to provide a base from which to continue learning about human behavior throughout our lives. If there were a single destination it would be that place at which we attain sufficient knowledge upon which to base action to remove barriers to achieving the full human potential of any person with whom we work.

Themes receiving special emphasis in this chapter include diversity, diversity within diversity, multiple diversities, and multiple perspectives on understanding differences. We explored the notion of developmental universals or commonalities in Chapter 4. In this chapter we will be much more concerned with developmental variation as not only acceptable, but as necessary for healthy individual human development and essential for a healthy society as well.

ALTERNATIVE AND POSSIBLE DEVELOPMENTAL THEORIES

The alternative/possible models we will explore focus on developmental approaches that include persons and conditions left out of or only peripherally addressed by traditional models. These approaches also reflect dimensions of the alternative paradigm for understanding HBSE outlined in Chapter 2.

We must recognize that no one alternative approach offers a model incorporating all the dimensions of alternative paradigms. Each, however, provides an alternative to traditional models along at least one, if not several, of the alternative paradigmatic dimensions. This diversity of focuses is in keeping with our search for multiple models and approaches that reflect the differing developmental experiences of diverse persons. Rather than any one alternative offering some complete and final answer, the alternatives we will explore reflect a variety of attempts to develop multiple answers to the developmental questions emerging from different persons, experiences, and conditions of concern to social workers.

Although the alternatives discussed differ from one another in many ways, they share some important dimensions and themes. They offer voices and visions that are important in responding to the exclusion of many persons from traditional paradigms. They address historical conditions of oppression. Other themes that emerge from some of the alternative perspectives we will explore include:

1. differences in experiences in carrying out the common developmental process of identity formation.
2. a lack of developmental mentors or role models for many oppressed and excluded persons.

3. impact on an individual's development of deficit or abnormal status often accorded excluded or oppressed persons by traditional models or by dominant society.

4. explicit attention to social environmental (SE) influences on individual development.

Another important structural characteristic of many of the alternative approaches is their **nonlinear, contextual quality.** This characteristic is most obvious in the non-stage-based nature of some of the alternatives we are about to explore. Even the models that emerge from or are adaptations of traditional stage-based models tend to be contextual and nonchronological. The approaches and models that follow attempt to include and reflect the dimensions (to varying degrees) of alternative paradigm thinking. They have also been chosen to address alternative perspectives on individual development throughout the life course. The alternative approaches that we explore, you will notice, often have their roots in traditional or dominant models, but they seek to transcend the limits of the traditional models in order to embrace diversity.

The following sections dealing with alternative perspectives on individual development and behavior are organized according to several "focuses"—people of color, women, sexual orientation, people with disabilities, elders, and men. These focuses are intended to highlight developmental issues and tasks faced by different groups but that are not focused on in traditional paradigm research. The concepts and issues dealt with within the specific "focus" sections, however, are not intended to apply exclusively to the persons or groups discussed in a specific section. As we have stressed, there is much overlap, interrelatedness, and similarity among developmental issues, conditions, and experiences of the groups discussed. We must also be extremely aware of **"diversity within diversity."** There are wide ranges of variability among members of specific groups. Unless we are aware of diversity within diversity, we risk denying the uniqueness of individuals. It is very important also to recognize the special developmental complexities faced by persons who are simultaneously members of more than one diverse group. **Intersectionality**, discussed in Chapter 3, is one emerging approach that focuses on the importance of understanding the complexity resulting from simultaneous membership in multiple oppressed groups.

SEHB and Individual Development

One of the themes especially significant in considering alternative perspectives on development is the role played by the larger social environment. As we noted in Chapter 4, few traditional theories of individual development attend to the significant influence of social environmental factors on development, yet the nature of interaction with the larger environment (for example, experiences of racism, homophobia, or sexism) has a significant influence on development throughout the life course. In addition, the availability of needed resources from the larger social environment for optimum development is a critical factor in developmental outcomes (nutrition, health care, housing, education, etc.). For example, Andrews and Ben-Arieh describe the critical importance of both positive interaction in and the availability of necessary material resources from the larger environment for optimal development. They point out that "material resources such as food, safe water, clothing, and housing are necessary but insufficient for holistic development. Stable, nurturing social relationships and safe, stimulating environments are essential" (Andrews and Ben-Arieh, 1999:110).

Poverty: The Social Environment and the Life Course

Practice Contexts

Professional social workers are expected to competently and proactively respond to the constantly changing contexts or environments that influence their practice. What is an example of how a change in a person's environment might have an impact on their individual development?

Poverty, especially as it affects children and women of childbearing years, often has a profound impact on individual development. Poverty results in a reduction of the resources available in the child's and the mother's environment necessary to provide for positive child development. **Poverty** is, of course, determined by income and "includes money income before taxes." The **poverty threshold** is a set of money income thresholds that vary by family size and composition to determine who is poor. For example, in 2008 the poverty threshold was $21,854 for a family of four with two children under age 18 (Population Reference Bureau 2008).

The U.S. Department of Health and Human Services uses "poverty guidelines" to determine who is poor in relation to its services and policies. Those guidelines for 2008 are included in the table below.

2008 HHS Poverty Guidelines

Persons in Family or Household	48 Contiguous States and D.C.	Alaska	Hawaii
1	$10,400	$13,000	$11,960
2	14,000	17,500	16,100
3	17,600	22,000	20,240
4	21,200	26,500	24,380
5	24,800	31,000	28,520
6	28,400	35,500	32,660
7	32,000	40,000	36,800
8	35,600	44,500	40,940
For each additional person, add	3,600	4,500	4,140

Source: Federal Register, Vol. 73, No. 15, January 23, 2008, pp. 3971–3972 (U.S. Census Bureau, 2008).

In addition, by studying patterns of income and participation in service programs using data from what are referred to as "panel studies" or long-term studies (up to 13 years' duration) of income patterns and program participation, new understanding about the likelihood of experiencing poverty in the United States is emerging. Using these data, researchers have discovered how likely it is that any one of us will experience poverty, the degree of the poverty, the length of time we are likely to be poor at any one time, and the differences in likelihood of experiencing poverty depending on whether we are white or African American.

Analyses of these long-term data reveal that poverty is not usually a continuous state for most people. For most people "spells of poverty are fairly brief." However, for those households only slightly above poverty, a fall back into poverty can happen quickly with the loss of a job or the exit of one of the breadwinners from the family. As a result many families will move in and out of poverty over time. Studies of these data also reveal significant differences between African Americans and white Americans. African Americans "were more likely to be touched by poverty and more likely to be exposed to poverty for substantially longer periods" than whites (Rank and Hirschl 1999:202).

Children under the age of 18 are the most likely age group to be poor in the United States at any point in time. However, analysis of panel-study data by Rank and Hirschl revealed some startling findings about poverty during the adult years. For example, they found that "60 percent of 20-year-olds in America will experience poverty" for at least a year at some point during their adult lifetime (Rank and Hirschl 1999:205). In other words, rather than poverty being an experience that only happens to others, "a clear majority of Americans" will experience poverty during their adult lifetime.

Of African American adults who reach the age of 75, 91 percent will have spent some time below the poverty line. Of white adults who reach the age of 75, 52.6 percent will have spent time below poverty level. A 1 in 2 chance of experiencing poverty seems large in a society with the affluence of U.S. society; a 9 in 10 chance seems intolerable. The duration of an episode of poverty is also dramatically different for African Americans than for whites. Rank and Hirschl define **dire poverty** as the "equivalent of spending a year below one-half of the official poverty line" (1999:208–9). For example, if the poverty level is $16,000 for a family of four, members of that family would spend at least one year with an income of no more than $8,000. One-third of all adult Americans will experience dire poverty. Sixty-eight percent of adult African Americans will experience dire poverty (Rank and Hirschl 1999:211–12).

Rank and Hirschl argue that since most of us will experience poverty during adulthood (to say nothing of the likelihood of childhood poverty) and since poverty underlies so many of the problems confronted by social workers, we should all take a very keen interest in reducing poverty. Rank and Hirschl point out, "for the majority of Americans, it is in their direct self-interest to have programs and policies that alleviate . . . the ravages of poverty." They point out that "for the majority of American adults, the question is not if they will experience poverty, but when" (1999:213–14).

Poverty and Human Development: Hunger in the United States and Globally

Among the most basic effects of poverty are hunger and malnutrition. Hunger and malnutrition play multiple and complex roles in human developmental outcomes. Adequate nutrition is necessary for a healthy and productive life. According to the United Nations Food and Agricultural Organization,

> taking age, gender, height, and weight into account, an adult needs about 1,300 to 1,700 calories per day just to maintain the basal metabolic rate (breathing, pumping blood, and so forth). To perform light activities a person needs about 1,720 to 1,960 calories. A person needs at least 2,100 calories to perform moderate levels of work. (Seipel 1999:417)

Chronic undernutrition results when the intake of calories is less than 1,900 per day (Seipel 1999:417). Malnutrition and hunger are widespread across the globe, including many persons in the United States. According to the Food Research and Action Council (FRAC), a national organization doing research and policy advocacy to reduce hunger in the United States, "approximately four million American children under age 12 go hungry and about 9.6 million more are at risk of hunger." Twenty-nine percent of these children "live in families that must cope with hunger or the risk of hunger during some part of one or more months of the previous year" (Food Research and Action Council, 2000). A total of almost 20 million

Professional social workers are expected to be able to engage in policy practice to improve social and economic well-being. Give an example of one U.S. policy or program that, as a social worker, you could use to assist a family in meeting its nutritional needs.

people in the United States experienced hunger during the 1980s (Seipel 1999:419).

Globally, hunger is pervasive and deadly. The World Health Organization (WHO) estimated that in 1998 "malnutrition was a causative factor in nearly half of the 10.4 million deaths among children under age five in developing countries." Hunger is also a major factor in disease and illness. WHO suggests that "30 percent to 40 percent of the 10 million incidents of cancer that occurred in 1996 could have been prevented by appropriate diets, along with other preventive measures" (Seipel 1999).

This situation is actually a significant improvement from the 1960s, when about 75 percent of people (about 1.6 billion people) "had a food supply that amounted to less than 2,100 calories per person per day." By the 1990s the percentage had dropped to about 10 percent. However, that number still amounted to a staggering 405 million people (Seipel 1999:416).

Seipel stresses that "malnutrition is not a simple problem with a simple solution. It results from the complex interplay of social and biomedical factors" (1999:418). **Food insufficiency** refers to inadequate food supplies or the inability of countries to produce enough food to meet the needs of their population. Approximately 800 million people still face this type of food insecurity or insufficiency. Poverty, of course, plays a significant role in hunger and malnutrition. Seipel also suggests that in many parts of the world gender inequality results in more hunger and malnutrition for women and girls than for men and boys "because of a cultural preference for men over women" (Seipel 1999:419).

These interconnected causes of poverty result in multiple consequences for human development. Malnutrition results in the inability of the body's immune system to fight infection. Malnutrition can result in growth faltering, or stunting and wasting—a failure to grow. Growth faltering is associated with impaired intellectual development and decreased learning opportunities. Also of major and long-term concern are the negative consequences of malnutrition for maternal and child health. Pregnant women who are malnourished are at significantly higher risks for "miscarriage, abortion, and stillbirth." Malnutrition and the associated lack of vitamin and mineral supplements can result in impaired health for both babies and their mothers. One of the most common results of malnutrition for infants is low birth weight. "Low birth-weight babies often do not survive, but if they do survive, their impaired immune systems make them more vulnerable to infection and disease" (Seipel 1999:420–1).

For social workers, a critical question is "what can be done to reduce hunger and malnutrition?" Seipel suggests a number of responses. At the macro and policy levels, one response is efforts to support nations in achieving food security or food sufficiency by either assisting in increasing production of sufficient food within the country or helping insure that nations have the economic capacity to import additional food. Helping to assure that available food supplies are distributed to those families most in need is another response. Of particular importance is creating support systems for women, including increasing educational opportunities, creating a women's support movement to enhance the rights of women, improving technology to reduce women's domestic workload, and promoting political participation by women. As social workers we can also use our skills to build awareness of hunger as a national and international concern and to promote the United Nations principles of human rights including the right of all persons to adequate nutrition (Seipel 1999:420–4).

War, refugees, and immigrants: Global influences on social work and human development

According to Nash, Wong, and Trlin, "social work is operating in an increasingly global environment. Nowhere is this more apparent than in work with immigrants, refugees and asylum seekers" (2006:345). They also note, "the movement of people (voluntary and forced) across borders is an international phenomenon, an expression of globalization with implications for national, economic and political stability and cultural identity" (Nash et al. 2006:345). For example, the context in which they discuss these issues is New Zealand.

In discussing the experiences of Bosnian refugees, Snyder, May, Zulcic, and Gabbard (2005) describe the impact on the development of children and families of war, becoming a refugee, and finding and settling in a new country. They note, for example, that during the Bosnian war "many women and children fled as refugees while men tended to stay behind to fight and protect property" (Snyder et al. 2005:614–615). The impact on these child refugees' development included numerous challenges. These included family separations, disruptions in socialization as a result of loss of familiar supports such as "schools and places of worship," and vulnerabilities to threats and actual experiences of violence. The results of having faced these challenges were many: difficulties developing trust and relating to peers, developmental delays, poor school performance, depression, post-traumatic stress disorder (especially for child victims of "rape, sexual abuse, and physical assaults"), nightmares and flashbacks, and survivor guilt (Snyder et al. 2005:615).

In addition to experiences related directly to having been in the midst of war, refugees also face a wide range of difficulties and vulnerabilities during resettlement and adaptation to new and unfamiliar environments during transit and after relocation. Snyder, et al delineate some of the stressors: "difficult transit experiences; culture shock; adjustment problems related to language and occupational change; and disruption in their sense of self, family, and community" (Lipson 1993 and Worthington 2001 in Snyder et al. 2005:616).

Refugees leaving their war-torn but home countries to settle in a new and unfamiliar place bring with them a history of multiple losses, including "severance from family and friends who have been left behind or killed, displacement from their homes and communities, social isolation, and the premature death of their children" (Snyder et al. 2005:616). There are many other complex challenges and issues facing refugees and the social workers who attempt to provide them services. In other chapters in this book we will continue to address these challenges for individuals, families, communities, and the international community.

Identity Development

Spencer and Markstrom-Adams (1990) remind us that according to Erikson, **identity development** is a major developmental task for which the stage is set during childhood and then played out during adolescence. Spencer and Markstrom-Adams (1990:290) suggest that the complexity of identity development increases "as a function of color, behavioral distinctions, language differences, physical features, and long-standing, although frequently not addressed social stereotypes." **Stereotypes** are generalizations about people based on such characteristics as those listed above. A **negative stereotype** is similar in many respects to **stigma** in that both terms refer to negative generalizations about people. In this case stereotypes are based on characteristics of members of minority groups considered negative by members of dominant groups.

In order to acknowledge this complexity, they believe that "new conceptual frameworks shaped by models of normal developmental processes are needed (i.e., as opposed to deviance- and deficit-dependent formulations)." New conceptual paradigms are necessary because "racial and ethnic groups have heretofore been examined through pathology-driven models" (Spencer and Markstrom-Adams 1990:304). In addition, traditional developmental theories often ignore the interplay of external societal factors with internal cognitive factors.

Throughout much of the rest of this chapter we will explore a variety of alternative concepts, models, and theories in order to present a more complete and inclusive picture of identity development. Next we will explore Self-Categorization Theory (SCT).

Self-Categorization Theory (SCT)

Hopkins (2008) reinforces the importance of the interplay of individual will and the environment or context in defining (and potentially redefining) who we are, both individually and in terms of group identity, especially in the context of minority status within a dominant society. For example, he notes, "Across the social sciences the significance of collective or social identities (e.g., ethnic and national) has attracted increasing interest" (2008:364). However, he also stresses that differences in power reflect that "people are not equally placed" in their ability to self-define either personal or group identity (2008:365).

Hopkins points to Self-Categorization Theory (SCT) as a helpful approach that recognizes the multiple levels at which individual identity is constructed. He notes, "According to the theory, the self may be defined at different levels of abstraction. Sometimes it may be defined in terms of individual uniqueness, at other times in terms of a specific group membership." In addition, according to SCT, individual and group identities "are not fixed or given" (2008:364). Specifically, he suggests, "Identities are not givens and we need an approach that recognizes the place for agency [individual will] and dialogue in identity-definition. Identities are not made and remade at will or in a rarefied public sphere. It is in the messiness of everyday practice that controversies arise and identities are invoked, defined and become meaningful" (Hopkins 2008:365). Once again, we see the complexity and ambiguity ("messiness") that must be appreciated in this alternative approach to creating, maintaining, or changing our identities as both individuals and members of specific groups.

Sanders Thompson addresses the complexity of African American identity development. She, like Hopkins, notes the multiple levels of identity that must be considered in efforts to understand African American identity and identity formation. In doing so, she calls for a "multidimensional approach to racial identification." She defines *racial group identification* as "a psychological attachment to one of several social categories available to individuals when the category selected is based on race or skin color and/or a common history, particularly as it relates to oppression and discrimination due to skin color." However, not all members of a group identify to the same extent with all elements of the group's identity (Sanders Thompson 2001:155). We will look more closely at the issues related to individual and group identity later in this chapter.

Diversity within diversity

Traditional developmental models assume homogeneity among group members. They assume that all members of a particular group share all characteristics such as family form, socioeconomic status, values, even color. Variations are often as extensive among group members as between one group and another. This diversity in diversity must be recognized in attempts to understand the development of members of minority groups (Spencer and Markstrom-Adams 1990:290–310). For example, we must recognize that there is wide variation among African American families from single parent, female-headed to traditional nuclear, two parent to large extended, multigenerational, and from low-income to middle-income to high-income families. Similarly, it is important to recognize the wide cultural and language variations among North American indigenous peoples. This group includes "all North American native people, including Indians, Alaska Natives, Aleuts, Eskimos, and Metis, or mixed bloods" (LaFromboise and Low in Spencer and Markstrom-Adams 1990:294). Among American Indians alone there are over 200 different languages. Likewise, one must recognize that there are significant differences in perspective among Japanese Americans of different generations in the United States. The "immigrant 'Issei,' the American born 'Nisei,' and the second generation of American-born Japanese called 'Sansei' " are seen by each other and themselves as very different (Nagata in Spencer and Markstrom-Adams 1990:294). In addition, there are wide variations among persons of Asian descent based on country or region of origin (Chinese, Korean, Vietnamese, Cambodian, among others). (See Chapter 2 for additional discussions of diversity within diversity.)

A call for alternative models

Traditional perspectives overlook patterns of coping and adaptation by focusing on deficits; strengths and abilities used to survive, cope, and excel in the face of major sociopolitical barriers are ignored. Orthodox perspectives fail to link unique ecosystem or multilevel environmental experiences with life-course models (which integrate historical, sociocultural, biological, and psychological components with behavior response patterns). (See discussion of life course in Chapter 3 and Chapter 6.) The standard or traditional models ignore the opportunity for furthering or broadening our understanding of resilience and risk for youth whose normative experiences require ongoing adaptive coping strategies as a function of race, ethnicity, and/or color (Gibbs and Huang 1989; Spencer and Markstrom-Adams 1990:290–310). (See Chapter 9 for a discussion of resilience and risk.)

Spencer and Markstrom-Adams suggest that to improve our understanding of minority children's development we need alternatives to traditional developmental models that reflect the minority child's developmental processes (identity formation) and that attend to specific needs emerging from the child's developmental context. They suggest that alternative models must:

1. incorporate and explain consequences of status characteristics of race/ethnicity, color, sex, and economic status;
2. address subjective experiences of stress and probable responses;
3. explore intermediate developmental processes to help better understand perception and cognition (ex. doll preference reinterpretation);
4. account for problem-solving patterns or coping strategies given the developmental context; and
5. link minority status, stress, and coping strategies with actual behavioral outcomes (1990:304).

Sexuality

A core element of our identity as human beings is sexuality. Traditional notions of sexuality tend to be binary in that they present sexuality only as either completely heterosexual or completely homosexual. Traditional notions also tend to see sexuality as synonymous with sexual behavior. In addition, traditional paradigm thinking makes the assumption that one's sexuality and the nature of its expression remain constant throughout an individual's life span. Many researchers in the area of sexuality have found significant evidence of a much greater variability among humans in terms of sexuality than indicated by traditional paradigm thinking in this area. Researchers have discovered wide ranges of sexual behaviors, sexuality expressed in many ways in addition to sexual behaviors or activities, and variations in sexual orientation at different points in the life span of many people. For example, Rothblum asks the questions: "Who is bisexual? Does sexual orientation fall on a continuum and, if so, which continuum: sexual feelings, sexual activity, self-identity?" (1994:631). Rothblum notes that "Golden (1987) presented a model of sexual orientation that is multidimensional" (1994:631). The dimensions are sexual identity, sexual behavior, and community participation. Golden suggested that at any point in time a person's sexual identity, behavior, and community participation may be congruent or incongruent with one another (Rothblum 1994:631).

Demo and Allen argue that "Gender and sexual orientation, though often paired, e.g., 'gay man,' are not essential, fixed categories but are emergent, fluid, changing and contested" (1996:416). Klein (in Demo and Allen 1996) reflects the complexity of the concept of sexuality by incorporating seven variables in the concept of sexual orientation and its possible variations:

1. sexual attraction,
2. sexual behavior,
3. sexual fantasies,
4. emotional preferences,
5. social preferences,
6. self-identification, and
7. lifestyle. (1996:417)

Other factors in understanding sexuality in more complex and alternative ways include not only the issue of a person's sexual behavior versus one's sexual identity but also the issue of "researcher-imposed definitions (which are often based on available and somewhat arbitrary classification schemes)" and may be considerably more narrow than an individual's self definition of his or her sexuality which often reflects much broader variation (Demo and Allen 1996:417).

Alfred Kinsey (1948:638) categorized the wide variations in terms of sexual orientation as a continuum from exclusive interest in same-sex relationships to exclusive interest in opposite-sex relationships. Kinsey created a scale, graduated between heterosexuality and homosexuality, to rate individuals on actual experiences and psychological reactions. The ratings are as follows:

0–Entirely heterosexual.

1–Predominantly heterosexual, only incidentally homosexual.

2–Predominantly heterosexual, but with a distinct homosexual history.

3–Equally heterosexual and homosexual.

4–Predominantly homosexual, but with a distinct heterosexual history.

5–Predominantly homosexual, only incidentally heterosexual.

6–Entirely homosexual.

Increasingly, scholars of sexual identity and sexual orientation are giving more attention to understanding the needs and realities faced by transgender persons. These and related issues facing transgendered persons are addressed in a section later in this chapter and are the focus of Illustrative Reading 5.1: Bending Gender, Ending Gender: Theoretical Foundations for Social Work Practice with the Transgender Community.

Multiple Intelligences

Like sexuality, the concept of **intelligence** is also a significant influence on individual identity development and plays a significant role in the way others define us. We explored traditional notions of intelligence in Chapter 4. Now we will turn to an alternative perspective on intelligence put forth by Gardner (1988; 1993). Gardner's theory of intelligences has important implications not only for understanding variation in individual development but for analyzing schools and other socializing institutions through which people learn. Gardner suggests that, rather than unitary IQ tests, we should "look instead at more naturalistic sources of information about how peoples around the world develop skills important to their way of life" (1993:7).

Gardner's alternative definition of intelligence

Gardner alternatively defines intelligence as "the ability to solve problems, or to fashion products, that are valued in one or more cultural or community settings" (1993:15). Gardner and his colleagues believe that "human cognitive competence is better described in terms of a set of abilities, talents, or skills . . . call[ed] 'intelligences.' All normal individuals possess each of these skills to some extent; individuals differ in the degree of skill and in the nature of their combination" (1993:15).

Gardner's approach is consistent with alternative paradigm thinking and some postmodern approaches in that rather than focusing only on the "norm" or "center," it focuses on people at the margins in an effort to develop new ways to understand the concept of intelligence and it emphasizes the notion of appreciating local or culture-based knowledge. Gardner notes that in his research he looks at special populations such as "prodigies, idiot savants, autistic children, children with learning disabilities, all of whom exhibit very jagged cognitive profiles—profiles that are extremely difficult to explain in terms of a unitary view of intelligence" (1993:8).

As a result of his research Gardner has posited a set of seven intelligences or "multiple intelligences." He suggests there may be more than seven and that the seven he has discovered are of equal value and not rank ordered in terms of importance (1993:8–9). The seven are:

1. Linguistic Intelligence: ability to use language as a form of expression and communication (for example, poets).

2. Logical-mathematical Intelligence: This is logical and mathematical ability as well as scientific ability. Much of the current IQ testing is based on skills in the areas of linguistic and logical-mathematical intelligence through its testing of verbal and mathematical skills.

3. Spatial Intelligence: the ability to form a mental model of a spatial world and to be able to maneuver and operate using that model (for example, sailors, engineers, surgeons, sculptors, and painters, he suggests have high spatial intelligence).

4. Musical Intelligence: the ability to appreciate and use music as a form of expression (for example, singers, composers, musicians).

5. Bodily-kinesthetic Intelligence: the ability to solve problems or to fashion products using one's whole body, or parts of the body (for example, dancers, athletes, surgeons, craftspeople).

6. Interpersonal Intelligence: the ability to understand other people: what motivates them, how they work, how to work cooperatively with them (for example, successful salespeople, politicians, teachers, clinicians, religious leaders. We might add social workers to this list as well.).

7. Intrapersonal Intelligence: a capacity to form an accurate, veridical [truthful] model of oneself and to be able to use that model to operate effectively in life (Gardner 1983:8–9).

Multiple intelligences and schools

According to Gardner and others who advocate this alternative definition of intelligence as multiple, "the purpose of school should be to develop intelligences and to help people reach vocational and avocational goals that are appropriate to their particular spectrum of intelligences." This notion of the purpose of schools runs quite contrary to what Gardner refers to as the uniform view of education. The **uniform view of education** is that "there is a core curriculum, a set of facts that everybody should know, and very few electives." Gardner argues instead for what he calls the individual-centered school. The **individual-centered school** takes a pluralistic view of education and recognizes "many different and discrete facets of cognition, acknowledging that people have different cognitive strengths and contrasting cognitive styles" (1993:6).

Creativity

Much of the alternative thinking about multiple intelligences is related to the notion of creativity. **Creativity** can be defined as the ability to solve problems in innovative ways. However, creativity is a multifaceted concept involving much more than simply problem solving. Gundry et al. (1994:23–24) look at creativity from four perspectives. These notions of creativity reflect a number of the dimensions of alternative paradigm thinking including interrelatedness, intuitiveness, heuristic approaches, and multiple ways of knowing. These multiple perspectives can help us appreciate the multidimensional nature of creativity. Through this appreciation we can increase our ability to recognize and nurture creativity in ourselves and in the people with whom we work.

Four theories of creativity

1. *The Attribute Theory:* "Most creative people have common attributes, such as openness, independence, autonomy, intuitiveness, and spontaneity."

2. *The Conceptual-Skills Theory:* Creative thought involves "solving problems through unconventional modes of thinking, as well as visualizing thoughts or whole models and then modifying them."

3. *The Behavioral Theory:* "A product or outcome is creative to the extent that it signifies a novel and useful behavioral response to a problem or situation. . . . Creative tasks are heuristic in nature, rather than algorithmic, meaning that there is typically no clear way to solve the given problem, so the problem-solver must learn a new path that will lead to a solution." (Note: Remember our exploration of heuristic thinking in Chapter 2.)

4. *The Process Theory:* "Creativity is a highly complex, multifaceted phenomenon that relies on individual talents, skills, and actions, as well as organizational conditions. . . . Creativity is a result of the interplay among the person, the task, and the organizational context" (Gundry et al. 1994:23–24).

> The division into "focus" sections that follow is simply intended to assist us in organizing the materials. It cannot be overstated, though, that we must not allow this organizational convenience to hide the interconnections among the individuals, groups, and experiences we explore. We do not want to obscure or oversimplify the reality that issues related to color, gender, sexual orientation, class, age, disabling conditions, and religion interact in powerful ways that influence the developmental experiences of different individuals in countless complex and different ways.

FOCUS: PEOPLE OF COLOR

Introduction

This chapter, and later chapters as well, present the work of a number of scholars from a variety of disciplines and perspectives who are people of color as well as dominant group scholars. In some cases these perspectives give an alternative voice to existing and traditional developmental models, and in some cases entirely alternative perspectives on development are suggested.

Often alternative perspectives on existing models and completely alternative models offered by these scholars are marked most notably by differences in themes running throughout and transcending developmental stages, phases, periods, or eras. The differences in theme seem to indicate the complex nature of differential life experiences of people of color and whites in U.S. society. Equally important, perhaps, are the similarities marked by shared conceptions of the developmental needs and milestones so fundamentally a part of the developmental journeys of all who are members of the human community. Once again we experience commonality and difference as simultaneous and inseparable elements of humans' developmental experiences. Before we look at specific alternatives, it may be helpful to consider some basic information about people of color in the United States.

Developmental Perspectives and People of Color: Emphasis on Children and Youth

There are a variety of general frameworks or models for understanding HBSE (several of which we explored in some detail in Chapter 3) that are particularly helpful in grasping the complexities of development for people of color. Gibbs and Huang (1989),* Spencer and Markstrom-Adams (1990), and others describe a number of frameworks for developing this understanding. Many of the applications of these frameworks are discussed here in the specific context

*The discussion of development perspectives and people of color, pgs. 250–257, is adapted with permission of the authors and publishers from the book, *Children of Color: Psychological Interventions with Minority Youth*, by Jewell Taylor Gibbs and Nahme Larke Huang and collaborators, pp. 4–12. Copyright 1989 by Jossey-Bass, Inc., a subsidiary of John Wiley & Sons, Inc.

of development of children of color. It is important to recognize, though, that many of these frameworks can be applied to developmental issues faced in adolescence and adulthood and in the contexts of families, groups, organizations, and communities as well. First we will explore a variety of perspectives and their implications for understanding the development of people of color. We will then explore the "Interactive Model" proposed by Gibbs and Huang and collaborators in *Children of Color: Psychological Intervention with Minority Youth* as an example of a model that integrates many of the key components of the several perspectives that follow.

Developmental perspective

Erikson's model of human development as a progression of developmental stages and crises is described in detail in Chapter 4 (see selection by Erikson in Chapter 4). A strength of Erikson's model, according to Gibbs and Huang (1989:5), is its assistance in helping to identify such important characteristics of the developing person as independence, competence, interpersonal skills, and a sense of identity.

Erikson's focus on the development of a sense of identity, for example, is a central concern of many developmental approaches, both traditional and alternative. Erikson's emphasis on identity formation reminds us how central our sense of "who we are" is to our development throughout life. This may be especially significant if we are attempting to develop a positive sense of who we are in the context of a hostile environment. Such a hostile environment exists for many members of the diverse groups with which we are concerned as social workers.

Another strength of Erikson's developmental perspective, according to Gibbs and Huang (1989:5), is its attention to the connections between the child's relationships to significant individuals in her/his life (parents, teachers, peers) and adjustment to the larger social environment (home, school, and community). Erikson's approach offers some assistance in appreciating the interconnectedness of the child, significant other individuals, and social institutions. Erikson's model does not, however, address the core social work concerns for social or environmental change and for the achievement of social and economic justice to remove barriers preventing individuals from reaching their fullest human potential.

Erikson's perspective also has significant shortcomings, according to Gibbs and Huang (1989:5–6), that render it less than appropriate as a comprehensive approach to understanding the complexities of the development of children of color (and women, poor persons, gay, lesbian, and bisexual persons, and persons with disabilities, we might add). It is biased toward children reared in nuclear families in highly industrialized societies. It is less applicable to children from extended families in nonindustrialized societies where different sets of psychosocial outcomes might be valued. This limit is especially important to recognize when thinking about recent immigrants or children reared on reservations or in "other homogeneous environments."

Another weakness in Erikson's approach is its assumption that self-concept and self-esteem of minority children are significantly affected by the stigma of membership in a devalued ethnic group. Gibbs and Huang remind us that there is considerable evidence that self-esteem and self-concept, essential ingredients in identity development, in children come more substantially and directly from families, close relatives, and friends than from broader society during childhood. Only later when the adolescent expands her/his radius of interaction beyond family and ethnic community does society seem to play a major role in self-esteem and self-concept, they argue. There is much recent research that finds self-esteem and self-concept of minority children and adolescents as high or higher than for their white counterparts (Powell 1985; Rosenberg and Simmon 1971; Taylor 1976, in Gibbs and Huang 1989:5).

Ecological perspective

Human
Behavior

As professional social workers, we are expected to understand the range of social systems and the ways these systems promote or deter persons in maintaining or achieving health and well-being. How can an ecological approach to understanding individual development assist us in achieving this expectation in relation to influences on the individual development of people of color?

The ecological perspective was discussed in conjunction with social systems thinking in Chapter 3 when we explored some of the tools used by social workers for approaching traditional and alternative perspectives about HBSE. Gibbs and Huang (1989:6–7) describe the ecological perspective as one in which the child and the adolescent are viewed as active agents in "interlocking systems" from family and school to government as it is reflected in social and economic policies. Each of the systems along this continuum from small to large presents risks and opportunities for individuals at each stage of their development.

This perspective is of value because it allows the incorporation of the multiple impacts of poverty, discrimination, immigration, and social isolation on the development of minority children and youth. For example, consistent with ecological thinking is the recognition that poverty has a negative impact on children's lives in multiple ways—in nutrition, housing, education, health, and recreation. The ecological model can also accommodate the accumulative impact of multiple characteristics and conditions on development. Although, as we noted in Chapter 3, ecological and social systems perspectives are less about social and political transformation of environmental systems than about describing and recognizing the interrelatedness of environmental and individual issues. When children are both poor and minority group members, the negative and long-term impact of poverty increases significantly. Recognition of the complex and damaging impacts of multiple stressors such as poverty, minority status, immigrant status, language problems, unemployment, and negative attitudes toward affirmative action efforts combine to significantly add to the challenges faced by low-income minority families in their efforts to provide a stable and nurturing environment for their children's development (Gibbs and Huang 1989:6–7). Gibbs and Huang (1989:7) stress, though, that despite these multiple and intractable ecological stressors, these families show tremendous strengths in their "remarkable resilience, creativity, and competence in meeting tasks of socializing their children in an often hostile and alien environment." We discussed the strengths perspective at some length in Chapter 3.

The ecological perspective also helps us understand the place of family, school, peer group, and community in minority child development and socialization. This perspective, for example, is helpful in understanding the kinds and intensity of conflict that can arise in families of recently arrived immigrants between values and norms in the home and those in the school and community. The impact of such conflicts can be very real and very damaging and may include physical health problems, behavior disorders, school adjustment problems, delinquency, depression, or suicide (Gibbs and Huang 1989:6–7).

Cross-cultural perspective

Gibbs and Huang (1989:7–8) find the cross-cultural perspective derived from anthropology helpful in providing a comparative framework for thinking about all human societies. This comparative approach can help us link the impact of large societal systems to individual human behavior. It assumes that all behavior has meaning and serves adaptive functions and that all behavior is governed by sets of rules and norms that promote stability and harmony in the society. It assumes also that behavior contrary to rules and norms disrupts social harmony and that the society will seek to control or regulate such behavior through such institutional mechanisms as shamans, spiritualists, faith healers, or mental health practitioners. We should recognize here that social workers are often key among the mental health practitioners and among other human service workers whom dominant society gives the responsibility for exercising this social control.

A human development alternative approach to identity development

D'Augelli argues that in contrast to linear and more internally-focused approaches to identity development, "from a human development perspective, identity is conceived of as the dynamic process by which an individual emerges from many social exchanges experienced in different contexts over an extended historical period—the years of his or her life" (1994:324).

Miller points out that "racial and ethnic identity are fundamental parts of the psychological profile of any individual who is a member of a racially or ethnically heterogeneous society. . . . Understanding the process by which individuals develop racial and ethnic identities is therefore an important part of understanding the total person" (1992:25). Racial and ethnic identity development take place in the context of intergroup relationships and social interactions within the larger environment. To fully understand racial and ethnic identity development we must consider these as critical elements or influencers of the overall identity development process. Some of the contexts of these intergroup relations are described below:

Intergroup Relations in Several Areas Need to be Taken into Account

Economics "Whether or not groups are economic competitors and economically interdependent, dependent, or independent affects the degree to which group relations are adversarial or cooperative. When one group controls the economic well-being of another, it is likely that the dependent group will be stigmatized."

Population Ratios "The frequency and probability of interracial contact will influence how often society will confront multiracial issues and how many multiracial people society will have to accommodate."

Societal Images "A group's status in society is reflected in popular images. The balance or imbalance of positive images of groups in society, a by-product of group relationships, affects multiracial or multiethnic experiences by communicating a sense of the value of the groups and by providing (or failing to provide) access to role models."

Socialization by the Collective "A theory of multiethnic or multiracial identification would need to account for the behavior of the collectives representing the multiethnic or multiracial individual in fostering group membership. The extent to which one group might actively socialize individuals into the collective and pass on the values and culture of the group while another group might be passive, disinterested, or even rejective will influence the individual's process of identification."

Historical Legacies "Individuals and groups live their lives in historical space. Both historical relations and alterations in present relations will be important aspects of understanding multiracial identity."

Rules for Intergroup Boundaries "A theory of ethnic identity development that could accommodate multiethnic or multiracial people would need to incorporate rules governing the rigidity or fluidity of boundaries surrounding social groups, principles for accommodating structural change, and rules to describe situational views of self. Identities may not be invariant properties, but may instead alter according to the social context."

Adapted from Miller, R. L. (1992). "The human ecology of multiracial identity." In Root, Maria P. P. (Ed.). *Racially mixed people in America.* Newbury Park, CA: Sage, 24–30.

An Interactive Model

Gibbs and Huang (1989:1–12) provide an analysis of some of the strengths and weaknesses of the approaches to human development described above. They then blend the results of this analysis into their "Interactive Model." They focus their analysis on race and ethnicity, with their attendant implications for social class, as the focal concerns when thinking about development of children of color. Specifically, they offer a synthesis of developmental perspectives, ecological perspectives, and cross-cultural perspectives that highlight and make central race and ethnicity rather than submerging these central elements as peripheral concerns in developmental thinking.

Gibbs and Huang (1989:11–12) propose an alternative, more holistic model they call **"interactive"** that both *incorporates and expands developmental, ecological, human development and cross-cultural perspectives as interacting dimensions of children's developmental life experiences.* They offer this model as a more appropriate and integrative approach to thinking about the development of people of color, specifically children and adolescents. The reader will note this model is characterized by concepts used to describe ongoing realities faced by children of color as they develop. These concepts become threads woven throughout the developmental fabric of these children's lives (and woven throughout their life span). This is an example of the non-stage-based nature of this alternative model.

Ethnicity

In the Gibbs and Huang alternative model, ethnicity is the overarching dimension of child development. It is a thread sewn throughout both internal and environmental experiences. Ethnicity provides a framework for perceiving and responding to the world. It shapes identity, both personal and social. It establishes values, norms, and expectations for appropriate behaviors. It defines parameters for choices and opportunities—social, educational, and occupational. Ethnicity provides the structures and contexts in which developmental tasks are approached. It also has significant impact on the way the external world of school, peers, and community perceive and treat the child (1989:8–12). These alternative developmental perspectives offer helpful definitions, clarifications, and comparisons of a number of concepts essential for social workers if we are to comprehend and respect the complexities of human behavior and development of diverse persons in a variety of social environments.

They offer the definition of **ethnicity** as "membership in a group of people who share a unique social and cultural heritage that is passed on from generation to generation. . . . Members of an ethnic group believe themselves to be distinctive from others in a significant way" (Gibbs and Huang 1989:9). Ethnic group membership provides "cultural identity and a set of prescribed values, norms and social behaviors"; a framework for forming a child's view of "self, the world and future opportunities"; "it gives meaning to the child's subjective experiences"; it structures interpersonal relationships; and gives "form to behaviors and activities." Ethnicity may determine the kind of family, language, neighborhood, church, school, and role models around which the child's development takes place (Gibbs and Huang 1989:9–10). (See discussion of ethnicity in Chapter 1.)

Biculturality

Ethnicity for children and families of color also results in requirements for dual socialization to both their ethnic world and the dominant white world in which they must interact and survive. The result of the dual socialization process is a person who is bicultural. **Bicultural socialization** is a process through which parents teach their children to function in two sociocultural environments. This process is influenced by a number of factors. These factors include the degree to which the two cultures share norms, values, perceptions, and beliefs; the availability of cultural translators, mediators, or models; the amount and kind of corrective feedback coming from each culture about one's behavior in that culture; the fit of conceptual and problem-solving style of persons of color with that of the dominant culture; the individual's degree of bilingualism; and the degree of similarity in physical appearance to that of the members of the dominant culture (Gibbs and Huang 1989:11–12).

The combination of race and ethnicity often results in dual developmental challenges due to the combination of differences in culture and visibility (physical or linguistic). The product of this is membership in a minority group. We explored this term in Chapter 3. Minority group membership is distinctive from, but often intertwined with, membership in ethnic or racial groups. **Minority groups** are "those groups that have unequal access to power, that are considered in some way unworthy of sharing power equally, and that are stigmatized in terms of assumed inferior traits or characteristics" (Gibbs and Huang 1989:10). One should note that this definition of minority group focuses on "power and privilege," not on numbers. Thus, women, a numerical majority, are members of a minority group in terms of their unequal access to power.

Social class and caste

The interactive model suggested by Gibbs and Huang includes the element of social class as an important developmental factor. **Social class** ascribes "a particular position and value to [the child's] family's socioeconomic status (SES)" (Gibbs and Huang 1989:10). Socioeconomic status, like ethnic, racial, or minority group status, is a major determinant of developmental environments and experiences. To a great extent it determines the developmental boundaries for the child's experiences and opportunities in social environment, life-style, level of education, and occupation. Some scholars suggest that the related concept *caste* or *castelike* status is a more accurate descriptor of the social standing and relationship to dominant groups for some members of minority groups in the United States. Ogbu (1978:23) suggests that African Americans have castelike status in the United States. **Caste minorities** are usually regarded by the dominant group as "inherently inferior in all respects. . . . In general, caste minorities are not allowed to compete for the most desirable roles on the basis of their individual training and abilities. The less desirable roles they are forced to play are generally used to demonstrate that they are naturally suited for their low position in society. Thus their political subordination is reinforced by economic subordination" (Ogbu 1978:23).

For many children of color in the United States, the combination of such characteristics as race, ethnicity, social class (or caste), [and gender] result in triple or even quadruple stigmatization. This is the case, for example, for a child who is nonwhite, non-Anglo-Saxon, non-middle-class, and female. This complex stigmatization, or negative labeling owing to such characteristics as race, ethnicity, class, and gender, presents enormous developmental barriers and challenges to be overcome (Gibbs and Huang 1989:10–11). Multiple stigmas can have significant impact on the experiences of the child throughout his or her developmental journey. (See discussion of multiple diversities in Chapter 2.)

Developmental Models and People of Color

Identity development theory, especially regarding African Americans, has progressed through several conceptualizations over the past 15 to 20 years. However, this has not been a linear progression. Existing conceptualizations can overlap and complement each other. This reflects the complexity and multidimensional nature of attempts to fully understand how identities are formed. For example, Sanders Thompson notes four different types of identity regarding African Americans. *Physical identity* refers to "a sense of acceptance and comfort with the physical attributes of African Americans." *Psychological identity* refers to "the individual's sense of concern for and commitment to and pride in the racial group." *Sociopolitical identity* refers "to the individual's attitude toward the social and political issues facing the African American community." Finally, *cultural identity* refers to "an individual's awareness and knowledge of as well as commitment to the cultural traditions of African Americans" (2001:159).

In addition, she describes three prominent conceptualizations of African American identity development: Nigrescence models, Africentric models, and group or social identity models (Sanders Thompson 2001). We will explore Nigrescence and Africentic models in the following sections. Group or social identity models were addressed earlier in this section, Self-Categorizations Theory (SCT).

Nigrescence/Black Identity Development Models

Cross's original model of African American identity development "emphasized that African Americans differ in their degree of identification with African American culture" (Parks et al. 1996:624). This differential identification was tied to stages of identity development.

Several scholars (Atkinson, Morten and Sue; Sue and Sue in Parks et al. 1996:624–625) have suggested the catalyst propelling individuals through the stages was societal oppression. Helms noted the "crucial role that the experience of the difference in 'social power' plays in the process of racial identity development" (in Parks et al. 1996:625). The above authors suggest that given the central place of oppression by the dominant group of nondominant group members, the model can be applied to other non-dominant groups. Recent revisions of the model "have shifted from stage-oppression focused development to sequential ego identity statuses and personality integration. Thus, stages have been replaced by statuses, and oppression as the essential feature has

Black Racial Identity Development

Ego-Status	Characterized By
Pre-encounter	Idealization of Whites and Whiteness.
	Denigration of Blacks and Black culture.
Encounter	Rejection of White culture.
	Beginning of search for Black identity.
	Confusion and intense affect mark this transitional stage.
Immersion-Emersion	Withdrawal into Black world.
	Idealization of Blackness.
	Embracing of stereotypical image of Blackness.
	Denigration of Whiteness.
Internalization	Internally defined positive Black identity.
	Transcendence of racism.
	Acceptance of positive aspects of White culture.

Adapted from Parks, Carter, and Gushue 1996: *Journal of Counseling and Development,* v. 74, 625. Copyright American Counseling Association. Reprinted with permission.

been replaced by ego differentiation and personality development" (Parks et al. 1996:625). The Cross model is summarized on the previous page.

An extension of "the Cross Model of Black Identity Development"

Parham (1989:187–226) presents a model of African American identity development that incorporates and expands upon "The Cross Model of Black Identity Development." Parham's extensions integrate Cross's stages of Black identity development with three chronological phases or periods: adolescence/young adulthood, middle adulthood, and later adulthood and they emphasize the high degree of variability among individuals as they struggle with Black identity development. Parham summarizes Cross's four-stage model in which an African American has a "conversion experience" that he refers to as a transformation from "Negro-to-Black." Cross's four stages are Pre-encounter, Encounter, Immersion-Emersion, and Internalization.

1. *Pre-encounter:* The individual views the "world from a White frame of reference" and devalues or denies her/his Blackness in thinking, actions, and behaviors. The person's frame of reference is referred to as "deracinated" and is characterized by a white normative standard in which attitudes are "pro-White and anti-Black."

2. *Encounter:* The individual experiences significant events or situations, such as housing discrimination because of skin color, that dramatically call into question previous attitudes and frames of reference. This stage involves the realization that his or her previous frame of reference is inappropriate and results in the decision to "develop a Black identity."

3. *Immersion-Emersion:* This involves a transition to a new Black identity in which the old frame of reference is discarded. This stage involves immersion in "Blackness" through intense attachment to elements of black culture and withdrawal from interactions with other ethnic groups. The tendency here is to glorify African American people and to denigrate white people.

4. *Internalization:* The person at this stage achieves a "sense of inner security and self-confidence with his or her Blackness." At this point there is a general decline of strong anti-white feelings, although African American is the primary reference group. "This person moves toward a more pluralistic, nonracist perspective" (Parham 1989:189–190; Cross 1971).

Patterns of identity development processes

Parham expands on Cross's stages by adding the dimension of life-cycle stages and their impact on the nature of movement through the Cross stages of Afrocentricity. In addition to identity development being a lifelong process, an individual may experience at least three different patterns for dealing with his or her racial identity as he or she moves along the life course (1989:211). These three alternative patterns of addressing issues of racial identity include the following:

1. *Stagnation:* According to this alternative, an individual maintains "one type of race-related attitude throughout most of [his or her] lifetime." That is, one could reach and maintain any of Cross's four stages—pre-encounter, encounter, immersion-emersion, or internalization—and remain in that stage for the remainder of his or her lifetime. For the most part, Parham considers this a liability for the individual since it results in a resistance to new experiences or ideas and it makes adjusting to change quite difficult. An exception to stagnation as a developmental liability would be the person who has reached "internalization" and remains at this level.

2. *Stagewise Linear Progression (SLP):* According to this alternative, a person moves from one stage to another—pre-encounter through internalization—in linear fashion. This is the developmental pattern most commonly suggested by Black identity development models. This pattern suggests a functional, continuing, and progressive movement toward growth and development. However, its linear nature somewhat oversimplifies the complexity of identity development for many individuals.

3. *Recycling:* This alternative involves "the reinitiation of the racial identity struggle and resolution process after having gone through the identity development process at an earlier stage in one's life." Parham suggests that recycling completely back to pre-encounter is unlikely, however. A more common pattern might be a person moving from "internalized attitudes into another encounter experience" (Parham 1989:213).

It is clear from the above discussion that development and refinement of Nigrescence theory, especially the Cross model, has received a great deal of attention and adaptation by scholars over the years. In Table 5.1, Worrell, Cross, and Vandiver (2001:202) present the progression of adaptations to the model.

Table 5.1   Cross's Nigrescence Stages and Identities

Model	Stage	Identity
1971 original model	Pre-Encounter	Pro-White/Anti-Black
	Encounter	
	Immersion-Emersion	Anti-White/Pro-Black
	Internalization	Humanist
	Internalization-Commitment	
1991 revised model	Pre-Encounter	Assimilation Anti-Black
	Encounter	
	Immersion-Emersion	Anti-White Intense Black Involvement
	Internalization	Black Nationalist Biculturalist Multiculturalist
2000 expanded model	Pre-Encounter	Assimilation[a] Miseducation[a] Self-Hatred[a]
	Encounter	
	Immersion-Emersion	Anti-White[a] Intense Black Involvement
	Internalization	Black Nationalist[a] Biculturalist Multiculturalist Racial Multiculturalist Inclusive[a]

[a]Subscale included in the Cross Racial Identity Scale.

Source: Worrell, F.C., Cross, W.E., & Vandiver, B.J. (July 2001). Nigrescence stages and identities. *Journal of Multicultural Counseling and Developement 29,* 2002.

Racial identity development through the life course

In addition to the above three alternative patterns for addressing African American identity development during one's life, Parham suggests that Cross's four stages—pre-encounter, encounter, immersion-emersion, and internalization—may occur at a number of different phases or stages of the life cycle beginning as early as late adolescence/early adulthood. He suggests that African American identity earlier on in life is largely a reflection of parental attitudes toward societal stereotypes. However, he suggests that home and social environments can influence the particular stage at which the adolescent begins the identity development process.

An individual may also experience any or all of Cross's four phases of Black identity development during middle or later adulthood, according to Parham (1989:197–209). During these periods, racial identity development struggles are complicated by the more traditional concerns of these development stages. He suggests, for example, that middle adulthood "may be the most difficult time to struggle with racial identity because of one's increased responsibilities and increased potential for opportunities" (1989:202). During late adulthood, traditional tasks include dealing with such social institutions as "social security and retirement, nursing homes, and community resources and recreation facilities." Parham stresses that "undoubtedly, the ways in which late-adulthood Black people interact with these institutions will be influenced by their racial identity attitudes" (1989:207).

Parham's perspective is strengths-based in that it suggests that while oppression is certainly an influence on the process, his model "assumes that Black/African self-identity is an entity independent of socially oppressive phenomena: Black/African identity is actualized through personal thoughts, feelings, and behaviors that are rooted in the values and fabric of Black/African culture itself" (1989:195). Parham's extensions are also consistent with our own social system's perspective and overall emphasis on human behavior and the social environment because they focus on identity development as an interactional process involving *both* internal (individual) and external (environmental) factors.

Parham's extensions help to articulate the complex and continuous nature of racial identity development processes. His extensions also stress the importance of recognizing the highly individualized nature of racial identity development. He emphasizes:

> recognizing that within-group variability is an important element in understanding Black people cannot be overstated. Tendencies to make between-group comparisons (Black vs. White) and/or to overgeneralize (all Blacks are alike) provides little, if any, conceptual clarity and should be avoided, or at least used with caution. (1989:223)

Africentric/African-Centered Models

Bent-Goodley (2005) provides a framework for approaching African American identity development at individual, family, and community levels based on an African-centered worldview that recognizes both the history of oppression and the strengths and principles of African-centered culture reflecting "the best of Africa." This approach is consistent with the definition of African-centered social work as "a method of social work practice based on traditional African philosophical assumptions that are used to explain and to solve human and societal problems" (Schiele 1997:804 in Bent-Goodley 2005:199).

Bent-Goodley presents eight principles central to this perspective in a linear fashion, but stresses that "they are connected as part of the larger African-centered paradigm." She further explains this connectedness, "collectively, the principles help individuals 'understand and respect the sameness of self and of other individuals, and to have a high sense of responsibility for the well-being and harmonious interconnection between self and community'" (Harvey and Hill, 2004:68 in Bent-Goodley 2005:199). The principles guiding this perspective are:

1. *Fundamental Goodness*: An important principle of the African-centered paradigm is that each person is fundamentally good.

2. *Self-Knowledge*: A fundamental social work principle is to begin where the client is. However, the African-centered principle of self-knowledge encourages the practitioner to begin where the practitioner is.

3. *Communalism* is defined as "sensitivity to the interdependence of people and the notion that group concerns transcend individual strivings" (Harvey 2001:227 in Bent-Goodley 2005:199).

4. *Interconnectedness*: The principles of interconnectedness and collective struggle are evident throughout the African American experience. Interconnectedness "recognizes that people 'are dependent upon each other; they are, in essence, considered as one'" (Graham 1999:258 in Bent-Goodley 2005:199)

5. *Spirituality* is another critical component of the African-centered paradigm. Spirituality can be defined as "the sense of the sacred and divine" (Martin and Martin 2002:1 in Bent-Goodley, 2005:200).

6. *Self-reliance*: Another essential component of the African-centered paradigm is self-reliance. . . . Although the collective experience is always at the center, members of the community are expected to make a contribution to the community and society.

7. *Language and the Oral Tradition* are also a part of the African-centered paradigm. Language brings people together and develops a basis of understanding. . . . The flow of communication or rhythm is also a part of the oral traditions.

8. *Thought and Practice*: The principle of thought and practice is primarily from the Black feminist tradition. . . . However, this principle is relevant to the African-centered perspective in that it emphasizes combining knowledge with social action. The idea of having knowledge of an injustice without engaging in planned change to eradicate the problem is antithetical to the African-centered paradigm (Bent-Goodley 2005:198–200).

Multidimensional model of racial identity

Another alternative model developed to help us understand the complexity of the development experiences and their influence on identities and behaviors of African Americans and potentially other groups with minority status (women, lesbians, gay men, and bisexuals) is the *Multidimensional Model of Racial Identity* (MMRI). The MMRI defines *racial identity* in African Americans as the significance and qualitative meaning that individuals attribute to their membership within the Black racial group within their self-concepts" (Sellers, Smith, Shelton, Rowley, and Chavous 1998:26–27). The MMRI is based on four assumptions that are the foundation of the model and four dimensions of racial identity that encompass the level of importance and the meaning of race for individual African American racial identity.

The four assumptions:

1. Identities are situationally [environmentally] influenced as well as being stable qualities of the person.

2. Individuals have a number of different identities and these identities are hierarchically ordered.

3. Individuals' perception of the racial identity is the most valid indicator of their identity.

4. MMRI is primarily concerned with the status of an individual's racial identity as opposed to its development. . . . [The focus is on] the significance and the nature of an individual's racial identity at a given point in time in the individual's life as opposed to placing an individual in a particular stage along a particular developmental sequence [stage] (Sellers et al. 1998:23).

Using the above four assumptions as a foundation, MMRI proposes four dimensions, along with subcategories in dimensions of *regard* and philosophies related to *ideology*. Two of the dimensions are *racial salience* and *the centrality of the identity*. These two dimensions focus on the importance of race as part of an individual's personal definition of self. The second two dimensions are *the regard in which the person holds the group associated with the identity* and *the ideology associated with the identity* (Sellers et al. 1998:24).

The four dimensions are described as follows, along with subcategories:

1. *Salience* refers to the extent to which one's race is a relevant part of one's self-concept at a particular moment in a particular situation.

2. *Centrality* refers to the extent to which a person normatively defines himself or herself with regard to race. Unlike salience, centrality is, by definition, relatively stable across situations.

3. *Regard* . . . is the extent to which the individual feels positively about his or her race (Sellers et al. 1998:25–26).

    a. *Private regard* refers to how positively or negatively an individual feels towards other African Americans and about being an African American.

    b. *Public regard* is "defined as the extent to which individuals feel other view African Americans positively or negatively" (Sellers et al. 1998:26).

4. *Ideology* . . . represents the person's philosophy about the ways in which African Americans should live and interact with society (Sellers et al. 1998:27).

    a. *Nationalist* ideology focuses on the "uniqueness of being Black." This "ideology posits that African American should be in control of the own destiny with minimal input from other groups." A person with this ideology is "more likely to participate in African American organizations" (Sellers et al. 1998:27).

    b. "The *oppressed minority* ideology emphasize the similarities between the oppression that African Americans face and that of other groups." A person with this ideology is keenly aware of oppression towards African Americans, but also sees a link between this oppression and that faced by other minority groups. This person "is more likely to view coalition building as the most appropriate strategy for social change" (Sellers et al. 1998:27–28).

    c. The *assimilationist ideology* focuses on the "similarities between African Americans and the rest of American society." A person with this ideology "can be an activist for social change; however, he or she is likely to feel that African Americans need to work with the system to change it" (Sellers et al. 1998:27).

d. "The *humanist* ideology emphasized the similarities among all humans. . . . [Persons with this ideology] are likely to view everyone as belonging to the same race—the human race. A humanist ideology is often concerned more with 'larger' issues facing the human race (such as the environment, peace, and hunger)" (Sellers et al. 1998:28).

Figure 5.1 provides a helpful overview of the model of racial identity.

Invisibility and microaggressions

Work, especially by professionals and scholars of African descent such as that described in the previous sections, continues to expand our understanding of the complexities of identity development for African Americans. Recent work by Franklin (1999) conceptualizing one source of challenge and opportunity influencing African American male identity development is that of an *invisibility syndrome.* Franklin defines **invisibility** as "a psychological experience wherein the person feels that his or her personal identity and ability are undermined by racism in a myriad of interpersonal circumstances" (1999). Franklin further explains that invisibility is "an inner struggle with the feeling that one's talents, abilities, personality, and worth are not valued or even recognized because of prejudice and racism." He suggests that understanding this concept is essential to understanding the lifelong developmental struggles faced by men of African descent. He further suggests that this concept can be applied to women of African descent as well. Franklin (1999) believes that racial identity development theory is important and complementary to the invisibility syndrome. However, he believes:

the scope of the invisibility syndrome paradigm is broader . . . than the racial identity model because it allows for interpretation of greater domains of human experiences that make up one's personal identity, as impacted by encounters of racism. In addition, the paradigm is intended to help assess personal self-efficacy and resilience in the face of encounters with racialized environments.

Specifically, the invisibility syndrome includes seven dynamic and interacting elements that represent intrapsychic processes experienced by African American men when faced with either a single racist encounter or the accumulation of racist encounters over time. Franklin uses Pierce's (1988, 1992 in Franklin 1999) concept of microaggressions to further clarify the nature of these encounters. According to Pierce, *microaggressions* are

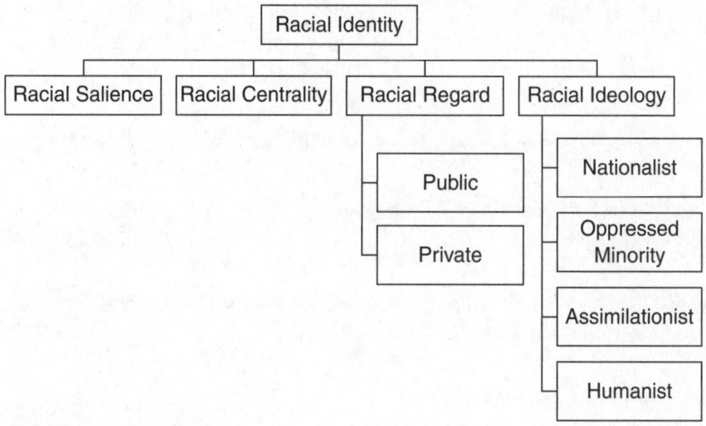

Figure 5.1
Schematic representation of the multidimensional model of racial identity. (Sellers, et al., Sage Publications)

verbal offensive mechanisms and nonverbal, sometimes kinetic offensive mechanisms that control 'space, time, energy, and mobility of the Black, while producing feelings of degradation, and erosion of self-confidence and self-image' (1988, p. 31), which, in their pervasiveness, have a cumulative deleterious psychological effect over time.

To take a closer look at themes, specific examples, messages through racial microaggressions, see Table 5.2.

Table 5.2   Examples of Racial Microaggressions

Theme	Microaggresion	Message
Alien in own land When Asian Americans and Latino Americans are assumed to be foreign-born	"Where are you from?" "Where were you born?" A person asking an Asian American to teach them words in their native language	You are not American. You are a foreigner.
Ascription of intelligence Assigning intelligence to a person of color on the basis of their race	"You are a credit to your race." "You are so articulate." Asking an Asian person to help with a math or science problem	People of color are generally not as intelligent as Whites. It is unusual for someone of your race to be intelligent. All Asians are intelligent and good in math/sciences.
Color blindness Statements that indicate that a White person does not want to acknowledge race	"When I look at you, I don't see color." "America is a melting pot." "There is only one race, the human race."	Denying a person of color's racial/ethnic experiences. Assimilate/acculturate to the dominant culture. Denying the individual as a racial/cultural being.
Criminality/assumption of criminal status A person of color is presumed to be dangerous, criminal, or deviant on the basis of their color	A White man or woman clutching their purse or checking their wallet as a Black or Latino approaches or passes A store owner following a customer of color around the store A White person waits to ride the next elevator when a person of color is on it	You are a criminal. You are going to steal/ You are poor/ You do not belong. You are dangerous.
Denial of individual racism A statement made when Whites deny their racial biases	"I'm not racist. I have several Black friends." "As a woman, I know what you go through as a racial minority."	I am immune to racism because I have friends of color. Your racial oppression is no different than my gender oppression. I can't be a racist. I'm like you.
Myth of meritocracy Statements which assert that race does not play a role in life successes	"I believe the most qualified person should get the job." "Everyone can succeed in this society, if they work hard enough."	Assimilate to dominant culture.
Pathologizing cultural values/communication styles The notion that the values and communication styles of the dominant/White culture are ideal	Asking a Black person: "Why do you have to be so loud/animated? Just calm down." To an Asian or Latino person: "Why are you so quiet? We want to know what you think. Be more verbal." "Speak up more." Dismissing an individual who brings up race/culture in work/school setting	Leave your cultural baggage outside.

Theme	Microaggresion	Message
Second-class citizen Occurs when a White person is given preferential treatment as a consumer over a person of color	Person of color mistaken for a service worker Having a taxi cab pass a person of color and pick up a White passenger Being ignored at a store counter as attention is given to the White customer behind you "You people. . ."	People of color are servants to Whites. They couldn't possibly occupy high-status positions. You are likely to cause trouble and/ or travel to a dangerous neighborhood. Whites are more valued customers than people of color. You don't belong. You are a lesser being.
Environmental microaggressions Macro-level microaggressions, which are more apparent on systemic and environmental levels	A college or university with buildings that are all named after White heterosexual upper class males Television shows and movies that feature predominantly White people, without representation of people of color Overcrowding of public schools in communities of color Overabundance of liquor stores in communities of color	You don't belong/ You won't succeed here. There is only so far you can go. You are an outsider/ You don't exist. People of color don't/ shouldn't value education. People of color are deviant.

Source: Sue et al. (2007). Racial microaggressions in everyday life: Implication for clinical practice, *American psychologist.* Washington D.C.: Amercian Psychological Association.

According to Franklin, when these encounters occur:

1. one feels a lack of recognition or appropriate acknowledgment;
2. one feels there is no satisfaction or gratification from the encounter (it is painful and injurious);
3. one feels self-doubt about legitimacy—such as "Am I in the right place; should I be here?";
4. there is no validation from the experience "Am I a person of worth?"—or the person seeks some form of corroboration of experiences from another person;
5. one feels disrespected (this is led to by the previous elements and is linked to the following);
6. one's sense of dignity is compromised and challenged;
7. one's basic identity is shaken, if not uprooted.

Franklin and others (Parham 1999; Yeh 1999) caution that, while these feelings cause confusion and alienation in the person experiencing them, they can also provide opportunities for growth, resolution, and increasing resiliency. However, they must be recognized and support, knowledge, and understanding on the part of culturally competent professionals or community members is often needed. For example, Franklin points out that, "Embracing the recognition and supportive identity attachments in the brotherhood of other African American men would be an example of a positive counterweight determining visibility." Development of a bicultural identity and worldview so important to the survival and thriving of people of color in a predominantly white environment is

> prevented by invisibility . . . because of racism's rejection and intolerance of the group of origin's defining attributes (e.g., skin color, intelligence, language, spiritual beliefs). Racism's unconditional rejection of people puts the individual's task of identity development in a quandary. There are social pressures on the individual, as a member of a minority group, to assimilate, and 'tolerance'—not acceptance—is the normative code of behavior of the dominant group.

Positive outcomes are influenced by three types of racial socialization. Protective, proactive, and adaptive racial socialization are identified as three distinct views of the world that Black male adolescents can acquire from messages and experiences given by caregivers.

1. Those having protective racial socialization beliefs view the world as distrustful and filled with racially hostile intents; they learn caution and are encouraged to succeed despite these circumstances.

2. Those who experience more proactive racial socialization are encouraged to focus on personal talent and cultural heritage, and less on racial hostility. Within proactive racial socialization are three important factors: spiritual and religious coping, cultural pride reinforcement, and extended family caring.

3. Adaptive racial socialization is represented as an integration of protective and proactive beliefs (Stevenson 1997 in Franklin 1999).

In commenting on Franklin's invisibility construct, Parham (1999) stressed the importance of a social change perspective, respect for spirituality and the importance of community in achieving positive outcomes leading to "visibility" in response to experiences of invisibility. He suggests that a powerful means of positively addressing invisibility is the development of a social advocacy or change perspective on the part of both the worker and the person experiencing the impact of invisibility to address the causes of racist encounters and environments. In addition, Parham (1999) points to the importance of a spiritual perspective:

> Still, there are dynamics associated with the energy and life force of African descent people that demand that the model address the spiritual dimension of the self as well. The African-centered worldview conceptualizes the world as a spiritual reality, where the manifestation of spiritness is the essence of one's humanity. From this viewpoint, it is therefore reasonable to believe that therapeutic healing must include a deliberate focus on the spiritness that permeates the cognitive, affective, and behavioral parts of the self.

The Adult Development of African American Men: An Extension of Levinson's Model of Adult Development

Herbert (1990) argues that theories of human development, in this case theories of adult development, must reflect people of color and the experiences of people of color. He suggests that this is necessary not only to acknowledge the existence of people other than whites, but also to acknowledge the impact of such issues as race and racism on the developmental experiences of people of color and whites alike. Herbert focuses on Levinson's study of the adult development of men. Levinson's model of adult development is described in Chapter 4. Herbert points out that, even though Levinson included five African American participants in his study, he did not examine racial development, and differences between the black and white groups were not systematically studied. Had these issues been explored, he argues, we could have learned important things about the influence of race and racism on blacks and whites alike. As Herbert reminds us, "racial identity is part of everyone's psychosocial development and is fundamental to how a person views self, others, environment, and the relationship of self to the environment" (1990:435).

Herbert's research was similar methodologically to that of Levinson with some important differences. Herbert's research used an all-black sample, was conducted by an African American researcher, and explicitly acknowledged race as an integral part of interviews and analyses. Herbert's results had a number of similarities to those of Levinson but included significant differences as well (1990:435–436).

African American men's development and racism

Developmental periods were experienced in similar chronological ranges for the African American men in Herbert's study and the respondents of Levinson. However, for Herbert's sample, race was an important factor for each individual from childhood through adulthood. For the men studied by Herbert, forming an adult identity was a complex task involving both conscious and "unconscious integration of race into their adult identity and the formation of a racial identity. They had to work at confronting race, racial discrimination, racial prejudice, and racism" (1990:437) as a significant part of their overall developmental experience.

Herbert documented, through the experiences of the men he studied, specific examples of the dynamics of race, discrimination, and racism across social system levels from individuals to social institutions (1990:436). These experiences included "Being denied a bank loan or promotion out of racial considerations; confronting racism in the military establishment, while serving one's country." Herbert also discovered that, unlike the men studied by Levinson, "the formation of *mentor* relationships was not significant for these men" (1990:438). A mentor is a more senior colleague who makes him- or herself available to junior colleagues for advice and guidance. A mentor offers his or her experiences for the benefit of the junior colleague.

In spite of the obstacles faced, the black entrepreneurs studied were successful in their enterprises; an accomplishment "truly remarkable when one considers that only four to six percent [of black-owned firms] survive to the second generation (Dewart 1988 in Herbert 1990), whereas the survival rate for white-owned firms has been estimated to be around 35 percent" (Backhard and Dyer in Herbert 1990:440).

Herbert dramatically illustrates that, while proceeding through similar processes of adult development outlined by Levinson, black men face greater stresses due to societal obstacles and diffuse contradictions and inconsistencies. He stresses that comparisons around the developmental similarities (similar sequences of age-specific periods, for example) between black and white men are greatly complicated when factors of race and racism are introduced, because there is no data on the effects of race and racism on the psychosocial development of white men. We must, Herbert concludes, begin to recognize the effects of race and racism on both white and black men (1990:441).

Herbert summarizes the importance for whites as well as for blacks of replacing traditional developmental theories with alternatives that include issues of racial discrimination, prejudice, and racism. He stresses that

> Modifying adult psychosocial developmental theory to account for the despicable forces and consequences of racial discrimination, racial prejudice, and racism should not be solely a black issue or agenda. White Americans are beneficiaries of the repugnant consequences of the these forces. . . . White people must begin to examine critically their own racial attitudes and behaviors to determine how they are shaped by and how they contribute to the forces of race and racism. . . . Any meaningful discussion about the continued expansion and development of adult psychosocial developmental theory must include consideration of the impact and consequences of racial dynamics, racial discrimination, racial prejudice, and racism on black people and on white people (1990:441–442).

New developmental tasks   To incorporate the powerful elements of race and racism into developmental theory for both blacks and whites, Herbert proposes two new developmental tasks. First, *"the formation of an explicit individual racial identity that both acknowledges and frees the individual of racism and prejudice."* Second, *"the formation of an individual self-concept dedicated to the eradication and abolition of racial discrimination, racial prejudice, and racism from our society"* (1990:442). These are tasks that need to be addressed at every developmental period throughout the life span. We will explore white racial identity development and the impact of racism below.

Herbert's work declares that the most urgent need of African American men in this society is to incorporate into developmental theory the "recognition, reversal, and abolition of racial discrimination and racism in this white-controlled society." His work also dramatically illustrates the developmental strength of African American men for whom "this most urgent need" is not being met. As he points out, the results of his study of the "total lives of black entrepreneurs" rather than of some more specific, traditional studies with limited and narrow concerns, "such as unemployment, drug abuse and dropout rates," illustrated the strengths of the black entrepreneurs he studied. His study participants "demonstrated an amazing ability not only to survive racial discrimination and racism, but to aspire and achieve under conditions of very few opportunities" (1990:442).

Multiracial Identities

The reality that U.S. society is becoming more and more diverse is reflected in the increasing attention to the experiences, strengths, and challenges of biracial and multiracial people. Kich stresses that "for biracial people, positive identification of themselves as being of dual or multiple racial and ethnic heritages has not been accepted or recognized in a consistent manner over the last several centuries" (1992:304). Yet Spickard argues that "people with more than one racial ancestry do not necessarily have a problem" (1992:13). However, they are faced with challenges both in developing a positive identity as multiracial individuals and in finding acceptance in the wider communities and cultures in which they live. These challenges are often filled with ambiguity and a sense of differentness on the part of the person and the larger community. For example, Kich points out, "The single most commonly asked question of biracial people—What are you?—continually underscores the experience of differentness" (1992:306).

Fong et al. stress the significant benefits and strengths that can accrue from positive identity as a multiracial person. They note that "At the individual level, psychological benefits may accrue to a multiracial individual from opportunities to adopt a multiracial consciousness. For individuals of mixed parentage, it is generally healthful and empowering to embrace both, or all, parts of themselves" (1996:24). The potential benefits at the individual level of identifying oneself as a multiracial person are not always shared by other members of communities of color.

Competing individual and community values

Fong et al. note the complex and often conflicting concerns about multiracial identity for communities of color. They note that

> Some African American civic leaders, for example, worry that if "biracial" and mixed become accepted ethnic identities, individuals with dual heritages will cease to identity as African American and that their numbers and talents will become unavailable to the African American community. Mass (1992) echoed this concern, reporting that there is fear in the Japanese American Community that it may "disappear" because mixed people may "hasten assimilation into mainstream culture." (Fong et al. 1996:24)

Biracial and multiracial identity development

Given the complexities, ambiguities, and competing concerns about biracial and multiracial identify at the community level, it is nevertheless important to explore the processes and struggles individuals must contend with in the development of positive multiracial identity. We will first explore a model for understanding the processes of biracial identity development across the lifespan. Then we will look at some processes and issues of specific concern for biracial and multiracial children and their parents.

Aldarondo (2001) suggests that the model of biracial identity development provided by Kerwin and Ponterotto (1995) is helpful, especially given that it is based on empirical research and incorporates a number of prior models. This model is outlined in the box below.

A Model of Biracial Development

1. Preschool Stage: Individuals become aware of racial and ethnic differences. The timing of awareness may be influenced by whether or not biracial children have exposure to multiple racial groups and whether or not their parents discuss racial and ethnic differences.

2. Entry to School: Biracial children face questions about their identity from other children in school. The child begins to place him- or herself into racial or ethnic categories. This experience is highly influenced by such contextual issues as the level of school integration or diversity and the availability of role models from different racial or ethnic groups.

3. Preadolescence: The biracial individual becomes sensitive to differences such as physical appearance, language, and culture.

4. Adolescence: This is often a difficult time for biracial persons "because of the external pressure to choose one group over another."

5. College/Young Adulthood: "During this time period identification is still primarily with one culture, but individuals are more likely to reject others' expectations for a singular racial identity and instead move toward appreciation of their multiple heritages."

6. Adulthood: "During this time individuals continue to integrate the disparate pieces of their own background to form their racial identity." As is the case with many linear stage theories, Aldarondo suggests that successful integration of a complete biracial identity depends on successful resolution of the prior stages.

Biracial and bicultural identity development in children

Jacobs argues that "it is possible to describe a developmental course for the formation of racial identity in biracial children" (1992:199–200). Central to Jacobs' formulation is the child's perception of skin color. Jacobs notes that skin color "is used in different ways by different biracial children, as well as by the same child at different times." He suggests that "preadolescent biracial children go through three qualitatively different stages of identity development" all involving their perception of their skin color.

Stages in the development of biracial identity in children

Stage I: *pre-color constancy:* During this stage children "experiment freely with color, as they have not yet classified people into socially defined racial categories and do not yet understand that skin color is invariant."

Stage II: *post-color constancy:* At this stage children have internalized a biracial label and have attained the concept of color constancy. This realization of color constancy forms the foundation for racial ambivalence, Jacobs believes. This ambivalence is "a consequence of a racial prejudice in society" and "experiencing and working through racial ambivalence is seen as a necessary task for people of color, including biracial children."

Stage III: *biracial identity:* At this stage ambivalence is diminished or absent. Jacobs believes it is at this point that "The child discovers that racial group membership is correlated with but not determined by skin color. Rather, racial group membership is determined by parentage" (Jacobs 1992:203–206).

Parenting biracial children

Parents can help children develop a positive biracial or multiracial identity by providing "their children the structure and the words that help them make sense of their experiences as they develop their self-concept and self-esteem. . . . Providing open communication about race and an interracial label validates and fosters the child's rudimentary interracial self-concept." ". . . In valuing each of the child's racial and ethnic heritages, parents structure emotional safety and confidence through a positive interracial label and through modeling an ability to discuss racial and ethnic differences openly" (Kich 1992:308).

A strengths-based approach

Parents of biracial children need special understanding of several important factors to help their child build a positive biracial self-concept:

1. *Fostering ego strength:* early ego-enhancing treatment of the child in the family including building "secure attachments, the support of individuation, the fostering of social and physical competencies, and encouragement of self-assertion."

2. *Biracial labeling:* presentation of a biracial label to the child by the parents assists in developing a biracial identity. This is not always necessary but is helpful often since the child "must assimilate a racial and ethnic label that is more complex and less readily available outside of his or her family than the labels of Black, White, Asian, Chicano, and so on."

3. *Ambivalence and racial material:* Parents need to realize that "their children's racial ambivalence is a developmental attainment that allows the continued exploration of racial identity."

Reflecting on this photo of President Obama and his maternal grandparents, what might be some examples of his grandparents' success in fostering ego strength, supporting biracial labeling, and providing a multiracial environment to support his positive identity development?

4. *Multiracial environment for parents and children:* A multiethnic community and social environment seems basic to positive biracial identity development. This is probably even more important for a biracial child than for either an African American or white child (Jacobs 1992:204–205).

FOCUS: WHITENESS/WHITE IDENTITY

As we learned from exploring the notion of paradigms and in our discussion of Whiteness in Chapters 1 and 2, the dominant group tends to measure and value worth in terms of standards of whiteness. However, the concept of whiteness itself is such a "taken for granted" dimension of the traditional paradigm that as a racial construct it is largely unexamined.

Janet Helms (in Parks et al. 1996:626), a scholar who has done extensive research on the development of identity, especially racial identity, "suggested that, as the socially powerful race in this country, Whites undergo a process of racial identity development that is very different from that of nondominant groups." Parks et al. suggest "for instance, as members of the dominant group, Whites are to some extent free simply to disengage from the development process through a change of job or locale, which eliminate their need to interact with members of other racial groups" (1996:626). In addition to being able to disengage from the white identity development process, Helms suggests that whites often deny "that a White *racial* group exists that benefits from White privilege" (1994:305).

Recognition of the importance of including content about whiteness and white privilege in social work education, specifically, is increasing. However, the importance of this content was recognized earlier by other disciplines, such as education and psychology. As a result, this content is available and can be adapted to social work education. For example, Abrams and Gibson (2007) have used content and educational approaches from other disciplines, as well as past models of social work diversity education, to argue for the importance of giving more attention to white privilege, white racial identity development, and whiteness in social work education.

Abrams and Gibson (2007:148) suggest:

> teaching about White privilege is fundamental to understanding the systematic oppression of people of color and raising self-awareness about practitioners' roles and responsibilities with culturally diverse clientele and communities. An additional benefit of this alternative model is the opportunity for the majority group of social work students (namely White students) to explore the meaning of their own ethnic and racial identities in relation to those whom they will encounter in their fieldwork and future professional practice.

They remind us of the social work profession's history of attempts to address diversity and oppression in education for practice. They describe three models used to attempt to provide content in this area. First, was the "assimilation" model that is considered by most to be outdated and has been largely rejected. This model "viewed ethnic racial minorities as deviant and encouraged them to acculturate to culturally dominant Anglo-Saxon norms." Second, the "culturally sensitive practice" model, popular in the 1980s, "targeted change in workers and agencies because of their ethnocentricity." In this model, the focus of changes shifted from the client to workers as well as their agencies. Third, was the "anti-racism" model. This model was more radical and proposed that "individuals in positions of power play a role in perpetuating the institutionally racist practices that systematically disadvantage ethnic and cultural minorities" (Abrams and Gibson 2007:149). They suggest, however, that none of these models incorporate the importance of white privilege and "its relationship to racial oppression, power, and inequities in access to resources" (Abrams and Gibson 2007:150). White privilege was defined and discussed at length in Chapter 2. In addition, these models did not address whiteness. Abrams and Gibson argue;

> The inclusion of content on oppression and social justice without mention of White privilege creates an imbalance in content as it silently maintains an assumption about the "hidden center" of White privilege. . . . In addition, the absence of content on Whiteness deprives White students of the opportunity to reflect on their own ethnic and cultural identities . . . or sift through ideas about how racism affects their own lives. (2007:150)

Further, they note, "in fact, most White people typically deny belonging to any racial or ethnic group and are unable to pinpoint how Whiteness occupies a center or mainstream position in society or even in their own personal lives" (Abrams and Gibson 2007:151). As a result, it is very important that significant attention to whiteness, white privilege, and white racial identity theory be included in our effort to more fully understand the complexities of human behavior and the social environment.

Carter and Jones suggest a rationale for White racial identity theory in that it "allows for an understanding of various psychological expressions or resolutions regarding a person's own racial group membership and provides insight into how a person's own view of a racial self influences in turn views of other racial groups" (1996:4). They also stress that "Understanding a person's racial worldview from the perspective of racial identity theory also reveals how a person participates in and understands individual, institutional and cultural racism" (see discussion of racism, Chapter 2). Carter and Jones argue that

> Every white person in the United States is socialized with implicit and explicit racial messages about him- or herself and members of visible racial/ethnic groups (i.e., American Indians and Hispanic, Asian, and black Americans). Accepting these messages results in racism becoming an integral component of each white person's ego or personality. Evolving a nonracist white identity begins with individuals accepting their "whiteness" and recognizing the ways in which they participate in and benefit from individual, institutional, and cultural racism. (1996:4)

White Identity Development Ego Statuses

Helms describes racial identity as "ego statuses that mature in a sequential manner" (in Carter and Jones 1996:4). There are a total of six ego statuses and while they may all be present in a person's ego structure at the same time, one status tends to dominate a white person's worldview at any given point. The statuses are as follows: **Contact** which is characterized by a naive denial that racism exists, acceptance of White values as "normal," and claims to be "color-blind." **Disintegration** is the stirring of internal conflict because of a recognition that racism exists; response to this status is often an overidentification or patronizing attitude toward African Americans. **Reintegration** is a reaction to disintegration and involves a withdrawal into white culture, denigration of African Americans, and belief in white superiority. **Pseudoindependence** is an intellectual, but not an emotional acceptance of African Americans, and often involves discomfort with close personal interaction with African Americans. **Immersion-emersion** is a search to recognize and rid oneself of personal racism and to define a nonracist white identity. **Autonomy** is the successful internal definition of a nonracist white identity characterized by openness to and interests in other cultures and the capacity for close personal relationships with African Americans, other people of color, and whites (Carter and Jones 1996:5–9; Helms 1994:304; Parks et al. 1996:625).

The statuses are summarized in Table 5.3.

Scott and Robinson (2001:418) provide a helpful summary of models of white racial identity development in Table 5.4.

Table 5.3	**Summary of White Racial Identity Ego Statuses**
Ego Status	Characteristics
Contact	Naiveté concerning people of color; lack of awareness of whiteness; claims to be "color blind"; racist without knowing it
Disintegration	Awareness that whites receive preferential treatment over people of color; confusion, guilt or shame about this differential treatment based on color
Reintegration	Attempts to reduce confusion by strongly identifying with whites as superior to people of color; in denial of white racial advantage; likely to hold more prejudicial attitudes about people of color
Pseudo-Independence	Period of questioning assumptions about the inferiority of people of color; have not come to terms with racism; intellectually recognized racism, but internally/emotionally not able to deal with it; period of distancing—"only 'bad' whites are racist"

continued

Table 5.3   Continued

Ego Status	Characteristics
Immersion-Emersion	Person begins to fully come to terms with racism both intellectually and emotionally; begins to seek out and question other whites about recognizing and reducing racism; begins personally to do something about the reality of racism; attempts to define a personal nonracist white identity
Autonomy	Nonracist white identity is achieved and integrated into thinking, feeling and behaving; race becomes an accepted part of white identity; person is open to new information about races and is much more capable of cross-racial relationships and interactions; values diversity.

Source: Adapted from Carter and Jones 1996; Parks et al. 1996; Helms 1994.

Table 5.4   White Racial Identity Models

Author	Component	Description
Helms (1990)	Stage 1: Contact	Unaware of own racial identity
	Stage 2: Disintegration	First acknowledgment of White identity
	Stage 3: Reintegration	Idealizes Whites: denigrates Blacks
	Stage 4: Pseudoindependence	Intellectualized acceptance of own and others' race
	Stage 5: Immersion/Emersion	Honest appraisal of racism and significance of Whiteness
	Stage 6: Autonomy	Internalizes a multicultural identity
Sue and Sue (1990)	Stage 1: Conformity	Ethnocentric, limited knowledge of other races
	Stage 2: Dissonance	Inconsistencies in belief system
	Stage 3: Resistance and Immersion	Person challenges own racism
	Stage 4: Introspection	Acceptance of being White
	Stage 5: Integrative Awareness	Self-fulfillment with regard to racial identity
Scott (1997)	Type I: Noncontact	Status quo; denies racism; seeks power and privilege
	Type II: Claustrophobic	Other races are "closing in" on him; disillusionment with the American dream; feels power and privilege are going to other races
	Type III: Conscious Identity	Dissonance between existing belief system and reality
	Type IV: Empirical	Questioning their role in racism and oppression and their struggle for unrealistic power from oppression
	Type V: Optimal	Person understands how his struggle for power and privilege has caused racism and oppression

Source: Adapted from Helms, J. (1990), Sue and Sue (1990), and Scott (1997).

FOCUS: WOMEN

As in the case of accounting for the developmental experiences of people of color, traditional approaches to research on human development have too often neglected or inaccurately portrayed women. However, a growing body of research on the developmental experiences and themes of women is emerging as a result of the work of a number of individuals and groups from a variety of disciplines and perspectives. The work of Sandra Harding, Evelyn Fox Keller, and others in the natural sciences (Harding 1986; Keller 1985); Nancy Chodorow in psychiatry and psychoanalysis (1978); Jean Baker Miller and her colleagues at the Stone Center for Developmental Services and Studies at Wellesley College in development and psychology (Jordan et al. 1991; Miller 1986); Mary Belenky and her coresearchers with the Education for Women's Development Project in education (1986); Carol Gilligan's work to increase our understanding of women's developmental experiences (1982); Patricia Hill Collins's work in the area of African American feminist thought (1990); and many others have created tremendously helpful resources to begin to include and understand the alternative perspectives of women. The work of these researchers and many others is unfolding and very much in process. We will look at a number of these efforts in the sections that follow.

Women and Development: A Different Voice

In current discussions of women's development, perhaps most often referred to and most commonly used by social workers is the work of Carol Gilligan (1982). It is important to recognize as we explore the work of Gilligan and other researchers working in the area of women's development that there is a great deal of mutual influence and integration of one another's work among many of the scholars working in the area of women's development. This cooperation, interconnectedness, and interrelatedness is consistent with the alternative paradigm generally. It also reflects a recurring theme or pattern in women's development itself. Through her own research and the integration of research of others, such as Jean Baker Miller and Nancy Chodorow, for example, Gilligan offers an alternative perspective on human development that seeks to focus on and include women's developmental issues to a much greater extent than the traditional developmental approaches of Freud, Erikson, Piaget, Kohlberg, and Levinson.

As a result of her research and that of others, Gilligan suggests the need for a paradigmatic shift that includes rather than excludes the perspectives, experiences, and views of the world of women. In her work she extends developmental paradigms to include and reflect the unique experiences of women. The importance of this extension of developmental paradigms to include women is underscored by the reality that women constitute between 52 and 53 percent of the population. As we have noted before, women are hardly a minority, although they have minority status in the United States and most other societies due to their unequal power and access to resources.

Gilligan's work to include and better understand women's development resulted in her discovery of a "different voice" that she found was characterized not necessarily by gender but by theme. She found this theme originally as a result of her efforts to understand the development of moral decision making among women. The voice, Gilligan asserts, is not necessarily exclusively male or female but reflects two different modes of thought. One mode focuses on individualization and rights, the other on connectedness and responsibility. In other words, one mode reflects the dimension of separateness and impersonality consistent with traditional paradigm thinking. The other mode reflects the dimension of interrelatedness and the value of personal experiences and relationships characteristic of alternative paradigm thinking. Although these themes are not necessarily tied to gender, according to Gilligan, they do seem to reflect the different developmental experiences of males and females. The theme of relatedness and connection has also been found by a number of other researchers working in the area of women's development. The work of Jean Baker Miller (and her colleagues), published in 1976, reported that "women's sense of self becomes very much organized around being able to make and then maintain affiliation and relationships" (1976:83). Miller and her colleagues at the Stone Center for Developmental Services and Studies at Wellesley College came to refer to this significant and recurring theme in the developmental experiences of women as "self-in-relation theory" (Jordan et al. 1991:vi).

Gilligan's work and the work of others takes us beyond traditional paradigms of development by presenting evidence that "normal" development may very well be different for females than for males for a variety of reasons. Gilligan suggests that traditional models and scales of human development based almost exclusively on the study of white males do not readily or necessarily apply to the development of females. She suggests that these differences in developmental experiences and patterns between males and females often result in depictions of females in traditional developmental models as developing "less normally" than males. Rather than women developing less normally, this alternative approach posits that "the failure of women to fit existing models of human growth may point to a problem in the representation, a limitation in the conception of human condition, an omission of certain truths about life" (Gilligan 1982:2). In other words, the problem is one of model not femaleness.

Women and identity formation

Gilligan's work focuses on women's identity formation and moral development. Her research focuses on adolescence and adulthood. However, she extends her approach to include assumptions about development during infancy and childhood as well. Gilligan's work is especially helpful in expanding understanding of the concepts of identity formation and moral development. These are central concepts in the traditional developmental models of Erikson and Kohlberg. As we will see, a shift in perspective, in this case from male to female, can result in dramatic shifts in the meanings attached to such apparently universal developmental issues as identity formation and moral development.

Gilligan reminds us that traditional models for explaining human development are often put forth as resulting directly from scientific, objective, and value-neutral processes. When we find that many of these models are based exclusively on the experiences of males, although their assertions about development are applied equally to females, the assumptions of objectivity and neutrality must be questioned. We are reminded of our earlier assertions about paradigms as human constructions subject to the limitations of the perspectives held by the humans creating them. This is essentially the case Gilligan makes about seeing life, specifically identity formation and moral development, through men's eyes only. As is the case with virtually all researchers concerned with individual development—both traditional and alternative—a primary concern of Gilligan's is that of identity formation. How do we come to see ourselves as we see ourselves? How we see ourselves has countless implications for how we behave.

Gilligan incorporated in her approach to understanding *identity formation* the alternative developmental perspective of Nancy Chodorow (1974, 1978). Chodorow tried to account for male/female personality and role differences by focusing on "the fact that women, universally, are largely responsible for early child care." Chodorow suggested that this early social environmental difference results in basic differences in personality development of girls and boys. She posited that personality formation is almost entirely set by three years of age, and that for both girls and boys the caretaker during the first three years is almost universally female. This early environment results in female identity formation taking place in a context of ongoing relationship, since "mothers tend to experience their daughters as more like and continuous with, themselves." Girls in turn see themselves as more "like their mother, thus fusing the experience of attachment with the process of identity formation" (in Gilligan 1982:7–8). This early environment also results in boys being experienced by their mother as male opposite. Boys "in defining themselves as masculine separate their mothers from themselves." By doing this, relatedness, connectedness, and empathy is less central in their early identity formation and definition of self. Individuation and separation is instead more central in males' identity formation (in Gilligan 1982:8).

Contrary to Freud's traditional notion of ego weakness in girls, Chodorow suggests that "girls emerge from this period [the first three years] with a basis for 'empathy' built into their primary definition of self in a way that boys do not." At the end of this early developmental process, "girls come to experience themselves as less differentiated than boys, as more continuous with and related to the external object-world, and as differently oriented to their inner object-world as well" (in Gilligan 1982:8).

Chodorow concludes that these different early experiences have significant consequences for the developmental experiences of both males and females throughout their lives. Attachment continues to be more important for female identity formation and separation and individuation remains more important for the development of masculinity in boys. Male identity tends to be threatened by intimacy, female identity, by separation. Males tend to have difficulty with relationships while females tend to have problems with individuation (in Gilligan 1982).

These different developmental paths are not necessarily problematic in themselves. They become problematic only when they are valued differently. For example, when the biases in the traditional literature of development defines "normalcy" as the "ability to separate." Empathy and connectedness then become "abnormal." When differences in development are valued differently *and* tied to gender, we see over half of the human family devalued because of different developmental experiences.

Sex differences in psychological research are neither new nor necessarily surprising. However, a problem emerges when "different" becomes defined as "better or worse than." When women do not conform to a standard based on men's interpretation of research data, the conclusion all too often is that there is something wrong with women, not with the standard (Gilligan 1982:14). In the case here of individuation and relatedness, the perspective of the observer has a good deal to do with the value accorded developmental experiences and behaviors of the observed. From Freud's and Erikson's male-centered perspective, identity constructed around attachment is ultimately a source of developmental weakness; from Chodorow's female-centered perspective, it is a source of developmental strength.

Women and moral development

Another core concern of researchers attempting to understand human behavior both from traditional and alternative perspectives is that of *moral development.* How do we come to define what is right and wrong and how do we come to base our decisions and actions on our definitions of what is right and what is wrong? Gilligan's approach to moral development emerged from looking at women's lives. Her alternative model is marked not by age-based developmental stages as are most traditional models—Kohlberg's for example—but by themes or principles. Her model integrates the following principles or themes:

1. Moral problems arise out of conflicting responsibilities rather than competing rights.

2. Moral problems require resolution through thinking that is contextual and narrative rather than formal and abstract.

3. Morality centers on the activity of care; it centers around responsibilities and relationships in the same way that morality as fairness centers on understanding rights and rules.

This framework's emphasis on context, relationship, and interrelatedness has much in common with several of the dimensions of alternative paradigm thinking that we explored earlier (Chapter 2).

In contrast, Kohlberg's is a morality focused on a reflective understanding of human rights. A morality of rights differs from a morality of responsibility in that it emphasizes separation rather than connection and sees the individual rather than the relationship as primary. Gilligan believes that a perspective on morality that emphasizes responsibility and relationship does not mutually exclude a sense of individuality or autonomy. She suggests, as Loevinger does, that we see autonomy in the context of relationship. Loevinger urges us away from traditional either/or dichotomous thinking about morality and suggests we replace this thinking with "a feeling for the complexity and multifaceted character of real people in real situations" (Loevinger in Gilligan 1982:21).

The responsibility perspective focuses on the limitations of any particular resolution and is concerned with the conflicts that remain. This conception does not focus on single solutions to single moral problems but focuses instead on the connectedness of any solution to an interdependent network of other problems and other solutions. In other words, it is an integrative, holistic, contextual approach consistent with one of the basic dimensions of our alternative paradigms and with social work purposes and values.

The gender implications of the two very different views of moral development are significant, Gilligan believes. Women's moral judgments show difference between the sexes but also give an alternate conception of maturity. Women bring to the life cycle a different and valuable point of view and a different and valuable ordering of priorities. For Gilligan (1982:23) "the elusive mystery of women's development lies in its recognition of the continuing importance of attachment in the human life cycle." Certainly such a perspective is an important one for social workers.

Gilligan cautions, though, that these different themes of moral development are not "gendered" in any absolute sense and should not result in generalizations about women's or men's development. Indeed, some women's sense of morality may be rights-focused and some men's may be responsibility-focused. However, given the differing findings of her work with female subjects and

Kohlberg's work with male subjects, it is understandable that these differing notions of morality would be sources of uncertainty, confusion, and fear for any person whose sense of determining what is correct and "right" behavior comes from the other perspective. She suggests, for example, that it is understandable that a morality of rights and noninterference may appear unsettling to women in its potential justification of indifference and unconcern. It is also clearly understandable that from a male perspective, a morality of responsibility appears inconclusive and diffuse, given its insistent contextual relativism (Gilligan 1982:23 and 123ff).

Another significant perspective that emerges from Gilligan's research is her notion of an *ethic of care,* more clearly delineated within women's identities and sense of morality. This ethic of care emphasizing relationship and responsibility for others is interconnected with the concept of "integrity" discussed by traditional paradigm researchers such as Erikson. *Integrity,* a focus of much adult developmental thinking, has a different (and richer, more complex) meaning for women, "because women's sense of integrity appears to be entwined with an ethic of care . . . to see themselves as women is to see themselves in a relationship of connection . . . the ethic or responsibility can become a self-chosen anchor of personal integrity and strength" (Gilligan 1982:171).

Gilligan believes that an "ethic of care" has significant implications for such societal concerns as aggression and hierarchy or inequality. She suggests that "women's development delineates the path not only to a less violent life but also to a maturity realized through interdependence and taking care." She points out that "just as the language of responsibilities provides a weblike imagery of relationships to replace a hierarchical ordering that dissolves with the coming of equality, so the language of rights underlines the importance of including in the network of care not only the other but also the self." She believes that "in the different voice of women lies the truth of an ethic of care, the tie between relationship and responsibility, and the origins of aggression in the failure of connection" (1982:172–173). Such a perspective on care, relationship, and responsibility has much in common with the historical mission and values of social work, with their emphases on inherent human worth and dignity and with social change to achieve social and economic justice and maximize individual and collective human potential.

The "ethic of care" is also consistent with our alternative paradigm's concern for integration and interrelatedness. The commonality is perhaps most evident in Gilligan's suggestion that it is essential to begin to integrate the two disparate voices reflected in traditional models and in her alternate model of human development. She believes the two voices are not mutually exclusive: "While an ethic of justice proceeds from the premise of equality—that everyone should be treated the same—an ethic of care rests on the premise of nonviolence—that no one should be hurt. In the representation of maturity, both perspectives converge in the realization that just as inequality adversely affects both parties in an unequal relationship, so too violence is destructive for everyone involved" (1982:174).

Criticism

Critics of Gilligan's approach and other researchers investigating interconnections among race, class, and gender in developmental experiences suggest that the experiences of the males and females in Gilligan's research can be assumed to reflect the experiences of persons who are white and relatively well-off financially (middle-class). These scholars are critical of Gilligan's work for not adequately addressing the diversity of characteristics, experiences, and environmental contexts among women. These criticisms have often focused also on the necessity of recognizing the interlocking nature of oppressions resulting from gender, class, and race in the United States and Western society.

Stack (1986:322), for example, finds that "the caste and economic system within rural southern communities creates a setting in which Black women and men have a very similar experience of class, that is, a similar relationship to production, employment, and material and economic rewards." Her suggestion is that in many cases women and men of color may have more in common with each other than do many white and black women because of the overriding impact of race and class. She suggests that for many African Americans "under conditions of economic deprivation there is a convergence between women and men in their construction of themselves in relationship to others, and that these conditions produce a convergence seen in women's and men's vocabulary of rights, morality, and the social good" (Stack 1986:322–323). However, Stack does not suggest that such work as Gilligan's should be discounted because of its lack of incorporation of factors of race and class along with gender. She suggests that future research should build upon this work by adding dimensions such as race and class (1986:324). Gilligan's later work reflects a very conscious attempt to integrate race, class, sexuality, and gender.

Models of women's identity development

In addition to the work of Carol Gilligan, Jean Baker Miller, and others concerned with understanding more fully the development and identity formation of women are models of women and development proposed by Helms and Conarton and Kreger-Silverman. The model developed by Helms was influenced by her work on racial identity development and is presented in Table 5.5. The model developed by Conarton and Kreger-Silverman was influenced by the work of Carol Gilligan as well as Jung and Dabrowski (Wastell 1996) and is presented in Table 5.6.

Table 5.5	**Womanist Identity**
Pre-encounter (Womanist I)	Acceptance of traditional sex roles; denial of societal bias.
Encounter (Womanist II)	Questioning and confusion about gender roles. Tentative exploration of solutions to role conflicts.
Immersion-Emersion (Womanist III)	Externally based feminist stance. Hostility toward men; idealization of women. Intense relationships with other women.
Internalization (Womanist IV)	Internally defined and integrated female identity without undue reliance on either traditional roles or feminist viewpoint.

Source: Adapted from: Parks, E. E., Carter, R. T., and Gushue, G. V. (1996, July/August). "At the crossroads: Racial and womanist identity development in Black and White women." *Journal of Counseling and Development, 74,* p. 625. Copyright American Counseling Association. Reprinted with permission.

Table 5.6	Conarton and Kreger-Silverman's Development Theory
Phase	Feature
1. Bonding	Interdependence with mother as unique and central relationship. This connectedness enables female children to enter early into nurturing roles.
2. Orientation to Others	Caring and connectedness to others with thin ego boundaries. May lead to difficulty in recognizing that some relationships are unbalanced.
3. Cultural Adaptation	It is during this phase that many women become "pseudomen" to adapt to Western cultural demands. This is when girls lose their "voice" (Gilligan 1991).
4. Awakening and Separation	During this phase, women begin to assert themselves in ways that are threatening to men (e.g., rejection of traditional views on women's roles in child rearing, putting themselves before others).
5. Development of the Feminine	Deeper exploration of needs. This involves the examination of the self and mobilizing the necessary will to implement the necessary changes.
6. Empowerment	This is not to have power over others but to have power to prevent themselves from being disempowered by others. Women use methods of "cooperation, consensus and mediation" (Conarton & Kreger-Silverman, 1988:58).
7. Spiritual Development	This phase involves the intuitive process of self-examination in which the younger naive self is put to rest. Power is again the focus but in the context of innermost sources, which can often frighten people around them.
8. Integration	The task is for women to be "teachers and healers" to undo the damage of unaware societies and groups. In this phase, women become oriented outward and inward at the same time. This means allowing their families to tend to themselves.

Source: Wastell, C. A. (1996). "Feminist developmental theory: Implications for counseling." *Journal of Counseling and Development, 74*, p. 578. © ACA. Reprinted with permission.

Adult Women and Developmental Experiences

As with traditional studies of women's development, studies of women's midlife experiences have been relatively few and have been too often generalized from studies of men at midlife done by men. McQuaide suggests that earlier studies of women's midlife experiences are also limited because women's experiences have changed radically as a result of the women's movement, feminism, greater reproductive choices, and more women entering the workforce. In addition, McQuaide argues that studies of women have been "problem-based" rather than "strengths-based." McQuaide's study of midlife, white women living in the New York area found that "midlife, for white, middle-class and upper middle-class women, at least, is not a time of torment" (McQuaide 1998:21–29). The reader should note that McQuaide clearly identifies the narrow scope of the population she used in her research. What are the limitations of this sample in terms of race and geographic representation?

McQuaide also found that well-being for the women she studied was increased by having a "confidante or a group of women friends, as well as having positive role models" (1998:29). She also found that for the women she studied, having a positive and strong self-concept in the face of a society marked by the social devaluation of mid-life women was important (McQuaide 1998:30).

Hunter and Sundel (1994) also argue for a more realistic and balanced appraisal of the realities of life for middle-aged women than has previously been presented in the literature and media. They do this by outlining current realities facing these women, both in terms of "Midlife Worries for Women" and in terms of "Midlife Advantages for Women."

Midlife Worries/Problems/Realities

"The middle years for women are often described as the worst—as a time of adolescent children, crises, suicides, the departure of husbands, empty nests, fading charms, melancholia, responsibilities for aging parents, and pressures to prepare for financial security in their final years. In addition, there are all sorts of physical reminders that one is not as young as one used to be" (Hunter and Sundel 1994:114).

- *Physical health:* Most women are healthy in midlife, but health risks do increase.

Three major threats to health

- Heart disease: number 1 killer of women in the United States
- Cancer: lung, breast, and colorectal cancer
- Stroke (MayoClinic.com 2009)

Poverty

- Among women, poverty rates are highest in families headed by a single woman, especially African American and Hispanic families (Spriggs 2006).
- According to the Census Bureau, in 2007, women made 77.5 percent of men's earnings. The median earnings of men in 2007 were $44,255, while for women the median earnings were $34,278.

Working caretakers and aging parents

- In 2001, an estimated 7 to 12 percent of all workers reported assisting an elderly parent or relative with daily living activities, arrangements for financial and health care, and residential moves (Moen 2001).
- Caring for elderly parents is a major stressor for midlife women.
- While both spouses are living, the wife is most likely to be caregiver for the ill elderly husband, but women and daughters are most likely to provide the care for most elderly.

Depression and Obesity

- Women who are obsese are twice as likely to be depressed.
- Women with depression are twice as likely to be obese (Simon et al. 2008).

Midlife strengths/realities

In addition to stressors and difficulties one must consider opportunities for midlife women.

> ❯ *Crisis is not likely:* No evidence to support midlife as necessarily a time of crisis for men or for women; most persons at midlife do not experience major crises, though questioning of goals may occur; midlife is not a time of increased divorce, neuroticism, suicide, or drastic career change.
>
> ❯ *Empty nest or menopause is unlikely to be a major trauma for midlife women:* On the contrary "for many women, midlife is a time of greater self-esteem and self-acceptance."
>
> ❯ *Prime Time: The 50s:* Mitchell and Helson (in Hunter and Sundel 1994:119) suggested "that the middle or early post-parental period is the best time, or prime of life, for women because of changes in roles and freed-up energies." They found women in their 50s to rate their quality of life the highest of any period. Sources of this high quality of life include:
>
> - *Economic status:* Income for many women and their families tends to peak in the pre-retirement 50s.
> - *Empty nest:* Rather than a source of trauma, "the children's departure is usually viewed with anticipation, and the available time and space are not seen as 'empty.'" Women are likely to have a greater sense of control and time to focus on their own development.
> - *Menopause:* "Major myth of menopause is that it causes emotional disturbance or a nervous breakdown and severe physical symptoms." There is significant evidence to suggest these claims are highly exaggerated and countered by positive elements of menopause: "few women at 50 see inability to have children as problem. There is also evidence that when controlling for income and employment status, mothers and women who never had children are no different in terms of happiness or satisfaction with life." Some researchers suggest changing the traditional descriptors of menopause, for example, changing the "symptoms" of menopause to the "signs" of menopause might help reduce the disease imagery.
> - *Sexual capacity and interest:* "whereas men's orgasmic capacity gradually decreases during the adult years, women's capacity does not decrease until about age 60."
> - *Intimate links with partners and friends:* intimacy and communication with partner and network of friends may very well increase (Excerpts from: Hunter and Sundel 1994:118–123).

Biology and reductionism

We explored the notion of reductionism and traditional developmental theories in Chapter 4. Hunter and Sundel (1994:123–124) suggest that much research on women's development has been reductionist in its overemphasis on biological factors and neglect of other critical factors. They posit that much of the imbalance and one-dimensional biological approach to stereotypes of midlife for women, results from sexism because such empowering and independent portrayals do not support male dominance. To counter this imbalance, Gergen suggested that "theoretical frameworks for studying women should emphasize other aspects of women's lives, such as the political, economic, moral, aesthetic" in order to "liberate women from 'biology'" (in Hunter and Sundel 1994:123–124).

FOCUS: SEXUAL ORIENTATION

Next we turn our attention to alternative models for understanding the special developmental issues and tasks faced by gay men, lesbians, bisexual, and transgender persons. Several different models of identity development are offered from a variety of perspectives for helping us develop a more holistic perspective on the development of persons with diverse sexual orientations and identities.

In addition to the significant number of gay men, lesbians, bisexual and transgender persons in the population, the significance of increasing our understanding of the developmental and environmental experiences of gay men and lesbians is underscored by the intensity of controversy surrounding many issues related to sexual orientation. Central to these controversies is the question of whether gay men and lesbians should have the same rights and protections as heterosexuals in all spheres of personal and social life. The rights in question include such basic ones as parenthood, the right to form and have legal recognition of gay- and lesbian-headed families (the right to marry), the right to serve in the military and other social institutions, the right to have access to housing without discrimination, and the right to have partners and family members covered by health insurance and other job-related benefits (domestic partnership rights) taken for granted by heterosexual workers and their families.

It is difficult to accurately determine the number of gay, lesbian, and bisexual persons in the general population. Part of this difficulty relates to how one defines gay, lesbian, or bisexual (see Kinsey continuum of sexual orientation earlier in this chapter). However, according to the American Community Survey, there "are an estimated 8.8 million gay, lesbian, and bisexual (GLB) persons in the U.S." (Gates 2006:1). According to Burgess, "the number of transgendered people is unknown" (in Burdge 2007:244). Burdge notes, however, that a 2003 report "suggested that self-identified transgendered people account for 2 percent to 3 percent of the overall lesbian, gay, bisexual, and transgender (LGBT) community" (Burdge 2007:244).

While traditional and dominant forces in society continue to struggle with discrimination, oppression, and social injustice in contrast to full acceptance at both personal and policy levels of persons with diverse sexual orientations and sexual identities, other cultures have historically been more successful in achieving full inclusion, as well as the provision of respected statuses for these persons. For example, in an article addressing caregiving practices among American Indians, the authors point out:

> Native LGBTQT-S (lesbian, gay, bi-sexual, transgender, queer, or two-spirit; hereafter referred to as two-spirit) people often have specific cultural roles and responsibilities tied to caregiving in indigenous communities.... Moreover, these roles are intimately tied to their identitites as Native LGBTQ or "two-spirit" people (Evans-Campbell et al. 2007:78).

The authors further note:

> Many indigenous societies in North America have historically acknowledged and incorporated the existence of diverse gender and sexual identities among community members. . . . Although there were exceptions, these community members tended to be well integrated with Native communities and often occupied highly respected social and ceremonial roles (Evans-Campbell et al. 2007:78).

Human Rights & Justice

As part of our professional practice of social work we are expected to advance human rights and social and economic justice. Give one example of what we can learn from another culture to assist us in advancing human rights and social and economic justice for persons with diverse sexual orientations and sexual identities within the dominant society.

Sexual Orientation and Biology

In addition, many questions remain about the origins and causes of homosexuality itself and about whether homosexuality is an orientation beyond the control of the individual or whether being gay or lesbian is a preference or a choice one makes. There is significant new evidence emerging from research in the natural sciences suggesting that biological factors operate in the determination of sexual orientation. These findings suggest that being a gay or lesbian person is no more chosen than being left-handed or brown-eyed is chosen. This is one of the reasons that the term *sexual orientation* is now preferred over the term *sexual preference. Preference* suggests one can choose to be or not be gay or lesbian. While one may choose not to openly acknowledge to self or to others one's homosexual identity, one's sexual *orientation* does not appear to be so clearly a matter of choice. This is perhaps best explained as the difference between acceptance of one's homosexuality and the choice not to accept or act on one's sexual feelings. The process of acknowledging gay or lesbian feelings and identity to self and/or others is often referred to as **coming out.**

In one study of gay men with twin and adopted brothers, substantial genetic influences in male sexual orientation were suggested. In this study homosexuality occurred among both brothers 52 percent of the time for identical twins who share their genes and 22 percent of the time among fraternal twins who share half the same genes. Among brothers with different biological parents but adopted into and raised in the same home, only 6 percent of the time did both brothers have a homosexual orientation (Bowers 1992:6). In another study, significant differences in the hypothalamus of the brain were found between gay men and nongay men, again suggesting a biological link in sexual orientation, but this time through a study using physiological evidence rather than the more sociological evidence in the study of twins and brothers (*Science* 1991:956–957). These studies are, of course, not proof in any final sense, but they do raise important questions about biology and sexual orientation. Since both of these studies included only gay men and excluded lesbians, the biological origins of lesbian orientation are even less certain. Even given the uncertainties about the biological origins of gay or lesbian orientation, there are a number of theoretical models available that can help us understand the developmental experiences and environments of gay men and lesbians. We explore some of these models next.

Perspectives on Lesbian, Gay Male, Bisexual, and Transgender Development

According to D'Augelli, perspectives on lesbian, gay male, and bisexual persons have changed dramatically "from mental illness to alternative life-style to sexual variation to diverse minority" (1994:328). D'Augelli suggests a human development model for understanding the development of gay men, lesbians, and bisexual persons. The phases of this model are outlined below.

1. *Exiting Heterosexual Identity:* "This set of concerns involves personal and social recognition that one's sexual orientation is not heterosexual. . . . Exiting from heterosexuality also means telling *others* that one is lesbian, gay, or bisexual. This 'coming out' begins with the very first person to whom an individual discloses and continues throughout life, decreasing only to the extent that the person is consistently and publicly identified with a non-heterosexual label."

2. *Developing a Personal Lesbian-Gay-Bisexual Identity Status:* "An individual must develop a sense of personal socioaffectional stability that effectively summarizes thoughts, feelings, and desires . . . such an initial status may be subject to revision as more experience is accumulated. . . . To a large degree, they cannot confirm their sexual-orientation status without contact with others."

3. *Developing a Lesbian-Gay-Bisexual Social Identity:* "This involves creating a large and varied set of people who know of the person's sexual orientation and are available to provide social support. This, too, is a lifelong process that has a profound effect on personal development."

4. *Becoming a Lesbian-Gay-Bisexual Offspring:* "Parental relationships are often temporarily disrupted with the disclosure of sexual orientation. . . . Generally, families show patterns of adaptation, with parents, siblings, and members of the extended family coming to overlapping, but not identical approaches."

5. *Developing a Lesbian-Gay-Bisexual Intimacy Status:* "The psychological complexities of same-sex dyadic relationships are made much more problematic by the invisibility of lesbian and gay couples in our cultural imagery. . . . The lack of cultural scripts directly applicable to lesbian, gay, and bisexual people leads to ambiguity and uncertainty, but it also forces the emergence of personal, couple-specific, and community norms, which should be more personally adaptive."

6. *Entering a Lesbian-Gay-Bisexual Community:* "This set of identity processes involves the development of commitment to political and social action. For some who believe their sexual orientation to be a purely private matter, this never happens. . . . To be lesbian, gay, or bisexual in the fullest sense—to have a meaningful identity—leads to a consciousness of the history of one's own oppression. It also, generally, leads to an appreciation of how the oppression continues, and commitment to resisting it" (1994:324–328).

Life Course Theory and Sexual Orientation

As discussed in Chapter 3 (with additional attention in Chapter 6), life-course theory is increasingly considered a significant alternative theory for understanding the complexities of human development because it is more contextual and fluid than traditional stage-based theories. In other words, it helps provide a more complete view of human behavior and the social environment. Hammack (2005) suggests that life course theory also offers an alternative and helpful approach to understanding developmental processes related to gay, lesbian, and bisexual persons, especially in terms of the impact of context, such as historical context, on the developmental trajectories experienced by different birth cohorts of gay, lesbian, and bisexual persons. He presents "A Model of Sexual Orientation Development in the Life Course Perspective." Using this perspective Hammack defines sexual orientation:

as the biologically based affective disposition of sexual desire which motivates behavior and assumption of identity. There are three important propositions embedded in this definition: (1) that individuals possess a biological disposition to respond affectively to members of a particular sex; (2) that this disposition is reflected in sexual desire, and (3) that a subjective understanding of one's desire in the context of a specific cultural model of human sexuality leads to behavioral practice and identity assumption (2005:276).

He also differentiates between the meanings of sexual orientation and sexual identity in terms of a life course developmental sexual orientation perspective. He notes:

> The conceptual distinction between sexual orientation and sexual identity is made explicit in this perspective. In contrast to the definition of sexual orientation, gay or lesbian identity is defined as a sexual identity category describing individuals who, by and large, have sex exclusively with members of the same sex. In making this terminological distinction, it is posited that biology, psychology, and society all assume pivotal roles in the formation of individual selves within a particular cultural context. In addition, the salience and significance of interpersonal relationships in the formation of a gay, lesbian, or bisexual identity cannot be underestimated (Hammack 2005:277).

The Figure 5.2 provides a visual depiction of Hammack's model.

In describing the impact of historical context on development of gay, lesbian, and bisexual persons in the United States, Hammack refers to "recent work on sexual orientation by Cohler and colleagues" that describes "the importance of birth cohort in the development of gay men and lesbians in the United States." These researchers identify "at least five cohorts with unique developmental experiences" (2005:275):

1. *Pre-War (World War II):* Gay persons' lives during this period were "characterized by massive secrecy, furtive sex, and the inevitability of marriage and reproduction."

2. *Post-War:* Persons in this cohort experienced "the post-War urban culture, increasingly populated by hordes of soldiers who had engaged in homosexual behavior, witnessed the birth of urban gay communities, with more gay men choosing to live a non-heterosexual lifestyle."

3. *Post-Stonewall:* Persons' experiences during this period were significantly influenced by "the Stonewall Inn riots of 1969 [which] provided significant maturation and momentum to the Gay Civil Rights Movement . . . [and marked] the political and social involvement of a generation."

4. *AIDS:* "With the discovery of AIDS in the early 1980s, this generation (along with the previous one) began to die en masse. . . . Those who came of age in the 1980s became highly educated about AIDS, and a cultural shift from promiscuity to monogamy occurred among gay men."

5. *Post-AIDS:* "Those who came of age in the mid and late 1990s witnessed the effectiveness of AIDS treatments, began to view HIV as a chronic, manageable illness (rather than the death sentence it was in the 1980s), and began to engage in unsafe sex in increasing numbers." In addition, the social climate, especially in the popular media, for many gay, lesbian, and bisexual

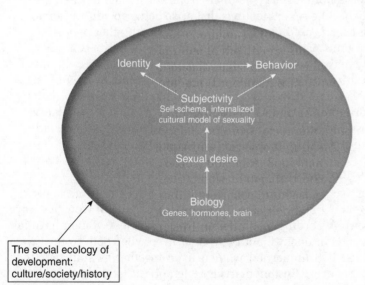

Figure 5.2
Schematic representation of the developmental pathway for sexual orientation.
Hammack, P.L. (2005). An Integrative Paradigm. *Human Development 48*(5):267–290.

persons in this cohort has become more accepting and inclusive. (Hammack 2005:274–275).

Through a life-course perspective on development and sexual orientation, we are able to better understand the many complex developmental experiences by more carefully considering both the person and the environment.

Multiple Meanings of Lesbianism

Rothblum (1994:630) asks the question: "What is a lesbian?" She notes, "Burch has differentiated between 'primary lesbians,' who have never had sexual relations with men, and 'bisexual lesbians,' who self-identified as heterosexual and had sexual relations with men before they had sexual relations with women. Very few women have had exclusively same-gender sexual experiences" (Rothblum 1994:630). Rothblum suggests, "Once women come out as lesbians, the lesbian community presumes that this will be permanent; in fact some lesbians subsequently become sexual with men" (1994:630). Rothblum also asks the important and often controversial question: "Is sexual orientation a choice or is it predetermined (e.g., genetic, hormonal)?" She indicates the varied perspectives on the answer to this question even between lesbians and gay men by noting that "generally, lesbians view sexual orientation as a choice (e.g., they state they became lesbians because it was more congruent with radical feminism), whereas gay men are more likely to view it as predetermined" (Rothblum 1994:630).

According to Rothblum, traditional definitions "of sexual activity, both the heterosexual and the lesbian/bisexual versions, focus on genital activity and thus ignore other, nongential sexual experiences that women may have had" (1994:633). She specifically points out that

> We have no terminology for the early sexual crushes that some girls develop on other people, usually a female friend or female teacher. We have no language for the sexual feelings that arise between adult friends, even when both friends are in sexual relationships with other people. In contrast, if the friends engage in genital sexual activity with each other, we immediately have language; they are having an affair. . . . In the lesbian communities, ex-lovers often remain friends and friends often become lovers . . . closeted lesbians may introduce their lovers to their family or co-workers as their friends. . . . Lack of language for sexuality that is not focused on genital contact means that such experiences are forgotten or cannot clearly be articulated (Rothblum 1994:633).

What is a lesbian relationship?

Rothblum points out that "the sex-focused definition of what constitutes a lesbian relationship" is extremely limited because it "ignores the reality of women's ways of relating" (1994:634). According to Rothblum, "for centuries, women have felt strong love, affection, and intimacy for other women, even when both women were married to men. When two unmarried women lived together as spinsters, they were considered to be in a '**Boston marriage**,' [emphasis added] a term that reflected the presumed asexual nature of the relationship (the word Boston usually referred to Puritan values)" (1994:635). Lillian Faderman (in Rothblum 1994:335) has described the passion and love between women in the 19th century:

> It became clear that women's love relationships have seldom been limited to that one area of expression, that love between women has been primarily a sexual phenomenon only in male fantasy literature. "Lesbian" describes a relationship in which two women's strongest emotions and affections are

directed toward each other. Sexual contact may be a part of the relationship to a greater or lesser degree, or it may be entirely absent.

McCarn and Fassinger (1996) reviewed multiple-stage models of both sexual identity development and racial identity development. They found both similarities and differences across the models. Based on their critical review, they suggested the need for less linear and more fluid models of sexual identity development, in this case, specifically lesbian identity development. Their approach is consistent with alternative paradigm thinking in its attempt to look at development from both fluid and multiple perspectives. Rather than a single-stage model, they provide a dual

Table 5.7   Proposed Model of Lesbian Identity Formation

Individual Sexual Identity	Group Membership Identity
(Nonawareness)	

1. Awareness

—of feeling or being different	—of existence of different sexual orientations in people

Self-Statement Examples:
"I feel pulled toward women in ways I don't understand." (I)
"I had no idea there were lesbian/gay people out there." (G)

2. Exploration

—of strong/erotic feeling for women or a particular woman	—of one's position regarding lesbians/gays as a group (both attitudes and membership)

Self-Statement Examples:
"The way I feel makes me think I'd like to be sexual with a women." (I)
"Getting to know lesbian/gay people is scary but exciting." (G)

3. Deepening/Commitment

—to self-knowledge, self-fulfillment, and crystallization of choices about sexuality	—to personal involvement with reference group, with awareness of oppression and consequences of choices

Self-Statement Examples:
"I clearly feel more intimate sexually and emotionally with women than with men." (I)
"Sometimes I have been mistreated because of my lesbianism." (G)

4. Internalization/Synthesis

—of love for women, sexual choices, into overall identity	—of identity as a member of minority group, across contexts

Self-Statement Examples:
"I am deeply fulfilled in my relationships with women." (I)
"I feel comfortable with my lesbianism no matter where I am or who I am with." (G)

model that takes into consideration both individual and group identity. Their proposed model will need continuing development and research in order to validate its ability to more fully explain lesbian development (see Table 5.7).

Bisexualities

Many of the issues about sexuality as a continuum and as expressed in multiple ways (see earlier section on sexuality) can be applied to thinking about bisexuality. For example, bisexual identity and bisexual behavior are not necessarily the same thing. The box below provides some answers to common questions about bisexuality.

Bisexual myths and stereotypes

Eliason (1996) points out a number of myths and stereotypes about bisexual persons. These myths and stereotypes reflect the complexities of a non-binary notion of sexual orientation. While there are few models and relatively little research on strengths-based approaches to understanding sexual orientation in relation to gay men and lesbians, there are even fewer resources available to assist us in understanding the complexities of bisexuality both individually across the lifespan and socially in terms of group and community attitudes and perspectives concerning bisexual persons. According to Eliason "Most people appear to have even more negativity and bewilderment about bisexuals than gay men or lesbians" (1996:131).

Stereotypes

- Bisexuals are just confused—they cannot decide whether to be homosexual or heterosexual.
- Bisexuals are promiscuous and must always have a partner of each gender.
- Bisexuals are afraid to admit that they are really lesbian or gay.
- Bisexuals are incapable of sustaining a long-term relationship and will always leave one person for someone of the other gender (Eliason 1996:131).

According to Eliason (1996:131), traditional myths and stereotypes about bisexual persons have more recently been exacerbated by misconceptions about the interrelationship of bisexuality and AIDS:

There is also a strong feeling among some people that bisexuals are responsible for bringing AIDS into the heterosexual community. Centers for Disease Control researchers found that risk behaviors, not risk groups, are the

---

Some Common Questions and Answers about Bisexuality

What do you mean by "bisexual" anyway?

Bisexuality means sexual or romantic attraction or behavior directed towards some members of more than one sex.

What is "a bisexual"?

A strict definition of a bisexual would be someone who has romantic and/or sexual relations with other people of more than one sex (though not necessarily at the same time). However, since not everyone has necessarily had the opportunity to act on their sexual/romantic attractions, some people prefer a looser definition; for instance, that a bisexual is a person who—in their own estimation—feels potentially able to have such attraction. This could be anyone who has erotic, affectionate, or romantic feelings for, fantasies of, and/or experiences with both men and women. A bisexual may be more attracted to one sex than the other, attracted equally to both, or find people's sex unimportant. The strength of their attractions to men and women may vary over time.

Source: Bisexuality. Available: http://www.biresource.org/

important variable. The lesbian, gay, and bisexual communities are among the most knowledgeable about HIV transmission and safer sex techniques. The greatest risk appears to be the large number of men who identify themselves as heterosexual but regularly engage in sex with men and do not inform their female lovers or do not engage in safer sex practices.

Bisexual research

Contrary to the misunderstandings and myths described above, there is some research that does help inform our understanding of the variation and complexity of bisexuality. Eliason (1994:131) points out, for example:

> Weinberg, Williams, and Pryor found that there were many different ways to experience bisexuality. Some were more attracted to women than to men (i.e., rarely is there a 50–50 distribution of sexual attractions); a few were simultaneous bisexuals (at any given time, having a lover of each gender), but most were serial bisexuals with one lover at a time. Bisexuals were no more confused about their identities than were lesbians or gay men, and even heterosexuals often experienced some confusion (70% of bisexuals, 65% of lesbians and gay men, and 28% of heterosexuals were confused about their sexual identity at some time in their lives).

Bisexuality may be much more common than most people think. Research carried out at the Harvard School of Public Health in 1994 found that 20.8 percent of the men and 17.8 percent of the women studied admitted to same-sex sexual attraction/behavior at some time in their lives (Harley 1996:www).

Transgender

As Burgess points out, since the 1990s persons who self-identity as transgender have begun to unite politically and socially "to demand the rights and respect" they deserve. As a result, transgender persons are increasingly visible in general society. This often results in a backlash from important external influences on transgender persons, including "families, schools, peer groups, places of employment and other institutions" (Burgess 2000:36). For social workers (or soon-to-be social workers), providing effective and respectful services to members of this population is increasingly important. However, Burgess suggests that we are often "ill-equipped with accurate knowledge" about the transgender population" (Burgess 2000:36). In an effort, to provide more accurate knowledge about this underserved population, Illustrative Reading 5.1 at the end of this chapter, "Bending Gender, Ending Gender: Theoretical Foundations for Social Work Practice with the Transgender Community," by Burdge, directly addresses important issues concerning social work and members of the transgender community.

In an earlier chapter, we discussed the importance and power of language and words in helping or hindering the well-being and quality of life of groups of people who face discrimination and oppression. We also noted the constantly changing nature of terms viewed as appropriate by members of these groups. In addition, the importance of accepting and respecting the self-definition of terminology by members of the groups themselves was discussed as an element of empowerment of group members. As is the case with other groups facing oppression and discrimination, a significant impediment to working effectively and respectfully with members of the transgender population is lack of knowledge of basic terms and definitions for describing and understanding this population. The following text box includes basic terms and definitions related to the transgender community.

Transgender Community: Terms and Definitions

Sexual Identity: An individual's sense of self as male or female from the social and psychological perspective.

Gender Identity: Refers to a person's innate sense of maleness or femaleness. Transgendered individuals report having experienced conflict over such gender assignment throughout childhood and adolescence.

Gender Role: The characteristics of an individual that are culturally defined as masculine or feminine.

Transgender: Transgender is an umbrella term encompassing the diversity of gender expression including drag queens and kings, bigenders, cross-dressers, transgenderists, and transsexuals. These individuals, many of whom cluster together to form their own communities, are people who find their gender identity—the sense of themselves as male or female—in conflict with their anatomical gender.

Gender Pronouns: He or She? How do I refer to this person? This is typically one of the first questions nontransgendered professionals and other interested people ask. The answer is: ask the person which pronoun he or she prefers.

MTF and FTM: These are acronyms that refer, respectively to "male to female" and "female to male" transitions. These designations reflect which direction of transition the person has taken.

Cross-Dressing: When a person dresses in the clothing of the opposite gender (i.e., males who wear traditionally female clothing, hairstyles, make-up, etc.). Cross-dressing is sometimes referred to as gender nonconforming behavior.

Transvestite: Men or women who wear clothing usually worn by persons of the opposite gender. Most transvestites are heterosexual, mostly married men, who "cross-dress" in the privacy of their own homes, for sexual or psychological gratification. Transvestites are not to be confused with female impersonators. Female impersonators are men who earn a living by "cross-dressing" and performing in nightclubs.

Drag Kings/Queens: These persons are heterosexual or gay/lesbian and are usually performers. There are some gay men or lesbians who "cross-dress" in public; this is referred to as "being in drag" and these men are often referred to as "drag queens." Men who dress as women for performance; women who dress as men for performance.

Transsexuals: Are individuals who feel an overwhelming desire to permanently fulfill their lives as members of the opposite gender. Transsexuals most commonly experience the most acute effects of gender dysphoria [anxiety and depression]. Many, though not all, opt for hormone therapy and genital reassignment surgery. These individuals can identify as heterosexual, gay or lesbian, or bisexual.

Intersexed or Hermaphrodite Individuals: Are those individuals with medically established physical or hormonal attributes of both male and female gender. When these conditions are detected at birth, these individuals are almost always assigned a gender solely on the basis of physical gender.

Source: Adapted from Mallon 2000:143–145

Cass's Model of Homosexual Identity Formation

Cass (1984:143) presents a model of homosexual identity formation that focuses "on the homosexual situation as experienced and perceived by homosexuals themselves." Themes common in a variety of models of homosexual identity development include change and growth as central to identity development. This is true of Cass's model as well. Her model differs from some others in that it takes a strengths perspective and does not operate from the assumption "that people perceive the acquisition of a homosexual identity in a negative light." It also differs from some other models in that it applies to identity formation for both gay men and lesbians.

Cass perceives identity development for homosexuals to proceed through six stages according to a variety of cognitive, behavioral, and affective dimensions (1984:147). At each stage, however, the decision not to proceed any further in the development of a homosexual identity may occur. Identity formation at any stage may take either a negative path away from acceptance and integration of a positive identity or a positive path toward acceptance and integration of a positive homosexual identity as part of one's total self-image. *Identity foreclosure* is the choice by an individual at any stage of homosexual identity development not to proceed any further. However, choosing identity foreclosure does not mean that homosexuality itself can be simply chosen or rejected. It simply means choices are made not to act upon feelings or continue to explore those feelings. Cass's model has significant limitations according to some researchers because it has not been thoroughly empirically tested. It is presented here because it is the most widely used model of gay identity formation. Cass's stages of homosexual identity formation are:

Stage 1: *Identity Confusion.* Persons at this stage face considerable confusion. Their previous identities in terms of sexual orientation are questioned as they perceive that their behaviors "(actions, feelings, thoughts) may be defined as homosexual."

Stage 2: *Identity Comparison.* The person accepts the possibility of a homosexual identity. He or she faces feelings of alienation with the recognition of clear differences between one's self and nonhomosexual others. If identity foreclosure does not occur, the individual may choose to make contacts with other homosexuals as a way of lessening feelings of alienation.

Stage 3: *Identity Tolerance.* Tolerance rather than acceptance of a homosexual self-image is characteristic of this stage. Increasing commitment to homosexual identity results in seeking out companionship of other homosexuals. Disclosure of one's homosexuality to heterosexuals or "coming out" is rare during this stage. The tendency is to maintain two identities, a public identity shared with heterosexuals and a private identity shared with homosexuals.

Stage 4: *Identity Acceptance.* "Increased contact with the homosexual subculture encourages a more positive view of homosexuality and the gradual development of a network of homosexual friends." One attempts to both fit into society and retain a homosexual life-style. "Passing" or pretending heterosexuality is practiced in some contexts while there is also likely to be some selective disclosure to heterosexual others, especially friends and relatives.

Stage 5: *Identity Pride.* Feelings of pride in one's homosexuality, strong "loyalty to homosexuals as a group," and devaluing heterosexuality is characteristic of this stage. This stage also often includes intense anger about society's stigmatization of homosexuals. This anger is often turned to disclosure to and confrontation with heterosexuals in attempts to gain validity and equality for homosexuals.

Stage 6: *Identity Synthesis.* Positive contacts with non-homosexuals helps create a sense of not being able to simply divide the world into good homosexuals and bad heterosexuals. With this comes a sense of "people having many sides to their character, only one part of which is related to homosexuality." One develops a way of life in which homosexuality is no longer hidden and public and private selves are integrated into a positive identity (1984:147–153).

FOCUS: ELDERS

Theories of Aging

In Chapter 4 we addressed the disengagement theory of aging as a very traditional approach to theories of aging. Here we will address some of the less traditional approaches to understanding aging. Schroots provides a summary of major theories of aging that have been developed since World War II (Schroots 1996:742).

First, regarding disengagement theory (see Chapter 4), Schroots argues that it presents "a one-sided view of the aged, given the significant proportion of older people who do not lose interest in life and do not withdraw from society" (1996:744). Baltes and colleagues attempted to take a more holistic or balanced view of human aging by presenting seven propositions to explain human aging and its variability:

1. there are major differences between normal, pathological, and optimal aging, the latter defined as aging under development enhancing and age-friendly environmental conditions;

2. the course of aging shows much interindividual variability (heterogeneity);

3. there is much latent reserve capacity in old age;

4. there is aging loss in the range of reserve capacity or adaptivity;

5. individual and social knowledge (crystallized intelligence) enriches the mind and can compensate for age-related decline in fluid intelligence (aging losses);

6. with age, the balance between gains and losses becomes increasingly negative; and finally,

7. the self in old age remains a resilient system of coping and maintaining integrity. (cited in Schroots 1996:745)

As a counterpoint to disengagement theory, Havighurst suggested *activity theory*, which states, "in order to maintain a positive sense of self, elderly persons must substitute new roles for those lost in old age. As such, activity theory presents a more realistic view of older people" (cited in Schroots 1996:744). While both of these theories have had significant influence on the study and perception of human aging, a newer, alternative, and somewhat more balanced theory it that of *gerotranscendence*. This theory, developed by Tornstam, suggests that as we move through old age, we experience "a shift in metaperspective from a materialistic and rational vision to a more cosmic and transcendent one, normally followed by an increase in life satisfaction." Gerotranscendence is related to "three levels of age-related ontological change." Remember from Chapter 3 that ontology refers our perspective about what is real. These three levels of ontological change, according to Tornstam, are:

1. *Cosmic level*—changes in the perception of time, space and objects, increase of affinity with past and coming generations, changes in the perception of life, disappearing fear of death, acceptance of the mystery dimension in life, and increase of cosmic communion with the spirit of the universe;

2. *Self*—discovery of hidden (both good and bad) aspects of the self, decrease of self-centeredness, self-transcendence from egoism to altruism, rediscovery of the child within, and ego-integrity;

3. *Social and Individual relations*—less interest in superficial relations, increasing need for solitude, more understanding of the difference between self and role, decreasing interest in material things, and increase of reflection (cited in Schroots, 1996:746–747).

Clearly, gerotranscendence offers an alternative to both disengagement and activity theory. It synthesizes elements of both, while adding significant attention to less concrete but important alternative notions of aging processes involving changing perceptions at the cosmic level (time, space, and objects), continuing self-discovery, and changes in perceptions of the importance of social and individual relations.

FOCUS: PERSONS WITH DISABILITIES

The Americans with Disabilities Act (ADA)

The Americans with Disabilities Act (ADA) is a significant piece of legislation and has multiple implications for social workers whether we are working at the individual, family, group, organizational, or community level. Orlin describes the significance of the act in that "ADA establishes that the nation's goals regarding individuals with disabilities are to ensure equality of opportunity, full participation, independent living, and economic self-sufficiency" (1995:234). The purpose of the act, then, is very consistent with the social work purpose of working to achieve social and economic justice.

What does the ADA cover?

- lodging
- facilities for public gathering:
  - exhibitions
  - entertainment
  - recreations
  - exercise
  - education
- stations used for public transportation
- service and social services establishments
- establishments serving food or drink (as long as they have contact with general public (Orlin 1995:234)

ADA: Definition of disability

According to the Americans with Disabilities Act (ADA), disability means "with respect to an individual, a physical or mental impairment that substantially limits one or more of the major life activities of such individuals, a record of such an impairment, or being regarded as having such an impairment" (Orlin 1995:234–235).

To appreciate the full meaning of this definition of disability we need to understand what is meant, according to the Act, by such terms as "major life activities," "record of" impairment, or "regarded as" having an impairment, "reasonable accommodation," and "undue hardship." **Major life activities** as defined by the ADA are listed in the box below.

Major Life Activities	
caring for oneself	breathing
performing manual tasks	learning
walking	working
seeing	
hearing	*Source:* Orlin M. The Americans with Disabilities Act: Implications for social services. Copyright 1995, National Association of Social Workers, Inc., Social Work. Adapted by permission.
speaking	

The term **record of** is a "provision [in the ADA] to protect people with a history of impairment such as persons with histories of mental illness or cancer and those who have been misclassified as having mental retardation or mental illness, for example." The term **regarded as** is intended in the ADA "to protect against discrimination based on the perceptions of others." For example, people with severe burns may not regard themselves as impaired, but encounter discrimination because others "regard" them as having a disability (Orlin 1995:235). Orlin distinguishes the ADA from other civil rights law by pointing out that "one concept that differs between public policy approaches to disability and race or gender discrimination is the concept of '**reasonable accommodation**'" (1995:236). This concept means the employer must make individualized accommodation "based on the specific needs of a qualified individual with a disability to enable that person to perform the essential functions of a job, unless such accommodation would be an 'undue hardship.'" **Undue hardship** is defined as "an action requiring 'significant difficulty or expense'" (ADA 1990). Any accommodation that would be unduly costly, extensive, substantial, or disruptive or that would fundamentally alter the nature or operation of the business or organization would be an undue hardship. Assessment of undue hardship existence varies from situation to situation depending on such factors as the resources of the organization available to make accommodation, for example, a small agency versus a large academic medical center (Orlin 1995:236). Often accommodations can be inexpensive and reasonably simple. (See Chapter 8 for examples of how some organizations have made "reasonable accommodations" for workers with disabilities.)

ADA protections for family, volunteers, and social workers

Family members or people otherwise associated with people with disabilities are also protected by ADA, "because discrimination against a person with an association or relationship with a person with a disability is also prohibited" (Orlin 1995:238). Examples are:

- A person who does volunteer work with people with AIDS is protected from discrimination by his/her employer because of the association.
- A person with a spouse with a disability cannot be refused a job by an employer concerned that the spouse's impairment will cause the person to miss too much work.
- A child with a sibling who has AIDS cannot be denied admission to a day care center. (Orlin 1995:238)

The protection provided in ADA in the above areas is especially important to social workers and other professionals who provide services to persons with disabilities. It is intended to prevent discrimination against these professionals in the course of carrying out their professional responsibilities.

Social Work, Developmental Disabilities, and Children

Increasing federal mandates require social workers to be knowledgeable and effective in working with children and families with or at risk of developmental disabilities. Malone et al. (2000) note that the Education of the Handicapped Act Amendments of 1986 (P. L. 99-457) required services not only to children with developmental disabilities or at risk for them but required family-centered services as well. Other related federal legislation includes the Developmental Disabilities Assistance and Bill of Rights Act. They note specifically that "we have moved to a definition of developmental disabilities that is inclusive of any number of conditions oriented to functional abilities and sensitive to family issues." Federal mandates also cover "young children with developmental concerns." This includes children from birth to five years old with a condition that without services "will likely result in substantial functional limitations in three or more major life activities." These life activities include the following:

- self care,
- receptive and expressive language,
- learning,
- mobility,
- self direction,
- capacity for independent living, and
- economic self-sufficiency if services are not provided.

Malone et al. point out:

Developmental concerns experienced by children can challenge typical development in the key domains: cognition, social and emotional growth, language and communication, and physical growth and skill. These concerns may be due to inherited genetic influences, environmental influences (or a combination of genetic and environmental factors) and have their genesis during the prenatal, perinatal, or postnatal period.

Malone et al. include both genetically or inherited conditions as well as environmental conditions that might result in developmental delays or disability.
Genetically based concerns:

- Down syndrome
- Fragile X syndrome
- phenylketonuria (PKU)
- Tay-Sachs disease

Environmentally based concerns:

- encephalitis
- meningitis
- rubella (German measles)
- fetal alcohol syndrome
- lead poisoning
- poor nutrition
- child abuse (Malone, et al. 2000)

Shonkoff, Hauser, Kraus, and Upshur (1992, in Malone et al. 2000) suggest three behavioral categories that should be assessed in determining the need for services:

1. meeting social expectations regarding social routines (adaptive behavior),
2. spontaneous interest in learning (play), and
3. developing interpersonal relationships (child–parent interaction).

In addition, Rubin (1990, in Malone et al. 2000) identified four major areas that can result in developmental difficulties after birth:

1. central nervous system infections,
2. accidents,
3. lead toxicity, and
4. psychosocial vulnerability.

These four areas reflect multiple system levels, including both individual and environmental contexts.

Persons with Disabilities and Social and Economic Justice

Kopels points out that in its research prior to passage of the ADA, "Congress found that the 43 million Americans who have one or more physical or mental disabilities, are, as a group, severely disadvantaged due to discrimination in the critical areas of employment, housing, public accommodations, education, transportation, communication, recreation, institutionalization, health services, voting, and access to public services" (1995:338). Kopels also reminds us, "People with disabilities are statistically the poorest, least educated, and largest minority population in America" (U.S. House of Representatives 1990). This extreme poverty results from both the types of jobs traditionally available and the lack of access to training and education: "Individuals with disabilities, however, have traditionally been employed in low-status, low-paying jobs. They have not had equal access to educational and training opportunities that could have prepared them for more gainful employment" (Kopels 1995:338).

ADA and Advocating for Social and Economic Justice

Orlin suggests, "Because the primary objective of the ADA is full participation of people with disabilities in the mainstream of American society, agencies should review the extent to which individuals with disabilities participate in their programs. A Louis Harris and Associate nationwide poll of people with disabilities conducted in 1986 found a high correlation of disability with poverty; joblessness; lack of education; and failure to participate in social life, shopping and recreation" (1995:238).

Kopels urges social work students to ask questions about the physical and policy environments in their field placement agencies. You might also adapt these questions to the colleges and universities you attend as well.

Physical

▶ Does agency have stairs, ramps, doorways, water fountains, restrooms, telephones, and other amenities that are accessible to clients with differing levels of abilities?
▶ What environmental modifications should be made?
▶ If the student became disabled while in field placement, would he or she be able to continue to work at the agency, or would "reasonable accommodations" need to be made?

Policy

▶ Does the agency provide sign language interpreters, if necessary, during counseling sessions?
▶ Can clients with visual impairments read their records?
▶ Is there a uniform policy for maintaining the confidentiality of client records, or do records of certain clients, like those with HIV/AIDS, illegally contain special, identifying notations? (1995:343).

FOCUS: MEN

Kimmel and Messner (1995:xiv–xv) point out that just as "white people rarely think of themselves as 'raced' people [and] rarely think of race as a central element in their experience. . . . men often think of themselves as genderless, as if gender did not matter in the daily experiences of our lives." They note though, that researchers have been studying masculinity for many years. These studies traditionally have focused on three models:

1. *Biological models* have focused on the ways in which innate biological differences between males and females programmed different social behaviors.

2. *Anthropological models* have examined masculinity cross-culturally, stressing the variations in the behaviors and attributes associated with being a man.

3. *Sociological models* have [until recently] stressed how socialization of boys and girls included accommodation to a "sex role" specific to one's biological sex. (Kimmel and Messner 1995:xv).

Men, Masculinity, and Identity

Kimmel and Messner (1995:xix–xx) argue that the traditional models for studying masculinity have increasingly come into question for assuming the definition of masculinity is universal across cultures; for omitting historical realities; and for failing to account for issues of power that are central to getting a fuller understanding of male identity development. Research on masculinity has undergone significant change in the last twenty years and has become more inclusive of elements and realities of masculinity omitted from earlier traditional perspectives. Newer alternative models have been heavily influenced by feminist research directed toward understanding the relationship between males and females. Most significant among the results of newer alternative approaches to studying masculinity was the realization that "power dynamics are an essential element in both the definition and enactment of gender." Traditional sex role research had ignored both the reality of power relations and of the reality that men held the dominant position within the power relations between genders. In addition, alternative models "looked at 'gender relations' and understood how the definition of either masculinity or femininity was relational, that is, how the definition of one gender depended, in part, on the understanding of the definition of the other" (Kimmel and Messner 1995:xix).

Kimmel and Messner believe:

the research on masculinity is entering a new stage in which the variations among men are seen as central to the understanding of men's lives. The unexamined assumption in earlier studies had been that one version of masculinity—white, middle-age, middle-class, heterosexual—was the sex role into which all men were struggling to fit in our society. Thus, working-class men, men of color, gay men, and younger and older men were all observed as departing in significant ways from the traditional definitions of masculinity (1995:xix).

White Male Identity Development

One effort to further understand some of the processes involved in white male identity development—in this case development in the areas of race, white male superiority, and gender—is presented by Scott and Robinson (2001) in a model referred to as the "Key Model." They note that rather than a linear, stage-based model as is the case with many traditional models of identity development, "the Key Model is circular in nature and suggests that movement occurs in multiple directions" (Scott and Robinson 2001:418). This model is presented in five "Types" of development dynamics. The Key Model is summarized below.

Type 1: Noncontact type

Description. Attitudes of individuals in this phase include little or no knowledge of other races or of their own race . . . and will either ignore, deny, or minimize the issues dealing with race and race relations. In addition, his attitudes about gender tend to be very traditional wherein gender roles are rigid and prescribed. . . . Individuals in this phase want to continue the status quo and are not aware of the need for legal steps to correct discrimination. Ethnocentrism characterizes this type as does a belief in the superiority of White males to women and to people of color.

Type 2: Claustrophobic type

Description. As the White man begins to realize that the American dream is not reality, he may start to look to "outsiders" (i.e., persons of color and women) to blame. The "Claustrophobic type" begins to feel that people of color and women are receiving unmerited advantages at his expense. During this phase, the person secures power for those like himself while seeking to restrict women and people of color from gaining access to their privileges. This position of privilege is inevitably gained at the expense of others. The person in this phase thinks there are too many groups vying for power and privilege. They feel "closed in" by the majority of the new workers in this twenty-first century: women, people of color, and immigrants. This person still views other races and women in a stereotyped and overgeneralized way. . . . White men may never exhibit attitudes other than the Type 1 and Type 2 attitudes. This stagnation in development can result from a failure to experience true dissonance.

Type 3: Conscious identity type

Description. This phase is characterized by a precipitating event, positive or negative, that creates dissonance between a person's existing belief system and real-life experiences with women and people of color that contradict this system. An example would be a professional woman or a person of color who intercedes significantly on the man's behalf, perhaps through surgery or adjudication of a difficult case. As a result, the man is required to reevaluate his culture, both as it exists around him and the extent to which he has internalized it. In doing so, he recognizes that both racism and sexism play an important role in how he views and blames others for the current social and economic situation. The person in this phase can either adopt the attitudes of the Claustrophobic phase or move into a phase (the Empirical type) in which he rationally and realistically looks at his feelings and actions toward women and people of other races and the overall struggle for power and privilege.

Type 4: Empirical type

Description. During this phase, the White man finally realizes that racism and sexism are real (i.e., not fabrications of people of color and women) and are involved in many aspects of his life. The person sees that he has been misplacing blame and that women and people of color are not responsible for discriminatory practices that may have directly affected him. The "Empirical type" is "forced" to again question the reasons for his disillusionment with the American dream. He recognizes that his privileged existence—earned through no effort of his own—is at the expense of many women and people of color who have been oppressed. At this phase, there is a growing, albeit disturbing, awareness of unearned privileges, due only to the color of his skin, that have allowed for easier negotiation of life. . . . The Person also questions his role in the Pervasive competition for power and privilege.

Type 5: Optimal type

Description. This person has changed his worldview into a holistic understanding of the common struggle of all people for survival. There is the realization that working with and interacting in other ways with all people independent of the constellation of one's identities (race and gender) is advantageous for truly meaningful existence. The person opens his lost and unexplored self to commune with self, family, and diverse others. There is an increased knowledge of race and gender relations and the roles they play. In this phase, the individual values all people for their intrinsic worth as human beings. The struggle for power over others in greatly minimized. The person is more aware of oppression in a general sense and works to eliminate specific instances of oppression. There is a pervasive understanding that survival is assured not by oppressing others but by living peacefully and harmoniously with self and others.

Masculinities

Newer alternative approaches see masculinity as multiple and present the newer notion of **masculinities** "the ways in which different men construct different versions of masculinity" (Kimmel and Messner 1995:xx). Kimmel and Messner suggest that more complete understandings of maleness and masculinity can be found through **social constructionist** approaches which seek to understand that one's identity as man "is developed through a complex process of interaction with the culture in which" one learns "the gender scripts appropriate to our culture, and attempt[s] to modify those scripts to make them more palatable"; through approaches that recognize "the experience of masculinity is not uniform and universally generalizable to all men in our society"; and through **life course** approaches which "chart the construction of these various masculinities in men's lives, and . . . examine pivotal developmental moments or institutional locations during a man's life in which the meanings of masculinity are articulated" (Kimmel and Messner 1995:xx–xxi).

NOMAS: An Alternative Vision of Maleness

An alternative perspective on masculinity and maleness is presented in the principles of the organization called NOMAS (National Organization of Men Against Sexism). NOMAS is an organization dedicated to enhancing men's lives and recognizes that:

> The traditional male role has steered many men into patterns such as isolation from children, lack of close relationships, denying of feelings, competitiveness, aggressiveness, preoccupation with work and success. NOMAS believes that men can live happier and more fulfilled lives by challenging, and un-learning, many of the old lessons of traditional masculinity. We are concerned with the full range of men's problems, and the difficult issues in men's lives. (1996:www)

Nomas: Statement of Principles

NOMAS advocates a perspective that is pro-feminist, gay affirmative, anti-racist, dedicated to enhancing men's lives, and committed to justice on a broad range of social issues including class, age, religion, and physical abilities. We affirm that working to make this nation's ideals of equality substantive is the finest expression of what it means to be men. We believe that the new oppurtunities becoming available to women and men will be beneficial to both. Men can live as happier and more fulfilled human beings by challenging the old-fashioned rules of masculinity that embody the assumption of male superiority. Traditional masculinity includes many positive characteristics in which we take pride and find strength, but it also contains qualities that have limited and harmed us. We are deeply supportive of men who are struggling with the issues of traditional masculinity. As an organization for changing men, we care about men and are especially concerned with men's problems, as well as the difficult issues in most men's lives. As an organization for changing men, we strongly support the continuing struggle of women for full equality. We applaud and support the insights and positive social changes that feminism has stimulated for both women and men. We oppose such injustices to women as economic and legal discrimination, rape, domestic violence, sexual harassment, and many others. Women and men can and do work together as allies to change the injustices that have so often made them see one another as enemies. One of the strongest and deepest anxieties of most American men is their fear of homosexuality. This homophobia contributes directly to the many injustices experienced by gay, lesbian and bisexual persons, and it is a debilitating restriction for heterosexual men. We call for an end to all forms of discrimination based on sexual-affectional orientation, and for the creation of a gay-affirmative society. The enduring injustice of racism, which like sexism has long divided humankind into unequal and isolated groups, is of particular concern to us. Racism touches all of us and remains a primary source of inequality and oppression in our society. NOMAS is committed to examine and challenge racism in our organizations, our communities, and ourselves. We also acknowledge that many people are oppressed today because of their class, age, religion and physical condition. We believe that such injustices are vitally connected to sexism, with its fundamental premise of unequal distribution of power. Our goal is to change not just ourselves and other men but also the institutions that create inequality. We welcome any person who agrees in substance with these principles to membership in the National Organization for Men Against Sexism. (http://www.nomas.org/principles)

Men and Violence

A key area of concern for understanding and changing traditional notions of masculinity is that of violence. We will examine violence in the context of families in Chapter 6. Here we will explore violence as a key issue and problem with which men must struggle, be accountable for, and address.

Violence against women

Stout suggests a model for appreciating the degree and extent of male controls and violence against women through the presentation of a continuum of male control and violence. Stout notes, "acts of violence against women are not isolated and social work professionals must examine the context and culture in which violence prevails when working with victims, survivors, and perpetrators" (Stout 1991:307).

In Stout's (1991:307) continuum model "control over women moves from subtle to overt forms of violence." The continuum proceeds in the following way:

1. Language, research bias, and differential treatment
2. Street hassling
3. Economic discrimination
4. Sexist advertising
5. Pornography
6. Sexual harassment
7. Battering

8. Sexual abuse and rape
9. Femicide (Stout 1991:307)

Rothblum stresses:

> Sex and violence against women are strongly associated in our society. . . . Most women, consciously or unconsciously, engage in a number of activities in order to avoid being raped by men (e.g., not listing their first name in the telephone directory, using a male voice on their telephone answering machine, not going out or driving or walking alone at night, taking self-defense courses, etc.). . . . Sex and fear of violence are so intertwined for most women that it is difficult to conceive of living a life free from that fear (1994:628–629).

Levy suggests the need to reconceptualize violence from a pathology-based perspective to one that recognizes violence is virtually normative in U.S. society. She suggests:

> If violence against women is a mainstream experience affecting a majority of women, then 21st-century social work strategies to deal with it must address this violence as a normative cultural phenomenon rather than as idiosyncratic pathology. . . . Rather than labeling battering as pathology or a family systems failure, [feminists] have challenged mental health practitioners to assume that violence against women, like that directed toward children, is behavior approved of and sanctioned in many parts of the culture (1995:317–318).

Levy urges:

> Society must redefine what normal masculinity is so that violent behavior toward women is seen as pathological and unacceptable. This change does not require categorization of violent behavior as a medically diagnosable pattern or disease but as behavior for which the perpetrator is held responsible. For example, young men in high school are generally ignored when they are seen pushing or hitting their girlfriends and are often surprised when accused of date rape. Their concepts of normal masculinity are shaken when confronted with the criminality of their behavior (1995:320).

Levy calls upon "Social work intervention in the 21st century [to] be guided by a definition of rape and battering as hate crimes against women, rather than seeing them exclusively as acts by 'a sick person.'" Further, she suggests that "Feminist social work practice that aims to eliminate violence against women must address the problem as a violation of human rights" (1995:321).

Violence and perpetrators

Levy (1995:323) offers suggestions for intervention in and prevention of violence in the 21st century. She suggests, for example, using models already available for teaching children and youth skills for building healthy relationships as a means of **preventing violence**. Skills include the following:

Skills for Teaching Anti-Violence Behavior

- Communication
- Problem solving

- Managing anger
- Assertiveness
- Mutual respect
- Flexibility
- Non-stereotyping of gender roles
- Empathy
- Stress management
- Conflict resolution
- Acceptance of variation of human sexuality
- Responsible and respectful sexuality (Levy 1995:323)

In addition, social workers can help prevent violence against women by

- Encouraging partnership rather than dominance and subordination in relationships
- Redefining masculinity and femininity
- Recognizing power dynamics and violence against women as a socially sanctioned abuse of power
- Recognizing victims' strengths rather than pathologizing their responses to violence
- Valuing the diversity of women's experiences
- Seeking solutions through community and social change as well as through individual change (Levy 1995:325)

Intervention for perpetrators of violence should include psychoeducational groups for rapists and batterers that emphasize the following:

1. The perpetrator's responsibility for and ability to control violent behavior
2. Awareness of the seriousness, danger, and consequences of violent behavior
3. Awareness of one's motivation (and sense of entitlement) to dominate and control women as socially sanctioned, and sometimes as an outgrowth of feelings of powerlessness displaced onto women
4. Anger management techniques
5. Empathy with women
6. Relationship skills, such as communication, assertiveness, and problem solving
7. Stress-reduction skills
8. Development of social support
9. Dealing with substance abuse (Levy 1995:323).

SUMMARY/COMMONALITIES

Myers et al. (1991) suggest that there are a number of important commonalities in developmental frameworks and models that address the experiences of members of diverse groups such as persons of color; women; gay men, lesbians, and bisexual persons, elders, persons with disabilities, and white men. Common developmental processes include:

a. a denial, devaluation, or lack of awareness of their oppressed identity;
b. a questioning of their oppressed identity;
c. an immersion in the oppressed subculture;

  d. a realization of the limitations of a devalued sense of self; and

  e. an integration of the oppressed part of self into their whole self-identity (1991:54–55).

It is important to note also as we conclude this chapter that developmental issues and alternative perspectives on other diverse persons and groups and the interrelationships of multiple diversities will continue to be dealt with as we proceed through the other chapters. This will be especially the case in relation to family as a major context of individual development, but diversities will continue to be a thread as well in regard to groups, organizations, communities, and globally as contexts in which individual developmental issues and tasks are played out.

Succeed with **PEARSON mysocialworklab**

Human Rights & Justice   Human Behavior   Policy Practice   Practice Contexts

Log onto **www.mysocialworklab.com** to watch videos on the skills and competencies discussed in this chapter. (*If you did not receive an access code to* **MySocialWorkLab** *with this text and wish to purchase access online, please visit* **www.mysocialworklab.com**.)

PRACTICE TEST

1. A central feature of the Cross Model of Black Identity Development is _____.
   a. the importance of the family in identity development
   b. a conversion experience which is also referred to as a transformation from "Negro to Black"
   c. differences in development experienced by people living in urban and rural areas.
   d. the impact of differences in educational level

2. Which of the following themes is NOT present in Gilligan's model of moral development?
   a. Moral problems require resolution through thinking that is contextual and narrative.
   b. Morality is focused on an understanding of human rights.
   c. Moral problems arise out of conflicting responsibilities.
   d. Morality centers on the activity of care.

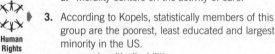

Human Rights & Justice

3. According to Kopels, statistically members of this group are the poorest, least educated and largest minority in the US.
   a. people with disabilities
   b. Hispanic persons
   c. African Americans
   d. Native Americans

4. In Herbert's study of identity development in African American men which of the following was NOT a significant finding?
   a. African American men proceeded through similar processes of adult development as the white men in the study by Levinson.
   b. Confronting race, racial discrimination and the formation of a racial identity was a significant part of their developmental experiences.
   c. Mentor relationships were a significant source of strength.
   d. African American men experienced greater stresses due to societal obstacles, and diffused contradictions and inconsistencies.

5. The theory of aging that suggests that as we move through old age we experience a shift in metaperspective from a materialistic and rational vision to a more cosmic and transcendent one, normally

followed by in increase in life satisfaction. This is referred to as_____.
   a. engagement theory
   b. gerotranscendence
   c. activity theory
   d. gerospirituality theory

6. In Cass's identity development model, a person who accepts the possibility of a homosexual identity, but may be experiencing feelings of alienation would probably fall into the stage _____.
   a. identity comparison
   b. identity confusion
   c. identity tolerance
   d. identity acceptance

Diversity in Practice

7. The principles of self-knowledge, interconnectedness, fundamental goodness, spirituality, language and oral tradition, and self-reliance are some of the principles found in what model of identity development?
   a. multidimensional model of racial identity
   b. Cross model of black identity development
   c. interactive model
   d. Africentric/African centered models

8. A key area of concern for understanding and changing traditional notions of masculinity is _____.
   a. eliminating stereotypes about gay men
   b. violence
   c. parenting
   d. socialization

9. This umbrella term is in reference to individuals who find their sense of themselves as male or female in conflict with their anatomical gender.
   a. gender role
   b. transvestite
   c. transgender
   d. cross-dressers

10. A social worker working with a client who is a refugee from a war zone might deal with issues such as _____.
    a. developmental delays
    b. poor school performance
    c. difficulty developing trust and relating to peers
    d. the client with the aid of the social worker might deal with all of these issues and more

---

Log onto **MySocialWorkLab** once you have completed the Practice Test above to take your Chapter Exam and demonstrate your knowledge of this material.

Answers

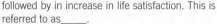

1)b 2)b 3)a 4)c 5)b 6)c 7)d 8)b 9)c 10)d

Bending Gender, Ending Gender: Theoretical Foundations for Social Work Practice with the Transgender Community

Barb J. Burdge

Gender is a ubiquitous social construct that wields power over every individual in our society. The traditional dichotomous gender paradigm is oppressive, especially for transgendered people whose sense of themselves as gendered people is incongruent with the gender they were assigned at birth. Transgendered individuals are targeted for mistreatment when others attempt to enforce conventional gender boundaries. This article discusses gender-based oppression and the resulting psychosocial difficulties experienced by many transgendered individuals. The discussion advances a critical analysis of the dominant gender paradigm using two alternative theoretical perspectives on gender—queer theory and social constructionism. The article argues that the transgender community is an at-risk population and that empowering practice with this population calls on social workers to target society's traditional gender dichotomy for change. An overview of practice implications and research needs is provided.

Key words: at-risk populations; gender; queer theory; social constructionism; transgender

This article puts forth a radical argument: Social workers should reject a dichotomous understanding of gender in favor of more accurate and affirming conceptualizations of gender. Best practices with the transgender population requires as much. In developing this argument, three central points will be defended: (1) transgendered people are oppressed in U.S. society (and, therefore, are a population of concern to social workers); (2) binary gender models are the foundation on which transgender oppression (and several other oppressive systems) depends; and (3) queer theory and social constructionism offer useful insights for social workers seeking an accurate understanding of gender.

Many disciplines have contributed to current knowledge of gender and the transgender community (for example, psychology, literature, medicine, sociology, anthropology, and philosophy). I have chosen to focus here on the sociological insights available at the intersection of social constructionism and queer theory. This conceptual site offers rich, thought-provoking considerations of gender, while creating fertile ground for no less than the elimination of gender-based oppression. As such, it offers alternatives to pathological models noted by several authors as historically dominant in psychological and medical thinking about transgendered people (Cooper, 1999; Gagné, Tewksbury, & McGaughey, 1997; Langer & Martin, 2004). Social constructionism and queer theory make a compelling case, and one consistent with social work's values and ethics, for the validity of transgender identities and the pursuit of gender rights.

The transgender community has its own distinct (but not homogeneous) culture. As with any culture, it has generated a unique language with which to communicate its reality. This language is somewhat fluid and continually evolving. Some terms have emerged organically from within the community; others have

---

Barb J. Burdge, MSW, LSW, is assistant professor and director, Social Work Program, Manchester College, 604 East College Avenue, Box 178, North Manchester, IN 46962; e-mail: bjburdge@manchester.edu.

Original manuscript received March 13, 2006 Final revision received September 8, 2006 Accepted October 16, 2006

been cast by science or academia. Keeping up with this quickly evolving lexicon can be challenging. Social workers must be able to appreciate ambiguous terminology—along with ambiguous genders. Self-definition is a matter of self-determination and social justice, which are basic values of the profession (NASW, 2000). As a result of this self-determined language, myriad terms have arisen. However, not all terms are accepted equally. "Transsexual" may be one person's label of choice. Another person, whose situation seems identical to the first, may reject transsexual in favor of "genderqueer." ("Queer" is an example of a previously negative term that is increasingly being reclaimed as a symbol of pride by the population it was once used against. In current usage, it generally refers to any person who transgresses traditional categories of gender or sexuality.)

Because it is empowering for oppressed groups to control the language representing them, social workers can honor the personal meaning of clients' chosen words, even when no "official" definitions exist.

Defining the Transgender Community

"Transgender" is an umbrella term (Lev, 2004; Mallon, 1999b) applicable to a range of individuals who express their gender in nontraditional ways. In general, transgendered people find their sense of self as female, male, or other to be in conflict with their assigned gender role (which was based on genital anatomy at birth). The term transgender can be accurately applied to self-identified bigenders, gender radicals, butch lesbians, cross-dressing married men, transvestites, intersex individuals, transsexuals, drag kings and queens, gender-blenders, queers, genderqueers, two spirits, or he-shes (Burgess, 1999; Hunter & Hickerson, 2003; Mallon, 1999b). These individuals may form their own social networks, hence the term "transgender community." For the purposes of this article, transgender is used to refer to people who claim the term on the basis of feelings that their assigned gender role is incongruent with their sense of self. Many people deviate from traditional gender norms. In the broadest sense, perhaps we all do, but most do not self-identify as transgendered. Lesbian, gay, and bisexual people, for example, may assume attitudes, behaviors, or clothes that do not fit their "appropriate" gender. However, I do not address these groups specifically here, as their identification rests on sexual orientation, not gender identity. Sexual orientation refers to one's emotional and sexual attractions, whereas gender identity refers to one's sense of self as being female, male, or otherwise gendered (perhaps transgendered or not gendered at all).

The number of transgendered people is unknown (Burgess, 1999). One report has suggested that self-identified transgendered people account for 2 percent to 3 percent of the overall lesbian, gay, bisexual, and transgender (LGBT) community (Rollins & Hirsch, 2003), but the inability to measure actual population size is a consistent theme in the literature. Until oppression of transgendered people is eradicated, we can never be certain of an exact count; many transgendered individuals may conceal their true gender identity given the lack of safety in the social environment.

The broad spectrum of people who fall under the umbrella of transgender also complicates attempts to estimate the size of this population. Prevalence rates have been estimated for two transgender subgroups: (1) intersex individuals (people born with ambiguous genitalia) and (2) postoperative transsexuals (people who have undergone sex reassignment surgery). Intersex people are frequently counted according to rates of infant genital modification surgeries. The Intersex Society of North America (2004) reported that each year approximately one to two infants out of every 1,000 born are surgically modified to "normalize" genital appearance. Prevalence estimates for postoperative transsexuals, based on number of sex reassignment surgeries performed in a given year, range from 1:500 to 1:2,500 (Conway, 2002). These ratios represent the combined estimations for both male-to-female (MTF) and female-to-male (FTM) surgeries, although MTF sex reassignment surgeries are more prevalent.

The Oppression of the Transgender Community

Transgendered people are among the most misunderstood and overlooked groups in our society (Burgess, 1999). Their very existence challenges the traditional gender dichotomy, and by stepping outside these fundamental social norms, they are vulnerable to discrimination and oppression. Young gender nonconformists face the complicated developmental task of building identities in a social environment that invalidates their reality and may even punish them for violating traditional gender roles (Bem, 1993; Brooks, 2000). Families cannot necessarily be depended on to offer a safe haven for transgendered youths. Parents are often ill equipped to understand their transgendered child (Burgess). Many transgendered youths' families may not only be unable to empower them, but may also perpetuate societal oppression. Likewise, transgendered adults can face severe social punishment—including harassment, social and familial rejection, workplace discrimination, denial of parental rights, and physical and sexual assault—for violating gender categories (Burgess; Donovan, 2001). Pierce (2001) suggested the term "shunning" to describe society's response to the transgender community.

In the face of this negative social environment, transgendered people try to adapt and survive. They may experience confusion, low self-esteem, and depression (Burgess, 1999). Many transgendered youths run away from home for self-preservation, but end up homeless and turn to prostitution (that is, "survival sex") in exchange for food, money, and shelter (personal communication with L. Davidson, former executive director, Indiana Youth Group, Indianapolis, April 12, 2005). Desperation to achieve consonance between gender identity and physical sex may drive transgendered individuals to self-mutilate or to use hormones obtained from the street (Swann & Herbert, 1999). Some transgendered individuals become suicidal (Burgess). Such behaviors, however, are too often viewed as the problem, when external factors (for example, rejection or assault by peers and family, hostile work or school environments, lack of supportive people and role models, pressures to conform to ill-fitting gender expectations) are the root cause (Burgess).

It is not surprising, then, that transgendered people seek social work services for a variety of reasons. Conversely, social workers may play different roles in the lives of transgendered clients. They may be case managers for transgendered youths in child welfare or youth services (see Mallon, 1999a). They may serve as therapists assisting families of transgendered people to respond affirmatively to their transitioning loved one (see Lesser, 1999). School social workers can create safe places for transgendered youths (see Burgess, 1999), and medical social workers could help sex reassignment surgery patients navigate the psychosocial aspects of their transition (see Bockting, Robinson, Benner, & Scheltema, 2004). Social workers can help transgendered victims of hate crimes (see Bush & Sainz, 2001). At a broader level, social workers join political advocacy efforts to ensure the civil rights of the transgender community (see Grise-Owens, Vessels, & Owens, 2004).

The NASW *Code of Ethics* (2000) obligates social workers to serve oppressed and vulnerable populations, eliminate discrimination based on sex, and seek social change to ensure the well-being of all people. (In anticipation of the 2005 NASW Delegate Assembly, the NASW Alaska Chapter conducted a petition drive to garner support for adding "gender orientation" to the list of vulnerable statuses named in the NASW *Code of Ethics*. This addition would have clarified social work's commitment to transgendered individuals, but the effort did not succeed.)

Service to the transgender community is a prime opportunity for social workers to fulfill this charge. With so many possibilities for working with the transgender community, social workers should be prepared. Effective social work with transgendered clients requires a high level of cultural competence, skills to create change at all levels, and sophisticated theoretical frameworks for understanding gender and gender-based oppression.

Deconstructing the Gender Binary

Gender is present in our lives from the time our genitals are first discernible—often in utero. It is the first "question" that is answered for us by the adults who welcome us at birth. Labeling a baby as either male or female (on the basis of visible genitalia) is generally seen as a simple matter, even though this label will be used to define the child and will have monumental implications for the course of the child's life (Cooper, 1999). The practice of assigning a gender label at birth operates with only two potential outcomes. Even in cases in which the genitalia are ambiguous, medical professionals and families generally pursue surgical modifications to **make** one gender fit (Cooper). Babies must fit within a label—either male or female. Very literally, our bodies must fit our words (Wilchins, 2004). We recognize no other options. Nonetheless, someone could look at an intersex infant and think, "Clearly, Nature [*sic*] has other things in mind" (Wilchins, p. 76).

Traditional gender assignment relies on three fundamental assumptions: (1) that anatomy determines identity (Cooper, 1999), (2) that reproductive functions accurately predict distinctive psychological and behavioral propensities in humans (West & Zimmerman, 1987), and (3) that only female and male genders exist (Bem, 1993). These assumptions, however, are consistently called into question by social research. Anthropological studies have described cultures that allow for gender-variant identities. Cooper cited certain Native American tribes, and Lorber (1994) illuminated certain cultures of Papua New Guinea and the Dominican Republic. The existence of transgendered people casts doubt on a binary, anatomical gender model.

In the classic article, "Doing Gender." West and Zimmerman (1987) made the enduring argument that gender is constructed by, and for, social interaction. Everyone "does" his or her gender (through dress, grooming, behavioral modifications, and so forth), not only to reflect one's internal self, but also to facilitate the social process. From this perspective, gender is a performance for which every person alters outward appearances to align with an internal sense of gender identity (Butler, 1990).

Gender becomes a powerful ideology to which people, as social actors, are held accountable (West & Zimmerman, 1987). To capture the ubiquitous nature of gender, Garfinkel (cited in West & Zimmerman) coined the term "omnirelevance." One implication of gender's omnirelevance is that any person can be held accountable for her or his status as a woman or a man during their performance of virtually any activity. In other words, we have no choice but to "engage in behavior at the risk of gender assessment" (West & Zimmerman, p. 136). The outcome of this assessment determines whether we are rewarded or sanctioned (for example, are ignored, receive awkward stares, receive threats, or experience violence). Children learn at an early age that they must accomplish gender successfully to be considered competent social actors (West & Zimmerman). This ideological system renews itself as individuals become entrenched in the myth of a gender binary and take it upon themselves to monitor and enforce the gender divide.

Another corollary of gender's omnirelevance is that "doing gender is unavoidable" (West & Zimmerman, 1987, p. 137); one cannot **not** do gender in our society. People will go so far as to do gender **for** someone who is not "appropriately" displaying her or his gender (Lucal, 1999). In other words, lacking traditional gender cues, observers will decide which gender category "should" apply and begin using it to conceptualize the gender-variant person.

As gender emerges out of social situations, it can be understood both as an outcome of and as a rationale for the division between two genders (West & Zimmerman, 1987). Doing gender both relies on and produces a societal belief in the reality of two distinct genders. The differences between groups are portrayed as "fundamental and enduring" (West & Zimmerman). The ensuing social arrangement, supposedly reflecting "natural differences," reinforces and authorizes hierarchical arrangements in which one gender category is valued above the other. Such a binary model, when under the influence of patriarchal culture, spawns a hierarchy of gender categories in which the nonmale category is devalued (Lucal, 1999). This misogyny fuels sexism, homophobia, and heterosexism (Brooks, 2000). In this way, women, gay men, lesbians, bisexuals, and transgendered people share the common prison of the dichotomous gender paradigm (Wilchins, 2004). Similarly, Lorber (1994) viewed gender as "a process of creating distinguishable social statuses for the assignment of rights and responsibilities" (p. 32). This process relies on individuals presenting their genders "clearly" so that privileges may be granted accordingly.

Queer Theory and the End of Gender

Lorber (1996) poignantly asked: "Why, if we wish to treat women and men as equals, there needs to be two sex categories at all" (p. 145). If gender categories are oppressing people, should we not dismantle them? Is this a worthwhile goal for social workers wanting to eliminate gender-based oppressions? I suggest the answer to these questions is "yes." However, to date, there has been no audible call for social workers to strike gender-based oppression at its heart by challenging the gender binary. Queer theory provides a useful postmodern analysis framing the subversion and potential elimination of dichotomous gender constructs. Despite its multidisciplinary roots, queer theory can be organized under a set of core assumptions. Stein and Plummer (1996) outlined four primary tenets of queer theory:

1. an idea that sexual power runs throughout social life and is enforced through boundaries and binary divides;
2. a problematization of sexual and gender categories as inherently unstable and fluid;
3. a rejection of civil rights strategies in favor of deconstruction, decentering, revisionist readings, and anti-assimilationist politics; and
4. a willingness to interrogate areas which normally would not be seen as the terrain of sexuality. (p. 134)

Consistent with queer theory, many authors suggest specific tactics for subverting gender (for example, Cooper, 1999; Lorber, 1994; Lucal, 1999; Morrow, 2004; Risman, 1998; West & Zimmerman, 1987; Wilchins, 2004). Wilchins offered a thoughtful deconstruction of gender, in which language becomes a primary target for social change. West and Zimmerman called concerned individuals to choose the paths of greater resistance and subvert gender by refusing to conform: Undermine gender by insisting on doing it differently. Lucal (1999) considered bending her own gender (for example, through dress, grooming, and body language), a personal contribution toward dissembling oppressive gender structures. At the same time, any person who wishes to undermine the binary gender system faces numerous interactional and structural barriers (Gagné et al., 1997). Gender activists will undoubtedly be met with awkward, and possibly dangerous, social moments.

If eliminating gender seems a dizzying proposal, be assured that it is. Risman (1998) studied families who transcended traditional gender categories and titled her subsequent book *Gender Vertigo*. This is an apt phrase reflecting the disorientation we will surely experience when society begins to transcend gender. Nevertheless, challenging oppressive gender structures and making gender rights a priority are critical steps toward universal freedom from punishment for gender nonconformity (Wilchins, 2004).

Implications for Social Work Practice

What does this mean for social work practice? My conclusion is that social workers must challenge the rigid gender binary, either by eliminating it or expanding it to include more gender possibilities. To accomplish this, it helps to remember our commitment to the person-in-environment perspective, which calls us to be prepared to target one or more systems for change. The following surveys possible applications for the theoretical perspectives discussed thus far.

Different authors (for example, Burgess, 1999; Langer & Martin, 2004) have advocated for eliminating gender identity disorder (GID) from the *Diagnostic and Statistical Manual of Mental Disorders* (4th edition, text revision) (American Psychiatric Association, 2000). This diagnosis is a mechanism by which a major social institution (that is, medicine) blatantly enforces gender role conformity (Brooks, 2000). GID bolsters gender stereotypes by pathologizing behaviors and attitudes that violate the rigid gender dichotomy. The diagnosis first appeared in 1980, shortly after homosexuality was removed from the DSM (Cooper, 1999). Langer and Martin suggested that GID was developed as an indirect way to treat suspected homosexuals. However, obtaining sex reassignment surgery requires a diagnosis of GID (Burgess). So, paradoxically, transgendered people desiring surgical intervention are dependent on being labeled with this diagnosis—one built on gender stereotypes. Authors who have argued for eliminating GID have suggested that the treatments of choice for gender-variant clients are to provide accurate information about gender, hormones, and sex reassignment surgery and help them (and their families) learn to love and accept their gender-variant selves (Burgess; Cooper; Langer & Martin).

Along these lines, social workers can present a transgender identity as a viable identity option for gender-variant clients. Cooper (1999) voiced concern that too many transgendered people internalize the socially constructed gender binary and, therefore, experience extreme intrapsychic pressure to pick either a male or female body or gender identity. Social workers can help relieve this pressure by educating clients about the sex—gender continuum and the social construction of gender and by giving them permission to identify themselves without reference to the traditional binary (NASW, 2003; Swann & Herbert, 1999). Health and mental health professionals are shifting from encouraging gender-variant individuals to adjust to one of two gender options to supporting self-identification as a transgendered person (Bockting et al., 2004). Today, more transgendered people are claiming space outside the gender binary (Cooper).

The emergence of a visible transgender community facilitated this paradigm shift (Bockting et al., 2004). The transgender community has become increasingly politically active in recent years. Groups such as the Intersex Society of

North America, GenderPac, and the National Transgender Advocacy Coalition are engaged in sophisticated public education and political advocacy efforts. Social workers are ethically obligated to take political action to create just and equitable laws. Therefore, social workers can advocate for workplace protections, relationship supports, immigration rights, and legal identity recognition for transgendered individuals and their families. At the same time, social workers can encourage transgendered clients to become politically involved, which can increase self-esteem and self-acceptance (Lombardi, 1999).

On a macrocultural level, we can empower our transgendered clients by working to alleviate the societal pressures they feel (Burgess, 1999). Ending gender oppression to help transgendered people is analogous to finding structural solutions to eliminate poverty, rather than trying to help individual poor people cope with their unfortunate plight in a hostile environment. We cannot end gender oppression by ignoring the inherent oppressiveness of the hierarchical gender binary (McPhail, 2004; Wilchins, 2004). Social workers can work to disrupt the traditional gender binary and advocate for gender rights—the freedom to be one's authentic self.

The first step for social workers in ending gender oppression is to challenge gender stereotyping unceasingly. Given the ubiquitous nature of gender stereotyping in our society, social workers need to be acutely perceptive and prepared to challenge gender stereotyping in any setting at any time. This may be accomplished in numerous ways depending on the specific context. Interpersonal strategies may include requesting clarification when gender-stereotyped jokes or comments are heard; reversing gender-stereotyped roles in everyday etiquette (for example, opening doors for others); or expressing reservations about gender-stereotyped assumptions of a person's appearance, personality, or sexual orientation. Introspective social workers can identify ways in which they may personally be conforming to gender stereotypes against their own sense of authenticity. With courage, they may choose to pursue a more genuine gender expression, thereby leading by example with their refusal to participate in an oppressive gender system.

In addition, social workers can educate the public on gender diversity (Bush & Sainz, 2001; NASW, 2003; Pierce, 2001). The specific manner in which this is done will depend on our community contexts and the nature of coalitions we build with entities that share our concerns. Our educational strategies may involve writing letters to the editor; talking with our elected officials; sponsoring a public lecture series; facilitating community discussion groups; creating professional development events; distributing educational materials at our local LGBT Pride Festivals; or hosting performances that challenge traditional notions of gender (for example, films, plays, and drag shows) and engaging the audience in discussions of the social construction of gender.

Whatever the forum, we must be capable of sophisticated conversations on gender if we hope to cure the social diseases of sexism, homophobia, heterosexism, and transphobia. In all our communications, we can intentionally inject the language of diversity and inclusivity into a gendered world. In doing so, we begin changing the broader gender discourse, lessening its oppressive power. Accomplishing this demands our adoption of accurate, albeit unconventional, theoretical frameworks for understanding gender (Bush & Sainz, 2001)—a significant intellectual challenge to our field. Two such frameworks—queer theory and social constructionism—have been suggested here as worthy of our consideration.

Future Research

Social work research can take many paths from this point. Although there is some consensus in the social work literature on best practices with transgendered people, most of these claims are based on anecdotal evidence. Such writings have emerged from an urgent need to jumpstart a gender-transgender dialogue among social workers. Of course, this is important information from social workers who have direct knowledge of the transgender community. Eventually, however, the profession will need the results of intentionally planned research projects to delve into the myriad facets of practice with transgendered people. There is also a need for more articles related to transgender issues in mainstream social work journals. Currently, such articles seem relegated to specialty journals, where they risk being read only by "the choir."

Fundamental questions regarding social work's role with the transgender community remain unanswered. For example, how often do transgender people seek services from social workers? How many social workers regularly provide services to this population? What do transgendered people want social workers to do? What are their lived experiences? What attitudes do social workers hold toward transgendered people?

Earlier studies have documented disturbingly high levels of homophobia and heterosexism among social workers (for example, Berkman & Zinberg, 1997; Wisniewski & Toomey, 1987). The links among sexism, homophobia, and heterosexism are well established in the literature, so, given the common root of gender stereotypes these oppressions share, we might expect to find discomfort or phobic responses among social workers toward transgendered people. Conversely, from a strengths perspective we need to identify trans-affirming social workers and learn from them. This could include assessing their skills, previous experiences, and theoretical frameworks and articulating what qualities make them trans-affirming. Ultimately, social work researchers need to establish alliances with the transgender community and create forums for transgender people to tell their own stories. There is much to learn from the transgender community about courage, resilience, authenticity, and social justice.

Social work students need to learn empirically supported and emerging theories of gender (McPhail, 2004). This will be no easy task. Not only is such content a radical departure from what many students perceive to be a fundamental certainty, it also conflicts with various religious and political beliefs. Nonetheless, we need to identify best educational practices for teaching about gender and gender theory, transgendered people, and cultural competence with this population.

To begin comprehending what a world with three or more genders (or even no genders) might look like, we could study people who are transcending the gender binary. Detailed case studies and phenomenological research would provide rich data to help social workers understand the nuances of being transgendered. From this, we may discover strategies for managing our own "gender vertigo" and envisioning a society beyond the gender binary.

Conclusion

I have argued that the transgender community is marginalized and misunderstood. They face discrimination at every turn, which too frequently leads to self-rejection or desperate acts to alleviate distress and survive. As the profession dedicated to serving vulnerable and disenfranchised populations, social work is positioned to take a closer look at the societal forces impinging on the lives of transgendered people and consider ways to dismantle the oppressive gender structure in society. Queer theory and social constructionism theoretical perspectives could effectively frame social work practice with the transgender community and our broader efforts to end all forms of gender oppression.

References

1. American Psychiatric Association. (2000). *Diagnostic and statistical manual of mental disorders* (4th ed., text rev.). Washington, DC: Author.
2. Bern, S. L. (1993). *The lenses of gender: Transforming the debate on sexual inequality.* New Haven, CT: Yale University Press.
3. Berkman, C. S., & Zinberg, G. (1997). Homophobia and heterosexism in social workers. *Social Work, 42*, 319–332.
4. Bockting, W., Robinson, B., Benner, A., & Scheltema, K. (2004). Patient satisfaction with transgender health services. *Journal of Sex & Marital Therapy, 30*, 277–294.
5. Brooks, F. L. (2000). Beneath contempt: The mistreatment of non-traditional/gender atypical boys. *Journal of Gay & Lesbian Social Services, 12*(1/2), 107–115.
6. Burgess, C. (1999). Internal and external stress factors associated with the identity development of transgendered youth. *Journal of Gay & Lesbian Social Services, 10*(3/4), 35–47.
7. Bush, I. R., & Sainz, A. (2001). Competencies at the intersection of difference, tolerance, and prevention of hate crimes. *Journal of Gay & Lesbian Social Services, 13*(1/2), 205–224.
8. Butler, J. (1990). *Gender trouble: Feminism and the subversion of identity.* New York: Routledge.
9. Conway, L. (2002). How frequently does transsexualism occur? Retrieved December 12, 2004, from http://ai.eecs.urnich.edu/people/conway/TS/TSprevalence.html
10. Cooper, K. (1999). Practice with transgendered youth and their families. *Journal of Gay & Lesbian Social Services, 10*(3/4), 111–129.
11. Donovan, T. (2001). Being transgender and older: A first person account. *Journal of Gay & Lesbian Social Services, 13*(4), 19–22.
12. Gagné, P., Tewksbury, R., & McGaughey, D. (1997). Coming out and crossing over: Identity formation and proclamation in a transgender community. *Gender & Society, 11*, 478–508.
13. Grise-Owens, E., Vessels, J., & Owens, L. W. (2004). Organizing for change: One city's journey toward justice. *Journal of Gay & Lesbian Social Services, 16*(3/4), 1–15.
14. Hunter, S., & Hickerson, J. C. (2003). *Affirmative practice: Understanding and working with lesbian, gay, bisexual, and transgender persons.* Washington, DC: NASW Press.
15. Intersex Society of North America. (2004). Frequency: How common are intersex conditions? Retrieved October 9, 2004, from http://www.isna.org/drupal/node/view/91
16. Langer, S. J., & Martin, J. I. (2004). How dresses can make you mentally ill: Examining gender identity disorder in children. *Child and Adolescent Social Work, 21*, 5–24.
17. Lesser, J. G. (1999). When your son becomes your daughter: A mother's adjustment to a transgender child. *Families in Society, 80*, 182–189.
18. Lev, A. I. (2004). *Transgender emergence: Therapeutic guidelines for working with gender-variant individuals and their families.* New York: Haworth Press.
19. Lombardi, E. L. (1999). Integration within a transgender social network and its effects on members' social and political activity. *Journal of Homosexuality, 37*(1), 109–126.
20. Lorber, J. (1994). *Paradoxes of gender.* New Haven, CT: Yale University Press.
21. Lorber, J. (1996). Beyond the binaries: Depolarizing the categories of sex, sexuality, and gender. *Sociological Inquiry, 66*, 143–159.

22. Lucal, B. (1999). What it means to be gendered me: Life on the boundaries of a dichotomous gender system. *Gender & Society, 13*, 781–797.
23. Mallon, G. P. (1999a). A call for organizational trans-formation. *Journal of Gay & Lesbian Social Services, 10*(3/4), 131–142.
24. Mallon, G. P. (1999b). A glossary of transgendered definitions. *Journal of Gay & Lesbian Social Services, 10*(3/4), 143–145.
25. McPhail, B. A. (2004). Questioning gender and sexuality binaries: What queer theorists, transgendered individuals, and sex researchers can teach social work. *Journal of Gay & Lesbian Social Services, 17*(1), 3–21.
26. Morrow, D. F. (2004). Social work practice with gay, lesbian, bisexual, and transgender adolescents. *Families in Society, 85*, 91–99.
27. National Association of Social Workers. (2000). *Code of ethics of the National Association of Social Workers.* Washington, DC: Author.
28. National Association of Social Workers. (2003). Transgender and gender identity issues. In *Social work speaks: National Association of Social Workers policy statements 2003–2006* (6th ed., pp. 345–349). Washington, DC: Author.
29. Pierce, D. (2001). Language, violence, and queer people: Social and cultural change strategies. *Journal of Gay & Lesbian Social Services, 13*, 47–61.
30. Risman, B. J. (1998). *Gender vertigo: American families in transition.* New Haven, CT: Yale University Press.
31. Rollins, J., & Hirsch, H. N. (2003). Sexual identities and political engagements: A queer survey. *Social Politics, 10*, 290–313.
32. Stein, A., & Plummer, K. (1996). "I can't even think straight": "Queer" theory and the missing sexual revolution in sociology. In S. Seidman (Ed.), *Queer theory/sociology* (pp. 129–144). Cambridge, MA: Blackwell.
33. Swann, S., & Herbert, S. E. (1999). Ethical issues in the mental health treatment of gender dysphoric adolescents. *Journal of Gay & Lesbian Social Services, 10*(3/4), 19–34.
34. West, C., & Zimmerman, D. H. (1987). Doing gender. *Gender & Society, 1*, 125–151.
35. Wilchins, R. (2004). *Queer theory, gender theory: An instant primer.* Los Angeles: Alyson Books.
36. Wisniewski, J. J., & Toomey, B. G. (1987). Are social workers homophobic? *Social Work, 32*, 454–455.

6

Perspectives on Familiness

CONNECTING CORE COMPETENCIES *in this chapter*

| Professional Identity | Ethical Practice | Critical Thinking | **Diversity in Practice** | **Human Rights & Justice** | Research Based Practice | **Human Behavior** | Policy Practice | Practice Contexts | Engage Assess Intervene Evaluate |

FAMILINESS

You may be wondering about the term *familiness* used in the title of this chapter. Why not "Perspectives on Family" or "Perspectives on *the* Family"? In this chapter, as throughout this book, our goal is to develop the most inclusive and varied set of perspectives that we can to think about family. To accomplish this we need to accept at the outset that *family* comes in many different shapes and sizes and accomplishes many different things for many different people. In order to respect this rich diversity, it is helpful to think not of *family* in the sense that there is one universal "best" or "most appropriate" family structure or set of family functions. Instead we want to begin with an expanded notion of *family* as multiple and diverse in both its forms and its functions.

The concept of *familiness* allows us to broaden what is often (traditionally) a quite limited notion of family. This concept reminds us as individuals and as members of particular families to think always about possible alternate structures and sets of functions that constitute *family* for others. The notion of familiness allows us to continue to respect the central role that family plays in virtually all our lives, but it also allows us room to accept that the family tasks fulfilled, the family needs met, the family structures (forms) used, and the environmental contexts in which family exists for us and for others are all subject to great variability and difference.

Our goal here is twofold. We want to develop more flexible, fluid, and multifaceted perspectives from which to learn about alternate family forms and structures. We also want to more fully understand traditional family structures and functions. Perhaps the most important implication of this somewhat unconventional term, *familiness,* is its use as a reminder to us that *family* as a social institution and *families* as the intimate and individualized arenas in which we carry out so much of our lives can and do change.

Familiness includes the traditional functions and responsibilities assigned by societies to families, such as childbearing, child rearing, intimacy, and security. It also recognizes the great diversity in structures, values, and contexts that define family for different people. In addition to traditional concerns when thinking about family, such as structure and function, *familiness* includes consideration of culture, gender, sexual orientation, age, disabling conditions, income, and spirituality.

This part of our journey toward understanding human behavior and the social environment within the context of familiness is not separate from, but is quite interconnected with, the concerns, issues, and perspectives we have explored in the previous chapters. The content of this chapter will be interwoven with the perspectives and information we explore in the chapters to come. We noted in Chapters 4 and 5 that families, groups, organizations, communities, and the international arena provide the environments or contexts in which individual behavior and development takes place. Familiness, our focus in this chapter, is a major context and has far-reaching influences on the developmental experiences and challenges of individuals. Individual members of families simultaneously have far-reaching and intense influences on the structure and functioning of families. Families and family issues simultaneously influence and are influenced by the groups, organizations, communities, and, increasingly, the global arena with which they interact and of which they are a part. This perspective is consistent with the systems perspective we explored in Chapter 3.

It is contended here, in fact, that familiness is a kind of intersection in our journey to more comprehensive understanding of HBSE. At this intersection our individual lives and experiences meet and are influenced by other individuals and other systems around us. Familiness has significant consequences for the choices we make about the travels we take later in life and for the quality of our experiences on those journeys. At the same time the issues related to familiness become major elements in our continuing developmental journeys.

In many ways, especially when we include alternative notions of *family* in our thinking, the boundaries between systems are blurred. It is often difficult to tell where family stops and group, organization, community, and the rest of the world begin. *Family* is sometimes considered a specific type of small group, for example. This interweaving should not be seen as troublesome, however. It is yet another example of the ambiguity that threads its way along our journey to understanding HBSE. We will attempt to use this ambiguity to appreciate the interdependence of these system levels and as a means of further developing a sense of strength in the ambiguous and interdependent nature of family and other system levels.

We will find, as we explore the various models of family in this chapter, that many of those approaches operate from similar assumptions to those of the approaches to understanding individual behavior and development. Many perspectives on family, for example, assume a stage-based, chronological, often linear progression of development. For example, in some cases we will find notions of family development to be strikingly similar to and consistent with Erikson's stage-based model for individual development. This is especially true of traditional perspectives on family. It is true to some extent also for some alternative approaches to family. As in the case of alternative models of individual development, we will find that alternative notions about family often begin with traditional models as departure points from which to then alter, expand upon, or offer contrasting perspectives on family functions and structures. Before exploring traditional and alternate perspectives on family we will consider some of the implications for social workers of how *family* is defined and some current issues and realities facing families today.

SOCIAL WORK AND FAMILIES

Social Work Implications

Hartman and Laird stress the importance to social workers of how *family* is defined. They note that the definitions of *family* that we use have a direct impact on the nature of the practice models we use for working with families. The definition of *family* also directly influences the kind of policies we have at local, state, national, and international levels regarding families. For example, as we noted in an earlier chapter, if the definition of *family* does not include gay and lesbian families or other persons living together as families but who are not legally recognized, the members of these families will not be eligible for benefits and rights typically available to family members. This can include such wide-ranging benefits and rights as coverage by health and life insurance policies or family visitation policies in hospitals. Hartman and Laird also stress how our personal definitions of *family* and our own experiences in families can be strong influences on how we deal with family issues in our practice of social work (1983:26).

Current Influences on Families

Perhaps the most significant reality facing families today is that of change. What this means for increasing numbers of families is that the so-called normal **nuclear family**—the husband as breadwinner, wife as homemaker, and their offspring all living in a residence apart from their other relatives—does not apply. Some of the forces propelling this climate of change include the feminist movement, economic insecurity pressing more families to have multiple breadwinners, immigration, rising rates of divorce, single-parent households, remarriage, domestic partnership, and gay marriage (Walsh 2003).

There is growing concern about many other changes as well. Walsh points out that one out of four babies is born to an unwed mother and one in four teenage girls gets pregnant. Over half of births to teenage girls overall and over 90 percent of births to African American teenage girls are nonmarital. The results of these "children having children" is that they are at a very high risk of long-term poverty, poor-quality parenting, and many other health and psychosocial problems of concern to social workers (2003). However, there are recent indications that rates of teen pregnancy are beginning to decline.

SEHB: The Social Environment and Family

Policy Practice

Professional social workers understand the significant role played by policy in service delivery. Do you think the family unit should drive so many of the policies that impact service to enhance human well-being and quality of life? Why? Why not?

Family as a policy instrument for social workers

The family (household) is one of the primary units of analysis used for policy development in the United States. For example, the family or household is a key unit of data collection and analysis of the U.S. Bureau of the Census. Census data are, in turn, used to define and set policy in such fundamental areas as the definition of poverty and the determination of eligibility for many human service programs. Family or household is the unit of study and analysis used by many researchers trying to understand a wide variety of conditions and patterns that influence quality of life or well-being at a number of system levels in addition to families, including individuals, communities, and society at large.

Family and poverty

The National Survey of America's Families (NSAF) conducted by the Urban Institute collected and analyzed data on a number of areas related to individual and family well-being by surveying over 40,000 households representing over 100,000 people in 13 different states (Adi-Habib, Safir & Triple n.d.). The NSAF findings included information that 46 percent of low-income nonelderly persons "lived in a family experiencing food problems in the previous year" (Zedlewski 2003). While family poverty cuts across race and ethnicity, whites are less likely than other groups to be poor. African American and Hispanic heritage families are about three times more likely to live in poverty than white families (Staveteig and Wigton 2000).

The Digital Divide: Technology and Families—The Influence of Race and Income

Assessing the distribution of and access to technology continues to be an important factor in economic and social well-being. While Internet access and use continues to increase among individuals and families, it is important to recognize that access and use varies considerably depending on a number of different individual demographic variables and household or family income. See Table 6.1. As technology becomes increasingly important in economic and social well-being, more attention is being given to the distribution of and access to technology across different groups within the population. Much of this attention is directed toward assessing the ability of families and households to acquire and use technology.

Kennedy and Agron point out that "equal opportunity has been a cornerstone of this nation for more than two centuries. But society has not always measured up to that ideal, and you don't have to go far to see the disparity between the exclusive suburban neighborhoods of the affluent and the decrepit slums of America's inner cities or the ramshackle homes of the rural poor" (1999). They also note the optimism among many educators and leaders that "the rapidly accelerating power of technology and the massive

Table 6.1   Demographics of Internet Users
Below is the percentage of each group who use the Internet, according to our December 2008 survey. As an example, 75% of adult women use the Internet.

	Use the Internet
Total adults	**74%**
Women	75
Men	73
Age	
18–29	87%
30–49	82
50–64	72
65+	41
Race/ethnicity	
White, Non-Hispanic	77%
Black, Non-Hispanic	64
Hispanic**	58
Geography	
Urban	71%
Suburban	74
Rural	63
Household income	
Less than $30,000/yr	57%
$30,000–$49,999	77
$50,000–$74,999	90
$75,000+	94
Educational attainment	
Less than High School	35%
High School	67
Some College	85
College +	95

Source: Pew Internet & American Life Project, November 19-December 20, 2008 Tracking Survey. N = 2,253 adults, 18 and older, including 502 cell phone interviews. Margin of error is ± 2%.

Please note that prior to our January 2005 survey, the question used to identify Internet users read, Do you ever go online to access the Internet or World Wide Web or to send and receive email? The current two-part question wording reads, Do you use the Internet, at least occasionally? and Do you send or receive email, at least occasionally?

**Figures for Hispanics in this survey include both English- and Spanish-speaking respondents.

Last updated January 6, 2009.

Human Rights & Justice

As professional social workers, we recognize the global interconnections of oppression. After reading the section, "Immigration Classifications, Preferences, and Categories" (on the next page), what is your conclusion about whether the U.S. immigration policy helps or hinders our efforts to address global oppression?

amounts of information available on the Internet . . . could close the chasm between the haves and the have-nots" (Kennedy and Agron 1999). Kennedy and Agron caution, however, that "technology won't be able to close the digital divide if the divide itself is preventing the have-nots from gaining access to the technology" (1999).

According to a report by the U.S. government called *Falling Through the Net: Defining the Digital Divide,* "information tools, such as the personal computer and the Internet, are increasingly critical to economic success and personal advancement" (National Telecommunications and Information Administration 1999). At the same time the **digital divide**—the gap between those who have access to these information tools and those who do not—is a serious and complex concern. Who has access to technology and who is equipped to use that technology are important factors in determining social and economic well-being, a central concern for social workers.

The digital divide is an example of the complex and multilayered impact of poverty on individuals, families, communities, and nations around the world, especially developing countries. The complex inter-relatedness of poverty and technology is a particularly dramatic example of how multiple factors must be assessed, understood, and addressed in order to reduce poverty. In the case of the digital divide, some of the most influential factors that must be understood are income, race/ethnicity, geographic location, and education.

While the digital divide may seem primarily a matter of newer information technology such as computers and the Internet, it is also very much about access to such basic technology as the telephone, because the primary means of accessing the Internet from home is either through telephone lines and modem connections (either regular or high speed DSL or through cable TV companies). While most homes have telephones today, there are still many homes without telephone service. The patterns associated with not having telephone service are closely linked to other factors associated with unequal access to information technology and to higher poverty rates such as race/ethnicity, education, income, and geographic location. This can also be the case with access to or the ability to afford cable TV service.

FAMILY AND GLOBAL ISSUES: IMMIGRATION

Immigration to the United States is considered in this chapter concerning families because the majority of people who immigrate do so in the context of families. According to the American Immigration Lawyers Association (AILA), "most legal immigrants, about 8 out of 11, come to join close family members." According to AILA, "family-sponsored immigrants enter as either immediate relatives—spouses, unmarried minor children, parents of U.S. citizens, or through the *family preference system,* for relatives of permanent residents and siblings of U.S. citizens." The AILA notes that "it is easy to see that family reunification is the cornerstone of our legal immigration policy. It is truly one of the most visible areas in government policy in which we support and strengthen family values. We acknowledge that family unification translates into strong families who build strong communities." The second priority is to allow in a relatively small number of immigrants with skills needed by businesses and industries when citizens with those skills are not available. The third priority of immigration policy is to allow oppressed persons fleeing religious and political persecution a haven. The intent is to offer protection to persons facing "ethnic cleansing, religious oppression, torture, and even death" because of their beliefs or practices (American Immigration Lawyers Association 1999).

Immigration Classifications, Preferences, and Categories

Social workers are often called upon to provide services to immigrants and their families. In order to provide service effectively, it is important to understand who can actually immigrate to the U.S. The U.S. Department of Justice, Immigration and Naturalization Service is the unit of government responsible for enforcing U.S. immigration statutes. In doing so, a set of immigration classifications, a list of preferences for types of immigrants, and a number of "categories" of persons eligible to apply for immigration are identified and defined. Table 6.2, Immigration Classifications, includes information on basic immigrant classifications and the U.S. government preferences associated with them.

Table 6.2   Immigration Classifications

Family-Based Immigration	*First Preference*
Immediate relatives	• Unmarried sons or daughters over 21 years of age of USC
• Spouses of US citizens (USCs)	*Second Preference*
• Unmarried children under 21 years of age of USCs	• Spouses and children of Legal Permanent Resident (LPR)
• Parents of USCs	• Unmarried sons or daughters over 21 years of age of LPR
	Third Preference
	• Married children of USC
	Fourth Preference
	• Siblings of adult USC
Employment-Based Immigration	*First Preference*
	• Priority Workers
	• Aliens of *extraordinary* ability in the sciences, arts, education, business, or athletics
	• Outstanding professors or researchers
	• Certain managers and executives transferred to the United States to work for their foreign employer or a U.S. affiliate or subsidiary firm
	Second Preference
	• Professionals with advanced degrees, and persons with exceptional ability
	Third Preference
	• Skilled workers, professional, and other workers
	Fourth Preference
	• Certain special immigrants (See descriptions in Table 6.3)
	Fifth Preference
	• Employment creation (investors)

Source: U.S Department of Homeland Security, U.S. Citizenship and Immigration Services. Available at: http://www.uscis.gov/portal/site/uscis/menuitem.5af9bb95919f35e66f614176543f6d1a/?vgnextoid=35e417d8d673e010VgnVCM1000000ec d190aRCRD&vgnextchannel=ca408875d714d010VgnVCM10000048f3d6a1 _____ Retrieved May 21, 2009

The "Special Immigrant" classification referred to in Table 6.2 is described in more detail in Table 6.3. In addition, some subcategories whose meanings are less self-evident are defined.

Immigrants and Oppression/Discrimination

Given the intent to address oppression through immigration policy, it is unfortunate that immigrants may actually face discrimination and oppression in this country because of their immigrant status. Immigration has become a divisive issue among many individuals and groups in the United States. Even though the United States is in many ways a nation of immigrants, many people tend

Table 6.3   Special Immigrant Categories

Basic Description	Additional Information
Employees of certain Panama Canal companies	N/A
Physicians	N/A
Foreign medical graduates who have been in the United States for a certain time	N/A
Foreign workers who were formerly long-time employees of the United States government	N/A
Retired officers or employees of certain international organizations who have lived in the United States for a certain time	N/A
Certain armed forces members	N/A
Afghani and Iraqi nationals who worked with the U.S. Armed Forces as a translator for at least 12 months	N/A
Amerasian	• An alien who was born in Korea, Vietnam, Laos, Kampuchea, or Thailand after December 31, 1950, and before October 22, 1982, and was fathered by a U.S. citizen
Special Immigrant Juvenile	• Is unmarried and less than 21 years old • Has been declared dependent upon a juvenile court in the United States or who such a court has legally committed to, or placed under the custody of, an agency or department of a state and who has been found eligible for long-term foster care • Has been the subject of administrative or judicial proceedings in which it was determined that it would not be in the juvenile's best interests to be returned to the juvenile's or his/her parent's country of nationality or last habitual residence

Basic Description	Additional Information
Self-petitioning battered or abused spouse or child of a U.S. citizen or lawful permanent resident	• Are now the spouse or child of an abusive U.S. citizen or lawful permanent resident • Are eligible for immigrant classification based on that relationship; are now residing in the United States; • Have resided in the United States with the U.S. citizen or lawful permanent resident abuser in the past • Have been battered by, or have been the subject of extreme cruelty perpetrated by • Your U.S. citizen or lawful permanent resident spouse during the marriage; or are the parent of a child who has been battered by or has been the subject of extreme cruelty perpetrated by your abusive citizen or lawful permanent resident spouse during your marriage; or your citizen or lawful permanent resident parent while residing with that parent; are a person of good moral character • Are a person whose removal or deportation would result in extreme hardship to yourself, or to your child if you are a spouse • If you are a spouse who entered into the marriage to the citizen or lawful permanent resident abuser in good faith

Workers for recognized religious organizations	• An alien who for the past two (2) years has been a member of a religious denomination which has a bona fide nonprofit, religious organization in the U.S.
	• Who has been carrying on the vocation, professional work, or other work described below, continuously for the past two (2) years; and seeks to enter the U.S. to work solely
	  • as a minister of that denomination
	  • in a professional capacity in a religious vocation or occupation for that organization
	  • in a religious vocation or occupation for the organization or its nonprofit affiliate

Source: U. S. Department of Justice. (2000). *Petition for Amerasian, Widow(er), or Special Immigrant: Form I-360.*

to be fearful and suspicious of immigrants. As is the case so often with prejudice and discrimination, many of the assumptions about immigrants are based on little fact. For example, some people argue that immigration should be reduced or ended because immigrants are a drain on the economy and public services. In fact, "immigrants pay more in taxes than they receive in public services, and are less likely to be on public assistance than U.S. born residents" (Hernandez and McGoldrick 1999:169). According to Hernandez and McGoldrick, "legal and undocumented immigrant families pay an estimated $70 billion a year in taxes while receiving $43 billion in services" (1999:169).

Others believe the majority of immigrants are in the United States illegally. AILA reports that "undocumented immigrants constitute only 1 percent of the total U.S. population and, contrary to popular belief, most of these immigrants do not enter the United States illegally by crossing our border with Canada or Mexico. . . . [Of those] here illegally, 6 out of 10 enter the U.S. legally with a student, tourist, or business visa and become illegal when they stay in the United States after their visas expire" (Hernandez and McGoldrick 1999).

Impact of Immigration on Families and Children

The process of immigration is stressful for all immigrant families and, depending on the circumstances that led to immigration, may be a challenge to the very survival of family members. Hernandez and McGoldrick point out that

> People immigrate for many reasons: for work, study, political and economic survival, or increased life options. Families may migrate to escape oppression, famine, or life without a future. Although migration has become the norm for many people worldwide, it is still a stressful and long-lasting transition and one that is generally not recognized by our society as a whole (1999:170).

The stresses that accompany immigration vary according to the family member and the point in the life course of family members. For example, "acculturation processes can threaten the family's structural composition by reversing hierarchies and family roles." Young children may acculturate more quickly than older family members. As children move out of the family into school and community, they may move away from both their parents and their original culture. In addition, as children move into the new culture more quickly than their parents do, they may "take on the task of interpreting the new

Table 6.4	**Children in Immigrant Families Expanded Their Share of All U.S. Children Between 1990 and 2007**	
	Children in Immigrant Families	
Year	Number (thousands)	Percent of all U.S. children
1990	8,331	13
2000	13,538	19
2007	16,548	22

Source: PRB analysis of decennial census and American Community Survey in Mather, 2009:2.

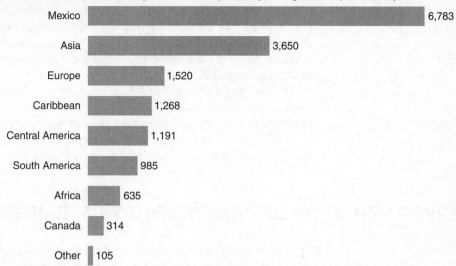

Figure 6.1
About two-fifths of children in immigrant families were born in Mexico or had a parent who was born in Mexico.
(PRB analysis of the 2007 American Community Survey in Mather, 2009:3)

culture for the parents," and parental leadership may be threatened (Hernandez and McGoldrick 1999). Given both the complexities and the potential for oppression as immigrant families make the transition to the United States, it is important for social workers to recognize and understand the impact of this social environmental context on the human behavior of family members.

Reading 6.1 addresses in some detail the impact of immigration on families and children. The author also provides a helpful summary of the stages of the migration/immigration process.

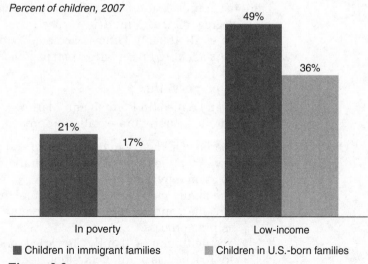

Figure 6.2
Children in immigrant families are much more likely than other children to live in low-income or poor families, which has negative long-term consequences.
(PRB analysis of the 2007 American Community Survey in Mather, 2009:2)

Mather defines children in immigrant families as "those under age 18 who were born outside of the United States or who reside with at least one foreign-born parent." In addition, she notes, "people are classified as 'foreign-born' if they are not U.S. citizens or if they are U.S. citizens by naturalization" (Mather 2009:2). Table 6.4 shows a quite dramatic increase in the number of children in immigrant families.

By far the largest increase in the number of children in immigrant families is among children from Mexico. Figure 6.1 shows the distribution of immigrant children in the United States and the countries of their origin.

Children in immigrant families experience poverty to a far greater extent than other children. This can be seen in Figure 6.2.

APPROACHES TO UNDERSTANDING FAMILINESS

Before proceeding to explore traditional and alternative perspectives on familiness, we will examine two approaches to understanding family complexity. First we will explore life-course theory, which can help us understand the many levels of individual development and interaction with the social environment that operate in families. Then we will explore a family-centered approach to working with families. Family-centered social work practice is an emerging perspective that has much in common with strengths-based social work, with appreciation for diversities and with a number of other dimensions of alternative paradigm thinking.

Family-Centered Practice

An alternative approach to thinking about and working with families is referred to as a **family-centered approach**. Rounds et al. point out that "In a family-centered approach, family members, not professionals, determine who constitutes the family" (1994:7). In addition, they explain that "A family-centered approach stresses family-professional collaboration, which requires a high degree of trust, mutual respect, and participation by both parties" (Rounds et al. 1994:9). Often associated with a family-centered approach to practice is a family preservation perspective.

Family preservation
Ronnau and Sallee (in Ronnau and Marlow 1993:540–541) describe the values that underlie a family preservation approach:

- People of all ages can best develop and their lives be enhanced, with few exceptions, by remaining with their family or relying on their family as an important resource.
- The family members' ethnic, cultural, and religious background, as well as values, and community ties are important resources to be used in the helping process.
- The definition of "family" is varied, and each family should be approached as a unique system.
- Policies at the local, state, and national levels should be formulated to strengthen, empower, and support families.
- The family members themselves are crucial partners in the helping process.

▶ Family members should be recognized as being in charge in order to resolve their own problems and avoid dependence upon the social service system.

▶ The dignity and right to privacy of all family members should be respected.

▶ Families have the potential to change, and most troubled families want to do so.

We will continue, as we proceed on our journey to understanding both traditional and alternative notions of family, to consider the social work practice implications of these changes occurring in families. For these and other reasons family provides the context for much social work practice. Families can be both barriers to and resources for reaching our potential as humans.

TRADITIONAL MODELS

The notion of family development as a series of predictable stages through which families pass is perhaps the oldest and most common framework for organizing traditional models for understanding family behavior and development. Duvall (1971:113–114) notes that some early stage models were quite simple. One early model consisted only of two stages:

1. the expanding family stage, taking the family from its formation to the time its children are grown; and
2. the contracting family stage, during which children leave the home and only the parents remain.

Duvall also describes a 1931 four-stage model. This model consisted of:

1. married couples just starting out;
2. couples with one or more children;
3. couples with one or more adult self-supporting children; and
4. couples growing old.

Another four-stage model she described focused on the formal education system as a major determiner of family developmental stages. This model consisted of:

1. preschool family;
2. grade school family;
3. high school family; and
4. all-adult family (Kirkpatrick et al. in Duvall 1971:114).

Some later stage-centered models of family life cycle included as many as twenty-four stages (Duvall 1971:114–115).

As noted above, many models of family development bear a striking resemblance to stage-based, chronological models of individual development, such as Erikson's model of individual psychosocial development. This similarity is not coincidental. Traditional approaches to family development are child focused or **child centered.** The developmental stages that an individual child passes through, according to many traditional models, in effect drive the development of the family. The family is pressed to change or react as a result of changes in the individual developmental stages of the child, usually the eldest child (Devore and Schlesinger 1991:274). For example, the birth of a child—the onset of the first stage of individual development—results in a shift from one developmental stage to another for the family. As we explore models of family development keyed to developmental stages of children, we will question the assumptions and inclusiveness of such models. For example, if all conceptualizations of family are premised on the bearing and rearing of children, are childless individuals or couples by definition excluded from having family (familiness)? We shall further explore this issue later in this chapter.

Traditional Definitions

Before exploring in more detail some models of family that are consistent with traditional paradigm thinking, it is perhaps helpful to define what is meant by *traditional family*. Traditional definitions of family have generally focused either on structure or function. Structural definitions focus on relationship among members that are based on marriage, blood, or adoption. Functional definitions focus on tasks performed by family for its members or for society, such as child rearing, meeting affectional needs of adults, and transmitting the values of the larger society (Hartman and Laird 1983:27–28).

Some traditional definitions have focused on both structure and function, such as Duvall's (1971) definition and list of family functions below. Here a family is defined as:

> a unity of interacting persons related by ties of marriage, birth, or adoption, whose central purpose is to create and maintain a common culture which promotes the physical, mental, emotional, and social development of each of its members. (1971:5)

She suggests that "modern" families implement this definition through six functions:

1. affection between husband and wife, parents, and children, and among the generations;
2. personal security and acceptance of each family member for the unique individual he [she] is and for the potential he [she] represents;
3. satisfaction and a sense of purpose;
4. continuity of companionship and association;
5. social placement and socialization;
6. controls and sense of what is right. (Duvall 1971:5)

Duvall suggests that this is a "modern" definition and outline of functions in contrast to "older" notions of the family. She suggests that it is modern because it replaces older notions of family in which "women 'slave over a hot stove,' preparing meals from foodstuffs they have grown and processed"; family members wear "homemade" garments; health and medical care is primarily provided by family members; education of children is done primarily by parents; children's play is supervised by parents rather than by day-care service staff; family protection is "dependent upon a rifle over the fireplace," instead of being provided by formal fire and police agencies (1971:3–4).

Such a "modern" definition suggests a great deal of historical change in notions of family arrangements and functions. Nevertheless both Duvall's notions of the "older" and the "modern" family reflect quite traditional perspectives on family. These notions suggest, for example, that a child-centered, two-parent, heterosexual white family with sufficient access to the resources necessary to carry out required family functions is the norm for family form and function. They suggest a definition of family with much in common with the "norm of rightness" we explored earlier (see Chapter 2) central to the "privilege" dimension of the traditional and dominant paradigm.

Neither the "older" nor the "modern" notion of family communicates a significant degree of potential for flexible alternatives in structure and function to include diverse family forms. Such family structures as extended families of multiple generations or "fictive kin" systems that include non-blood-related members of many African American families are not likely to be included. (We will explore the concept of fictive kin in more detail later in this chapter.) Functional definitions also present problems because of the lack of agreement in society about what functions family must or should fulfill. The controversies over who should be responsible for sex education, discipline, and care of children, and care of aged persons, persons with disabilities, and sick persons are examples of the uncertainties about what functions are included in functional definitions of the family (Hartman and Laird 1983:26–28). Recognizing the difficulties with traditional structural or functional definitions of family, we will next consider some traditional models of family and familiness. These models are based on relatively narrow structural and/or functional perspectives.

Duvall and Hill: National Conference on Family Life Model

Evelyn Duvall and Reuben Hill (in Kennedy 1978) cochaired a committee for the National Conference on Family Life in 1948 out of which emerged a model consisting of a sequence of eight stages. This model is child-centered and has been widely used and adapted since its creation. A major assumption of this model is that parenting children is the central activity of adult family life (Kennedy 1978:70).

This model of a family life cycle incorporated three criteria into eight stages. The three criteria included 1) a major change in family size; 2) the developmental age of the oldest child; and 3) a change in the work status of "father." The eight stages of the original model (Kennedy 1978:70) are as follows:

Stage 1: Establishment (newly married, childless)

Stage 2: New Parents (infant—3 years)

Stage 3: Preschool family (child 3–6 years and possible younger siblings)

Stage 4: School-age family (oldest child 6–12 years, possible younger siblings)

Stage 5: Family with adolescent (oldest child 13–19, possible younger siblings)

Stage 6: Family with young adult (oldest 20, until first child leaves home)

Stage 7: Family as launching center (from departure of first to last child)

Stage 8: Post-parental family, the middle years (after children have left home until father retires).

This model was adapted slightly by Hill in an article appearing in 1986. The passage of almost forty years resulted in virtually no substantive changes in the model itself (Hill 1986:21), although, as we shall see, significant changes were occurring in the form and function of family for many members of society. The most substantive change between the two models is perhaps the recognition in the final or eighth stage of the 1986 adaptation of the model that the producer of family income (breadwinner) is not necessarily the father as was the implication in the earlier model.

Family developmental tasks

The family life cycle approach, of which the Duvall and Hill model above is perhaps the most used example, was also influenced a great deal by the concept of developmental tasks. The notion of developmental tasks, if you recall from our earlier discussion of individual models of development, was a fundamental element used by Erikson and others to describe the activities individuals engaged in and struggled with as they moved through their various developmental stages. This concept was also a central organizing element used by family developmentalists to describe the activities and struggles faced by whole families as they moved along their developmental journeys. Eleanor Godfrey as early as 1950 defined family developmental tasks as "those that must be accomplished by a family in a way that will satisfy (a) biological requirements, (b) cultural imperatives, and (c) personal aspirations and values, if a family is to continue to grow as a unit" (in Duvall 1988:131). Duvall describes these basic family tasks as:

1. providing physical care;
2. allocating resources;
3. determining who does what;
4. assuring members' socialization;
5. establishing interaction patterns;
6. incorporating and releasing members;
7. relating to society through its institutions; and
8. maintaining morale and motivation. (Duvall 1988:131)

These basic tasks, according to family developmentalists, are addressed by every family at every stage of its life cycle. However, each family accomplishes these tasks in its own ways. If it does not, society steps in in the form of some agent of social control (including social workers) to try to ensure the accomplishment of the necessary tasks (Duvall 1988:131).

Changes in Traditional Family Life Cycle Models

In 1980 Carter and McGoldrick offered another traditional model of family development from a life cycle perspective. Their model was directed toward use by family therapists in interventions with families. Carter and McGoldrick originally published their model as *The Family Life Cycle.* They published an adaptation of their original model in 1989 as *The Changing Family Life Cycle.* In 1999 they published a new edition called *The Expanded Family Life Cycle.* As the title indicates, in this edition the authors recognize more fully many family issues consistent with alternative paradigm thinking.

The most recent edition retains the focus on traditional family life cycle stages (see Table 6.5). It also maintains the overall child-centered focus of traditional family stage models—coupling, the family with young children, the family with adolescents, the "launching" phase, and post-parental families. In this respect the model remains quite traditional and continues to have similarities to the much earlier models described earlier (see Duvall and Hill model above).

However, their expanded perspective on familiness emphasizes much more the diversity of family forms. They note in the Preface that

> we celebrate diversity as we welcome the multiculturalism of the twenty-first century. We refer not only to cultural diversity, but also to the diversity of family forms. There are many ways to go through life in a caring,

productive manner, and no specific family structure is ideal (Carter and McGoldrick 1999: xv).

In addition, Carter and McGoldrick recognize more fully the impact of discrimination and oppression on families: "vast differences in family life cycle patterns are caused by oppressive social forces: racism, sexism, homophobia, classism, ageism, and cultural prejudices of all kinds" (1999: xv). This recognition is reflected in increased attention to families of color, gay and lesbian families, and single adults.

Table 6.5   The Stages of the Family Life Cycle

Family Life Cycle Stage	Emotional Process of Transition: Key Principles	Second-Order Changes in Family Status Required to Proceed Developmentally
1. Leaving home: Single young adults	Accepting emotional and financial responsibility for self	a. Differentiation of self in relation to family of origin b. Development of intimate peer relationships c. Establishment of self re: work and financial independence
2. The joining of families through marriage: The new couple	Commitment to new system	a. Formation of marital system b. Realignment of relationships with extended families and friends to include spouse
3. Families with young children	Accepting new members into the system	a. Adjusting marital system to make space for child(ren) b. Joining in childrearing, financial, and household tasks c. Realignment of relationships with extended family to include parenting and grandparenting roles
4. Families and adolescents	Increasing flexibility of family boundaries to include children's independence and grandparents' frailties	a. Shifting of parent child relationships to permit adolescent to move in and out of system b. Refocus on midlife marital and career issues c. Beginning shift toward joint caring for older generation
5. Launching children and moving on	Accepting a multitude of exits from and entries into the family system	a. Renegotiation of marital system as a dyad b. Development of adult to adult relationships between grown children and their parents c. Realignment of relationships to include in-laws and grandchildren d. Dealing with disabilities and death of persons (grandparents)

Continued

Table 6.5   Continued

Family Life Cycle Stage	Emotional Process of Transition: Key Principles	Second-Order Changes in Family Status Required to Proceed Developmentally
6. Families in later life	Accepting the shifting of generational roles	a. Maintaining own and/or couple functioning and interests in face of physiological decline: exploration of new familial and social role options
		b. Support for a more central role of middle generation
		c. Making room in the system for the wisdom and experience of the elderly, supporting the older generation without overfunctioning for them
		d. Dealing with loss of spouse, siblings, and other peers and preparation for own death. Life review and integration.

Source: Betty Carter and Monica McGoldrick, *The Expanded Family Life Cycle.* Copyright © 1999 by Allyn and Bacon. Reprinted by permission.

In their 1989 discussion of the family life cycle, Carter and McGoldrick recognized that many changes had occurred in the family in the recent past and more and more families, even American middle-class families, were not fitting the traditional model. Among the influences resulting in changes in the family life cycle were a lower birthrate, longer life expectancy, the changing role of women, and increasing rates of divorce and remarriage (1989:10–11). In addition to these influences, Carter and McGoldrick asserted that while in earlier periods "child rearing occupied adults for their entire active life span, it now occupies less than half the time span of adult life prior to old age. The meaning of the family is changing drastically, since it is no longer organized primarily around this activity" (1989:11). Recognition of this shift continues in their 1999 work. This recognition of movement away from a solely child-centered focus on family life is especially significant in light of our observations about this as a central feature of virtually all traditional models of family.

Divorce, remarriage, and stepfamilies

One especially significant change noted by Carter and McGoldrick was the rapidly growing rates of divorce and remarriage. Divorce and remarriage had in fact become so common in American families, they observed, that "divorce in the American family is close to the point at which it will occur in the majority of families and will thus be thought of more and more as a normative event" (1989:21).

Given the extent of divorce and remarriage occurring in U.S. society, the family forms that come about as a result of divorce are treated here as traditional family configurations. It is important to note, though, that for the family members going through divorce and remarriage, these transitions represent dramatic alternative family configurations. In recognition of the increasing frequency of divorce and remarriage, Carter and McGoldrick (1999) offer models for both the family in the process of divorcing and for the processes occurring in a family as a result of remarriage. These models are presented as Tables 6.6 and 6.7.

Because divorce touches the lives of so many family members today, efforts to understand the dynamics and impact of divorce have flourished. Most traditional studies of divorce, for example, have emphasized the difficulties and problems created for members of divorcing families, especially for the children in those families. More recent studies, however, note that there can be a wide range of responses to divorce on the part of family members. This range still

Table 6.6   An Additional Stage of the Family Life Cycle for Divorcing Families

Phase	Emotional Process of Transition *Prerequisite* Attitude	Developmental Issues
Divorce		
The decision to divorce	Acceptance of inability to resolve marital tensions sufficiently to continue relationship	Acceptance of one's own part in the failure of the marriage
Planning the breakup of the system	Supporting viable arrangements for all parts of the system	a. Working cooperatively on problems of custody, visitation, and finances b. Dealing with extended family about the divorce
Separation	a. Willingness to continue cooperative coparental relationship and joint financial support of children b. Work on resolution of attachment to spouse	a. Mourning loss of intact family b. Restructuring marital and parent-child relationships and finances; adaptation to living apart c. Realignment of relationships with extended family; staying connected with spouse's extended family
The divorce	More work on emotional divorce: Overcoming hurt, anger, guilt, etc.	a. Mourning loss of intact family: giving up fantasies of reunion b. Retrieval of hopes, dreams, expectations from the marriage c. Staying connected with extended families
Post-divorce family		
Single-parent (custodial household or primary residence)	Willingness to maintain financial responsibilities, continue parental contact with ex-spouse, and support contact of children with ex-spouse and his or her family	a. Making flexible visitation arrangements with ex-spouse and his [her] family b. Rebuilding own financial resources c. Rebuilding own social network
Single-parent (noncustodial)	Willingness to maintain parental contact with ex-spouse and support custodial parent's relationship with children	a. Finding ways to continue effective parenting relationship with children b. Maintaining financial responsibilities to ex-spouse and children c. Rebuilding own social network

Table 6.7   Remarried Family Formation: A Developmental Outline*

Steps	Prerequisite Attitude	Developmental Issues
1. Entering the new relationship	Recovery from loss of first marriage (adequate "emotional divorce")	Recommitment to marriage and to forming a family with readiness to deal with the complexity and ambiguity
2. Conceptualizing and planning new marriage and family	Accepting one's own fears and those of new spouse and children about remarriage and forming a stepfamily Accepting need for time and patience for adjustment to complexity and ambiguity of: a. Multiple new roles b. Boundaries: space, time, membership, and authority c. Affective Issues: guilt, loyalty conflicts, desire for mutuality, unresolvable past hurts	a. Work on openness in the new relationships to avoid pseudo-mutality. b. Plan for maintenance of cooperative financial and coparental relationships with ex-spouses. c. Plan to help children deal with fears, loyalty conflicts, and membership in two systems. d. Realignment of relationships with extended family to include new spouse and children. e. Plan maintenance of connections for children with extended family of ex-spouse(s).
3. Remarriage and reconstitution of family	Final resolution of attachment to previous spouse and ideal of "intact" family; Acceptance of a different model of family with permeable boundaries	a. Restructuring family boundaries to allow for inclusion of new spouse-stepparent. b. Realignment of relationships and financial arrangements throughout subsystems to permit interweaving of several systems. c. Making room for relationships of all children with biological (noncustodial) parents, grandparents, and other extended family. d. Sharing memories and histories to enhance stepfamily integration.

*Variation on a developmental scheme presented by Ransom et al. (1979)

Source: Carter, B., and McGoldrick, M., *The Expanded Family Lifecycle.* Copyright © 1999 by Allyn & Bacon. Reprinted/adapted by permission.

includes the possibility of severe problems for some family members, but it also includes recognition of the potential for divorce and remarriage to bring quite positive results as well. For example, divorce may result in relief from intense conflict and life-threatening abuse for some people. Remarriage for many may present opportunities for forming satisfying and harmonious new relationships. Even when choosing to remain single, for many persons divorce provides an opportunity for personal growth and development (Hetherington, Law, and O'Connor 1993:208–209).

As divorce rates have climbed, remarriage rates and the number of persons living in stepfamilies have risen dramatically as well. A **stepfamily** is broadly defined as "a household containing a child who is biologically related to only one of the adults." In 1987 it was estimated that 35 percent of all adults were in step situations as "stepparents, parents who had remarried, or adult stepchildren." In addition, 20 percent of all children under nineteen years of age were stepchildren or half-siblings. Overall, this meant that in 1987, 33 percent of the entire population of the United States was in a step situation. (Visher and Visher 1993:235). It is expected that by 2010 "stepfamilies will be the most prevalent type of family in the United States" (Carter and McGoldrick 1999: 417).

Even given the numbers of persons living in step situations, to be in such a situation is still to live with a variety of negative stereotypes. The term *stepchild* is still used to indicate poor treatment or second-class status in many situations. Fairy tales often perpetuate the notion of the "wicked stepmother" or the "mistreated stepchild," for example (Visher and Visher 1993:244).

Visher and Visher stress that for many individuals and families the transition through remarriage to stepfamily life is a challenging but satisfying journey. They note, though, that only recently has remarriage and stepfamily research moved away from a "deficit" or problem-focused approach. They suggest that there are several characteristics of successful stepfamilies. Among these characteristics are the following:

1. *Expectations are realistic:* They recognize that instant love and adjustment is a myth and that emotional bonding takes time. They allow each member to come to accept the new relationship at his or her own pace; recognizing, for example, that young children are likely to develop close relationships with stepparents more easily than teenagers, who may be struggling with their identities and moving toward independence from the family.

2. *Losses can be mourned:* They allow recognition and grieving of relationships lost through divorce. Adults in the stepfamily realize the sadness resulting from this loss that may be displayed by children who have no control over the changes that have occurred in their lives.

3. *There is a strong couple relationship:* The couple works as a team and understands the importance of providing an atmosphere of stability for children. The couple relationship can also serve as a model for children as they move toward adulthood.

4. *Satisfactory step relationships have formed:* The stepparent has taken the time necessary to take on the parenting role. The couple works together as a team and the parent initially takes the more active parenting role but supports the development of a parent role by the stepparent. (It is possible that stepparents and stepchildren will not form a close interpersonal relationship, but the relationship will be one of tolerance and respect nevertheless.)

5. *Satisfying rituals are established:* The family will accept that there is no right or wrong way for family rituals, which may be different for each member. For example, members will develop a flexible and compromising approach to such things as the proper procedures for doing laundry, or celebrating a birthday, or cooking the holiday meal.

6. *The separate households cooperate:* Satisfactory arrangements will be worked out between the children's households. A "parenting coalition" on the part of all involved parents will be developed for the benefit of the children (Visher and Visher in Walsh 2003:164–169).

In addition to changes in families as a result of divorce, remarriage, and stepfamily arrangements, Carter and McGoldrick recognized several other "variations" that would have an impact on the family life cycle. These variations included differences from the American middle-class norm due to poverty and due to cultural differences (1989:20–25). They also recognized the potential for significant variations in the family life cycle as a result of differences such as sexual orientation (1989:60–61). That these variations were recognized in the context of a traditional perspective on the family is significant. These differences were still seen, however, only as variations on the "normal" or traditional model.

Grandparents as Parents

Grandparents provide regular care for grandchildren or assume other parental roles either formally through court orders or decisions or informally where the grandchild lives with or spends a regular portion of his/her day with a grandparent (Jendrek 1996:206). The grandparent-as-parent role is a form of kinship care (see discussion of kinship care later in this chapter).

Parental roles

The role of parent from a legal perspective includes both legal and physical custody:

> ♦ Legal custody is "the right or authority of a parent, or parents, to make decisions concerning the child's upbringing" (Schulman and Pitt in Jendrek 1994:207). Ex. Decisions about medical care, education, discipline.

Using data from the most recent Census (2000), the American Association of Retired Persons (AARP) points out the following:

♦ 6.3% (4.5 million) of children in the United States under age 18 are growing up in grandparent-headed households. Approximately one-third of these children have no parent present in the home.
♦ The numbers of children in grandparent-headed households have increased 30% since 1990, and 105% since 1970.
♦ The majority of grandparents raising grandchildren are between ages 55 and 64; approximately 20 to 25% are over 65.
♦ Ethnicity crosses all lines:

Ethnicity	Grandparents	Grandchildren
White	51%	44%
African American	38%	36%
Hispanic	13%	18%

♦ While grandparent-headed families cross all socio-economic levels, these grandparents are more likely to live in poverty than other grandparents.
♦ There are eight times more children in grandparent-headed homes than in the foster care system.

Source: Baker n.d.

- ▶ Physical custody is "the right to physical possession of the child, i.e., to have the child live with the . . . parent" (Schulman and Pitt in Jendrek 1994:207).

Combining the traditional parent roles regarding legal and physical custody results in three possible categories of "**grandparents-as-parent**" roles:

1. *Custodial grandparents:* "A legal relationship with the grandchild (adoption, full custody, temporary custody, or guardianship). . . . These grandparents assume the functions typically linked to parenthood in our society; they become the grandchild's physical and legal custodians." Grandparents typically assume custodial care of grandchildren because of severe problems in the grandchild's nuclear family including financial, emotional or mental health, and substance abuse problems (Jendrek 1994:207).

2. *Day-care grandparents:* These grandparents "are not casual baby-sitters; they provide grandchildren with daily care for extended periods. Day-care grandparents assume responsibility for the physical care of their grandchildren but assume no legal responsibility" (Jendrek 1994:207).

3. *Living-with grandparents:* These grandparents "assume a parenting role that falls between that of the custodial and day-care grandparent. Living-with grandparents do not have legal custody but provide some, if not all, of the daily physical care for the grandchild." Two categories of living-with grandparents:

- ▶ those who have one or more of the grandchild's parents living with them
- ▶ those who have neither parent in their household (Jendrek 1994: 207–208).

As Laird (in Walsh 1993:286) points out, "most studies of 'minorities' . . . start from a majority perspective (usually white, middle-class, male), comparing and searching for 'difference,' measuring the population of interest against some accepted norm and describing how it is different, exotic, or deviant." In the remainder of this chapter we will explore differences in familiness as alternatives to, as well as variations on, traditional models of family. Whenever possible we will present alternative notions on familiness from the perspective of the persons who represent those alternatives. In some cases, even presentation of alternative perspectives by persons representing an alternative perspective is limited because there is no language in traditional definitions and conceptualizations of family to describe alternative elements.

THE ALTERNATIVE/POSSIBLE

As indicated earlier in this chapter, many alternative approaches to understanding familiness are extensions or adaptations of traditional models or perspectives. Other alternative approaches include perspectives that offer striking contrasts to traditional approaches. The alternative approaches to understanding familiness that we are about to explore will provide us with a number of concepts important for understanding human behavior in the social environment more generally, in addition to their usefulness in helping us to expand our understanding of familiness.

The alternative approaches we are about to explore tend to be more flexible and more pluralistic than are traditional approaches to thinking about families and familiness. They tend to accept that changes occurring in the environment often require changes in the structures and functions of families. They do not assume that all families do or should look and behave the same or that the same family will or should look and behave the same way at different times. These approaches tend to place greater emphasis on the environmental and social forces that influence family structures and functions. A number of the models also stress the interdependence of families with other related systems—individuals, groups, organizations, and communities.

Alternative Definitions

We are often presented with images that suggest that the only viable definition of family is one consistent with the traditional two-parent, child-centered, nuclear, white heterosexual, stage-based portrayals we visited in the preceding sections. While this perspective on family is an accurate portrayal of many families (though, as we noted earlier, the number of families fitting this definition is rapidly decreasing), there are many, many families not reflected in this portrayal.

Other, more flexible and pluralistic ways of defining family are needed to represent the great diversity of current family forms. These ways of defining family and familiness are more likely to include or reflect dimensions of alternative paradigm thinking that we have been exploring throughout this book, such as recognition of a diversity of family forms.

If multiple or diverse definitions of family forms are not available, great numbers of very real functioning families can be rendered invisible. Scanzoni and Marsiglio (1991), for example, remind us that Stack (1974) could not find any families in her research work in an urban African American community "until she redefined family as 'the smallest organized, durable network of kin and non-kin [i.e., friends] who interact daily, providing the domestic needs of children and assuring their survival.' "

Seligman suggests a basic and quite flexible alternate definition of families (in Scanzoni and Marsiglio 1991:117) based on the findings from his national survey in which 75 percent of the respondents, when asked to define "the family," defined it as "a group of people who love and care for each other." The central place of the quality of the relationships that constitute family is also stressed in a court ruling regarding the definition of family in a case supporting gay rights. In this case the judge concluded: "It is the totality of the relationship, as evidenced by the dedication, caring, and self-sacrifice of the parties which should, in the final analysis, control the definition of family" (Stacey in Walsh 1993:17). Another quite flexible definition of family is that of D'Antonio (in Scanzoni and Marsiglio 1991:117): "A unit comprising two or more persons who live together for an extended period of time, and who share in one or more of the following: Work (for wages and house), sex, care and feeding of children, and intellectual, spiritual, and recreational activities."

Toward an integrative approach

Hartman and Laird urge not only a flexible definition for family, but they remind us that most of us are really members of multiple families simultaneously. Their approach to defining family integrates traditional notions of family and alternate perspectives on family. They suggest that there are two categories of family: One is biologically based; the other is based on relationship. The first type they define as **family of origin.** By family of origin they mean:

> that family of blood ties, both vertical (multigenerational) and horizontal (kinship), living or dead, geographically close or distant, known or unknown, accessible or inaccessible, but always in some way psychologically relevant. Also included in the family of origin are adopted members and fictive kin, people who, although not related by blood, are considered and have functioned as part of a family.

The second type of family they refer to is **family as intimate environment.** This second type of family, they say, is:

> that current family constellation in which people have chosen to live. Such a family group in our context consists of two or more people who have made a commitment to share living space, have developed close emotional ties, and share a variety of family roles and functions. (Hartman and Laird 1983: 29–30)

Examples of this second type of family include "a middle-aged married couple whose children are reared; two elderly sisters, one a widow and the other a spinster, who share an apartment in a retirement community; a group of biologically related and unrelated adults and children who have formed a group or communal family in which a range of commitments exists." Hartman and Laird suggest that "a family becomes a family when two or more individuals have decided they are a family" by creating an environment in which they share emotional needs for closeness, living space, and the roles and tasks necessary for meeting the biological, social, and psychological needs of the members. They do not limit the definition of family only to those recognized by courts of law (1983:30–31).

Family structure and diversity

In addition to the two types of family relationships described by Hartman and Laird, the types of family structures within which we live reflect a great deal of diversity. The National Survey of American Families (NSAF) reported information on family structure by race and ethnicity. The findings indicated that while most white (71 percent) and Asian American (77 percent) children lived in two-parent families, "slightly more than half of Hispanic children and half of Native American children lived in two-parent families. In contrast, only about one-third of [African American] children lived with two parents" (Staveteig and Wigton 2000). Figure 6.2 provides details and definitions of differences in family structures by race and ethnicity. The diversity of family structures combined with variations in structure according to the race/ethnicity of families is another clear example of "diversity within diversity" (see discussion of diversity with diversity and multiple diversities in Chapter 2).

As we continue our journey toward more comprehensive ways to understand familiness, we will keep in mind these multiple and flexible notions of family. The following exploration of alternative notions of familiness is organized according to several "Focus" areas. This arrangement is similar to that used in Chapter 5 for alternative perspectives on individual development. The cautions suggested in that chapter concerning false divisions and oversimplification of multidimensional and interacting factors apply here as well.

Life Course Theory and Familiness

Human Behavior

Social workers are knowledgeable about human behavior across the life course. How does Life Course theory assist us in gaining, organizing, and using this critical knowledge? How is Life Course theory different from traditional life-span theories?

Life course theory, as an independent and evidence based theory, has also often been considered an important approach to understanding more fully family development and the intersections of family development with the developmental patterns of the individuals who make up the family along with the larger environmental contexts that have significant influence on family development and well-being. We explore the family-focused application of life course theory here. We consider terms and concepts central to the theory and four contexts: temporal, socio-structural, process and change, and family diversity that provide the organizing framework for the theory.

Demo and Allen (1996:426) consider life course theory helpful because it looks at families with greater attention to the complexity and variability that are part of people's lives. According to Demo and Allen, "this framework focuses on the multiple trajectories and social contexts (e.g., family, employment and community) shaping individual lives and the unique and overlapping pathways and trajectories within families." They note that "by examining social age, developmental age and historical age, researchers can identify cohorts who experience similar slices of history from different developmental vantage points, thereby illuminating the intersections of biography and history" (Demo and Allen 1996: 426-27). **Life Course** theory is a contextual, processual, and dynamic approach. It looks at change in individual lives and in family units over time by tracing individual developmental *trajectories* or paths in the context of the development of family units over time. Life course theory is concerned with the interconnections between personal biographies or life stories and social-historical time (Bengston and Allen 1993:469-499). Glen Elder, one of the early leaders in research that resulted in the development of life course theory, defines another central concept of the theory: human agency. According to Elder, the "principle of . . . *human agency* states that *individuals construct their own life course through choices and actions they take within the opportunities and constraints of history and social circumstances*" (1998:4).

Temporal context

The **temporal context** is used to describe the multiple timeclocks that affect family life. Life course theory itself reflects a timeclock that is **sociogenic** in that it is concerned with the entire lifetime of individuals and families as they develop in the context of the larger society. Another sense of timeclocks within family development is referred to as ontogenetic time and ontogenetic events. The term **ontogenetic** describes the developmental levels of individuals as they grow, change, and age from birth to death and is indexed most simply but quite inexactly by chronological years. As we have noted elsewhere, some psychologists (Piaget, Kohlberg, Erikson, and Valliant) use age period or level or stages that describe that the behavior of individuals in families is in part a function of the individual's ontogenetic development level and of other family members' ontogenetic levels. **Ontogenetic time** and **ontogenetic events** are ways of describing that the behavior of individuals in families is in part a function of the individual's ontogenetic development level and of other family member ontogenetic levels (Bengston and Allen 1993:470–472; 480–481).

Another temporal or time-related concept that is important in understanding life-course theory is that of generation. **Generation** refers to the position of individuals in the ranked descent within a biosocial family of procreation and succession. Related concepts are **generational time** and **generational events,** which are a way of depicting that the behavior of individuals in families is also a function of generational placement with attendant roles and expectation. Generational time is also called family time. **Generational** or **family time** is indexed not only by biogenetic statuses within families (grandparent, parent, child), but also by the roles, expectations, and identities related to those statuses (Bengston and Allen 1993:471; 481).

Still another temporal context helpful in understanding life course theory is historical time and place events. Elder notes, *"empirical research findings . . . affirm the principle of . . . historical time and place: that the life course of individuals is embedded in and shaped by the historical times and places they experience over a lifetime"* (Elder 1998:3). The concepts of **historical time** and **historical events** reflect that the behavior of individuals and families, and of families as units, is also a function of secular or period events, especially geopolitical or economic events. This temporal context is usually indicated in terms of events, periods, or eras dominated by watershed geopolitical or economic events: the Civil War Period, the Depression, the Vietnam era (Bengston and Allen 1993:481–482). We should note, though, that some alternative theorists would argue that "real" historical impact is best understood in terms of the impact of these watershed events on the individual and family. In other words, the local or personal consequences of these events on day-to-day life must be considered central.

Sociostructural context

The **sociocultural context** is a way of understanding the social ecology of families in terms of several dimensions. Sociostructural context includes the concept of **social structural location** or the location of families in the broader social structure. This location of the family within the larger society influences the events they experience as the family and its members develop and interact over time. The sociostructural context also includes the **social construction of meaning** in that families and their members attach meaning to events that occur and interact at multiple levels: individual life span, generational, and historical events are interpreted through meanings adapted from social structure location and developed through family interaction (Bengston and Allen 1993:482–483).

Examples of the social construction of meaning might include: norms about the right time to marry, give birth, become a grandparent, and retire. The meanings attached to events also are influenced within families by their **cultural context.** Shared meanings reflected in cultural values both create and interpret life span, generation, and historical events as they impinge on families. Cultural values give meaning to change in families and those meanings may be quite different from one cultural context to another (Bengston and Allen 1993:483).

Continuity and change

Life course theorists see families influenced significantly by both stability and change which are often referred to as homeostasis and adaptability or the dialectics of continuity and change. Families and members respond over time to individual developmental, generational, and historical events and their responses to this range of events reflect both change (adaptability) and continuity (homeostasis), or innovation and transmission. The concept of **diachronic analysis of families** is a process of analyses of processes over time—focusing on dynamic, as contrasted with static, elements of phenomena. Family processes are examined in addition to family structure. The notion of simultaneously attending to both continuity and change also implies that we cannot understand or explain development from just one point in time. Interactions among age, period, and cohort phenomena influence behaviors of families and individual members over time. Life course theorists stress the dynamic, nonlinear notion of change and its impact. For example individual, generational, and historical changes combined with the social context of those changes mutually effect members, families and the larger community, or social context (Bengston and Allen 1993:483–484).

Heterogeneity and diversity among families

Life course advocates also emphasize diversity among families and note that there is considerable diversity in the ways families react to and give meaning to individual developmental, generational, and historical events. These theorists also suggest that heterogeneity or diversity in families increases over time. They note that, for example, a family kinship network is increasingly diverse over time, adding and changing members through birth and marriage. In addition, life course theory recognizes there is considerable variation in family structure as a result of differences in location within the social structure: gender, race/ethnicity, or socioeconomic status (Bengston and Allen 1993:484).

FOCUS: PEOPLE OF COLOR

Harrison et al. use an ecological framework as a departure point for developing an alternative approach to familiness. This approach emphasizes the interaction of individuals with the social environment. Harrison et al. focus on the ecological challenges faced by the families of people of color in their interactions with social systems and institutions in the larger environment (1990:347). Others have stressed the importance of using a strengths-based approach to dealing with families of color as well (Attneave in McGoldrick, Pearce, and Giordano 1982:81–82; Boyd-Franklin in Walsh 2003:268–269). A strengths-based perspective for understanding families of color is consistent with the principles of the strengths-based perspective on social work described in Chapter 3. Central to a strengths-based approach to families of color is the notion of adaptive strategies.

Adaptive Strategies

Families of color develop a variety of adaptive strategies to overcome environmental barriers to their (and their members') well-being and development (Ho 1987). Harrison et al. describe **adaptive strategies** as observable social behavioral "cultural patterns that promote the survival and well-being of the community, families, and individual members of the group" (1990:350). Adaptive strategies recognize the interdependence of community, individual, and family systems. This interdependence offers an example of family as the intersection at which a variety of systems come together and interact with one another.

A strengths-based adaptive-strategies approach to studying and understanding families of color and their children offers an alternative to traditional deficit- or pathology-focused approaches. The specific groups with which we are concerned include African Americans, American Indians/ Alaskan Natives, Asian/Pacific Americans, and Latino Americans (Harrison et al. 1990:348).

An adaptive-strategies approach highlights the interconnectedness of the status of families of color, adaptive strategies, socialization goals, and child outcomes (Harrison et al. 1990:348). Through this approach we can delineate a number of contextual or environmental issues that interact to result in the need for adaptive strategies on the part of these families and their members. Specific issues addressed through this approach include racism and oppression, extendedness of families, role flexibility within families, biculturalism, and spirituality and ancestral worldview. While there are some differences in the nature of these strategies from one group to another, the strategies themselves seem to be strikingly similar across the groups (Boyd-Franklin in Walsh 2003; Harrison et al. 1990:350; Ho 1987).

Response to racism and oppression

Diversity in Practice

Social workers recognize the extent to which a culture's structures and values may oppress, marginalize, alienate, or create or enhance privilege and power. How does the section, "Islam: Family and Spirituality," help us to understand this when working with families who are Islamic?

A number of statuses or conditions interact in the social environments of families of color and result in the need to create adaptive strategies to respond effectively to those conditions. Basic among these is the status of minority group itself. As you may recall, minority group status is not necessarily determined by size of group, but by subordinate status ascribed to members of the group by majority or dominant groups in society. Harrison et al. remind us that a crucial variable "in majority-minority relations is the differential power of one group relative to another" (Yetman in Harrison et al. 1990:348).

In addition to the variable of differential power, ethnocentrism and competition for resources to meet human needs combine to form systems of ethnic stratification (Harrison et al. 1990:348). **Ethnocentrism** is defined by Logan (1990:18) as an individual's view that "their own culture [is] the most important way of life in the world and therefore [is] the context for measuring all other significant experiences and acts." The concept of ethnocentrism was discussed earlier in our more general discussions about traditional and alternate paradigms.

Another important concept is ethnic stratification. **Ethnic stratification** is "a system or arrangement where some relatively fixed group membership (e.g., race, religion, or nationality) is used as one of the standards of judgment for assigning social position with its attendant differential rewards" (Noel in Harrison et al. 1990:348). In other words, ethnic stratification is a system of differential treatment based on minority or majority group status.

Caste or castelike status is a specific form of ethnic stratification. You might recall that we explored this notion in the context of individual development in Chapter 5. As suggested by our discussions of social class in Chapter 5, caste and class are often compared and contrasted in discussion of social status. Caste and class are similar in that they both represent social positions held by persons or groups in a society. They differ, however, in that social class implies a position or status from which one can move as various conditions change. For example, increasing a family's educational level, income, or moving from one neighborhood to another may result in movement from a lower social class to a middle-class status. Caste status, however, is not nearly as amenable to such movement. You might recall again from our discussion in Chapter 5 that castelike status, especially in U.S. society, is much more ascribed. An **ascribed status** is permanent and based on characteristics or conditions not subject to the control of the individual, such as skin color, or, as Ogbu notes, historic conditions of slavery, conquest, or colonization.

For Ogbu, castelike groups in the United States may differ in many ways, but all have in common the element of being treated as exploitable resources. Examples of this treatment for specific groups include:

a. the enslavement of Africans and, after emancipation, their segregation and perceived inferior status based on race;

b. military conflicts over land and territory between American Indians and European Americans, and the forced removal and transfer of Indians to reservations;

c. Asian Americans whose recent immigrants from Indochina sometimes suffer from the same subordination and exploitation endured by earlier immigrants from China, Philippines, and Japan (the latter were incarcerated during World War II); and

d. Hispanics who were incorporated through conquest and displacement. (in Harrison et al. 1990:348)

Again, we see that while specific experiences vary considerably among different groups in this society, many conditions that result from these experiences are often shared by the members of different groups. Underlying these conditions is a theme of racism and oppression.

Effective adaptive strategies for families of color include recognition of the realities of racism and oppression for members in a society in which the traditional/dominant paradigm prevails in the existing social hierarchy (Boyd-Franklin in Walsh 2003; Harrison et al. 1990:347–348). Harrison et al. stress, for example, that "historically, ethnic minority children were not included in samples of subjects studied for establishing normative trends or investigating theoretical questions. Most often data on ethnic minority children came from comparative studies with a controversial deficit explanation" (1990:348). Such findings offer dramatic examples of the invisibility or "abnormality (pathology)" accorded diverse persons (non-European descended) in much traditional paradigm research we explored in Chapter 2. Boyd-Franklin stresses that dealing with racism and oppression is central to family life for African Americans. For African American parents "normal family development" is a complex process that involves educating their children to recognize and deal with racism, discrimination, and negative messages from society about African Americans. African American parents must simultaneously help their children not to internalize the negative messages from society, but to be proud of who they are and believe that they can achieve in spite of racism and discrimination (in Walsh 2003:262).

The challenges faced by ethnic minority families result from long and shared histories of oppression and discrimination. The impact of these conditions on social and economic well-being of ethnic minority families has very real consequences in poverty, high unemployment, substandard or no housing, and poor health. All of these are of intense concern to social workers, for they present major barriers to families and their members reaching their fullest human potential. These obstacles, however, do not prevent ethnic minority families from pursuing goals of "educational achievement, economic development in the community, political power, affordable housing, and maintaining cultural and religious traditions" (Harrison et al. 1990:349). One significant source of strength and support for pursuing these goals is the extended family.

Extended and augmented or "fictive" family networks

The specific nature or makeup of extended families differs considerably among ethnic minority groups. This family type is, however, found as an adaptive strategy and a strength across all the ethnic minority groups discussed here. The concept of extended family refers to multiple dimensions of familiness. **Extended family** as we use the term refers to more than traditional definitions of extended family as the nuclear family plus grandparents, aunts, uncles, and other kin related by blood or marriage. Included as members are not only parents and their children, but other relatives related by blood or marriage as well as non-blood or non-marriage-related persons who are considered by other family members, and consider themselves, family. Extended family for many families of color is really an "extensive kinship network." This network helps family members survive "by providing support, encouragement, and 'reciprocity' in terms of sharing goods, money, and services" (Boyd-Franklin in Walsh 2003:268–269).

For many African American families this network "might include older relatives such as great-grandparents, grandmothers, grandfathers, aunts, uncles, cousins, older brothers and sisters, all of whom may participate in child-rearing, and 'non-blood relatives' such as godparents, babysitters, neighbors, friends, church family members, ministers, ministers' wives, and so forth" (Boyd-Franklin 1993:368). African American extended familiness expand family into community relationships through fictive kinship. **Fictive kinship** is "the caregiving and mutual-aid relationship among nonrelated blacks that exists because of their common ancestry, history, and social plight" (Martin and Martin 1985:5). Andrew Billingsley (1968) referred to this extended family form as **augmented family.** Billingsley (1992) more recently referred to this arrangement as **"relationships of appropriation."**

For many Native American families, extended family consists of a "collective, cooperative social network that extends from the mother and father union to the extended family and ultimately to the community and tribe" (Harrison et al. 1990:351). In many traditional Native American families, parenting is shared by several adults. In these traditional extended families "uncles and aunts often had particular disciplinary responsibilities toward their nieces and nephews, freeing biological parents for a much looser, more pleasure-oriented association with offspring" (Attneave in McGoldrick, Pearce, and Giordano 1982:72–73).

"The traditional Asian/Pacific-American family is characterized by well-defined, unilaterally organized, and highly interdependent roles within a cohesive patriarchal vertical structure" in which "prescribed roles and relationships emphasize subordination and interdependence . . . and esteem for . . . the virtue of filial piety" (Harrison et al. 1990:351). **Filial piety** is an intense sense of respect for and obligation to one's parents and ancestors.

Latino family extendedness emphasizes "strong feelings of identification, loyalty, and solidarity with the parents and the extended family" and involves "frequent contact and reciprocity among members of the same family." It has some similarities with the African American family "in that it is bilaterally organized and includes nonrelative members (e.g., *compadres*)" (Harrison et al. 1990:351–352).

All of these forms of extended family offer a variety of sources of strength and support in addition to that offered by one's most immediate or nuclear family. It is crucial to recognize that there is great variation within groups (diversity-in-diversity) in the importance placed on extended family. These variations might be related to the number of generations a family has lived in the United States or whether or not one has access to extended family members.

Some Native Americans who have moved to urban areas from their reservation communities to find employment, for example, may have great difficulty gaining access to their extended family support networks. Many first-generation or recent Asian and Latino immigrants may have had to leave their extended family in their country of origin.

Kinship care

Closely associated with the adaptive strategy of extended family networks described above is the concept of **kinship care**. Scannapieco and Jackson describe the history of the concept. They note that the concept of kinship care has emerged from the research of a number of African American scholars (Billingsley 1992; Stack 1974) who "documented the importance of extended kinship networks in the African American community. As we noted earlier, the term 'kin' often includes any relative by blood or marriage or any person with close nonfamily ties to another" (1996:191). Billingsley referred to "augmented family" (1968) and "relationships of appropriation" (1992:31) to describe "unions without blood ties or marital ties. People become part of a family unit or, indeed, form a family unit simply by deciding to live and act toward each other as family." The history of kinship care is connected to the strong history of extended kinship in African and African American history: "The primary family unit in West Africa at the time of slavery in the United States was the extended family, which incorporated the entire community. Children belonged to, and were the responsibility of, the collective community" (Scannapieco and Jackson 1996:191). In West Africa, according to Yusane, " 'kinship relations were the foundation of social organization' and the 'extended family system is based on interdependent functions' that also serve as protection from calamities. African children were valued and viewed as an investment in the future" (in Scannapieco and Jackson 1996:191).

Scannapieco and Jackson also note that "Africans saw children as part of their immortality, and there were no 'illegitimate' children. All children were the shared concern of the community, and children were expected to care for their parents when the parent got old (respect for elders in the family and community continues as an African tradition" (1996:191).

Definition of kinship care   African American families continue to face extreme challenges to their well-being and existence in the late 1990s. African American children placed in out-of-home care have increased dramatically for a variety of reasons: drug and alcohol abuse, teenage parenting, crime, and violence (Edelman 1987; Scannapieco and Jackson 1996).

The African American community is responding in a resilient manner through the adaptive response of informal and formal "kinship care." Grandparents are often the extended family members who assume responsibility for kinship care (see discussion of grandparents as parents earlier in this chapter). *kinship care* has been defined as "the full-time nurturing and protection of children who must be separated from their parent by relatives, members of their tribes or clans, godparents, step-parents, or other adults who have a kinship bond with a child" (Child Welfare League of America in Wilhelmus 1998:118). This adaptive response is consistent with the strong history of African American extended family and community responsibility to the well-being of children (Scannapieco and Jackson 1996:190–192). Kinship care is sometimes referred to in two ways:

1. Private Kinship Care: Custody remains with the family member. Relative caregivers are not eligible for child-care payments, although other

assistance might be available. Private kinship arrangements take various forms:

- The [relative] is caretaker, but the parent retains legal custody and can make any decisions regarding the kids.
- The [relative] has temporary legal custody, which public housing and some school districts require of caregivers. Legal custodians make decisions concerning daily care of the child, but parents are still involved in major decisions.
- The [relative] adopts the child, and rights of the birth parent are terminated. Few grandparents choose this option because it can end a relationship with their own child.

2. Foster Kinship Care: Relatives become the foster parents, but the state retains custody. (Gebeke 1996)

Today there are more African American children in kinship care than in traditional foster care. Social workers must recognize and support this important form of resilience (see Chapter 3) in the African American family and community. Central to effective practice in this area is learning to work with the "'kinship triad,' made up of the children, the biological parents, and the caregiver relatives. . . . The social worker must keep in mind that the caregiver relative does not consider himself or herself a foster parent in the traditional sense. The caregiver relative is responding to the needs of the family, not the needs of the child welfare system. His or her decision is preserving the African American family" (Scannapieco and Jackson 1996:193–194).

How does this image reflect the discussion of "social role flexibility" and "fluidity of roles" in the narrative?

Social role flexibility/fluidity of roles

This concept applied to ethnic minority families means that "familial social roles can be regarded as flexible in definition, responsibility, and performance. Parenting of younger siblings by older siblings, sharing of the breadwinner role among adults, and alternative family arrangements" are examples of this role flexibility (Harrison et al. 1990:352). Freeman (in Logan et al. 1990:57ff) refers to this flexibility as **fluidity of roles** and suggests that it has historically been a significant source of strength for African American families as they faced survival in a hostile environment that often required family members to shift from one family role to another.

Pinderhughes points out that the flexibility of roles, although a source of strength and survival for many African American families, has often been viewed as a deficit "because it was different from the White middle-class nuclear family model" of very specific role expectations for males and females (in McGoldrick, Pearce, and Giordano 1982:112–113). Hines and Boyd-Franklin suggest that role flexibility results in a greater sense of equality for African American couples. They suggest that the emphasis put on equality between men and women by the women's movement has long been a reality for many African American women. Having a working mate is much less threatening for many African American men than for many white men because of this history of role flexibility (in McGoldrick, Pearce, and Giordano 1982:89–90).

Biculturalism

We explored this concept briefly in Chapter 5 as it related to individual development. This important concept carries even more significance in the context of family. **Biculturalism** is "the ability to function in two worlds" (Pinderhughes in McGoldrick, Pearce, and Giordano 1982:114). However, Harrison et al. stress the complexity of this process for people of color because of the devaluing of their original cultures by the majority group in U.S. society. People of color and their families are put in the position of accommodating or changing behaviors or beliefs to make them consistent with those of the majority culture, and simultaneously engaging in a complex process of keeping and giving up parts of the culture of origin. The result is a person who learns to "function optimally in more than one cultural context and to switch repertoires of behaviors appropriately and adaptively as called for by the situation" (Laosa 1977 in Harrison et al. 1990:352). Freeman refers to the virtual requirement of biculturality on the part of African American families as the "dual perspective." She notes that African American parents have the double responsibilities of socializing their children "to adapt to and function well in a larger society that often views their racial and cultural background in a derogatory manner. ... [and] to retain a positive racial identity and meet expectations of their racial group that may be in conflict with expectations of the society" (in Logan et al. 1990:61).

Socialization is central to the process of becoming bicultural. We have discussed the concept of socialization in a variety of contexts so far in this book. We discussed socialization as a core concept in social systems thinking. We discussed the importance of socialization in many models of individual development. **Socialization** "refers to the processes by which individuals become distinctive and actively functioning members of the society in which they live" (Harrison et al. 1990:354). Thus socialization is a central and ongoing part of our individual development. Family is the context in which a great deal of socialization takes place.

A family's ethnicity and the socialization of its members are intricately interconnected. Ethnicity is an important factor in such general aspects of socialization as "values, social customs, perceptions, behavioral roles, language usage, and rules of social interactions that group members share" (Harrison et al. 1990:354).

In addition to the importance of socialization in the process of becoming bicultural, Harrison et al. present the notion of "socialization for interdependence" as an important socialization goal of the ethnic minority groups they studied. Ethnic minority children are socialized in the context of their family to develop a cooperative view of life in which cooperation, obligation, sharing, and reciprocity are central elements of their beliefs and behaviors (1990:355). This focus on interdependence and cooperation is in sharp contrast to the traditional or dominant paradigm's primacy on competition and independence.

An additional strength of biculturalism, most notably found in studies of bilingualism, is cognitive flexibility. The greater cognitive flexibility of bilingual children is reflected in their enhanced abilities "to detect multiple meanings of words and alternative orientations of objects" and "to attend to language as an object of thought rather than just for the content or idea" (Harrison et al. 1990:356).

Given the benefits of biculturality and the virtual necessity of ethnic minority families socializing their children to be bicultural in order to survive, what of biculturality and white people? James Leigh suggests that it is necessary for all people in the United States to become bicultural, not only members of ethnic minority groups. A major step in this direction is an acceptance and expectation of bilingualism. Leigh suggests that we all need to recognize that Black English, Spanish, and Native American languages are not "foreign languages." They are multiple languages reflecting the multicultural realities of U.S. society. In addition to incorporating multiple languages, Leigh suggests that we must also incorporate diverse "histories" into our understanding of the complex society in which we live. We must tell the history of America from the perspectives of its native peoples as well as from the perspective of Columbus and subsequent newcomers (1989:17–19).

Biculturality is not an option for social workers, it is a necessity. To be able to enter into the culture of another person is an essential skill for social workers living in a multicultural pluralistic society. Biculturality is very similar at the cultural level to empathy at the interpersonal level. Empathy at the cultural and at the interpersonal level should not be considered separate skills but two components of the same essential skill necessary for competent practice on the part of any social worker.

Spirituality and ancestral worldviews

As we learned in Chapter 1, worldviews are extremely influential in the way we see ourselves, others, and the world around us. Our worldviews are also strong influences on our families. We discovered, in our earlier exploration of worldviews, that the dominant worldview or paradigm was characterized by an emphasis on individualism and separateness in which every person is separate from every other person and is solely responsible for her or his own well-being. This Eurocentric individualistic worldview is contrary to the ancestral worldviews of many ethnic minority groups. For many minority groups a worldview emphasizing the interrelatedness of the self or the individual with other systems in the person's environment such as families, households, communities, and the ethnic group as a whole is held (English 1991:20–24; Harrison et al. 1990:353; Martin and Martin 1985).

Ancestral worldviews are reflected throughout the institutions responsible for imparting the beliefs and values of the group. In addition to and in conjunction with the family, religious and spiritual institutions hold and pass along the philosophical standpoints or worldviews of the people. Many African Americans hold a worldview with roots in an African philosophical position that stresses collectivism rather than individualism. The worldviews of many Native Americans perceive all aspects of life as interrelated and of religious significance although there is no single dominant religion among the many Native American cultures. Asian/Pacific American families stress a belief system in which harmony is a core value. Latino religious beliefs reinforce a belief system in which familism is a central tenet (Harrison et al. 1990:354). Such worldviews as these suggest much more in common with the core concerns of social work; with the principles of social systems and ecological thinking and with the growing emphasis in social work on the roles of spirituality and religion in understanding the lives of the people with whom we work.

The church often plays an important and supportive role for families of color. Church provides a sense of community and interrelatedness for many families. Family and church are so interrelated for some African Americans, for example, that church members may refer to other members as their "church family." One's church family may provide such important supports as role models for young family members and assistance with child rearing. For families trying to survive in what is likely a hostile environment, "churches often provide an alternative network for friends, junior choir, after school and summer activities, babysitting, and male and female adult role models." These role models are likely to include "the minister, minister's wife, deacons, deaconesses, elders, and trustee boards" (Boyd-Franklin 1993:369). Social workers need to be aware that such sources of strength and support as the "church family" may be available to assist African American families. Boyd-Franklin (1993:369–370) suggests that social workers need to become "acquainted with the ministers in African-American communities as these individuals have a great deal of power and influence" and can often provide a wide range of support for families.

Even for African American families that do not belong to a formal church, spirituality may play a significant role. This spirituality can be quite distinct from a "religious orientation." Consistent with an Afrocentric worldview that sees reality as both spiritual and material at the same time, spirituality is a part of every person (Myers 1985:34–35). This spirituality "is often a strength and a survival mechanism for African-American families that can be tapped, particularly in times of death and dying, illness, loss, and bereavement" (Boyd-Franklin 1993:370).

Islam: family and spirituality

The events of 9/11/2001 and the subsequent wars in Iraq and Afghanistan have reinforced the importance of having accurate information about members of the populations with which we work, in this case the Muslim/Arab population. This is especially true of this population because of the tendency of many, post-9/11, to see all persons who are Muslim or of Arabic ancestry as terrorists or supporters of terrorism because of their adherence to fundamentalist Islam. This is certainly not the case for the great majority of persons who are Muslim.

The Muslim population is growing rapidly around the world and in the United States. There are between 6 and 8 million Muslims living in North America (Rehman and Dziegielewski 2003:32). In addition, as noted earlier in this chapter, "special immigrant status" may now be granted to some citizens of Iraq and Afghanistan who have worked for the U.S. government in connection with the wars. Yet as social workers and in general we know little about Muslim culture or religion. In Chapter 10, we will look more closely at Muslim culture and community. Here we address Islamic spirituality in relation to its influence on family.

> The term 'Islam' . . . refers to the religion based on the doctrine that Muslims believe was revealed in the year AD 610 to the Prophet Muhammad in the city of Mecca. People who adhere to the religion of Islam are called Muslims. . . . The basis of Islam is the Koran, a Holy Book . . . 'it is the eternal, uncreated, literal word of God, sent down from heaven, revealed . . . to the prophet Muhammad as a guidance for human kind.' . . . A second valid religious authority is the *Hadith,* the tradition of the Prophet Muhammad's words and deeds as well as those of many of the early Muslims" (Al-Krenawi and Graham 2000:82).

Values recognized by the Koran include the following:

- Hospitality and generosity in giving and spending;
- Respect for elders and parents;
- Wealth and preeminence of male children;

◗ Subordination of women to men;
◗ Modesty;
◗ Intensive religiosity;
◗ Equality of all human beings; and
◗ Health and strength. (Hall and Livingston 2006:144)

These basic values are central influences on the organization and behaviors of Muslim families.

> Arab families place high value on spirituality in the form of Islam. The patriarchal arrangement is its traditional family structure. Both recent and not so recent Arab immigrants who follow Islam conform to a hierarchical organization of authority that extends to roles, obligations, and status. The welfare of the family supersedes the welfare of the individual, making the family the basis of identity. . . . Furthermore, family is a reference point for behavior and spiritual directives (Hall and Livingston 2006:143).

> In addition, "in Arab families, where Islam is the spiritual tradition, reverence for the patriarch, as well as concern for the family's status, provides a strong sense of solidarity and loyalty" (Hall and Livingston 2006:144).

However, it is very important to understand that Muslim/Arab families are quite diverse in terms of which and to what extent values and behaviors within Islam are emphasized. As a result, it is crucial that social "workers should be aware that no particular set of beliefs and values exists that is representative of all Muslims" (Hodge 2005:164).

As indicated above:

> The basic social unit for Muslims is the family. . . . However, "family" is often conceptualized broadly to include relatives or even the whole Islamic community. It is the family, most specifically the husband and wife, that is understood to be responsible for reproducing spiritual and social values. Thus, family, both nuclear and extended, is essential to the spiritual and social health of the broader ummah [community] (Hodge 2005:165).

As noted above, we will look more closely at Muslim community and culture in Chapter 10.

In summary, Al-Krenawi and Graham suggest that social workers who work with Muslim families should:

1. Have an understanding of Muslim family arrangements as more hierarchical and less flexible.

2. Have an understanding of the implications of gender construction within Muslim society, which limits women's movements outside the home.

3. Appreciate that the client may be reluctant to work with a practitioner of the opposite sex.

4. Have a basic understanding of Islam . . . and Islamic movement traditions, as well as their common practices and implications. (2000:299)

Familiness and Multiracial Realities

As we discovered in Chapter 5, as U.S. society becomes more diverse the boundaries between and among diversities are becoming more and more blurred. One example of this is the growing population of biracial and multiracial people. The issue of multiracial identity and heritage has special implications for families, both in the area of adoption/foster care and in the area of special challenges for parenting multiracial children (see Chapter 5 for a discussion of parenting challenges for multiracial children).

Multiracial adoption and foster care

Same race adoption   Fong et al. note that the existence of substantial numbers of racially mixed people "suggests that social workers may have to recast the dialogue about what have been regarded as 'transracial' adoptions" (1996:22). *Transracial adoptions* are also referred to as "interracial," "interethnic," or "transethnic" adoptions (Hollingsworth 1998:104). They point out that the position taken by social work since the 1970s has been that children should be placed for adoption with parents of like ancestry. This policy was advocated initially and most strongly by the National Association of Black Social Workers [NABSW]. The formal position, put forth in 1974 by NABSW was: "Only a black family can transmit the emotional and sensitive subtleties of perception and reaction essential for a black child's survival in a racist society" (Smith in Fong et al. 1996:22). "Similar arguments can be made for placement of American Indian, Mexican American, and Asian American children" (Fong et al. 1996:22). The Indian Child Welfare Act of 1978 recognized the importance of maintaining cultural and community relationships as well as family relationship decisions about the welfare of Native American children. It gave "tribal courts exclusive jurisdiction over American Indian child custody proceedings" (Hollingsworth 1998:105).

Policy and practice in the area of multiethnic and multiracial adoption and foster care have remained unsettled. Since passage of the Multiethnic Placement Act of 1994, social workers and others concerned with child welfare have continued to struggle with fundamental issues about how to achieve what is best for children of color who may need out-of-home placement either temporarily (foster care) or permanently (adoption). Hollingsworth found five themes that have emerged from the ongoing struggle among organizations concerned with child welfare and transracial adoption:

1. That ethnic heritage is important;
2. That children be raised preferably by their biological parents or, when not possible, by other biological relatives;
3. That economic need alone is not an acceptable reason for children to be deprived of their biological parents;
4. That efforts should be made to ensure that adoptive parents of the same race as the child are available and systemic barriers should not interfere; and
5. That placement with parents of a different race is acceptable and even preferable when the alternative means a child is deprived of a permanent home and family. (Hollingsworth 1998:113)

Clearly the issue of multiethnic adoption is complex and must be considered from multiple perspectives. Hollingsworth argues that "seeking to solve the problems associated with the overrepresentation of children of color in the child welfare system by protecting transracial adoption is simplistic and fails to protect those who are most vulnerable in this society—the children dependent on that society." She suggests that "a more responsible approach is to understand and eliminate the circumstances that constitute the cause of the situation" (Hollingsworth 1998:114). One of the most significant circumstances that cause out-of-home placements is poverty.

Family poverty, diversity, and out-of-home placement   As indicated earlier in this chapter (and in other chapters), poverty is closely related to many other conditions that impede individual and family well-being. In addition, families of color (especially African American, Hispanic, and Native American families) are much more likely to experience poverty than white families. Hollingsworth argues that "living in poverty" is one of the reasons large numbers of children of color are in out-of-home placements. She notes that "over 46 percent of all African American children lived in poverty in 1993, as did 41 percent of all Latino children; only 14 percent of white children lived in poverty" (Children's Defense Fund in Hollingsworth 1998). In addition, "56 percent of children living with their mothers only were poor, compared to 12 percent of those living with married parents, and children of color were more likely than white children to live in mother-only households" (Hollingsworth 1998:111).

Poverty is closely associated with "circumstances that result in out-of-home placements." For example, the National Incidence Study of Child Abuse and Neglect found that

> Children from families with annual incomes below $15,000 were 22 times more likely to experience maltreatment than children from families whose incomes exceeded $30,000. They were 18 times more likely to be sexually abused, almost 56 times more likely to be educationally neglected, and over 22 times more likely to be seriously injured. Children of single parents had an 87 percent greater risk of being harmed by physical neglect and an 80 percent greater risk of suffering serious injury or harm from abuse and neglect (Hollingsworth 1998:113–14).

Multiracial adoption and foster care   Fong et al. (1996:22) suggest that for the many racially mixed children and people today, this policy, which assumed that everyone was a member of only one race, may be insufficient. They describe the Multiethnic Placement Act of 1994 as one example from the policy arena of dealing with this complex issue.

> The Multiethnic Placement Act of 1994 (P.L. 103-382) challenges the traditional practice of using race and ethnicity as the deciding factor in adoption. The act bans discrimination in placement decisions based solely on race, color, or national origin. . . . It allows agencies to consider the cultural, ethnic, or racial background of children and the capacity of the prospective foster or adoptive parents to meet the needs of the children based upon their background; and stipulates that agencies engage in active recruitment of potential foster or adoptive parents who reflect the racial and ethnic diversity of the children needing placement (Smith in Fong et al. 1996:23).

The issue of the best family arrangement for mixed race children is complex and emotional for many reasons (see Chapter 5, Competing Individual and Communal values), Fong et al. do not take a side in the debate about adoption of children who are clearly of one race by parents of that race. However, they argue "that a child who is mixed Mexican and Chinese probably belongs as much with a Chinese family as with a Mexican family" (1996:23). They note, though, that others might legitimately argue "that children of African American heritage, for example, should be reared by black families because only those families can sufficiently nurture children's positive black identities" (Fong et al. 1996:23). Fong et al. add that this position is not universally accepted by African American scholars and human service professionals. They point to the position of African American psychologist, Prentice Baptiste:

> Biologically, these [biracial] children are neither Black nor White, but equally a part of both races. But the Jim Crow traditions and laws will

attempt to define all of them as Black regardless of their phenotypic appearance. Parents of interracial children must counter this attempt by teaching them that they are and culturally can be members of both races. Positive models of both races must be very apparent to these children during early years of development (in Fong et al. 1996:23).

Fong et al. stress that "this is an issue that policymakers and practitioners in adoptions and foster care will continue to ponder and debate" (1996:23).

FOCUS: WOMEN

Feminist Perspectives on Families and Familiness

Rather than offering a single perspective or model for thinking about and understanding the interrelatedness of women and familiness, Ferree (1990) offers a synthesis of feminist issues and perspectives related to the family that she refers to as a **gender model**. Hers is perhaps an appropriate approach to take when exploring women and familiness. The family arena has traditionally created and enforced very different and often confining, oppressive, and exploitative roles and expectations for women members at the same time that women are central figures in virtually all traditional (and most alternate) notions of family.

Demo and Allen remind us that "Feminists have exposed the sexist and heterosexist underpinnings of any definition of family that takes as given that there is one type of family that can stand in for all other types and that the identities and behaviors of family members can be described by using the concept of 'gender role' " (1996:427). They assert that

> Reducing gender to a role ignores the structural features of gender and its interconnectedness to other dominant ways in which groups are differentially provided opportunities and oppressed. . . . A role . . . reduces gender to the more narrow and depoliticized realm of interpersonal relationships. . . . Sociologists do not describe class or race inequality as "class role" or "race role," recognizing that such descriptions hide the power relations of social stratification beyond individual experience or interpersonal interaction (Demo and Allen 1996:427).
>
> Ferree states that "a feminist perspective redefines families as arenas of gender and generational struggles, crucibles of caring and conflict, where claims for an identity are rooted, and separateness and solidarity are continually created and contested" (Demo and Allen 1996:427; Ferree in Demo and Allen 1996:428).

Consistent with our attempts to explore alternatives to traditional approaches to thinking about familiness and its implications for understanding HBSE, the alternatives we explore here reflect efforts to recognize the often complex and oppressive forces emerging from traditional family arrangements. This part of our journey represents another point at which we can rethink or revision familiness in ways that empower all members of families, in this case specifically women members, to reach their full human potential. This, of course, has important implications for social workers' concerns about and responsibilities for assisting all humans in reaching their fullest human potential.

Ferree's synthesis of feminist thinking about the family sphere reflects several dimensions of alternate paradigm thinking in addition to the feminist dimension. It critically examines a number of the dimensions of traditional paradigm thinking. Her synthesis addresses issues of separateness versus inter-relatedness; diversity; oppression; privilege; and masculinity/patriarchy.

Ferree describes a number of common themes of feminist premises in thinking about women and familiness. She notes that "male dominance within families is part of a wider system of male power." This patriarchal family arrange-ment is damaging to women and "is neither natural nor inevitable" (1990:866). Feminist analyses of family question the notion of family as separate from other social institutions such as political and economic institutions. They question notions of family as a "separate sphere" that is a safe and private haven unconnected to the public or outside world. On the other hand, feminist analyses remind us that violence and inequality characteristic of the public world also permeate in significant ways the family sphere. Feminist perspec-tives suggest that there are very different and often conflicting interests inside families that are associated with gender. Feminist critiques of traditional per-spectives on the family suggest "a new approach that (a) defines families as fully integrated into wider systems of economic and political power and (b) recog-nizes the diverging and sometimes conflicting interests of each member" (1990:867). With this perspective in mind we will explore a number of issues and concepts important for understanding familiness and that have significant consequences for women in the context of family. These issues and concepts will include family violence, gender or sex roles, family work, and dual wage earner families.

Women, families, and violence

Feminist analyses of family have been particularly important in documenting and analyzing the widespread violence that occurs in the family context. Many of these analyses have described the connections between violence against women and the inequalities that characterize traditional families. Miller (1986) notes that violence against women in families has implications for everyone, not just for women.

Miller offers disturbing information on the extent and types of violence against women. She notes, for example, that based on current information avail-able, estimates are "that rape occurs to one out of four women in the United States, that one third of female children and adolescents under the age of eigh-teen experience significant sexual abuse, and that violence occurs in one third to one half of U.S. families" (Miller 1986:xxi–xxii). Even women who have not directly experienced such forms of violence must live each day "with the per-vasive threat of violence" (Miller 1986:xxiii).

Miller suggests that study of this context of inequality and violence or the threat of violence has resulted in important information about strengths of women who must survive in this context. She stresses that the increasing attention to and knowledge about violence in families has come about in large part as a result of the strength of survivors of violence against women and of the efforts of women directly involved in action to reduce family violence. The incredible strengths of women who live with violence or the threat of violence are perhaps most dramat-ically reflected in their continuing efforts "to create growth-fostering interactions within the family." Miller concludes that "women, as a group, struggle to create life-giving and life-enhancing relationships within a context of violence and life-destroying forces" (Miller 1986:xxiii). This complex and often contradictory family context in which goals of safety, peace, and security are sought in an environment often characterized by inequality and violence must be recognized in our attempts to more fully understand family. (See Chapter 5 for an addi-tional discussion of violence.)

Globally, one of most serious human rights issues related to violence against women and girls is the cultural practice of female genital mutilation or cutting. The text below defines and summarizes the evolution of terms related to this form of violence against women and girls.

Women and Forced Migration

Ross-Sheriff (2006) points out the central role that women play in the complex processes involved in migration, refugee status, and immigration, especially in the context of war and conflict. She points out:

> Women and their dependent children constitute more than 80% of refugees and displaced persons. . . . They suffer the agonies and turmoil of war while playing significant roles in diverse capacities as mothers, sisters, wives, widows, wage earners, and caretakers of their families. . . . Refugee women bear a disproportionate share of the suffering. They must provide for their children in an atmosphere in which their security is threatened and the likelihood of sexual violence is increased (Ross-Sheriff, 2006:206).

In her research with Afghan women in exile, she was able to document four stages "of uprooting and displacement" across three categories. The four stages or time periods are:

1. The last days prior to leaving their homes to seek asylum, [which she refers to] as pre-uprooting.
2. During the flight from their homes to the country of asylum (uprooting).
3. During the time in exile in [this case] Pakistan.
4. After repatriation back to Afghanistan (Ross-Sheriff 2006:208–209).

The three categories that cut across all four stages of uprooting and development based on her research were:

1. Experiences and traumatic events.
2. The roles of women as social actors.
3. Coping and support (Ross-Sheriff 2006:209).

Deciphering the Terms: Mutilation, Cutting, or Circumcision?

Female genital mutilation/cutting (FGM/C), also known as female circumcision (FC), female genital cutting (FGC), and female genital mutilation (FGM), involves the cutting or alteration of the female genitalia for social rather than medical reasons.

The term FC was widely used for many years to describe the practice; however, it has been largely abandoned as it implies an analogy with male circumcision. Various communities still use the term FC because it is a literal translation from their own languages. Female genital mutilation/cutting is a far more damaging and invasive procedure than male circumcision. FGM/C is often perceived as a way to curtail premarital sex and preserve virginity.

FGM is the term most commonly used by women's rights and health advocates who wish to emphasize the damage caused by the procedure. In the mid-1990s, many organizations decided to shift to the use of the more neutral term, female genital cutting, because they considered FGM to be judgmental, pejorative, and not conducive to discussion and collaboration on abandonment. The U.S. Agency for International Development currently uses the term FGM/C.

Sources: Anika Rahman and Nahid Toubia, *Female Genital Mutilation: A Guide to Laws and Policies Worldwide* (London and New York: Zed Books, 2000): 4; and *Abandoning Female Genital Mutilation/Cutting: Information From Around the World* (Washington, DC: Population Reference Bureau, 2005).

In Tables 6.8 through 6.11, she provides detail that demonstrates challenges faced and issues addressed by the women in her study (Ross-Sheriff 2006:209–216).

Gender or sex role?

Traditional notions of sex roles in families emerge out of and along with traditional notions of family and of the "proper" roles of family members, especially the roles of males and females. The traditional notion of family was based largely on the observations by social scientists of "white, middle-class suburban families of the 1950s." As we discovered earlier, what emerged was the nuclear family structure portrayed as the ideal or the norm. Within this structure men were to play the instrumental/breadwinner/leader role and women were to play the socioemotional/homemaker/supportive role (Walsh 2003:10).

Subsequently, we have begun to realize that this model of family caused significant problems for families and their individual members. Wives and mothers were overburdened with responsibilities for the well-being of husbands and fathers, as well as children, at the same time that society undervalued (and in monetary terms attached no value to) their contributions. Fathers and husbands, on the other hand, were seen as head of the household but were in fact on the margins of the family as a result of the demands of their breadwinner role. This placed even more responsibility for the family on wives and mothers. What

Table 6.8   Pre-Uprooting Period

Experiences and Traumatic Events That Precipitated Flight
    Constant fear of persecution from other ethnic groups
    Lack of freedom and restrictions of movement
    Bombardment, air raids, shooting
    Fear of arrest of husband, son, brother, or father
    Harassment or persecution by the government and opposition forces
    Explosion of bombs in the neighborhood
    Rocket launching in front of residence
    Worry about reaching the hospital to deliver a baby
Role of Women as Social Actors
    Family decision makers and/or pressuring and influencing family decisions
    Protectors of family members
    Facilitators of daily living activities of family members
    Providers of home schooling
    Protecting, hiding, securing family possessions
Active Coping and Support
    Vigilance
    Information sharing
    Moving to homes of relatives in safer neighborhoods
    Sharing own home with relatives who lived in more dangerous areas or had lost homes
    Sharing food
    Controlling children
    Serving elders
    Waiting and praying

Source: Ross-Sheriff, F. Afghan women in exile and repatiation: passive victims or social actors? *Affillia 21*(2) 14.

Table 6.9   Flight from Afghanistan

Traumatic Experiences and Events
    Fear of being caught and punished severely
    Fear of bandits
    Encounters with the border patrol (harassment, persecution, being turned back, and detention)
    Risking unknown and dangerous paths to evade the border patrol
    Encounters with police who tortured male family members
    Difficult conditions walking through mountainous terrain and thorny unpaved paths
    Challenges of escaping after dark by difficult means (i.e., on foot, on donkeys/horses, by bus or truck)

Roles of Women as Social Actors
    Protecting children
    Hiding male family members
    Getting information from diverse sources about alternate routes when stopped
    Moving on despite pain and encouraging family members not to give up (i.e. motivating men, children, and elderly family members)

Active Coping and Support
    Traveling by night and resting during the day at hotels that were recommended as safe spaces
    Staying during the day with people who they had known and who would provide refuge
    Learning about alternate routes where they would not encounter the border police
    Using different modes of travel and alternate routes
    Bribing to get safe passage
    Multiple means of travel
    Staying together with the family throughout the journey

Source: Ross-Sheriff, F. Afghan women in exile and repatriation: passive victims or social acors? *Affilia 21*(2) 14.

appeared functional from the perspective of the masculine-focused dominant perspective "proved quite dysfunctional for women in families. . . . The disproportionate responsibility for maintaining the household and the well-being of husband, children, and elders, while sacrificing their own needs and identities, proved detrimental" to women's physical and mental health (Walsh 1993:20; 2003:14–16).

The traditional perspective on sex roles as equal and complementary made invisible the very real power differentials inherent in the perspective. The failure to recognize power differentials built into traditional notions of sex roles—men as strong and women as weak, for example—supported the continuing oppression of women within the structure of family. The analysis of power inequalities within traditional definitions of family has helped to recognize and bring into the open the abuses and inequalities of power and conflict that result in wife battering, marital rape, and incest (Walsh 1993:380). Not only do narrow, inflexible, and inequitable sex role definitions result in threats to the health of many women, but we know from the all-too-familiar cases of sexual and physical assault within the context of families that the result for many women can be fatal.

We have noted at a number of points in our journey that issues related to power and inequality are essential to understanding more comprehensively the complexities of HBSE. A gender model is helpful in this regard because it focuses on issues of domination, categorization, and stratification—all fundamental and necessary concepts for understanding power.

Table 6.10   During Exile

Experiences and Traumatic Events
 No shelter or poor shelter
 Lack of funds for basic living expenses (i.e., rent, gas, electricity, and food)
 Poor and miserable living conditions
 Police raids and extortion
 Fear of male family members being accused and actually being jailed
 Hard labor and poor working conditions
 Inclement weather
Roles of Women as Social Actors
 Establishing contacts with family members, neighbors, and coethnics who had come earlier and seeking their support
 Managing the home and taking responsibility for all family members, including extended family members, until they managed to rent their own rooms
 Motivating husbands, sons, and brothers
 Managing the family and meeting the family's needs with limited resources
 Inquiring and learning about NGOs and religious organizations that would help find jobs, health care, medicine, schools, and so on
 Helping family members, neighbors, and coreligionists with whatever they could share (i.e., information, food, and medicine)
 Managing emotions such as anger, sorrow, and feelings of helplessness
Active Coping and Support
 Hard work
 Relief for having survived the journey and determination to manage until war ends
 Living with little resources
 Child labor as a source of survival
 Networking to find most effective means of survival
 Accessing support
 Providing mutual support and solidarity with the family, ethnic community, and people from the local *Masjid* (place of worship)
 Keeping faith and depending on Allah

Source: Ross-Sheriff, F. Afghan women in exile and repatriation: passive victims or social actors? *Affilia 21*(2) 14.

Table 6.11   Prior to and During Repatriation

Feelings That Facilitated the Decision to Return and Future Aspirations
 Feelings of exhilaration for the end of the war
 Feelings of joy for the prospects of returning home, coupled with fear about the conditions at home
Roles of Women as Social Actors
 Gathering and sharing information
 Giving and receiving support for daily survival during the initial resettlement period
 Making decisions within the family context
 Supporting children with schooling
 Supporting elderly members of the family
Active Coping and Support
 Providing mutual support for the preparation to depart
 Providing mutual solidarity within the family and community
 Doing hard work by oneself and providing encouragement to members of the family
 Maintaining hopes and aspirations for regaining normalcy

Source: Ross-Sheriff, F. Afghan women in exile and repatriation: passive victims or Social actors? *Affilia 21*(2) 14.

Ferree summarizes the problems with use of the traditional concept of "sex roles" for explaining family members' statuses, behaviors, and traits:

> The role approach . . . obscures the dimension of power and the ongoing processes of conflict associated with change. Feminist explorations of family relationships are therefore increasingly cast in a fundamentally different theoretical context, that of gender. (1990:868)

Ferree notes the fundamental difference between sex role explanations and gender explanations of human behaviors: "While the sex role model *assumes* a certain packaging of structures, behaviors and attitudes, the gender model analyzes the *construction* of such packages" (1990:868).

Family work

The issue of work is another central element in a gender model for understanding familiness. Gender is intricately interconnected with determining the division of labor or work (both paid and unpaid) in families and households. A gender model calls upon us to recognize the interconnections of work and family. It suggests that both men and women must be considered simultaneously workers and family members. A gender model also requires that a historical perspective be introduced into any efforts to understand the place and nature of work and gender in the family.

The term *family work* is a helpful concept for thinking about work in the context of family. **Family work** refers to "the household chores and childcare tasks that must be performed by families to maintain the household and its members" (Piotrkowski and Hughes 1993:191). Traditional views of family see men as the only paid workers in the family and therefore men are seen as the "providers" for the other dependent family members—women and children. Women, on the other hand, are responsible for family work. A gender model suggests that such a version is not only inaccurate today but has historically not been an accurate portrayal (Ferree 1990:871).

How might the experiences of the woman in this photo reflect the concept of "second shift" described in the narrative? Might this woman need a "wife" in the sense described by Ferree in the discussion of "dual-wage-earner" families?

The gender perspective points out historical inaccuracies as a source of the "male provider myth." "It recognizes that women have always contributed significantly to the household economy, including through paid employment in and out of the home." Despite the male provider myth, women's "economic contributions have been substantial. . . . The social association of masculinity with the role of sole provider is new, not 'traditional.' " The construct of the "self-made man" emerged only in the nineteenth century. Ferree suggests that the self-made man was not self-made at all but was the result of "a gendered process in which mothers and wives have clearly prescribed, supporting roles" (1990:871–873). The picture of a household in which the ideal arrangement is a single (male) wage-earner with a support system (women and children) at home freeing him of responsibilities other than wage earning has important implications for women in current economic conditions requiring two wage earners rather than one in order to make ends meet.

Dual-Wage-Earner families

For many women, entering the work force has resulted in what some writers have referred to as a "second shift." As more and more women have entered the full-time work force to share breadwinning responsibilities, there has not been a corresponding sharing of family work responsibilities by their husbands. Several studies have found that working women in two-wage-earner households continue to carry up to 80 percent of household and child-care responsibilities (Walsh 2003:16). The amount of family work done by husbands varies by ethnic group. Some data suggest that African American men do more of the family work than white men. This is an example of the greater role flexibility in African American families than in white families (Piotrkowski and Hughes 1993:192).

Ferree suggests that "women who enter conventionally male defined careers . . . need a wife . . . because the expectations built into the structure of the job and the workplace take such a full-time support system for granted." A two-"husband" family, in which both wage earners focus on career and have little time or energy left over to invest in family life, needs in effect to hire a wife. There are at least two possible responses to this need. One has implications for race and class because the "wife" hired is "typically a woman of color and/or a new immigrant" (1990:873). As indicated above, a second, and more likely response is for the wife who becomes a wage earner to simply add this role to her other responsibilities for the well-being of the family—often to the point of exhaustion. Some single mothers suggest that losing a husband actually *decreases* time pressures in housework (1990:874–875).

Yet another and seldom discussed response is the role of children in performing unpaid labor when both mothers and fathers work for pay outside the household. Several scholars suggest that children may do more housework than their fathers when their mothers work outside the home. The division of labor among children in the household is also gendered in that "daughters are still more likely to be given housework than sons, and among sons and daughters who do housework, daughters do more hours of work" (Ferree 1990:874–875).

The gender perspective also suggests that income coming into a household from wage earners is subject to gendering processes. It is not safe to assume that money coming to the household all goes into a common pot that is equitably divided based on family and individual needs. For example, women's earnings may be earmarked specifically for child care, while men's "bonuses" may be considered the man's alone. Still other evidence, especially evidence generated from studies of battered wives who have left their husbands, suggests that even in households generating substantial earnings, some members may in fact be living below poverty level owing to lack of access to the income generated by a husband unwilling to share that income fairly with his wife and children. Such gender inequities inside households are rarely accounted for in official data-gathering efforts:

> Social policy continues to be driven by the implausible assumptions that all family members are equally well-off, that above-poverty-line household incomes imply no below-poverty-line individuals within them, and that increasing total family income has the same effect if it derives from a rise in male or female income (Ferree 1990:878).

The gender perspective suggests that both micro and macro transformation is needed in the "work-family" system. For us as social workers, this perspective helps us appreciate the implications for women and families in the areas of HBSE, practice, research, and policy. Such transformations need to include:

> changes in transportation systems, home design, normal work schedules, recruitment and promotion structures, and national job creation policies [as well as more] traditional demands for affordable child care, more flexible work opportunities, and enforcement of equal opportunity policies for women. Because men's jobs and career paths are gendered and built upon a structure of family support that is also gendered, changes for women necessarily also imply changes for men, and men's reactions to change should be understood in these terms (Ferree 1990:874).

Summary

The gender perspective to increasing our understanding of alternate approaches to thinking about family is helpful in two ways that are especially important for us as social workers. It suggests that family systems are intricately interconnected with the other environmental systems that form the context in which individuals live and develop. It also suggests that family as a social construction is neither all good nor all bad; it is a complex arena with the potential for both supporting and putting up significant barriers to the well-being of its members.

As Ferree suggests, "both family and household are ever more firmly situated in their specific historical context, in which they take on diverse forms and significance. Race and class are understood as significant structural features underlying the diversity of family forms." She also urges that "rather than insisting on a dichotomous view of families as either solidary or oppressive, the gender model suggests that family relationships may be altruistic, or self-seeking, or carry an inseparable mix of motivations; that they may be simultaneously supportive and oppressive for women in relation to diverse others; that there is not one dimension of family power, but many" (1990:879).

FOCUS: SEXUAL ORIENTATION

Familiness from a Lesbian/Gay Perspective

Traditional approaches to family not only assume a nuclear, two-parent, white, child-centered family form, they also assume a heterosexual pairing/partnership as the foundation upon which family is built. Slater and Mencher (1991) and other scholars point out that such assumptions neglect a significant portion of the population and deny legitimacy to the family forms and functions that exist among gay and lesbian families. Like a number of other diverse family types, gay and lesbian families have for the most part been treated as if they were either deviant and dysfunctional or as if they did not exist at all. Our notion of familiness, along with our search for inclusiveness consistent with our notions of alternate paradigm, recognizes the need to understand family issues related to gay and lesbian families.

Slater and Mencher describe the neglect in traditional approaches to family of lesbian and gay male families in the areas of family life cycle models, predictable stresses of family life, and societally sanctioned rituals recognizing a family's successful negotiation of stressors and tasks presented at various stages of its life cycle (1991:373–375).

To begin to remedy these problems, Laird suggests that gay and lesbian families must be included in efforts to understand familiness. She suggests further that lesbian and gay families can "teach us important things about other families, about gender relationships, about parenting, about adaptation to tensions in this society, and especially about strengths and resilience" (1993:284). Gay and lesbian families are both similar and different in many ways from heterosexual families.

To more completely understand gay and lesbian families, as in the case of heterosexual families, they must be viewed *intergenerationally:* "Each partner, child, and other family member is influenced by and must come to terms with the specific history and culture of his or her own family of origin and its sociocultural context" (Laird 1993:285). Also like heterosexual families, gay and lesbian families are not a monolithic group. They display a wide range of diversities. As Laird points out, gay men and lesbians vary in terms of race, class, sex, age, religion, political affiliation, and all the other differences displayed among any group of individuals. As a result, gay and lesbian families reflect this wide array of individual differences as well (Laird 1993:286). However, the general movement for gay liberation has been criticized by many of its diverse members for its lack of diversity and inclusiveness. Carrier, for example, suggests that gay liberation in the United States has been primarily a white, middle-class movement (in Laird 1993:291).

Slater and Mencher (1991) note several specific problems for lesbian (and less directly for gay) families when we are limited to traditional heterosexually based models of family. Traditional models provide a life cycle process and context that is multigenerational and begins with the launching of a young adult who then couples, raises her or his children, and launches them as young adults. This model is not applicable to the young lesbian woman. Her experiences in her family of origin with its heterosexual focus provide no image from which she can launch her own family. Traditional models also take for granted a system of social supports to assist families as they move through their life cycles. For lesbians there are no socially accepted rituals to support and recognize these passages. Because there are few studies of gay familiness or parenthood we are left to assume that similar dynamics operate for gay men as well.

Traditional models of family are also child-centered (see earlier discussion of traditional models). Slater and Mencher note that while some lesbians have and wish to have children, lesbian life is not as child-centered as traditional models of family life. They remind us that childless heterosexual couples also experience this lack of a place in traditional models. Childless couples and lesbian and gay couples do nevertheless "establish and maintain a family unit which passes through discrete stages with their attendant stresses, transitions, and accomplishments" (1991:376).

Lesbian families certainly share many of the common stresses and patterns of heterosexual families. This may be in large part because the heterosexual family is the only role model for familiness available to most lesbians. There are, however, significant differences in the family-related issues, experiences, and realities faced by lesbians. Slater and Mencher stress that many of the issues facing lesbian families are not stage-based, as is the case with traditional models, but are contextual and consist of recurrent themes regardless of stage. Prominent among these contextual issues is the reality of creating and sustaining family in a continually hostile environment that refuses any legitimacy for your form of family. Lesbian families must continually face issues related to their very viability as a family. Larger society portrays lesbian families as "unconnected individuals" rather than related family members. Lesbian couples are most often treated as "roommates" or "friends living together" (1991:376). Again, we are left to assume that similar issues arise concerning gay men and their families.

Verification and validation of lesbian (or gay) familiness are dependent almost totally on the couple themselves, for they receive no validation from the larger society as is the case for heterosexual families. In fact to seek public recognition for lesbian (or gay) familiness through social exposure is often to risk the members' jobs, families of origin, housing, safety, or child custody (Slater and Mencher 1990:376–377).

Traditional Family Development Theories: Implications for Gay and Lesbian Families

In Chapter 3 we explored a number of traditional theories for understanding and explaining human behavior and social environment. These theories included structural functional, psychoanalytic, social learning, social exchange, and human development theories. Demo and Allen (1996) examined these same theories specifically for their implications for gay and lesbian families. Their objective was not to dismiss any other theories or to claim one grand theory. Their purpose was

1. To demonstrate that heterosexuality is a foundation for many theories of human and family development
2. To argue that a multiplicity of theories is necessary to understand ever-increasing family diversity (Demo and Allen 1996:423).

Demo and Allen "argue that traditional family theories, rooted in positivist assumptions of objectivity and neutrality, are insufficient in and of themselves and that *in addition* to mainstream approaches we need theories that posit the social construction of reality and recognize the inevitability of differences and the instability of concepts" (1996:423).

A need for multiple approaches

Traditional family theories tend to stress clarity of stages and linear progression through them, clarity of roles, and clarity of family boundaries. They tend to see ambiguity in these areas as inherently problematic. They have neglected, however, to consider that the gay and lesbian families who struggle with ambiguities in these areas may result in creating "new ways of relating that are positive for postmodern family functioning" (Demo and Allen 1996:426). Demo and Allen suggest the need for multiple perspectives "to incorporate new insights and thus revise knowledge about families by including what was formerly invisible or excluded. In our view, a promising direction is to use the insights and applications of both positivist and post-positivist; traditional and alternative approaches" (1996:428).

Defining Gay and Lesbian Families

While gay and lesbian families have much in common with heterosexual families, they are also difficult to define because of their differences from traditional notions of family. Laird (1993:294) suggests that gay and lesbian families might be best referred to as **families of choice** *because they combine blood relatedness with love and choice.* Gay and lesbian families are "formed from lovers, friends, biological and adopted children, blood relatives, stepchildren, and even ex-lovers, families that do not necessarily share a common household. In fact, in some lesbian communities, the boundaries between family, kinship, and community become quite diffuse." A basic definition of **lesbian or gay family** is the "intimate, enduring interaction of two or more people who share a same-sex orientation (e.g., a couple) or by the enduring involvement of at least one lesbian or gay adult in rearing a child. . . . Many lesbian and gay adults simultaneously live in two worlds—their heterosexual family of origin and the lesbian or gay family they maintain as adults—creating an extended family environment that may be termed a 'mixed gay/straight' or 'dual-orientation family'" (Demo and Allen 1996:416). Given all these variations we must recognize that there is no "uniform or normative definition for 'gay family' any more than there is for 'American' family." In addition, Laird argues, "definitions of family are political and ideological, created and recreated in social discourse and shaped in social relations of power" (Laird in Walsh 2003:178). However, this lack of a single or clear definition of gay and lesbian family may suggest some significant strengths from which heterosexual family studies and social workers working with families might benefit:

> With their relatively fluid boundaries and varied memberships, their patterns of nonhierarchical decision making, their innovative divisions of labor, and the relative weight given to friendship as well as blood relatedness, such families offer further challenge to dominant notions of family structure and function and present an opportunity for mental health professionals to assess the limitations in current definitions of family and kinship (Laird in Walsh 2003:179).

Contested Terrain: Gay and Lesbian Marriage

As I write this, intense political and social debates are taking place concerning the rights of gay men and lesbians to form families through marriage or civil unions that provide the same benefits and responsibilities as those accorded heterosexual couples and their families. The context of these debates in terms of outcomes to date has been primarily at the state level, though the debates themselves are also taking place at a national level. In addition to the right to marry or form legally recognized civil unions, related issues of rights to adopt or become foster parents are also part of the current discourse.

At this writing, for example, very recently lawmakers approved same-sex marriage in New Hampshire and Maine (effective September 14, 2009). In

How might these partners and their families reflect diversity and "diversity within diversity" in some of the ways discussed in this chapter?

addition, same-sex marriages are legal in Vermont (effective September 1, 2009), Massachusetts, Iowa, and Connecticut. New Hampshire and New Jersey currently allow civil unions that "provide state-level spousal rights to same-sex couples" (CNN 2009). However, the debates are still ongoing and some reversals have occurred. For example, in May 2008 the California State Supreme Court ruled that it is illegal to discriminate against same-sex couples by denying them the right to marry, "after which 18,000 gay and lesbian couples got married there." However, in November 2008 California voters "approved Proposition 8, which amended the state constitution to ban gay marriage" (CNN 2009). The 18,000 couples who married prior to the passage of Proposition 8 were allowed to retain their marital status.

Adoption and foster care by gay or lesbian families have also been areas of significant debate. For example, the American Academy of Pediatricians has

Policy Practice

Social workers are expected to use evidence-based interventions in their practice. How could additional empirical research such as that described in this section assist social workers in our policy practice efforts to create policies that do not discriminate against gay and lesbian families?

endorsed adoption by gay and lesbian persons (Laird in Walsh 2003:182). However, some states have reacted to the issue of gay adoption and foster care by passing legislation making it illegal for gay and lesbian persons to adopt or provide foster care. Adoption by gay and lesbians is currently illegal in Florida. In the November 2008 elections, Arkansas voters approved Act 1, which restricts adoption or foster care to married couples. While this applies to both homosexual and heterosexual persons, it in effect reduces significantly the number of persons available for adoption or foster care at a time when the state is experiencing a shortage of available adoptive and foster parents. This act is currently being contested by the Arkansas American Civil Liberties Union.

Unfortunately, there is little empirical research to guide decision making in the areas of gay and lesbian marriage, adoption, and foster care provision. As a result, the debate has primarily centered on emotional and value-laden conflicts over what are often referred to as appropriate "family values." Langbein and Yost (2009:292) have conducted research to begin to address some of the issues surrounding gay marriage in terms of whether or not same-sex marriage "has any adverse impact on societal outcomes specifically related to 'traditional family values.'" Specifically, these researchers tested "the claim of the Family Research Council that same-sex marriage will have negative impacts on marriage, divorce, abortion rates, the proportion of children born to single women, and the percent of children in female-headed households." In carrying out their research they considered "(1) whether gay marriage (or its equivalent) was legally permitted in that year; (2) whether the state offered some level of similar rights to same-sex partnerships; and (3) whether gay marriage was expressly forbidden by a state's law in that year." (2009:293) In their research they used "state-by-state data from 1990, 2000, and 2004 to analyze the impact of each of these legal frameworks on five outcome variables (marriage, divorce, abortion, BOW [born out of wedlock] rates, and children in female-headed households)" (Langbein and Yost 2009:293).

Based on their research, they found "no statistically significant adverse effect from allowing gay marriage" (Langbein and Yost 2009:292). In addition, they concluded specifically:

> Allowing gay marriage has no significant adverse impact on the family values variables. . . . It appears that any positive external effects of laws banning gay marriage are accompanied with similar or larger positive effects from laws that allow it. The implication is that laws allowing gay marriage, and the individual choices they reflect, have no significant adverse external effects, and may have positive effects. It follows that there can be no rational argument against these laws based on the alleged negative consequences of gay marriage for "family values" (Langbein and Yost 2009:293).

In addition, they argue that government (local, state, or national) bans on same-sex marriage have unintended adverse economic consequences. They posit, "for example, the ban on gay marriage induces failures in insurance and financial markets. Because spousal benefits do not transfer (in most cases) to domestic partners, there are large portions of the population that should be insured, but instead receive inequitable treatment and are not insured properly. Larger insurance pools reduce costs for all" (Langbein and Yost 2009:307).

More empirical research such as this is clearly needed, if we are to move away from making decisions in this arena based on value conflicts and divergent personal belief systems.

Lesbian and gay families: diversity within diversity

Lesbian and gay family diversity is of interest to scholars because:

1. These families have been stereotyped as a monolithic group, so their heterogeneity reveals diversity within diversity.

2. Their diversity helps to illustrate and elaborate our understanding of how diverse all families are.

3. Lesbian and gay families pose serious challenges and exciting opportunities for testing, revising and constructing family theories (Demo and Allen 1996:415–416).

There is little research on this configuration of "multiple minorities." Most research on gay or lesbian persons and families or children raised by lesbian or gay parents use study samples that are overwhelmingly either "white, well-educated, middle-class male[s]" or "white, middle- to upper-middle-class, formerly married lesbians." This tendency "obscures multiple layers of diversity within lesbian and gay families and restricts our ability to document the special problems as well as the special strengths of lesbian and gay families" (Demo and Allen 1996:420).

Differences among lesbian and gay families   Demo and Allen (1996:416) outline a number of areas in which lesbian and gay families differ in order to illustrate that gay and lesbian families are clearly not a monolithic whole but are highly diverse. They list and describe differences in composition and structure, family processes, social stratification, interfamily diversity, and gender among gay and lesbian families. It is important to note that families with bisexual members, though very little research has been conducted on them, are likely to exhibit even higher degrees of variability in a number of these areas. It is also important to note the areas of diversity among gay and lesbian families that are also evident among heterosexual families. The degree of commonality between many gay and lesbian families and heterosexual families is significant. Demo and Allen (1996:416–417) list a variety of differences among gay and lesbian families:

▶ *"Composition and structure of lesbian and gay families differ according to* number, gender, and sexual orientation of adult(s) heading the household, length of couple relationship, household size, the presence and number of children, and sibling structure."

▶ *Family processes differ among families in nature of members'* interactions with one another in terms of the "nature and degree of involvement, support, nurturance, communication, conflict, tensions, and stresses."

▶ *Family differences in terms of social stratification and diversity* include "gender, sexual orientation, generation, age, race, and ethnicity."

▶ *Interfamily diversity* regardless of number and degree of sexual orientation variation, it is important to recognize that "changes in sexual orientation over time and over stages in the life course add further complexity to the task of understanding how family relationships are influenced by sexual orientation and how diverse family structures evolve."

Family roles

The issue of negotiation of roles within the lesbian family both represents a source of stress and demonstrates creativity and strength on the part of lesbian family members. Heterosexual family members have been socialized since birth to the appropriate family roles expected of them. These roles almost exclusively emerge according to one's gender. Contrary to popular myths about lesbian and gay couples, most couples do not simply adopt traditional heterosexual versions of family roles. Lesbians' family roles tend to demonstrate greater role flexibility and divide tasks and responsibilities more according to individual preferences, abilities, and needs than is the case with prescribed gender-based traditional roles. This flexibility often requires repeated renegotiation as situations change and time passes, which is more complex than in traditional heterosexual families. However, this continuous renegotiation and evaluation may very well be outweighed by the increased liberation from rigid, confining traditional roles (Slater and Mencher 1991; Laird 1993).

Lesbian and gay couples and relationships

Faced with recurring stressors in an often inhospitable social environment, lesbian families create innovative responses to meet their needs for familiness. These responses emerge both from the couple relationship and from the lesbian community. This loose community network not only offers a source of support and legitimation for lesbian families, it also in many ways functions as an extension of lesbians' families.

Lacking supports from the larger society, lesbian couples often adopt a particular sense of closeness not experienced by heterosexual couples. This intense connectedness is often described in heterosexual family therapy literature as "fusion" and usually carries a negative or pathological connotation. Even though this intense closeness is sometimes the source of some difficulties in maintaining separateness of individual identities for lesbian couples, it is more often found to be functional in its nurturance of a high degree of intimacy and interconnectedness when the larger environment provides little or no validation of individual couple identity (Laird 1993; Slater and Mencher 1991:379).

While lesbian couples have been stereotyped as forming relationships that are too close, gay men are often stereotyped as unable to form lasting couple relationships at all. As Laird points out, "the gay couple is tainted by social images that portray gay males as promiscuous, flamboyant, bar-hopping clones, with coupleness itself an anomaly" (1993:312). A number of researchers have attempted to move beyond these stereotypes to look more closely at the relationships and sexual behaviors of gay couples. The results have varied. Some research indicates that "openness" or extra-couple relationships seem to enhance couple longevity. Some research indicates that closed couples were more "happy." Other research indicates that there are no differences "between open and closed couples together 3 years or longer, in intimacy, satisfaction, security, or commitment" (Laird 1993:312). We should note that what is important is the meaning of sexual relationships outside the couple for the couple themselves. "For some couples, an extra couple sexual encounter or affair may feel like the ultimate betrayal; for others it may be interpreted as an experience that has little to do with and does not contaminate the couple relationship" (Laird 1993:313).

Blumstein and Schwartz, in extensive research on the sexual behaviors of heterosexuals and homosexuals, found that regardless of the type of relationship, men tend to have more outside partners than women (in Laird 1993:313). This suggests that monogamy (relationships with no outside sexual partners) may "be more related to gender socialization than to sexual orientation." In gay relationships, it seems that "outside sex in the gay male couple is not related to gay men's overall happiness or commitment to the relationship." Laird reminds us that although gay men (like heterosexual men) are more likely to have sex outside of a couple relationship than are lesbians (or heterosexual women), "AIDS has and is shaping a trend toward more sexual exclusivity and more stability in gay male couple relationships" (1993:313).

Family and community

As noted earlier, the lesbian community has created many innovative and positive responses to the general hostility and lack of support for lesbian familiness in the society at large. The lesbian community may often "offer the lesbian family its only source of positive public and social identity" (Slater and Mencher 1990:380). The lesbian and gay community allows members to discover and to communicate with each other and among families what is normal and typical for lesbian or gay families and individuals. The community allows members to begin to identify common experiences in meeting challenges and accomplishing family developmental tasks. Lesbian and gay communities are also a source of family rituals specific to the experiences and needs of lesbian and gay families. The community may, for example, offer a context for carrying out rituals borrowed from heterosexual culture, such as exchanging rings or anniversary cards. The lesbian community has also created its own unique validation rituals in recognition of the contextual issues faced by lesbian individuals and families. These include rituals to recognize "coming out" and lesbian commitment ceremonies.

Gay and lesbian communities are as diverse as heterosexual communities. Laird cautions that "we not assume, from experiences with one community, that we understand gay or lesbian 'culture' or 'norms' for all such communities." In addition, she stresses that we must also recognize that different members of the same community relate to the community differently and have very different perspectives on that community (1993:293).

Children of lesbian and gay parents

Increasing research attention is being focused on the children of lesbian and gay parents. This new emphasis can be accounted for by several factors:

1. The need on the part of gays and lesbians considering parenthood to understand the issues and challenges they may face;
2. The concerns of social scientists with how such families and their children cope with oppression;
3. The impact of this nontraditional family form on psychosocial development; and
4. The provision of more accurate information to a legal system that has operated largely on prejudice and mythology in custody situations and in addressing questions concerning the rights of gay and lesbian parents and their children. (Laird in Walsh 2003:199)

The findings of this research suggest that the children of gay and lesbian parents face special difficulties, such as social discrimination, ridicule, and even isolation. Adolescent children are especially vulnerable to peer pressure and harassment as they struggle with the development of their own identities. However, in spite of difficulties such as these "the peer and other social relationships of children of lesbian and gay parents do not differ significantly from those of any other children" (Laird 1993:313–315).

Perhaps the most often raised concern or myth about children of gay or lesbian parents is whether the children are more likely than the children of heterosexual parents to grow up gay or lesbian. "A number of researchers (Bozett 1981, 1987, 1989; Golombok et al. 1983; Hoeffer 1981; Huggins 1989; Kirkpatrick et al. 1981; Miller 1979; Paul 1986; and Rees 1979) have concluded that the sexual orientations/preferences of children of gay or lesbian parents do not differ from those whose parents are heterosexual." Laird suggests that "this makes sense since it is equally clear that most homosexual adults were themselves reared in heterosexual families" (Laird in Walsh 2003:201).

Children of gay and lesbian parents seem to grow and develop quite well in spite of the prejudice and discrimination they face. Some research on children of lesbian parents even indicates that they may benefit. They tend to be more flexible and tolerant than other children. One might also ask if there are not benefits to be gained by children of lesbian parents who are not raised in the traditional patriarchal family structure.

FOCUS: FAMILIES AND DISABILITY

Social workers are expected by federal mandates as well as our values and ethics to provide services to families and their members with disabilities. In order to do so effectively it is important to understand a range of issues facing these families with whom we work. In addition, we must develop a keen understanding of social environmental issues influencing these families and their members. Some of these issues include culture, income or poverty, and accessibility of services. All these factors can be interrelated for many families of children with disabilities.

Harry (2002) provides a helpful historical overview of approaches used in working with families with children with disabilities. She notes that

> prior to the 1970s, the emphasis was on psychoanalytic approaches to parents, particularly mothers, an approach that for the most part presented the mother as a victim or patient in severe psychological crisis who needed to go through certain stages of reaction before a point of 'acceptance' could be reached.

Harry (2002) notes that this approach may have had some relevance in its attempt to help parents come to terms with their child with a disability. However, she also points out that this approach was limited in several ways. It "focused almost totally on White, middle-class families who could access the kinds of services offered by the psychoanalytic model." It promoted a "pathological view of families of children with disabilities," and it totally ignored cultural differences in the ways families may react to and deal with a child with a disability.

The passage of P.L. 99-457 in the 1986 Education of the Handicapped Amendments brought us to the present point where parents were to be partners or collaborators with service providers for their children. As noted in Chapter 5 and elsewhere, the fundamental approach was to be family-centered practice (Harry 2002). This approach has also reinforced the importance for social workers of culturally competent practice with families.

Harry (2002) contrasts the current approach to the early years of the disability movement, which she refers to as highly ethnocentric. The primary concern of the leaders of this movement was the fight for recognition by people with disabilities as a minority group or culture with distinct needs and issues. As a result, Harry posits that adding a multicultural focus would have diluted the movement's drive for recognition of its own.

Bailey et al. (1999) point out that "almost all parents experience challenges in learning about and gaining access to services if they have a child or family member with a disability." These challenges for parents include:

1. learning about their child's disability,

2. becoming aware of their child's educational and therapeutic needs,

3. identifying the range of services that potentially could help support them and their child, and

4. gaining access to those services.

Additional interacting factors include:

1. characteristics of the child (e.g., severity of disability, specialization of needs for services or equipment, known features of the disability),

2. characteristics of the family (e.g., education of parents, knowledge of services, advocacy efforts), and

3. characteristics of the community (e.g., availability of resources, attitude of professionals, interagency collaboration) (Bailey et al. 1999).

Bailey et al. (1999) studied Latino/a access and use of the service system provided through P.L. 99-457. They noted that for Latino/as, like parents of many nondominant ethnic groups, there were special challenges to successfully accessing and using services for their children. Some of these challenges included:

- difficulties due to language barriers,
- lack of familiarity with cultural expectations for appropriate helpseeking behavior, or
- professionals who do not understand or appreciate fully the implications of cultural and ethnic variation in values, goals, and behavior.

With the passage of P.L. 99-457 in 1986 and its call for family-centered practice, cultural differences among families of children with disabilities became a significant concern of both researchers and practitioners. For example, in 1993 Weisner studied the differences between European American families and East African families in concerns about caring for their children with disabilities and found

> that European American parents were very concerned about the difficulty of maintaining equality of treatment toward the siblings and felt discomfort with allotting 'undue' responsibility to the nondisabled siblings. By contrast, such matters were found not to be a cause for concern among the East African parents, in whose family systems sibling equity was not a predominant value and for whom responsibility for younger or less competent siblings was a matter of tradition (Weisner in Harry 2002).

Additional research on diverse families in the United States has produced four themes important for understanding and working with families of children with disabilities:

1. the fact that social groups construct disability differently from one another and from professionals,

2. the differential expectations for childhood development and differential interpretations of the etiology and meaning of disabilities,

3. the role of culture in parental coping styles, and

4. the effects of any of the foregoing factors on parental participation in the special education process (Harry 2002).

Harry urges professionals to be cautious of stereotyping that may result from overgeneralizing cultural patterns of constructing disability when working with individual families. For example, she notes that

> it is well known that traditional cultural patterns have been described for particular groups, such as the attribution of disability to spiritual retribution or reward among many Asian groups, an emphasis on the wholeness of the spirit within a disabled body among Native American groups, and the belief that conditions such as epilepsy are reflections of spiritual phenomena within the individual (Fadiman 1997 in Harry 2002).

However, the degree to which these constructions are held by any one family is subject to great variation. Harry also calls for service providers to develop an understanding of the disability perspective of the family with whom they are working, rather than impose their own perspective on the family. For example, Atkin (1991) pointed out that, "Service provision for disabled people usually embodies the views of the provider rather than the user" (p. 37), and called for research and service provision policies that are informed by "an account of disability in terms of black people's perceptions without these perceptions being seen as pathological" (p. 44 in Harry 2002).

Harry (2002) describes six challenges professionals face in providing effective services to culturally different families:

1. cultural differences in definitions and interpretations of disabilities;
2. cultural differences in family coping styles and responses to disability-related stress;
3. cultural differences in parental interaction styles, as well as expectations of participation and advocacy;
4. differential cultural group access to information and services;
5. negative professional attitudes to, and perceptions of, families' roles in the special education process; and
6. dissonance in the cultural fit of programs.

Malone et al. (2000) provide a helpful list of the types of services social workers can provide to families with children or other members with disabilities:

1. conduct home visits to assess living conditions, patterns of parent–child interaction, and special instruction to child and family;
2. conduct psychosocial developmental assessment of the child in the family context;
3. assess and provide services related to basic family needs and problems in family functioning;
4. investigate allegations of child neglect and maltreatment;
5. provide individual and family counseling;
6. plan and implement family services such as parent support groups and appropriate social-skills building activities for child and parent;
7. identify, mobilize, and link families to available supports;
8. help families to interface necessary social systems (conduct "boundary" work);
9. facilitate linkages among home, school, and community;
10. evaluate community resources or supports and factors that contribute to risk;

11. advocate for family rights and access to community resources;
12. provide information and education to families and professionals;
13. assist with transition planning;
14. serve as a family liaison or negotiator on the assessment and evaluation team;
15. consult with other professionals on family issues.

In addition to delivering culturally competent services in the areas above, social workers must also understand the impact of poverty on these families. Recent studies have found a significant link between poverty and risk for disability in children (Fujiura and Yamaki, 2000; Kaye, LaPlante, Carlson, and Wenger, 1996; Seelman and Sweeney, 1995 in Park et al. 2002). In addition, "among children with disabilities aged 3 to 21 in the United States, 28% are living in poor families. By contrast, among the children without disabilities in the same age range, only 16% are living in poverty" (Fujiura and Yamaki, 2000 in Park et al. 2002).

Park et al. (2002) note:

the fact that households with a family member with developmental disabilities have significantly lower income and greater dependence on means-tested income support indicates that poor families of children with a disability will be affected by poverty more severely than either poor families of non-disabled children or affluent families of children with a disability (Fujiura and Yamaki 1997).

SUMMARY/TRANSITION

In this chapter we explored some significant current influences on families. We have considered some social work implications of familiness. Traditional perspectives on family were examined, including definitions, historical perspectives on the family, family developmental tasks, life cycle notions of family, and some changes that have occurred in traditional perspectives on family. Divorce, remarriage, and stepfamilies were explored as traditional because of the number of individuals and families struggling with divorce and remarriage. It was recognized, though, that for the individuals struggling with the challenges of divorce, remarriage, and the formation of stepfamilies, these family constellations are in all likelihood considered alternative.

In this chapter we also explored alternative perspectives on familiness. We surveyed some alternative definitions of *family* or *familiness* and examined multifaceted definitions of *familiness* that attempt to integrate both traditional and alternative aspects. We explored a number of issues related to families and people of color. We employed an ecological approach to better understanding families of color. This approach included investigation of adaptive strategies employed by people of color to deal with the consequences of racism and oppression. Among the adaptive strategies explored were family extendedness, social role flexibility, biculturalism, and spirituality and ancestral worldviews. We also explored the impact of migration and immigration on families.

This chapter addressed issues and concerns related to women in families. This included a feminist perspective on family and familiness. Within the feminist perspective we explored gender and sex roles, the concept of family work, family violence, and issues of concern in dual-wage-earner families.

In this chapter we explored the issues of familiness from the perspectives of gay and lesbian families. We struggled with definitions of gay and lesbian families. We looked at family roles, gay and lesbian couples and relationships, and the place of gay and lesbian community in considerations of familiness. We also examined some of the findings of research on the status of children of gay and lesbian parents.

Finally, we explored the importance of understanding and competently working with families with members who have disabilities. The next chapter will focus on traditional and alternative notions about small groups. We will also consider the social work implications of a variety of approaches to understanding small-group structures and dynamics.

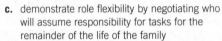

PRACTICE TEST

1. What is a major assumption of the Duvall and Hill Model of family development?
   a. A strengths based approach to family development.
   b. Parenting is the central activity of adult family life.
   c. That families can come in many different forms.
   d. That families may include non-related members.

2. The definition of _____ is family membership based on blood ties, as well as adopted members and people who are considered as and have functioned as part of a family.
   a. extended family
   b. family as intimate environment
   c. nuclear family
   d. augmented family

3. A social worker who looks at family development in four contexts: temporal, socio-structural, process and change, and family diversity is using _____.
   a. family life model
   b. family socialization theory
   c. life course theory
   d. social-structural model

4. Which of the following statements is NOT consistent with a family-centered approach?
   a. Family members, not professionals, determine who constitutes the family.
   b. Family norms are important in determining intervention.
   c. Family-professional collaboration requiring a high degree of trust, mutual respect and participation is stressed.
   d. A family preservation perspective is often associated with a family-centered approach.

Diversity in Practice

5. This unit, which can be helpful to social workers working with African American families, is made up of the biological parents, the children, and caregiver relatives.
   a. kinship triad   c. fictive family
   b. augmented family d. church family

6. Lesbian families tend to _____.
   a. adopt traditional heterosexual versions of family roles
   b. demonstrate role flexibility and divide tasks and responsibilities according to individual preferences and abilities

   c. demonstrate role flexibility by negotiating who will assume responsibility for tasks for the remainder of the life of the family
   d. none of the statements describe lesbian families

7. According to Hartman and Laird the definition of family used has an impact on us as social workers. How can this affect our practice with families?
   a. The definition of family used can impact the nature of the practice model used for working with families.
   b. The definition of family influences policies at the state, local, national and international level regarding families.
   c. Our personal definition of family and our own experiences in families can be strong influence on how we deal with family issues in practice.
   d. All of these can affect our practice with families.

8. Which of the following statements would not prove helpful to a social worker that is working with a Muslim family?
   a. A social worker should have an understanding of Muslim family arrangements as more hierarchical and less flexible.
   b. The social worker should have an understanding of the implications of gender construction within Muslim society.
   c. The basic social unit for Muslims is the Mosque.
   d. Appreciate that the client may be reluctant to work with a practitioner of the opposite sex.

Human Rights & Justice

9. A source of strength and support for ethnic minority families in facing the challenges of a long history of oppression and discrimination is _____.
   a. family relationships within the nuclear family
   b. the extended family
   c. the education system
   d. civil rights legislation

10. A social worker should be aware that divorced families have additional life cycle issues that families who do not experience divorce do not. The decision to divorce involves which developmental issue?
   a. working cooperatively on problems of custody
   b. acceptance of one's own part in the failure of the marriage
   c. giving up fantasies of reunion
   d. mourning loss of intact family

Log onto **MySocialWorkLab** once you have completed the Practice Test above to take your Chapter Exam and demonstrate your knowledge of this material.

Answers

1)b 2)d 3)c 4)b 5)a 6)b 7)d 8)c 9)b 10)b

Effective Child Welfare Practice with Immigrant and Refugee Children and Their Families

Barbara A. Pine and Diane Drachman

This article presents a multistage migration framework to broaden the lens through which child welfare personnel can view immigrant and refugee families and their children. By better understanding the family's experiences in both emigration and immigration, including reasons for leaving their home country, experiences in transit, and reception and resettlement experiences in the United States, child welfare personnel are better equipped to assess their needs and provide effective prevention, protection, permanency, and family preservation services. Case examples illustrating the application of the framework and guidelines for program and practice are included.

Immigrant children constitute one of the fastest growing groups in the United States today, with their numbers increasing to an estimated 9 million by 2010 (Fix & Passel, 1994). Some of these children, by reason of their families' experiences in migration and resettlement, are likely to need child welfare services, which in the United States are designed for the most vulnerable children—those at risk of neglect, abuse, abandonment, or separation from their families and placement in out-of-home care. Typically, child welfare services include prevention, child protection, family preservation, foster care, adoption, and preparation for emancipation (Maluccio, Pine, & Tracy, 2002).

Until recently, however, little attention has been given in the literature to the needs of immigrant children. Moreover, the social work literature on immigrants and immigration has mainly emphasized only one part of the migration process: the immigrants' experience in this country (Drachman & Paulino, 2004).

Social workers who provide child welfare services must identify sources of support and stress in the relationships between families and their environment, and develop their intervention strategies accordingly. To provide effective services for immigrants that are family-centered and culturally competent, child welfare practitioners must understand the child and family's experiences in both emigration and immigration.

This article uses a multistage framework on the migration and resettlement experience to demonstrate how understanding the migration experiences and different immigrant groups— transnational, circular, return, and undocumented—is critical for effective services to families and their children (Drachman, 1992; Drachman & Paulino, 2004). The framework, which emphasizes the circular processes of the migration experience, includes an examination of the premigration experience and the reasons for leaving the country of origin, the journey to the resettlement country, the reception from the resettlement country, and in some cases, the return to the country of origin.

After an overview of the numbers and needs of immigrant families and children in the United States, attention is given to immigrant families' status, a critical aspect of their reception and eligibility for needed services during

Barbara Pine, PhD, is Professor and Diane Drachman, PhD, is Associate Professor, School of Social Work, University of Connecticut, West Hartford, CT. The authors thank Catherine Ward, master of social work candidate at the University of Connecticut School of Social Work, for her invaluable research assistance.

Source: Pine, B. & Drachman, D. (2005). Effective child welfare practice with immigrant and refugee children and their families. *Child Welfare 84*(5), 537–550, 557 & 562.

their resettlement. Because a number of risk factors emanate from recent immigration policies, those most related to child welfare services will be delineated.

A discussion of the multistage framework follows this overview. The framework has been used to analyze the experiences of various immigrant groups, including Southeast Asians (O & Porr, 1990), Haitians (DeWind, 1990), Cubans (Gil, 1990), Russians (Drachman & Halberstadt, 1992; Mandel, 1990), Koreans (Drachman, Kwon-Ahn, & Paulino, 1996), and Dominicans (Drachman et al., 1996). Its implications for child welfare practice, however, have yet to be explored.

The article concludes with a set of guidelines for program and practice with immigrant families that emphasize a "humanitarian voice" in helping them secure the welfare of their children (Drachman, in press) and find services that embody the principles of prevention, permanency, protection, and family preservation.

Scope of the Challenge

Demographics

Unprecedented numbers of immigrants and refugees arrived in the United States during the past two decades, creating a wave of immigration not unlike the first wave at the turn of the 20th century more than 100 years ago. Then as now, social workers were in the forefront, advocating for and providing services to the new arrivals. As Giovannoni (2004) noted, "American social work developed largely around the provision of services to immigrants" (p. xi).

Child welfare services had their inception in major urban areas with large immigrant populations. Charles Loring Brace, the father of foster care, launched the orphan trains as a way of finding rural families for large numbers of homeless and dependent children, mainly the offspring of immigrants. The Societies for the Prevention of Cruelty to Children (SPCC), which grew out of the organization to protect animals, were designed to "save" mostly immigrant children (Hacsi, 1996; McGowan, 1983). So feared was the SPCC in immigrant communities that children often played a bogeyman type of game about the "Cruelty" coming to get you.

Unfortunately, the needs of immigrants in today's wave have outpaced the ability of mainstream institutions and professions to meet them, including child welfare agencies and schools (Fix, Zimmerman, & Passel, 2001). Although the network of services and supports in the six major immigrant receiving states (California, Florida, Illinois, New Jersey, New York, and Texas) is fairly well developed, the fastest growth of the immigrant population—through either direct immigration or secondary migration from one of the six—has been in 22 other states, where there has yet to be developed the needed capacity for linguistic or cultural competence.[*]

During the 1990s, nearly one million legal immigrants arrived in the United States, as well as an estimated 300,000-500,000 undocumented immigrants. In addition, between 70,000 and 125,000 refugees resided in the United States (Capps, Passel, Periz-Lopez, & Fix, 2003). Today, one in 10 people (more than 10% of the U.S. population) is foreign born, a figure that has doubled since 1970 (Fix et al., 2001; Healy, 2004). More than 31 million people in the United States are foreign born (Capps et al., 2003). Although immigrants have come from nearly 100 different countries, most are from Latin America and

---

[*]Ten states with the fastest growing immigration populations are North Carolina, Georgia, Nevada, Arkansas, Utah, Tennesseen, Nebraska, Colorado, Arizona, and Kentucky (Capps et al., 2003).

Asia. Mexico alone represents 30% of all foreign-born people in the United States today, with Asia at 26% and other Latin American countries at 22% (Capps et al., 2003). Moreover, the proportion of the foreign-born population that is undocumented may have climbed to an estimated 28% (Fix et al., 2001). Most of the future population growth in the United States may be driven by immigration and births to immigrants.

Immigrants and their families tend to be young. According to the 2000 U.S. Census, one out of every five children is either an immigrant or has an immigrant parent (Shields & Behrman, 2004). As of 1997, 20% of school-aged children had at least one immigrant parent (Ruiz-de-Velasco & Fix, 2000). Most immigrants to the United States—80%—enter either as part of a family unit or come to join a family member already here (Fix et al, 2001). Family unity is a strength among immigrants. Nearly 40% of immigrants' children live with extended family members, as compared with 22% of U.S.-born children. They also are more likely to live with both of their parents (Shields & Behrman, 2004).

Although immigrant families have many strengths, they do face many challenges. Their reasons for leaving their home country, their experiences on the journey, their reception in the United States, and, in particular, their legal status, are critical in creating effective services.

Legal Status as a Critical Challenge to Family Well-Being

The various immigration statuses carry different entitlements to benefits and services and different legal rights (Drachman, 1995). Some scholars assert that one's status structures the immigration experience, which ultimately has implications for families' and children's adaptation (Suarez-Orozco & Suarez-Orozco, 2001). The categories most pertinent for families coming to the attention of child welfare agencies include legal permanent resident, undocumented immigrant, refugee, special immigration juvenile status, and mixed-status families.

A legal permanent resident is a person who has been admitted legally to the United States following a successful application process and usually under the sponsorship of a close family member or, in some cases, an employer. Legal permanent residents receive permission to work, certified by what is commonly known as a "green card." This largest group of immigrants is eligible to become naturalized citizens three to five years after receiving a green card.

Undocumented immigrants (also called illegal immigrants) are those who do not have valid immigration documents. They may have expired temporary visas or may have entered the country without the knowledge of immigration authorities.

Refugees are admitted to the United States because of a "well-founded fear of persecution" in their own country. Although refugee status is usually accorded to groups of people, each individual must qualify. Refugees are eligible to apply for legal permanent resident status after a year (Capps et al., 2003).

Special immigration status can be accorded to some minor immigrants under Special Immigrant Juvenile Status, enacted under Section 203 (b)(4) of the Immigration and Nationality Act. Under this legislation, immigrant visas can be issued to juveniles who are eligible for long-term foster care because they have been abused, neglected, or abandoned, and for whom reunification with their birthfamily is not possible (U.S. Citizen and Immigration Services [USCIS], 2004).

A mixed-status family is one in which members are in different legal categories. The family can include citizen children (children born in the United

States), undocumented children, an undocumented parent or parents, and a parent or others with legal permanent residence.

Especially following the 1996 restructuring of immigration and welfare policies, legal status has a strong effect on families' social and economic characteristics and their likelihood of coming to the attention of child welfare personnel. Current immigration policies emphasize self-sufficiency, barring even legal immigrants from obtaining welfare benefits, food stamps, disability payments, and publicly funded health insurance during their first five years in the country. Those accorded refugee status can receive these benefits, while those who are undocumented enjoy neither protection nor benefits with the exception of education and emergency health care (Greenberg & Rahmanou, 2004).[*]

The mixed-status family is of special significance to child welfare agencies. Eighty-five percent of noncitizen households with children contain citizen children. Although mixed-status families make up 9% of all families, they constitute 14% of low-income families (Fix & Zimmerman, 1999). In California and New York, where the immigrant population tends to be larger, the proportion of poor immigrant families is larger. In New York, one in five low-income families is a mixed-status family; in California, 40% of low-income families is mixed status. Moreover, children in mixed-status families represent 21% of all children lacking health insurance nationwide; more than half of those are in California (Fix & Zimmerman, 1999).

Families with mixed status present a number of problems. An undocumented parent's fear of deportation may prevent that parent from seeking services for a citizen child who is eligible, especially when the household is composed of both citizen and undocumented children. Thus, the undocumented status of one member can have a chilling effect on other family members using services, even when they are eligible. Furthermore, mixed status creates inequality among children and divisiveness in the family, because citizen children have the same rights and service eligibility as other U.S. children, while their undocumented siblings do not. Child welfare personnel must understand these differences and barriers to services, which some have dubbed "structural discrimination," to find effective ways of meeting families' needs while ensuring family stability and integrity.

Other Challenges to Family Stability and Well-Being

The lack of English language proficiency of parents is among the biggest risks to the well-being and successful integration of immigrant families. The lack of such proficiency is associated with a host of other risks, including limited labor market opportunities and less desirable jobs, lower income, poorer health, more crowded housing, and poverty (Capps et al., 2003). The poverty rate among children of immigrants is 22%, as compared to 14% of those with U.S.-born parents (Greenberg & Rahmanou, 2004). One in four low-income children lives in an immigrant family (Fix & Zimmerman, 1999). Although immigrant families have higher rates of employment and higher incidences of two-parent families, they are more likely to be poor (Nightingale & Fix, 2004). The children of immigrants are twice as likely to be in fair or poor health as those of U.S.-born parents (Capps et al., 2003). Hernandez (2004) noted that the greatest risk factors for immigrant children or the children of immigrant parents are a parent with low educational attainment (no high school diploma),

---

*For a more complete discussion of legal status and benefits under new immigration legislation, see Drachman and Ryan, 2001.

low family income, or no proficiency in English, and being a member of a single-parent family.

Stages of Migration: Critical Variables

Knowledge of the migration experience is necessary to effectively provide services to immigrant families in the child welfare system. Multiple and cumulative stresses surround the migration experience, especially those caused by leaving family members, friends, community, home, and homeland. Many immigrants stay in transition after their departure from their native country, living in a refugee camp or holding in a detention center for a short or long period of time. After arriving in the destination country, immigrants need to find housing. Some need to learn a new language and secure education for their children. Others need to find employment and become familiar with the country's cultural ways, as well as learn new systems of health, education, transportation, and so on. Although immigrant populations have many strengths, stresses can render them vulnerable and at risk for problems in resettlement. The stresses are also exacerbated for families and children in contact with the child welfare system.

To facilitate child welfare workers' understanding and assessment of the immigration experience, we offer a conceptual frame-work that views migration as a process versus migration as an event (Marquez & Padilla, 2004). The framework links the migration experiences that occur in the country of origin with experiences in an intermediate country (or place) and finally in the destination country. Because child welfare workers are not in contact with immigrant families and children until they are living in the United States, the framework offers a way for workers to consider the intermingling between experiences in earlier phases of migration with resettlement experiences. Ultimately, an understanding of the immigration experience requires an understanding of the emigration experience, as both are parts of a unitary process.

Figure 1 outlines the stages of migration, the critical variables in the stages, and common factors that influence each stage. It expands on the framework applied to the diverse immigrant populations previously cited. Recent work on transnationals, circular migrants, and return migrants has furthered its development (Drachman & Paulino, 2004)

Premigration or Departure Stage

Social, political, economic, and educational factors in the premigration and departure stage are significant. This phase may involve abrupt flight (Southeast Asians, Bosnians, Somalians, Liberians), exile, or a situation in which individuals choose to depart (Koreans, many Caribbean islanders). Some of the issues individuals face in this stage include expectation for a better future; separation from family and friends; withdrawal from a familiar environment; decisions regarding who leaves and who is left behind; experiences of persecution, violence, loss of significant others, or a long wait; and living in limbo prior to departure. After resettlement, other issues emerge: concern for those left behind, depression associated with the multiple losses, incongruity between expectations and the reality of life in the new land, and survivor guilt and post-traumatic stress for people who witnessed and experienced violence and the loss of others.

Transit or Intermediate Stage

In the transit phase, experiences may range from a perilous sea journey on a fragile boat (e.g., Haitians and Cubans) to an uncomplicated arrangement for

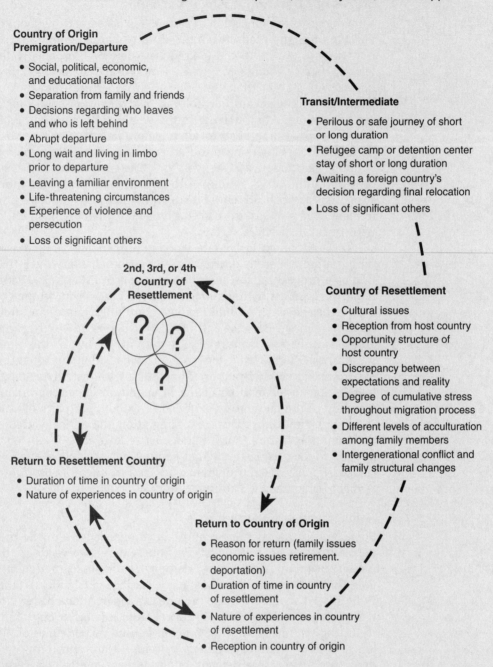

Factors That influence Each Migration Stage
Age, family composition, urban/rural background, race, education, culture, socioeconomic background, occupation, belief system, social support.

Country of Origin
Premigration/Departure

- Social, political, economic, and educational factors
- Separation from family and friends
- Decisions regarding who leaves and who is left behind
- Abrupt departure
- Long wait and living in limbo prior to departure
- Leaving a familiar environment
- Life-threatening circumstances
- Experience of violence and persecution
- Loss of significant others

Transit/Intermediate

- Perilous or safe journey of short or long duration
- Refugee camp or detention center stay of short or long duration
- Awaiting a foreign country's decision regarding final relocation
- Loss of significant others

2nd, 3rd, or 4th Country of Resettlement

Country of Resettlement

- Cultural issues
- Reception from host country
- Opportunity structure of host country
- Discrepancy between expectations and reality
- Degree of cumulative stress throughout migration process
- Different levels of acculturation among family members
- Intergenerational conflict and family structural changes

Return to Resettlement Country

- Duration of time in country of origin
- Nature of experiences in country of origin

Return to Country of Origin

- Reason for return (family issues economic issues retirement. deportation)
- Duration of time in country of resettlement
- Nature of experiences in country of resettlement
- Reception in country of origin

Figure 1
Stages of Migration: Critical Variables
Source: Drachman & Paulino. (Eds.). (2004). *Immigrants and social work: Thinking beyond the borders of the United States.* Binghamton, NY: Haworth.

travel on a commercial flight (many Asians, Caribbean islanders, and Europeans). The duration of the transit phase may vary from hours to years. An individual might live in limbo in a refugee camp for years while awaiting a final destination (Southeast Asians, Somalians). The transit phase also could involve a long stay in a detention center while awaiting the decision of a receiving country regarding entry or deportation (Haitians). On the other hand, an individual may leave the country of origin and, within hours, connect with family or friends in the new country (many Asians, Caribbean islanders, and Europeans).

Resettlement Stage

Common issues in resettlement include the degree of cumulative stress experienced by the family, the discrepancy between expectations and actual quality of life in the United States, the reception in the new country (e.g., policies about inclusion or exclusion), and the opportunity structure of the receiving country. Reunification in a different family structure with new members, such as stepparent and half- or stepsiblings, may generate conflict. Changes in power relationships between parent and child also may foster conflict. Cultural issues assume prominence and include different views between the home and host country on health, mental health, help-seeking behavior, education, child-rearing practices, gender-role behavior, and different levels of acculturation among family members. Cultural issues also surface in the interactions between service personnel and immigrant families. Depression, suicide ideation and suicide attempts, substance and chemical abuse, parent-child conflict, and wife and child abuse are among the commonly reported problems. As men and women shift in their traditional marital roles (particularly when wives are employed and husbands are unemployed or earn less than the wives), marital conflict or dissolution may surface even among cultures where divorce is rare.

Immigration status is subsumed under the factor of reception in the resettlement phase. Undocumented status is particularly important to understand for effective child welfare practice. As previously noted, this status carries limited legal rights and limits in service eligibility. Furthermore, the undocumented person is subject to deportation because of a provision in the 1996 Illegal Immigration Reform and Immigrant Responsibility Act (IIRIRA), which removes the right to judicial review for groups of undocumented individuals. The groups include people convicted of an offense involving drugs, child abuse, child neglect, child abandonment, immigration law, aggravated felony, and misdemeanors such as shoplifting (Medina, 1997). This provision of the law also is retroactive. Thus, an undocumented single mother who arrived in the United States as a child and committed an offense years ago may be deported despite the years following her conviction when she was productively raising a family and working. Her removal from the family leaves her children without supervision, which would cause the child welfare system to intervene and place the children in foster care. Unfortunately, family separation overrides family preservation in this instance (Committee on Children and Families, 2002).[*]

---

[*]The reader is urged to consult this document for a heart wrenching, but most informative presentation of immigrants' experiences with the child welfare system in New York through this published testimony before the New York State Assembly's Committee on Children and Families, Task Force on New Americans, dated July 11, 2002.

Return to the Country of Origin

Contrary to common beliefs, immigrants may return to their home country (Drachman & Paulino, 2004). Thus, the migration process may continue beyond resettlement. The reasons for returning vary. Some immigrants involuntarily return to their native country because of deportation. If a parent is deported, the action can initiate a child's entry into the foster care system. On the other hand, a child may accompany the deported parent while other family members remain in the United States, but then the family is separated. If the deported parent is the primary wage earner, family members who remain in the United States may be catapulted into economic jeopardy. Although a parent may be deported to his or her country of birth, it may not be the country in which the parent was raised. Thus, the parent is returned to an unfamiliar land, where he or she may not even speak the language.

Immigration status varies for a sizeable immigrant population of transnationals. Some are legal permanent residents. Others are undocumented. Transnationals are people whose net-works, activities, and patterns of life encompass both home and host countries (Charles, 1992; Glick-Schiller, Basch, & Blanc-Szanton, 1992; Wiltshire, 1992). They return to their native land for long or short periods of time. Their contacts with family members in the home country may involve them in decisionmaking on health care or education for children. During their home country stays, they may take part in political, social, or religious activities. Concurrently, these immigrants are involved with their U.S. families. They are involved in their places of employment, religious organizations, and ethnic communities in the United States (Drachman & Paulino, 2004).

An awareness of the two-country social field of transnationals will help social workers consider family relationships where significant members are living in another country. A service provider, for example, could explore the degree and nature of family contacts despite members' separation and develop helping plans to include members separated by national borders.

Finally, the immigration experience is influenced by factors embedded in all phases of the migration process, including age, family composition, culture, race, education, social supports, occupation, and socioeconomic and urban or rural backgrounds. Although the factors are common to all phases, they can lead to different immigration experiences. A young child, an adolescent, a middle-aged adult, or a senior may experience migration differently. Migrating as a family is likely to be different from migrating as an individual. Immigration can be traumatic for an unaccompanied minor because of age and the absence of parents. A person of color commonly experiences a different reception from that of a Caucasian. Significant differences in culture and belief systems between sending and receiving countries can alter the experience. Social supports from the ethnic community can mitigate the stresses of migration while their absence can heighten the stress. The experience of people arriving from a fishing or rural village into a technological society is likely to be different from that of highly educated individuals. Child welfare workers should consider all factors to facilitate effective assessment for immigrant families and children.

Guidelines for Program and Practice

The following set of recommendations for program and practice points the way forward for child welfare agencies as they seek to preserve and protect immigrant families and their children.*

- Develop educational programs on child welfare practice with immigrant children and families. The migration framework could guide the curriculum. Areas of inquiry could segment into phases of migration and factors associated with those phases. Using the framework, case material on families from different nations could be presented so that workers could learn about different immigrant populations, using a conceptual vehicle that generalizes but still extracts specific information.
- Develop a manual for immigrant families to familiarize them with the different immigration statuses. The rights and benefits of each status would be identified. The manual could be translated into the languages of the different client groups.
- Establish a relationship between child welfare agencies and legal service organizations familiar with immigration law for consultation and training of social workers. Lawyers could train workers on relevant and changing immigration laws and procedures, while agencies would obtain consultation on unique client situations. The collaboration and the joining of forces between legal and child welfare organizations also would strengthen advocacy efforts on behalf of immigrant families.
- Recruit foster families from immigrant groups, translate agency materials into immigrants' languages, hire translators, and employ consultants from immigrant communities to provide cultural knowledge and information.
- Offer cross-cultural training programs for child welfare workers. Members of immigrant communities could serve as "cultural consultants."
- Develop collaborative relationships and form teams between public and private agencies and community agencies that serve immigrants. With family members' permission and an assurance of confidentiality, community agencies could invite representatives from public agencies to team meetings when cases involving immigrant families are discussed, including case reviews of foster families, family group conference meetings, and regular staff meetings. To protect confidentiality, all identifying information would be deleted.
- Send agency representatives to key locations in the community where immigrants and leaders could be reached (e.g. social clubs, places of worship) to present information about the agency, its mission, and its operation as a social service organization.
- Offer forums on conflicting policy perspectives that affect child welfare, such as the disagreement between child welfare and immigration law. Through discussions, agencies can develop strategies toward strengthening family preservation while respecting immigration law. Discussion groups would include members of immigrant communities,

---

*For further reading on ways to support immigrant children and their families, see the *Future of Children: Children of Immigrant Families, 14* (2) (Summer 2004).

child welfare workers and other service providers, lawyers, and personnel associated with government immigration organizations

▶ Offer discussion groups for social workers to focus on ethical dilemmas arising from competing obligations, such as honoring client confidentiality, supporting social justice, and meeting basic human needs vis-a-vis reporting un-documented persons (in some circumstances) and denying them needed services.

▶ Use the migration framework to guide the assessment of immigrant and refugee families. The factors in each of the migration stages would be considered and transposed into areas for exploration. In the departure stage, for example, practitioners could explore with clients the reasons for leaving the home country, the circumstances surrounding their departure, decisions about who would leave and who would remain in the home country, and the nature of losses experienced. A similar procedure would explore immigrants' experiences in subsequent phases of the migration process. The common factors associated with all phases, such as age, race, culture, social supports, and family composition, would be examined.

Finally, the authors believe that social workers must become more international through a better understanding of global issues, especially those affecting their clients; through cross-national communication with other social workers, especially—when working with immigrants and refugees—those in "sending" countries; and through both knowledge about immigration policy and advocacy for humane treatment of immigrants and refugees (Healy 2004).

References

1. Bowles, A. (2005, January 2), Settling in, restlessly. *New York Times, Connecticut,* p. 6,
2. Capps, R., Passel, J. S., Periz-Lopez, D., & Fix, M. (2003). *The new neighbors: A user's guide to data on immigrants in U.S. communities.* Washington, DC: The Urban Institute.
3. Charles, C. (1992). Transnationalism in the construct of Haitian migrants' racial categories of identity in New York City. In N. Glick-Schiller, L. Basch, & C. Blanc-Szanton, (Eds,), *Towards a transnational perspective on migration: Race, class, ethnicity, and nationalism reconsidered* (pp. 101–123). New York: New York Academy of Sciences.
4. Committee on Children and Families. (2002). *Public hearing on problems facing immigrant families in the child welfare system.* (July 11, 2002). New York: New York State Assembly.
5. DeWind, J. (1990). Haitian boat people in the United States: Background for social service providers. In D. Drachman (Ed.), *Social services to refugee populations* (pp. 7—56). Washington, DC: National Institute of Mental Health.
6. Drachman, D. (in press). Recurring forces that shape United States immigration policy. *The Caribbean Journal of Social Work.*
7. Drachman, D, (1995). Immigration statuses and their influence on service provision, access, and use. *Social Work, 40,* 188–197.
8. Drachman, D, (1992). A stage of migration framework for services to immigrant populations. *Social Work, 39,* 68–72.
9. Drachman, D., & Halberstadt, A. (1992). Stage of migration framework as applied to recent Soviet émigrés. In A. S. Ryan (Ed.), *Social work with immigrants and refugees* (pp. 63–75). Binghamton, NY: Haworth..
10. Drachman, D., Kwon-Ahn, Y. H., & Paulino, A. (1996). Migration and resettlement experiences of Dominican and Korean families. *Families in Society, 77* (10), 626–638.

11. Drachman, D., & Paulino, A, (2004), Introduction: Thinking beyond the United States' borders. In D. Drachman & A. Paulino (Eds,), *Immigrants and social work: Thinking beyond the borders of the United States* (pp. 1–9). Binghamton, NY: Haworth.

12. Drachman, D., & Ryan, A. S. (2001), Immigrants and refugees. In A. Gitterman (Ed.), *Handbook of social work practice with vulnerable and resilient populations* (pp. 651–686). New York: Columbia University Press.

13. Fix, M., & Passel, J. (1994). *Immigration and immigrants: Setting the record straight.* Washington, DC: The Urban Institute.

14. Fix, M., Zimmerman, W., & Passel, J. S. (2001). *The integration of immigrant families into the United States.* Washington, DC: The Urban Institute.

15. Fix, M., & Zimmerman, W. (1999). *All under one roof: Mixed-status families in an era of reform.* Washington, DC: The Urban Institute. Accessed October 29, 2004, from www.urban.org.

16. Gil, R. (1990). Cuban refugees: Implications for clinical social work practice. In D. Drachman (Ed.), *Social services to refugee populations* (pp. 57–72). Washington, DC: National Institute of Mental Health.

17. Giovannoni, J. (2004). Foreword. In D. Drachman & A. Paulino (Eds.), *Immigrants and social work: Thinking beyond the borders of the United States* (pp. xi–xii). Binghamton, NY: Haworth.

18. Glick-Schiller, N., Basch, L., & Blanc-Szanton, C. (1992) Transnationalism: A new analytic framework for understanding migration. In N. Glick-Schiller, L. Basch, & C. Blanc-Szanton (Eds.), *Towards a transnational perspective on migration: Race, class, ethnicity and nationalism reconsidered* (pp. 1–24). New York: New York Academy of Sciences.

19. Greenberg, M. H., & Rahmanou, H. (2004). Looking to the future, commentary 1. *The Future of Children,* 14(2), 139–145.

20. Hacsi, T. (1996). From indenture to family foster care: A brief history of child placing. In E. P. Smith & L. A. Merkel-Holguin (Eds.), *A history of child welfare* (pp. 155–173). Washington, DC: Child Welfare League of America.

21. Healy, L. (2004). Strengthening the link: Social work with immigrants and refugees and international social work. In D, Drachman & A. Paulino (Eds.), *Immigrants and social work: Thinking beyond the borders of the United States* (pp. 49–67). Binghamton, NY: Haworth.

22. Hernandez, D. J. (2004). Demographic change and life circumstances of immigrant families. *The Future of Children,* 14(2), 17–47.

23. Maluccio, A. N., Krieger, R., & Pine, B. A. (1990). Adolescents and their preparation for life after foster family care: An overview. In A. N. Maluccio, R. Krieger, & B. A. Pine (Eds.), *Preparing adolescents for life after foster care* (pp. 5–17). Washington, DC: Child Welfare League of America.

24. Maluccio, A. N., Pine, B. A., & Tracy, E. M. (2002). *Social work practice with families and children.* New York: Columbia University Press.

25. Maluccio, A. N., Pine, B. A., & Warsh, R. (1994). Protecting children by preserving their families. *Children and youth services review,* 16(5/6), 295–307.

26. Maluccio, A. N., Warsh, R., & Pine, B. A. (1993). Family reunification: An overview. In B. A. Pine, R. Warsh, & A. N. Maluccio (Eds.), *Together again: Family reunification in foster care* (pp. 3–19). Washington, DC: Child Welfare League of America.

27. Mandel, Y. (1990). Soviet refugees. In D. Drachman (Ed.), *Social services to refugee populations* (pp. 79–90). Washington, DC: National Institute of Mental Health.

28. Marquez, R., & Padilla, Y. (2004) Immigration in the life histories of women living in the United States—Mexico border region. In D. Drachman & A. Paulino (Eds.), *Immigrants and social work: Thinking beyond the borders of the United States* (pp. 11–30). Binghamton, NY: Haworth.

29. McGowan, B. G. (1983). Historical evolution of child welfare services: An examination of the sources of current problems and dilemmas. In B. G. McGowan &

W. Meezan (Eds.), *Child welfare: Current dilemmas, future directions* (pp. 45–90). Itasca, IL: F. E. Peacock.

30. Medina, I. (1997). Judicial review—A nice thing? Article III, separation of powers and the illegal immigration reform and immigrant responsibility act of 1996. *Connecticut Law Review, 29,* 1525–1563.

31. Nightingale, D. S., & Fix, M. (2004). Economic and labor market trends. *The Future of Children,* 74(2), 49–59.

32. O, S. L., & Porr, P. (1990). Social work practice with Indochinese refugees. In D. Drachman, (Ed.), *Social services to refugee populations* (pp. 9–20). Washington, DC: National Institute of Mental Health.

33. Pecora. P. J., Whittaker, J. K., Maluccio, A. N., & Barth, R. P. (2000). *The child welfare challenge: Policy, practice, and research.* New York: Aldine de Gruyter.

34. Pine, B. A. (1986). Child welfare reform and the political process. *Social Service Review, 60* (3), 339–359.

35. Sherraden, M. S., & Segal, U. A. (1996). Multicultural issues in child welfare. *Children and Youth Services Review, 18* (6), 497–504.

36. Shields, M., & Behrman, R. E. (2004). Children of immigrant families: Analysis and recommendations. *The Future of Children,* 14(2), 4–15.

37. Suarez-Orozco, C, & Suarez-Orozco, M. (2001). *Children of immigration.* Cambridge, MA: Harvard University Press.

38. Ruiz-de-Velasco, J., & Fix, M. (2000). *Overlooked and underserved: Immigrant students in U.S. secondary schools.* Washington, DC: The Urban Institute.

39. U.S. Citizen and Immigration Services (2004). *Memorandum #3: Field guidance on special immigrant juvenile status petitions.* Accessed January 11, 2005, from www.uscis.gov.

40. Wiltshire, R. (1992). Implications of transnational migration for nationalism: The Caribbean example. In N. Glick-Schiller, L. Basch, & C. Blanc-Szanton (Eds.), *Towards a transnational perspective on migration: Race, class, ethnicity and nationalism reconsidered* (pp. 175–188). New York: New York Academy of Sciences.

7

Perspectives on Groups

CONNECTING CORE COMPETENCIES *in this chapter*

| **Professional Identity** | Ethical Practice | Critical Thinking | **Diversity in Practice** | Human Rights & Justice | Research Based Practice | Human Behavior | Policy Practice | **Practice Contexts** | Engage Assess Intervene Evaluate |

Knowledge about small groups is essential for social workers. Much of social work practice takes place in the context of small groups. Whether your practice is directed primarily toward individuals, families, organizations, or communities, much of what you do on a day-to-day basis will be done in the context of small groups. Addressing the needs of individuals and families will almost certainly require work in the context of some type of team. Medical social workers working with individuals and families, for example, are often members of multidisciplinary care teams made up of physicians, nurses, dieticians, physical therapists, and others. These teams are small groups and require understanding of the dynamics of small groups. Social workers practicing in an administrative or management context carry out much of their day-to-day practice through such small groups as work groups and committees. If your practice setting is at the community level, you are almost certain to be involved in task forces and consumer groups.

Certainly if you practice as a generalist social worker, you will be involved in small group efforts at many levels, including any combination of those described above. Practice in a public social services setting, for example, may require you to be involved in interdisciplinary teams, staff work groups, support groups for clients, community task forces, and any number of other types of groups. Our involvement as social workers in such a variety of group settings as those described above will require sufficient knowledge about small groups to be effective as both a group member and a facilitator or leader.

DEFINITIONS

A very basic definition of a group is "a small, face-to-face collection of persons who interact to accomplish some purpose" (Brown 1991:3). Another definition suggests that a group is "two or more individuals in face-to-face interaction, each aware of his or her membership in the group, each aware of the others who belong to the group, and each aware of their positive interdependence as they strive to achieve mutual goals" (Johnson and Johnson 1991:14). Both of these definitions' concern for shared purpose and common interaction clearly differentiate a group from what is often referred to as an aggregate or a mere collection of individuals with no common purpose and little or no mutual interaction. An example of an aggregate or mere collection of people is the people with whom you might ride an elevator. These definitions also suggest a compatibility with the core purposes and values of social work and the assumptions we make about ourselves, others, and social work in this book.

HISTORICAL PERSPECTIVE

The small group as an important context for understanding and influencing human behavior has a multidisciplinary history. It has roots in the disciplines of education, psychology, sociology, and social work. Concern for understanding the influences of groups on individual and collective behavior is primarily a product of the twentieth century, although through much of modern history important questions about the place of groups in our individual and collective lives have been raised.

History of Group Theory and Practice

Professional Identity

An element of our professional identity as social workers is knowledge of the profession's history. What part of group work history adds to our body of knowledge about the profession's history?

Twentieth-century researchers' concerns have been multifocused, including the role of groups in democracy, leadership, decision making, work, leisure, education, and problem solving. Social workers have focused their interests in small-group behavior in a range of areas from social reform to the role of groups in education, leisure, therapy, and citizenship.

An early institution through which the influences of groups on individual and community life were studied and used for problem solving was the settlement house movement of the early twentieth century. Later on social workers turned their interests in groups to the therapeutic or treatment potential of groups for dealing with mental illness and other problems in living. More recently, social workers have extended their interests in and work with groups to their use as a means of self-help and support for the persons with whom we work. Self-help and support groups are used to address a great variety of issues, from increasing political awareness, as in consciousness-raising groups in the women's and civil rights movements, to groups for dealing with addictions, physical or sexual abuse, and other personal difficulties that can benefit from the assistance of others with similar experiences (Brown 1991; Johnson and Johnson 1991; Worchel, Wood, and Simpson 1992).

History of a Group

Just as it is important to have some sense of the emergence in history of concern for small groups as a unit of study and as an important environment within which human behavior occurs, it is important to recognize the impact of historical factors on the development of any particular small group. Every small group with which we deal or to which we belong is heavily influenced by the past experiences of the members of the group. Group members do not enter group situations from a vacuum. We come to groups having had past experiences in groups—both positive and negative. We come to groups with perspectives on other people based on our past experiences with others. Depending on the quality of our past individual and group experiences, it is possible that two different people can join the same group at the same time and have diametrically opposed perceptions about what their shared experience in the new group will be like. Andrea can enter a group for the first time and see in the faces of the other group members rich and exciting possibilities for new friendships, new ideas, and new solutions to her problems. Mitchell can look at the same faces and see a terrifying collection of strangers and potential enemies waiting to create many more problems for him than they could ever solve. It is out of this diversity of perceptions, based on radically different pasts, that the challenge of groupness emerges. As social workers, we are often charged with guiding these very different people to share their differences in an attempt to confirm the hopes of Andrea and to allay the anxiety and the fears of Mitchell so both can benefit from each other's experiences and come closer to fulfilling both their potentials as humans. We cannot hope to do this unless we are aware of the history and experiences we bring to the group ourselves. What, then, is this mysterious entity called the small group?

Before we explore specific approaches and concepts for understanding small groups, it may be helpful to recognize some similarities among models and concepts used for understanding human behavior in group environments and approaches to understanding human behavior at other levels with which we are concerned in this book. Models for understanding small-group development, for example, share a number of things with models for understanding individual and family development. Perhaps the most apparent similarity is that of stage-based models of group development. Many approaches to understanding the development of any particular group include some framework based on developmental stages. Many of the concepts for explaining small-group structures and functions also can be applied to organizational and community levels of human behavior. Such concepts as leadership, roles, norms, and socialization are examples of concepts used for understanding small groups that we will see again as we explore organizations and communities.

TRADITIONAL AND ALTERNATIVE PERSPECTIVES

We will examine a number of basic dimensions and concepts commonly used to explain small-group structures and dynamics, whether discussing traditional or alternative perspectives on groups. As we explore these basic dimensions and concepts we will examine the different emphasis placed on the concepts in traditional and alternative paradigm thinking.

Process and Product Dimensions

One way of thinking about a group is to consider whether the group is product or process focused. Some students of groups have emphasized the product or outcome dimension, while others have been primarily concerned with internal group processes that occur during the life of a group. The dimensions of outcome and process are also sometimes referred to as **task** and **maintenance,** or **instrumental** and expressive (Anderson and Carter 1990; Napier and Gershenfeld 1985; Worchel, Wood, and Simpson 1992). All these terms suggest that groups operate simultaneously on two levels. **Task level** is concerned with the accomplishment of the concrete goals of the group—a task force must complete a grant application to begin a service to people with AIDS or who are HIV positive, for example. The **process dimension** is concerned with the socioemotional needs of the task force members—task force members must develop effective processes for relating to one another and for addressing their individual feelings related to AIDS and HIV in the group context in order to effectively complete the task. The members must be able to work together.

Goals and Purposes

Most researchers and practitioners agree that all groups must have elements of both outcome and process. There is a good deal of disagreement, however, on which element of this dimension should be of primary concern. The amount of attention to task or process is influenced by the goals or purposes of the group. A **group goal** is most simply defined as a place the group would like to be (Napier and Gershenfeld 1985:181–225).

Traditional perspectives would suggest that a task-oriented group such as the one discussed above might give precedence to accomplishing its goal of completing the grant application over concerns for how well the group members were able to "get along" with each other. Alternative perspectives would suggest, however, that the group is not driven so exclusively by its stated goal or purpose at all times. The group cannot be successful in accomplishing its stated task if its members disagree about or are too anxious about their own feelings about the controversial issue of AIDS/HIV to focus on that task. The group cannot accomplish its task unless members can get along with each other well enough to unite in their efforts to accomplish the task and unless they are comfortable enough as individuals with the group's goal to invest their individual energies in pursuit of that group goal. These are process and socioemotional dimensions that cannot be separated from the product or task dimensions.

Some groups have purposes or goals that are more process or socioemotionally oriented than task or outcome oriented: a men's consciousness-raising group formed to address members' concerns for developing ways of relating to and behaving toward each other and to women in ways that are nonsexist, for example. Such a group is concerned primarily with changing members' ways of thinking, relating, and behaving. Its focus is process oriented. However, it also requires that the group accomplish concrete tasks as well. Members will need to determine tasks they will undertake to operate the group—when, where, and how often they will meet, for example. However, the task dimension is clearly secondary to the process concerns of the group for focusing on socioemotional and relationship dimensions.

Goals and purposes of groups, whether process or product focused, may be determined externally or internally. The task force goal to develop a grant application for AIDS/HIV services may have resulted from an agency board of directors' decision to develop services in this area and the board's direction to the staff to form a task force to implement its directive. It might have emerged as a result of external concerns raised by persons in the community who were HIV positive, who had AIDS, or who provided care for persons with AIDS. It might also have emerged from discussions among the persons who were members of the task force about the needs for such services and about the possible mechanisms for funding services. The men's consciousness-raising group's goals or purposes may also have been determined externally or internally. The group might have been created by agency management as a result of complaints by women coworkers, for example, of sexist behavior and sexual harassment by their male colleagues. The group might also have emerged out of its members' own recognition of their difficulties in relating to and behaving toward the women in their lives in nonsexist ways.

Whether groups' goals and purposes come about as a result of external or internal forces has important consequences for the ways groups will operate. As social workers we are likely to find ourselves in the position of facilitating or being a member of groups with externally imposed as well as internally determined goals and purposes.

Membership

The examples of external and internal determination of goals for a group also suggest that members of groups come to be members in different ways. The different sources of goal setting for the AIDS/HIV task force and the men's group illustrate that membership might be voluntary or involuntary. The task force members called upon by the board of directors of their agency and the men required to be members of the consciousness-raising group because of their coworkers' complaints probably felt very different about being a part of their respective groups than did the task force members and the men's group members who decided among themselves that they wanted to become members of their group.

Membership describes the quality of the relationship between an individual and a group. Group members, whether they are in the group voluntarily or involuntarily, know they are members of the group. How we come to be a group member and how we feel about our membership in a group influences the level of membership we will have in the group. It influences how much of ourselves we will invest in the group.

Group membership can be differentiated by levels. **Formal or full psychological membership** suggests that we have invested ourselves significantly in the group and its goals; we feel a high degree of commitment to the group's goals and to the other group members. The other members of the group likewise see and accept us as full members of the group. When we are voluntarily a member of a group, and when we participate directly in determining the group's goals, we are more likely to experience full psychological membership.

We do not have this degree of membership in all groups to which we belong. We might be a marginal member of some groups. **Marginal members** are not willing to invest themselves fully in the group. They may do what is necessary to remain a member of the group, but only what is minimally necessary. Marginal members do make contributions to groups, but to a much lesser degree than full psychological members. There are a number of factors that result in marginal membership. We may be in the group involuntarily. We may not feel that we were a part of the process of forming the goals of the group. If the goals of the group were determined externally, for example, we may feel less ownership in its goals and therefore be more marginal as a member. We may also be a marginal member if we simply do not have time to become a full member but wish to support the goals of the group and contribute what we can in support of the group goals. In other words, marginal membership is not necessarily negative for the group or member. Marginal members can provide valuable services to groups.

Another level of membership in groups that is worthy of note is aspiring membership. An **aspiring member** is one who is not formally a member of a group but wishes to be a member. As an aspiring member we might identify strongly with the goals of the group, but we may not be able to become a formal member of the group for a variety of reasons. The group may not have room for us or we may not meet membership criteria for the group (Napier and Gershenfeld 1985:74–111).

As group facilitators and members, social workers need to be particularly aware of this level of membership. Aspiring members offer a rich potential source of new group members who are likely to invest a great deal of energy in helping the group to achieve its goals. As social workers, we should also be concerned that aspiring members are not being excluded from membership in a group because of barriers that deny them access. If an aspiring member has a disability that makes it impossible for her or him to get to the group meetings and therefore does not apply for formal membership, we must act to move that aspiring member to full membership. If a member aspires to be a part of a group but finds or believes that her or his gender, sexual orientation, income, or other difference prevents him or her from being a full member, we must act to remove such barriers to membership.

Leadership, Followership, and Decision Making

Bass (in Gastil 1994:954–955) provides a **general definition of leadership** as "an interaction between two or more members of a group that often involves a structuring or restructuring of the situation and the perceptions and expectations of the members. . . . Leadership occurs when one group member modifies the motivation or competencies of others in the group. Any member of the group can exhibit some amount of leadership." Gastil argues that leadership is "only *constructive* behaviors aimed at pursuing group goals" (1994:955). One traditional approach to leadership put forth by Lewin suggests three styles of leadership:

1. *Democratic leadership* focuses on group decision making, active member involvement, honest praise and criticism, and comradeship. (We will examine in more detail democratic leadership later in this section);

2. *Autocratic leadership* characterized by domineering and hierarchical leader behavior; and

3. *Laissez-faire leadership* characterized by an uninvolved, non-directive approach to leading (in Gastil 1994:955).

Other traditional notions of leadership tend to frame this element of group life as a set of inborn traits, as the product of the situation or environment, or as emerging from the position of leadership held by the person. The **trait** notion suggests that leaders are born. It implies that leadership is possible only for people who have the traits of leadership and that these people (leaders) are somehow destined for greatness or influence well above the rest of us. **Situational leadership** suggests that leaders emerge out of the requirements of a particular situation. If a person has the necessary expertise required to solve a particular problem, the requirements of the situation create the leader. **Positional leadership** suggests that leaders are created by the positions they hold. The position of chair or president will evoke from its holder the qualities necessary to lead. The authority or influence necessary for leadership comes out of the position or title. Trait, situational, and positional notions of leadership are incomplete or either/or perspectives. Either you have the magical traits of leadership or you do not; either you find yourself in a situation requiring your expertise or you do not; either you end up in a leadership position or you do not. These traditional notions are incomplete and leave out some important considerations. They suggest that leaders and followers are mutually exclusive roles (Napier and Gershenfeld 1985:227–296). In Chapter 8 we will address traditional and alternative types and styles of leadership in the context of organizations.

Functional leadership

An alternative perspective on leadership suggests that leaders and followers are not so dichotomous or separate from each other. A functional definition of leadership suggests that leadership is simply behavior that assists a group to achieve its goals. Such a definition recognizes the potential for anyone in the group to be a leader. Leadership is demonstrated simply by doing what is necessary to help the group reach its goals, whether they be process or product related. Such a definition recognizes that sometimes people have the necessary characteristics or traits to lead in a particular context. One member's temperament may allow him or her to more readily lead the group in efforts to resolve conflict than others in the group, for example. A functional definition also suggests that a person with a leadership position such as chair or president may more readily lead the group in some formal activities—convening or adjourning the group, for example. A functional perspective also suggests that there are times when the environment or situation may call upon the expertise of a particular member to lead the group, such as a group facing a financial crisis calling upon a member with accounting skills to lead it through the crisis. Functional leadership offers an alternative notion of leadership that recognizes

Practice Contexts

The provision of leadership to improve the quality of social services is an expectation of the profession for its members. After reading this section, which of the types or styles of leadership do you think is the most consistent with social work values and principles?

leadership within a group as mobile and flexible. A functional definition makes it difficult to distinguish leaders from followers, because everyone is viewed as having the potential for leadership. Functional leadership might be effectively practiced through a rotating rather than a fixed structure of leadership in groups. Rotating leaders also reduces tendencies toward hierarchical and positional group structures. Alcoholics Anonymous groups are examples of group efforts in which functional and nonhierarchical forms of leadership are emphasized.

The potential for leadership on the part of all group members, however, may not necessarily be realized. Unless group members recognize the existence of this potential in each other and unless they allow each other to act on their potential, it will not be realized. In effect, this alternative notion of leadership suggests that, contrary to traditional notions, leaders are not simply born or created by positions or situations; leaders are created by followers. Other members of the group allow leaders to lead by accepting the leadership behavior of the member who leads (Napier and Gershenfeld 1985:227–296).

Some researchers suggest that the concept of leadership as traditionally understood, especially trait or "great person" notions, is alienating. Gemmill and Oakley (1992: 120) suggest that by accepting the necessity of a leader or of a hierarchy with leaders at the top, we "de-skill" everyone else in the group. We relinquish our potential for developing our own "critical thinking, visions, inspirations and emotions" when we define leadership as a special quality or set of qualities held only by some special person (or select group of persons) other than ourselves. By turning over decision making and power to someone else through traditional ways of defining leaders we *are* able, however, to remove much of the uncertainty and ambiguity we are likely to experience in small groups with functional, rotating, or nonhierarchical leadership approaches. In doing so we—the followers—are relieved of making risky, sometimes frightening decisions. In turning ourselves over to a leader, we are, unfortunately, also relieved of the opportunity to participate equally in addressing issues that directly affect us (Gemmill and Oakley 1992:117–123).

This notion of leadership is compatible with the dimensions of alternate paradigm thinking. It replaces hierarchy with equality. It incorporates a feminist perspective in redefining power from "power over" to "power as the ability to influence people to act in their own interests, rather than induce them to act according to goals and desires of leaders" (Gemmill and Oakley 1992:124). It "re-visions" or reconceptualizes leadership as supportive and cooperative behaviors rather than impersonal and competitive behaviors. It redefines leadership as "people taking the initiative, carrying things through, having ideas and the imagination to get something started, and exhibiting particular skills in different areas" (Bunch and Fisher 1976 in Gemmill and Oakely 1992:124–125).

Democratic Groups

As has been the case with other alternate or "new" perspectives, this alternative view of leadership has a great deal in common with what we historically have defined—although we have rarely practiced it—as democracy or democratic decision making. This reconceptualization also is more compatible with the core concerns of social work. It emphasizes several elements of what has been defined as **unitary democracy**—cooperation, common ground, relationship, and consensus (Gastil 1992:282).

Gastil (1992:278–301) defines small-group democracy and the decision-making processes that must take place in democratic groups. According to

Gastil, **democratic groups** have power and they distribute that power among members equally. They are inclusive and their members are fully committed to democratic process. They are based on relationships among members that acknowledge their individuality while also recognizing mutual responsibilities as group members. Democratic groups operate through processes that ensure each member equal and adequate opportunities to speak and participate. These opportunities are coupled with a willingness on the part of members to listen to what others have to say. The element of listening is perhaps harder to ensure than that of guaranteeing the opportunity to speak. One is meaningless, however, unless the other is present. This decision-making process also protects a member's right to speak and be heard in dissent from a position taken by the group as well (Gastil 1992).

Democratic leadership/followership

A definition of **democratic leadership** is "behavior that influences people in a manner consistent with and/or conducive to basic democratic principles and processes, such as self-determination, inclusiveness, equal participation, and deliberation" (Gastil 1994:956). Gastil specifies that "leadership is behavior, not position" (1994: 957). A democratic group is called a *demos.*

Three primary functions of democratic leadership behavior:

1. *Distributing responsibility:*
   - "Seeks to evoke maximum involvement and the participation of every member in the group activities and in the determination of objectives"
   - "Seeks to spread responsibility rather than to concentrate it" (Krech et al. in Gastil 1994:958).

2. *Empowerment:*
   - Requires a politically competent membership skilled at speaking, thinking, organizing, and many more tasks
   - Democratic leaders avoid behaviors associated with a "great man" [*sic*] model of leadership
   - Democratic leaders show genuine care and concern for members without being paternalistic
   - Democratic leaders seek to make members into leaders; seek to make themselves replaceable.

3. *Aiding deliberation:*
   - Through constructive participation, facilitation, and maintenance of healthy relationships and a positive emotional setting
   - Through careful listening and respectful acknowledgment of others' views (Gastil 1994:958–961).

Facilitation Gastil (1994:961) differentiates the concept of facilitation from participation. **Facilitation,** according to Gastil, is a form of **metacommunication,** which is communication *about* the group's deliberation. Facilitation involves:

1. Keeping deliberation focused and on track

2. Encouraging free discussion and broad participation, sometimes needing to discourage verbosity and draw out shy or marginalized voices (at the community level this may mean outreach to isolated or marginalized groups who have not, but should have a voice in public debate)

3. Encouraging "members to observe the norms and laws that the demos has adopted"

4. Maintaining a healthy emotional setting, positive member relationships, and a "spirit of congeniality" (Gastil 1994: 961).

Distribution of leadership   Gastil stresses that democratic leadership should be distributed widely among the group members. He believes that diffusing leadership does not make a group "leaderless," instead it makes the group "leaderful." This "leaderful" or diffused leadership is reflected in the suggestions below:

- In the ideal demos, more than one person serves every leadership function, no individual does an inordinate amount of the leading, and every group member performs leadership functions some of the time
- In most cases it is possible to rotate leadership functions among the membership so that individual members become capable of serving a variety of leadership functions (Gastil 1994:962).

Follower responsibilities   The wide distribution of democratic leadership behaviors among all members requires significant follower responsibilities. **Followers:**

1. Must take responsibility for the well-being of the demos

2. Must be accountable for their actions and decisions

3. Are ultimately responsible for maintaining their autonomy (independence)

4. Recognize ways they can function as leaders

5. Must be willing to work with those leading (Gastil 1994:963–964).

When is democratic leadership not appropriate?

This alternative approach to democratic leadership is not appropriate for all group settings. **Democratic leadership is not appropriate**

- When the problem is clearly defined and has an obvious technical solution, e.g., setting a broken bone
- When an "executive" or "judge" is needed to interpret a decision of the demos, but judge/executive must remain accountable to demos
- If group is indifferent to a problem
- When the problem is not within the jurisdiction of the group (Gastil 1994: 964–965).

Why do people reject democratic leadership?

- Because the democratic structure threatens their undemocratic authority. To move toward democracy would cost status, power, money.
- Some people have authoritarian values and have a strong belief in "the justness and efficiency of powerful, directive authorities."
- "Most people have, to some degree, an unconscious and conscious desire for a hero, a charismatic figure capable of solving our problems and sweeping away confusion."
- Some people reject the very notion of leadership and do not believe in the necessity of leaders (anarchic) (Gastil 1994:970).

This decision-making process is very different from traditional autocratic approaches to decision making based on hierarchical structures in which leaders have sufficient power and authority to impose their position and will on members. It is also quite different from traditional notions of democratic leadership styles of decision making in which only majority rule is emphasized. This model's emphasis on high degrees of participation and efforts to achieve consensus seeks decisions that respect the concerns and standpoints of all members. It does not suggest that every member will agree equally with every decision made by the group, but that every member will feel sufficiently heard to abide by the decision of the group. Such decision-making processes take considerably more time than traditional autocratic or simple majority rule processes, but both process and product are beneficiaries of the responsible participation and resources of all members rather than of a few in leadership positions (Gastil 1992).

Implementing alternative models of leadership, followership, and decision making is quite challenging and demands a great deal from group members. These models require a high degree of self-awareness on the part of all members. Members must be aware, for example, of limits on the group's time. Members must be careful to ensure that others have time to speak and be heard. Members are challenged through these processes to be as concerned with the collective good as they are with their individual well-being. These cooperative, collective, and highly participative processes are often very difficult to learn and to implement. This is especially the case for many of us who have been socialized into competitive, individualistic, and hierarchical structures and processes for group decision making.

While cooperative, collective, and participative leadership and decision-making processes seem at odds with the competitive, individualistic, and hierarchical leadership and decision-making approaches consistent with the dominant paradigm, alternative approaches have a long history of use by many American Indian tribes in North America. Attneave reminds us that for many of these tribes:

> Tribal histories never suggested the impatient solution of majority vote so revered by "democracies." If a sizable portion of the band, tribe, or village dissented, discussion continued until some compromise could be reached. Except when asked specifically to do so, no one spoke for anyone else, and each was expected to participate. Discussions could last for hours, even days, until all were heard and a group decision was reached (Attneave in McGoldrick, Pearce, and Giordano 1982:66–67).

Attneave (1982:67) notes that even today the influence of the old alternative approaches can be seen and that "tribal meetings still last for hours, and tensions can be high as one faction seeks consensus while another pushes for a majority vote." This is an indication of the challenges to be faced when alternative perspectives and traditional ones meet.

Roles and Norms

Other basic concepts that help us to understand human behavior in the context of groups include roles and norms. **Roles** are expectations about what is appropriate behavior for persons in particular positions. Roles may be formally assigned, such as president or recorder, or they may be informal and based on the interests and skills of individuals such as harmonizer (someone the group looks to to keep the peace) or summarizer (someone skilled in restating the key elements from a discussion).

As members of groups we play multiple roles, depending on the current needs and demands of the group. Sometimes our multiple roles tend to contradict each other. When we find ourselves in this situation we are experiencing role conflict. **Role conflict** "refers to the disparity which an individual experiences among competing roles" (Brown 1991:75). We are likely to experience role conflict, for example, if we are assigned by our agency administrator to facilitate a group and we attempt to play roles to facilitate a functional, democratic, and consensus-oriented leadership style, but we are given a very short time to accomplish the goal set for the group by the administrator. We experience a conflict between the demand of the alternate roles required to be a consensus builder and the traditional and more time-saving leadership roles based on majority rule or even autocratic leadership.

Such conflicts are often not easily resolved. In most instances resolution requires a compromise between what we would prefer ideally and what is possible practically. For example, if there is insufficient time to reach complete consensus, we can still emphasize the need for everyone to participate in discussions and decision making to the maximum extent possible. We can also look to the other group members for ways to make the process as participative as possible, given the time constraints, rather than shifting entirely to an autocratic approach.

Norms are the "group's common beliefs regarding appropriate behavior for members." Norms guide group members' behaviors in their interactions with each other (Johnson and Johnson 1991:16–17). They help members know what to expect of others and what is expected of them. Roles and norms are important concepts for understanding both traditional and alternative perspectives on groups. The specific nature of the roles and norms that structure a group may serve either to maintain power inequality and restrict diversity or they may serve to guide groups to ensure that power is shared equally and that diversity is sought and respected. Norms for a specific group emerge over time and must be learned by new members entering the group. This process of learning the norms of the group is referred to as socialization. We have discussed socialization processes previously in the context of individual development and as a process through which families transmit to their children the values and rules of behavior of the family and the society in which the family lives.

Conformity and Deviance in Groups

Two factors related to roles and norms important to consider in groups, both as a leader or facilitator and as a group member, are the concepts of conformity and deviance in groups. Conformity refers to "bringing one's behavior into alignment with a group's expectations" (Sabini 1995:A3). **Deviance** is defined as violation of "norms or rules of behavior" (Curran and Renzetti 1996:10). We will explore these concepts by looking more at the related concepts of idiosyncrasy credit, groupthink, and team think.

Idiosyncrasy credit

Hollander defines idiosyncrasy credit as "the potential for individuals to behaviorally deviate from group norms without being sanctioned," and also as the "'positively disposed impressions' a person acquires as a member of a group" (in Estrada et al. 1995: 57). Idiosyncrasy credit or the ability to deviate from group norms without negative sanction from other group members can be gained in a number of ways. It can be gained by importing it from external sources (you secure outside funding for your group to reach its goals); by being assigned a high-status role within the group (your status as group chair); by displaying competence (your negotiating skills allowed you to settle a troubling conflict within the group); by conforming to group norms (you almost always adhere to group norms, so you are occasionally allowed to violate a norm, with the group trusting that based on your history you will return to adhering to the norms); or by being group-oriented in your motivation (the group trusts that your deviance will be good for the group because you have in the past worked for the good of the group). Hollander noted that there are limits to the extent and use of idiosyncrasy credits that group members will allow. Hollander posited that "members will only allow them to act differently in a manner that is consistent with their high-status roles" (in Estrada et al. 1995:58–59).

Groupthink

The concept of idiosyncrasy credit is an example of groups allowing members to deviate from their norms or rules. Group researchers have also noted the power of groups to press members to conform to group decisions, even when the group's decision may not be the best possible decision. Neck and Manz note that "excessive emphasis on group cohesiveness and conformity" can interfere with effective thinking processes" (1994: 933). Janus (1982) called this phenomenon *groupthink.* **Groupthink** is "a mode of thinking that people engage in when they are deeply involved in a cohesive in-group, when the members' striving for unanimity override their motivation to realistically appraise alternative courses of action . . . a deterioration of mental efficiency, reality testing, and moral judgment that results from in-group pressures" (Janus 1982:9).

Neck and Manz note that "groups exert enormous pressures on their members to conform to the norms established by the group social system." They suggest that these pressures can be either negative or positive depending on the nature of conformity being pressured (1994:944). Groupthink is a term used to indicate when the outcome of pressure to conform results in a decision by the group that has a negative outcome. A number of researchers have explored the conditions that lead to groupthink as well as ways to prevent groupthink.

Neck and Manz (1994:933) also point out that groupthink can result from faulty decision-making processes within the group.

Some tendencies toward groupthink also come about as a result of what Neck and Moorhead (1995:550) refer to as a **closed leader style.** *Closed leader style:*

1. Does not encourage member participation
2. Does state his/her opinions at the beginning of the meeting
3. Does not encourage divergent opinions from all group members
4. Does not emphasize the importance of reaching a wise decision

Symptoms of Groupthink

1. Direct social pressure placed on a member who argues against the group's shared beliefs
2. Members' self-censorship of their own thoughts or concerns that deviate from the group consensus
3. An illusion of the groups' invulnerability to failure
4. A shared illusion of unanimity
5. The emergence of self-appointed mind guards that screen out adverse information from outside the group
6. Collective efforts to rationalize
7. Stereotyped views of enemy leaders as weak or incompetent
8. An unquestioned belief in the group's inherent morality (Neck and Manz 1994:932–933).

Decision-Making Defects

1. Incomplete survey of alternatives
2. Incomplete survey of objectives
3. Failure to examine the risks of the preferred choice
4. Failure to reappraise initially rejected alternatives
5. Poor information search
6. Selective bias in processing information at hand
7. Failure to work out contingency plans

Teamthink and avoiding groupthink   If we are aware of the symptoms and the faulty decision-making processes that lead to groupthink, we can work to avoid it in our work in groups. Neck and Manz (1994:940) suggest the concept of **teamthink** as an alternative to groupthink and as a way to prevent group-think. *Teamthink* includes:

1. Encouragement of divergent views
2. Open expression of concerns/ideas
3. Awareness of limitations/threats
4. Recognition of member's uniqueness
5. Discussion of collective doubts.

Other mechanisms for avoiding groupthink included using **methodical decision-making procedures** to "ensure that the group adheres to a highly structured and systematic decision-making process . . . [and make groupthink less likely] by promoting constructive criticism, nonconformity, and open-mindedness within the decision-making group" (Neck and Moorhead 1995:549). Miranda suggests that the effective use and management of **conflict** in a group can help prevent groupthink: "Productive conflict leads to group satisfaction with outcomes and a perception that the conflict has been useful. Productive conflict also leads to an improved group climate and greater group cohesion and is likely to enhance the quality of the group's decision" (1994:124).

Individual and Group Dimensions

Traditionally, some researchers have directed their interest toward the individuals who constitute groups, while others have concentrated on the group as an entity in itself, separate in many ways from the individuals who make it up

How to Avoid Groupthink

1. Assignment of role of critical evaluator to each member
2. Leader impartiality in setting goals and directions for group
3. Setting up of several independent policy-planning and evaluation groups to work on the same problem
4. Periodic division into separate outside groups and reconvening to work out differences
5. Member discussion and deliberations outside the group with trusted colleagues and reporting back of their findings (This suggestion does not apply to groups with a norm of confidentiality within the group.)
6. Invitation of one or more outside experts (non-core group members) to each meeting
7. Assignment of one member to the role of devil's advocate at each meeting
8. Spending time attending to interrelationships among group members
9. After consensus is reached, holding a "second chance" meeting to express doubts and rethink as necessary. (Janus 1983: 262–271)

(Johnson and Johnson 1991:15; Worchel, Wood, and Simpson 1992:2). Alternative perspectives on groups suggest that we must recognize the importance of groups both for the individuals who make them up and the group as a whole.

Process and outcome, goals and purposes, and levels of membership may all look very different, depending on whether one is looking at the dimension from the perspective of the individual group member or from that of the group as whole. Much of what must happen in a group involves striking a balance between what is best for the individuals who make up the group and what is best for the group as a whole. At all levels groups must struggle to achieve an optimum balance between meeting the individual needs of the members and the needs of the group as an entity.

As social workers who will be responsible for facilitating and practicing in groups, we must recognize the need to help blend the goals of individual members with the purposes of the group in such a way that one does not constrain the other but actually complements the other. All the concepts and dimensions of groups we have explored thus far must be considered in our efforts to help individual members and the group as a whole to accomplish their goals. We must recognize that whether a group's goals are set internally or externally and whether its membership is voluntary or involuntary will influence how well individuals who constitute the group can come together as a group and operate as a unit. A group in order to be a group must create a bond among its members, often referred to as cohesiveness. This is a complex and difficult task that cannot be accomplished without the support of group members.

As we discussed in our examination of membership, individuals come to groups with a range of levels of commitment and investment in the group. Individuals come to groups with their own goals for being there. For involuntary members, the goal may be simply to put up with and put into the group enough to survive until they can leave. For voluntary, full psychological members the individual goal may be to do whatever is necessary to see the group's purposes fulfilled. Their individual goal may be virtually the same as the group's goal. This is of course more likely if the members feel they have a part in fashioning the group's goal and if they can therefore see themselves and their individual goals reflected in the group's goal. Alternative perspectives on groups that place a premium on process and participation, cooperation, consensus decision making, and shared or functional leadership tend to be more able to blend individual and group interests and needs.

Agendas

Achieving a balance between the needs of the individual and those of group, however, cannot be achieved effectively unless members feel able to state and make known to other members their own goals, interests, and reasons for participating in the group. This process is sometimes referred to as agenda setting in groups. If individuals are able to voice their individual agendas for the group, the members can then work to effectively blend members' individual agendas with the purposes or goals of the group to create more integrated **surface agendas.** When agendas are not brought to the surface in this manner they are referred to as **hidden agendas.** You have probably heard this term in reference to groups with which you have been associated. One member may suggest to another (usually outside the context of the group meeting) that one of the other members has a hidden agenda. What they really mean is that that member has individual goals he or she wishes to achieve through the group that have not been brought to the surface and shared with the other members of the group. A hidden agenda is not necessarily damaging to the group, but hidden agendas often create difficulties for groups. They are often sources of confusion and interfere with group progress in setting and moving toward shared group goals. On the other hand, if a member has an unspoken individual goal that he or she wishes to achieve through the group that is not contrary to the goals of the group, it need not be problematic. For example, in the men's group we discussed earlier, if a member has as an individual and unspoken goal, improving his ability to use what he learns in the group to help him socialize his young son to behave in nonsexist ways, this hidden agenda will not likely interfere with the group's overall goal of reducing its members' sexist behaviors.

Just as individual and group goals must be blended and can become problematic if they conflict, roles played by members in groups may serve to advance the interests and needs of the group or they may serve to further individual interests and needs and conflict with the well-being of the group. Napier and Gershenfeld (1985:238–244) discuss individual and group roles in their discussion of leadership behavior in groups. They suggest that any member may exercise leadership by assuming roles conducive to the group's accomplishment of its tasks. They differentiate between group task (or product) and group maintenance (or process) focused roles. They also suggest that roles that serve the individual's interests over those of the group tend to create problems in the group's functioning.

Product-focused roles

Napier and Gershenfeld list a number of task- or product-oriented roles that serve to help the group select and move toward common outcomes. The **initiator** gets the ball rolling by proposing tasks or goals to the group. The **information** or **opinion seeker** requests facts and seeks relevant information about a group concern. The **information** or **opinion giver** offers information about group concerns. The **clarifier** or **elaborator** interprets and reflects back to the group ideas and suggestions to clear up confusion and offer alternatives. The **summarizer** pulls together related ideas and restates the suggestion after the group has discussed them and offers a decision or conclusion for the group to accept or reject. The **consensus tester** checks with the group periodically to see how much agreement there is to find out how close the group is to reaching a consensus. The product-oriented roles can be found to differing degrees in different groups. Not all groups are characterized by all of these roles (1985:238–244).

Process-focused roles

Group maintenance, process, or socioemotional roles that help the group move forward as a group are also suggested by Napier and Gershenfeld (1985). The encourager demonstrates warmth, friendliness, and responsiveness to others and gives recognition and opportunities for others to contribute to group efforts. The **expressor of group feelings** attempts to feed back to the group his or her sense of the mood or affective climate of the group. The **harmonizer** attempts to reconcile differences and reduce tensions by helping group members to explore their differences. The **compromiser** is willing to try to reconcile their differences. The **gatekeeper** attempts to keep channels of communication open by helping to bring all members into participation to help the group solve its problems. The **standard setter** suggests standards for the group to use and tests group efforts against the standards of the group. It is important to restate here that these different roles do not necessarily represent separate members of groups (Napier and Gershenfeld 1985:239–244, 279–280). Our functional definition of leadership implies that different members of the group demonstrate or play these roles at different times depending on the needs of the group and its individual members. As in the case with product-oriented roles, not all groups display all of these process-oriented roles.

Individual-focused roles

Individual roles represent sets of behaviors that serve the needs of individuals, often at the expense of the well-being of the group. Individuals playing these roles are concerned with meeting their own needs and interests. Napier and Gershenfeld (1985: 241–242) suggest several individual roles that interfere with a group's ability to reach its goals. The aggressor tends to attack and belittle the positions and contributions of others, often sarcastically. The **blocker** suggests why a suggestion will not work and why his or her position is the only one worthy of attention. The **self-confessor** uses the other group members to ventilate about personal problems and to seek sympathy. The **recognition seeker** offers his or her personal response to a problem as exemplary of what should be done in the current group situation. The **dominator** attempts to take over the proceedings of the group by interrupting others, by flattering other members, or by asserting his or her superior status. The **cynic-humorist** uses double-edged humor to remind the group of the pointless nature of its efforts. The **special interest pleader** attempts to sway the group to his or her individual preference by suggesting that his or her position is representative of an entire group of similarly minded people outside the confines of the group.

It is important to recognize that some of the behaviors associated with individual roles described above are not inherently harmful to the group's efforts. Certainly at times confrontation, conflict, discussion of personal problems, comparing a current group predicament to similar past individual experiences, humor, and reminding group members of the interests of persons outside the immediate group can be quite helpful to groups. These roles and their associated behaviors become harmful only when they are played at the expense of the good of the group and serve to help individuals gain power over the group for their individual interests and needs.

Stage Theories and Models

Johnson and Johnson (1991:19) note that there are many different approaches that incorporate the notions of stages or phases through which groups pass. These approaches, they suggest, can be divided into two types. "*Sequential-stage theories* specify the 'typical' order of the phases of group development" and "*recurring-phase theories* specify the issues that dominate group interaction which reoccur again and again" (Johnson and Johnson 1991:19). Sequential theories are more prescribed and less flexible approaches to the study of groups. They are more consistent with traditional paradigm thinking. Recurring-phase theories are more emergent and fluid and are more compatible with alternative notions of groups.

Hare (1994:441) addresses the diversity of opinions about groups evolving through a series of predictable phases or stages. "Even when phases can be identified, group members may need to recycle through the initial phases several times before they are ready to deal with the task at hand" (Hare 1994:441).

Sequential-stage theories

Traditional notions of group life have much in common with traditional notions of individual development. This is especially the case in their conceptualization of groups as a relatively fixed sequence of stages, each of which the group must pass through in a fixed order as it develops and pursues its purposes or goals. There are a number of different models of groups based on sequential-stage theories.

A common sequential-stage model of groups is that of Tuckman and Jensen (1977 in Johnson and Johnson 1991:395; Napier and Gershenfeld 1985:467). They based their model on an extensive review of the literature on group development. This model includes five stages referred to as forming, storming, norming, performing, and adjourning.

1. *Forming* is a stage of uncertainty and some discomfort as new group members come together for the first time in a new situation.

2. *Storming* occurs as group members raise questions and display resistance to the demands of the group. This is a period of conflict and rebellion.

3. *Norming* is the group's establishment of mechanisms for resolving conflict, working together as a group, and accomplishing the group purpose. Order is established.

4. *Performing* is the actual carrying out on the part of the group and its members of the tasks necessary to accomplish its purpose.

5. *Adjourning* is the termination phase of the group. It occurs as the task is completed and the group members make preparations to end their work together.

Another sequential stage model posits seven stages through which groups pass during their development (Johnson and Johnson 1991:395):

1. defining and structuring procedures and becoming oriented;

2. conforming to procedures and getting acquainted;

3. recognizing mutuality and building trust;

4. rebelling and differentiating;

5. committing to and taking ownership for the goals, procedures, and other members;

6. functioning maturely and productively; and

7. terminating.

Brown (1991:69–74) synthesizes the work of a number of researchers on small groups, including a number of social work researchers (Garland, Jones, and Kolodny 1973; Hartford 1971; Sarri and Galinsky 1985 in Brown 1991). His model also incorporates some aspects of the Tuckman and Jensen model outlined above. Brown's synthesis is summarized below:

1. *Origin Stage:*   This is also referred to by some as a pregroup stage. This stage occurs as an idea for a group, and the sharing of that idea with others is transformed into the decision to create a group.

2. *Formation:*   This phase includes people's feeling of uncertainty upon entering a group situation. This phase recognizes that people bring to a new group their past experiences—both positive and negative—with groups.

3. *Power and control:*   Differences and conflicts emerge during this stage as people struggle to maintain their personal interests and values at the same time that they are asked to submit to the needs and purposes of the group. An informal structure begins to form, with members taking a variety of task and maintenance or socioemotional roles.

4. *Intimacy:*   This stage occurs when the socioemotional climate of the group is able to incorporate the differences in personality and experiences of

the members. Norms or accepted patterns of behavior begin to take shape. Also, an informal status hierarchy may emerge as people demonstrate leadership behavior that assists the group in achieving its purposes.

5. *Maturation:* Not all groups progress to this stage because of their inability to negotiate the differences necessary to problem-solve or because of insufficient time within which to accomplish the necessary tasks. Groups that reach this stage experience a balance of socioemotional and task activities. They are able to effectively attend both to the product and process dimensions of the group in order to get the work of the group done. People feel able to express their differences and have them respected. At this stage conflict is likely to occur, but it is not counterproductive to the group's continuance as it was in the power and control phase. There is a high degree of cohesiveness or feelings of connectedness to each other on the parts of group members.

6. *Separation:* This is the termination or ending phase. This phase may not be experienced by all groups or it may not be experienced by all group members at the same time in any final sense. Separation occurs most noticeably in time-limited groups that meet for a specified purpose or purposes and then disband. In groups that are not time limited, but are ongoing, members come and go in a more fluid way. Separation may be occurring for some members at the same time that other members are newly joining the group in such open-ended groups. Ambivalence characterizes the group or members undergoing termination.

Recurring-stage alternatives

Many alternative notions of groups accept that groups tend to develop in stages. However, alternative perspectives place much more emphasis on circular or looping patterns within the overall framework of stages or phases. Alternative perspectives are less linear than traditional notions and they are more multidimensional. They accept and even expect that developmental stages are subject to recurrence throughout the life of a group.

Recurring-stage perspectives accept that change and movement are ongoing and necessary in groups. These alternative approaches, however, accept that often for groups to progress they must return to previous stages and revisit past issues. Going forward often means going backward. Conflict may recur periodically in the group's development, for example. Changes in the larger environment may cause the group to change its goals or its membership. These external changes may in turn cause the group to return to internal issues of origin, or conflict. External changes may also cause the group to jump ahead to consider termination or separation issues.

Both external and internal changes make it necessary for a group to revisit previous phases or to jump ahead nonsequentially to new stages. These many uncertainties are part of the reality of change that groups must face and they raise important questions about the reliability of a traditional, linear, fixed-stage perspective on groups. They suggest that an alternate recurring-phase perspective might be more appropriate.

Social Systems/Ecological Perspectives

Social systems or ecological perspectives on groups offer another often used alternative approach to groups. As we discussed in Chapter 3, social workers have found social systems or ecological perspectives helpful frameworks for incorporating some of the important social and environmental influences on human behavior. A systems framework is helpful in our attempts to understand group behavior more completely for this same reason. It recognizes the dynamic nature of groups and the interrelatedness of the larger environment, the group itself, and the members of the group.

Small groups can be viewed as social systems (Anderson and Carter 1990; Brown 1991). In doing so we are able to take advantage of the emphasis in social systems thinking on recognizing the interrelatedness and mutual influence of one entity, in this case the small group, with entities or systems in the larger environment. Systems thinking also allows us to look inside the system of concern or focal system, the small group in this context, to see the interrelatedness and mutual influences of the component parts or subsystems on one another. This is especially helpful in thinking about small groups because it provides us a framework within which to place a number of things we have been learning during this part of our journey toward more comprehensive understanding of HBSE.

For example, a social systems framework allows us to fit the personal and historical experiences gained by group members in their interactions with the larger environment prior to joining a group with the impact of these experiences on the person's perceptions and behaviors inside the group. The impact of racism or sexism that a member experiences outside the group is very likely to influence the behavior of the member inside the group. A systems approach also recognizes the influence of events that occur in the larger environment or suprasystem during the life of a group on the behavior of the group. If cutbacks in agency funding cause the layoff of one or more members of the task force seeking funds to create services for people who are HIV positive and people with AIDS, that small group will be forced to respond in some way. Reducing the scope of its goals, reorganizing responsibilities or tasks within the group, spending time processing the confusion and disruption caused by the change in membership, or perhaps even terminating for lack of sufficient human resources to continue its work are all possible responses within the group to the change occurring in the environment external to the group. This environmental change in turn has a major impact on the subsystems or component parts of the task force. Some individuals not only must leave the group, but they are now out of work entirely. Other members are faced with additional work and attendant stress as a result of the loss of other members.

Other concepts from systems thinking can also help us to understand small groups. The concept of *holon* (Anderson and Carter 1990) appropriately applies to small groups. It defines a critical characteristic of systems as being both a whole and a part at the same time. Certainly our task force on AIDS/HIV and our men's group can be seen as simultaneously whole entities and parts of other systems—agencies, communities, professions. Energy and linkage (Anderson and Carter 1990) are other helpful concepts in thinking about small groups. Energy, defined as the "capacity for action," (Anderson and Carter 1990) aptly describes the potential for groups to act and move to solve problems and to develop. Linkage or the ability to connect with other systems to exchange or transfer energy is another helpful way of understanding how small groups do their work. The subsystems, the individual members, of small groups connect with each other and exchange energy as they attempt to define issues, acquire resources, and bring about desired changes. At the same time small groups link with systems in the larger environment to exchange energy. The very goal of the AIDS/HIV task force was to link with other systems external to it in order to acquire funding. The purpose of the men's group was to allow group members to more effectively link or interact with women in the larger environment in nonsexist and nonexploitative ways.

Anderson and Carter (1990) also describe organization as an essential characteristic of social systems. *Organization* is the ability of a system to put its parts together into a working whole. Certainly the characteristics of leadership, followership, membership, and roles and norms all reflect the efforts of small groups to organize or structure themselves to achieve their goals.

Traditional perspectives on small groups and alternate approaches when considered together offer us a great deal of information from which to choose as we attempt to lead, facilitate, and be members of groups. In addition to these perspectives, it is essential that issues of diversity and oppression be considered in conjunction with any perspective or framework for understanding human behavior in a group environment.

Diversity, Oppression, and Groups

Diversity in Practice

Effective social work group work practice involves attention to both diversity and oppression in the context of groups. How can the section, "Diversity, Oppression, and Groups," assist you in appropriately attending to both diversity and oppression in the context of groups?

Groups: Oppression and social and economic justice

Understanding group behavior in the social environment requires serious attention to issues of diversity. Successful group membership or group facilitation requires knowledge of and respect for the differences that we and other group members bring to the group. Groups also can be effective contexts for addressing oppression.

Garvin (in Sundel, Glasser, Sarri, and Vinter 1985:461ff) suggests a number of group formats that might be helpful in efforts to empower oppressed people. Groups can be appropriate for addressing needs of members of such diverse groups as gay men and lesbians, elderly persons, persons with disabilities including persons with mental illnesses, and persons living in poverty. The history of social work with groups has its origins in social reform and the settlement house movement (see historical perspective section above). This history reflects the potential for social work in group contexts to address the needs of oppressed persons.

Garvin describes a number of group formats for use in working with oppressed persons. These formats illustrate more generally the kinds of groups social workers use in their work. We have mentioned some of these group types previously. They include:

1. *Consciousness-raising groups.* Time limited groups that help members share their experiences and explore their feelings about their oppressed status. These groups also help members explore possible avenues to empowerment.

2. *Treatment groups.* Groups that attempt to modify dysfunctional behaviors, thinking, and feelings. For example, a treatment group for gay men might assist the members to deal with feelings of depression and low self-esteem that can result from harassment and other forms of discrimination. It is essential that the group facilitator have a positive perspective on gay and lesbian sexual orientation. This reinforces again the need for social workers to be self-aware and to address our own tendencies toward homophobia (fear of homosexuality).

3. *Social action groups.* Groups directed to bringing changes in the larger environment in order to reduce oppression. Such groups can also teach members valuable skills in working with others and can help members increase their self-esteem.

4. *Network and support groups.* These groups can assist members in reducing feelings of social isolation and in recognizing their strengths by helping members to connect with others in similar situations to provide mutual support and to seek resources.

As a member of or facilitator for the group in this photo, what are some examples of knowledge about the diverse groups represented might you need to be respectful and effective?

5. *Skill groups.* These groups have as goals development of members' empowerment skills. Empowerment skills learned and practiced in these groups might include group leadership, social change, communication, and networking (Garvin in Sundel, Glasser, Sarri, and Vinter 1985:466–467).

Groups and people of color

Davis (1985) outlines a number of important considerations both for persons of color and white persons as group members and as facilitators. Davis (1985:325) stresses that issues of color affect all group contexts and perspectives. He urges that "those practitioners who believe their particular group work orientation transcends race and culture would perhaps do best by minorities to refrain from working with them" because race and culture are such powerful forces in this society.

Davis outlines a number of areas related to group dynamics in which race or color plays an important part. These areas include:

1. *Group composition.* Should groups be racially homogeneous or heterogeneous? The purpose of the group should be considered carefully in answering this question. Traditionally, groups purposefully composed of racially similar persons have been formed to enhance ethnic identity. Groups composed of people of different racial and ethnic backgrounds have often been formed to reduce racial prejudice. Davis suggests that a more complex question of racial composition is raised when race is unrelated to the group's purpose. Preferences of group members vary markedly by color. African Americans have been found to prefer group composition to be approximately half white and half nonwhite. Whites appear to prefer African Americans to compose no more than 20 percent of the members. These findings suggest that for African Americans it is important to feel, in the context of the small group, that they are not in the minority. Whites, on the other hand, appear to be threatened when they are not in the majority. Davis (1985:328–332) suggests that because neither minority persons of color nor majority whites prefer to be in a minority, workers should attempt racial balance in group composition.

Racial balance will also help avoid tokenism in group composition. **Tokenism** is the practice of giving the appearance of representation and access to resources or decision making without actually doing so. For example, one low-income-neighborhood person is placed on a task force to decide whether a potentially lucrative convention center project should be allowed to displace residents of the low-income neighborhood. All the other task force members are wealthy business executives and land developers who are likely to benefit financially from the project. While the task force composition might give the appearance that the neighborhood is represented, it is highly unlikely that the neighborhood person will be able to counter the interests of the other members. The low-income-neighborhood resident is a token (Davis 1985:328–332).

2. *Culture and communication.* It is important to recognize that cultural communication styles are important influences in any group. Davis illustrates the contrast between the high value placed on restraint and humility by Asian culture and the value placed on confrontation as a means of testing the validity of one's point of views by many African Americans. Davis suggests that such differences do not mean that different cultures should avoid being mixed in small groups, but that these differences must be taken into account in group process (1985:332).

3. *Trust.* Issues of trust among members and between members and facilitators must receive special attention when dealing with groups composed of whites and persons of color. Experiences brought to the group from the external environment often result in persons of color hesitating to disclose information about themselves to whites out of feelings of distrust based on discriminatory treatment by whites in the larger society. Persons of color also assume, often justifiably so, that white persons know so little about them because of segregation in society that whites have little of value to offer in understanding or solving their problems. On the other hand, whites often are unwilling to accept or trust that minority persons of color, even when in the position of expert, have anything of value to offer (Davis 1985:332–334).

4. *Status and roles.* Groups composed of persons of color and of whites must attend carefully to issues of status and roles in the group. There is often a tendency to attach statuses and roles within groups according to the patterns of minority/majority relations in the larger society. This is especially problematic when white group members are unaware of changes in status in the larger society of many persons of color who have overcome obstacles and barriers to attain statuses and roles equal to those of whites (Davis 1985:334).

Diversity and creativity in groups

Concerns are often raised about the difficulties and problems that flow from diverse groups, especially racially mixed groups. McLeod et al. remind us, to the contrary, that the theme of "'value-in-diversity,' rests on a hypothesis that ethnic diversity, at least when properly managed, produces tangible, positive effects on organizational outcomes" (1996:249). In the corporate context for example, scholars "suggest that ethnic diversity may be related to increased organizational creativity and flexibility . . . [and] that the insights and sensitivities brought by people from varying ethnic backgrounds may help companies to reach a wider variety of markets" (McLeod et al. 1996:249).

A key argument underlying the notion of diversity as a positive factor in small groups "is that the variety of perspectives and experiences represented on heterogeneous teams contributes to the production of high-quality ideas. Moreover, the variety in perspectives can stimulate further idea production by group members" (McLeod et al. 1996:250). In other words, diversity in perspectives and thought processes results in increased creativity in problem solving in groups. McLeod et al. note that Kanter refers to this as **kaleidoscope thinking,** "twisting reality into new patterns and rearranging the pieces to create a new reality. . . . Having contact with people from a variety of perspectives is one condition necessary for kaleidoscope thinking" (1996:250).

The conflict that may emerge in groups as a result of member diversity may also be an asset. Nemeth, for example, suggests that "minority dissent appears to stimulate exactly what theorists have recommended for improved performance and decision making, that is, a consideration of the issue from multiple perspectives" (in McLeod et al. 1996:250).

However, there is relatively little empirical research testing this "value-in-diversity" hypothesis and some research suggests advantages of homogeneous groups. For example, Watson, Kumar, Michaelsen found that "during the early stages of group development, ethnically homogeneous groups perform better than heterogeneous groups" (in McLeod et al. 1996:249). McLeod et al. conducted research using ethnically diverse groups of graduate and undergraduate students from a large midwestern university. [Note: Using your skills at paradigm analysis, deconstruction, and critical thinking, what might be the limitations of this research?] McLeod et al.'s hypothesis was: "Ethnically diverse groups will produce higher quality ideas than will all-Anglo groups." Their "preliminary analyses showed that the ideas produced by the groups with four ethnic groups represented were judged significantly more feasible than the ideas produced by the groups with three ethnic groups represented and by the all-Anglo groups. . . . The ideas produced by the heterogeneous groups were judged as significantly more feasible . . . and more effective . . . than the ideas produced by the homogeneous groups." However, "the members of homogeneous groups reported marginally significantly higher levels of interpersonal attraction than did members of heterogeneous groups" (1996:252–258).

McLeod et al. concluded that their findings supported the hypothesis "that diverse groups will have a performance advantage over homogeneous groups on a creativity task requiring knowledge of different cultures. On the other hand, . . . [they] also found evidence suggesting that members of heterogeneous groups may have had more negative affective reactions to their groups than did members of homogeneous groups" (1996:257).

The researchers in this study suggest therefore that diversity in groups is complex and that both increased numbers (quantity) of diverse members and quality of the interaction among members or "proper management of diversity" are equally important in reaping the potential benefits of an increasingly diverse workforce (McLeod et al. 1996:260–261).

Researchers have continued to attempt to unravel the complexity of diversity in the context of work with small groups. Attempts have been made to better understand the interplay of diversity with product or outcome dimensions of groups and the process or socio-emotional dimensions. For example, Knouse and Dansby (1999) studied the impact of work-group diversity and work-group effectiveness. While their findings were similar in some ways to previous research, they also posited some additional issues regarding diversity in small groups. They found as others have (Kanter, 1977; McCleod et al., 1996), that group effectiveness seems to decline and conflict is more likely to increase in groups that include over 30 percent membership from diverse groups. However, they suggest that effectiveness or group product is likely related to other more complex factors, such as status and power differences as Davis (1985) has suggested. They note that "groups that contain powerful higher status minorities or women tend to have less conflict than those with less powerful members of subgroups" (Tolbert et al., in Knouse and Dansby 1999). These authors suggest that, rather than looking only at the physical proportion of diverse members in a group, we need to seek a more sophisticated overall measure of diversity that also considers such factors as status, power, differences in ability, and psychological differences. Time together as a group may also be an important factor. They note, for example, that Harrison, Price, and Bell (1998, in Knouse and Dansby 1999) "found that as the time increased that group members worked together, the effects of surface-level diversity decreased. . . . Group members had greater opportunities over time to interact and thus better understand each other and form interpersonal relationships."

In another recent study, Oetzel (2001) found that an independent or interdependent self-image (belief and comfort in working individually versus collectively, often connected to cultural background) and communication processes (participation, cooperation, respect) are important elements of understanding diversity in small groups. Oetzel found that the self-image of group members in terms of having an individualistic or collectivistic perspective was more explanatory of group communication processes than group composition. He also found that interdependent perspective was positively associated with participation and cooperation in small groups. In addition, he found that equal participation and respect resulted in a member giving more effort to achieving group outcomes and more group member satisfaction.

Research in the area of groups and diversity continues to produce both interesting and sometimes conflicting results. Thomas et al. conducted research on creativity and group enjoyment related to heterogeneous and homogeneous groups. The task before their groups was to develop a creative ending to an open-ended short story (Thomas 1999). Their findings were both interesting and confounding. For example, they found, "teams composed primarily of ethnic minorities resulted in more positive emotions and fewer negative ones" (1999:145). However, Thomas also found that "there was no significant difference in creativity between groups composed mainly of ethnic minorities and those composed mostly of Caucasians" (1999:145). This finding contradicts the findings of McLeod et al. (see above), who concluded that diverse groups did have an advantage over homogeneous groups on a creativity task that required knowledge of different cultures. It is important to recognize there are many factors that influence groups and diversity. For example, the tasks required in these two studies were quite different. Another interesting finding of the Thomas study was that "teams composed mainly of ethnic minorities reported having a better time [group enjoyment] than teams composed mostly of Caucasians" (1999:152). Thomas further notes that while "there were no advantages in creativity, there were no disadvantages either. This suggests that greater group enjoyment was not achieved at the cost of performance on the task" (1999:152).

Thomas concludes that his "research findings are important both theoretically and practically. They provided evidence for the overall effects of ethnic composition regardless of individual race/ethnicity. Ethnic composition can truly be more than the sum of its individual members. Asians, non-Asian ethnic minorities, and Caucasians all enjoyed working in minority-dominated teams more. . . . All other things (like performance) being equal, it seems that groups dominated by minorities are more enjoyable for everyone" (1999:152).

Practice implications of diversity in groups

Davis et al. stress that "race is such an emotionally charged area of practice that leaders may fail to identify and deal with racial issues because they wish to avoid racial confrontations, are anxious, or perhaps are unsure about how to proceed" (1996:77). Davis et al. stress that the "color blind" approach that says race is transcended when different people come together in a group for a common purpose denies the significance of race (1996:78). These scholars point out, instead, that "whenever people of different races come together in groups, leaders can assume that race is an issue, but not necessarily a problem" (Davis et al. 1996:77). However, due to the history of race relations, individuals' perceptions of racial difference, and issues in the larger environment, race can be a significant source of tension in these groups. Both leaders and members need to be prepared to understand and address racial tensions in racially mixed groups.

Davis et al. (1996:83) suggest there are three basic sources of racial tension within racially mixed groups of people of color and white people. These sources of tension are from:

1. Within individual group members
2. The nature of the group itself
3. The environment of the group

In order to deal with racial tensions, Davis et al. (1996:83–84) suggest the leader needs "trifocal" vision. This trifocal vision requires leaders to:

1. Consider issues related to individuals such as:
   - Have general knowledge of how different populations tend to view power, authority, status, interpersonal boundaries, typical cultural and family expectations, but must be careful not to overgeneralize in these areas
   - Be sensitive to the specific racial makeup of the group and the number of persons from each group: unequal numbers can lead to subgrouping and domination by members of one group; equal numbers may not be perceived as balanced on the part of group members used to being a majority (e.g., whites).

2. Consider issues related to the group itself such as:
   - Group purpose and goals, especially if different members from different races have different expectations of focus or purpose

- Norms that promote recognition and respect for differences, member equality, and open discussion of racial issues can help prevent members from being cautious, mistrustful, and guarded.

3. Consider issues related to the larger environment such as:
   - Climate of society
   - Events in the members' neighborhoods
   - The sponsoring organization's reputation for responsiveness to racial concerns
   - The way member's significant others view the group.

Within racially mixed groups, according to Davis et al. (1996:85), problems concerning racial issues can occur at three levels:

1. *Between members and leaders:* If the leader is the only representative of a particular race, he/she can feel isolated; leaders can be insensitive; members can doubt the leader's ability due to race; leaders who are people of color may find their competence challenged by whites and members of other races.

2. *Between members:* Racist behaviors/comments leading to verbal or physical attacks; subgroup formation by race to dominate; members who avoid discussing sensitive topics; members don't participate because they feel isolated or under attack because of their race.

3. *Between member and environment:* Institutional racism in community and society; member's reluctance to attend meetings in unfamiliar territory; sponsoring organizations perceived as unresponsive.

Groups and gender

Just as the patterns of interaction and treatment in larger society impact on small-group dynamics around issues of race and color, group behavior is influenced powerfully by issues related to gender. Social workers must respect and understand the impact of gender on group dynamics. Rosabeth Moss Kanter has studied the interactions of males and females in small group and organizational contexts extensively.

Kanter has found evidence that "the presence of both men and women in the same group heightens tension and may put women at a disadvantage" (1977:372). She also suggests that power and status differentials between men and women in society tend to be replicated in small mixed-gender groups. Since "males have generally higher status and power in American society than females . . . when men and women are ostensible peers, the male's external status may give him an advantage inside the group. . . . In mixed groups of 'peers' men and women may not, in fact, be equal, especially if their external statuses are discrepant" (1977:373).

Kanter also describes differential impacts of gender in leadership of work groups. Kanter (1977:374) suggests that "even if women have formal authority, they may not necessarily be able to exercise it over reluctant subordinates." She cites the example of a case in which a woman "had formal leadership of a group of men, but the men did not accept this, reporting informally to her male superior."

Kanter suggests a number of strategies for reducing the inequalities and difficulties faced by women in mixed-gender work groups. She suggests that the most important means of addressing this problem is to "change the sex ratio in the power structure of organizations, to put more women in positions of visible leadership" (1977:381).

She suggests, more importantly, and similar to Davis's observation about the racial composition of groups, that

> the relative proportion of men and women in work groups and training groups should . . . be taken into account in designing programs. Whenever

possible, a 'critical mass' of females should be included in every working group—more than two or three, and a large enough percentage that they can reduce stereotyping, change the culture of the group, and offer support without being a competitive threat to one another. If there are only a few women in the sales force, for example, this analysis suggests that they should be clustered rather than spread widely. (1977:383)

Only if we attend carefully to issues of diversity in the groups we create, those we facilitate, and those to which we belong will our efforts result in effective groups.

Relationship of feminist perspectives and social work with groups   Lewis notes that principles of social work with groups have a number of commonalities with principles of feminism (1992:273):

1. A *common consciousness* of the embedded details of victimization
2. The systematic *deconstruction* of negative and disadvantaging definitions of reality
3. The process of *naming,* of identifying the consequences of established structures and patterns
4. Trust in the *processes within the group* to reconstruct a new reality and to provide the context within which to test and practice new language, behaviors, expectations, and aspirations
5. A belief in the *power of the group,* united to bring about desired changes in the context, however small these may be
6. A *sense of community* through the experience of reaching out and discovering allies and "same-thinkers and doers" in the wider social context

Groups and persons with disabilities

As we noted in Chapter 3, there are 43 million persons with disabilities in the United States. Given the number of persons with disabilities in the population and given the special needs of this group, it is very likely that social workers will work with persons with disabilities in virtually all kinds of small group situations. As a result it is important to be sensitive to the needs, feelings, and strengths of persons with disabilities. Brown (1995) outlines a specific set of rights of people with disabilities in groupwork. This "Bill of Rights" can help us make sure we are respectful and inclusive of persons with disabilities in our work in groups. The first two sections of the table reflect ADA standards. "The third section on ethics and accommodation [is] . . . based on 'due care' in standards of practice and the accommodation process" (Brown 1995:73).

Helpful suggestions for insuring that persons with disabilities are able to exercise their full rights within group contexts are included in what Patterson et al. (1995:79) refer to as:

Disability Etiquette for Groups

1. It is appropriate to acknowledge that a disability exists, but asking personal questions is inappropriate unless one has a close relationship with the person with the disability.
2. It is important to speak directly to the person with a disability, even when a third party (e.g., attendant, relative, interpreter) is present.
3. It is appropriate to use common words such as *look* or *see,* for individuals with visual impairments, as well as *running* or *walking* with people who use wheelchairs.

4. It is appropriate to offer assistance to a person with a disability, but one should wait until it is accepted before providing the assistance. Clarification should be sought from the individual with the disability if the group leader is unsure of how or what type of assistance is needed.

In addition, Patterson et al. provide a listing of suggestions for use by group leaders in groups where some members have disabilities including blindness, mobility impairment, deafness, or speech impairment.

Rights of People with Disabilities in Group Work

Places of Public Accommodation and Telecommunication	• The right to access and full utilization of all public accommodations • The right to access and full utilization of telecommunication • The right to access and full utilization of public ground transportation
Inclusion and Accommodation	• The right not to be discriminated against on the basis of disability when being referred or requesting participation in group work • The right not to be discriminated against on the basis of being regarded as a person with a disability • The right of the individuals to be judged for inclusion in the group on their own merits • The right to be tested fairly • The right to request and to be provided with reasonable accommodation that is not an undue hardship • The right not to be disqualified from group membership based on the inability to perform nonessential role functions • The right not to be limited, segregated, or classified as a person with a disability • The right not to be discriminated against as a direct threat to the safety or the health of others, unless certain standards are met • The right of individuals not to be retaliated against because they made a charge, testified, assisted, or participated in any manner in an investigation, proceeding, or hearing to enforce any provision of ADA or other legislation that was developed to protect their rights • The right not to be discriminated against because of an association with people with disabilities • The right not to be discriminated against by a third party contract
Ethics and Accommodation	• The right and responsibility to initiate discussion with the facilitator about any accommodation needs • The right to reveal a disabling condition to the group leader and to members without begin discriminated against • The right to expect the development of group norms that recognize the value of diversity within the group, the distribution of group roles based on abilities, and the value of accommodation to maximize use of resources • The right to receive feedback about what can be changed, rather than feedback about what is personally degrading because of a disability • The right not to be the target of scapegoating because of disability as the group negotiates power and communication distribution within the group

Adapted from Brown 1995 *The Journal for Specialists in Group Work,* v. 20 (2), 73–75. Copyright American Counseling Association. Reprinted with permission.

Specific Suggestions for Four Common Disabilities a Group Leader Might Encounter

Blindness	• If the person seems to need assistance, identify yourself and let the person know you are there by a light touch on the arm.
	• Let the person take your arm and follow the motion of your body.
	• When seating the person, place his or her hand on the side or back of the chair.
	• Use verbal cues and specificity in giving directions (e.g., left, right, three steps down).
	• Early in the group have each member identify him- or herself upon speaking until the person with blindness has learned to recognize members' voices.
Mobility Impairment	• When conversing for any length of time with someone who uses a wheelchair, sit down to have the dialogue at eye level.
	• Leaning or hanging on the individual's wheelchair should be avoided because this is part of the person's body space.
	• If a group member uses a manual wheelchair, it is appropriate to offer assistance if any distance is involved or when carpeting makes propelling the wheelchair more difficult.
Deafness	• The group members and leader should be positioned in such a way that the individual with the disability has a clear view of the speaker's mouth.
	• Speak clearly, without exaggerating, and use a regular speed and tone of voice.
	• When an interpreter is used, both eye contact and speech should be directed toward the individual with deafness and not the interpreter (e.g., "John, I look forward to having you in our group" vs. "Tell John I look forward to having him in our group").
	• The interpreter's ethical code includes confidentiality.
Speech Impairment	• Maintain eye contact and be patient.
	• Do not interrupt or finish sentences for the group member.
	• Do seek clarification if you do not understand the individual's speech.

Note: Adapted from Patterson et al. 1995 *The Journal for Specialists in Group Work*, v. 20 (2), 79. Copyright American Counseling Association. Reprinted with permission.

Effective Groups

Groups can be said to be effective if they accomplish three things: 1) goal achievement; 2) maintenance of good working relationship among members; and 3) adaptation to changing environmental conditions that allow effectiveness to be maintained. Johnson and Johnson offer a model of effective groups that includes nine dimensions:

1. Group goals must be clearly understood, be relevant to the needs of group members, highlight the positive interdependence of members, and evoke from every member a high level of commitment to their accomplishment.

2. Group members must communicate their ideas and feelings accurately and clearly.

3. Participation and leadership must be distributed among members.

4. Appropriate decision-making procedures must be used flexibly to match them with the needs of the situation.

5. Conflicts should be encouraged and managed constructively. . . . Controversies (conflicts among opposing ideas and conclusions) promote

involvement in the group's work, quality and creativity in decision making, and commitment to implementing the group's decisions. Minority opinions should be accepted and used.

6. Power and influence need to be approximately equal throughout the group. Power should be based on expertise, ability, and access to information, not on authority.

7. Group cohesion needs to be high. . . . Cohesion is based on members liking each other, desiring to continue as part of the group, and being satisfied with their group membership.

8. Problem-solving adequacy should be high.

9. The interpersonal effectiveness of members needs to be high. Interpersonal effectiveness is a measure of how well the consequences of your behavior match your intentions. (1991:21–24)

SUMMARY/TRANSITION

All of the perspectives, concepts, and dimensions we have considered in this chapter are important to help us understand groups. Currently as students and teachers and as social workers and future social work practitioners, we do and will continue to conduct much of our work in the context of small groups. We create groups, we facilitate groups, and we can expect on almost a daily basis to spend time as a member of some small-group effort.

In this chapter we have explored groups as contexts in which both process and product are inextricable concerns. We have examined a number of issues involved in the formation and achievement of group purposes and goals. The interrelated and interdependent nature of membership, leadership, followership, and decision making was considered. A variety of roles and norms played by group members and their significance for the individuals playing them and for the group as a whole have been investigated. We have outlined a number of stage-based models of group development, recognizing that while stages are a part of group development they do not occur only in linear or fixed sequences. Social systems or ecological frameworks for explaining many aspects of groups have been sketched, along with recognition of some of the limitations of this common approach used by social workers to understand groups. We have stressed the absolute necessity of considering issues of oppression and of diversity in our work with and in groups. We noted that regardless of purpose or goal, serious attention must be given to issues concerning persons of color, persons with disabilities, and gender in all the groups with which we are associated.

Only by attending to the multiple, complex, interdependent, and interrelated dimensions of groups can we be effective in our group work. By doing so we can gain a much more complete and holistic picture of groups than we can from concentrating on any one perspective. This multiple-perspective approach is consistent also with our attempts in this book to develop a worldview that is inclusive and that incorporates a "both/and" rather than an "either/or" approach to understanding HBSE.

As throughout this book, the knowledge we explored here about groups is interdependent and interconnected with the things we have learned about individuals and familiness on our voyage toward understanding human behavior and the social environment. The information we gathered during this part of our journey is related to and interconnected with our explorations in the chapters on organizations and communities that follow.

Succeed with PEARSON **mysocialworklab**

 Professional Identity   **Diversity in Practice**   **Practice Contexts**

Log onto **www.mysocialworklab.com** to watch videos on the skills and competencies discussed in this chapter. (*If you did not receive an access code to* **MySocialWorkLab** *with this text and wish to purchase access online, please visit* www.mysocialworklab.com.)

PRACTICE TEST

Professional Identity

1. One of the earliest uses of small groups by social workers was
   a. as part of friendly visiting.
   b. in schools.
   c. in settlement houses.
   d. for treatment of mental illness.

2. _____ are expectations about what is appropriate behavior for persons in particular positions.
   a. Norms
   b. Roles
   c. Purposes
   d. Recurring phases

3. The notion that leaders are created by followers is consistent with what type of definition of leadership?
   a. situational leadership
   b. functional leadership
   c. democratic leadership
   d. unitary leadership

4. A group that operates through processes that give each member equal and adequate opportunities to speak and participate and where members show a willingness to listen to what others have to say would refer to a_____
   a. democratic leadership group
   b. functional group
   c. consciousness-raising group
   d. laissez-faire group

5. According to Brown's model of small groups, the stage of group development where members are able to attend to both product and process dimensions of the group in order to get the work of the group done and show a high degree of cohesiveness is _____.
   a. intimacy
   b. norming
   c. performing
   d. maturation

6. Two things that differentiate a group from an aggregate or collection of people are
   a. goals and objectives.
   b. a leader and followers.
   c. shared purpose and common interaction.
   d. an agenda and roles.

7. Which of the following is NOT a factor in the development of groupthink?
   a. closed leadership style
   b. faulty decision-making processes
   c. methodical decision-making processes
   d. a deterioration of mental efficiency, reality testing, and moral judgment that results from in-group pressures.

8. The internal group processes that occur during the life of a group are referred to as _____.
   a. the maintenance/expressive dimension
   b. group norms
   c. roles in groups
   d. the task/instrumental dimension

Diversity in Practice

9. Which of the following would not be a source of racial tension with a racially mixed group of people of color and white people?
   a. within the individual group members
   b. the nature of the group itself
   c. the environment of the group
   d. the roles of the group

10. _____ refers to bringing one's behavior into alignment with a group's expectations.
    a. groupthink
    b. the compromiser role
    c. norming
    d. conformity

Log onto **MySocialWorkLab** once you have completed the Practice Test above to take your Chapter Exam and demonstrate your knowledge of this material.

Answers

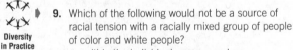

1) c 2) b 3) b 4) a 5) d 6) c 7) c 8) a 9) d 10) d

Group Work Practice with Australia's Asylum Seekers

Val Clark

Australia's asylum seekers have been rendered voiceless by the circumstances in which they find themselves, circumstances that include being subjected to punitive government policies, denial of basic rights and needs, economic impoverishment and social disadvantage. The Asylum Seekers Centre (ASC) in Sydney provides an individualised casework service to asylum seekers. The ASC also provides opportunities for asylum seekers to improve their circumstances through attending English classes and participating in other educational and social group programmes. The present paper is concerned with small group facilitation of mutual aid processes at the ASC. It focuses on one group programme, 'Open Forum', to illustrate a strengths-based empowerment practice. The paper concludes with some suggestions for extending group work practice with and on behalf of asylum seekers.

Keywords: Asylum Seekers; Group Work; Mutual Aid

Introduction

The *Tampa* incident in August 2001 marked a turning point in Australia's consciousness of 'asylum seekers'. Nightly television footage showed the crowded deck of the *Tampa* and detailed the progressive manoeuvres of the Australian government to block the would-be refugees from setting foot on Australian soil. Australians were polarised in their response. Some were horrified at the prospect that Australia could be swamped by floods of unwanted refugees, whereas others were shocked to witness the lack of compassion being shown by their government and fellow citizens toward so obviously traumatised people.

The media coverage of the *Tampa* incident brought the plight of asylum seekers to the attention of Australians across a wide socioeconomic spectrum and sparked the formation of many groups aimed at reversing, or at least softening, the government's harsh treatment of asylum seekers (Jupp, 2002; Haddad, 2003; Devetak, 2004; Moorehead, 2005). It also resulted in a deluge of offers of support to the Asylum Seekers Centre (ASC) in Sydney from people wanting to 'do something' to help asylum seekers.

The Asylum Seekers Centre

The ASC is a non-government not-for-profit organisation staffed by a small core of paid employees (equivalent to five full-time positions) and a current pool of approximately 80 volunteers. The ASC commenced operation in 1993 under the auspices of the Jesuit Refugee Service. It is now sponsored by the Good Shepherd Sisters and The Mercy Foundation and is assisted by many other groups and individuals from volunteer, academic, and professional organisations.

The ASC provides case management and other services to asylum seekers who are awaiting the final determination of their application for refugee

Correspondence to: Val Clark, Lecturer, Social Work, School of Humanities and Social Science, The University of Newcastle, NSW 2308, Australia. Email: val.clark@newcastle.edu.au

ISSN 0312-407X (print)/ISSN 1447-0748 (online) © 2006 Australian Association of Social Workers DOI: 10.1080/03124070600985962

Source: Clark, V. (2006). Group work practice with Australia's asylum seekers. *Australian Social Work* 59(4), 378–390.

379

protection and who are living in the community. Volunteers at the ASC provide a wide range of services, including teaching English, catering lunches, pro bono professional services (e.g. medical and legal), assistance with transport, occasional emergency accommodation and social support.

The asylum seekers who visit the ASC are an extremely vulnerable population. Many have been awaiting a final determination on their applications for protection for many years. They have fled persecution and other dangers in their countries of origin and, in many cases, they have also been persecuted in countries through which they have transited on their journey to Australia. Many have experienced torture or other forms of trauma associated with organised violence or exile.

Lengthy periods of immigration detention (after arrival in Australia) have caused extreme mental stress for many of the asylum seekers who had previously coped well with the enormity of dislocation from their homes, communities and former ways of life. The harsh conditions and lack of psychiatric services in detention have also exacerbated pre-existing mental illness for some asylum seekers, making it even harder for them to survive in the community after their release.

Increasingly, it is being recognised that, as a result of their experiences, asylum seekers have a high incidence of both physical and mental health problems (Sinnerbrink et al., 1996; Harris & Telfer, 2001; Smith, 2001; Steel & Silove, 2001; Kisely et al., 2002). Owing to changing conditions of the visas held by many asylum seekers (e.g. the restrictions associated with Bridging Visa E), the majority of ASC clients lack Medicare and Centrelink entitlements and do not have permission to work, in either a paid or voluntary capacity. They usually have no family supports in Australia and are entirely dependent on the charity of individual community members and voluntary organisations such as the ASC.

During sabbatical leave in February–May 2005, I spent time at the ASC. I observed how naturally occurring small group processes among the asylum seekers there assisted in realising the ASC's aim of being a place of welcome for all. This paper arises from these observations and reflections on my facilitation of four sessions of one group at the ASC known as Open Forum. Before discussing this work with Open Forum, it may help to locate it within the broader context of group work activities at the ASC and provide a rationale for group work as a method of choice when working with asylum seekers.

Group work at the ASC

Group work offers opportunities unavailable in individual casework for assisting asylum seekers in their common struggle to gain some control in their lives. Working with people in groups contrasts with the dominant individualist approach of professional social work practice. Group work provides the potential for all group members to become helpers and thereby to rise above the position of dependent recipient of other people's acts of kindness.

My aim in the present paper is to describe a simple open-ended group that I worked with at the ASC and show how this group provides possibilities for client empowerment. The group meets for approximately 50 minutes once a week and provides an opportunity for all asylum seekers, volunteers, staff and visitors to the Centre to discuss issues that are of mutual interest; hence, the group's name, 'Open Forum'. Other groups in the ASC's programme include those oriented towards educational aims (e.g. learning English, computer skills) or social aims (e.g. conversation, art, music).

Group work at the ASC is a powerful method for assisting people who share a common experience: seeking asylum. Both formal and informal groups at the ASC foster a tolerance of diversity among asylum seekers and those who work with them. Asylum seekers originating from a dozen different countries sit down to lunch together and this simple act serves to break down the divisions among them, even when their home countries are traditional enemies.

The asylum seekers share many common concerns and hopes for the future. They willingly engage in collaborative processes of learning, with English teachers tapping this force to good effect in the classroom. One volunteer, an experienced professional teacher, told me of her delight to discover students who were keen to help each other to learn and her admiration for how they provided each other with high levels of emotional support. Mutual support is a common feature of programmes at the ASC and it is very evident that asylum seekers use the opportunities provided at the Centre to connect with one another and make friends.

Theory and practice issues in group work with asylum seekers

One of the most salient features of work at the ASC is that the client population is multi-ethnic, multi-cultural and multi-linguistic. A review of literature about group work with multi-ethnic populations conducted by one American author (Saino, 2003) found that articles tend to focus on groups where members are of a single ethnicity or, divided among two ethnicities, or where the ethnic differences between the worker and the group are a feature. Articles reviewed by Saino tended to stress the benefits of homogeneity within a group, thereby serving as a mirror for the wider society where racial and cultural diversity is avoided. Saino only located a small number of articles that actually dealt with multi-ethnic groups (i.e. groups where members are from multiple ethnicities).

Saino's article is of particular interest here because it describes group work practice quite similar to that at the ASC. In both cases the work is with a truly multi-ethnic group; it is conducted in English and yet English is not the first language of the participants. Although this may seem, on the face of it, to be a recipe for failure and group breakdown, it is not necessarily so. It can also serve as a stimulus for some valuable bonding and group achievement (Saino, 2003, p. 275):

> 'While the members were able to share their anxieties and frustrations over expressing themselves in English, conversing in English also helped them to increase their confidence.'

However, varying English language levels can obscure conflicts or issues for and between members. The group facilitator may be 'in the dark' to a greater extent than occurs in other groups in which everyone speaks the same language, simply because members have a limited capacity to express themselves.

Saino emphasises the facilitator's role in building trust and safety in the group so that members may be supported to share their issues and concerns. She also makes the point that, although the process of working with a multi-ethnic group is difficult for the facilitator, the group members are actually quite resilient, have expertise in adapting to new situations, tend to be enthusiastic learners and can teach others (including the facilitator) a great deal about their cultures. Although Saino does not use the term, it is apparent that she is describing the concept of 'mutual aid' as it operates within her group.

Mutual aid

Mutual aid is an important and overlooked theme within the group work literature. Steinberg (2002, p. 33) defines mutual aid in the following way:

> '. . . As a social ideal it states that possibilities for helping others and being helped are limitless; as a social work ideal it states that possibilities

for catalyzing such a process are limited only by lack of understanding or imagination.'

Perhaps a partial reason for overlooking the importance of mutual aid is the reworking and inclusion of this concept within the group work literature such that it becomes a taken-for-granted feature of practice with groups. Many social workers would have experienced the phenomenon of working with a group where the members help each other as much as, if not more than, the help they receive from the professional group facilitator.

Mutual aid is evident in many approaches to group work practice, including empowerment-oriented practice (Shulman, 1994, 2005) and the strengths perspective (Saleebey, 2002). These approaches were the foundations of my work at the ASC. Shulman's conceptualisation of groups as forums for the enactment of mutual aid processes is empowering of group members, because it encourages them to form helping relationships with one another, rather than relying solely on assistance provided by a formal group facilitator. My social work practice, guided by a strengths perspective, is focused on discovering, embellishing, exploring and exploiting the strengths and resources of the people with whom I work. Saleebey (2002, p. 1) argues that it is through this focus on strengths and resources that the social worker can assist people '. . . to achieve their goals, realise their dreams and shed the irons of their own inhibitions and misgivings, and society's domination'.

Steinberg (2002, p. 33) describes mutual aid as a process of empathy, as '. . . subtle as a nod of recognition from a fellow group member at just the right moment'. She views all people as having a right to mutual aid processes to assist them to have a say over their own affairs and to enhance their estimation of their own capacity to not only help themselves, but also to help others. Steinberg (2002, p. 35) refers to the 'magic' of mutual aid:

> '. . . It is always magical to discover the things about ourselves that are seen as truly helpful by others and to discover the things about others that are truly helpful to us.'

The small acts of kindness and empathy undertaken by asylum seekers at the ASC are of great significance to them because they are able to connect with each other via their common humanity. They know first-hand about the asylum-seeking experience. For them, the security and peace of mind that come from being a member of a mutually supportive group at the ASC may be in stark contrast to their daily lives. These are daily lives that are characterised by great poverty, exclusion from many of the most basic of social engagements that come with employment and many acts of hostile rejection by the broader Australian community.

Groups at the ASC provide opportunities for asylum seekers to connect with and help each other. Although Open Forum at the ASC may appear to be a simple group with limited scope for enacting mutual aid processes, it is my contention that all group structures offer valuable opportunities in which mutual aid can occur. I now move, in the next section of the paper, to a closer consideration of the Open Forum sessions in which I was involved during my time at the ASC.

Open Forum: Using Mutual Aid to Support Strengths-Based Empowerment Practice

Open Forum at the ASC is held once a week on Wednesdays just before lunch; attendance is open to anyone who is at the Centre. Open Forum has been facilitated in the past by a succession of volunteers and paid staff. I facilitated Open

Forum for four sessions during March/April 2005. I also observed two other sessions of Open Forum that were facilitated by ASC staff.[1] Although formal ethics approval was not sought, I was granted permission by the ASC Coordinator to submit this paper for publication.

I had only visited the Centre on a few occasions before taking on the facilitation of Open Forum. In the following account of my practice, the impression could be given that what I did was well planned, well thought out and smoothly executed. This was often far from the case. My actual facilitation at the time involved much learning on the run, trial and error and constant refinement of my thinking.

Because Open Forum is open-ended, membership can change considerably from week to week as people come and go at the Centre. A total of 15 asylum seekers attended the four sessions I facilitated, but only two came to all four sessions, whereas six attended only once. The actual numbers attending each session ranged from five to 11. Languages spoken by group participants included Farsi, Arabic, Spanish, Nepalese, Korean, Mongolian, Vietnamese, Chinese (dialect unknown) and French. As noted previously, most participants did not share a common language with others, with the exception of their limited English. Other people present at these forums included a volunteer English teacher who prepared lunch while also listening in and occasionally contributing to discussions, a member of the paid staff and a high-school work-experience student who came to one session.

Open Forum has been a regular part of the ASC programme since the earliest days of the Centre. Many current and former volunteers spoke to me about how attendance at Open Forum had helped them to appreciate the range of ASC services and activities and gave them an understanding of some of the issues confronted by asylum seekers. They also spoke of Open Forum as one of the happenings at the Centre representing the coming together of people from many lands in a spirit of tolerance and mutual support.

The stated purpose of Open Forum is to give all who spend time at the ASC the opportunity to exchange information and discuss issues of common interest. It is a time for making announcements about upcoming events, changes to the various ASC programmes and services and other developments in the wider community. It can also be a place where developments in asylum-seeker policies and current news are discussed. For example, during one session, discussion of the Cornelia Rau situation was of great interest to the asylum seekers, many of whom could not understand the coverage of this in the media owing to their limited English.

Although Open Forum is not defined as being a therapeutic group, it could be expected to have considerable therapeutic value for asylum seekers. Many asylum seekers are isolated and lonely and have limited opportunities for companionship outside the Centre. Companionship has been shown to be an important healing factor for asylum seekers (Kelsey, 2004); forming friendships also allows people to join together in their own interests (Donaldson, 2004).

Yalom (1995) proposes that a number of therapeutic factors can operate within all groups and these can be seen to operate to a greater or lesser extent within Open Forum. These therapeutic factors include the instillation of hope, universality ('all in the same boat' phenomenon), imparting of relevant and important information and altruism. Yalom (1995) also lists possible therapeutic factors as including those associated with learning about new situations and relating to others. One small example of how the Open Forum group would be useful is that it provides a safe place for asylum seekers to learn interpersonal skills for communicating in English.

A major challenge of my work with Open Forum was to balance two key considerations. The first was my desire to have a planned and purposeful approach to my practice; the second was my desire, and the group's need, to be spontaneously responsive to moment-by-moment interactions. Lang (2004) states that if the social worker remains flexible and responsive to happenings within the group, then the group itself will implement its own powerful influences on the members. This was evident to me when members of Open Forum would interrupt a pre-set agenda as circumstances required. For example, latecomers would be welcomed and introduced no matter what the group was in the midst of discussing. This was no mere indulgence: there was very little continuity of group membership from week to week, making each session rather like a single-session group. The practice of welcoming newcomers regardless of what is occurring in a group setting is also a culturally sensitive practice that can facilitate bonding, inclusion and the development of group cohesion.

I found that the best strategy was to have a simple plan that gave participants a clear sense of the purpose for each session, to ensure continuity across sessions so that attendees would know what to expect even if they had not been to Open Forum previously and to maintain a flexible permissive response to whatever interruptions occurred on the day. In view of the constantly changing membership of Open Forum from session to session, my plan also involved thinking about each meeting as being a single-session group.

It may help to expand a little here on my rationale for the single-session strategy. As the name suggests, 'single-session groups' are groups that meet only once. Although Open Forum is a weekly meeting at the ASC, its open-ended nature means that each meeting is of a new group, where some members may have been present at the previous week's meeting and others were not. Facilitating such a group requires the worker to 'tune in' to the needs of the particular population (asylum seekers), use group facilitation skills in a focused and flexible way, and manage the stages of the group's development within a tight time-frame (Shulman, 1999; Kosoff, 2003). A pitfall for workers leading single-session groups is not allowing sufficient time for the group to work through each of its development stages. More specifically, the leader needs to establish a supportive atmosphere, move into and work with the middle stage and then have enough time for a positive ending and transition (Clemens, 2004).

Facilitating Open Forum while attending to the stages of group development was a major challenge for me given the barriers to effective communication within the group. Despite the difficulties, I decided to focus on what I felt were the most important aspects of the four stages that could be seen to operate in each meeting of Open Forum. I turn now to a summary of each of these four stages.

Welcome, Purpose of the Meeting and Introductions

The commencement of each meeting of Open Forum holds within it the essential message of welcome. This message has particular significance for asylum seekers because it contradicts the message of rejection contained in current government policies and in the responses to asylum seekers by many in the Australian community. I therefore chose a form of words to commence each meeting that would convey that everyone in attendance was welcome.

I then provided a simple explanation of the purpose of the meeting. This needed to be done at the beginning of every meeting because some participants had not attended Open Forum previously. I also realised that there was value in reminding everyone present that this is a meeting that encourages freedom of speech. This may have been an unfamiliar idea to some asylum seekers who had little or no experience, in their countries of origin, of exercising a right to speak freely in public.

I was careful to explain the purpose of Open forum, as I understood it, because I felt such an explanation would help to lower the usual anxiety that exists for members at the beginning stage of a group. Additional anxiety may have existed for the asylum seekers owing to the fact that I was a new person at the Centre and had little prior contact with any of them.

After outlining the purpose of Open Forum generally and the agenda for the day's meeting specifically, my next task was to initiate introductions. I repeated each person's name to get the pronunciation right and used the white-board to ensure correct spelling. This repetition and recording also helped everyone to remember the names of those present. I was sensitive to possible concerns asylum seekers may have about publicly stating their names and thereby disclosing their identity. What was important here was that I was not taking an official record of correct names but, rather, that everyone had choice about the name by which they preferred to be known within the context of this group and that I would take care to do as they wished in this regard. Sometimes I invited participants to talk to each other in pairs for a couple of minutes and then introduce their partner to the whole group. This helped them to connect with one other person to gain support before speaking up in the large group.

The introductions section of each Open Forum meeting was crucially important in that each asylum seeker's right to individuality was respected through the simple act of using their preferred names. Bauman (1997, p. 33) sees such simple actions as central to the 're-empowerment of strangers'. The asylum seekers were strangers to me at the beginning of Open Forum and my focus on learning and using their names was an essential step for me to build a relationship of trust with them.

I aimed to use the beginning stage of each meeting to lower participants' anxiety by ensuring that everyone knew what to expect as the meeting unfolded. This first stage required a larger allocation of meeting time than would be the case for less culturally and linguistically diverse groups.

Open Discussion

In the second stage of the meeting, I aimed to open up discussion on matters relevant to the Centre and the lives of the asylum seekers. Sometimes discussion topics were my choice, but I also encouraged participants to raise topics of their own. A common theme was related to the ASC weekly programme: which parts of it were asylum seekers finding useful, which less so and ideas for changes.

I initiated discussion in a number of ways depending on who was present, their level of English proficiency, recent events in the Centre and in the broader community. For example, one meeting occurred after a Centre picnic day. I started the conversation by asking the simple open-ended question, 'What did you like most about the picnic?' Those who had not been present were told by the others about the various aspects of the picnic, including the food, the games and the weather, and this led to some exchange of information about 'free' public spaces in Sydney, such as the Botanical Gardens and Centennial Park, and also about how to get to these locations using public transport. One of the asylum seekers was puzzled about how public parklands came to exist and this led to a discussion about public facilities being funded through the taxation system.

Discussion topics would sometimes arise in unexpected ways. For example, in response to my question, 'What would you like to discuss today?', one asylum seeker asked for help in getting his spectacles fixed. He had spoken to one of the caseworkers about this and was frustrated that he had been waiting for some time for the repairs to be organised. I commented on how frustrating it can sometimes be when you are waiting for someone else to do something that is important to you. The following group discussion focused on common experiences of waiting for the determination of their refugee status and their frustrations arising from having to depend on charity and being denied incomes of their own. We also talked about the procedure for making a complaint about services at the Centre.

During this second stage of Open Forum, mutual aid processes occurred as asylum seekers shared with each other their common experiences and strategies for problem solving and coping. The focus on issues of mutual concern helped build a sense of community within the group of asylum seekers at the ASC and bridge the gulf of their cultural and linguistic diversity.

Announcements and Information Exchange

The third stage of Open Forum was largely devoted to announcements about events at the Centre and about other services (e.g. English classes available through other organisations). I made a point of following up my announcements with an invitation for the participants to make announcements of their own. My aim was to encourage them to actively share information among themselves rather than remaining as passive recipients.

In practice, there was often a back and forth movement between the third and second stages of the meeting. For example, an attempt by me during the second stage to initiate group discussion might fall quite flat but then, when I moved on to making announcements about upcoming events, this information could trigger some lively group discussion.

Closure

My main task during the fourth and final stage of each Open Forum was to bring the group to an orderly and timely close. This stage was usually fairly brief and, in most cases, I began the process of closure with an announcement that Open Forum was about to finish. I then summarised any issues of concern that had been discussed and any decisions that had been made for follow-up action. I was careful to reinforce at this time any positive interactions that had occurred during the group meeting. This focus on positive interactions near the end of a single-session group can encourage individual group members to connect further with one another outside the group (Kosoff, 2003). Finally, I concluded the meeting by reminding members of the next Open Forum, thanking everyone for participating and issuing an invitation to lunch.

This final stage could easily slip into being a 'taken-for-granted' and unexamined practice. However, as I reflected each week on my experience of facilitating Open Forum, I found that it was often this final stage that would indicate for me what I needed to attend to differently in the next meeting. For example, when I experienced the end stage of one session as being rushed and emotionally flat, it was a signal that I needed to manage time more effectively and encourage more interactions between asylum seekers during the meeting.

Extending Group Work with and on Behalf of Asylum Seekers

Group work has long been seen as a core social work method and yet it receives significantly less attention than other methods in the social work literature

(Brown, 1997). This limited focus on group work is unfortunate, given the capacity of groups to unleash powerfully therapeutic forces of mutual aid and self-empowerment.

The group work method provides social workers and other helping professionals with a way of engaging asylum seekers in collaborative efforts to help themselves. Group work can directly challenge a 'top-down' approach to practice (Ife, 1997) that privileges the knowledge of the professional over that held by clients. Such a challenge seems nowhere more needed than when the clients in question are asylum seekers. Another important challenge offered by group work is to the dominant individualist approach to service delivery. When applied to asylum seekers, this approach can serve to isolate them from one another and entrench a view of their personal troubles as being disconnected from political and social realities.

Numerous possibilities exist for extending group work practice with asylum seekers. Despite the communication difficulties in working with a multi-cultural and multi-linguistic population, asylum seekers can readily be engaged in self-help projects. Examples already in operation at the ASC include learning English, learning job-related skills and participating in social activities. Other therapeutic programmes could be developed to address the various legacies of asylum-seeking experience, such as the stress arising from previous torture and trauma.

Work with asylum seekers should not be limited to situations in which they are constructed as clients in need of professional services. Including asylum seekers in mainstream community groups and activities is a practice that contrasts markedly with the exclusionary practices of the current government. Churches and TAFE colleges are providing examples of how asylum seekers can be included as equal members in local congregations and educational programmes.

In addition, asylum seekers should be considered for leadership roles, such as group facilitator, educator and consultant, in programmes on asylum-seeker issues. They could be involved in these capacities in community education programmes, political lobbying and activism. Although many asylum seekers have informally taken on such leadership roles, there are significant structural barriers to their being able to do so in more formal ways. A major limitation would seem to be the actual state of impoverishment in which most asylum seekers find themselves; another, is the constraints imposed by visa conditions, often including an embargo on work both of a paid and voluntary nature. For many organisations, the ASC included, elevating asylum seekers to higher status roles requires significant shifts in the way that services are planned, developed and resourced over time. Positive discrimination recruitment strategies, in favour of those who have been asylum seekers, could be one way of elevating the position of individual asylum seekers.

Apart from group work with asylum seekers themselves, the group work method is also of great relevance in work about asylum seekers. For example, training and supervision groups for staff and volunteers provide valuable opportunities to challenge individualistic and paternalistic approaches to practice with asylum seekers. Such groups can use experiential learning exercises (e.g. role-plays based on asylum seeker scenarios) to develop practice skills and enhance a capacity for empathy. These groups can also be used to foster a culture among workers of interdependence and mutual support and, most importantly, a strengths-based orientation towards asylum seekers.

Conclusion

The ASC provides services to some of the most socially marginalised and disadvantaged people in Australia today; people who have often experienced great trauma both in their countries of origin and while in Immigration detention in Australia. Social workers, given the profession's commitment to social justice, have roles to play in protesting against harsh and punitive government policies, advocating for fairer treatment for asylum seekers and supporting the work of the non-government agencies (such as the ASC) that currently provide the bulk of services to asylum seekers.

This paper has presented a practice example of group work with asylum seekers at the ASC. The single-session group, Open Forum, provided opportunities for asylum seekers to engage in mutual aid. Mutual aid is central to effective group work with any population. In the case of asylum seekers, mutual aid is particularly significant. It provides a means for them to escape from passivity and dependence on others and to engage in self-help and altruism.

In many ways, Open Forum stands in stark contrast with groups I have previously worked with. I had never previously facilitated a group in which the members were so united in their common experiences of threats to life, freedom and human dignity. Many would have experienced, at first hand, the horrors of war and the tortures of brutal regimes. All had suffered extremes of loss; loss of country, culture, language, home, intimate relationships, possessions, status and role. In the face of such deprivations, these people exhibited a kind of resilience, serenity and generosity of spirit that I found inspiring. They helped me to more fully appreciate the mutuality component of mutual aid. In the face of major religious, cultural, ethnic and language differences, they took obvious pleasure in one another's company and in helping one another. In addition, they exhibited great tolerance and patience towards me in my efforts to understand their situations.

Note

[1] I acknowledge here the contributions that ASC staff and volunteers have made to my work. In particular, I thank Tamara Domicelj and Fiona Keast for sharing their practice and ideas about Open Forum.

References

1. Bauman, Z. (1997), *Postmodernity and its Discontents,* New York University Press, New York.
2. Brown, A. (1997), Groupwork, In Davies M (ed.), *The Blackwell Companion to Social Work,* Blackwell, Oxford, pp. 223–230.
3. Clemens, S. E. (2004), Recognizing vicarious traumatisation: A single session group model for trauma workers, *Social Work with Groups,* 27 (2/3), 55–74.
4. Devetak, R. (2004), In fear of refugees: The politics of border protection in Australia, *International Journal of Human Rights,* 8(1), 101–109.
5. Donaldson, L. P. (2004), Toward validating the therapeutic benefits of empowerment-oriented social action groups, *Social Work with Groups,* 27(2/3), 159–175.
6. Haddad, E. (2003), Refugee protection: A clash of values, *International Journal of Human Rights,* 7(3), 1–26.
7. Harris, M. & Telfer, B. (2001), The health needs of asylum seekers living in the community, *Medical Journal of Australia,* 175, 589–592.
8. Ife, J. (1997), *Rethinking Social Work: Towards Critical Practice,* Longman, South Melbourne.
9. Jupp, J. (2002), *From White Australia to Woomera: The Story of Australian Immigration,* Cambridge University Press, Cambridge.
10. Kelsey, A. (2004), Healing through companionship, *Social Work with Groups,* 27(2/3), 23–33.

11. Kisely, S., Stevens M., Hart B. & Douglas C. (2002), Health issues of asylum seekers and refugees, *Medical Journal of Australia,* 26(1), 8.
12. Kosoff, S. (2003), Single session groups: Applications and areas of expertise, *Social Work with Groups,* 26(1), 29–45.
13. Lang, N. C. (2004), Concurrent interventions in multiple domains: The essence of social work with groups, *Social Work with Groups,* 27(1), 35–51.
14. Moorehead, C. (2005), *Human Cargo: A Journey Among Refugees,* Henry Holt, New York.
15. Saino, M. (2003), A new language for groups: Multilingual and multiethnic groupwork, *Social Work with Groups,* 26(1), 69–82.
16. Saleebey, D. (2002), *The Strengths Perspective in Social Work Practice,* Allyn & Bacon, Boston.
17. Shulman, L. (1994), *Mutual Aid Groups, Vulnerable Populations and the Life Cycle,* Columbia University Press, New York.
18. Shulman, L. (2005), *The Skills of Helping Individuals, Families, Groups and Communities,* Thomson Brooks/Cole, Melbourne.
19. Sinnerbrink, I., Silove, D. & Manicavasagar V. (1996), Asylum seekers: General health status and access to health care, *Medical Journal of Australia,* 165, 634–637.
20. Smith, M. (2001), Asylum seekers in Australia: The medical profession can assist by reinforcing the principle of health care as a right, and opposing policies that contribute to poor health, *Medical Journal of Australia,* 175, 587–589.
21. Steel, Z. & Silove, D. (2001), The mental health implications of detaining asylum seekers, *Medical Journal of Australia,* 175, 596–599.
22. Steinberg, M. D. (2002), The magic of mutual aid, Social Work with Groups, 25(1/2), 31–38.
23. Yalom, I. (1995), *The Theory and Practice of Group Psychotherapy,* Basic Books, New York.

8

Perspectives on Organizations

![Connecting Core Competencies icon]

CONNECTING CORE COMPETENCIES *in this chapter*

| Professional Identity | Ethical Practice | Critical Thinking | Diversity in Practice | Human Rights & Justice | Research Based Practice | Human Behavior | Policy Practice | Practice Contexts | Engage Assess Intervene Evaluate |

Organizations form the contexts in which much of our daily lives are carried out. They form the environments in which a vast array of human behaviors take place. For many of us, virtually all aspects of our lives are intertwined with and influenced by organizations. To give us some idea of how much of our own and others' lives are touched by organizations from the time we are born until the time we die, let us consider some examples of organizations. We very likely were born in or with the assistance of an organization—a hospital, public health agency, prepared childbirth program. We are likely to be socialized or educated in the context of organizations—day care, preschool/Headstart, grade and high schools, higher education institutions, vocational/technical schools. We very likely play in the context of organizations—organized sports, girls'/boys' clubs, Scouts, Jack and Jill, health/exercise clubs, fraternities/sororities. We may carry out much of our spiritual life in and mark major life events with rituals in the context of formal religious organizations—church, synagogue, temple, mosque. We probably do or will work in an organizational context—human service agencies, corporations, health and mental health organizations. We get many of our basic subsistence needs met through organizations—grocery, clothing, drug and department stores, food banks, housing authorities, banks, restaurants. We probably will grow old in the context of organizations—senior centers, home health or chore services, nursing homes, and assisted living organizations. We may very well die in an organizational context—hospital, hospice. While this sampling is not intended to be an exhaustive list of the organizations that influence us throughout life, it does give us a place to start in considering the far-reaching impact of organizations on our individual and collective lives (Etzioni 1964).

If you reflect on the examples of organizational contexts above, it is not difficult to recognize that many of the organizations through which human needs are met are also contexts in which social workers work. Whether we are working to meet our own needs or those of other individuals, families, groups, communities, or nations we are very likely to be acting in or through an organizational environment. We are concerned here, of course, with what organizations do to help us meet human needs. We are also concerned with how organizations can and do present barriers to or may even prevent us from meeting our needs and reaching our full potential as humans. We are concerned, especially, with the role of organizations in helping or hindering diverse persons as they proceed through the life course. And we are concerned with the roles that diverse persons have in constructing the organizations that impact, so directly and comprehensively, their lives.

Organizations reflect and are reflected in the paradigms or worldviews of the persons who construct and operate them. Since organizations have such a high degree of influence on our day-to-day lives throughout our lives, it is imperative that we all share in creating and operating them. Only in this way will organizations be responsive to the needs of diverse persons.

As we begin to explore organizations, we need to recognize that much of the information on small groups from the previous chapter will apply to organizations as well. Much of the activity that organizations are engaged in happens through a variety of small groups. If you think about an organization in which you are involved, you can probably recognize that much of your involvement in relation to the organization is carried out through different small groups. You are likely, for example, to be a member of a committee or work group within the organization. You are also likely to have membership in informal groups within the organization—a group of organization members you eat lunch with on a regular basis, for instance. So much of an organization's activity is carried out in small groups that it begins to look as if the organization is really a collection of small groups. Because of this it is important that we use what we know about small groups to help us better understand organizations.

In this chapter we will explore a number of perspectives on formal organizations. We will explore the notion of organizational culture. We will look to history for some perspective on how we came to be a society and a world so reliant on the structures and processes of formal organizations. We will look to traditional notions of organizations for understanding about the nature of the existing organizations with which we and the people with whom we work must deal every day. We will explore alternative notions of how organizations might/can be changed or structured to meet human needs and accomplish the core concerns of social work. We hope to use the understanding we gain about organizations in order to make them more responsive to our needs and to the needs of others. We seek avenues in this part of our journey to create and re-create organizations that are inclusive of the visions and voices of all the peoples with whom social workers are concerned.

HISTORICAL PERSPECTIVE ON ORGANIZATIONS

We may think of a society characterized by so many different kinds and sizes of organizations directed toward a dizzying range of purposes and goals as a modern phenomenon. However, organizations have long been a basic context within which a wide range of human behavior and interaction takes place. It is true that the number and variety of organizations has increased greatly in the twentieth century. However, organizations and the study of organizations have been with us for a long, long time. Etzioni reminds us that the pharaohs employed organizations in the creation of the pyramids. Chinese emperors over a thousand years ago made use of organizations to build irrigation systems. The first popes created the universal church as an organization to manage a world religion (Etzioni 1964:1). Iannello (1992:3) notes that the philosophers of ancient Greece were interested in the study of organizations as a means of achieving specific goals and purposes.

Shafritz and Ott (1987:1) suggest it is safe to say that humankind has been creating organizations ever since we began hunting, making war, and creating families. Organizational study as a deliberate and focused field of exploration, especially in terms of managing large organizations, is largely a product of the twentieth century, however. Much of the study of organizations during the twentieth century has been done focusing on business or profit-making organizations. There is, though, a growing body of information that focuses on not-for-profit or public service organizations. Most students of organizations agree that the rise of industrial (and more recently the emergence of postindustrial) society in the twentieth century has resulted in great increases in the quantity, size, and type of formal organizations in almost every area of life. This proliferation of formal organizations directed toward achieving a multitude of goals has greatly increased our interest in understanding formal organizations.

As we have learned about paradigms in general, our beliefs about what organizations are, what they do, and how they do it have not come about in a vacuum. They have been greatly influenced by the people, times, and cultures associated with their development. Shafritz and Ott (1987:2) suggest that "the advent of the factory system, World War II, the 'flowerchild'/anti-establishment/self-development era of the 1960s, and the computer/information society of the 1970s all substantially influenced the evolution of organization theory." We can add to this list important recent and currently unfolding influences, such as the reorganization of Eastern Europe; the organizations involved in the tragedy of September 11, 2001, in New York, Washington, and Pennsylvania and its aftermath; the hurricane Katrina disaster in New Orleans and the surrounding Gulf Coast; the wars in Iraq and Afghanistan; and the growing recognition that we are all citizens of one global and interdependent society. Current concerns about the impact of modern organizations on the environment of our planet, and such important movements as the women's movement and other human rights movements also reflect the influence of organizations on our lives. As we explore traditional and alternate perspectives on organizations, we will travel a route that parallels many of the historic influences of the early, middle, and late twentieth century, as well as the early twenty-first century. To begin to understand organizations we need some basic concepts and definitions.

BASIC CONCEPTS/DEFINITIONS

Whether exploring traditional or alternative notions about organizations, it is helpful to have at least a very general definition from which to explore differences in perspectives on organizations. Etzioni (1964:3) uses Talcott Parsons's basic definition of **organizations** as "social units (or human groupings) deliberately constructed and reconstructed to seek specific goals." Another common definition is that "an organization is a collection of people engaged in specialized and interdependent activity to accomplish a goal or mission" (Gortner, Mahler, Nicholson 1987:2). Iannello (1992:8) suggests that one might simply define organizations "as systems of continuous, purposive, goal-oriented activity involving two or more people." All three of these basic definitions differ slightly, but they share some essential common ground. All three recognize organizations as collectivities of people working together to accomplish a goal (or goals).

Within this common ground, however, there is a wide range of possibilities for differences in perspectives. The characteristics of the people involved in the organization, how those people are arranged in relation to one another, the nature of the goal (or goals), and the specific parts different organizational members play in accomplishing the goal (or goals) are just some of the sources of different perspectives on organizations.

An organizational **goal** can be defined simply as the desired or intended ends or results to be achieved by an organization (Neugeboren 1985:27) or as a "desired state of affairs which the organization attempts to realize" (Etzioni 1964:6). The nature of goals varies greatly from organization to organization and may even vary within the same organization over time. Different human service organizations may share a basic mission or purpose of improving the quality of life for people in the communities they serve. Human service organizations may vary greatly, however, in the specific goals they pursue in order to improve the quality of life.

Neugeboren (1985:5–17) suggests that there are three kinds of goals pursued by human service organizations. **Social care** goals are those directed toward changing the environment in order for people to improve the quality of their lives and reach their maximum potential. **Social control** goals are those directed toward controlling the behavior of people who are deemed to be deviant and who interfere with the ability of others to maximize their potential and improve the quality of their lives. **Rehabilitation** goals are those directed toward changing individuals so they will have improved quality of life and better opportunity to reach their fullest potential. Organizations may have multiple goals. Human service agencies such as state departments of social or human services may encompass social care (day-care licensing to ensure high-quality environments for young children, provision of concrete services such as food stamps), social control (legal consequences for parents when child-abuse allegations are substantiated), and rehabilitation (parenting classes for abusive parents to assist in changing parenting behaviors that led to child abuse).

Goal displacement is characteristic of an organization that is pursuing goals contrary to the goals it originally and officially proclaimed. An example of organizational goal displacement is an adolescent group home originally begun to rehabilitate troubled teens that becomes a social control institution to incarcerate adolescents. Organizations may also be characterized by **goal succession.** This is the replacement of one goal by another goal when the original goal has been accomplished or it has declared itself unable to accomplish its original goal. The March of Dimes was an organizational effort originally directed to obtaining resources necessary to find a cure for polio. Upon the virtual elimination of the threat of polio—in no small way a result of the efforts of the March of Dimes—the organization adopted a new goal that included combating birth defects. Goal succession is likely to be a functional change in goals; goal displacement is likely to be dysfunctional (Etzioni 1964:10ff).

Organizations with multiple goals may experience conflict over the amount of organizational resources or energy to devote to their various goals. Such conflict may be especially pronounced if an organization is undergoing goal displacement in a situation in which the organization's stated goals are different from and may compete with its actual goals. Think about the potential for conflict within the adolescent group home in the example above. If some staff want the home to rehabilitate troubled teens so they can return to their families and the community, while other staff see the goal as removal from the community and incarceration, the potential for significant conflict in the organization is very great.

Types of Organizations

What type of organization is represented by this photo of President Obama addressing a joint session of Congress?

There are three types of organizations or organizational sectors with which social workers are most likely to work and need to understand. One type, **private-for-profit** organizations, sometimes referred to as **market sector organizations,** include businesses and corporations organized with the primary goal of making an economic profit. A second type of organization is the **governmental** organization. Governmental organizations comprise the **public sector** and include local, state, national, and international (the U.N., the European Union, for example) governmental organizations. Public health, education, and human service organizations are some of the most common public sector organizations. A third type of organization is the **private-not-for-profit** organization. These organizations are also referred to as **non-governmental organizations** or **NGOs.** (NGO is a term more often used to describe this

Engage Assess Intervene Evaluate

Professional social workers have the knowledge and skills to practice with organizations. For each of the "Types of Organizations" discussed in this section, give one example of a role a professional social worker might play.

type of organization outside the United States.) Non-governmental organizations comprise what is often referred to as the **voluntary** or **civil sector.** They include a wide range of organizations that provide civic and human services (Urban League, Lions Clubs, League of Women Voters, for example) which are funded by private citizens (donations), fund-raising organizations (United Way, for example), or privately funded foundations (Ford or Kellogg Foundations, for example). Historically social workers have been more involved in public sector and voluntary or not-for-profit sector organizations. However, increasingly social workers are both working in or in partnership with market sector organizations in order to achieve human well-being and reduction of poverty and oppression (Rifkin 1998).

Differing perspectives on organizational concepts and types result in very different notions about what organizations are like, what they should be like, and what they might be like. These differences have significant implications and consequences also for the organizations' ability to respond positively to the core concerns of social work we are addressing in this book. As in the chapters dealing with each level of human behavior we explore in this book, we will address notions about organizations from both traditional and alternative paradigmatic perspectives.

There are several traditional models of or approaches to organizations that have had major influences on the way the organizations we deal with every day are structured and operated. These perspectives did not emerge in a vacuum. They emerged from and along with the larger historical context of the twentieth century. As we learned about paradigms generally, the different traditional paradigms often emerged as reactions to or extensions of prior notions of what organizations should be and do.

TRADITIONAL PARADIGMS

There are several broad categories of traditional perspectives on organizations. These broad areas are sometimes referred to as schools of thought. They include classical approaches (scientific management or machine theory and bureaucracy), human relations, systems, and contingency theory. Within these broad categories there are a number of basic concepts that can help us to understand the nature of the organizations with which we deal on a day-to-day basis. These theories and concepts also will help us, as social workers, to better understand the organizational context within which we work and through which the people with whom we work seek services to improve the quality of their lives. The organizational context, then, has important implications for both the quality of our own lives—for we spend so much of our time in this context—and the quality of life of the people with whom we work—for the organizational context is pivotal in determining whether or not people will receive the basic resources necessary to improve the quality of their lives. Once again we see that our interests and those of the people with whom we work are interconnected.

Scientific Management or Classical Theory

Scientific management is a conceptual framework (or body of theory) for defining, structuring, and managing organizations that is consistent with the positivistic, scientific, objective, and quantitative dimension of the traditional paradigm. As its name implies, it is closely connected to and relies on the assumptions of science as the ideal approach to understanding organizations. Scientific management was put forward as a theory about organizations by Frederick Taylor in the very early part of the twentieth century. (He presented a paper outlining his approach to the American Society of Mechanical Engineers as early as 1895.) This school of thought has been tremendously influential in defining the structures and processes that make up much organizational life today. This is perhaps understandable, given the influence and power accorded scientific approaches to understanding human behavior generally during the twentieth century (Pugh, Hickson, and Hinings 1985).

Taylor's scientific management was directed toward maximizing efficiency in industry. Efficiency is an important basic concept related to organizations and is a major concern in virtually all organizational theories. **Efficiency** is defined as the production of the maximum amount of output for the least amount of input. It is, in other words, doing the most with the least possible amount of resources. Efficiency is often discussed in conjunction with another basic organizational concept, effectiveness. **Effectiveness** is defined simply as the degree to which the goals or purposes of an organization are accomplished. As we noted above, a primary concern of organizations is attainment or accomplishment of goals (Pugh, Hickson, and Hinings 1985).

According to Taylor, scientific management could achieve maximum effectiveness and efficiency in the attainment of organizational goals through four basic principles. Faithful adherence to these four principles would result in finding the "one best way" to perform a task, do a job, or manage an entire organization. The first principle involved creating a **"science of work"** for each worker's job or task. This was accomplished by taking what was typically known about each task and objectively or scientifically studying what was known and what needed to be done to accomplish the task. This new information was recorded, tabulated, and reduced to formal laws, rules, or even mathematical formulas that defined and standardized each task necessary to do a job. This process of studying, recording, and codifying work tasks is sometimes referred to as a "time and motion study." Time and motion studies sought to create a perfect match between the actions of workers and the activities carried out by machines. They sought to unite workers and machines into one smooth and efficient process for carrying out necessary tasks. While this principle applied in Taylor's model almost exclusively to production in factory settings, it was extended over the years to many other organizational settings as well. For example, studies of human service offices procedures to reduce unnecessary movement or effort in order to increase the number of clients seen is an example of this principle in a nonfactory environment. Task analysis, work load analysis, and time studies are all examples of efforts to scientifically analyze tasks and processes in social work agencies to make operations efficient (Taylor in Grusky and Miller 1981).

The second principle focused on the **scientific selection and training of workers.** The process of objectively studying each of the workers for their fitness for a particular task, then training them very deliberately to efficiently accomplish that task was quite different from traditional arrangements in which workers determined what they were suited for doing and then set about to train themselves as best they could to do the work for which they were hired. This was yet another means of making work scientific. This concern for careful selection and training of workers was adapted far beyond the factory system. In social work education and practice, the education and selection processes used to ensure that individuals are suited and prepared for the professional jobs they will carry out is an example of this concern. The specific requirements for education of social workers as reflected in the Council on Social Work Education (CSWE), accreditation requirements, the continuing education requirements of many social work agencies, and the requirements for specific amounts and kinds of continuing education activities for renewal of social work licenses in many states are all examples of how this principle has influenced social work education and practice. If you have been through or will go through an application or screening process to be fully admitted to the social work program or school in which you are taking this course, your experience is consistent with this principle of scientific management (Taylor in Grusky and Miller 1981).

Taylor's third principle focused on **bringing together management and workers to ensure that the scientific principles resulting from the study of the tasks to be completed and the careful selection and training of workers to carry out those tasks were successfully implemented in the work setting.** This principle involved management's taking responsibility for closely monitoring the workers to make sure they were performing their jobs in accordance with scientific principles. This principle also required that workers be rewarded appropriately for adhering to the standardized rules for carrying out specific tasks. Most often this reward took the form of economic benefits, specifically increases in pay. Taylor, though, suggested that there were other "plums" that could be offered, such as better or more kind treatment of workers and allowing workers greater say in what they preferred as rewards for adhering to scientific principles. There is some confusion about Taylorism—as scientific management is sometimes called—in respect to notions of reward. This theory is often described as seeing economic reward as the only motivator for workers. It is safe to say that economic rewards were considered the primary source of motivation, but as Taylor suggests above, workers might also consider better treatment by management a kind of reward as well. Regardless of the kind of reward, the purpose of "plums" was to ensure that workers performed in accordance with the scientific standards for their jobs. The notion of supervision and evaluation of social workers and the relationship of salary increases to evaluation results as determined by managers or supervisors in agencies are examples of how this principle applies in social work settings (Taylor in Grusky and Miller 1981).

The fourth principle of scientific management focused on **expanding the role played by managers in the overall production process.** Taylorism saw managers as having many responsibilities previously thought to be within the purview of the workers themselves. As can be seen from the preceding three principles, managers became responsible for studying, defining, standardizing, and monitoring the tasks carried out by workers. Managers in effect took over from workers planning, decision making, and judgments about what jobs were to be done and how those jobs were to be carried out. This change resulted in a redivision of labor in the work setting. In many ways a new class of managers was created within work organizations. These managers, while assuming new responsibilities previously held by workers themselves, simultaneously took away some of the freedoms workers had previously held. Examples of this new division of labor can readily be seen in social work settings today. Especially in large agency settings, the promulgation of regulations and procedures by managers about how tasks are to be carried out and the expectation that direct service workers will then implement those regulations and procedures is an example of this principle. The supervision, evaluation, and establishing of rewards in the form of salary increases by management are all examples of this new division of labor between workers and managers (Taylor in Grusky and Miller 1981; Taylor in Shafritz and Ott 1987; and Pugh, Hickson, and Hinings 1985).

Organizations operating according to the principles of scientific management are characterized by several themes. These themes include:

- high degrees of specialization in jobs and the qualifications and training of personnel,
- clear division of labor,
- distinct hierarchy of authority, and
- assumptions that workers are motivated primarily by economic rewards.

Bureaucracy

Another classic model of organizations was put forth by Max Weber in his formulation of bureaucracy. Weber (1864–1920) formulated the structure and characteristics of bureaucracy during approximately the same time period that Taylor's scientific management was emerging. Bureaucracy, in one form or another, defined in one way or another, and often symbolizing the shortcomings of organizational life, is almost a synonym for organizations today. Bureaucracy in a number of respects has similarities with the scientific management theory we explored earlier. Bureaucracy values highly two dimensions of the traditional or dominant paradigm. It puts a premium on many of the elements of the positivistic, scientific, objective, and quantitative dimension of the traditional paradigm and on rationality and impersonality (Pugh, Hickson, and Hinings 1985; Shafritz and Ott 1987).

Weber outlined a number of **characteristics of bureaucracy.** First is the notion of a stable and officially stated structure of authority. Areas of authority within a bureaucracy are explicitly spelled out by rules or administrative regulations. Second, there is a clear "pecking order" or hierarchy of authority. This hierarchy clearly delineates who is responsible to whom within the bureaucratic organization. It provides a graded system of supervision in which lower offices are responsible to higher offices. Third, the organization's management is based on extensive written records of transactions, regulations, and policies that are kept over time. It is these written records that provide standardization and stability to the management of the organization. However, many people believe this emphasis on written records of activities and transactions is often taken to such extremes that workers' ability to do their jobs effectively is hindered. This over-emphasis on paperwork is disparagingly referred to as "**red tape.**" Fourth, the persons who fulfill management functions—those who run the organization—have specialized training and expertise that specifically prepares them for their jobs. Fifth, organizational responsibilities take precedence in the day-to-day life of personnel. In other words, one's official duties come first. Sixth, management of a bureaucracy follows a system of stable and comprehensive rules learned by managers through specialized education for their positions. Seventh, employment in a bureaucracy is seen as a "vocation" or career for which the person is specially trained and that the person sees as a duty to perform. Eighth, the persons who manage a bureaucratic organization should be separate from those who own the means of production. This prevents individual interests from interfering with decision making for the good of the organization and helps ensure rational decision making. To make sure this is the case, managers receive a fixed salary for their work rather than an hourly wage. Ninth, the resources of the organization must be free from outside control in order for managers to allocate and reallocate resources purely on the basis of the needs of the organization. This includes resources in the sense of personnel as well as financial resources. In other words, administrators must have the authority to hire, fire, and move personnel from one position to another within the organization (Pugh, Hickson, and Hinings 1985; Shafritz and Ott 1987).

Weber's framework for bureaucracy was conceptualized as an **"ideal type."** By this it is meant that this structure is one toward which organizations should strive. It is not assumed that this type necessarily exists in any complete or perfect way in any given organizational setting. However, it was assumed in this framework that the closer an organization can come to this ideal structure, the more efficient and effective it will be in accomplishing its goals. We know from systematic study of existing organizations, as well as from our individual personal experiences, that no single organization is likely to include all the characteristics of a bureaucracy. We also know from the many criticisms of bureaucratic organizational life that incorporating the ideal characteristics of bureaucracy does not necessarily guarantee that the organization will reach its goals, nor that it will do so with maximum efficiency (Grusky and Miller 1981; Pugh, Hickson, and Hinings 1985; Shafritz and Ott 1987).

There are a number of other considerations in addition to the characteristics of bureaucracies that are important to think about as we attempt to develop more comprehensive understanding of HBSE in organizational contexts. Many of these other characteristics take us in the direction of alternative paradigm thinking. They include consideration of nonrational factors in organizational life, consideration of the impact of linkages to the external environment on the internal life of the organization, and consideration of personal as well as impersonal factors on our organizational experiences. Recognition of these other considerations lead to some approaches significantly different from those of scientific management and bureaucracy with their central concerns for rationality and efficiency.

These different approaches include human relations, decision theory, and systems models. While these approaches differ markedly from the classic approaches we have explored thus far, they are nevertheless considered here under traditional paradigms because they have more in common with traditional and dominant paradigmatic assumptions than with the dimensions of alternative paradigms we have outlined in this book. We might best think about these models as middle-range perspectives along a continuum leading us toward newer alternative or possible views of organizations.

Characteristics of Bureaucracy

1. Stable and official structure of authority.
2. Clear hierarchy of authority ("pecking order").
3. Written records kept over time.
4. Specialized training and expertise.
5. Official duties come first.
6. Stable and comprehensive system of rules.
7. Career employment.
8. Managers separate from "owners" of organization.
9. Managers free to allocate and reallocate resources.

Human Relations

What has come to be known as the human relations theory of organizational behavior emerged from and in many ways became a reaction to the focuses on rationality, machinelike precision, planning, and formality of classical scientific management and bureaucratic theory. Human relations thinking, however, did not discount entirely the traditional concerns of organizational life such as efficiency, effectiveness, and goal centeredness. Nor did it suggest that scientific management approaches be done away with entirely. It suggested instead that these concerns were insufficient to understand the complexities of modern organizational life (Etzioni 1964).

The Hawthorne studies

Human relations thinking emerged directly from classical scientific approaches. Elton Mayo (1880–1949) is considered by many to be the founder of the human relations school. It was in the process of seeking to extend understanding of the necessary factors for truly efficient and productive organizations that human relations emerged somewhat unexpectedly. In the process of carrying out a series of studies that have come to be referred to as the Hawthorne Studies, Elton Mayo and his colleagues happened upon the basic concepts of human relations approaches. Two of the studies within the Hawthorne series illustrate some of the fundamental "surprises" that became the human relations school. One study involved exploring the effect of lighting or illumination in the work area on worker productivity. In this study, illumination was manipulated according to the hypothesis that optimum illumination would result in improved worker output. Contrary to this hypothesis, the researchers found that whether illumination was increased, decreased, or left alone, worker output increased. This led to the finding that the attention given the workers in the experiment and their interpretation of this attention as symbolic of the organization's interest in and concern for their perspectives was a crucial factor in their productivity. This has come to be known as the **Hawthorne effect.** In other words, workers were motivated to produce by other than purely economic rewards. They were also motivated by informal factors such as individual attention and concern for their input in the operation of the organization (Etzioni 1964; Pugh, Hickson, and Hinings 1985).

A second experiment in the Hawthorne series resulted in an equally "surprising" finding. This study is referred to as the Bank Wiring Room study because it involved observing and manipulating factors in a work setting in which telephone switchboards (called "banks") were being wired. This study resulted in the finding that not only informal factors such as individual attention affected worker productivity, but that groups of workers developed informal systems of managing output quite separate from the direction provided by management. The effect of this **informal group structure** was to set production norms or expectations about what were appropriate levels of production. On the one hand the group was concerned with not overproducing in the belief that overproduction would lead to layoffs of workers. On the other hand the group was concerned that production be "fair" in the sense that management and owners were not taken advantage of by unfairly low levels of production (Etzioni 1964; Pugh, Hickson, and Hinings 1985).

A number of the **basic concepts of human relations thinking** emerged from these studies and many others carried out since the original Hawthorne studies. First, the importance of individual attention and positive social interaction as well as economic rewards in worker productivity and satisfaction uncovered a virtually unexplored level of organizational life that centered on informal, nonrational, emotional, and unplanned interactions. Second, the pivotal role of informal social groups in efficiency and productivity was discovered. These groups functioned according to informal and internal norms, leadership structures, communication patterns, and levels of participation that had not been considered at all important to the scientific management proponents (Etzioni 1964; Gortner, Mahler, and Nicholson 1987; Grusky and Miller 1981; Pugh, Hickson, and Hining 1985).

It is helpful to note here that these early studies of organizational life out of which the human relations school emerged significantly increased interest in understanding the role and behavior of small groups in our day-to-day lives. Many basic group concepts such as small-group norms, leadership, decision making, roles, communication, and goals, which are explored in Chapter 7, have direct linkages to efforts to understand organizational life. This is consistent with our perspective in this book that sees human behavior and the social environment as an interlocking and overlapping network of mutually interdependent processes and contexts.

The tendency here may be to see only the differences between scientific management and human relations perspectives. We need to keep in mind, though, that neither of these schools of thought questioned in any fundamental ways the traditional and dominant forms of organizational life. Both schools saw maximum efficiency and productivity as the consuming purpose of organizations. Both schools accepted hierarchies of power and control (whether they be formal or informal) as givens in organizational life. Neither of these schools saw significant conflict among the interests of the various groups within organizations. It was assumed in these traditional approaches that what was good for the organization's owners and managers at the top of the hierarchy was good for its line of lower-level workers at the bottom of the organizational hierarchy. In short, neither of these schools provided fundamentally new or alternative models within which to carry out our organizational lives.

Theory X and Theory Y

Ethical Practice

Professional social workers are knowledgeable about the value base of the profession. In your opinion, is Theory X or Theory Y more consistent with social work values? What elements of the theory you chose support your opinion?

As researchers continued to seek ways to maximize organizational efficiency, productivity, and goal achievement, the concerns of behavioral scientists began to influence organizational studies. Douglas McGregor (1906–1964), a social psychologist, became interested in the influence of managers' underlying assumptions about human behavior on their management practices. McGregor was specifically interested in managers' basic assumptions about what motivated people to behave as they do. His work led him to formulate two sets of assumptions about human motivation. One set he called **Theory X.** It reflects a belief on the part of managers that their role was to direct and control the activities of workers. The second set of assumptions he referred to as **Theory Y.** These assumptions reflected the beliefs of managers that their role was one of creating supportive relationships in which organizational members could exercise their inherent tendencies to grow, develop, and learn for their own benefit and that of the organization. McGregor's **Theory X assumptions are:**

1. The average human being has an inherent dislike for work and will avoid it if he[she] can.

2. Because of this human characteristic of dislike for work, most people must be coerced, controlled, directed, or threatened with punishment to get them to put forth adequate effort toward the achievement of organizational objectives.

3. The average human being prefers to be directed, wishes to avoid responsibility, has relatively little ambition, wants security above all. (Pugh, Hickson and Hinings 1985:167)

McGregor's Theory Y posits a very different perspective on what motivates us. **Theory Y assumptions follow:**

1. The expenditure of physical and mental effort in work is as natural as play or rest. The ordinary person does not inherently dislike work.

2. [Humans] will exercise self-direction and self-control in the service of objectives to which [they] are committed.

3. The most significant reward that can be offered in order to obtain commitment is the satisfaction of the individual's self-actualizing needs. This can be a direct product of effort directed towards organizational objectives.

4. The average human being learns, under proper conditions, not only to accept but to seek responsibility.

5. Many more people are able to contribute creatively to the solution of organizational problems than do so.

6. At present the potentialities of the average person are not being fully used. (Pugh, Hickson, and Hinings 1985:167–168)

Theory X is more consistent with the assumptions of scientific management and traditional paradigm thinking. Theory Y assumptions about human motivation are much more in line with the core concerns of social work. In addition, Theory Y assumptions are philosophically more consistent with the dimensions of alternative paradigms we have outlined in this book than are those of Theory X.

Systems Perspectives

Systems theories or perspectives on organizational behavior have much in common with general social systems structures and processes we discussed earlier in this book (Chapter 3). As in the case of our earlier discussion of social systems approaches, systems approaches to organizations represent a kind of middle ground between traditional and alternative paradigms. Systems perspectives on organizations, for example, have a significant reliance on scientific and quantitative tools consistent with traditional paradigm thinking used to analyze organizational systems. However, systems approaches also present integrated holistic perspectives on organizations and their environments consistent with alternative paradigm thinking. (This is especially true of open-system perspectives on organizations and the related contingency perspective on organizations. See below.)

Systems approaches to organizational analysis represent attempts to synthesize the classic or scientific management schools (emphasis on detailed scientific, empirical, quantitative study of organizations) and the human relations school (recognition of the reality of unplanned events and informal structures). Organizational systems thinkers differentiate between closed- and open-systems perspectives. A **closed-system** perspective views organizations as total units in and of themselves with occurrences in the environment surrounding the organizations having little impact on the organization itself. It is often suggested that Weber's machinelike bureaucratic structure with its completely rational planning and decision making separate from environmental influences represents a closed-system approach. **Open-systems** perspectives see organizations as units very much influenced by the larger environment in which they exist (Katz and Kahn in Shafritz and Ott 1987:252–254).

The systems school views an organization as a complex and interconnected set of elements interacting in dynamic processes influencing both internal elements and the environment surrounding the organizations. Organizations as systems must change or adapt as the environment in which they exist changes. Katz and Kahn (in Shafritz and Ott 1987:254–259) outline nine characteristics of open systems that they believe apply to organizations as open systems:

1. *Importation of energy:* Organizations must bring in energy from the external environment in the form of material and human resources. Organizations are neither self-sufficient nor self-contained.

2. *Through-put:* Organizations use the energy they import to produce products, train people, or provide services.

3. *Out-put:* Organizations send products into the external environment.

4. *Systems as cycles of events:* The pattern of energy exchange which results in out-put is cyclical. An organization takes in raw materials (energy), uses that energy to produce a product or service (through-put), returns that product or service to the environment (out-put) in exchange for money to purchase additional raw materials with which to begin repetition of the cycle.

5. *Negative Entropy:* A process necessary for organizations to fight off entropy (tendency for a system to lose energy or decay) and to build up energy reserves. (Anderson and Carter (1990) use the term synergy in a very similar way. Synergy, the use of energy through increased interaction of the system's parts to create additional energy, may be a more "manageable" concept.) In an organization, a for-profit organization in particular, this is the process of making a profit on out-put.

6. *Information Input, Negative Feedback, and the Coding Process:* Set of processes through which organizations develop mechanisms to receive information on their performance in order to correct problems. Organizations develop selective processes through which they code information input to filter out unnecessary or extraneous information.

7. *The Steady State and Dynamic Homeostasis:* A movable balance established by organizations taking in energy and information, using it, then exporting it in return for needed resources in a functional way. It is a movable balance in the sense that it represents a continuous but dynamic state of change rather than a static state.

8. *Differentiation:* Tendency of organizations to develop toward greater complexity and greater specialization of functions. (In organizations, this concept is consistent with the notion of division of labor we explored in our discussion of bureaucracy.)

9. *Equifinality:* The possibility of a system to attain its goals through a variety of different processes or paths.

You have very likely by now noticed a great deal of commonalty between the open-systems concepts used in relation to organizations above and the more general social systems concepts we explored earlier in this book. This is an example of the widespread influence that systems thinking has had in the natural, social, and behavioral sciences.

Contingency Theory

Before we leave systems perspectives on organizations, we should visit briefly a close "relative" of organizational systems thinking. This is contingency theory. **Contingency theory** suggests that the effectiveness of any organizational action— a decision, for example—is determined in the context of all the other elements and conditions in the organization at the time the action is taken. Contingency theory posits that everything is situational and that there are no absolutes or universals. Contingency theorists assert that organizations always act in a context of relative uncertainty. In other words, they make decisions at any given point based on incomplete information. Given the incompleteness of the information, organizations must make the best decision they can with the information they do have.

Both systems and contingency theorists have as a major concern the processes of and variables influencing decision making in organizations. A significant component of systems and contingency theories is decision making. Shafritz and Ott (1987:234–238) suggest that use of complex quantitative tools and techniques to assist in gathering and processing the most information possible in order to make the best decision possible in an uncertain environment is a central theme of systems and contingency theorists. Such decision-making processes based on the assumption of incomplete information and uncertainty has been referred to as "satisficing" (March and Simon 1958 in Gortner, Mahler, and Nicholson 1987:258).

Organizational Life Cycle Theories

Yet another traditional perspective on organizations, as is the case with individuals, families, and groups, is that of the life cycle. Researchers and theorists, primarily in the business disciplines, have posed a number of theories of organizations based on life cycles or stages. Howard and Hine (1997) suggest that, while there are differences in these theories, there are also similarities. They see these similarities as first a struggle for autonomy, followed by expansion, then stability.

More specifically, Hanks (1990 in Dodge and Robbins 1992) outlines four organizational life cycle stages:

1. startup or entrepreneurial stage;
2. growth or expansion stage;
3. a domain protection stage and/or expansion stage;
4. a stability stage.

A third perspective on organizational life cycle theories (Miller and Friesen 1980 in Jawahar and McLaughlin 2001) suggests the following stages that tend to occur in sequence:

1. birth,
2. growth,
3. maturity, and
4. revival.

While these stage theories reflect a good deal of similarity, Miller and Friesen see organizations not only progressing to stability, but also having the potential to revitalize themselves after reaching maturity or stability. This approach is perhaps the least traditional of the three, given its less linear approach that allows for a rebirth or revitalization even at the later stages of the cycle.

STRENGTHS, WEAKNESSES, CRITICISM

Before considering alternative paradigmatic perspectives on organizations, it is helpful first to consider some things that the traditional and dominant perspectives do and do not tell us about the realities of human behavior in organizational environments. The traditional perspectives on organizations we have explored so far tell us much about this level of human behavior that will be helpful in our social work practice and in our personal lives. These traditional notions, however, leave much untold or unclear about this important arena as well.

Classical traditional perspectives such as scientific management and bureaucratic theory (also referred to as rationalistic or mechanistic perspectives because of their concern with rational goal setting and decision making aimed at achieving machinelike efficiency in organizations) told us much about the formal structure of organizations. Human relations thinking, with its concern for the nonrational and social elements of organizations, revealed much about the informal aspects of organizations. Systems and contingency theories presented us with perspectives that recognize both the formal and the informal aspects of organizations in addition to acknowledging the influences of the larger social environment on organizations.

However, Hasenfeld (in Patti 2009:65) notes limitations of systems or ecological perspectives as they have been applied to organizational theory. He points out, for example, that research on organizations from an ecological perspective has not examined closely enough strategies to address macro-level system issues and changes such as changes "in the social, political, and economic environment in which [human service] agencies are embedded." In addition, he argues that too little ecologically based organizational theory has focused on "the role organizations play, individually and collectively, in constructing the environment in which they operate."

In other words, he suggests that ecological theory has not paid enough attention to "suprasystem" issues that form and continuously change the larger environment in which organizations exist and function. He has also posited that the theory has not been responsive enough to the ability of individual organizations to influence or change that larger environment in order for the organization to function better and more effectively meet its goals. Consistent with the perspective in this book, ecological or systems perspectives on organizations have not sufficiently accounted for the interdependence and interplay between the "focal" system (the individual organization) and elements in the larger macro-environment (the "suprasystem"). See Chapter 3 for a description of the more general systems perspective terms: focal and suprasystem.

These traditional perspectives, however, leave much unsaid about other important dimensions of organizational life. Classical perspectives (scientific management and bureaucracy) as well as human relations perspectives all assume, for example, that hierarchy is a necessary prerequisite for efficient and effective goal achievement in organizations. Systems approaches also assume some degree of hierarchy, although its specific characteristics may change in response to environmental conditions. Some alternative perspectives question the essential nature of hierarchy in organizations (Iannello 1992).

Flowing from the assumption of hierarchy of traditional perspectives—classical, human relations, and systems—is the assumption that power must be divided unequally among the members of the organization. Power here is defined as the ability to influence movement toward accomplishment of goals. Whether this is according to formal and rational structures in bureaucracy, informal and nonrational networks in human relations approaches, or flexible and changeable arrangements based on environmental conditions in systems thinking, all of these traditional approaches include an inherent power differential among members.

In addition, these traditional perspectives see inequality or unequal distribution of power as basically functional for organizational members. In scientific management, lower-level workers benefit from power differences by having their basic economic needs met even though management and owners benefit materially to a greater extent in proportion to their greater power. In human relations thinking, not only are formal differences in power recognized, but the informal social networks reflect differences in power among network members as well. These formal and informal power inequities serve different, though overall functional, purposes. They support the realization of the organization's formal goals and they support the informal (social or personal) goals of members.

System's approaches see power differences as necessary and of mutual benefit in service to overall system goals and the goals of subsystems. Systems approaches do recognize the necessity for power (authority) distribution to be rearranged periodically in response to changes in the environment. It is interesting to note that traditional organizational paradigms rarely use the term *power. Power* is instead referred to as authority over persons and resources within the organization that is necessary to maintain itself and to reach goals. Some alternative perspectives explicitly address issues of power and power inequities in organizations and seek ways to make power distribution within organizations more apparent so that it can be redistributed more equitably. Alternative perspectives also tend to approach power differences among organizational members as problematic rather than functional.

Another area in which alternative and traditional perspectives differ is that of conflict. Scientific-management approaches see truly rational and formal organizations as basically nonconflictual. Human relations approaches when optimally implemented see informal structures as reducing the need for conflict to the point that these organizations have sometimes been referred to as "big happy families." Systems approaches go a bit further in recognizing that organizational conflict exists but they suggest that effective organizational systems will be "self-righting" in that they will make whatever adjustments are required to address and reduce conflict in order to return to a positive and mutually beneficial balanced state. Systems approaches, while recognizing the existence of conflict, see it as an exception, not a norm. (Buckley has addressed issues of conflict—he calls it "tension"—as a more "normal" part of systems behavior than most other systems thinkers.) Most systems approaches, nevertheless, operate from assumptions of cooperation and harmony (Barnard and Simon in Abrahamsson 1977:151).

What is needed are alternative organizational perspectives that recognize the reality of differences or conflicts among members and that create mechanisms for using conflict resolution processes as an ongoing avenue for strengthening the organization (Abrahamsson 1977; Iannello 1992).

ALTERNATIVE PARADIGMS

As we begin to explore alternative paradigms we emphasize that we do not want to exclude information provided by traditional perspectives. We want to extend that information in order to gain more comprehensive, inclusive perspectives on organizations. We are reminded here that alternative paradigms, while often critical of traditional perspectives, also often use traditional thinking as a departure point. In this respect it is helpful to recall the importance of historical perspective and the notion of continuum in our thinking about HBSE. Our goal, as we proceed on our journey to explore alternative perspectives on organizations, is to fill in some of the gaps in our knowledge and to clarify some of the areas left unclear by traditional organizational thinking. We are especially concerned with finding perspectives that are consistent with the core concerns of social work. Alternative perspectives are more "in process" than many traditional perspectives. Because many of the alternative perspectives are only now emerging, there are fewer examples of them around us. These alternative perspectives are also less "finished" in that their potential for improving the quality of our organizational lives has not been thoroughly studied or tested and can only be estimated in many respects. We begin our exploration of alternative perspectives with the notion of organizational culture as a way to think about organizations in more holistic ways.

Organizational Culture/Climate

Regardless of whether an organization is in line with traditional paradigm or alternative paradigm thinking, it can be thought of as having an organizational culture that reflects and supports its prevailing view of the world. Earlier in this book we defined *culture* as the accumulation of customs, values, and artifacts that are shared by a group of people.

Schein (1992:7–15) suggests that organizations have many of the characteristics commonly associated with culture. He especially emphasizes that organizations are cultures by virtue of the shared experiences that organizational members hold in common. These shared experiences merge into a whole pattern of beliefs, values, and rituals that become the "essence" of the **organization's culture** and help provide stability. Organizational members adhere to these patterns, but they are not likely to be conscious of them in their day-to-day activities. This invisible or "taken for granted" aspect accounts for some of the difficulty outsiders have in fully understanding a given organization. It also accounts for some of the confusion and discomfort that new organizational members are likely to experience when they first enter the organization. This taken-for-granted aspect also helps explain why longtime members of an organization have difficulty explaining to new members or to outsiders exactly how the organization operates.

Schein (cited in Austin and Claassen 2008:341) suggests there are three levels of culture, in this case organizational culture: (1) basic assumptions, (2) values and beliefs, and (3) cultural artifacts. Austin and Claassen (2008:342) summarize Schein's definition of levels of organizational culture in Figure 8.1.

Schein (1992:11–12) stresses that all organizations do not develop smoothly integrated cultures shared equally by all organization members. When this integration is lacking the results are likely to be ambiguity and conflict. Lack of an integrated culture can come about because of turnover in organizational membership or because of the different experiences from outside the organization that its members bring with them. As a result, such organizations may be continuously trying to create an integrated whole from the shared and unshared experiences of members. Some organization members, leaders for example, are likely to play a larger role than others in the processes of creating or changing the culture.

What does this image portray about the "organizational culture" and "organizational climate" in which these men work?

This perspective on organizational culture can help us understand both stability and change in social work and human service organizations. This notion of culture combined with our perspective on traditional and alternative paradigms can help us to understand some of the problems within organizations and

Three Levels of Culture

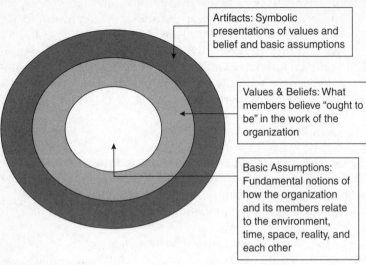

Artifacts: Symbolic presentations of values and belief and basic assumptions

Values & Beliefs: What members believe "ought to be" in the work of the organization

Basic Assumptions: Fundamental notions of how the organization and its members relate to the environment, time, space, reality, and each other

Figure 8.1

Three Levels of Culture (Austin, M. J., & Claassen, J. (2008). Impact of Organizational Change on Organizational Culture: Implications for Introducing Evidence-Based Practice. *Journal of Evidence-Based Social Work, 5*(1/2), 321–359.)

between organizations and the people they attempt to serve. For example, how can an organization with a culture characterized by patriarchal, white, quantitative, competitive, and privileged perspectives respond effectively to consumers and new organizational members whose worldviews are characterized by feminist, multicultural, qualitative, or cooperative perspectives? The concept of organizational culture can help us understand the difficulty faced by women, people of color, or persons with disabilities when they enter organizations (and they typically enter as lower-ranking members, rather than as members in formal leadership positions) that have historically been made up only of privileged able-bodied white males with a traditional paradigm perspective. It can also help us appreciate how important it is that the organizational culture of social work organizations reflect and respect the larger culture of the communities and people they serve.

In addition to the somewhat invisible but highly influential concept of organizational culture is the concept of organizational climate. These two concepts are highly interrelated. They both communicate the "feel" of an organization. *Organizational culture* includes such basic components as the fundamental beliefs and values of the organization. **Organizational climate,** on the other hand, reflects how organization members communicate organizational culture in more visible or observable ways. For example, how members interpret or communicate to others the organization's policies, practices, and procedures (Schneider et al. 1996:7–9). It is important to assess the climate of an organization in order to determine the nature of the culture communicated to consumers, other organizations, and the larger community of which the organization is a part. Schneider et al. identify **four key climate dimensions:**

1. *The nature of interpersonal relationships.*   Is there mutual sharing and trust or conflict and mistrust? Are relationships between . . . units cooperative or competitive? Does the organization support socialization of newcomers or a sink-or-swim approach? Do people feel that their personal welfare is important to those around them and to top management?

2. *The nature of the hierarchy.*   Are decisions affecting work and the workplace made only by top management or are they made with participation from those affected by the decision? Is the organization characterized by a team approach to work or strictly an individualistic competitive approach? Does management have special perquisites that separate them from their subordinates, such as special parking or dining facilities?

3. *The nature of work.*   Is the work challenging or boring? Are jobs adaptable by the people performing them, or are they rigidly defined so that everyone must do them the same way? Does the organization provide workers with the necessary resources (tools, supplies, information) to get the work done?

4. *The focus of support and rewards.* Are the goals of work and the standards of excellence widely known and shared? What gets supported: being warm and friendly to [consumers] or being fast? Is getting the work done (quantity) or getting the work right (quality) rewarded? On what basis are people hired? To what goals and standards are they trained? What facets of performance are appraised and rewarded? (1996:10–11)

The "Iron Law of Oligarchy"

An alternative to traditional approaches to organizational behavior emerged at virtually the same time that Taylor's perspectives (discussed earlier) on scientific management and rationality in organizations were gaining prominence. This alternative appeared also at about the same time that Weber's notions about bureaucratic structure were being introduced. This alternative perspective preceded the more recent notions of organizational culture and climate. However, as you read this section, keep in mind the concepts of organizational climate and culture which can help you understand the kind and feel of the organization Michels described. Robert Michels published his work describing the "Iron Law of Oligarchy" in its original German in 1911. Scientific management and the theory of bureaucracy gained prominence roughly during the period from the turn of the century to 1930. Michels's work, however, took a decidedly contrary and pessimistic approach to the kinds of organizations Taylor and Weber were heralding as the answer to the organizational needs of the time.

Michels suggested that rather than organizations striving to meet the rationally specified needs of the organization as a whole, they instead serve the needs only of an elite few who gain control of the organization. He became convinced that formal organizations made democracy (participation and decision making by a majority of organizational members) impossible and inevitably resulted in **oligarchy**—government or control by the few.

As organizations grew in scale their original goals would always end up being displaced by the goal of maintaining the organization in service to the interests of a small group of controlling elites. As an organization grew and became more bureaucratic it would employ a "ruling class" of managers or leaders. Their self-interests in maintaining the prestige and influence that accompanied their leadership positions resulted in a growing gap between the top and the bottom of the organizational hierarchy. Leaders no longer represented the interests of followers (Iannello 1992; Michels in Grusky and Miller 1981; Pugh, Hickson, and Hinings 1985).

Michels originally based his theory on his studies of revolutionary democratic political parties that grew into conservative political bureaucracies far removed from their original democratic goals. He came to believe that the development of oligarchy would happen to any organization regardless of its original purpose because oligarchy was a function of growing size or scale and the accompanying emergence of specialization and hierarchy. He was convinced that bureaucracy and democracy were inherently in opposition to one another (Michels in Grusky and Miller 1981; Pugh, Hickson, and Hinings 1985).

As the self-interests of the organizational ruling class began to take precedence over original, more democratic goals of organizational members, Michels suggested that the leaders of the organization would stress the need for internal unity. The harmony of ideas and views, along with the need to avoid or suppress tension and conflict, would become paramount. He also suggested that the ruling elite would put forth notions about dangers and hostility in the environment surrounding the organization, underscoring the need to hide internal differences from those outside the organization in order to maintain the status quo of the organization (Pugh, Hickson, and Hinings 1985:207–210).

Michels's view of the difficulty (the virtual impossibility, he came to believe) of large organizations' goals remaining consistent with democratic ideals was indeed a pessimistic one. Whether it was entirely justified is perhaps open to some argument. However, his alternative perspective does suggest that traditional models of organization are far from ideal and entail significant problems and risks in terms of ethics and values of which social workers need to be aware.

The tendency toward serving a select few powerful and prestigious leaders rather than the needs of all organizational members (and consumers of organizational services, as well, we might add) is certainly inconsistent with a number of core concerns of social workers. This tendency is contrary to concerns about maximum participation, self-determination, rights to resources, social and economic justice, and respect for diversity. As social workers and members of organizations (both as leaders and as followers), we need to recognize and act to prevent tendencies toward organizational oligarchy.

A Critical Perspective

Kathleen Iannello (1992) presents a contemporary alternative perspective on organizations that follows in part from her belief that Michels's iron law of oligarchy, while criticized by a number of students of organizations, certainly has not been refuted. Indeed, she suggests that it is out of the hierarchical nature of traditional organizations that Michels's oligarchy grows (Iannello 1992:3–25). If you recall, from our earlier exploration of traditional perspectives, hierarchy is considered a necessary component of modern organizational structures. This is especially so in a bureaucracy, perhaps the most common modern organization form (Iannello 1992:3–7, 12).

Iannello's critical perspective suggests that alternatives to hierarchy are possible. However, to create alternatives we must first recognize that hierarchy is embedded throughout the values, norms, and ideologies of the larger society.

This critical perspective expands on traditional open-systems theory (explored earlier) in its emphasis on the interrelatedness of organizational structure and the values, norms, and ideologies of the surrounding environment. Iannello (1992:7–10) suggests that this critical perspective goes beyond traditional open-systems theory in recognizing the entire *society* as the environment having an "important and pervasive" influence on the nature of the organization. This perspective is in contrast to open-systems notions of an environment consisting only of those systems having a direct impact or influence on the organization, for example, other competing organizations in the immediate environment of the focal organization.

The critical perspective goes beyond open systems and much other traditional organizational thinking in another respect. It incorporates historical perspective as an additional pivotal consideration necessary for developing alternative models of organizations (Iannello 1992:10). This perspective suggests, for example, that much is to be learned by asking "why," in a historical sense, an organization is structured as it is. How did it come to be the way it is? This questioning can engage us in paradigm analysis at the organizational level. For example, we might ask who founded the organization? What was their worldview? What were their values? Did they recognize the importance of difference? Did they see the organization's purpose as preserving or restoring human dignity and assisting members to reach their maximum potential? How was power distributed within the organization?

The critical perspective questions the necessity and inherent nature of hierarchy in organizations. It offers a different perspective on the meaning of hierarchy, and from this alternative perspective it calls attention to some of the problems created by hierarchy. Through its alternative analysis of hierarchy, the critical perspective raises a number of issues related to the dimensions of traditional and alternative paradigms with which we are concerned here. Specifically, it addresses such issues as power, domination, and privilege. It offers a definition of **hierarchy** as "any system in which the distribution of power, privilege and authority are both systematic and unequal" (Iannello 1992:15).

This perspective's critique of hierarchy includes the concept of alienation of lower-level workers resulting from their lack of access to and participation in decision-making processes. The critique also questions the social control directed toward lower-level members of the hierarchy by those at the top in order to maintain their positions of power.

By looking beyond traditional narrow or closed-system organizational perspectives to include societal values and historical influences, the critical perspective reflects several dimensions of alternative paradigm thinking. This critical view allows the incorporation of a feminist perspective. It allows us to question the influence of patriarchal and masculinist societal values on organizational structures such as hierarchy.

Its historical perspective allows inclusion of broader interpretive, personal, experiential standpoints in addition to traditional "great person" accounts for thinking about the past and present structures of organizations. It allows serious consideration, for example, of power relations in organizations based on the experiences of all organization members rather than only the experiences of "key" administrators or decision makers (Iannello 1992:3–13). In this respect it more readily allows for the inclusion of women's perspectives in thinking about organizations. For it is at lower levels in organizational hierarchies—clerical and administrative assistant positions, for example—that women have historically been concentrated.

Consensus Organizations

Iannello develops a model of nonhierarchical organizations she refers to as consensus organizations. These organizations operate "primarily through a consensus decision-making process." The decision-making process followed in consensus organizations operates in a much more participative way in contrast to the centralized and alienating decision making by managers and leaders at the top levels of the hierarchy in traditional organizations. **Consensus decision making** occurs only after an issue has been widely discussed, with participation of a broad base (ideally all) of the organization members. After this discussion takes place, "one or more members of the assembly sum up prevailing sentiment, and if no objections are voiced, this becomes agreed-on policy" (Iannello 1992; Mansbridge in Iannello 1992:27).

Iannello notes that consensus organizations are also referred to by some as cooperative or collective organizations. She defines **consensus organization** as "any enterprise in which control rests ultimately and overwhelmingly with the members-employees-owners, regardless of the particular legal framework through which it is achieved" (Iannello 1992; Rothschild and Whitt in Iannello 1992:27). Consensus organizations attempt to "humanize the workplace, to put meaning and values back into jobs in order to reconnect the worker with society." To accomplish this goal these organizations focus on maximizing the level of commitment on the part of all workers to this primary goal. The means used to increase commitment and reduce alienation in consensus organizations is reducing hierarchy.

Examples of existing models of consensus organizations include the Israeli kibbutzim and a number of historical American Indian tribal organizations. However, we should be careful not to overgeneralize. We need to recognize that different kibbutzim and current American Indian tribal government organizations operationalize consensus principles to different degrees. Ideally, a kibbutz operates on consensus assumptions and principles. These include shared and egalitarian decision making in all aspects of organizational life. This principle is implemented through weekly meetings of the entire organizational membership and a complex system of committees. This allows face-to-face decision making. Leadership positions within the organization are elected and rotated among members to discourage hierarchy. Leadership positions offer no individual rewards for the individuals who hold them. Rewards within the organization are linked to achievement of collective rather than individual goals (Iannello 1992:32).

As noted in the earlier discussion of consensus-based decision making in small groups, Attneave stresses the central role played by consensus in many American Indian tribal government organizations. While the earlier discussion focuses on a preference for consensus in small-group decision making, Attneave stressed that this form of decision making operated whether the group was "the tribe, the band, the family or any other coherent cluster of people." Attneave noted that "tribal histories never suggested the impatient solution of majority vote so revered by 'democracies'" (Attneave 1982:66–67).

Comparison of consensus and bureaucratic organizations

How do consensus and bureaucratic organizations compare in terms of some of the basic issues and concerns of organizations generally? Rothschild and Whitt studied a number of consensus organizations, and Iannello used their findings to compare consensus and hierarchical bureaucratic organizations along several dimensions. A summary of this work follows:

1. *Authority:*　In contrast to the ideal bureaucratic structure, in which authority is vested in the individual according to position or rank within the organizations, authority in the consensual organization rests with the collectivity.

2. *Rules:*　In the consensual organization, rules are minimal and based on the "substantive ethics" of the situation. In the traditional organizations, rules are fixed, and emphasis is placed on conformity to the rules.

3. *Social control:*　For the consensual organization, social control is based on something akin to peer pressure. Social control rarely becomes problematic, because of the homogeneity of the group. . . . Within a bureaucracy, social control is achieved through hierarchy and supervision of subordinates by their superiors, according to the formal and informal sanctions of the organizations.

4. *Social relations:*　For the collective, social relations stem from the community ideal. "Relations are to be holistic, personal, of value in themselves." In the traditional model, the emphasis is placed on impersonality, which is linked to a sense of professionalism. "Relations are to be role based, segmental, and instrumental."

5. *Recruitment and advancement:* In the consensual organization, recruitment is based on friendship networks, "informally assessed knowledge and skills," and compatibility with organizations' values. The concept of advancement is generally not valued, since there is no hierarchy of positions and related rewards. Within the bureaucratic model recruitment is based on formal qualifications and specialized training. The concept of advancement is very meaningful for an individual's career and is based on formal assessment of performance according to prescribed rules and paths of promotion.

6. *Incentive structure:* For the consensual organization, "normative and solidarity incentives are primary; material incentives are secondary." For bureaucracy, "remunerative incentives are primary."

7. *Social stratification:* The consensual organization strives to be egalitarian. Any type of stratification is carefully created and monitored by the collectivity. In the bureaucracy, there are "differential rewards" of prestige, privilege, or inequality, each justified by hierarchy.

8. *Differentiation:* In the consensual structure, division of labor is minimized, particularly with regard to intellectual versus manual work. Jobs and functions are generalized, with the goal of "demystification of expertise." Bureaucracy maximizes division of labor to the extent that there is a "dichotomy between intellectual work and manual work and between administrative tasks and performance tasks." Technical expertise is highly valued and specialization of jobs is maximized. (Iannello 1992:28–29)

Limits of consensus organizations

There are a number of factors that limit the ability of organizations to successfully implement nonhierarchical structures. Some of these are summarized below:

1. *Time:* Consensus-style decision making takes more time than bureaucratic decision making, in which an administrator simply hands down a decision. . . . The idea of consensus, in which every member of an organization must agree to a decision, conjures up the picture of long, drawn-out sessions in which members may never agree. However, real-world experience has demonstrated that the endless rules and regulations of bureaucracies can also lead to protracted disputes. . . . It is important to recognize that both bureaucracies and consensual organizations are capable of making decisions quickly or slowly, depending on the nature of the issue.

2. *Emotional intensity:* There is more emotional intensity in the consensual setting. Consensual organizations provide face-to-face communication and consideration of the total needs of the individual. As a result, conflict within the organization may exact a much higher personal cost; individuals are held more accountable for their actions. In the bureaucratic organization, impersonality and formality make conflict less personal and therefore easier to handle. But bureaucratic procedure also alienates people and is less satisfying personally. . . . [The] degree of emotional intensity has positive and negative aspects for members of both organization types.

3. *Non-democratic habits and values:* As members of a hierarchical society, most of us are not well prepared to participate in consensual styles of organization. Our earliest contact with organizational life in educational and other settings is bureaucratic.

4. *Environmental constraints:*   Environmental constraints—economic, political, or social pressures from the outside—are more intense in consensual organizations because such groups often form around issues that run counter to the mainstream of society. . . . Consensual organizations can also at times benefit because they provide a service or offer an avenue of participation that is not available through other organizations. This has been true, for example, of organizations providing alternative health care or food co-ops providing natural or organically grown foods.

5. *Individual differences:*   While bureaucracies are able to capitalize on differences in the attitudes, skills, and personalities of individual members, such differences may pose a problem for organizations based on consensual process. For consensual organizations such diversity may lead to conflict. Yet while this point has merit, it paints a somewhat false picture of both bureaucratic and consensual organization. . . . Some argue that bureaucracy breeds sameness, encourages lack of creativity, and provides little in the way of reward for anyone attempting to break out of set patterns. When such rewards exist they are reserved primarily for those at the top of the organization. Yet others have pointed out that bureaucracies, or at least public bureaucracies, have the most diverse membership of any institutions. Thus, it is unsurprising that members of consensual organizations, which are frequently homogeneous, are likely to agree on issues that face the organization. (Rothschild and Whitt, Iannello in Iannello 1992:29–31)

An alternate perspective would suggest that it is possible for similarity and difference to coexist. For example, it would seem that there can be homogeneity in terms of shared philosophy and values simultaneous with diversity in ethnicity, gender, and sexual orientation. However, the above limitations do leave the issue of conflict as a potential source of growth and strength somewhat unaddressed.

Modified Consensus Organizations

Based on the assumptions and principles of consensus organizations, their comparison with hierarchical/bureaucratic organizations, and the limitations of both models, along with her study of three different consensus organizations, Iannello develops an organizational type she refers to as "modified consensus." The elements of this model have a good deal of consistency with core concerns of social work. Modified consensus organizations are characterized by alternative structures and processes from those of traditional models. These differences include the areas of decision making, nonhierarchical structures and processes, empowerment, and clarity of goals.

Modified consensus organizations assure broad-based participation in decision making, but are also conscious of the need to make timely decisions for the sake of operational efficiency. This is accomplished by differentiating between critical and routine decisions. Critical decisions are those that involve overall policy and have the potential for change in the fundamental direction of the organization. Critical decisions are made by the entire membership; in hierarchical organizations, only those at the top make critical policy decisions. In modified consensus organizations, routine decisions are those that are important in the day-to-day operation of the organization. Routine decisions are delegated horizontally within the organization according to the skills and interests of organizational members.

A second area of difference between modified consensus and traditional organizations is in concern for process. Process issues include concern for consensus, emerging leadership, and empowerment. Central to process is trust. This essential trust is fostered by maintaining consensus through the participation and agreement of all organization members in the critical decisions faced by the organization. The trust built through consensus on critical decisions in turn engenders sufficient trust among members to allow routine decisions to be delegated. Without mutual trust among members, the domination of some by others in the organization, characteristic of traditional hierarchical organizations, would be difficult to avoid.

Leadership is essential in both traditional and alternative organizations. The nature of leaders and the processes for development of leadership varies significantly between traditional and modified consensus organizations, however. Modified consensus organizations look within their membership and recognize its variety of abilities and expertise as the source of leadership. Efforts are made to maximize the skills of members. Members with specific skills provide ongoing education and training of other members who want to learn these skills. Central to this process is rotation of members through various positions of leadership within the organization. The assumption is that all members have the potential for leadership in a wide range of areas. This perspective is very different from traditional notions of leadership that hold leadership to be characteristic only of the specialized experts at the top of the hierarchy. (See discussion of traditional and alternative notions of leadership in Chapter 7 for a detailed discussion of different perspectives on leadership.)

Modified consensus organizations also seek to minimize power and maximize empowerment. Iannello (1992:44–45) describes power as "the notion of controlling others, while empowerment is associated with the notion of controlling oneself." Therefore, within organizations based on empowerment, members monitor themselves. In organizations based on power, there must be an administrative oversight function. This perspective is consistent with our earlier discussions of empowerment as power to accomplish one's goals or reach one's potential rather than "power over" others.

Iannello argues that power "is a relational concept that has a win/lose element to it" (1992:120). The members of the women's organizations she studied and found most consistent with modified consensus structure and operation rejected the idea of voting on major decisions for this reason. To vote meant there would always be some members who perceived themselves to have "lost" (unless voting was unanimous). "With consensus decision making, based on the concept of empowerment, it is perceived that everyone 'wins' because all members agree to the final decision" (Iannello 1992:120).

Organizational leadership

In Chapter 7, we examined several leadership types and styles in the context of groups. While there are certainly similarities in the types and styles of leadership needed for effective group work practice and organizational practice, there are also differences. For example, the definition of leadership as "a process by which an individual influences a group of individuals to achieve common goals," clearly applies to both organizational and group contexts (Packard in Patti 2009:144). However, leadership in the context of an organization, especially if it is a large, complex organization, is quite different from leadership in the context of a small group.

In Chapter 7, trait-based leadership theory was briefly described. However, even though this theory lost a good deal of its influence since its introduction in the first part of the 20th century, Packard notes that there has been renewed interest recently in efforts to understand traits associated with effective leadership. The more recent research in this area suggests the importance of a number of traits associated with effective organizational leadership. These include:

- A high energy level and tolerance for stress
- Self-confidence (including self-esteem and self-efficacy)
- An internal locus of control orientation [a sense that you, rather than external forces, control your destiny]
- Emotional stability and maturity
- Personal integrity (in Patti 2009:156)

Packard cautions that "traits are important only to the extent that they are relevant to a particular leadership situation" (in Patti 2009:146). In other words, as is so often the case—context matters.

Leadership skills and competencies have also received increased attention on the part of researchers and scholars. *Leadership competencies* are defined as "the combination of knowledge, skills, traits and attributes that collectively enable someone to perform a certain job." Competencies found to be associated with leadership effectiveness include:

- Character (displaying integrity and honesty)
- Technical and professional expertise
- Problem-solving and analytical ability
- Innovation
- Self-development
- A focus on results
- Setting "stretch" goals
- Taking personal responsibility for outcomes
- Effective communication
- Inspiring and motivating others
- Trust and interpersonal effectiveness
- Concern for others' development
- Collaboration and organizational change skills
- Ability to champion change
- Ability to relate well to outside stakeholders (Packard in Patti 2009:146–147)

Leadership styles

In Chapter 7 several traditional leadership styles applicable to small groups—autocratic, laissez faire, and democratic—were presented. Here we will address leadership styles within an organizational context with a focus on emerging or alternative styles. There has been considerable criticism of research in the area of leadership styles, especially in terms of its inconclusive nature. However, Yukl (cited in Patti 2009:147) observes, "the overall pattern of results suggests that effective leaders use a pattern of behavior that is appropriate for the situation and reflects a high concern for task objectives and a high concern for relationships." Behaviors related to tasks, relationships, and a newer behavioral area that specifies "change-oriented" behaviors are presented in Table 8.1.

Charismatic leadership styles have been addressed in past research and from a traditional paradigm perspective of "larger than life heroes," newer notions of charismatic leadership are less traditional and recognize that charismatic style can be displayed by leaders who are not "strongly charismatic" as those implied in the example above. "A charismatic leader is a strong role model who demonstrates competence and confidence, articulates goals, and communicates high

Professional Identity

An important part of developing our professional identity as social workers is to practice person reflection to assure continual professional development. Reflect on the leadership styles discussed in this section. Which style or styles reflect the style(s) of leadership you want to develop in continuing your development as a professional social worker?

Table 8.1	Examples of Task-, Relations-, and Change-Oriented Behaviors

Task-Oriented Behaviors

- Organize work activities to improve efficiency.
- Plan short-term operations.
- Assign work to groups or individuals.
- Clarify what results are expected for a task.
- Set specific goals and standards for task performance.
- Explain rules, policies, and standard operating procedures.
- Direct and coordinate work activities.
- Monitor operations and performance.
- Resolve immediate problems that would disrupt the work.

Relations-Oriented Behaviors

- Provide support and encouragement to someone with a difficult task.
- Express confidence that a person or group can perform a difficult task.
- Socialize with people to build relationships.
- Recognize contributions and accomplishments.
- Provide coaching and mentoring when appropriate.
- Consult with people on decisions affecting them.
- Allow people to determine the best way to do a task.
- Keep people informed about actions affecting them.
- Help resolve conflicts in a constructive way.
- Use symbols, ceremonies, rituals, and stories to build team identity.
- Recruit competent new members for the team or organization.

Change-Oriented Behaviors

- Monitor the external environment to detect threats and opportunities.
- Interpret events to explain the urgent need for change.
- Study competitors and outsiders to get ideas for improvements.
- Envision exciting new possibilities for the organization.
- Encourage people to view problems or opportunities in a different way.
- Develop innovative new strategies linked to core competencies.
- Encourage and facilitate innovation and entrepreneurship in the organization.
- Encourage and facilitate collective learning in the team or organization.
- Experiment with new approaches for achieving objectives.
- Make symbolic changes that are consistent with a new vision or strategy.
- Encourage and facilitate efforts to implement major change.
- Announce and celebrate progress in implementing change.
- Influence outsiders to support change and negotiate agreements with them.

Source: Yukl (2006), Table 3-1, p. 66.

expectations." However, researchers also caution that "charismatic leadership is risky: Power can be misused, and followers can become inappropriately dependent upon a charismatic leader" (Packard in Patti 2009:151).

Two additional leadership styles that often combine with charismatic styles are transactional and transformational styles. *Transactional* style, the more traditional of the two, includes an exchange process through which the leader and followers agree "to accommodate each others' needs." Transformational leadership is a more alternative but increasingly influential style. A *transformational* style "transforms and motivates followers by (1) making them more aware of the importance of task outcomes, (2) inducing them to transcend their own self-interest for the sake of the organization or team, and (3) activating their higher order needs" (Yukl cited by Parker in Patti 2009:151). Researchers caution that "transformational leadership can be confused with 'pseudotransformational leadership,' which focuses on personal power, manipulation, threat, and punishment" (Avolio and Bass cited by Parker in Patti 2009:152).

Other emerging and more alternative leadership styles include Exemplary Leadership, Visionary Leadership, and Servant-Leadership. According to Kouzes and Posner (cited by Parker in Patti 2009:153), *exemplary leadership* includes "five practices" and "ten commitments." See Table 8.2.

Visionary leadership includes the ability to develop, articulate, and communicate a clear organizational vision. "A vision is 'a realistic, credible, attractive, and inspiring future for the organization''' (Nanus and Dobbs cited by Parker in Patti 2009:153). Parker notes, "while a mission statement describes why an organizations exists (its purpose) and what it does (its unique niche of programs and activities), a vision statement represents where the organization wants to be, its ideal future" (in Patti 2009:153).

Servant leadership is an alternative style with its roots in philosophical, ethical, and moral principles and it presents "the unorthodox idea that the leader should first serve followers." This model seems particularly well suited to social work organizations. This is evident in its ten characteristics: "listening, empathy, healing 'broken spirits' and 'emotional hurts,' general and self-awareness, using persuasion rather than positional authority, broad conceptual thinking and visioning, learning from the past and foreseeing future outcomes, stewardship

Table 8.2   Leadership Practices and Commitments

Practices	Commitments
Model the way	Clarify personal values Set an example by aligning actions with values
Inspire a shared vision	Envision the future Enlist others in a common vision
Challenge the process	Find opportunities to innovate, change, and grow Experiment and take risks
Enable others to act	Foster collaboration through trust and cooperative goals Sharing power and discretion
Encourage the heart	Show appreciation for individual excellence Celebrate victories through a spirit of community

Source: Parker in Patti, 2009:153

('holding their institutions in trust for the greater good of society'), commitment to the growth of people, and building community." Interestingly, this style was developed by a retired executive, Robert Greenleaf of AT&T, an organization most would consider very traditional (Parker in Patti 2009:153–154).

Feminist Approaches to Organizations

As indicated in the discussion of consensus-based organizations, feminist theory offers an important alternative perspective on organizational behavior. This theoretical perspective is increasingly being applied to thinking about organizational life. For example, Gilligan's theory that women's development (see Chapter 5) is based on an ethic of care and the centrality of relationships has been applied to organizational life and business enterprises. Liedtka notes that "Gilligan's metaphor of the web to represent feminine thinking, has been juxtaposed against the use of hierarchy to represent masculine thinking" (1996). Burton also suggests that "in one sense it might be said that traditional, economics-based approaches to management have concentrated on the legalistic, contractual, masculine side of human existence" (1996). These alternative organizations based on relationships and caring "are not bureaucracies. . . . The rules in a bureaucracy become, over time, the ends rather than the means. Thus, caring, even for the customer or client, is subordinated to perpetuation of the organization in its current state" (Liedtka 1996).

Core concepts from Gilligan's theory are associated with other new management theories such as **stakeholder theory** and the notion of learning organizations (see discussion of learning organizations in this chapter). "Stakeholder theory, like the ethic of care, is built upon a recognition of interdependence." Stakeholder theorists suggest that "the corporation is constituted by the network of relationships which it is involved in with employees, customers, suppliers, communities, businesses and other groups who interact with and give meaning and definition to the corporation" (Liedtka 1996).

According to Burton, newer approaches such as "stakeholder theory might then be said to be the feminine counterpart to traditional management" theories (1996).

How do the women in this photo, who are distributing water and ice to hurricane survivors, portray an "ethic of care" and the "centrality of relationships" put forth in the theory of Carol Gilligan?

Stakeholder Theory and Feminist Perspectives

Stakeholder theory seems to promote a more cooperative, caring type of relationship. Firms should seek to make decisions that satisfy stakeholders, leading to situations where all parties involved in a relationship gain. The inherent relatedness of the firm under stakeholder theory forces firms to examine the effect of their decisions on others, just as the inherent relatedness of humans in feminist theory forces us to examine the effect of our decisions on others. (Burton and Dunn 1996)

The concept of the learning organization, another alternative approach to organizational management, also reflects elements of feminist theory, especially the ethic of care. The learning organization also appreciates the importance of relationship and interconnectedness characteristic of much alternative paradigm thinking, including feminist perspectives. For example, the learning organization is closely linked with "communities that share a sense of purpose that connects each member to each other, and to the community at large. Learning organizations are characterized by an ability to maintain an open dialogue among members, that seeks first to understand, rather than evaluate, the perspectives of each. . . . Care-based organizations would seem ideally suited for such processes" (Burton and Dunn 1996).

Caring organizations recognize the importance of employees and frontline workers as the primary providers of services to consumers: "It is the employees who deal directly with these customers who ultimately determine the firm's success or failure. The rest of the organization, including senior management, exists to support and respond to, rather than control and monitor, these frontline workers" (Liedtka 1996). Such organizations will be characterized by listening to the needs of their consumers and by willingness to experiment to meet the changing needs of consumers. As Liedtka points, out, "they will need to listen, to inquire, and to experiment. They will be collaborative enterprises . . . which value the diversity of their workforce, and who work in partnership with their suppliers and in the communities in which they reside" (Liedtka 1996). Certainly these perspectives are important approaches to consider in designing and operating social work organizations.

Women and career phases

Research by O'Neil and Bilimoria (2005) resulted in uncovering recurring patterns and phases in the careers and life courses of women that differ from those of men. These differences emerge from three major factors:

1. The differential impact of family responsibilities on men's and women's careers [see "Family Work" section in this chapter]

2. Findings from women's developmental psychology . . . suggest a distinctive relational emphasis may pervade women's career development [see Chapters 4 and 5 for detailed discussions in this area]

3. Women's relative under-representation and subsequent token status at higher organizational levels uniquely constrain their career progress (O'Neil and Bilimoria 2005:169)

With the above information as context, O'Neil and Bilimoria found, through their research, three general phases of career development among the women in their study. These phases are summarized below.

Career Phase 1: Idealistic Achievement—The driving force of phase 1, early career (ages 24–35), is idealistic achievement. Women in the idealistic achievement phase will most likely base their career choices on their desires for career satisfaction, achievement and success, and their desires to positively impact others. . . . Women in this phase are most likely to see themselves in charge of their careers and will doubtless be proactive in taking strategic steps to ensure their career progress. . . . They believe their futures are replete with unlimited possibilities to "do and have it all" and they see their careers as opportunities to realize their dreams.

Career Phase 2: Pragmatic Endurance—The driving force of phase 2, mid-career (ages 36–45), is pragmatic endurance. Women in this phase are pragmatic about their careers and are operating in production mode, doing what it takes to get it done. Their career patterns are reflective of both ordered and emergent tendencies. They have a high relational context and are managing multiple responsibilities both personally and professionally. . . . These women are most likely to be dissatisfied and disenfranchised with their workplaces and stalled at the middle management level after having worked for 10 to 20 years. The staggering impact of negative organizations and managers, and discrimination and sexual harassment combine to produce a bleak environment for many mid-career women. These women may likely divert their full energies and talents from their careers to other areas of their lives that provide them with a sense of satisfaction, self-worth, achievement and recognition because the circumstances of their careers are not in and of themselves fulfilling.

Career Phase 3: Reinventive Contribution—The driving force of phase 3, advanced career (ages 46–60) is reinventive contribution. The women in this phase are focused on contributing to their organizations, their families and their communities. They are most likely to attribute personal and professional others as having had input into the direction of their careers (external career locus) and are likely to reflect a stable, planned career path (ordered career pattern). . . . Success for these women is about recognition, respect and living integrated lives. Women in the reinventive contribution phase of their careers will be more likely to work in arenas that provide them an opportunity to contribute meaningfully through their work. (O'Neil and Bilimoria, 2005:182–184)

The authors conclude that research on women in organizations "strongly suggests that organizations need to understand, recognize and support women's career and relationship priorities in order to retain talented professional women." However, in this particular study the researchers "found strong evidence that while organizations may agree on the importance of that support, they often fall short in practice, resulting in a lack of women who reach the higher rungs of management" (O'Neil & Bilimoria, 2005:185).

Next, we explore network organizations and social change theories of organizations (critical theory and empowerment theory). These theoretical approaches also share tenets of feminist theory consistent with the discussions in the previous section, "Feminist Theory and Organizations."

Network organizations

Another emerging organizational theory is that of the network organization. This has been especially true for human service organizations. The increasing prominence of such organizational realities as privatization of services and managed care approaches have created the need, even the requirement, for human service organizations to devote more attention building and maintaining networks both internally and externally. *Network organizations* create network exchange relations, collaborations, and alliances with other organizations. In addition, "innovations in information technology, especially the Internet, have supported the transformation from traditional models of bureaucracy to network organizations" (Hasenfeld in Patti 2009:61). Think, for example, about the organization of networks formed through such social networking sites such as Facebook, YouTube, and MySpace. Hasenfeld notes, "research suggests that in addition to external networks, internal networks, rather than hierarchical structures, may have greater advantages, especially in reducing costs and improving quality." However, he also notes that "despite the critical importance of networks to human services administration, they receive limited attention" (in Patti 2009:61).

Social change theories and organizations

Critical theory is an alternative approach to social change in and through organizations. Alvesson and Deetz describe critical theory as an approach to understanding and changing organizations. They suggest, "the central goal of critical theory in organizational studies has been to create societies and workplaces which are free from domination, where all members have equal opportunity to contribute to the production of system which meet human needs and lead to the progressive development of all" (cited by Hasenfeld in Patti 2009:71).

According to Alvesson and Deetz, critical theory as an approach to organizational analysis and change includes four major themes or premises:

1. Organizational forms need not be accepted as the natural order of things.
2. Management interests are not universal.
3. The emphasis on technical rationality represses understanding and mutual determination of the desired ends.
4. The organizational culture fosters the hegemony of dominant groups. (cited by Hasenfeld in Patti 2009:71–72)

Another important alternative approach to organizational theory is empowerment theory which is based on feminist theory of organizations. Some basic premises of an *empowerment approach* include:

1. Creating a structure that ensures participation of clients in organizational decision making;
2. Making all program beneficiaries (clients, staff, board members) equal partners;
3. Reducing cultural, ethnic, and gender barriers;
4. Ensuring that managers are committed to an empowerment ideology;
5. Promoting the use of teams;
6. Involving all constituencies in program evaluation and renewal; and
7. Mobilizing power to increase the political influence of all beneficiaries. (Hardina, Middleton, Montana, and Simpson cited by Hasenfeld in Patti 2009:73–74)

The empowerment approach as an organizational theory is both quite difficult to implement and maintain and has very limited empirical evidence (see also sections on Consensus Based Organizations and Feminist Approaches to Organizations in this chapter) (Hasenfeld in Patti, 2009:73–74).

Chaos/Complexity Theory and Organizations

In Chapter 3 we explored alternative theories that were extensions of social systems thinking. Included in these discussions were chaos and complexity theories. Students of organizations have begun to explore the application of these two theoretical perspectives to organizational behavior. These perspectives are increasingly presented as alternatives to traditional bureaucratic approaches to organizations. One of the most significant differences in the newer approaches of chaos and complexity is their focus on the importance of recognizing the positive aspects of change and flexibility, while traditional bureaucratic approaches seek stability and standardization. Evans points out, for example, that "traditional systems theorists have held that equilibrium or stability is the desirable state for an organization," but chaos theorists contend "that a condition of loosely bounded instability appears necessary to enable existing structures and patterns of interaction to respond to environmental demands." New paradigm managers focus more on developing "organizational processes and systems that support the agency's capacity, self-renewal, and self-organization" (1996). Wheatley suggests that consistent with newer extensions of systems thinking, organizations can be described as "living systems."

For social workers, a particularly helpful aspect of newer organizational thinking is its focus on the benefits and need for diversity in organizations. Evans stresses that "one excellent source of creative disorder is work force diversity. Organizational culture traditionally works to smooth out, if not eliminate, difference, but public managers can endeavor to counter this tendency by flexible job assignments, creating diverse work groups, and recognizing the unique contributions of individual women and men" (Evans 1996).

Another element of new-paradigm organizational thinking is its emphasis on understanding the multiple layers and complexity of organizational life. Zhu discusses the complementary nature of Eastern philosophical recognition of complexity and interconnectedness within organizations. Zhu points out that complex "systems involve multiple dimensions which are at once differentiated and interconnected." From this "Oriental systems approach" the organizational environment is closely connected to the larger social environment in "a dynamic web of multiple relations: relations within the complexity of 'the world,' relations between the human mind and that world, and relations among human beings" (Zhu 1999).

These newer approaches also incorporate a more spiritual approach to organizational management. They shift the focus "from structural and functional

Organizations as Living Systems

As living systems, organizations possess all of the creative, self-organizing capacities of other forms of life. The people within all organizations are capable of change, growth, and adaptation—they do not require outside engineering or detailed design. People are capable of creating structures and responses that work, then moving into new ones when required. We possess natural capacities to work with change in a creative and effective way. (Wheatley and Kellner-Rogers 1996) aspects of organization to the spiritual characteristics and qualities of organizational life." Overman suggests these managers focus "on energy, not matter; on becoming, not being; on coincidence, not causes; on constructivism, not determinism; and on new states of awareness and consciousness" (Overman 1996).

Alternative approaches to management stress the importance of relationships, social networks, and small groups. One approach is referred to as "the **network organization,** in which individuals or small groups use networks of personal contacts and contractual relationships to bring together the resources needed for each venture" (Hendry 1999). See previous section for details about network organizations.

Theory Z

We included in traditional approaches to understanding organizations a discussion of Theory X and Theory Y. These were organizational theories based on sets of assumptions about people held by managers. Douglas McGregor proposed Theory X as an approach to management based on the assumption that people were basically lazy and irresponsible. Theory X held that because people would naturally seek to avoid work and responsibility, a major part of the manager's responsibility was to constantly watch workers to make sure they were working and fulfilling their responsibilities. Theory Y, on the other hand, held that people "are fundamentally hardworking, responsible, and need only to be supported and encouraged" (Ouchi 1981:58–59).

William Ouchi (1981) developed an alternative theory of organizational management that he termed Theory Z. Like Theories X and Y, Theory Z was an approach to management premised on assumptions about humans. However, Theory Z had its basis not in traditional Western assumptions about humans, but in assumptions about humans based on Japanese culture and reflected in many Japanese organizations and approaches to management. While not all Japanese firms displayed all Theory Z characteristics to the same degrees, Ouchi found a significant number of Japanese firms that reflected a Theory Z perspective. Ouchi compared U.S. corporations with these Japanese firms and found fundamental differences in the assumptions underlying the business enterprises in the two countries. He contrasted the elements of the two approaches as follows:*

Japanese Organization	U.S. Organization
Lifetime employment	Short-term employment
Slow evaluation and promotion	Rapid evaluation and promotion
Non-specialized career paths	Specialized career paths
Implicit control mechanisms	Explicit control mechanisms
Collective decision making	Individual decision making
Collective responsibility	Individual responsibility
Holistic concern	Segmented concern

The Theory Z emphasis on job security, collective decision making, and collective responsibility for decisions, along with a holistic perspective, has a good deal of similarity with the consensus and modified consensus models described above. Unlike consensus and modified consensus notions, Theory Z has been applied to very large profit-making organizations, including major U.S. and multinational business corporations.

Ouchi suggests that participative or consensus decision making is perhaps the best-known feature of Japanese organizations. A consensus approach has also been widely researched and experimented within the United States and Europe.

A group or team approach is a central mechanism for implementing consensus-based decision making in Theory Z organizations. A **team** approach, sometimes referred to as **quality circle** or **quality control circle,** is a cohesive work group with the ability to operate with a significant degree of autonomy in the areas for which it is responsible. While teams are often formal and official work groups, many times these teams are not officially created but simply form from among organization members to address a problem or issue that arises. Ouchi describes the function of quality control circles:

> What they do is share with management the responsibility for locating and solving problems of coordination and productivity. The circles, in other words, notice all the little things that go wrong in an organization—and then put up the flag. (1981:223)

A team approach is central to Theory Z–type organizations in both the United States and Japan. In the United States, the Theory Z organization's focus on consensus decision making is usually implemented at the small-group level within the large organization. Ouchi describes the typical participative decision-making structure and process as it has been adapted in the West:

> Typically, a small group of not more than eight or ten people will gather around a table, discuss the problem and suggest alternative solutions. . . . The group can be said to have achieved a consensus when it finally agrees upon a single alternative and each member of the group can honestly say to each other member three things:
>
> 1. I believe that you understand my point of view.
> 2. I believe that I understand your point of view.
> 3. Whether or not I prefer this decision, I will support it, because it was arrived at in an open and fair manner. (Ouchi 1981:36–37)

Our earlier discussion of organizational culture suggested that there is less ambiguity and conflict when there is an integrated and homogeneous organizational culture. In addition, it suggested that there is less organizational conflict when the external cultural experiences of organization members are similar to and compatible with the culture of the organization. The Japanese cultural value of collective decision making and collective responsibility is reflected in and quite compatible with Japanese organizational culture based on long-term employment, trust, and close personal relationships.

A significant limitation of Theory Z organizations both in Japan and in the United States is their difficulty in dealing with cultural diversity. They tend to depend on a homogeneous internal organizational culture. This in turn makes it unlikely that people will be brought into the organization if they come from external cultures that are diverse. The consensus and modified consensus approaches discussed earlier also depended on or assumed a high degree of homogeneity among organizational members, at least in terms of organizational goals, philosophy, and values. While consensus, modified consensus, and Theory Z organizations reflect many values consistent with alternative paradigm perspectives and with the core concerns of social work, their reliance on similarity rather than diversity is a major limitation.

Total Quality Management (TQM)

Total Quality Management (TQM) "is a management approach to long-term success through customer satisfaction. TQM is based on the participation of all members of an organization in improving processes, products, services, and the culture they work in" (Bennett et al. in Colon 1995:105). *TQM principles* include:

1. A focus on the consumer of the organization's services
2. Involvement of everyone in the organization in the pursuit of quality
3. A heavy emphasis on teamwork
4. Encouragement of all employees to think about and pursue quality within the organization
5. Mistakes are not to be covered up but are to be used as learning experiences/opportunities
6. Workers are encouraged to work out problems solvable at their level and not to pass them along to the next level
7. Everyone is on the quality team and everyone is responsible for and encouraged to pursue quality (Ginsberg 1995:20).

Learning Organizations

The concept of a learning organization is an attempt to go beyond the notions of total quality management, especially the notion of adapting to changes as they occur. According to Hodgetts et al. **learning organizations** "not only *adapt* to change, but they *learn and stay ahead of* change" (1994:12). A learning organization is characterized by:

1. An intense desire to learn about itself
2. A strong commitment to generating and transferring new knowledge and technology
3. Openness to the external environment
4. Values that emphasize shared vision and systems thinking
5. Focus on interrelationships among factors and long-term rather than short-term approaches to problems (Hodgetts, et al. 1994:12–13).

Learning culture

Barrett (1995:40) provides a helpful list of competencies characteristic of organizational cultures that support and nurture a learning environment. These competencies include:

1. *Affirmative Competence.* The organization draws on the human capacity to appreciate positive possibilities by selectively focusing on current and past strengths, successes, and potentials.
2. *Expansive Competence.* The organization challenges habits and conventional practices, provoking members to experiment on the margins, makes expansive promises that challenge them to stretch in new directions, and evokes a set of higher values and ideals that inspire them to passionate engagement.

3. *Generative Competence.* The organization constructs integrative systems that allow members to see the consequences of their actions, to recognize that they are making a meaningful contribution, and to experience a sense of progress.

4. *Collaborative Competence.* The organization creates forums in which members engage in ongoing dialogue and exchange diverse perspectives.

These levels of competence are quite compatible with alternative paradigm thinking generally and alternative thinking about organizational life more specifically. For example, they focus on strengths-based thinking and collaborative approaches. These competencies also reflect a postmodern or deconstructive tone in their call to focus on the margins of organizational discourse in order to be more inclusive of diverse perspectives and as a source of creative solutions beyond the status quo.

Global Issues

In addition to changing realities about organizational and work life in the United States, we must begin to recognize and respond to the global nature of our everyday lives. We are more than ever citizens of the planet Earth, in addition to being inhabitants of the United States. For example, Illustrative Reading 8.1 provides detailed information on the organization and implementation of refugee camps internationally. One approach to thinking globally within the corporate world which seems applicable to social workers seeking excellence in the organizations we work for and administer is that of the world-class organization.

World-Class Organizations

A number of researchers and futurists interested in the rapidly changing and increasingly international and global nature of organizational environments are advocating the concept of world-class organization. Hodgetts et al. define a **world-class organization** as "the best in its class or better than its competitors around the world, at least in several strategically important areas" (1994:14). Thus, these writers believe that "any organization, regardless of size or type, can be world-class." World-class organizations include the characteristics of both total quality organizations and learning organizations (see discussions of TQM and the learning and intelligent organization). According to Hodgetts et al. (1994:14–18) world-class organizations, however, can be distinguished by additional characteristics or additional emphasis on characteristics of both total quality and learning organizations. Such organizations have:

- A customer-based focus, similar to a TQM organization, but also include:
  - Shared vision for customer service
  - Shared ownership of the customer service tasks and solutions
  - Organizational structure, processes, and jobs designed to serve the customer
  - Empowered teams for generating new ideas and approaches to improve customer service
  - Information systems designed to monitor and predict the changing needs of the customer
  - Management systems that ensure prompt translation of the customers' requirements to organizational actions

- Compensation systems designed to reward employees for excellent service to customers
▶ Continuous improvement on a global scale
  - Emphasize global nature of learning
  - Utilize global networking, partnerships, alliances, and information sharing
▶ Fluid, flexible or "virtual" organization
  - Respond quickly, decisively, and wisely to changes in the environment
  - Depend on outside partnerships and temporary alliances
  - Develop a fluid, flexible, and multiple-skilled workforce
▶ Creative human resource management
  - Effectively energize employee's creativity in decision making and problem solving
  - Constant training ("goof around and learn")
  - Effective reward systems: positive recognition for success; recognition is open and publicized throughout the organization; recognition carefully tailored to the needs of the employee; rewards are given soon after they are earned; relationship between performance and reward is understood by everyone in the organization
▶ Egalitarian climate
  - Value and respect for everyone: employees, consumers, owners, suppliers, community, and environment
  - Shared vision/information
  - Holistic view of employees
  - Open communication
  - Business ethics, community citizenship
  - Environment-friendly systems
  - Mentoring, coaching, buddy system
  - Employee involvement participation
  - Sponsor of community, wellness, and family programs
▶ Technological support
  - Computer-aided design (CAD) and manufacturing
  - Telecommunications networks
  - Database systems
  - Interorganizational communication systems
  - Multimedia systems
  - Continuous technical training (adapted from Hodgetts et al. 1994: 14–18).

Managing Diversity

R. Roosevelt Thomas, Jr., a scholar who addresses diversity in organizations, has done extensive research and consultation related to the realities of diversity in American corporations. Based on this research and experience he has developed an approach to organizations and management called "managing diversity" (MD). He defines this approach as a "'way of thinking' toward the objective of creating an environment that will enable all employees to reach their full potential in pursuit of organizational objectives" (Thomas 1991:19). Other proponents of MD suggest that it means recognizing that individuals are different and that this diversity can be a strength rather than a weakness for organizations. Advocates of MD also stress that managing diversity is necessary to deal with current labor force and workplace realities.

Thomas (1991) suggests that managing diversity goes beyond affirmative action approaches and recognizes the growing tendencies among employees to celebrate their differences. He suggests that while affirmative action was and continues to be necessary, it can only help get minorities and women into an organization. It cannot ensure that once in an organization they will be able to reach their full potential. The goal of managing diversity is "to develop our capacity to accept, incorporate, and empower the diverse human talents of the most diverse nation on earth" (Thomas 1990:17). MD is an approach that can pick up where affirmative action leaves off.

More recently Thomas (1996) has extended his work on managing diversity to include what he refers to as "redefining diversity" from an organizational perspective. He suggests that a full definition of diversity must include not only differences, but similarities as well. "Diversity refers to any mixture of items characterized by differences and similarities," according to Thomas. He stresses the importance of understanding the "diversity mixture," which includes not only people but any other aspects of the organization as well. These other aspects can include product lines (or services), functions, marketing strategies, or operating philosophies.

Thomas also "has suggested that current notions of diversity need to be broadened to go beyond mere representation to a focus on diversity management: 'making quality decisions in the midst of difference, similarities, and related tensions.' " He suggests additionally that leaders of diverse organizations need to "become comfortable with tension and complexity" and "more strategic in their thinking, considering diversity issues in the context of mission, vision, and strategy" (2006, cited by Packard in Patti 2009:160).

This expanded notion of diversity is helpful in thinking about human behavior in the context of organizational environments because it requires us to be more completely inclusive in our thinking and actions. It requires us to include similarities as well as differences in the diversity mixture. In addition, it requires us to think about differences not only in terms of people, but also in terms of all of the activities of the organization. These activities include the services we provide to consumers, the marketing of those services, and the philosophies used by the organization to plan, deliver, and evaluate its operations.

The increasingly pluralistic workplace

According to the Hudson Institute, "the U.S. labor force will continue its ethnic diversification in the twenty-first century."

Labor Force Projections

- The number of persons working or looking for work is projected to increase by 17.4 million over the 2002–2012 period, reaching 162.3 million in 2012.
- The projected labor force growth will be affected by the aging of the baby-boom generation—persons born between 1946 and 1964.
- The growth rate of the 55 and older group is projected to be 4.1 percent, nearly 4 times the rate of growth of the overall labor force.
- It's anticipated that in 2012 youths will constitute 15 percent of the labor force.
- Prime-age workers—those between the ages of 25 and 54—will make up about 66 percent of the labor force.
- The 55 and older age group will increase from 14.3 percent to 19.1 percent of the labor force.

- Due to faster population growth resulting from a younger population, higher fertility rates, and increased immigration levels, the Hispanic labor force is expected to reach 23.8 million.
- White non-Hispanics will continue to make up about 66 percent of the labor force.

Principles of pluralistic management

Using the work of Crable, Kunisawa, Copeland, and Thomas, Nixon and Spearmon* outline a number of principles of pluralistic management. They define **pluralistic management** as "leadership that aggressively pursues the creation of a workplace in which the values, interests, and contributions of diverse cultural groups are an integral part of the organization's mission, culture, policies, and procedures and in which these groups share power at every level" (1991:156–157). Principles of pluralistic management include the following:

- Achieving a pluralistic work force is not only a moral imperative but a strategic one.
- Top management must make a commitment to create a pluralistic work force before fundamental structural and systemic changes can occur in the organizations.
- A genuinely pluralistic workplace means changing the rules to accommodate cultural differences in style, perspectives, and world views.
- The contemporary definition of diversity embraces groups of individuals by race; ethnicity; gender; age; physical characteristics; and similar values, experiences, and preferences.
- Cultural awareness and appreciation at the individual or group level are necessary but not sufficient conditions to transform an organization into a pluralistic workplace. Fundamental changes must take place in the institution's culture, policies, and administrative arrangements.
- Pluralistic managers value their own cultural heritage and those of others in the workplace.
- Pluralistic managers understand the value of diversity and seize the benefits that differences in the workplace offer.
- Pluralistic managers work to overcome barriers that hinder successful and authentic relationships among peers and subordinates who are culturally different from the mainstream stereotype.
- The empowerment of employees through career development, team building, mentoring, and participatory leadership is a cornerstone of the pluralistic workplace.
- Pluralistic management incorporates issues of diversity in organization-wide policies and practices and is not restricted to equal employment opportunity (EEO) policies and procedures.
- Skill in pluralistic management is an integral component of managerial competence.
- The ultimate goal of pluralistic management is to develop an organization that fully taps the human-resources potential of all its employees.

Nixon and Spearmon note that these principles "resonate with two central values of the social work profession: respect for the dignity and uniqueness of the individual and self determination" (1991:157).

*Nixon, R., and Spearmon, M. *Building a Pluralistic Workplace.* Copyright 1991, National Association of Social Workers, Inc. "Skills for Effective Human Services Management." Adapted by permission.

Diversity in Practice

Professional social workers understand how diversity characterizes and shapes the human experience, they are knowledgeable about the way social systems promote or deter people in maintaining and achieving health and well-being, and they use conceptual frameworks to guide assessment processes. Using Nixon and Spearmon's typology or framework, assess the level of pluralism that you believe best describes your college or university. Provide examples to support your assessment.

A typology of organizational progression to pluralism

Nixon and Spearmon (1991:157–158) offer a helpful four-level typology to assess an organization's level of progress toward being a truly pluralistic workplace.

Level 1: Token EEO organization. Hires people of color and women at the bottom of the hierarchy; has a few token (see definition of token in Chapters 7 and 9) managers who hold their positions only as long as they do not question organization policies, practices, mission, and so on.

Level 2: Affirmative Action Organization. Aggressively recruits and supports the professional development of women and people of color and encourages non-racist, non-sexist behaviors; to climb the corporate ladder, women and people of color must still reflect and fit in with policies, practices, and norms established by dominant white men.

Level 3: Self-renewing Organization. Actively moving away from being sexist and racist toward being pluralistic; examines its mission, culture, values, operations, and managerial styles to assess their impact on the well-being of all employees; seeks to redefine the organization to incorporate multiple cultural perspectives.

Level 4: Pluralistic Organization. Reflects the contributions and interests of diverse cultural and social groups in its mission, operations, and service delivery; seeks to eliminate all forms of oppression within the organization; workforce at all levels (top to bottom) reflects diversity; diversity in leadership is reflected in policymaking and governance structures; is sensitive to the larger community in which it exists and is socially responsible as a member of the community (Nixon and Spearmon 1991:157–158).

TECHNOLOGY, ORGANIZATIONS, AND SOCIAL POLICY

As in so many areas, technology is having a profound impact on the nature of organizations and organizational life. Technology may be seen as blurring the boundaries between organizational and community life in some ways. However, it might be more accurate to say that technology is providing organizations with alternative avenues for influencing community life and achieving organizational goals within communities. For example, the Internet can offer voluntary or civic sector organizations a very direct mechanism for communicating and achieving their purposes within communities.

Common concerns about the U.S. political process include decreasing voter turnout and increasing costs of campaigning, which make political office unattainable for many moderate- and low-income citizens. Both of these trends are particularly important to social workers, because political participation is a primary means of influencing social policy to improve the well-being of the populations we serve. Technology may offer help in increasing citizen involvement in the political process and making campaigning more affordable. Westen points out that "a 1996 AT&T poll reported that two-thirds of all Americans would use the Internet to find out more about political candidates if the information were available, and nearly half would rather vote by computer than from a polling booth" (Westen 1998).

However, as Westen notes, technology cannot determine the future and health of our democracy because "in the end, that outcome is determined by the spirit and skills of the people themselves. But technology can provide the electorate with the ability to make improved decisions" (Westen 1998). Clearly, the 2008 presidential campaign, especially the campaign of Senator, now President Barak Obama, used Internet connectivity (email, texting, Facebook, YouTube) to an unprecedented extent in organizing, funding, and promoting his campaign. For example, many have suggested that the greatly increased voter turnout among young people was in large part a result of his campaign's significant investment in communication and networking through the Internet.

SUMMARY/TRANSITION

In this chapter we explored definitions and historical perspectives on organizations generally, in addition to discussing a number of specific traditional and alternative perspectives on organizations. In considering traditional perspectives, scientific management, bureaucracy, human relations, and Theory X and Theory Y were discussed. Theory Y, systems, and contingency theory perspectives were discussed as somewhat mid-range perspectives having some characteristics or qualities of both traditional and alternative paradigms.

We addressed alternative organizational approaches within the framework of organizational culture. Using organizational culture as a backdrop, Michel's "Iron Law of Oligarchy," Iannello's critical perspective, consensus, and modified consensus organizational approaches were addressed. Network organizations, social change theories of organizations, and organizational leadership theories were also addressed as alternative to traditional organizational thinking. Theory Z, teams or quality circles, and managing diversity perspectives were also presented as alternative perspectives on organizations.

We concluded this chapter with the recognition that no single alternative perspective was entirely consistent with alternative paradigm principles or social work core concerns. The challenge we were left at the end of this chapter was to continue to search for newer alternatives that incorporate the separate strengths of alternative and traditional models while avoiding their shortcomings.

Professional Identity · **Ethical Practice** · **Diversity in Practice** · **Engage Assess Intervene Evaluate**

Log onto **www.mysocialworklab.com** to watch videos on the skills and competencies discussed in this chapter. (*If you did not receive an access code to* **MySocialWorkLab** *with this text and wish to purchase access online, please visit* www.mysocialworklab.com.)

PRACTICE TEST

1. In _____, managers are responsible for studying, defining, standardizing, and monitoring the tasks carried out by workers.
   a. bureaucracy
   b. management by objectives
   c. scientific management
   d. systematic management

2. Which of the following is consistent with Theory Y thinking?
   a. The average human being learns, under proper conditions, not only to accept but seek responsibility.
   b. Whether or not I prefer this decision, I will support it, because it was arrived at in an open and fair manner.
   c. The average human being has an inherent dislike for work and will avoid it if he/she can.
   d. none of the above

Practice Contexts

3. Organizations make decisions at any given point based on incomplete information and must make the best decision they can with the information they do have. This statement best describes _____.
   a. human relations theory   c. contingency theory
   b. decision theory   d. Theory Y

4. The notion of the entire society as the environment having an important and pervasive influence on the nature of organizations is an example of _____.
   a. the critical perspective
   b. open-systems theory
   c. organizational culture
   d. traditional paradigm perspective

5. How organization members communicate or interpret to others the organization's policies, practices and procedures would be an example of _____.
   a. Hawthorne effect
   b. organization culture
   c. organizational climate
   d. organizational communication norms

6. This type of organization is characterized by an expanded customer based focus, egalitarian climate, technical support and fluid, flexible or "virtual" organization:
   a. managing diversity
   b. intelligent organization
   c. pluralistic organization
   d. world-class organization

Diversity in Practice

7. This approach to organizational analysis and change includes the following themes: management interests are not universal, organizational forms do not have to be accepted as the natural order of things and organizational culture fosters the hegemony of dominant groups.
   a. empowerment approach
   b. critical approach
   c. social change approach
   d. diversity approach

8. Women in this career phase tend to focus on contributing to their organizations, families, and communities, and success for women in this career phase is about recognition, respect and living integrated lives.
   a. pragmatic endurance
   b. generative fulfillment
   c. reinventive contribution
   d. idealistic achievement

9. Some of the characteristics of the _____ leadership style include: listening, empathy, using persuasion rather than positional authority, broad conceptual thinking and visioning, a commitment to the growth of people, and building community.
   a. servant   c. visionary
   b. charismatic   d. transactional

10. An organization in which critical decisions are made by the entire membership and routine decisions are delegated horizontally within the organization would be an example of a _____.
    a. consensus organization
    b. modified consensus organization
    c. bureaucratic organization
    d. Theory X organization

Log onto **MySocialWorkLab** once you have completed the Practice Test above to take your Chapter Exam and demonstrate your knowledge of this material.

Answers

1) c 2) a 3) c 4) b 5) d 6) d 7) b 8) c 9) a 10) b

Shelter and Site Planning

Médecins Sans Frontières/Doctors Without Borders, Refugee Camp Project

Introduction

Refugees arriving in any specific area tend to settle down in different ways: often, they concentrate on an unoccupied site and create a 'camp'; at other times, they spread out over a wide area and establish rural settlements; and sometimes they are hosted by local communities (rural or urban). The latter two situations, also called 'open situations', occur less frequently than the first (see below and the Introduction to Part II).

A poorly planned refugee settlement is one of the most pathogenic environments possible. Overcrowding and poor hygiene are major factors in the transmission of diseases with epidemic potential (measles, meningitis, cholera, etc.). The lack of adequate shelter means that the population is deprived of all privacy and constantly exposed to the elements (rain, cold, wind, etc.). In addition, the surrounding environment may have a pronounced effect on refugee health, particularly if it is very different from the environment from which they have come (e.g. presence of vectors carrying diseases not previously encountered).

Camps usually present a higher risk than refugee settlements in open situations as there is more severe overcrowding, and less likelihood that basic facilities, such as water supply and health care services, will be available when refugees first arrive.[2,7] Relief work is more difficult to organize for very large camp populations, such as some of the Rwandan refugee camps in Zaire (Goma, 1994) which contained more than 100,000 refugees.

In order to reduce health risks, it is essential that site planning and organization takes place as early as possible so that overcrowding is minimized and efficient relief services are provided. Shelters must be provided as rapidly as possible to protect refugees from the environment, and infrastructure installed for the necessary health and nutrition facilities, water supply installations, latrines, etc. All this must be initiated within the first week of intervention.[3]

Relief agencies are usually faced with one of two possible situations: either the camp is already established with a refugee population that has spontaneously settled on a site prior to the arrival of relief agencies, or site planning is possible prior to their arrival, for example, when they are being transferred to a new camp.

Whichever is the case, prompt action must be undertaken to improve the site and its facilities; poor organization in the early stages may lead to a chaotic and potentially irreversible situation in regard to camp infrastructure, with consequent health risks. For example, lateral expansion of a site must be accounted for from the beginning in order to avoid overcrowding if refugee numbers increase.

Two possibilities: a refugee camp or integration into the host population

There is always a lot of discussion as to whether the formation of a refugee camp is acceptable, or whether resources would be better directed to supporting local communities who host refugees. The two main types of refugee settlement—camp or integration into the local population—each offer both advantages and disadvantages as laid out below:

Camp or Integration into the Local Population: Advantages and Disadvantages[7,8]

CAMP ADVANTAGES:
- Provides asylum and protection
- More suitable for temporary situation

Source: Reprinted with permission of Médecins Sans Frontières USA.

‣ Easier to estimate population numbers, to assess needs and monitor health status
‣ Some basic services are easier to organize (e.g. distributions, mass vaccinations)
‣ Allows visibility and advocacy
‣ Repatriation will be easier to plan

CAMP DISADVANTAGES:

‣ Overcrowding increases risk of outbreaks of communicable diseases
‣ Dependence on external aid, lack of autonomy
‣ Social isolation
‣ Little possibility of realizing farming initiatives
‣ Degradation of the surrounding environment
‣ Security problems within the camp
‣ Not a durable solution

INTEGRATION ADVANTAGES:

‣ Favors refugee mobility, easy access to alternative food, jobs, etc.
‣ Encourages refugee survival strategies
‣ Possibility of refugee access to existing facilities (water, health etc.)
‣ Enhances reconstruction of social/economic life and better integration in the future

INTEGRATION DISADVANTAGES:

‣ Population more difficult to reach, leading to difficulties in monitoring health needs
‣ Implementation of relief programs more complex, requires knowledge of local situation
‣ Risks destabilizing the local community, risk of tensions between local community and refugees

Health agencies are generally not involved in deciding between the two options. Every refugee situation is specific to itself. The main factors influencing the way in which they eventually settle are the number of refugees, the capacity for the local community to absorb them, the ethnic and cultural links between the refugee and local communities and the political and military situation. In practice, the predominant factor is the relationship between refugees and the local population.

It should, however, be pointed out that relief programs, particularly food aid may well play a role in attracting refugees into a camp situation even when integration would probably be a better option for them.

It is camp situations that are dealt with more specifically here, because camp populations are exposed to greater health risks. However, most of the principles described below may also be applied to open situations.

Site Planning

Site planning must ensure the most rational organization of space, shelters and the facilities required for the provision of essential goods and services. This requires supervision by experts (e.g. in sanitation, geology, construction, etc.) which must be integrated into the planning of other sectors, especially water and sanitation. It is therefore essential that there is coordination from the beginning between all the agencies involved and between the different sectors of activity, especially in an emergency situation when time is generally in short supply.

Site planning in refugee situations is normally the responsibility of UNHCR (or an agency delegated by UNHCR). As UNHCR is usually not present where there is an internally displaced settlement, another agency will have to take charge. Although health agencies will not always be involved in organizing a site, they should nevertheless make sure that this is undertaken correctly because of its direct influence on the subsequent health situation; it is therefore necessary to have an understanding of the basic principles of site planning.

As stated above, the possibilities in regard to site planning depend largely on which of the two refugee situations described will be encountered.

1. In most cases refugees have already settled on a site and planners may well be faced with chaotic conditions. The immediate priority must be to improve or reorganize the existing site, and in rare instances it may even be advisable to move the refugee population to another site (see below).

2. The ideal but far less frequently encountered situation is that where site planning can be carried out before the arrival of refugees on a new site. The most appropriate site layout may then be worked out in advance and in accordance with guidelines.

In both situations, the following principles must be respected as far as possible.

- Sufficient space must be provided for everybody: space for every family to settle with the provision of amenities (water and latrines) and other services, and access to every sector. High density camps should be avoided because they present a higher risk for disease transmission, fire and security problems.[2]
- Short-term site planning should be avoided, as so-called temporary camps may well have to remain much longer than expected (e.g. some Palestinian refugee camps have been in existence since 1947).[2] This means that consideration must be given to the possibilities for expansion should the population increase.[1]
- A few small camps (ideally circa 10,000 people) are preferable to one large camp because they are easier to manage and because they favor a return to self-sufficiency.[2] Unfortunately, this is rarely possible when there is a massive influx of refugees (e.g. the refugee movements in Rwanda and Burundi, 1993-94).
- Refugees should be involved and consulted. Their social organization and their opinions should be taken into account wherever possible.
- Local resources (human and material) and local standards should be employed whenever feasible. Seasonal changes (e.g. the rainy season) must also be taken into consideration.

Site Selection

The ideal site, responding to all requirements, is rarely available. The choice is generally limited, as the most appropriate areas will already be inhabited by local communities or given over to farming. In any case, relief agencies are seldom on the spot to select a site before refugees arrive.

However, there are certain criteria in regard to site selection which must still be taken into account.[1,9]

- Security and protection: the settlement must be in a safe area (e.g. free of mines), at a reasonable distance from the border, and from any war zones.
- Water: water must be available either on the site or close by.
- Space: the area must be large enough to ensure 30m^2 per person (see Table 1).
- Accessibility: access to the site must be possible during all the seasons (e.g. for trucks).
- Environmental health risks: the proximity of vector breeding sites transmitting killer diseases should be avoided as far as possible (e.g. tsetse fly for trypanosomiasis). Where such areas cannot be avoided, they must be treated.
- Local population: every effort should be made to avoid tensions arising between local and refugee communities; for instance, legal and traditional land rights must be respected.
- It is important that the terrain should slope in order to provide natural drainage for rainwater off the site[4].

Energy sources should also be considered when selecting a site, particularly as deforestation resulting from using wood for cooking fuel entails politico-ecological problems.

Site Organization

Once the site has been secured, the planning and location of the required infrastructure must be worked out. A map should be used and the road network drawn onto it. The area should then be divided into sections and locations decided for the different facilities. Good access by road to every section and each installation is essential for the transport of staff and materials (e.g. food and drugs) in order to ensure the different services are able to function.

Several factors should be taken into account in deciding the spatial organization of facilities and shelters (location and layout):

- space required per person and for each installation
- accessibility of services
- minimum distance required between facilities and shelters (see table 1)
- cultural habits and social organization of the refugee population (clans and extended families)
- ethnic and security factors, relationships among different sections/members of the community, etc.

Table 1	Some Quantified Norms for Site Planning[1,2]
Area available per person	30 m^2
Shelter space per person	3.5 m^2
Number of people per water point	250
Number of people per latrine	20
Distance to water-point	15 m max.
Distance to latrine	30 m
Distance between water-point and latrine	100 m
Firebreaks	75 m every 300 m
Distance between two shelters	2 m min.

Cultural and social traditions are a determining factor in ensuring refugee acceptance of the infrastructure and services provided, particularly in regard to housing, sanitation, burial places, etc. However, as the layout that might be preferred by the refugees is not always the one that would allow the most efficient delivery of aid, site planning generally requires compromise solutions that take into account the different points of view.[2]

Essential Installations

Essential installations are described in Table 2. Some are likely to be centralized:

▶ reception center
▶ health center
▶ hospital
▶ meeting place for home-visitors, etc.

Other facilities, such as health posts, latrines, washing areas, etc., should be decentralized. Care must be taken to ensure that there is sufficient space for such decentralized services in all the camp sub-divisions.

The location of health facilities must be carefully determined.

▶ The central health facility should be located in a safe and accessible place, preferably on the periphery of the site in order to avoid overcrowding and allow for future expansion. The space required depends on the type and desired capacity of the medical services to be provided.
▶ The hospital, if one is necessary, is usually an expansion of the in-patient service of the central facility. The criteria are thus similar but more space is required (in line with the number of beds). It is particularly important to plan space for water and sanitation facilities, as well as room for eventual expansion (e.g. outbreaks of disease).
▶ The peripheral health facilities should be centrally located within the areas they are to serve so as to ensure easy access. The number required depends mainly on the size of the population (e.g. 1 health post per 3,000–5,000 refugees).
▶ A site for a cholera camp must be identified in advance, separate from other health facilities. It must be large enough to ensure sufficient capacity for potential needs and be provided with adequate water and sanitation facilities.[6]

The Layout of Shelters

The way shelters are grouped has an important influence on the re-establishment of social life, on the use of latrines and water-points, and on security.

Table 2	Main Installations Required on Refugee Sites

- Roads and firebreaks
- Water supply and sanitation facilities (defecation areas, latrines, waste disposal pits, washing places, etc.)
- Health facilities: health center, health posts, hospital, pharmacy and site for cholera camp.
- Meeting place for home-visitors
- Nutritional facilities: therapeutic and supplementary feeding centers
- Distribution site and storage facilities (in separate locations)
- Administrative center, reception area
- Other community facilities: market, schools, cemetery, meeting places, etc.

In general, the site should be divided into smaller units for management purposes. For example, it could be divided into sectors of 5,000 and sections of 1,000 people. However, the formation of such units must take into account the existence of any groups within the population which may be mutually hostile.

Two main ways of grouping shelters are described:

1. The preferred method is to organize the site into basic community units, constituted by a number of shelters and community facilities (latrines, water-points and washing areas).[1,3] These basic units should correspond in design as closely as possible to that with which the refugees are most familiar. Examples for designing such community units are available in several reference books.[2,4,9]

2. Laying out shelters in lines and rows is another possibility, but is usually not recommended because this deprives families of personal space, and increases the distances to latrines and water-points. On the other hand, such a layout can be implemented quickly and is often preferred when there is a sudden and massive influx of refugees to cope with.

Since in most cases the population will have settled on a site before any site planning can be carried out, solutions will have to be sought for improving the situation.

- Usually, the site may be improved without moving all the shelters. A better organization of facilities, improving access to all sections of the camp, and carefully planning sections for new arrivals will decrease health risks and improve camp management,

- A thorough reorganization of the site (and most shelters) may sometimes be necessary, although radical change is usually not advised. Such reorganization should be considered when there is a real threat to refugee health from overcrowding or a danger of fire, etc. For example, it was decided to move and reorganize all shelters in the Rwandan camps for refugees from Burundi in 1993, in order to counter the high fire risk and to facilitate the management of relief assistance.

- Critical problems, such as a lack of water in the area, insecurity or potential danger resulting from the camp's proximity to the border, may present major obstacles to the camp remaining where it is. A move to a new site could then be considered, but the operational problems involved in a move and the social and psychological consequences for the population must be carefully weighed up in advance,

Shelter Provision

The objectives of providing shelters are: protection against the elements and against vectors, provision of sufficient housing space for families, and restoring a sense of privacy and security. Shelters are required in every refugee emergency; but the type and design of shelter, who constructs it and how long it should last will vary in every situation.[2]

However, some general principles may be concluded:[2]

- Shelters that have already been built by refugees or buildings occupied by them (e.g. schools) must be assessed. It is important that consideration is given to the amount of space available for each person, to ventilation (e.g. risk of respiratory infection) and for protection against rain, as these factors may entail significant health risks.

- Wherever possible, refugees should construct their own shelters and should receive material (including appropriate tools) and technical support to assist them in doing so.

▶ It is best to use suitable local materials where available. Special emergency shelters (e.g. tents) and pre-fabricated units have not yet proven practical because of their high cost and the problems of transporting them. It is also difficult to persuade refugees to accept something which is not within their cultural traditions. However, some types of prefabricated shelter are still being tested and may be suitable for use in the first weeks of an emergency.

▶ A minimum sheltering space of $3.5m^2$ per person is recommended in an emergency. However, different cultures have different needs.—Single-family shelters are preferable (unless multi-family units are traditional).

When Refugees First Arrive

The provision of shelter is a high priority. Immediate action should be taken to assess the arrangements already made and provide material for temporary shelters[2].

There are several common solutions for temporary shelters:

▶ Shelters built by the refugees themselves, with material found locally or distributed by agencies, are the most common solution.

▶ Tents may be useful when local material is not available and as very short term accommodation, but they are expensive and do not last long.

▶ Plastic sheeting may be used for constructing temporary shelters or to protect them. Methods for setting up plastic temporary shelters are described in guidelines.[5]

▶ Local public buildings, such as schools, may provide shelter initially but are not usually suitable for large numbers. They are a very temporary solution.

The Post-Emergency Phase

Temporary shelters should no longer be used after the emergency stage has passed; an early start must be made to constructing shelters made of more permanent material.

However, it must be acknowledged that there are certain constraints involved in such shelter construction programs.[10]

▶ Any shelter building or rehabilitation program takes time.

▶ Such programs are costly (although they may produce savings in other sectors).

▶ As there is a vast range of options for building shelters and a wide range of criteria have to be taken into account, such programs are complex to manage. This is a specialized job and requires expertise.

This can often become a highly political issue with local authorities obstructing the building of (semi-) permanent housing when they want to prevent refugees settling for a long period of time. Longer-term housing should be similar to that with which refugees are already familiar, but should also reflect local conditions.[2] The use of local material is preferable, but its availability may be problematic (e.g. degradation of the environment through deforestation).

In countries such as Afghanistan or the countries of Eastern Europe, where very low temperatures may be experienced in winter, shelter provision is essential for protection against the cold. Although a few solutions have been proposed (e.g. winter tents and the provision of heaters), this is a particularly difficult problem to deal with in an emergency situation.

Once time allows, traditional housing may be built, if the materials are available, and there are sufficient financial resources.

Principal Recommendations Regarding Shelter and Site Planning

▶ Site planning and improvement should take place as early as possible in order to minimize overcrowding and make it possible to organize efficient relief services.

▶ A site should be selected with a view to security, access to water, the provision of adequate space, environmental health risks, and the local population.

▶ Site planning must ensure the most rational organization of the available space in regard to shelters and the necessary facilities and installations. Where refugees have already settled on a site before any planning could be envisaged, it is not usually advisable to institute radical changes, but improvements and reorganization should be carried out.

▶ Small sites are preferred. The cultural and social patterns should be taken into account.

▶ The provision of material for temporary shelters is a high priority when refugees first arrive. These should preferably be single-family shelters, constructed out of local material (when available) by the refugees themselves.

Key References

1. Médecins Sans Frontières. *Public health engineering in emergency situations.* Paris: Médecins Sans Frontières, 1994.
2. UNHCR. *Handbook for Emergencies.* Geneva: UNHCR, 1982.

Other References

3. Toole, M J, Waldman, R J. Prevention of excess mortality in refugees and displaced populations in developing countries. JAMA, 1990, 263(24): 3296–302.
4. Simmonds, S, Vaughan, P, William Gunn, S. *Refugee community health care.* Oxford: Oxford University Press, 1983.
5. Oxfam. *Plastic sheeting.* Oxford: Oxfam, 1989.
6. Médecins Sans Frontières. *Prise en charge d'une épidémie de choléra en camp de réfugié.* Paris, Médecins Sans Frontières, 1995.
7. Harell-Bond, B, Leopold, M. *Counting the refugees: The myth of accountability.* [Symposium] London: Refugee Studies Programme, 1993.
8. Van Damme, W. Do refugees belong in camps? Experiences from Goma and Guinea, *The Lancet,* 1995, 346(8971): 360–2.
9. Kent Harding D. *Camp planning.* [draft]. Geneva: UNHCR, 1987.
10. Govaerts, P. *Report on UNHCR shelter workshop,* February 1993. [Internal report]. Brussels: Médecins Sans Frontières, 1993.

9

Perspectives on Community(ies)

CONNECTING CORE COMPETENCIES *in this chapter*

| Professional Identity | **Ethical Practice** | **Critical Thinking** | Diversity in Practice | **Human Rights & Justice** | Research Based Practice | Human Behavior | **Policy Practice** | Practice Contexts | Engage Assess Intervene Evaluate |

Each stop along our journey toward understanding human behavior and the social environment, thus far, has been important. In some respects, though, this chapter on community may be the most important. Such an assertion is not intended to lessen the importance of understanding human behavior at individual, family, group, organizational and global levels. Instead, the notions of community we explore here highlight the importance of these other levels by bringing them together into one arena.

In a sense we have been talking about community all through this book. Who we are as individuals is influenced greatly by the community contexts within which we live. Who we are as individuals significantly influences the nature of the communities in which we live. Families, groups, and organizations also carry out their lives and seek to fulfill their potential and goals in the context of community. Communities are an important element in complex global issues. All of these levels of human behavior are intricately intertwined with community. The core concerns of social work are interconnected with and define qualities of community to which social workers aspire. The dimensions of both traditional and alternate paradigms reflect ways of viewing community—albeit very different views. The very concept of paradigm or worldview reflects the elements that together form community (regardless of the nature of the specific elements). When Kuhn (1970) discussed paradigm shifts in the natural sciences (see Chapter 1), he did so using the language of community. The assumptions we made at the beginning of our journey about the relationships among ourselves, social work, and the people with whom we work are also essential relationships to consider in defining and giving meaning to community.

It is not an exaggeration to say that we cannot talk about social work in the spirit in which we have done so here without also talking about community. It is always within the context of community that we practice social work. The individuals, families, groups, and organizations with which we work are fundamental building blocks of community. Communities are also fundamental building blocks of nations around the globe. It is in response to the needs and demands of humans at these levels that we construct and reconstruct community.

Community is an inclusive but somewhat elusive concept for many of us today. Much has been written about the "loss of community" and about the "search for community." These notions suggest the significant changes occurring in people's views of community. They are also consistent with our attempts in this book to embark on a journey in "search" of more holistic ways of understanding HBSE. In this chapter we embark on a journey in search of community.

Community is where the individual and the social environment come together. An inclusive perspective on community can help social workers answer the perennial question confronting our field: "Should the resources and interests of social workers best be directed toward individual or social change?" The answer, it seems, is a resounding yes! We must focus on both—and that focus must simultaneously be directed internally to us and externally to the world around us. We can do nothing else, for each is contained in the other. We must change ourselves in order to change the world. As the world changes, we change (Bricker-Jenkins and Hooyman 1986). Community represents that level of human behavior at which we as individuals connect with the social or collective world around us.

As we explore notions of community both from traditional and alternative perspectives, we will see that as has been the case with paradigms generally, the kinds and quality of communities are influenced more by the worldviews of some of us than others. It will be our quest here to explore notions of community that will allow all members of communities to participate, learn from one another, and be represented in this important sphere of life. For community provides important opportunities and challenges to expressing individual and collective human differences as well as similarities.

HISTORICAL PERSPECTIVES ON COMMUNITY

How people have thought about community in the past was influenced by the dominant worldviews in place at the time. The ways in which we think about community presently are greatly influenced by the dominant paradigms of the historical periods in which we live, as are the ways we think about human behavior and the social environment generally.

The revolutionary changes in perspectives on the individual brought about by the Renaissance in Western Europe had a great impact also on perspectives on the individual's place in much of the larger collective world of community. Again, we are reminded that the individual and the social are indeed closely (even inseparably) interrelated. These revolutionary changes occurring in Western Europe had influence far beyond this relatively limited geographic region of the globe. The new paradigms of the Renaissance (you might recall from our discussion in Chapter 1) came to define and dominate the modern world. Central to this revolution was the belief in the centrality of the individual rather than of society or the collective.

Anthropologist David Maybury-Lewis (1992:68ff) believes this shift from the centrality of the collective to the individual had significant implications, positive and negative, for both family and community.

In addition to the implications of the Renaissance view of the supremacy of the individual, the emergence of modern science in the nineteenth century also had significant influence on the global environment of which human communities are a part. The emergent philosophy of science was based in large part on the assumption that the natural world existed to be mastered by and to serve humans. A belief in humans' right to exploit nature had religious roots as well. "Medieval Christianity also taught that human beings . . . were created in God's image to have dominion over this earth." These beliefs in the supremacy of humans over nature were in stark contrast to the worldviews of many tribal peoples, who saw strong interconnections and mutuality between humans and the other elements of the natural world as well as the spiritual world (Maybury-Lewis 1992:73).

A worldview focusing on mutual interdependence of individuals, families, communities, and the larger world rather than one based on individuality and exploitation of nature results in significantly different perspectives on the

From Community to Individual as Paramount

The glorification of the individual, this focus on the dignity and rights of the individual, this severing of the obligation to kin and community that support and constrain the individual in traditional societies . . . was the sociological equivalent of splitting the atom. It unleashed the human energy and creativity that enabled people to make extraordinary technical advances and to accumulate undreamed of wealth. (Maybury-Lewis 1992:68) place of community in the scheme of things. A worldview based on interdependence has much to teach us about how to live together with each other; how to create "a sense of community through intricate and time-tested webs of inclusion" (Utne 1992:2).

These alternative and historically older perspectives, from which we can learn much, have continued to exist, although they have been largely ignored in dominant worldviews. These alternatives represent, for the most part, roads not taken by the constructors of dominant paradigms as they defined what community is or should be. Examples of alternative perspectives continue to exist in the beliefs about and views of community held by many indigenous peoples in the United States and around the globe. Many of the alternate notions about community that we will explore here as "new" ways of thinking about community actually have their roots in ways of thinking about community that are much "older" than those views currently dominant. This is another way of recognizing that our journey to a more holistic understanding of community represents a completing of a circle through which we can begin anew to think about HBSE, rather than a linear notion of a journey that ends at a specific destination "at the end of the line" in the present.

DEFINING COMMUNITY

Community is a complex and multifaceted level of human behavior. It is made even more complex, and hence somewhat more difficult to define, because it is such an inclusive (and, as noted earlier, a somewhat elusive) concept. Definitions of community need to incorporate human behavior at the individual, family, group, and organizational levels. To do this we take the position here that there are multiple ways of defining community. Different definitions focus on different facets of communityness. Different definitions may also reflect varying degrees of consistency with the dimensions of traditional or alternative paradigms.

As we explore traditional and alternative perspectives on community, we will encounter a number of basic elements used to think about community. These basic elements will include such notions as **community as a collective of people.** This *includes individuals, groups, organizations, and families; shared interests; regular interaction to fulfill shared interests through informal and formally organized means; and some degree of mutual identification among members as belonging to the collective.*

Anderson and Carter (1990:95–96) suggest that community is a perspectivistic notion. This notion of multiple "perspectives," rather than a "single definition of" community is perhaps appropriate here because it implies that community is different things to different people. This broad notion allows inclusion of traditional as well as alternative perspectives as individuals, families, groups, and organizations come together or separate in distinct communities. It allows us to incorporate the multiple perspectives we have explored on all the other levels of human behavior throughout this book into our thinking about communities. For example, when we discuss the important roles of individuals in community, we can now think about the important roles played by all individual members, including women and men; people of color and white people; people with disabilities and temporarily able-bodied people; poor people and people who are financially well-off; old and young people; gay men, lesbians, bisexual, transgender, and heterosexual people. When we discuss the important roles played by families within the context of community, we can now think about alternative and diverse family forms, including gay and lesbian families and augmented or fictive families, as important elements of community in addition to traditional nuclear or simple extended family forms.

TRADITIONAL PERSPECTIVES

Community as Place

Perhaps the most traditional perspective on community is one that associates community first and foremost with a geographical location—a place, in which we carry out most of our day-to-day activities. Our hometown or our neighborhood, for example. Reiss offers a typical example of place-focused perspectives on community. He suggests that "a community arises through sharing a limited territorial space for residence and for sustenance and functions to meet common needs generated in sharing this space by establishing characteristic forms of social action" (1959:118).

Traditional perspectives on community as territory or space were used as a basis to describe both small rural communities and large urban cities. Dwight Sanderson (in Warren and Lyon 1988:258–260) described a rural community geographically as the rural area in which the people have a common center of interest (such as a village or town center) and a common sense of obligation and responsibility. Sanderson suggested a method developed by Galpin to locate the boundaries of rural communities. You locate the rural community by beginning at the village or town center and mark on a map the most distant farm home whose members do their business there (Sanderson in Warren and Lyon 1988:259).

Weber defined *city* as an economic marketplace or market settlement that was a specific geographic space. He defined **city** as a place where local inhabitants could satisfy an economically substantial part of their daily wants on a regular basis in the local marketplace. He saw city as a place in which both urban (city dwellers) and nonurban (people from the surrounding rural area) could satisfy their wants for articles of trade and commerce. These articles of trade were produced primarily in the local area surrounding the city or were acquired in other ways and then were brought to the city for sale (Weber in Warren and Lyon 1988:15–17). These notions of rural communities and cities as geographic locations (places) in which we carry out a variety of activities or functions to meet our needs are probably the most traditional ways we think of community.

Community as Function

Warren extends the perspective on community as place by describing in more detail the nature of the functions that are carried out in the place or space that is community. He suggests that **community** is *"that combination of social units and systems that perform the major social functions having locality relevance. In other words, by community we mean the organization of social activities to afford people daily local access to those broad areas of activity that are necessary in day-to-day living"* (1978:9).

Warren describes these activities or functions as five types:

1. local participation in production-distribution-consumption of necessary goods and services by industry, business, professions, religious organizations, schools, or government agencies.

2. socialization or the transmission of knowledge, social values, and behavior patterns to members by families, schools, religious organizations, and other units.

3. social control to influence members' behaviors to conform to community norms through laws, the courts, police, family, schools, religious organizations, and social agencies.

4. social participation in activities with other members through religious organizations, family and kinship groups, friendship groups, business, government programs, and social agencies.

5. mutual support for community members in times of need through care for the sick, exchange of labor to help members in economic distress, and assistance for other needs by primary groups such as families and relatives, neighborhood groups, friendship groups, local religious groups, social service agencies, insurance companies, and other support units. (Warren 1978:10–11)

Community as Middle Ground, Mediator, or Link

Community has often been viewed as a kind of "middle ground" or context in which individuals' "primary relationships" such as those in family and close friendship groups come together with their "secondary relationships," which are more specialized associations such as those in formal organizations (work, school, religion). This notion of community suggests that community is that place where the individual and the society meet.

Warren (1978:9) stresses the linkages between the people and institutions of a local community and the institutions and organizations of the larger society. Another aspect of this approach, especially when combined with the notion of community as that location in which all our daily needs are met, is that community is a microcosm of society. It is an entity in which we can find, on a smaller or local basis, all the structures and institutions that make up the larger society (Rubin in Warren and Lyon 1983:54–61). As we will see later when we explore alternative perspectives on community, significant questions have been raised about whether this is a realistic or necessary way of perceiving community.

Community as Ways of Relating

Another traditional approach to community shifts the central focus on community from the relatively concrete or instrumental notions of geographic place or a set of specific functions to a much more interactional or affective focus on community as ways people relate to each other. This is a much more affective- or "feeling"-focused way of defining community. As we will see, this perspective on community offers a number of avenues for expanding our notions of community to include alternative, more inclusive views of what community means.

This approach to community focusing on the ways members relate to one another emphasizes identification or feelings of membership by community members and feelings by others that a member is in fact a member. This notion also stresses sharedness. It emphasizes feelings of connectedness to one another on the part of community members. This perspective on community can be referred to as a sense of "we-ness" or a "sense of community" that is felt by members.

Ferdinand Tönnies (in Warren and Lyon 1988:7–17) formulated what has become a classic way of describing two contrasting ways people relate to each other as members of collectivities. His formulations have often been used in relation to discussion of different ways people relate to each other in different community contexts. Tönnies's conceptualization is helpful here because while it focuses on ways of relating, it also lends itself to thinking about the nature of relationships that predominate in large urban communities compared to those in small rural communities. In other words, it allows us to incorporate place as well as relationships in our feelings about community. In addition, Tönnies's approach suggests a historical perspective on changes in the ways people have tended to relate to one another within community over time.

Tönnies's formulation is based on two basic concepts. One he referred to as gemeinschaft, the other he termed gesellschaft. **Gemeinschaft relationships** are ways of relating based on shared traditions, culture, or way of life and on a sense mutual responsibility arising out of that shared tradition. He associated gemeinschaft relationships with the ways people related to each other in small stable rural communities where people knew each other well, shared many past experiences, and expected to continue long relationships with each other into the future. He suggested gemeinschaft relationships were based on what he called natural will. **Natural will** reflected a quality of relationship based on mutuality in which people did things for one another out of a sense of shared and personal responsibility for one another as members of a collective.

Gesellschaft relationships, on the other hand, were ways of relating to each other based on a contractlike exchange in which one member did something for another in order for that person to return the favor in the form of needed goods, money, or services. This way of relating was based in what Tönnies referred to as rational will. **Rational will** reflected impersonal ways of relating not based on shared culture, tradition, or personal relatedness over time. Gesellschaft relationships were founded on the rational reality that people needed things from each other to survive, and to get those things one had to exchange goods, services, or money for them. Gesellschaft relationships were more likely to characterize life in large urban cities where people were not likely to know one another well or share a past with the people with whom they had to interact to get their needs met (Tönnies in Warren and Lyon 1988:7–17).

Tönnies believed that gesellschaft and gemeinschaft relationships could and often did exist simultaneously. Some needs were met contractually based on rational will and some were met out of a sense of mutual responsibility based on natural will. One form tended to predominate, however, depending on whether the community context was traditional and rural (gemeinschaft) or impersonal and urban (gesellschaft). Tönnies saw the emergence of capitalist industrial urbanized societies to replace traditional societies dominated by agrarian rural communities as a historical movement from gemeinschaft relationships predominating in collective life to their replacement by gesellschaft relationships (Tönnies:7–17 and Warren:2–3 in Warren and Lyon 1988).

Community as Social System

Notions of community as a social system offer a somewhat more comprehensive or holistic view of community than many of the other traditional notions. Like notions of community as relationship, approaches to community as a social system offer some helpful avenues to pursue as we search for more comprehensive and inclusive alternatives to traditional notions of community.

The advantages of a systems view of community are similar to the advantages of a systems view of some of the other levels of human behavior we have explored. A systems view allows us to see the various components or subsystems of communities—the individuals, families, groups, and organizations that make up communities. A social systems view allows us to recognize the influence on communities of other systems and subsystems in the larger environment—the influence of state and national governments on the local community, for example. A systems approach also acknowledges that influences among systems components and between communities and the environment are reciprocal. A systems view suggests that a community influences the larger environment at the same time that the community is influenced by the larger environment. In recognizing these reciprocal influences, a systems view can help us to appreciate the reality of ongoing change in community life. Perhaps an illustration of these reciprocal influences will help.

Prior to the Civil Rights Act of 1964, it was common practice for various community subsystems—local restaurants, hotels, service stations, or bus companies, for example—to deny their services or to provide inadequate services to African Americans. This discrimination had a direct impact on the day-to-day lives of many individuals in local communities. In response to this discrimination, individual African Americans began to organize themselves within their local communities and across many different communities and they began to demand equal access to community services. As more and more people began to demand change, their collective influence began to be felt at state and national levels.

At the state level a number of individual states reacted to these demands by attempting to silence the calls of their citizens for equal rights. At best, many states responded by doing nothing and continuing their discriminatory practices. The civil rights movement continued to grow from the acts of individual people in individual communities to a national movement that would not accept the unwillingness of state and local systems to change and provide equal services to African Americans. Instead, participation in the civil rights movement demanded that the national government intervene and stop the continued discrimination at the state and local level.

After much conflict and much time passed, the national government responded by creating and beginning enforcement of the Civil Rights Act. This national legislation had a direct influence on states and localities by making it unlawful to discriminate against people of color in public accommodations and services. In turn, as the Act began to be enforced, its influence was felt by many individual citizens. Individuals who had practiced discrimination against people of color in the areas covered by the Civil Rights Act now had to suffer consequences if they were found breaking the law. Individuals who had been discriminated against now knew they had the support of federal law in their efforts to obtain equal services.

ALTERNATIVE PERSPECTIVES ON COMMUNITY

Our efforts to explore alternative ways of knowing and viewing community will involve a number of the dimensions of alternative paradigms we outlined in Chapter 2. It will include interpretive, intuitive, qualitative, subjective approaches, feminist perspectives, diversity-focused visions, personal and integrative perspectives, and perspectives addressing oppression and discrimination in community. Our journey will use as points of departure a number of the elements of traditional perspectives on community as well. Some parts of our journey will involve looking in different ways at some of the traditional perspectives on community. In our search for alternatives, as was suggested earlier, we will return to some older visions of community held by indigenous peoples in various parts of the globe.

Alternative Approaches to Community

Ethical Practice

Professional social workers are knowledgeable about the value base of the profession. As you read and reflect on the alternative approaches to community that make up this section, give an example for each approach to illustrate how it reflects specific social work values. Did you find any approaches that you believe are inconsistent with social work values?

As the 1990s became the early 2000s, a number of exciting developments emerged in thinking about community and its role in the daily life of individuals and families and in the larger society of which community is a building block. This new thinking (or rethinking) about community presents some important possibilities for social workers as we work to assist communities and their members in using their assets to achieve both individual and collective well-being. This new thinking offers more holistic or comprehensive approaches to understanding many interrelated elements of community life than in the past. These approaches have far-reaching implications for virtually all the competencies and professional practice behaviors (see Table 1.1 on page 4) that make up social work education and practice: not just human behavior and the social environment. These new developments integrate theoretical approaches to understanding community (the knowledge base) with policy and practice approaches to bring about positive community changes that are consistent with social work values and ethics. In addition, these alternative approaches reinforce the connections to well-being at the individual, family, group, organization, community, and global levels. Among the concepts and approaches that make up this exciting new direction for understanding and intervening in and with communities are:

- Community building
- Community renewal
- Community assets and strengths
- Social capital
- Civic ethic and civil society

SEHB and Community: Poverty Reduction

One of the most promising themes that flows through these concepts and approaches is of fundamental concern to social workers: poverty reduction. As we have indicated in other chapters, the theme of poverty reduction is of critical importance to social work because it is at the core of so many of the other concerns that social workers attempt to address such as infant mortality, substance abuse, violence, racism and sexism, child abuse and neglect, hunger, homelessness, and teen pregnancy. Poverty reduction is also a theme that unites our efforts across all system levels—individual, family, group, organization, community, and society.

As is so often the case, many of these newer alternative approaches to community strengths and needs by addressing the overarching issue of poverty really take us back to social work history—a history that was first and foremost about addressing human needs resulting from lack of physical and social resources. However, these alternative approaches also integrate new developments in strengths-based and assets-based theory and practice that have emerged in the profession only recently. Next we will explore some of these alternative developments in thinking about community.

Community Building/Community Renewal

A new response to poverty reduction at the community level is "known as **community building**; its goal is overhauling the nation's antipoverty approach and creating communities that work for the low-income families who live there" (Walsh 1997). Community building is also referred to as **community renewal**. Walsh stresses that community building takes a more comprehensive approach to poverty in theory and practice because it goes beyond analyzing poverty only in terms of jobs or income "but [also] as a web of interwoven problems—poor schooling, bad health, family troubles, racism, crime, and unemployment—that can lock families out of opportunity, permanently." In addition, community-building initiatives work toward poverty reduction at multiple levels to address economic, social, and political marginalization that locks people and communities into poverty (1997).

Ewalt, a social worker, stresses that "it is clear that redeveloping impoverished communities requires a multifaceted approach that addresses the physical and economic conditions of neighborhoods as well as the social and cultural aspects" (1998b). Such strategies also acknowledge the "linkages and interconnectedness among the various strands of an individual's life and of the importance of family and neighborhood influences in determining individual level outcomes" (Connell et al. in Naparastek 1998:12). This recognition of the multilayered and ever-changing influences of the larger social environment on individual development is consistent with life-course theory discussed in Chapter 5.

Central to community building or community renewal is the idea "that the path toward individual, neighborhood, and corporate renewal is indivisible from or, at the very least, dependent on efforts to rebuild a sense of community. Ultimately, the culture of renewal represents the individual American's revived search for meaning—but within the context of community" (Louv 1997).

Strengths/assets

The concept of community building also conveys an asset rather than a deficit approach to poverty reduction consistent with alternative paradigm thinking. For example, it uses a metaphor of "building"—a constructive concept—rather than earlier and traditional metaphors, such as that used in 1960s-era approaches to poverty reduction which often referred to as "the war on poverty." As Walsh points out, "war is about destruction, community building is about creation" (1997). Community building uses the existing assets of poor communities as the foundation for development. This approach focuses first "on the strong institutions, associations, and individuals that still exist in poor communities—from schools and churches to the corner grocer who employs teenagers and the stay-at-home mom who watches latchkey kids—rather than focusing solely on deficits like crime, unemployment, or school failure" (Walsh 1997).

People- and Place-Based Strategies

Another indication of the comprehensive or holistic approach taken by community builders is the attempt to reunite what Walsh refers to as the traditional split "between 'people' and 'place' strategies." Traditional antipoverty approaches tended to be divided into two parts: "human services—the 'people'

people, [that] focused on the education, family support, and health care needs of the poor—and the 'place' strategists, the community development field that focuse[d] more on rebuilding neighborhoods—with housing, retail development, and attempts at job creation—than on human development" (Walsh 1997).

Naparastek points out the mutually reinforcing nature of an approach integrating both people- and place-based strategies: "A community-building approach looks at the whole picture, acknowledges the interconnectedness of people- and place-based strategies, and recommends a course of action in which solutions are tied together in such a way that they reinforce one another" (1998:11). Such approaches can help improve the effectiveness of community-based social work practice. "Linking place- and people-based strategies through community-building has significant implications for social work, because it means improving the delivery and quality of human services, strengthening community organization, stimulating economic development, and in every possible way improving the quality of life of residents while affecting physical improvements," according to Naparastek (1998:11).

Community Building and Physical Environment

Policy Practice

Part of our responsibility as professional social workers is to analyze, formulate, and advocate for policies to advance social wellbeing. How do the preceding approaches to community building and revitalization reflect policies or programs that advance social wellbeing at the community level? Give two specific examples.

A significant part of place-based community building involves the actual physical design of homes and neighborhoods. Community building strives for physical construction of homes and neighborhoods that support the creation of a "sense of community." This focus on physical design is referred to as an architecture of community renewal. Examples of these innovative design changes include:

- Placing the garage or carport around back, or hiding it on the side of the structure
- Building houses with front porches to increase interactions with neighbors and a sense of community
- Clustering housing and offices closer together so workers might be able to walk to their jobs
- Using mass transit rather than cars (Louv 1996)

Louv suggests that the design of schools today should support a sense of community but often do not: "Schools in the late 19th and early 20th centuries strove for stateliness and grandeur. . . . Looking at the typical suburban school, one wants to exhort it: 'Buck up! Show some pride! Remember that you're crucial to the community!' " Another innovative design approach is to "allow each single-family house to have a garage apartment or cottage at the rear of its lot. . . . [So grandparents] may be available for baby-sitting and other household assistance, but without the frictions of sharing their children's living quarters 24 hours a day. . . . These apartments also can be used by grown sons and daughters, especially after a divorce or a job layoff" (1996).

Comprehensive Community Initiatives

Holistic and integrative approaches to community building and renewal are often referred to as **comprehensive community initiatives (CCIs)**. Ewalt cites the definition of comprehensive community initiatives (CCIs) by Kubisch, Weiss, Schoor, and Connell.

Comprehensive Community Initiatives (CCI) Definition

CCIs contain several or all of the following elements and aim to achieve synergy among them: expansion and improvement of social services and supports, such as child care, youth development, and family support; health care, including mental health care; economic development; housing rehabilitation and/or construction; community planning and organizing; adult education; job training; school reform; and quality-of-life activities such as neighborhood security and recreation programs. (Ewalt 1998b:3)

To make these new comprehensive community-building approaches work and for social workers to become effective in helping them work, Naparastek and Dooley suggest the need for linking community building "to social work practice in a form that requires competence in the processes of place-based and people-based strategies; . . . the need for social work practitioners who are familiar with community theory and community organizations, who understand the processes of physical and economic development, and who have core knowledge of social work values and commitment to grassroots participation" (Naparastek 1998:14).

Community-building principles

The National Community Building Network, formed in 1993 by a number of private foundations (Ford, Casey, and Rockefeller) and other community-building initiatives, developed a set of eight principles to guide community-building efforts:

1. Integrate community development and human service strategies. Traditional antipoverty efforts have separated "bricks and mortar" projects from those that help families and develop human capital; each approach needs the other to be successful.

2. Forge partnerships through collaboration. Building community requires work by all sectors—local residents, community-based organizations, businesses, schools, religious institutions, health and social service agencies—in an atmosphere of trust, cooperation, and respect.

3. Build on community strengths. Past efforts to improve urban life have too often addressed community deficits; our efforts build on local capacities and assets.

4. Start from local conditions. There is no cookie-cutter approach to building community; the best efforts flow from and adapt to local realities.

5. Foster broad community participation. Many urban programs have become professionalized and alienated from the people they serve; new programs and policies must be shaped by community residents.

6. Require racial equity. Racism remains a barrier to a fair distribution of resources and opportunities in our society; our work promotes equity for all groups.

7. Value cultural strengths. Our efforts promote the values and history of our many cultural traditions and ethnic groups.

8. Support families and children. Strong families are the cornerstone of strong communities; our efforts help families help themselves. (Walsh 1997)

These eight principles provide a framework for understanding newer approaches to community development and revitalization.

Economic Perspectives on Community: Capital/Assets

Driving these new approaches to community renewal is a growing recognition on the part of social workers and others that poverty reduction at the individual, family, and community level is to a very great extent about assessing, using, and growing assets. "Asset building is a new way of thinking about antipoverty strategies; its emphasis on resources rather than problems has much in common with the strengths perspective in social work practice and policy development" (Page-Adams and Sherraden 1997:432). Assets involve multiple types: human, physical, and fiscal. The concept of assets and asset development is closely related to the concepts of human, economic, and social capital discussed in sections that follow. A shift to an assets-based practice and policy framework would cause a paradigm shift in the profession that would result in social workers advocating for policies that "invest in people instead of programs" (Beverly 1997:23ff).

A number of years ago, "Sherraden (1988, 1990, 1991) suggested that households and communities develop not by income alone (the dominant theme of the welfare state), but also by savings and asset building. In this usage, the term 'assets' is restricted to the concept of wealth, including both property and financial holdings" (Page-Adams and Sherraden 1997:423). "Sherraden proposed a system of individual development accounts (IDAs)—matched savings for purposes such as education, home ownership, and small business development" (Page-Adams and Sherraden 1997:423–24). Based on evaluation of asset development programs, Yadama and Sherraden concluded that "it appears that assets lead to more positive attitudes and behaviors, and the same attitudes and behaviors lead to more assets" (in Ewalt, 1998a:68).

In addition to Individual Development Accounts (IDAs) to be used for home ownership, educational investments, or small business development, Sherraden also foresees other types of asset development accounts such as Individual Training Accounts (ITAs) to be used by individuals to invest in human capital development through education and training chosen by individuals to meet their education and training needs. Beverly and Sherraden note that the Council on Adult and Experiential Education and participating employers who set up ITAs for their employees "have found that workers make much better use of these training funds than of training that is offered *en masse* to all employees. Because the money is 'theirs' workers make careful choices about how to invest in themselves, and they are committed to the training" (1997:24).

Types of Capital: Financial, Human, Social, and Cultural

Consistent with the community-building principle of combining or integrating both "people-" and "place-based" strategies is the increasing concern over the multiple types of capital necessary to comprehensively address poverty at the personal, family, and community levels. While there are numerous types of capital, perhaps the three most common and relevant for social workers are: financial (or economic), human, and social capital. Cultural capital is a more recent addition to the types of capital.

Financial capital

Financial capital refers to money or property that is available for investment or "use in the production of more wealth" (*Webster's* 1995). In other words, financial capital is resources available to use to create more resources. It is interesting that for a profession with a long history of concern for reducing poverty, we have been so hesitant to incorporate the concept of financial capital and capital or asset creation in the policies and programs we support. It would seem fundamental that many of the multitude of difficulties poor people face result from inadequate financial capital—they do not have access to the resources necessary to accumulate financial capital. A growing number of social workers are working to incorporate concepts such as capital and assets into social work programs and policies. For example, growing interest in social development in social work, both in the United States and internationally, reflects this increasing recognition of the importance of economic assets to individual and collective well-being. Midgley points out that "social development is characterized by the integration of social and economic processes and the promotion of the social welfare of all. At the same time, social development is 'particularly concerned with those who are neglected by economic growth or excluded from development'" (Midgley in Beverly and Sherraden 1997:3).

Human capital

Human capital refers "to an individual's skills, knowledge, experience, creativity, motivation, health, and so forth. . . . Like other forms of 'capital,' human capital is expected to have future payoffs, frequently in the form of individual employment opportunities, earnings, and productivity in market and non-market sectors" (Beverly and Sherraden 1997:1–2). Beverly and Sherraden suggest that unlike financial capital, human capital can be used, but it cannot be used up because "individuals cannot be separated from their knowledge, skills, and other individual attributes" (Beverly and Sherraden 1997:2).

The concept of human capital is of significance to social workers interested in alternative approaches and policies concerned with poverty reduction because it "represents a broad social development strategy" and because it is strengths- and assets-based (Beverly and Sherarden 1997:3). Beverly and Sherraden argue that "because social workers have traditionally advocated for improvements in social welfare and have a particular concern for those who are marginalized, it is particularly appropriate to promote investments in human capital [and] . . . investments in human capital have the potential to integrate economic development with improvements in social welfare" (1997:25–26).

Human capital is also an important concept for social workers because there is a great deal of empirical evidence that building human capital has positive outcomes for people in areas such as improved employment opportunities, higher wages, and better fringe benefits (health insurance, retirement benefits, etc.). In addition, other assets accrue for individuals as a result of increases in human capital, including increased savings, improved health outcomes, and improved access to and use of social resources such as information and influence. Communities also benefit from increases in the human capital held by their members. For example, Beverly and Sherraden note that community members with higher levels of education are more likely to volunteer, make charitable donations, and participate in political activities in their communities. Communities with better-educated members also tend to be more economically viable. Finally, Beverly and Sherraden also note intergenerational benefits to increases in human capital holdings. Increased levels of human capital on the part of mothers has a positive impact on the health of their children. Children of parents with higher levels of education generally obtain more education for themselves than their peers with less well educated parents (Beverly and Sherraden 1997:3–10).

All these positive outcomes suggest that social workers would do well to use human capital theory as a significant policy and practice framework. Beverly and Sherraden argue that the social work "profession should consider the formation of human capital as a central commitment and organizing theme. . . . Social work practice . . . should be viewed not merely as an endeavor to solve problems, but also as an opportunity to build human capital—in knowledge, skills, experience, credentials, position, health, physical ability, mental cap[a]city, and motivation—that can contribute to future well-being" (1997:16). These authors also suggest some quite specific and concrete areas in which social workers can help the people with whom we work build their human capital at both policy and practice levels. These areas include working to increase investments in early childhood development, including advocating for basic nutrition and health care for all preschool children because good nutrition in infancy and early childhood can offset some of the learning difficulties faced by many poor children. Advocating for increased financial support for college education, vocational education and training (including computer and information technology training), and lifelong learning is also important (Beverly and Sherraden 1997:17–23).

Social capital

One of the most engaging concepts and a cornerstone of the new or alternative community theory is that of social capital. Understanding the meaning, significance, and use of this core concept can help us link social work principles and values to the new work on community building and renewal. It can also help us appreciate the mutually reinforcing and interrelated nature of human behavior at the individual, family, group, organizational, community, and societal levels.

"The term **social capital** has been used for about forty years to describe resources that are neither traditional capital (money or the things money buys) nor human capital (skills or know-how). . . . *Social capital refers, then, to resources stored in human relationships, whether casual or close*" (emphasis added, Briggs 1997). It "is the stuff we draw on all the time, through our connections to a system of human relationships, to accomplish things that matter to us and to solve everyday problems" (Briggs 1997). "Defined simply, it consists of networks and norms of civic engagement" (Wallis et al. 1998). Social capital means "the sum of our informal, associative networks, along with social trust—the degree to which we feel we can expect strangers to do right by us" (Lappé and DuBois 1997).

Social capital is closely related to both financial and human forms of capital. For example, "businesses have never thrived, nor have economies flourished, without social capital. Not that social capital is an adequate substitute for the other kinds of capital. . . . Rather, social capital makes the other kinds work well. It greases the gears of commerce, along with other areas of life" (Briggs 1997).

The concept of social capital is important in helping us understand both poverty and community development. It also has a significant role to play in empowerment approaches to reducing poverty and building strong families and communities (Wallis et al. 1998). According to Wallis et al., "in both the public and nonprofit sectors, there is growing belief that programs that empower communities strengthen the resources they can provide to individuals. From this perspective, community development and individual development are intertwined, and social capital suggests the substance that is both binding and created between them" (1998).

Robert Putnam, one of the early scholars to introduce the concept of social capital in the social sciences, stressed the connections between economic and social capital. Putnam concluded,

> after studying the role of informal relationships in economic success in Italy, that the "norms and networks of civic engagement contribute to economic prosperity and are in turn reinforced by that prosperity. . . . Chief among these norms is reciprocity, the willingness of people to help one another with the expectation that they in turn can call for help." (Wallis et al. 1998)

Warner suggests that the concept of social capital evolved from an initial individual and family emphasis to a community focus: "Early work on social capital focused at the individual or family level in an effort to understand how stocks of social capital contribute to individual education or economic achievement." However, Warner notes that Putnam later explored the nature of social capital at the community level or "public" capital which resides in groups or networks of groups within communities. This public- or community-based form of social capital comes about in the community through "organized spaces for interaction, networks for information exchange, and leadership development" (1999:375).

According to Briggs, the concept of social capital is now used in connection with family, neighborhood, city, societal, and cultural system levels.

A number of scholars and practitioners who study and use the concept of social capital in their work stress that while the concept itself is value-neutral, the uses and impacts of social capital may be either negative or positive: "as a resource or means, social capital has no right or wrong to it until some judgment is made about the ends to which we put it. We covet social capital for the reasons that many people covet money: not for what it is but for what we can do with it" (Briggs 1997).

Wallis, for example, points out that "although social capital helps facilitate actions, those actions may be either beneficial or harmful. Social capital that benefits a narrowly defined social group may not benefit a larger social group or society in general" (1998). Briggs stresses that "social capital that benefits

Social Capital Helps Us "Get By"

It is used by individuals . . . to "get by" (for social support), that is, to cope with the everyday challenges that life presents, from flat tires to divorces. When we confide distress to a friend or listen as a confidante, social capital is at work, directly serving the person in distress but also renewing the relationship in ways that will, over time, be used by the speaker and the listener. When poor moms share caregiving tasks and rides to church along networks of relatives, friends, and acquaintances, they each draw on social capital. . . . These kinds of support often, but not always, come from people who are alike in race, class, and other terms. What is more, we are born into many of these supportive ties (to kin, for example). (Briggs 1997)

Social Capital Helps Us "Get Ahead"

Social capital is used for social leverage, that is, to change or improve our life circumstances, or "opportunity set." When we ask a friend who is "connected" to put in a good word as part of a hiring or grantmaking decision, or when an inner-city kid, through a personal tie, gets a shot at a life-changing scholarship, this too is social capital. (Briggs 1997) me may not benefit my neighbors. That is, individuals may further their own aims through social capital without doing much for the community at large" (1997). Briggs illustrates "that profitable youth gangs and mafia rings depend on social capital. Sweetheart corporate deals, including those that cheat taxpayers, depend as much on off-the-books social capital as they do on mountains of legal paperwork. The now impolitic 'old boy network' functioned, and still functions in many places, through trusting ties among the 'boys' involved, to the detriment of those excluded" (1997). Just as social capital can be used for negative or positive purposes, it is also not equally distributed among individuals and communities: "not all groups have equal access to social capital. Reserves of social capital are unevenly distributed and differentially accessible depending on the social location of the groups and individual who attempt to appropriate it" (Schulman and Anderson 1999).

Warner helps us understand both the multiple levels and linkages of social capital across system levels and its unequal distribution by outlining three forms of social capital:

1. Horizontal social capital is found "in communities where horizontal ties within community are strong and norms of broad community participation exist and tend to produce more egalitarian and robust democratic structures."

2. Hierarchical social capital "is characterized by patron—client relations (and gangs) which can stifle development and skew governmental and economic structure to the interests of a particular group."

3. Absence of social capital "is found in communities with few networks among residents: wealthy 'gated communities,' which substitute economic capital for social networks, and poor and isolated communities characterized by insecurity, fear, and isolation." (1999:374–5)

If social capital is to be a useful concept for social work policy and practice, two questions need to be asked. *First, can social capital be consciously created? Second, given the unequal distribution of social capital among individuals and communities, can the creation of social capital be facilitated by external entities such as governments?* Warner points out that government certainly has played a role in decreasing community opportunities and resources for social capital development, such as its "abandonment of inner city public institutions" and in rural areas through school consolidation, which results in loss of the personal, family, and local community networks necessary for social capital construction (1999:379–80). This being the case, she argues that governments can and should be active in supporting social capital development for poor rural and urban communities.

She suggests that "at the individual level [social capital is] formed within the bounds of family, work, and school. . . . In communities where forums for interaction no longer emerge as natural extensions of work, school, or play, they can be intentionally created and designed to encourage development of social capital to enhance community problem solving." Warner provides examples of intentionally creating or supporting "public spaces" that act as places for citizens to engage in conversations and activity to enhance community effectiveness and democracy. She suggests "these spaces may be incidental (sidewalks), voluntary (clubs and associations), or quasi-official (planning board hearings), but they must be relatively participatory to enable the communication essential for public democratic discourse." Through these mechanisms "the citizen becomes a producer as well as a consumer of community" (Warner 1999:376–379).

To facilitate the creation of social capital, governments must undergo a paradigm shift in the way they relate to communities: "Local government must shift from acting as controller, regulator, and provider to new roles as catalyst, convener, and facilitator. . . . Government programs are most effective in promoting community level social capital when they develop a facilitative, participatory structure and involve participant as partners, not clients, in program design." Warner illustrates the difference in traditional and alternative roles played by government entities by contrasting Head Start with its requirement that parents be involved in decision making through its policy councils with traditional hierarchical school decision making where most decisions are made by professionals rather than by parents (Warner 1999:384–9).

Warner also suggests the need for professionals, including social workers, to make fundamental changes in both their roles and their policies/programs. She suggests, for example, that programs which narrowly focus on individual social capital development such as parenting skills or job training "are unlikely to connect participants to broader community or extra-community resources." These kinds of "social services and community development programs are designed to address deficits rather than assets in communities. Highly professionalized services assume that the professional has the expertise while the client has the problem." Shifting to participatory, partnership-based management on the part of traditional social service agencies and schools will involve a significant paradigm shift. Warner notes that "participatory management represents a major organizational innovation for hierarchical, professionalized government structures" (Warner 1999:384–9).

The process of building social capital is similar to the concept of *synergy* in social systems thinking (see Chapter 3) in that "social capital is built up through repeated exchanges among people (or organizations) over time. It depends on regular borrowing and lending of advice, favors, information, and so on, and "depends on making regular deposits and withdrawals into a system of relationships, some of them quite casual, others very intimate" (Briggs 1997). The destruction or loss of social capital results from processes similar to those involved in entropic systems (see Chapter 3) in that "it breaks down through disuse as much as through the distrust that alienates" (Briggs 1997).

Spiritual Capital: Religion and Social Capital

Houses of worship build and sustain more social capital—and social capital of more varied forms—than any other type of institution in America. Churches, synagogues, mosques, and other houses of worship provide a vibrant institutional base for civic good works and a training ground for civic entrepreneurs. Roughly speaking, nearly half of America's stock of social capital is religious or religiously affiliated, whether measured by association memberships, philanthropy, or volunteering. Houses of worship run a variety of programs for members, from self-help groups to job training courses to singles' clubs.

Houses of worship also spend $15 to $20 billion each year on social services, such as food and housing for the poor and elderly. Regular religious services attenders meet many more people weekly than nonworshipers, making religious institutions a prime forum for informal social capital building.

Better Together: Report of the Saguaro Seminar on Civic Engagement in America, John F. Kennedy School of Government, Harvard University (Cambridge, MA: 2000). Available on-line from *bettertogether.org*

Bridging capital versus localized social capital

An important concept for understanding the dynamics of social capital creation and use for positive outcomes is **bridging capital**. In poor and "disenfranchised neighborhoods, there are often significant amounts of social capital. The problem is the lack of **bridging capital**, *or connections with people and institutions throughout the wider community*" (emphasis added, Wallis et al. 1998). Wallis notes that "Putnam distinguishes two types of social capital: **Localized social capital** 'accumulates in the course of informal social interactions that families and people living in communities engage in through their daily lives.' *Bridging capital* 'connects communities and organizations to others' (Wallis et al. 1998). Bridging capital also connects social capital with financial, physical (community buildings, businesses, schools, material goods, equipment, etc.), and human capital and serves to mobilize these resources toward attaining larger social objectives" (Wallis et al. 1998).

Wallis stresses that "the distinction between [local and bridging capital] is important in explaining why a community rich in informal social interactions might still be poor in its capacity to provide economic opportunities. For example, people living in a poor inner-city neighborhood or rural village can participate in rich daily social interactions yet still be socially isolated from the larger city or region within which they reside" (1998).

Civil Society, Civic Culture, and Civic Ethic

The concept of social capital is often associated with the concept of *civil society*. Bradley suggests that "**civil society** . . . is the sphere of our most basic humanity—the personal, everyday realm that is governed by values such as responsibility, trust, fraternity, solidarity, and love" (emphasis added in Wallis et al. 1998). "The common element binding local and bridging capital is a norm of civic engagement (or civic ethic)" (Wallis et al. 1998).

The multiple layers that interact in the creation and use of social capital which result in and flow from civil society are sometimes referred to as a *"nested structure."* This nested structure comes about in the following way: "The civic ethic begins with personal affinities and relationships that build trust, and it then brings small groups of citizens together in common purpose. These private networks in turn form the basic building blocks of civic culture, creating a climate that supports the growth of cooperative problem solving" (Wallis et al. 1998).

Using the nested structure concept, "family, neighborhood, and community represent basic levels of social organization. Social interaction, social capital, civic infrastructure, and a civic culture are the elements critical to building a healthy civil society. Each of these four elements is present in some form at each of the levels of social organizations and links different levels of social organizations together" (Wallis et al. 1998).

Social Capital and Diversity

Social capital is a useful concept in understanding and addressing issues of diversity, discrimination, and oppression in communities. For example, people who work in community building suggest that social capital is "often created and expressed differently according to how it was influenced by race, class, and ethnicity" and stress that people who work in the area of community building in communities with diverse populations "need to have extensive familiarity with work in different cultural contexts to successfully identify and use social capital effectively" (Wallis et al. 1998).

In addition, to be effective in community building and renewal in poor and disenfranchised communities with populations of persons of color, efforts must include "addressing the impact of racism as part of their problem solving effort in community building" (Wallis et al. 1998). Racism and discrimination can "be tied in with the theme of social capital, especially in recognizing that some groups organize around racial prejudice and that this is a negative form of social capital" (Wallis et al. 1998). Individual and institutional racism are fundamental barriers to the creation of effective relationships among individuals, families, groups, organizations, and communities so essential to the creation and positive use of social capital.

Cultural Capital

Cultural capital and the related concept of cultural wealth are used to help more completely understand social and racial inequalities. Culture was defined in Chapter 1 as "the accumulation of customs, values, and artifacts shared by a people." Yosso notes, "Franklin (2002) defines cultural capital as 'the sense of group consciousness and collective identity' that serves as a resource 'aimed at the advancement of an entire group'" (2005:81). Bourdieu (in Yosso 2005:76), who originally developed the concept, defines *cultural capital* as "an accumulation of cultural knowledge, skills and abilities possessed and inherited by privileged groups in society." He also posited that cultural capital must either be inherited or gained through formal schooling. However, Yosso argues that cultural capital is not only inherited, possessed, and used by privileged groups, but also is widely available among members of communities of color. She suggests the traditional description of cultural capital as available only to privileged groups who either inherit it or gain it through their access to formal education reinforces a deficit view of communities of color. For example, she notes that Bourdieu's "theory of cultural capital has been used to assert that some communities are culturally wealthy while others are culturally poor. This interpretation of Bourdieu exposes White, middle class culture as the standard, and therefore all other forms and expressions of 'culture' are judged in comparison to this 'norm'" (Yosso 2005:76). She argues that to the contrary communities of color possess large amount of cultural capital ("cultural wealth") and it appears in various forms. She outlines several types of cultural wealth or capital that can be found in abundance in communities of color. These types are summarized below.

1. *Aspirational capital* refers to the ability to maintain hopes and dreams for the future, even in the face of real and perceived barriers. This resiliency is evidenced in those who allow themselves and their children to dream of possibilities beyond their present circumstances.

2. *Linguistic capital* includes the intellectual and social skills attained through communication experiences in more than one language and/or style. . . . Linguistic capital reflects the idea that Students of Color arrive at school with multiple language and communication skills. In addition, these children most often have been engaged participants in a storytelling tradition, that may include listening to and recounting oral histories, parables, stories (*cuentos*) and proverbs (*dichos*). . . . Linguistic capital also refers to the ability to communicate via visual art, music, or poetry.

3. *Familial capital* refers to those cultural knowledges nurtured among *familia* (kin) that carry a sense of community history, memory and cultural intuition. . . . This form of cultural wealth engages a commitment to community well being and expands the concept of family to include a more broad understanding of kinship.

4. *Navigational capital* refers to skills of maneuvering through social institutions. Historically, this [implies] the ability to maneuver through institutions not created with Communities of Color in mind. . . . Navigational capital thus acknowledges individual agency within institutional constraints, but it also connects to social networks that facilitate community navigation through places and spaces including schools, the job market and the health care and judicial systems.

5. *Resistant capital* refers those knowledges and skills fostered through oppositional behavior that challenges inequality. . . . This form of cultural wealth is grounded in the legacy of resistance to subordination exhibited by Communities of Color. . . . Furthermore, maintaining and passing on the multiple dimensions of community cultural wealth is also part of the knowledge base of resistant capital. For example, even from within internment camps, Japanese communities resisted racism by maintaining and nurturing various forms of cultural wealth (Yosso 2005:78–81).

Critical Race Theory

"Critical race theory (CRT) has been defined by a number of scholars as a legal counter-discourse generated by legal scholars of color concerned about issues of racial oppression in the law and society" (Lynn 2004:155). Since its emergence in the late 1980s in the context of law and racial inequities within the legal system, CRT has been applied in critiques of the U.S. education system to examine its deficit-based treatment of people of color. It has received little attention within social work and social work scholarship (Abrams and Moio 2009:252).

Within the arena of education and the preparation of teachers, Yosso outlines five basic tenets of CRT that are important in its understanding and are relevant to social work as well:

1. *The intercentricity of race and racism with other forms of subordination.* CRT starts from the premise that race and racism are central, endemic, permanent and a fundamental part of defining and explaining how US society functions.

2. *The challenge to dominant ideology.* CRT challenges White privilege. . . . CRT challenges notions of "neutral" research or "objective" researchers.

3. *The commitment to social justice.* CRT is committed to social justice and offers a liberatory or transformative response to racial, gender and class oppression.

4. *The centrality of experiential knowledge.* CRT recognizes that the experiential knowledge of People of Color is legitimate, appropriate, and critical to understanding. . . . CRT draws explicitly on the lived experiences of People of Color by including such methods as storytelling, family histories, biographies, scenarios, parables, *cuentos* [stories], *testimonios*, chronicles and narratives.

5. *The transdisciplinary perspective.* CRT goes beyond disciplinary boundaries to analyze race and racism within both historical and contemporary contexts, drawing on scholarship from ethnic studies, women's studies, sociology, history, law, psychology, film, theatre and other fields. (Yosso 2005:74–75)

Abrams and Moio note, "CRT acknowledges the intersectionality of various oppressions and suggests that a primary focus on race can eclipse other forms of exclusion." They further note that reconciling the dilemma presented by placing a central focus on race, while also recognizing the importance of a "multidimensional framework" when addressing issues of oppression, is a subject of continuing ambivalence and discussion among CRT scholars (2009:251–252). The next section addressing "differential vulnerability" and an "equality of oppressions" paradigm within social work and social work education also directly relates to this dilemma, but does not resolve it.

Differential Vulnerability Versus "Equality-of-Oppressions" Theory

Critical Thinking

An important component of our development as professional social workers is our ability to think critically and be able to distinguish, appraise, and integrate multiple sources of knowledge. Use your critical thinking skills (you may want to consult the "Critical Thinking" section in Chapter 1), to weigh the evidence in this section for and against the assertions made. Based on your analysis do you accept, reject, or suspend judgment on the assertions and arguments made?

The meaning and importance of "Cultural Competence" in social work was addressed in Chapter 1. Here we address two theoretical positions that raise questions about the appropriateness and efficacy of the current "Cultural Competence" approach in social work education and practice. The following discussion demonstrates the complexity and multifaceted nature of approaches to effectively address oppression and social injustice within the social work community.

Scheile (2007:83–84) argues that because the accreditation standards of the Council on Social Work Education (CSWE) make no distinction "about the frequency, intensity, or pervasiveness of the various forms of oppression" among the ... categories of persons and groups that face oppression, social work has adopted what he calls an "equality-of-oppressions" paradigm. It should be kept in mind that the CSWE accreditation standards must be met by any social work education program in the United States wishing to receive or retain accredited status. In other words, all accredited social work programs are required to address all ... categories of diverse persons and groups through their classroom and field curricula as well as the broader learning context (implicit curriculum) in which the programs are located. These categories are age, class, color, culture, disability, ethnicity, gender, gender identity and expression, immigration status, political ideology, race, religion, sex, and sexual orientation (CSWE 2008:5).

According to Schiele, the *equality-of-oppressions* paradigm "assumes that every source of oppression is equal to others in its severity, frequency, and production of human degradation." He contends that this paradigm "has weakened social work education's capacity to enhance content on people of color" (2007:84).

Schiele offers a different diversity/oppression model that is founded on "concept of differential vulnerability." *Differential vulnerability* would provide "a model to prioritize the various forms of oppression important to social work education" (2007:84). The concept of differential vulnerability originated within the public health discipline in which it is defined as "the recognition that 'at risk' populations vary in their level of susceptibility to stressful life events." Schiele contends, "if oppression is viewed as a stressful life event, the disadvantage generated by it may produce substantial variance." While recognizing that oppressed populations have similarities with each other, some oppressed groups may be at more risk than others for the damaging effects of oppressions (Schiele 2007:93).

Young outlines five different attributes or "faces" of oppression. These different elements of oppression may help clarify the concept of differential vulnerability. They are summarized below:

1. Exploitation is "a steady process of the transfer of the results of the labor of one social group to benefit another."

2. Marginalization can be defined by thinking in terms of a "group of people referred to as 'marginals.' Marginals are persons who lack, or who are blocked from obtaining, the training and skills necessary to locate and sustain gainful employment." Examples include the nonworking poor, persons who are severely disabled, or persons who are intensely stigmatized.

3. Powerlessness can be defined "as the extra liabilities endured by nonprofessionals, who are those with little or no advanced training or education." These persons "have less power in the workplace" and "often work for or are supervised by professionals"

4. Cultural imperialism speaks to the inequality in human values, experiences, and interpretations . . . that some groups have more power over determining which human values, experiences, and interpretations are valid. . . . [C]ultural imperialism is "the universalization of a dominant group's experience and culture, and its establishment as the norm." . . . Those whose culture and experience are most different from the dominant group are assumed to be the most marginalized in society.

5. "Violence implies physical abuse and harm." Examples of oppressed groups who are more vulnerable to violence include hate crimes, rape, and domestic abuse. Violence also includes "lesser forms of aggression, such as harassment, intimidation, and ridicule." (cited in Schiele 2007:93–94)

Schiele points out limitations of the differential variability model. He suggests, "the most obvious limitation" of the model "is that it might lead some to engage in ruthless competition to underscore their group's subjugation." Such competition could lead to both intergroup and intragroup conflict that could have the effect of causing "some to deny the oppression of others" and lead some to the conclusion that the "lesser" types of oppression need not be addressed.

Schiele argues that the "five faces of oppression" model may help reach a balance between "recognizing the importance of all forms of oppression" and "prioritizing specific forms of oppression." At the same time it is necessary to recognize that "any one of the five faces is enough to consider a group oppressed." However, we also need acknowledge that "not all the faces are applicable to all groups." On the other hand, because of the history and power of racism in the United States, "Blacks and Latinos . . . often suffer all five forms of oppression" (Young 1990 in Schiele 2007:95). Schiele concludes as a result that people of color, especially African Americans and Hispanic Americans, "may need to receive additional attention in social work education" (Schiele 2007:95).

Certainly, issues surrounding either an "equality-of-oppression" paradigm or the "differential vulnerability" model are controversial and unresolved in social work. It is necessary, though, to continue to think critically about how we address all oppressions and the related differing "faces of oppression."

Nonplace Community

A **nonplace community** is a community in which attachment to a specific place or geographic territory is absent and is not considered essential for community to exist. Nonplace communities are sometimes referred to as "**communities of the mind,**" "**communities of interest,**" or "**identificational communities**" (Anderson and Carter 1990; Longres 1990). It is perhaps difficult to perceive of community as not primarily associated with a place because we are socialized from early on to think of community primarily as a place (e.g., our "hometown"). Nonplace perspectives of community are also a bit more difficult to grasp because of our more general socialization to traditional paradigm thinking. If we cannot see, feel, hear, or observe objectively an entity through our senses (consistent with scientific thinking), we have difficulty accepting that that entity in fact exists.

On the other hand, this notion of community might be a bit easier to grasp if we recall that a number of aspects of traditional approaches to community have not been primarily place-based. When we talk about community in terms of relationships, or functions, or networks of linked subsystems, we are not talking primarily about place. However, we do usually assume that those relationships, functions, or networks exist in some more or less constant relationship to a place. Nonplace notions of community suggest that one need not associate these aspects of "communityness" with a specific or constant place. Community as social network is discussed as a special type of nonplace community later in this section.

The notion of nonplace communities as "identificational communities" can be a helpful one. It suggests that a central feature of a nonplace community is a feeling of commonalty or identification with the other members of the community. This perspective is a helpful way to conceptualize many diverse communities—the African American community, the gay or lesbian community, the Catholic community, the community of cancer survivors. Nonplace notions of community can help us to recognize that it is possible, indeed likely, that we are members of several communities simultaneously. **Identificational communities include** "groups such as ethnic/cultural/religious groups, patient groups, friendship groups, and workplace groups. While membership in these communities often overlaps with geographic communities, membership is not determined by place, but by interest or identification with the group" (Longres 1991; Germain 1991 in Fellin 1993:60)

Professions can also be thought of as nonplace communities or "communities of interest"—the social work community, for example. As social workers, we share common interests with other members of the profession. We identify with and are identified by others as members of the social work professional community. If we think about the basic elements of community we began this chapter with, we can compare the social work profession with these elements and assess whether social work reflects these community elements. Certainly social workers form a collective of people (primarily comprised of individuals and groups rather than entire families and organizations) with shared interests. Our shared interests are even codified in the Code of Ethics of the profession. As social workers we interact regularly on an informal basis with other social workers—with our colleagues in our agency or with colleagues we went to school with and with whom we continue to maintain contact, for example. We also have formally organized mechanisms for fulfilling our shared interests—the National Association of Social Workers (NASW) sponsors state and national conferences and meetings for its members to share their common professional interests, for example. The Council on Social Work Education holds an Annual Program Meeting each year that brings together members of the social work education community from around the country to share their interests. Such meetings as these not only provide opportunities to share professional interests, but they also serve to allow members of the community to maintain their personal relationships with other members of the social work community. They help reinforce our feelings of membership in the larger social work community. The purpose of NASW itself is focused on furthering the professional interests of social workers. We mutually identify ourselves as members of the social work community and others identify us as members of the social work community (both other social workers and members of other communities). In all these ways we nurture our sense of community.

Nonplace perspectives on community can help us maintain a sense of community and can give us reassurance and security even when we are separated from other community members or when we move from one geographic location to another. A Cambodian refugee can "reunite" with his or her community by connecting with other Cambodian people in the new location. Even if there are no other Cambodian people in the new location, one's sense of identity as a member of the Cambodian community can remain with the person and help the person have a sense of belonging although separated from other community members.

In this respect our nonplace communities can have a historical dimension. Some of what provides us with a sense of belonging, a sense of community, does not exist in the present. Past experiences of community upon which we build our current beliefs about community exist primarily as memories. These memories of the past are important avenues for determining the nature of community for us today. Stories of ancestors and friends who have died also help provide a sense of community or communalness—connectedness to other humans—that is an essential part of community.

Community, technology, and social and economic justice

Another important consideration in nonplace notions of community is that of technology. Much of the ability to maintain a sense of community regardless of whether it is place-based or not is the ability to communicate with other members of the community. The communication technology available to many of us today enables us to maintain and access community relationships almost instantly. Modern transportation systems allowing us to physically travel from one place to another quickly and temporarily (air travel, freeway systems, high-speed rail, etc.) enable us to maintain some face-to-face contact with the members of our nonplace communities over time.

It is important to recognize that such avenues to expanded visions of community are unequally available to different members of the human community. Much of the technology necessary to maintain nonplace community is expensive. Think about the concerns most of us have about the amounts of our cell phone bills from month to month or of the cost of air travel or of owning and maintaining an automobile. Think about the reality that many of us do not have access to telephones at all and certainly cannot afford air travel or the cost of owning and maintaining a car. Consider that for some of us with disabling conditions the ability to create and maintain nonplace community may be essential to our survival, but unattainable without access to expensive technology or modes of transportation. If we are unable to move about freely in order to participate in place community to meet our daily needs, nonplace relationships and networks and the resources necessary to maintain them become

What might this photo communicate about technology and social and economic justice? What might this photo communicate about the "digital divide"?

extremely important means of establishing and maintaining a sense of belonging or any sense of community.

Virtual community

One of the more recent notions of nonplace community is that of the virtual community created through the world wide web of the Internet.

Porter defines a *virtual community* as an aggregation of individuals or business partners who interact around a shared interest, where the interaction is at least partially supported and/or mediated by technology and guided by some protocols or norms (Porter 2004). She provides a Typology of Types of Virtual Communities in Figure 9.1.

Parrish suggests that "virtual communitarians," advocates for and members of virtual communities, focus on a number of areas that are similar to more traditional ideas of community. These include:

- personal intimacy, moral commitment, and social cohesion
- goals, fears, and interests in common
- the recognition by individuals of other individuals who have goals, interests, and fears in common with themselves, and who manifest both recognition that these can best be dealt with interpersonally, and desire to do so. (2002:262–263)

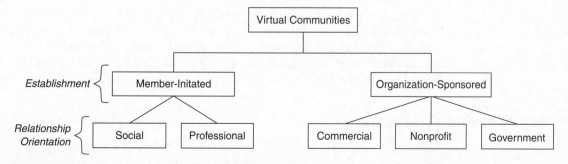

Figure 9.1
Types of Virtual Communities

In addition, Parrish suggests that advocates for virtual community also focus on elements that distinguish virtual from traditional notions of community:

1. transcendence of Cartesian [geographic] space;
2. emphasis on choice;
3. fluidity of identity;
4. evaluation by communication; and
5. equality (Parrish 2002:273).

Parrish summarizes his assessment of virtual communities as presented by a number scholars:

> Virtual communities are . . . exciting new forms of community which *liberate* the individual from the social constraints of embodied identity and from the restrictions of geographically embodied space; which *equalize* through the removal of embodied identity structures; and which promote a sense of connectedness (or *fraternity*) among interactive participants. (Parrish 2002:279)

Virtual community is also often associated with and overlaps the increasing popularity of social networking sites such as Facebook, MySpace, and Twitter. The following table ranks the popularity of these three currently popular sites by the number of monthly visits. These data were reported in February 2009.

Rank and Site	Monthly Visits
1. Facebook.com	1,191,373,339
2. MySpace.com	810,153,536
3. Twitter.com	54,218,731

Source: Compete.com, 2009

It is important that social workers understand that virtual communities exist and that for a growing number of people virtual communities can provide a significant opportunity for acquiring a meaningful "sense of community." It is equally important that we recognize both the advantages and disadvantages that virtual communities hold for individual and community life including those listed above. For social workers, it is especially important to recognize and continually evaluate the implications of technology and technological advances for the core social work concern of social and economic justice.

Notions of nonplace community highlight that community involves many important qualitative elements. Community is not necessarily a place and a place is not necessarily a community. Such a multidimensional and qualitative perspective on community does not rely on place, although it may be created from and associated with any number of places. A nonplace perspective on community allows us to create individualized communities that have meaning for us personally. Such perspectives are subjective and interpretive, but very valuable ways to think about community.

Community as Social Network

Both CSSNs and the concept of social capital discussed earlier reflect an alternative approach to community as a social network. A social network approach is a nonplace perspective on community. The notion of social network represents somewhat of a middle ground between traditional and alternative paradigm thinking about community. Some suggest that it is not in itself a community, but that it is an important component of community for many people. Netting, Kettner, and McMurty (1993:103–104), in their discussion of the importance of social networks as community resources, use Balgopal's definition:

> Social networks such as kin, friends, neighbors, and coworkers are supportive environmental resources that function as important instruments of help. . . . Social networks provide emotional resources and strength for meeting the need of human relatedness, recognition, and affirmation. They also serve as mutual aid systems for the exchange of resources such as money, emotional support, housing, and child care.

Certainly this perspective suggests that social networks include many of the supports and resources commonly thought of as part of community whether it is a place or nonplace community.

Other researchers have attempted to trace or map social networks as a means of understanding community. This approach, referred to as network analysis, has included attempts to describe community by focusing on interpersonal relationships. This alternative was used by Wellman and Leighton (in Warren and Lyon 1988:57–72) to try to discover if large urban *gesellschaft*-like communities had completely done away with personal *gemeinschaft*-like ways in which community members might relate to one another. They were especially concerned with if and how these personal and primary relationships could exist in the large and relatively impersonal urban context. Based on their analysis, they determined that personal relationships remained strong and important to urban dwellers but these relationships often extended well beyond the geographic boundaries of neighborhoods or communities and included relatives and friends in distant places. Although the primary personal relationships were not necessarily territorially or place based, people were able to maintain them through modern communications technology and transportation systems. This approach to network analysis concluded that a more workable alternative perspective on community was one that included both place, in terms of neighborhood or geographically defined community, and nonplace community networks that functioned to meet primary mutual support and identification needs not met in the urbanized and mobile environment characteristic of much of modern society.

Qualitative Aspects of Community

McKnight (1987:54–58) posits an ideal community vision that is inclusive of all community members and offers a qualitatively different experience in living from that possible in organizational or institutional life. McKnight suggests a number of other ways that communities can be defined by considering their differences from formally constructed and explicitly goal-directed organizations or institutions (see discussion of organizational goals, Chapter 8). McKnight sees community and formal organizations as oppositional in many ways. He suggests that institutions operate to *control* people while the means of association through community is based on *consent.*

McKnight's vision is inclusive in that he finds a place even for those who have been excluded from community and labeled as in need of institutionalization either in the traditional sense of a mental (or other social control) institution or in the more contemporary sense of human service systems that he sees as the equivalent of institutions without walls. The themes of community, he suggests, include:

1. *Capacity.* Recognition of the fullness of each member because it is the sum of their capacities that represents the power of the group. Communities are built upon recognizing the whole depth—weaknesses and capacities [strengths] of each member.

2. *Collective Effort.* The essence of community is people working together. One of the characteristics of this community work is shared responsibility that requires many talents. Thus, a person who has been labeled deficient can find . . . support in the collective capacities of a community that can shape itself to the unique character of each person.

3. *Informality.* Transactions of value take place without money, advertising, or hype. Authentic relationships are possible and care emerges in place of its packaged imitation: service.

4. *Stories.* In universities, people know through studies. In businesses and bureaucracies, people know by reports. In communities, people know by stories. These community stories allow people to reach back into their common history and their individual experience for knowledge about truth and direction for the future.

5. *Celebration.* Community groups constantly incorporate celebrations, parties, and social events in their activities. The line between work and play is blurred and the human nature of everyday life becomes part of the way of work. You will know you are in community if you often hear laughter and singing. You will know you are in an institution, corporation, or bureaucracy if you hear the silence of long halls and reasoned meetings.

6. *Tragedy.* The surest indication of the experience of community is the explicit common knowledge of tragedy, death, and suffering. (1987:57–58. Copyright © 1987 by Social Policy Corporation. Used with permission.)

"To be in community is to be a part of ritual, lamentation, and celebration of our fallibility. Knowing community is not an abstract understanding. Rather it is what each of us knows about all of us. . . . It is only in community that we can find care" (McKnight 1987:58; McKnight 1992:90).

African American community qualities

Barbara Solomon's (1976:57) discussion of ways of defining African American community questions the appropriateness of traditional place-based and quantitative definitions. She suggests a way of defining African American communities that is much more qualitative in focus:

The physical proximity of peoples in some geographical location is not enough to define community. A degree of personal intimacy must also be present among the residents of the physical space. This aspect of community has generally been ignored by social scientists whose image of community has been colored by those characteristics amenable to quantitative analysis, e.g., income level, crime rate, or incidence of hospital admissions. Personal intimacy, however, is indicated through the existence of such relationships as friendship and marriage and such feelings as confidence, loyalty, and interpersonal trust (1976:57).

McKnight's and Solomon's community visions, with their recognition of the value of qualitative dimensions, including personal strengths and fallibilities; informality; collective efforts and responsibility; stories as avenues to knowing and understanding; accepting as real and legitimate both celebration and tragedy; and the importance of personal intimacy, relationships, confidence, loyalty, and trust have much in common with many of the dimensions of our alternative paradigm. Even though McKnight's vision is set in opposition to modern human service organizations, and Solomon's vision is offered in part as a critique of existing social science definitions of community (among which can be included those created and used by many social workers), they both include much that is consonant with the core concerns and purposes of social work.

INTENTIONAL COMMUNITIES

Communes

Both McKnight's and Solomon's perspectives on community suggest that the boundary between community and family and small group often blurs. This is especially true when we consider intentionally formed communities, specifically communal perspectives on community. Communal living has often been studied as an alternative approach to traditional family forms. Communal living has also been studied as an intentional effort to construct new forms of community living. For our purposes this difference in perspective is not problematic. It helps us realize that the boundaries between different levels of human behavior are blurred and change according to the perspective of the observers and participants involved. It might be helpful to reconsider levels of human behavior as not mutually exclusive but existing on a continuum that is not linear but spiral. For example, as family forms change and expand from nuclear to extended or networks of fictive kin (see Chapter 6 on families) they spiral into forms that resemble community almost as much as (or perhaps more than) they resemble traditional family forms. So, while we consider communal living here as a form of alternative community, keep in mind that in many ways we might just as appropriately have included it in our chapter on families.

Whether viewed from the perspective of family or community, efforts in communal or communitarian living represent efforts to create alternatives to traditional arrangements for living together. Aidala and Zablocki (1991:89) define a commune as

> any group of five or more adults (with or without children) most of whom are unrelated by blood or marriage, who live together without compulsion, primarily for the sake of some ideological goal for which a collective household is deemed essential.

Marguerite Bouvard (1975 in Warren 1977:561, n. 1) adapts a definition of the Federation of Intentional Communities and includes both family and community:

> Communes are free as opposed to blood-related families. . . . [A commune] must include a minimum of three families and also common economic, spiritual, and cultural institutions.

Communitarian movements tend to come about during times of social and cultural transition. Such movements have occurred periodically throughout history and have included religious, political, economic, and alternative family foundations. The most recent and most studied flurry of activity in communal-living experiments occurred in the United States during the 1960s and 1970s.

Aidala (1989:311–338) suggests that communes allow conditions of social and cultural change in which old patterns of living are questioned and new patterns have not yet emerged. She suggests that they are "intense ideological communities [which] allow limited experimentation with alternatives in work, family, politics, religion, and their intersections." She believes that "communal experiments functioned for their participants, and one might argue, for the larger society as well, as part of the process of changing norms for family life" (1989:312). She notes that commune members "were concerned with working out norms, justifications, and habitual practices to support cohabitation, delayed childbearing or childlessness, assertive women, emotionally expressive men, working mothers, child-tending fathers, and relationships based upon discussion and negotiation rather than predefined, obligatory roles" (1989:334). It is interesting to compare these goals with the core concerns and values of social work, such as self-determination, rights for each person to reach their fullest human potential, social and economic justice, and equality. Aidala suggests also that the very existence of communal experiments, whether they ultimately failed or succeeded in achieving their purposes, were important voices questioning the status quo of traditional family forms and human relationships (1989:335).

Aidala and Zablocki also find evidence that significant numbers of commune members were not explicitly seeking new family forms but joined communal groups in search of "consensual community" in which "to live in close relationship with others with whom one agreed about important values and goals. Communes were attempts to intentionally expand networks of emotional support beyond conventional bonds of blood and marriage" (1991:88). Nevertheless, the boundaries of family and community often merged in communal life. "Forming a communal household had to do not only with common location but with a particular type of relationship among members characterized by holistic, affectional bonds, and equally important dimensions of *shared belief and conviction*" (1991:113). Note the elements of family, groups, and community in these descriptions of communes. Aidala (1989) and Aidala and Zablocki (1991) refer to these communal arrangements as "wider families." This is perhaps a helpful way to appreciate the intersection of the several levels of human behavior reflected in these experiments.

Rosabeth Moss Kanter (in Warren 1977:572–581) perhaps best summarized the core issues and concerns faced by communes or utopian communities. The central issue, she believed, was that of commitment. The basic concerns were how members arranged to do the work the community must have done to survive as a group, and how the group managed to involve and satisfy members over a long period of time.

The issue of commitment Kanter referred to reflects the important search for a fit between individual needs and interests and those of the community that is central to communal struggles. She suggested that "commitment . . . refers to the willingness of people to do what will help maintain the group because it provides what they need." When a person is committed, what that person wants to do is the same as what that person must do. The person gives to the group what it needs to maintain itself and receives in turn what the person needs to nourish her/his sense of self (1977:574).

Kanter listed several specific problems with which communes must deal in order to ensure both their survival and group and individual commitment:

1. How to get work done without coercion.

2. How to ensure decisions are made, but to everyone's satisfaction.

3. How to build close, fulfilling relationships, but without exclusiveness.

4. How to choose and socialize new members.

5. How to include a degree of autonomy, individual uniqueness, and even deviance.

6. How to ensure agreement and shared perception around community functioning and values. (Kanter in Warren 1977:572)

These perspectives on communes may run counter to many of the stereotypes we might hold about communes as rather normless contexts for excessive and irresponsible behaviors such as drug abuse and irresponsible sexual activity. While these excesses may have been a part of some communal experiences (as they are a part of noncommunal life), those who have studied communal life have found that these intentional communities are much more likely to be serious attempts to find workable alternatives to the historic needs of individuals, families, groups, and communities.

New towns

Communes are almost exclusively efforts on the part of private individuals and groups to find new visions of community by creating intentional communities. There have been government-assisted experiments in the creation of intentional communities as well. Government efforts to create new communities or "new towns" began as an effort to respond to the "urban crisis" that erupted during the 1960s. This crisis of community came about in large part because of the history of oppression and exclusion of many community members, especially persons of color and low-income persons, from meaningful participation in the life of the community. These individuals and groups had been denied access to participation in the locality-relevant functions of community necessary to meet individual and family needs (see Warren, above).

New towns were an effort to build new communities that would not be characterized by the oppression and discrimination that had been so harmful to so many people and had culminated in the explosions that were the urban crisis of the 1960s. New towns were sanctioned by the federal government in the form of loan guarantees to private developers who would literally build new communities. The federal government loan guarantees came with the requirement that new towns provide plans for including a wide representation of people as potential community members—people of color, low-income people, older persons, persons with disabilities. The fundamental concern was for new communities to ensure optimum "quality of life" or "the well-being of people—primarily in groups but also as individuals—as well as the 'well being' of the environment in which these people live" (statement from 1972 Environmental Protection Agency conference quoted in Campbell 1976:10). Many people have pointed out that few if any new towns actually lived up to these high expectations.

The basic concept of new towns was not really new when it received renewed interest in the late 1960s. The "Garden City" concept had been in place in Britain since the turn of the century. In the United States new towns emerged after World War I, and government support for several so-called greenbelt towns began in 1929. The new towns of the 1960s were comprehensive efforts to build community with consideration for both physical and social environments. They were planned "to provide for a broad range of social, economic, and physical activities within a defined area of land and within a predetermined time period" (Campbell 1976:17). Socially they were to include a full range of educational services and health, recreation, civic, and religious organizations. Economically they were to include businesses, industry, and professional endeavors. Physically they were to include "infrastructure" of roads and utilities as well as housing for a wide range of income levels. This comprehensive range of services was to be carried out in economically viable, environmentally sound, and socially interactive ways. Citizens of new towns were to have meaningful participation in governance and decision making throughout the development process (Campbell 1976:17).

Government support for new town development decreased to virtually nothing by the end of the 1970s. As a result, this experiment in government-supported intentional community development probably was not in place long enough even to effectively evaluate its success or failure. Certainly, as noted earlier, there is little doubt that new towns failed to reach the lofty potential declared for them by their proponents. New towns, like other experimental intentional communities, held great promise for the quality of life they hoped to provide and might serve as helpful models of what community life might be like under varying conditions. Campbell suggests that the greatest challenge of new towns was:

> to structure and maintain an environment . . . in which human potential is enhanced, and finally, one where people irrespective of age, sex, race, religion, or economic condition can positively interact with each other and nature. (1976:266)

Community: Social and Economic Justice and Oppression

Human Rights & Justice

Professional social workers are expected to understand the forms and mechanisms of oppression and discrimination. How do the forms and mechanisms of oppression and discrimination add to your understanding of oppression and discrimination at the community level?

The challenges faced by new towns reflect the need to undo existing patterns of oppression and unequal distribution of power in traditional communities. Our alternative paradigm requires us to recognize and work toward the reduction of existing oppression at all levels of human behavior. Community, because of its inclusiveness of other levels of human behavior, is a critical context for recognizing—with the goal of reducing—oppression and unequal distribution of power.

An essential first step to reducing oppression and unequal distribution of power is the recognition of their existence. One way to begin to recognize the existence of oppression and inequality in communities is to think about the physical structure of the traditional communities within which we live. How are they arranged? How segregated are community members from each other in terms of color and income or class? How does this segregation come to be? How is it maintained?

Community and discrimination

Where we live is a powerful influence on much of what we experience in other spheres of our lives. Where we live is a powerful influence on whom we have as friends; on whom we have as role models and associates; on where and with whom we go to school; on the kinds of jobs and resources to which we have access; and on the quality of our housing. Segregation in housing results in different people having fundamentally different experiences in relation to the influences we listed above. In the United States segregation is most often based on color and/or income. While segregation based on color in many areas of life (schools, public accommodations, jobs, housing) has been made illegal through such legislation as the 1964 Civil Rights Act and the 1954 Supreme Court ruling (Brown versus Topeka Board of Education) we need only to look around us to become aware of the continuing reality of segregation in our communities.

Logan (in Warren and Lyon 1988:231ff) and Feagin and Feagin (1978:85ff) describe several types of institutionalized discrimination in communities that serve to create and maintain oppression and unequal distribution of power. These mechanisms of oppression include blockbusting, racial steering, and redlining.

Blockbusting is a practice followed by some real estate brokers in which the racial fears of whites about African American families are used to manipulate housing markets. Blockbusting can happen when a previously all-white neighborhood begins to become integrated. After a few African Americans move into the neighborhood, white home owners are manipulated into selling their property, often at lower than market value, out of fear. These same homes may then be sold at significantly inflated prices to new incoming African American persons. **Racial steering** is a process that perpetuates existing patterns of segregation. Racial steering involves realtors or rental-property management agents steering people to specific areas of communities in order to maintain racial or economic segregation. **Redlining** is a form of discrimination used by some banks and other lending institutions that declares certain areas or sections of communities as bad investment risks. These areas often coincide with poor neighborhoods or neighborhoods with larger populations of people of color. The term *redlining* came from the practice by some institutions of actually outlining in red on a map the areas in which they would not approve home loan or mortgage applications. This practice prevents low-income people or people of color from acquiring loans in order to become home owners rather than renters. It also negatively affects communities because it prevents community people from purchasing and rehabilitating deteriorating rental housing (Logan 1988:231–241; Feagin and Feagin 1978:85–115).

These practices provide examples of mechanisms for creating and maintaining segregation, discrimination, and oppression in communities. These processes are all directly related to housing. Housing is only one element of community life. However, because where we live influences so many of the other sectors of our lives, it seems fundamental that we recognize housing as a cornerstone of systems of oppression in communities. Housing segregation directly influences other patterns of segregation; perhaps most fundamental among these is school segregation. It can be argued that until we are willing to—indeed, until we insist on the opportunity and right to—live in truly integrated neighborhoods and communities we will most likely never be able to eliminate oppression and discrimination in this or the other sectors of life. All of us as humans must have the right to live in the communities and neighborhoods we choose.

By living close to others we come to know, respect, and understand the complexities of those persons different from ourselves. By living among people different from ourselves we can learn to compromise, to respect, and learn from difference, to celebrate and be strengthened by difference. The examples we have used here focus on low-income people and people of color. They can readily be applied also to people different from us in other ways—in sexual orientation, religious beliefs, disabling conditions, or age, for example.

Social development approach

One approach to community building and improvement with a global perspective is that of social development. **Social development** has been defined in multiple and interrelated ways. It has been described as:

▶ "the process of planned change designed to bring about a better fit between human needs and social policies and programs." (Hollister)
▶ "directed towards the release of human potential in order to eliminate social inequities and problems" (Meinert, Kohn, and Strickler)
▶ "an intersystemic and integrated approach designed to facilitate development of the capacity of people to work continuously for their own welfare and the development of society's institutions so that human needs are met at all levels especially the lowest" (Billups and Julia)
▶ aiming "to foster the emergence and implementation of a social structure in which all citizens are entitled to equal social, economic, and political rights and equal access to status, roles, prerogative and responsibilities, regardless of gender, race, age, sexual orientation, or disability" (Chandler). (Sullivan 1994:101)

All of these definitions share a concern for gaining access to basic resources to fulfill human needs for community members. Sullivan argues, however, for an expanded notion of basic human needs from the traditional notion of needs for housing, food, clothing, etc. to include "the provision of opportunities, the ability to maximize individual and collective potential, assurance of equal rights and protection of the natural environment" (Sullivan 1994:107–108). This expanded notion of the goals of a social development approach are certainly consistent with social work values and ethics, respect for human diversity, and social and economic justice. Asamoah et al. provide a summary of social development specifically in the context of social work. They suggest:

> Social development emphasizes the values of human rights, social justice, equity in resources, and parity between human and economic development . . . values consistent with those of social work. Similarly, social development's focus on strengths, empowerment, self-sufficiency, and development support the change and growth orientation of social work. The broad applicability of social development provides a common worldwide identity for the profession (Asamoah, Healy, and Mayadas 1997).

The definitions of social development above and the more inclusive notion of basic human needs are also consistent with such approaches as strengths, feminist, and empowerment perspectives on bringing about the necessary changes at the community and individual levels to accomplish the goals and fulfill the requirements of the definitions (see Chapters 1, 2 and 3).

Diversity and Community

Recognizing and removing barriers to help create community environments in which the benefits of diversity can be realized are fundamental concerns for social work at the community level. The intentional communities we explored earlier, such as communes and new towns, reflect significant concerns for diversity in a number of respects. Certainly a central concern for us as social workers (or soon-to-be social workers) is the degree to which human diversity is respected and incorporated in community. Perspectives on communities consistent with the alternate paradigms we consider in this book will attempt to maximize and respect diversity among community members as a source of strength. At the same time, alternate perspectives must balance the importance of diversity in communities with the importance, especially for many members of oppressed groups, of living around and within communities of people with whom we have much in common and that can provide us with a sense of positive identity, security, and history.

Religion and community

A significant element of community life for many people is that of religious institutions. Maton and Wells describe the potential for both positive and negative contributions of religion to community well-being. They define **religion** very broadly as "encompassing the spectrum of groups and activities whose focus extends beyond the material reality of everyday life (i.e., to a spiritual reality)" (1995:178). You might want to compare this definition of religion with our earlier definitions of religion and spirituality.

Religious institutions and community development   Maton and Wells (1995) point out the role that many religious organizations have played in community development efforts. They note:

> Religious organizations, especially those in urban areas, have a vested interest in revitalizing surrounding neighborhoods and communities. This form of environmental change may have a preventive effect by reducing stress related to urban infrastructure decay and enhancing supportive resources (Maton and Wells 1995:182).

Religious institutions and social action   In addition to community development directed toward improving the physical structures and well-being of community members, religious organizations have often played significant roles in social action to bring about social and economic justice in communities. Church involvement in social action has an especially rich history and tradition in the African American community. Maton and Wells point out:

> especially in the South, black churches functioned as the institutional centers and foundation of the [civil rights] movement. . . . Black churches provided the movement with the leadership of clergy independent financially from the white society and skilled at managing people and resources, an institutionalized financial base, and meeting place where strategies, tactics and civil rights organizations were developed. Furthermore, black churches supplied the movement with "a collective enthusiasm generated through a rich culture consisting of songs, testimonies, oratory and prayers that spoke directly to the needs of an oppressed group." (1995:187–188)

Religious institutions as a negative force in community life   We must be aware that while churches and other religious institutions have played very positive roles in community life, they have also historically contributed to individual and community problems in a variety of areas. Maton and Wells point out:

> some religious principles and values can lead to inappropriate guilt and anxiety, or a limited view of the nature of emotional problems. . . . Organized religion's . . . considerable psychological and economic resources, can be used to subjugate and disempower rather than empower groups, such as women and racial minorities. . . . Religion's focus on helping the "less fortunate," while generating many volunteer and economic resources, can lead to

a paternalistic, disempowering approach to those in need. Also, because mainstream religion is part of the current power structure in society, it often does not take part in empowerment activities that challenge the current structure (1995:189).

Social workers need to be aware of the significant potential for churches to assist communities and their members. At the same time we need to recognize their potential for exacerbating individual and community problems.

Community and people with disabilities

Mackelprang and Salsgiver (1996:9ff) describe two alternative paradigms for achieving social and economic justice for people with disabilities: the Minority Model and the Independent Living Perspective. The minority model was the foundation for "the birth of disability consciousness" in the United States and arose out of the civil rights turbulence of the 1960s. Mackelprang and Salsgiver (1996) assert that this movement matured with the development of the independent living concept in the early 1970s.

Independent living perspective　Mackelprang and Salsgiver stress, "Independent living encourages people with disabilities to begin to assert their capabilities personally and in the political arena" (1996:10).

Some principles and examples of the independent living model

1. Independent living proponents view people with disabilities not as patients or clients but as active and responsible consumers.
2. Independent living proponents reject traditional treatment approaches as offensive and disenfranchising and demand control over their own lives.
3. Independent living proponents retain their own personal responsibility to hire and fire people who provide attendant or personal care rather than allowing formal structures to provide and control the professional care givers.
4. Independent living proponents prefer attendants who are trained by the individuals with disabilities themselves instead of licensed providers like registered nurses.
5. Independent living proponents see empowerment as self-developed and not bestowed by someone else. For example, social workers are viewed only as consultants, not as prescribers of care or treatment plans.
6. Independent living proponents believe that the greatest constraints on people with disabilities are environmental and social.
7. Independent living proponents espouse a philosophy that advocates natural support systems under the direction of the consumer. (Mackelprang and Salsgiver 1996:10–12)

Independent living: strengths and limitations　Mackelprang and Salsgiver suggest that social work has much to learn from the independent living perspective and "can benefit greatly from a shift in focus from case management in which clients are labeled 'cases' to a consumer-driven model of practice that acknowledges self-developed empowerment and not empowerment bestowed from others" (1996: 12–13). They also note, however, that "the independent living approach can be criticized as viewing problems too much from an external perspective. Independent living may be too quick to assume that consumers already have knowledge and abilities rather than recognizing that they may need assistance to develop their strengths" (1996:12). They recommend a partnership between social work and independent living proponents in which social work can contribute its multi-systems and ecological approach and the disability movement "can help social work enhance approaches to clients, better empower oppressed and devalued groups, and understand the needs of people with disabilities" (1996:13).

Community and sexual orientation

Special issues exist for lesbians or gay men in the community context. Urban areas may offer more opportunity for persons to accommodate diversity within diversity than do small or rural communities. Some research suggests that "for most lesbians and gay men, partners and friends are more reliable and constant sources of social and emotional support than family of origin members. As a result, relations within the community assume a special significance for lesbian and gay individuals and their families" (Demo and Allen 1996:420). Homophobia both in the community and internalized homophobia have significant consequences for individual and community life for gay men and lesbians:

> On a daily basis, lesbian and gay parents and stepparents must confront internalized and externalized homophobia when they come out to their children's teachers, the parents of their children's peers and other members of the community. Even routine tasks, such as filling out forms at a child's day-care center that ask for information about "mother" and "father" are daily reminders that mainstream heterosexual society neither recognizes the child's family . . . nor accommodates lesbian or gay stepparents. (Crosbie-Burnett and Helmbrecth 1993 in Demo and Allen 1996:420)

Toward a strengths approach to community

Perhaps an ideal community is one in which individual identity and identity as a member of the community are integrated. Myers (1985:34–35) finds such a holistic-perspective in an Afrocentric worldview. The African concept of "extended self" actually includes community. Self and community are not separate or distinct systems. She notes that "self in this instance includes all of the ancestors, the yet unborn, all of nature, and the entire community" (Myers 1985:35). Utne (1992:2) suggests the benefits and strengths of a non-Western, more inclusive perspective on community. He recommends that "perhaps we in the West will listen to what [indigenous] people have to teach us and start making different choices. Perhaps someday our children will know the experience of community conveyed by this common phrase of the Xhosa people of southern Africa: 'I am because we are.'"

Collins (1990) offers an important feminist perspective on community and diversity. Her perspective reflects the strength of African American women in creating and maintaining communities in which they and their families have historically been able to survive in the struggle against oppression in the surrounding environment. Her perspective reflects an Afrocentric worldview in which holism and unity are central. Collins's (1990:53) perspective also recognizes the critical influence on African American individuals, families, organizations, and communities of the slavery and oppression comprising so much of the history of African peoples in the United States. She suggests that these historical conditions resulted in significant differences between African American and white communities. She describes an alternative to traditional white communities in which family, extended family, and community merged and in which "Black communities as places of collective effort and will stood in contrast to the public, market-driven, exchange-based dominant political economy in which they were situated" (Bethel in Collins 1990:53).

Black women played significant roles in the creation and maintenance of this alternative community. Women provided the stability necessary for these communities, whose primary concern was day-to-day survival (Collins 1990:146). The empowering, but not overpowering, role played by African American women in their communities and families is portrayed in the following excerpt:

> African American women worked to create Black female spheres of influence, authority, and power that produced a worldview markedly different from that advanced by the dominant group. Within African American communities Black women's activities as cultural workers is empowering. . . . The power of Black women was the power to make culture, to transmit folkways, norms, and customs, as well as to build shared ways of seeing the world that insured our survival. . . . This power . . . was neither economic nor political; nor did it translate into female dominance (Radford-Hill in Collins 1990:147).

Collins also summarizes the alternative meaning of community that emerges from an Afrocentric worldview as one that stresses "connections, caring and personal accountability." This historical worldview, combined with the realities of oppression in the United States, resulted in alternative communities that empowered their members. These communities were created not through theorizing, but instead they came about "through daily actions" of African American women. These alternative communities created:

> sanctuaries where individual Black women and men are nurtured in order to confront oppressive social institutions. Power from this perspective is a creative power used for the good of the community, whether that community is conceptualized as one's family, church community, or the next generation of the community's children (Collins 1990:223).

Resiliency and community

We explored the concept of individual resiliency earlier. This concept is also relevant to understanding human behavior in the community environment, for individual resilience is heavily influenced by the quality of community life. Saleebey (1996:300) notes that community is more and more recognized as critical to individual resiliency. Communities can help or hinder resiliency and have been referred to in two ways as they relate to resiliency:

1. *Enabling niches:* places where individuals become known for what they do, are supported in becoming more adept and knowledgeable, and can establish solid relationships within and outside the community.

2. *Entrapping niches:* individuals are stigmatized and isolated. Membership in the community is based on collective stigma and alienation. (Saleebey 1996:300)

Specific characteristics of communities that "amplify individual resilience" include:

- Awareness, recognition, and use of the assets of most members of the community
- Information networks of individuals, families, and groups
- Social networks of peers

◗ Intergenerational mentoring relationships that provide succor, instruction, support, and encouragement

◗ Many opportunities to participate and make significant contributions to the moral and civic life of the community and to take a role as a full-fledged citizen

◗ High expectations of members (Saleebey 1996:300)

Community: Wellness and resilience

All of the above characteristics are reciprocal for improving the well-being of the individual and the community. Saleebey also notes the relation of wellness and resilience to community. They both:

> suggest that individuals are best served, from a health and competence standpoint, by creating belief and thinking around possibility and values, around accomplishment and renewal, rather than centering exclusively on risk factors and disease processes. . . . Both indicate that health and resilience are, in the end, community projects, an effect of social connection, the aggregation of collective vision, the provision of mentoring, and the reality of belonging to an organic whole (Saleebey 1996:301).

SUMMARY/TRANSITION

In this chapter, within the larger context of traditional and alternative approaches to community, we explored a variety of different but often interrelated types of, and perspectives on, communities. Historical perspectives on community were reviewed. Issues related to defining community were discussed.

Within the arena of traditional perspectives on community, a number of ways of thinking about community were presented. Community as a specific place and community as a set of functions was explored. Community was discussed as a middle ground, mediator, or link between small systems such as individuals, families or groups, and larger societal systems. Community as ways of relating or as patterns of relationships and community as a social system were described.

Alternative perspectives on community included the notion of nonplace community. Community as a social network or web of relationships and resources through which members meet needs and face challenges in life was discussed as an alternative to more traditional notions. Qualitative aspects of community were explored, including discussion of some qualitative aspects of African American communities. Intentional communities, including communes and new towns, were presented.

Issues of oppression and power at the community level were included among alternative perspectives. The notion of heterogeneity or diversity and community life was presented. In this discussion a strengths approach to community was included.

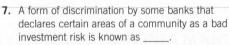

Succeed with PEARSON **mysocialworklab**

Ethical Practice **Critical Thinking** **Human Rights & Justice** **Policy Practice**

Log onto **www.mysocialworklab.com** to watch videos on the skills and competencies discussed in this chapter. (If you did not receive an access code to **MySocialWorkLab** with this text and wish to purchase access online, please visit **www.mysocialworklab.com**.)

PRACTICE TEST

1. Socialization and mutual support for community members in time of need are examples of community _____.
   a. functions
   b. networks
   c. social systems
   d. structures

2. _____ are an example of government assisted efforts to create intentional communities that would not be characterized by the oppression and discrimination that lead to the "urban crisis" of the 1960s.
   a. Communes
   b. New towns
   c. Utopian communities
   d. Suburbs

3. Ways of relating based on shared traditions, culture, or way of life and on a sense of mutual responsibility arising out of that shared tradition are known as _____.
   a. social networks
   b. gesellschaft relationships
   c. gemeinschaft relationships
   d. augmented families

4. A social worker might encounter a community that has rich informal interactions but can still be poor in its capacity to provide economic opportunities—for example, people living in a poor inner city neighborhood yet socially isolated for the larger city. The concept to describe this is a lack of _____.
   a. economic capital
   b. bridging capital
   c. vertical capital
   d. community capital

Diversity in Practice

5. Membership in ethnic, cultural, or religious groups, or workplace groups are examples of _____.
   a. utopian communities
   b. intentional communities
   c. social communities
   d. indentificational communities

6. Holistic and integrative approaches to community building and renewal are often referred to as _____.
   a. community regeneration
   b. comprehensive community initiatives
   c. the war on poverty
   d. civil ethic or civil society

Human Rights & Justice

7. A form of discrimination by some banks that declares certain areas of a community as a bad investment risk is known as _____.
   a. blockbusting
   b. racial steering
   c. redlining
   d. community isolation

8. The sense of group consciousness and collective identity that serves as a resource aimed at the advancement of an entire group is referred to as _____.
   a. cultural capital
   b. social capital
   c. community identification
   d. community consciousness

9. This approach to community building and improvement has a global perspective and focuses not only on gaining access to basic resources to fulfill human needs but also on the provision of opportunities, assurance of equal rights and the ability to maximize individual and collective potential.
   a. global community development
   b. community organizing
   c. social development
   d. comprehensive development

10. An aggregation of individuals or business partners who interact around a shared interest where the interaction is at least partially supported and/or mediated by technology and guided by some protocols or norms is referred to as _____.
    a. cyberspace community
    b. social community
    c. a technologically advanced community
    d. virtual community

Log onto **MySocialWorkLab** once you have completed the Practice Test above to take your Chapter Exam and demonstrate your knowledge of this material.

Answers

1) a 2) b 3) c 4) b 5) d 6) b 7) c 8) a 9) c 10) d

Media Labeling *versus* the US Disability Community Identity: A Study of Shifting Cultural Language

Beth Haller[a]*, Bruce Dorries[b] and Jessica Rahn[a]

[a]Towson University, USA; [b]Mary Baldwin College, USA

This study examines disability terminology to explore how the news media frame cultural representations of the disability community. More specifically, the paper examines the impact of the Americans with Disabilities Act on journalist's language choices about disability topics. A content analysis of news stories using disability terms in The Washington Post *and* The New York Times *during the past decade was conducted. The paper illustrates that disability community identity continues to be formed, transformed and maintained through news media presentations of disability terminology. The paper argues that the US Disability Rights Movement had some success during the 1990s in putting forth language that advances its aims, though the study also suggests that some journalists continue to use terms that perpetuate limiting, narrow stereotypes about people with disabilities.*

Language has always had power to define cultural groups, and the past 15 years have ushered in a new era in the USA for framing disability via the media because of the passage of the Americans with Disabilities Act (ADA). The Act, primarily crafted by disability rights activists, tried to bring about significant change in the USA by eliminating many societal barriers that people with disabilities faced.[1] In light of the law's effort to change US society, this study assesses how or if the US news media have absorbed any of these shifts in US society because of the ADA. Specifically, the study looks at the terms the media use to refer to people with disabilities. Numerous studies already exist that have assessed other aspects of media coverage of disability issues (Clogston, 1989, 1990, 1991; Cumberbatch & Negrine, 1991; Haller, 1993, 1995, 1999a, 1999b, 2000; Johnson, 2000; Barnartt et al., 2001). Our focus on disability terminology is specifically narrow because the US Disability Rights Movement has been advocating appropriate language use for a number of decades; like all social groups, they contend that what they are called is part of their identity as people with disabilities and they should decide these terms. In addition, we argue that looking at terminology is significant because it gives us a way to understand whether a more disability-aware US society is manifesting itself in changes in media behaviors as well. We suggest that even something as mundane as the words used to refer to a group are important because they have ramifications both for the self-perception of people with disabilities and what the general public believes about disability.

This study assesses the impact of disability rights efforts as the movement embodies what Longmore (1995) termed 'The second phase', a move toward strengthening disability culture through self-definition. Phase one shifted people with disabilities into the mainstream by outlawing discrimination and

Source: Haller, B., Dorries, B. & Rahn, J. (2006). Media labeling *versus* the US disability community identity: a study of shifting cultural language. *Disability & Society 21*(1), 61-75.

mandating access—it argued for social inclusion. In phase two, both activists and theorists consider media coverage and the language used by journalists to represent disability issues to be central to this process.

Language, Framing and Disability Identity

The concept of framing gives a useful perspective for this study because it 'offers a way to describe the power of a communicating text' (Entman, 1993, p. 51). Media texts contain frames, 'which are manifested by the presence or absence of certain keywords, stock phrases, stereotypical images, sources of information, and sentences that provide thematically reinforcing clusters of facts or judgments' (p. 52). Through their selection of certain words over others, the media make certain terms more salient or memorable for their audiences. This study looks at one small, but powerful, element of media framing of people with disabilities—how they are referred to as a social group.

Language about groups engaged in a social movement has always been a site of contested terrain (Allen, 1990; Smith, 1992; Stewart et al., 1994). As society changes, certain terminology falls out of favor, such as the continuum in the USA from 'colored' to Black to African Americans. The dominant culture, or majority, generally resists these language shifts, often derogatorily labeling them as 'just political correctness' (Reiser, 2001). Often the media have been sluggish in assimilating new terms. Accordingly, activists for social movements have had to push their language changes into media frames, usually with only moderate success.

For decades, both overt and implied references to people with disabilities have concerned disabilities studies scholars and the Disability Rights Movement because they are so integral to disability culture and identity. Disability policy consultant June Isaacson-Kailes explains: 'A significant element in the struggle for basic human rights is what people call themselves. . . . Disability culture is the commonality of the experience of living with a disability, and language is one of the keys to acknowledging this culture' (1985, p. 5). British disability studies scholar Mairian Corker (1998, p. 225) explained 'that the process of defining is bound up in "matters of identity" and therefore with action, political and otherwise, which is taken'.

For example, since the 1980s, the Disability Rights Movement has been trying to move from the term 'handicapped', which many feel associates people with disabilities with beggars (Barnes, 1992) (although recent research reports that derivation of the word is inaccurate, (Crowley & Crowley, 1999)), to 'people with disabilities', which is known as 'people-first' terminology. The passage of the ADA tried to push out the term 'handicapped' because activists were involved in writing the legislation and made sure it included the 'people-first' terminology. As political scientist Art Blaser (2002, p. 26) notes: 'With the term "disability," we have a major advantage because it's been used for decades, and was used by an almost unanimous Congress in passing the Americans with Disabilities Act'. The preferred disability terminology was a way that activists infused some disability culture into the ADA.

Disability culture as an outgrowth of identity is imbedded with political activism. Since the 1960s, US disability rights activists have advocated for a 'frame' in which society views them and their issues as a legitimate minority group that faces societal barriers and discrimination (Fleischer & Zames, 2001). Journalist Joseph Shapiro (1993), in his book, *No pity. People with disabilities forging a new civil rights movement,* explained that the recent history of the US Disability Rights Movement had an emphasis on activists coming together to push for federal legislation such as the Rehabilitation Act in the 1970s, which was a precursor to the ADA. Johnstone (2004) argues that formalized education and the recent growth of Disability Studies college programs forged modern disability identity. He argues that disability identity is becoming a formalized part of US society:

> The common voice and other empowering identities for people with disabilities are emergently receiving support by formalized structures. These structures publicize and communicate the notion of disability identity to the larger population. Messages such as: people come before disability, disability as a social and political issue, and promotion of disability culture are found in formal education, organizations and communications. . . . Publications have institutionalized the disabled identity into mainstream society. Narrative accounts of disability have brought the reality and complexity of disability to a wide readership, some with no previous experience with the notion of identity. (Johnstone, 2004, online)

The narrative accounts to which Johnstone refers are personal accounts within memoirs and other books about personal stories, rather than the mass media. Media reports, too, prefer these personal stories that are fashioned into narratives of 'overcoming the odds' or exceptional accomplishments (Thomson, 2001); however, in the hands of the media, these narratives serve to undermine disability identity with their syrupy messages infused with pity. Therein lays the tension between the internal pride, identity and culture of the Disability Rights Movement and the misinterpretation by the wider society, represented by the media, that active people with disabilities are 'inspirational' or are 'superior' in the face of 'tragedy'. The Disability Rights Movement is trying to move forward a serious political agenda, and the media focus on blind people who go bowling or a teen with a severe facial disfigurement who copes with life gracefully (Haller, 2001).

These issues underpin the discussions of disability terminology, the terms preferred by the Disability Rights Movement, and what is actually used by the news media. For decades, publications intended primarily for the disability community have noted that much media coverage of disability issues often does not include language that reflects current usage within the community (Birenbaum, 2000). The disability rights magazine, *The Disability Rag*, noted in 1990, the year the ADA passed, that 'even as we begin to see more "real" disability reporting', media coverage illustrates a seeming lack of awareness and context when addressing disability issues (p. 7).

Some disability activists criticize the Disability Rights Movement for the 'media problem', saying it stems from lack of a single, national voice for the movement, lack of training in conveying the importance of language choice to the media, as well as lack of framing issues in ways that emphasize people-first and other standards for addressing disability issues ('What we say', *Ragged Edge*, 1999). However, many in the disability community say they are hampered by the negative associations that already exist inherently in the words 'disabled' and 'disability'. As activist Bill Bolt argued in *Ragged Edge* (formerly *The Disability Rag*):

> The name that we've insisted on for ourselves—the word 'disabled'— sends journalists into a tailspin. If we are 'disabled,' that is, 'without abilities,' then what is this demand for equal employment, journalists likely think. On the other hand, if we can work with only minimal special

arrangements, then why do we need all kinds of government funds to live on? (Bolt, 1999, p. 24)

US disability studies scholar Simi Linton, in her book *Claiming Disability* (1998), also notes the problematic nature of the prefix 'dis', which connotes separation or taking apart. It has numerous denotative meanings:

> absence of, as in disinterest; opposite of, as in disfavor; undo, do the opposite of, as disarrange; and deprive of, as in disenfranchise. The Latin root dis means apart, asunder. Therefore, to use the verb disable, means in part to deprive of capability or effectiveness. The prefix creates a barrier, cleaving in two, ability and its absence, its opposite. Disability is the 'not' condition, the repudiation of ability. (Linton, 1998, p. 30)

Yet, disability activists and scholars also counter that any new terms promoted by the movement, regardless of journalists' practices and intentions, would soon be stigmatized by the larger culture; therefore, efforts should concentrate on improving perceptions of people with disabilities. Over time such efforts might erase the stigma associated with 'disabled' and similar terms. 'Old habits die hard, in part because they are reinforced by the media', notes Blaser, adding, 'But they do die' (2002, p. 25). He disagrees with those who consider negativity inherent in the words 'disabled' and 'disability' and public perception of the terms as unalterable. Decades of work by the movement has been changing the meaning of disability, much as African Americans transformed the term 'black' and the gay and lesbian movements altered 'queer'. Blaser says the disability community is fighting the same fight as these other social groups: 'I'm not convinced that our task in changing language is more difficult than Malcolm X's was, or unusually difficult when compared with other groups'. But I'll really be surprised if it's not still being fought by my children's grandchildren' (p. 26).

Some rhetorical and linguistic theorists agree with Blaser. Although disability has long been equated with tragedy, suffering and weakness in the minds of many in the general public, the Disability Rights Movement continues to battle for a new understanding of the word over many years or decades to come. British disability studies scholar Jenny Corbett (1996) maintains that language, as a primary source of power and control, must be contested—words, for example, disabled, must be won by the 'voice of enlightened modernity' in debates about political correctness, so that old usages are redefined. Language that retains a metaphorical suffering, pathos and dependency needs to be challenged. For example, by reclaiming 'cripple', disabled activists take the image in their identity that scares outsiders and make it a source of militant pride.

In the same vein, Linton maintains that wrestling for control of language and attempting to reassign the meaning of terminology used to describe disability and disabled people is vital to show how language reinforces the dominant culture's views of disability. She argues that since roughly 1980, people with disabilities themselves have gained more control over definitional issues, including within the news media. 'Less subtle, idiomatic terms for people with disabilities, such as: "cripple", "vegetable", "dumb", "deformed", "retard", and "gimp" have generally been expunged from public conversation though they appear in discourse. . . . Cripple as a descriptor of disabled people is considered impolite, but the word had retained its metaphoric vitality, as in "the expose in the newspaper crippled the politician's campaign"' (Linton, 1998, p. 16). However, Ben-Moshe says that even the metaphoric use of disability terms stigmatize people with disabilities:

> When we use terms like 'retarded,' 'lame,' or 'blind'—even if we are referring to acts or ideas and not to people at all—we perpetuate the

stigma associated with disability. By using a label, which is commonly associated with disabled people to denote deficiency, a lack, or an ill-conceived notion, we reproduce the oppression of people with disabilities. (Ben-Moshe, 2005, pp. 108–109)

Other types of negative terminology that remain in the media reinforce a 'sick role' or the medicalization of the disability identity. The news media sometimes refer to people who had contracted polio earlier in life as having been 'stricken' with polio. People with AIDS are sometimes referred to as 'AIDS sufferers', 'suffering from' AIDS, 'AIDS patients', or 'victims of' AIDS. Activist Jo Bower explains how dislike of this language has been a bond between many people with different disabilities: 'All of us have rejected the terms "victim" and "patient" to describe our relationship to our conditions and instead have chosen terms with dignity, which underline our personhood primarily and our condition second, as in people with HIV or people with disabilities' (Bower, 1994, p. 8). Linton adds that phrases found in media writing, such as, 'the man is a victim of cerebral palsy', makes the disease an agent that acts upon a helpless victim. Use of 'victim' implies criminal action while also giving life, power and intention to the condition while rendering the person passive and helpless. Problematic assumptions also apply to terms such as 'suffering from' or 'afflicted with'. If the person's condition is germane to the story, language such as 'he has cerebral palsy', serves as a better descriptor because it doesn't impose extraneous meanings while more accurately reporting the facts.

With regard to the stereotyping phrases 'wheelchair bound' or 'confined to a wheelchair', Linton notes that these common descriptions in the print media grant more power to the chair than the person. To report instead that someone uses a wheelchair 'not only indicates the active nature of the user and the positive way that wheelchairs increase mobility and activity but recognizes that people get in and out of wheelchairs for different activities: driving a car, going swimming, sitting on the couch, or occasionally, for making love' (1998, p. 27).

Peters (1999) believes such sociolinguistic changes that aim to empower people with disabilities will result in the most positive consequences. Media framing though negative terminology can even prove detrimental to the self-images of people with disabilities. Such practices result in significant negative consequences and barriers to productive living. Many disabled people (particularly youth) internalize labels and language used to inculcate them as passive recipients of state welfare, Peters says. 'They develop a false consciousness as they internalize the oppressors' image conveyed through language. This cultural invasion leads many disabled people to a silent world of passive acceptance where they adapt to the status quo . . .' (p. 103). Corker reaches similar conclusions, but optimistically notes that around the world disabled people have been using language to create a 'new disability discourse', and that issues of linguistic and cultural difference go well beyond '"nice" words and the "nasty" words relating to disability that are in cultural circulation' (p. 193). To effectively produce sociocultural change, the US Disability Rights Movement continues to directly engage media and other powerful institutions by calling attention to the linguistic frames used to characterize disability.

The Significance of the ADA as an Agent of Change

The first director of the National Council on Disability recalled what he said was the most important media event in the US Disability Rights Movement—the international Cable News Network (CNN)'s decision to carry the signing of the Americans with Disabilities Act live on TV. He said this one media event may have even been the most significant aspect of the ADA because 'laws are as much perception as reality' (Fleischer & Zames, 2001, p. 210). This one event thrust disability rights before the eyes of a huge TV audience and in turn, got journalists thinking about disability issues as a legitimate news story.

This study of disability terminology selected a time frame of analysis after the passage of the ADA because as strong disability rights legislation, it had the potential to shift US society to be more barrier-free. Linguistically, the ADA helped create a message about people with disabilities that contrasted with narrow stereotypes and misleading myths of the past. The Disability Rights Movement had long been battling a medical or social welfare representation, that the media often reinforced, which views disability as a physical problem alone residing within an individual (Scotch, 1988). The activists have long pushed for the disability rights model of representation (similar to the British disability studies Social Model), which acknowledges physical differences while shifting the focus from the disabled individual as 'the problem' to societies that have yet to modify their architectural, occupational, educational, communication and attitudinal environments to accommodate everyone.

One of the greatest accomplishments of activists in getting the ADA passed was maintaining the narrative of civil rights and minority group politics in the law (Watson, 1993). The disability community established a strong narrative for the ADA: "That its protections were an issue of civil rights rather than a charitable obligation or some other rationale" (Watson, 1993, p. 29). The ADA was 'civil rights regardless of cost' (p. 30). With that narrative secure in the legislative language, government sources and disability-related sources gave the news media the same information. For decades, disability has been defined and framed by government through legislation on war veterans, rehabilitation, education and social security (Liachowitz, 1988), but this time the Disability Rights Movement had the rhetorical power to craft the ADA. As Scotch explains: 'The disability rights movement is one in which the way an issue was framed had serious effects on both movement participation and the ability of the movement to influence public policies' (1988, p. 168).

Haller (1999a, 1999b, 1995, 2000) has argued that the ADA and the US news media's coverage of it in the early years helped place the disability rights model before the broader public. Disability rights activists helped construct the wording of the ADA and with those words flowing through the US government to the media, a more rights-oriented frame of disability was presented to the public. Therefore, in one sweeping legislative action, the disability rights perspective was forced onto the media radar and the public agenda of the USA, possibly shifting the media frames of people with disabilities.

It should be noted that mass media may be even more significant in presenting people with disabilities and their issues because many Americans have less interpersonal contact with people with disabilities because of barriers that still exist in society. Much of society is exposed to views of disability almost exclusively through mass media (Louis Harris and Associates Inc., 1991).

The media's coverage of the ADA probably promoted an awareness of the preferred terminology with which to refer to people with disabilities because the news media parroted the government's 'people-first' language in the coverage (Haller, 1995). Past research has confirmed that most journalists give high credibility to government information (Olien et al., 1989). For example, after the ADA, some local or state governments embraced 'people-first' language. Pennsylvania Governor Robert P. Casey mandated 'people-first' language in an executive order barring discrimination based on disability in state government (1992). Examples of people-first language are saying 'a professor with a disability' rather than 'a handicapped professor', saying 'uses a wheelchair' not 'confined to a wheelchair', or 'non-disabled' not 'normal' (Temple University Institute on Disabilities, 1992).

Therefore, this study seeks to understand whether this carefully crafted disability rights wording for ADA has begun to influence how two elite members of the US news media refer to people with disabilities.

Analysis of Disability Terminology in Two Elite Newspapers

This study conducted a content trend analysis of two major US newspapers to look at disability terminology use over a ten-year period. *The New York Times* and *Washington Post* were selected primarily because of their large circulations and their prominence as agenda-setting, elite media in the USA. Although content analysis makes judgments about content, not media effects, the assumption is that elite media act as opinion leaders about disability information and disability terminology in their stories. Most Americans say they use elite news media for information and these media are extremely important to them, according to a 1996 Gallup poll. Although Americans use more network TV news as a source, they are more likely to value the information from newspapers (Schwartz, 1996).

All the print stories in the data set were collected from the Lexis-Nexis newspaper database. The search terms used were: 'disabled', 'disability', 'disabilities', 'handicapped', 'cripple' and 'crippled'. All the stories with these terms were evaluated. The unit of analysis was an individual newspaper story, not the terms, so one story might contain several different terms. Also, any stories that used metaphorical disability terms that were not connected to disability issues or people with disabilities were eliminated from the sample. Restaurant listings referring to 'handicapped accessible' facilities were eliminated. Also, any story in which the only use of the disability term was in an organization's name, such as the President's Committee on the Employment of People with Disabilities, was eliminated because the use of the term reflected no decision-making on the part of the newspaper. However, stories that had any disability term, even one reference unconnected to the rest of the story, were still included in the sample. The limitation of this search is that it missed stories about individual disabilities if there was no use of one of these terms, such as a story about a blind person that never used the term 'disability'. However, because the focus of this study is specifically disability terminology, using the six terms above was the most viable option.

The samples consisted of stories in the two newspapers during October and November 1990, 1995 and 2000. October and November were selected because October is Disability Awareness Month and during November most activities in American life continue to occur, such as school and government meetings. Table 1 illustrates the number of stories per publication per year that were evaluated. The analysis of the terminology looked at the ways in which the terms were used, such as 'The disabled', 'disabled person/people', disability as a noun, 'people with disabilities', 'handicapped', 'cripple' or 'crippled'. The study does not pretend to give an all-encompassing picture of disability terminology but by using these two months hopes to show trends in the use of the terms.

A separate analysis looked at three other terms, specifically; 'confined to a wheel-chair', 'wheelchair-bound' and 'wheelchair user'. The analysis of these terms covered the entire years of 1990, 1995 and 2000, so the findings on those terms were the universe of uses for those years rather than samples. They are included in Table 2.

Table 1   **Disability-Related Terms in *The New York Times* and *Washington Post***

Terms	Oct-Nov 1990 (N = 140)[*]	Oct-Nov 1995 (N = 224)[*]	Oct-Nov 2000 (N = 186)[*]
	New York Times	*New York Times*	*New York Times*
'The Disabled'	28	71	41
Disabled person (as adjective)	41	59	61
Become disabled (as adverb) or other	22	19	20
Disability (as noun)	36	49	33
Person with disability/persons with disabilities	13	21	37
Handicapped (any use not part of organization's name)	38	37	26
Cripple (noun, referring to disability)	0	3 (in quotes)	1 (in quote)
Crippled (verb or adverb, referring to disability)	10	6	0
	Washington Post	*Washington Post*	*Washington Post*
'The Disabled'	34	66	44
Disabled person (as adjective)	55	70	81
Become disabled (as adverb) or other	25	37	30
Disability (as noun)	34	43	65
Person with disability/Persons with disabilities	19	24	45
Handicapped (any use not part of organization's name)	32	21	17
Cripple (noun, referring to disability)	1	1	0
Crippled (verb or adverb, referring to disability)	10	5	7

[*] Several terms may appear in one story. N = number of total stories.

Findings

A significant finding from the trend analysis is that these two US agenda-setting newspapers seem to be learning to eliminate the term 'handicapped'. Table 1 shows that *The New York Times* used the term 38 times in 1990 and by 2000 that had dropped to 26 uses; *The Washington Post* used the term 32 times in 1990 and by 2000 that had dropped to 17 uses. This change possibly illustrates the inroads the Disability Rights Movement is making in educating news media about preferred terminology. In addition, because 1990 saw the passage of the ADA, many in the media were only beginning to become aware of disability terminology changes. For example, two 1990 *New York Times* stories in preparation for ski season used phrases such as ski 'clinics for the handicapped' (Nelson, 1990, p. 15) and 'expanded handicapped skiers' program' (Carr, 1990, p. 8). Whereas in 2000, a *New York Times* story that had several references to 'handicapped children' was headlined 'Parents make toys for disabled children' (Brenner, 2000, p. 22). So there seems to be a transition occurring in the news media to replace the term 'handicapped' with 'disabled' in some instances. In addition, both newspapers appear to understand that the term 'crippled' is no longer appropriate, although *The Washington Post* used the term occasionally.

Table 2	**Wheelchair-related Terms in *The New York Times* and *Washington Post***		
Terms	1990 (complete years)	1995 (complete years)	2000 (complete years)
	New York Times	*New York Times*	*New York Times*
Wheelchair-bound	12	19	18
Confined to a wheelchair	16	14	21
Wheelchair user	4	16	13
	Washington Post	*Washington Post*	*Washington Post*
Wheelchair-bound	9	10	21
Confined to a wheelchair	9	13	10
Wheelchair user	5	8	13

Another positive finding is the increased use of the 'people-first' terms, 'person with a disability' or 'people with disabilities'. In the *Washington Post*, this term increased from 19 references in 1990 to 45 in 2000. Part of this increase is probably due to prevalent use of 'people-first' terminology among government and disability organizations, and the media are using verbatim references to terms given to them by these groups. For example, a *Washington Post* education story uses the phrase 'students with disabilities', which is probably how the Council for Exceptional Children's report—the source of the story—referred to them (*Washington Post*, 2000, Nov. 7, p. A18.)

However, general disability terminology that is not preferred by the disability community also had increases over the years. Use of the term, 'The Disabled' increased in both newspapers, especially in 1995. The reason this noun phrase is not preferred is that these nouns created from adjectives define people with disabilities in terms of their disabilities, rather than as people first (Longmore, 1985). This type of language subjugates people and presents them only in terms of their disability, rather than as multidimensional people. Not unsurprisingly, Dajani (2001) confirmed that a now defunct Disability News Service rarely used 'the disabled' but that *The Associated Press* used the term more often than 'people with disabilities' or 'disabled people' over a six-month period.

However, it is speculated that most media do not know or understand this problem with the term 'the disabled'. 'The disabled' fits with the norms of journalism because it is shorter than 'people with disabilities' in space-sensitive newspapers. Also, many times the newspapers used 'the disabled' in combination with other groups, such as 'housing for the homeless, the disabled and people with mental problems' in *The New York Times* (Brenner, 1995, p. 1). These uses of the terms illustrate another problem in how 'the disabled' is used—it seems to be partnered with powerless societal groups. In fact, the majority of US people with disabilities between the ages of 21 and 64 (57%) are employed; therefore, it is inappropriate to identify them as poor or homeless (US Census, 2002, online).

Finally, the most problematic terminology use in the two newspapers is the continued and increased use of 'wheelchair-bound' and 'confined to a wheelchair'. *The AP Stylebook*, the 'bible' on language use for print journalists, tells journalists not to write about a person's disability unless it is pertinent to the story (Goldstein, 2002). The *Stylebook* admonishes writers not to use the terms 'confined to a wheelchair' or 'wheelchair-bound' because 'people use wheelchairs for independent mobility' (Goldstein, 2002, pp. 74–75). Therefore, in using incorrect language about disability, the journalists have rejected some of the rules of their profession. Imbedded cultural beliefs seemed to overtake the professional norms of journalists. Even as recently as the death of Christopher Reeve in October 2004, *The Washington Post* continued to use 'wheelchair bound' in an editorial about stem cell research and Reeve, and in a story about the arrest of an elderly protestor (Thackeray, 2004, p. A17).

The Washington Post was found to be a prevalent user of the term 'wheelchair-bound', with use of the term increasing from nine instances in 1990 to 21 instances in 2000. Although this is a small number for the entire year, the term is never supposed to be used at all. The term is typically used as an adjective to describe someone, such as 'her wheelchair-bound sister' (Toscano, 2000, p. M24) or 'two wheelchair-bound New Yorkers' (Kurtz, 2000, p. A8). The use of 'confined to a wheelchair' assigns blame to a disease or medical condition that caused the 'confinement'. For example, the *New York Times* called 'Carol Rosenwald, frail and confined to a wheelchair by multiple sclerosis' (Ryan, 2000, p. 1).

As language use, both terms are incorrectly applied because confined means 'to keep shut up, as in a prison' and bound means 'tied' (*Webster's New World Dictionary of the American Language*, 1977), and everyone who uses a wheelchair leaves the chair for activities such as sleeping. When journalists use these terms, they misrepresent disability, as well as showing their misunderstanding of the disability experience. Wheelchairs are not binding or confining but actually increase mobility, speed and ability. For many people, wheelchairs increase their personal freedom (Issacson-Kailes, 1986).

A number of disability studies scholars argue that this inappropriate language use reflects the fears of non-disabled people about disability. Human fears of an 'imperfect body' that might need to use a wheelchair are great. Feminist disability studies scholar Susan Wendell (1989) says that it is more than just fear of physical difference at work here: 'Suffering caused by the body, and the inability to control the body, are despised, pitied, and above all, feared. This fear, experienced individually, is also deeply imbedded in our culture' (Wendell, 1989, p. 112). One study showed that 29% of Americans surveyed felt wheelchair use was a tragedy (Patterson & Witten, 1987). Journalists are inculcated with these same cultural fears.

Even in light of these cultural fears, this study of terminology in *The Washington Post* and *New York Times* does provide some evidence that journalists are learning to integrate new, more favorable terms into their stories. Both newspapers are using the term, 'wheelchair user' more often. The use of the term more than doubled in *The Washington Post* and more than tripled in *The New York Times*. Considering that entire years of stories were analyzed, there is not much use of the term, but the fact that 'wheelchair user' grew in prevalence in 1995 and 2000 means two major newspapers are aware it exists.

Conclusions

As with other oppressed groups in society, language is a site of struggle. And for people with disabilities, issues of identity are tied to media labeling. Even the slight improvement of disability terminology in the news media, that is, less use of 'handicapped' and more use of 'wheelchair user', serves to illustrate the growing political influence and identity of the U.S Disability Rights Movement. Susan Scheer, formerly a deputy director in New York's Mayor Office for

People with Disabilities, explains that the growth of an educated, professional class of disability rights advocates has meant a more sophisticated approach to changing media coverage of disability issues:

> Litigating cases and lobbying elected officials were the traditional techniques that the community used in the past. But now these techniques are used in combination with establishing connections with television, radio, and newspaper reporters and educating them. The language in the news accounts and editorials, although far from perfect, is much improved; for example, 'wheelchair user' is finally beginning to replace 'wheel-chair bound.' Also, stories have more balance, and the result is that the public is beginning to understand disability issues. (Susan Scheer, quoted in Fleischer & Zames, 2001, p. 208)

Although Scheer's comments are slightly more optimistic than this study found, many who follow media reporting are seeing that American journalism has a better understanding of disability topics. The hope is that deep within media practices, changes are percolating—changes that will begin to see people with disabilities and their issues in the same way as other social, cultural, and civil rights issues. This study offers no definitive proof that the media are beginning to understand disability rights and disability terminology, but the trends found do indicate that their labeling of people with disabilities has improved. For example, if the trends found by this study continue, the word 'handicapped' may no longer appear in US news media within a decade or so.

Therefore, studies such as this one that track media labeling of people with disabilities help us understand how far the US news media have come and how far they must go to reach a higher level of disability understanding. This paper illustrates that changes in disability language use within the media can signal a new paradigm in the way people with disabilities will be framed in the future.

Note

1. As this paper is about disability terminology in the US media, the preferred term in the USA, 'people with disabilities', will be used. It is understood that other English-speaking countries have other preferred terms.

References

1. Allen, I. L. (1990) *Unkind words: ethnic labeling from Redskin to WASP* (New York, Bergin & Garvey).
2. Barnartt, S., Schriner, K. & Scotch, R. (2001) Advocacy and political action, in: G. L. Albrecht, K. D. Seelman & M. Bury (Eds) *Handbook of disability studies* (Thousand Oaks, CA, Sage), 430–449.
3. Barnes, C. (1992) *Disabling imagery and the media: an exploration of the principles for media representations of disabled people* (Derby, The British Council of Disabled People).
4. Barnes, C. & Mercer, G. (2001) Disability culture: assimilation or inclusion?, in: G. L. Albrecht, K. D. Seelman & M. Bury (Eds) *Handbook of disability studies* (Thousand Oaks, CA, Sage), 515–524.
5. Ben-Moshe, L. (2005) 'Lame idea': disabling language in the classroom, in: *Building pedagogical curb cuts: incorporating disability into the university classroom and curriculum* (Syracuse, NY, Syracuse University Press), 107–115.

6. Birenbaum, A. (2000, July–August) Once again, for the first time, people with disabilities are recruited into the workforce, *Ragged Edge.* Available online at: http://www.raggededgemagazine.com/0700/0700medge1.htm (accessed 18 October 2002).
7. Blaser, A. (2002) Changing the meaning of 'disability', *Ragged Edge,* 25–26.
8. Bolt, B. (1999, July–August) The media don't 'get it' because we don't know what 'it' is, *Ragged Edge,* p. 24.
9. Bowe, F. (1978) *Handicapping America* (New York, Harper & Row).
10. Bower, J. (1994) HIV & disability, *The Disability Rag & Resource,* 15(2), 8–14.
11. Brenner, E. (1995, October 15) Unease persists over housing mandates, *New York Times,* section 13WC, p. 1.
12. Brenner, E. (2000. November 26) Parents make toys for disabled children, *New York Times,* section 14WC, p. 22.
13. Carr, S. (1990, November 11) Winter in the snow; stretching dollars on the slopes, *New York Times,* section 5, p. 8.
14. Casey, R. P. (1992, July 22) *Commonwealth of Pennsylvania Governor's Office executive order,* (Harrisburg, PA, Commonwealth of Pennsylvania), 1–2.
15. Clogston, J. (1989) A theoretical framework for studying media portrayal of persons with disabilities, paper presented at the annual meeting of *AEJMC,* Washington, DC, August.
16. Clogston, J. S. (1990) *Disability coverage in 16 newspapers* (Louisville, KY, Advocado Press). Clogston, J. (1991) *Reporters' attitudes toward and newspaper coverage of persons with disabilities.* Ph.D. dissertation., Michigan State University.
17. Corbett, J. (1996) *Bad-mouthing: the language of special needs* (Bristol, Falmer Press).
18. Corker, M. (1998) Disability discourse in a postmodern world, in: T. Shakespeare (Ed.) *The Disability Reader* (London, Cassell), 221–233.
19. Corker, M. (1999) New disability discourse, the principle of optimization and social change, in: M. Corker & S. French (Eds) *Disability discourse* (Philadelphia, PA, Open University Press).
20. Crowley, M. & Crowley, M. (1999) Spotlight on handicap, *Take our word for it,* 66. Available online at: http://www.takeourword.com/Issue066.html (accessed 13 July 2005).
21. Cumberbatch, G. & Negrine, R. (1991) *Images of disability on television* (London, Routledge).
22. Dajani, K. F. (2001) What's in a name? Terms used to refer to people with disabilities, *Disability Studies Quarterly,* 21(3), 196–209.
23. Entman, R. M. (1993) Framing: toward clarification of a fractured paradigm, *Journal of Communication,* 43(4), 51–58.
24. Finkelstein, V. (1980) *Attitude and disabled people* (New York, World Rehabilitation Fund 47).
25. Fleischer, D. Z. & Zames, F. (2001) *The Disability Rights Movement: from charity to confrontation* (Philadelphia, PA, Temple University Press).
26. Goldstein, N. (Ed.) (2002) *The Associated Press stylebook and briefing on media law* (Cambridge, MA, Perseus).
27. Haller, B. (1993) Paternalism and protest: coverage of deaf persons, *The Washington Post* and *New York Times, Mass Comm Review,* 20, 3–4.
28. Haller, B. (1995) *Disability rights on the public agenda: news media coverage of the Americans with Disabilities Act.* Unpublished doctoral dissertation. Temple University, Philadelphia.
29. Haller, B. (1999a) How the news frames disability: print media coverage of the Americans with Disabilities Act, in: *Research in social science and disability* (vol. 1) (Rockville, MD, JAI Press).
30. Haller, B. (1999b) *News coverage of disability issues: a final report for the Center for an Accessible Society,* San Diego Center for an Accessible Society, July.
31. Haller, B. (2000) If they limp, they lead? News representations and the hierarchy of disability images, in: D. Braithwaite & T. Thompson (Eds) *Handbook of communication and people with disabilities* (Mahwah, NJ, Lawrence Erlbaum).

32. Haller, B. (2001, April 29) Confusing disability and tragedy, *The Baltimore Sun,* p. 4C.
33. Isaacson-Kailes, J. (1985) Watch your language, please! *Journal of Rehabilitation,* 22, 68–69.
34. Isaacson-Kailes, J. (1990) Language is more than a trivial concern [Self-published article, Los Angeles, CA]. Available online at: http://www.jik.com/resource.html.
35. Johnson, M. (2000) *Make them go away* (Louisville, KY, Avocado Press).
36. Johnstone, C. J. (2004) Disability and identity: personal constructions and formalized supports, *Disability Studies Quarterly,* 24(4). Available online at: http://www.dsq-sds.org/_articles_html/2004/fall/dsq_fall04_johnstone.html (accessed 12 November 2004).
37. Kurtz, H. (2000, October 20) In the Senate race, what's past is present, *Washington Post,* p. A8.
38. Liachowitz, C. (1988) *Disability as social construct* (Philadelphia, PA, University of Pennsylvania Press).
39. Linton, S. (1998) *Claiming disability* (New York, New York University Press).
40. Longmore, P. K. (1985) A note on language and social identity of disabled people, *American Behavioral Scientist,* 28(3), 419–423.
41. Louis Harris and Associates, Inc. (1991) *Public attitudes toward people with disabilities. National poll conducted for National Organization on Disability* (New York, Louis Harris and Associates, Inc.).
42. Nelson, J. (1990, November 11) Winter in the snow; Breckenridge's wealth of choices, *New York Times,* section 5, p. 15.
43. Olien, C., Tichenor, P. & Donohue, G. (1989) Media and protest, in: L. Grunig (Ed.) *Monographs in environmental education and environmental studies* (Troy, OH, North American Association for Environmental Education).
44. Patterson, J. & Witten, B. (1987) Myths concerning persons with disabilities, *Journal of Applied Rehabilitation Counseling,* 18(5), 42–44.
45. Peters, S. (1999) Transforming disability identity through critical literacy and the cultural politics of language, in: M. Corker & S. French (Eds) *Disability discourse* (Philadelphia, PA, Open University Press).
46. Ragged Edge (1999, July–August) *What we say. What they hear,* 19–23.
47. Reiser, R. (2001, October) Does language matter? *Disability Tribune.* Available online at: http://www.daa.org.uk/e_tribune/e_2001_10.htm (accessed 11 July 2005).
48. Ryan, B. (2000, December 31) Snapshots of their lives, *New York Times,* Section 14CN, p. 1.
49. Schwartz, J. (1996, July) Local news matters, *American Demographics,* p. 18.
50. Scotch, R. K. (1988) Disability as the basis for a social movement: advocacy and politics of definition, *Journal of Social Issues,* 44(1), 159–172.
51. Shapiro, J. (1993) *No pity. People with disabilities forging a new civil rights movement* (New York, Times Books/Random House).
52. Smith, T. W. (1992) Changing racial labels: from 'colored' to 'Negro' to 'Black' to 'African American', *Public Opinion Quarterly,* 56, 496–514.
53. Stewart, C., Smith, C. & Denton, R. (1994) *Persuasion and social movements* (3rd edn) (Prospect Heights, IL, Waveland).
54. Temple University Institute on Disabilities (1992) *People first: a language guide.* Brochure available from IOD/UAP, Ritter Annex, Temple University, Philadelphia, PA, 19122.
55. Thackeray, B. (2004, October 30) Wheelchair users not bound, *Washington Post,* p. A17.
56. Thomson, R. G. (2001) Seeing the disabled: popular rhetorics of popular photography, in: P. K. Longmore & L. Umanski (Eds) (2001) *The new disability history: American perspectives* (New York, New York University Press).
57. Toscano, M. (2000, December 21) Music rocks into town, *Washington Post,* p. M24.
58. US Census (2002) 12th anniversary of Americans With Disabilities Act (press release). Available online at: http://www.census.gov/Press-Release/www/2002/cb02ff11.html (accessed 18 October 2002).

59. Washington Post (2000, November 7) *Extra credit,* p. A18.
60. Watson, S. D. (1993) A study in legislative strategy, in: *Implementing the Americans with Disabilities Act* (Baltimore, MD, Paul H. Brookes).
61. *Webster's New World Dictionary of the American Language* (1977) (New York, Popular Library).
62. Wendell, S. (1989) Toward a feminist theory of disability, *Hypatia,* 4(2), 104–124. (1999, July–August) What we say, What they hear, *Ragged Edge,* pp. 19–23. (2000, November 7) Extra credit, *Washington Post,* p. A18.

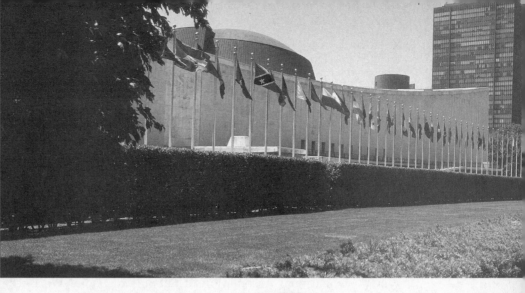

10

Global Perspectives and Theories

CHAPTER OUTLINE

CONNECTING CORE COMPETENCIES *in this chapter*

| Professional Identity | Ethical Practice | Critical Thinking | Diversity in Practice | **Human Rights & Justice** | Research Based Practice | Human Behavior | Policy Practice | Practice Contexts | Engage Assess Intervene Evaluate |

This chapter addresses traditional and alternative as well as emerging approaches to theories and knowledge about international or global social work. It is important, as we begin to ground ourselves in knowledge about human behavior and the social environment in an international context, that we begin by looking at what exists currently at international and organizational levels. This chapter presents some of the fundamental thinking about international social work past, present, and future.

Specifically, it presents in full the fundamental document guiding much of the thinking about international social welfare, the U.N. Universal Declaration of Human Rights. While adopted in 1948, this essential document has received scant attention in U.S. social work education until recently.

This chapter will also introduce you to the missions and purposes of three of the major international organizations for social workers—the International Association of Schools of Social Work, the International Federation of Social Workers, and the International Council on Social Welfare. Becoming familiar with all these documents is critical to gaining a basic understanding of the current context of international social work. The reader is encouraged to visit the Web site citations for each of these organizations to learn about current plans and activities, as well as how to become a part of the international social work community. Clearly, human behavior and the social environment in a global context calls for a life-long learning approach because the world is constantly and rapidly changing. The technological resources (Web sites) referenced in this chapter can provide access to the world of global social work as it responds to rapid change around the globe.

Certainly the events of September 11, 2001, and the resulting wars in Iraq and Afghanistan had an impact on individuals, families, groups, organizations, and communities throughout the United States and the world. These tragic events also presented an urgent reminder of the interrelationship of international concerns, needs, hatred, and actions with the well-being of people in the United States. It is safe to say that virtually every person in the United States was touched by these tragic events either directly or indirectly. It is also safe to say these events touched the lives of countless people and nations around the world. Social workers, because of our special concerns for the person *and* the environment, human dignity and worth of all people, and social and economic justice, have a special responsibility to understand and act to address such issues as those leading to and following September 11.

SOCIAL WORK AND ISLAM

In the aftermath of 9/11, it has become increasingly clear how little the U.S. public in general, and social workers specifically, know about the Muslim or Arab world and Islamic religion and culture. In Chapter 6 we addressed Islam in the context of family. Here we will address some of the basic tenets of an Islamic worldview or culture that guide the lives of Muslims and that are important for improving social workers' understanding of Islam both from religious and societal vantage points. However, it is very important that the reader understand that Muslims and Muslim communities, like all humans and communities, differ in the degree to which the various tenets of Islam are perceived and practiced by different individuals and communities.

As Al-Krenawi and Graham note, "Ethnic Arab societies are highly diverse and consist of heterogeneous systems of social differentiation based on ethnic, linguistic, sectarian, familial, tribal, regional, socioeconomic, and national identities." They also note that at a societal level the greater emphasis is on "the collective over the individual, having a slower pace of societal change, and a greater sense of social stability" (2000a:10).

Rehman and Dziegielewski present seven basic beliefs that are included in an Islamic worldview:

1. the belief in one God, Allah . . . as the one and only Creator/Sustainer of the heavens and the earth;
2. the belief in Divine Will (Al-Qadr/ fatalism);
3. the belief in the angels of Allah;
4. the belief in the revealed books of Allah (the Torah, the Psalms, the Qur'an and the Gospel);
5. the belief in the messengers of Allah [prophets];
6. the belief in the day of judgment; and
7. the belief in life after death (2003:33).

Al Krenawi and Graham describe what are referred to as the "Five Pillars of Islam." These pillars are integrated in life of followers of Islam:

1. The *shahada,* or profession of faith, is the belief that there is no other god but Allah and that Muhammad is His last prophet.
2. The *salat* is the imperative to pray five times daily: at dawn, noon, mid-afternoon, sunset and evening.
3. The *zakat* is the requirement to pay alms to the needy on behalf of one's family and business. It was customarily calculated as an annual payment of two and one half percent of all capital, assets, savings, and current income above a specified threshold.
4. The *siam* is the imperative to fast from food, drink and sex during daylight hours during the month of Ramadan, which immediately precedes the celebration of the date upon which Allah revealed the Koran to the Prophet Muhammad.
5. The *Hajj* is a pilgrimage to Mecca, a holy city of Islam located where Allah revealed the Koran to the Prophet Muhammad. The pilgrimage should be undertaken at least once in a Muslim's lifetime, if financially, mentally and physically capable. (Al-Krenawi and Graham 2000b:294–295)

In addition, "there are certain dietary rules in Islam. Muslims are not permitted to eat pork or consume alcohol or any other drugs that have the potential of impairing normal functioning" (Rehman and Dziegielewski 2003:33).

DEFINING INTERNATIONAL AND GLOBAL CONTEXTS

Asamoah et al. (1997) note that the terms "international" and "global" are often used interchangeably. However, these scholars differentiate between the two. They consider the general term *international* to be "the narrower term, referring to anything involving two or more nations, whereas 'global' [generally] refers to a mode of thinking about the planet as a whole and the interactive effects of social phenomena, linking domestic and international concerns in a seamless web." Healy, on the other hand links the terms more specifically to issues of social welfare.

Healy (1995 in Midgley 1997:9–10) differentiates between the terms *international* and *global*. She refers to *international* as "a broad umbrella term that refers to comparative accounts of social welfare activities in many countries." She defines *global* as "referring comprehensively to welfare activities that affect the planet as a whole" (1995 in Midgley 1997:9–10). We will keep these differences in mind as we explore international and global perspectives on social work.

HISTORICAL CONTEXT OF INTERNATIONAL SOCIAL WORK: TRADITIONAL AND ALTERNATIVE PERSPECTIVES

Mayadas and Elliot (1997) trace the history of international social work through four phases. Phase One they refer to as the Early Pioneers (1880s to 1940s). During this period there was a great deal of international exchange between Europe and the United States. This phase focused on the transfer of new social welfare approaches from Europe, primarily England to the United States. The two primary approaches were the Charity Organization Societies and Settlement Houses. Midgley describes the theory of the Charity Organization Society movement as follows:

> The Charity Organization Society was critical of the practice of giving aid to anyone who claimed to be poor, and it used women volunteers to investigate and verify the circumstance of the applicant for poor relief. These volunteers also formulated plans to rehabilitate their clients and to ensure that they became self-sufficient. This approach . . . was believed to be based on scientific principles (1997:162).

He describes the Settlement House Movement as follows:

> The settlements were not concerned with treatment but with neighborhoods and other activities that helped poor people improve their circumstances. Settlement houses relied extensively on student volunteers, who ran adult education classes, youth clubs, and recreational activities that catered to the needs of deprived people living in the slums of European and North American cities. Settlement workers were also engaged in community organizing (1997:162).

Mayadas and Elliott (1997:175–176) suggest that the professional values underlying these approaches "were paternalism, ethnocentrism, and protectionism, and were based on service models of charity, philanthropy, and social control of the poor."

Phase Two, according to Mayadas and Elliott, was Professional Imperialism (1940s–1970s). This phase focused on the development and export of social work education from the United States to other countries. Underlying values remained primarily paternalistic, ethnocentric, and colonialistic. Services were based on social control, remedial, medical, and crisis-oriented approaches. It was not sensitive to the cultural differences between the United States and the countries to which it exported a social work education model focused on practice with individuals, even though many of the cultures of the other countries were more collectively and group focused (Mayadas and Elliott 1997:176).

Phase Three, the reconceptualization and indigenization of social work (1970s–1990s) was a response to the lack of fit between indigenous (native) people's needs and the model being exported in Phase Two. The extreme poverty and political repression in many countries of the developing world led to a rejection of Western models and the development of more radical, liberationist, and social development oriented models. During this phase underlying values included regionalization, polarization, separation, and localization. This is consistent with a rejection by developing countries of Western-focused models (Mayadas and Elliott 1997:177).

Phase Four, international social development in the 21st century is still in process, and represents a paradigm shift in international social work. Approaches to international social work are becoming more social development oriented, comprehensive, and sensitive to the needs of the cultural and social contexts of different countries and regions. Values underlying the emerging approach are mutual exchange of ideas, multicultural, and focused on democracy, diversity, social, cultural, and ethnic interchange (Mayadas and Elliott 1997:177). We will look more closely at the social development approach later in this chapter.

Social Work in a Global Context: Debates/Critiques

The issues surrounding social work in a global context are difficult, complex, and a source of disagreement and controversy in the profession. Midgley (2001 in Gray and Fook 2004:625) notes several of the issues that face social workers in their efforts to understand social work in a global context:

- the nature of international social work;
- the profession's commitment to internationalising social work education and practice;
- the universality of social work values;
- internationalism as a desirable normative position; and
- on the nature of social work itself, that is, whether the profession should be committed to remedial, activist or developmental forms of practice.

Part of the overall debate surrounding social work in a global context is the issue of "professional imperialism." Gray and Fook (2004:626) note:

Many social workers across the world are becoming ever more vocal about the forces of "professional imperialism," particularly in the developing world. Over the past 30 years social work writers have been trying to raise awareness of the dominance of Western influences on social work and have been stressing the need for social work in the developing world to free itself from the 'in-built assumptions and cultural biases of first world theories and models of practice' . . . and to develop indigenous education and practice.

Below is a discussion of indigenization flowing from and part of the position taken in the "professional imperialism" debate.

Indigenisation debate

The indigenisation debate rests on two central premises:

Human Rights & Justice

As professional social workers, we are expected to recognize the global interconnections of oppression and discrimination and undertake strategies to promote human and civil rights. After reading this section, do you believe Western social work is part of the solution or part of the problem in developing a truly global approach to social work? Do you believe a truly global approach to social work is possible and beneficial? Why or why not?

1. Social work is a Western invention and a product of modernity. The notion of progressive change fits this paradigm. The question here is "whether or not, for example, Western perspectives on practice are really responsive to the personal and social needs of the population of other regions."

2. Indigenisation is postmodern to the extent that it questions the dominance of "social work as a Western invention" and seeks to relate it to local culture, history, and political, social and economic development. Implicit in the indigenisation side of the debate is the question of "whether it is incumbent on particular nations to develop their own orientations to social work practice." . . . This can also be extended into the question of whether national boundaries or commonalities make the most responsive basis for "localised" practice, or whether in fact there might be less structural or static boundaries, based on shared experiences, which provide a more appropriate framework for practice. (Gray and Fook 2004:634–635)

The two premises of the debate described above are addressed at more specific levels below:

1. The globalisation–localisation debate: The arguement "that alongside the process of globalisation was a counter tendency towards the development of locally based solutions."

2. The Westernisation–indigenisation debate: Is western social work relevant "to third world or developing contexts, such as Africa and Asia. Is Western social work capable of addressing developing world issues "such as poverty, AIDS/HIV, hunger, drought, and war."

3. The multicultural–universalisation debate: What are the "implications of built-in cultural biases . . . within social work's multicultural or culturally sensitive perspective, the notion that its values are universalisable and the potential conflict with non-Western and traditional cultures with collectivist values based [among other things] on kinship, community networks and the extended family system." (Gray and Fook 2004:627)

TECHNOLOGY AND INTERNATIONAL SOCIAL WORK

Increasingly, technology and access to technology are significant issues in the global environment and in international social work. New technologies can provide many opportunities for international social work and social development. However, their availability and access can also be serious barriers for people who lack the resources or countries that lack the infrastructures to acquire and use them. Midgley (1997:33) for example, notes that "many experts believe that the rapid expansion of information technology in recent decades has played a much more important role in fostering globalization than political or economic development." In other words, technology, particularly information and communication technology, can and does play a major role in the ability of people around the globe to communicate, in many cases instantly. The result of this is believed by many to be movement toward global integration and a world culture. The challenges, however, are significant in the area of technology and its potential for bringing people together. As is so often the case, lack of resources, education, and equal access create what has been referred to several times in this book as the digital divide—a world of "haves" and "have nots" with great disparities among people and countries in their ability to acquire and use technology to communicate and improve the quality of their lives. Technology is certainly a central consideration in international social and economic development efforts. In her recent book, Healy (2001) addresses the potential for new technologies to advance international social work practice and education.

INTERNATIONAL SOCIAL DEVELOPMENT

Social development is "an approach for promoting human well-being that seeks to link social programs directly with economic development efforts. Its proponents argue that economic development should be harnessed for social purposes." Rather than the remedial and "band aid" approaches to social programs, advocates for social development suggest that "social programs should contribute positively to economic development" (Midgley 1997:75–76). This approach has been used widely in the developing world and is increasingly being used in vulnerable areas of the developed world. The concept of social development was addressed briefly in Chapter 9. It has much in common with the assets approaches to community development and poverty reduction discussed in Chapter 9 as well. In the global context social development has become of increasing interest to nations and organizations struggling to overcome dire poverty and great disparities in who benefits from economic development around the world.

As we have noted several times throughout this book, social work, especially social work in the United States, has historically struggled to balance its stated responsibilities in the areas of both individual and social change or micro and macro approaches. As we have also noted several times, this historic struggle is also present in the arena of human behavior and the social environment (HBSE). Within HBSE, this struggle often results in much more attention to human behavior at the individual or small system level than to the social environment or the larger systems, such as organizations, communities, and the global environment, that form the context of human behavior at the individual or small system levels. Some have suggested that a social development approach might offer a way to bring more balance to these competing responsibilities within the profession.

For example, Asamoah et al. note, "the United Nations Development Program links human development and sustainable development, both of which are elements of social development. This linkage of the micro and macro is reflected in Lowe's definition of social development as "an encompassing concept that refers to a dual-focused holistic, systemic-ecologically oriented approach to seeking social advancement of individuals as well as broad-scale societal institutions" (Lowe, 1995 quoted in Asamoah, Healy, and Mayadas 1997).

Next, we will explore the U.N. Universal Declaration of Human Rights.

UNITED NATIONS UNIVERSAL DECLARATION OF HUMAN RIGHTS

This declaration of universal human rights is perhaps one of the most important documents guiding international social work organizations. It has been used widely to develop principles and missions of social work organizations around the world. Note that given the time periods in which it was created male pronouns are used predominantly. However, note also the inclusion of "sex" in Article 2. Adopted in 1948, its implementation in much of the world is far from complete, including in the United States.

Articles of UN Declaration of Human Rights

Article 1. All human beings are born free and equal in dignity and rights. They are endowed with reason and conscience and should act towards one another in a spirit of brotherhood.

Article 2. Everyone is entitled to all the rights and freedoms set forth in this Declaration, without distinction of any kind, such as race, colour, sex, language, religion, political or other opinion, national or social origin, property, birth or other status. Furthermore, no distinction shall be made on the basis of the political, jurisdictional or international status of the country or territory to which a person belongs, whether it be independent, trust, non-self-governing or under any other limitation of sovereignty.

Article 3. Everyone has the right to life, liberty and security of person.

Article 4. No one shall be held in slavery or servitude; slavery and the slave trade shall be prohibited in all their forms.

Article 5. No one shall be subjected to torture or to cruel, inhuman or degrading treatment or punishment.

Article 6. Everyone has the right to recognition everywhere as a person before the law.

Article 7. All are equal before the law and are entitled without any discrimination to equal protection of the law. All are entitled to equal protection against any discrimination in violation of this Declaration and against any incitement to such discrimination.

Article 8. Everyone has the right to an effective remedy by the competent national tribunals for acts violating the fundamental rights granted him by the constitution or by law.

Article 9. No one shall be subjected to arbitrary arrest, detention or exile.

Article 10. Everyone is entitled in full equality to a fair and public hearing by an independent and impartial tribunal, in the determination of his rights and obligations and of any criminal charge against him.

Article 11. (1) Everyone charged with a penal offence has the right to be presumed innocent until proved guilty according to law in a public trial at which he has had all the guarantees necessary for his defence. (2) No one shall be held guilty of any penal offence on account of any act or omission which did not constitute a penal offence, under national or international law, at the time when it was committed. Nor shall a heavier penalty be imposed than the one that was applicable at the time the penal offence was committed.

Article 12. No one shall be subjected to arbitrary interference with his privacy, family, home or correspondence, nor to attacks upon his honour and reputation. Everyone has the right to the protection of the law against such interference or attacks.

Article 13. (1) Everyone has the right to freedom of movement and residence within the borders of each state. (2) Everyone has the right to leave any country, including his own, and to return to his country.

Article 14. (1) Everyone has the right to seek and to enjoy in other countries asylum from persecution. (2) This right may not be invoked in the case of prosecutions genuinely arising from non-political crimes or from acts contrary to the purposes and principles of the United Nations.

Article 15. (1) Everyone has the right to a nationality. (2) No one shall be arbitrarily deprived of his nationality nor denied the right to change his nationality.

Article 16. (1) Men and women of full age, without any limitation due to race, nationality or religion, have the right to marry and to found a family. They are entitled to equal rights as to marriage, during marriage and at its dissolution. (2) Marriage shall be entered into only with the free and full consent of the intending spouses. (3) The family is the natural and fundamental group unit of society and is entitled to protection by society and the State.

Article 17. (1) Everyone has the right to own property alone as well as in association with others. (2) No one shall be arbitrarily deprived of his property.

Article 18. Everyone has the right to freedom of thought, conscience and religion; this right includes freedom to change his religion or belief, and freedom, either alone or in community with others and in public or private, to manifest his religion or belief in teaching, practice, worship and observance.

Article 19. Everyone has the right to freedom of opinion and expression; this right includes freedom to hold opinions without interference and to seek, receive and impart information and ideas through any media and regardless of frontiers.

Article 20. (1) Everyone has the right to freedom of peaceful assembly and association. (2) No one may be compelled to belong to an association.

Article 21. (1) Everyone has the right to take part in the government of his country, directly or through freely chosen representatives. (2) Everyone has the right of equal access to public service in his country. (3) The will of the people shall be the basis of the authority of government; this will shall be expressed in periodic and genuine elections which shall be by universal and equal suffrage and shall be held by secret vote or by equivalent free voting procedures.

Article 22. Everyone, as a member of society, has the right to social security and is entitled to realization, through national effort and international cooperation and in accordance with the organization and resources of each State, of the economic, social and cultural rights indispensable for his dignity and the free development of his personality.

Article 23. (1) Everyone has the right to work, to free choice of employment, to just and favourable conditions of work and to protection against unemployment. (2) Everyone, without any discrimination, has the right to equal pay for equal work. (3) Everyone who works has the right to just and favourable remuneration ensuring for himself and his family an existence worthy of human dignity, and supplemented, if necessary, by other means of social protection. (4) Everyone has the right to form and to join trade unions for the protection of his interests.

Article 24. Everyone has the right to rest and leisure, including reasonable limitation of working hours and periodic holidays with pay.

Article 25. (1) Everyone has the right to a standard of living adequate for the health and well-being of himself and of his family, including food, clothing, housing and medical care and necessary social services, and the right to security in the event of unemployment, sickness, disability, widowhood, old age or other lack of livelihood in circumstances beyond his control. (2) Motherhood and childhood are entitled to special care and assistance. All children, whether born in or out of wedlock, shall enjoy the same social protection.

Article 26. (1) Everyone has the right to education. Education shall be free, at least in the elementary and fundamental stages. Elementary education shall be compulsory. Technical and professional education shall be made generally available and higher education shall be equally accessible to all on the basis of merit. (2) Education shall be directed to the full development of the human personality and to the strengthening of respect for human rights and fundamental freedoms. It shall promote understanding, tolerance and friendship among all nations, racial or religious groups, and shall further the activities of the United Nations for the maintenance of peace. (3) Parents have a prior right to choose the kind of education that shall be given to their children.

Article 27. (1) Everyone has the right freely to participate in the cultural life of the community, to enjoy the arts and to share in scientific advancement and its benefits. (2) Everyone has the right to the protection of the moral and material interests resulting from any scientific, literary or artistic production of which he is the author.

Article 28. Everyone is entitled to a social and international order in which the rights and freedoms set forth in this Declaration can be fully realized.

Article 29. (1) Everyone has duties to the community in which alone the free and full development of his personality is possible. (2) In the exercise of his rights and freedoms, everyone shall be subject only to such limitations as are determined by law solely for the purpose of securing due recognition and respect for the rights and freedoms of others and of meeting the just requirements of morality, public order and the general welfare in a democratic society. (3) These rights and freedoms may in no case be exercised contrary to the purposes and principles of the United Nations.

Article 30. Nothing in this Declaration may be interpreted as implying for any State, group or person any right to engage in any activity or to perform any act aimed at the destruction of any of the rights and freedoms set forth herein.

Source: http://www.un.org/Overview/rights.html

Millennium Goals

Consistent with principles outline in the U.N. Declaration of Human Rights, in 2000 the United Nations Development Program, in collaboration with numerous countries, private-for-profit, nonprofit, non-governmental (NGOs), and public governmental organizations, set an agenda for ending world poverty by the year 2015. In his foreword to the United Nations Millennium Development Goals Report 2008, Secretary-General Ban Ki-Moon noted the lofty purpose of the goals: "in adopting the Millennium Declaration in the year 2000, the international community pledged to 'spare no effort to free our fellow men, women and children from the abject and dehumanizing conditions of extreme poverty.' We are now more than halfway towards the target date—2015—by which the Millennium Development Goals are to be achieved."

The Secretary-General also notes that the grand intentions of the Millennium Development Goals (MDGs) "encapsulate the development aspirations of the world as a whole. But they are not only development objectives; they encompass universally accepted human values and rights such as freedom from hunger, the right to basic education, the right to health and a responsibility to future generations" (U.N. 2008:3). The eight goals are as follows:

1. Goal: Eradicate extreme poverty and hunger
2. Goal: Achieve universal primary education
3. Goal: Promote gender equality and empower women
4. Goal: Reduce child mortality
5. Goal: Improve maternal health
6. Goal: Combat HIV/AIDS, malaria and other diseases
7. Goal: Ensure environmental sustainability
8. Goal: Develop a Global Partnership for Development (U.N.)

Progress and challenges

The 2008 report addresses both accomplishments and work still to be done to achieve the goals. The report noted, "there has been sound progress in some MDG areas . . . and a number of targets are expected to be reached by their target dates, mostly 2015."

Progress

- The overarching goal of reducing absolute poverty by half is within reach for the world as a whole;
- In all but two regions, primary school enrolment is at least 90 percent;
- The gender parity index in primary education is 95 per cent or higher in six of the 10 regions, including the most populous ones;
- Deaths from measles fell from over 750,000 in 2000 to less than 250,000 in 2006, and about 80 per cent of children in developing countries now receive a measles vaccine;
- The number of deaths from AIDS fell from 2.2 million in 2005 to 2.0 million in 2007, and the number of people newly infected declined from 3.0 million in 2001 to 2.7 million in 2007;
- Malaria prevention is expanding, with widespread increases in insecticide-treated net use among children under five in sub-Saharan Africa: in 16 out of 20 countries, use has at least tripled since around 2000.
- The incidence of tuberculosis is expected to be halted and begin to decline before the target date of 2015;

- Some 1.6 billion people have gained access to safe drinking water since 1990;
- The use of ozone-depleting substances has been almost eliminated and this has contributed to the effort to reduce global warming;
- The share of developing countries' export earnings devoted to servicing external debt fell from 12.5 per cent in 2000 to 6.6 per cent in 2006, allowing them to allocate more resources to reducing poverty;
- The private sector has increased the availability of some critical essential drugs and rapidly spread mobile phone technology throughout the developing world. (U.N. 2008:4)

Challenges remaining

The report also identified "targets that are likely to be missed unless additional, strengthened or corrective action is taken urgently." These targets include:

- The proportion of people in sub-Saharan Africa living on less than $1 per day is unlikely to be reduced by the target of one-half;
- About one quarter of all children in developing countries are considered to be underweight and are at risk of having a future blighted by the long-term effects of undernourishment;
- Of the 113 countries that failed to achieve gender parity in both primary and secondary school enrolment by the target date of 2005, only 18 are likely to achieve the goal by 2015;
- Almost two thirds of employed women in the developing world are in vulnerable jobs as own-account or unpaid family workers;
- In one third of developing countries, women account for less than 10 percent of parliamentarians;
- More than 500,000 prospective mothers in developing countries die annually in childbirth or of complications from pregnancy;
- Some 2.5 billion people, almost half the developing world's population, live without improved sanitation;
- More than one third of the growing urban population in developing countries live in slum conditions;
- Carbon dioxide emissions have continued to increase, despite the international timetable for addressing the problem;
- Developed countries' foreign aid expenditures declined for the second consecutive year in 2007 and risk falling short of the commitments made in 2005;
- International trade negotiations are years behind schedule and any outcome seems likely to fall far short of the initial high hopes for a development-oriented outcome. (U.N. 2008:4)

Clearly much progress has been made, but much remains to be done in accomplishing these critical goals. It is important to note that the report identifies losses or potential losses in movement to attain a number of the goals due to the declining world economy. This report was produced in 2008, prior to the tremendous decline in world economies as the decline became a full-blown recession in the fall of 2008 and into the first half of 2009. Both the U.N. Universal Declaration of Human Rights and the Millennium Goals are founded on the fundamental belief in human rights. In the following section, we explore the notion of social work as a human rights profession.

Social Work as a Human Rights Profession

There are different definitions of human rights, but they all have much in common, as the definitions and discussion provided below reflect. In 1988 the International Federation of Social Workers (IFSW; see information on IFSW in a following section) declared, "social work was and always has been a human rights profession." Healy presents the basic tenet associated with the IFSW declaration as "the intrinsic values of every human being and as one of its main aims the promotion of equitable social structures, which can offer people security and development while upholding their dignity." Healy provides a basic definition of *human rights* as "those rights that belong to all just because we are human." She finds Articles 22 and 25 of the U.N. Universal Declaration of Human Rights particularly applicable to social work as a human rights profession (see these articles in the preceding section, "United Nations Universal Declaration of Human Rights") (Healy 2008:735–737). In addition, Lundy and van Wormer provide the *Social Work Dictionary*'s definition of social justice: "an ideal condition in which all members of a society have the same basic rights, protection, opportunities, obligations, and social benefits" (Barker quoted in Lundy and Van Wormer 2007:727).

The concepts of social and economic justice are also fundamental elements of social work's purpose and are closely related to the concept of human rights, but are not the same thing. Lundy and van Wormer, for example, argue, "economic justice is a narrower concept, referring to the standard of living that ideally should be equitable. All persons ought to have opportunities for meaningful work and an income that provides them with adequate food, shelter, a level of living that contributes to good health." They further explain, "whereas social and economic justice is a general term that relates to society in general, human rights is a term that, from the point of view of the people, refers to specific universal standards relevant to freedom and well-being, personal and collective rights" (Lundy and Van Wormer 2007:727–728).

In their discussion of the "potential for human rights to serve as a unifying framework" for the profession, Asamoah et al. note that the UNDHR (see preceding section) actually defines four categories of human rights:

1. Recognition of human dignity.
2. Recognition of civil and political rights.
3. Economic and social rights—including government responsibility to guarantee that human needs for shelter, health care, education, and old age security will be met.
4. Solidarity rights "stress the need for individual and international cooperation to realize such rights as a clean environment, peace, and international distributive justice." (Asamoah, Healy, and Mayadas 1997)

These scholars argue that in the United States the first two categories of rights have been considered "as the totality of human rights." However, they also argue, "for social work as a global profession . . . the other two categories are equally or more important" (Asamoah et al. 1997).

One of the greatest violations of human rights is torture. In Illustrative Reading 10.1: A Plague of Our Time: Torture, Human Rights, and Social Work, the authors address this egregious violation of human rights. They present information on the prevalence of torture and they note that social workers in the United States are often ill prepared to deal with survivors of torture, though many immigrants and refugees who come to the United States have been victims of torture. In addition, they provide information on intervention approaches and outline resources that may be helpful to social workers who work with victims of torture.

Next, we explore the major international social work organizations that are actively engaged in the struggle to bring human rights and social and economic justice to the forefront of social work in a global context.

INTERNATIONAL SOCIAL WORK ORGANIZATIONS

Professional Identity

Part of our identity as professional social workers is our commitment to the profession's enhancement. Give two examples of how international social work organizations reflect our commitment to the profession's enhancement.

Professional Identity

Professional social workers serve as representatives of the profession, its mission, and its core goals. Compare the international definition of social work and the related components outlined in this section with the U.S. definition (see Chapter 1 for a refresher on the CSWE definition of social work in terms of its mission, goals, and purposes). What are the differences? Similarities?

There are a number of international social work organizations concerned with the implementation of the U.N. Universal Declaration of Human Rights. In addition, these organizations share many concerns about the mechanisms for and responsibilities of social workers in effectively creating a global environment consistent with social work ethics and values, especially those concerned with social and economic justice and well-being for all people. Three of the major international organizations of social workers are the International Federation of Social Workers (IFSW), the International Council on Social Welfare (ICSW), and the International Association of Schools of Social Work (IASSW). These organizations often work collaboratively to provide leadership and direction for the development of effective international approaches to social work education and practice. For example, IFSW and IASSW worked jointly to put forth an International Definition of Social Work in 2001. It is included below after the missions and principles of these organizations.

The International Association of Schools of Social Work (IASSW) is an international association of institutions of social work education, organizations supporting social work education, and social work educators. Its mission is:

a. To develop and promote excellence in social work education, research, and scholarship globally in order to enhance human well-being.

b. To create and maintain a dynamic community of social work educators and their programs.

c. To support and facilitate participation in mutual exchanges of information and expertise.

d. To represent social work education at the international level.

In fulfilling its mission, IASSW adheres to all United Nations Declarations and Conventions on human rights, recognizing that respect for the inalienable rights of the individual is the foundation of freedom, justice and peace.

Members of IASSW are united in their obligation to the continued pursuit of social justice and social development. In carrying out its mission, IASSW fosters cooperation, collegiality, and interdependence among its members and with others.*

The International Council on Social Welfare (ICSW), founded in Paris in 1928, is a nongovernmental organization which now represents national and local organizations in more than 80 countries throughout the world. Our membership also includes a number of major international organizations.

*http://www.iassw.soton.ac.uk/Generic/Mission.asp?lang=en

Mission: The International Council on Social Welfare (ICSW) is a global nongovernmental organization which represents a wide range of national and international member organizations that seek to advance social welfare, social development and social justice.

ICSW's basic mission is to promote forms of social and economic development which aim to reduce poverty, hardship and vulnerability throughout the world, especially amongst disadvantaged people. It strives for recognition and protection of fundamental rights to food, shelter, education, health care and security. It believes that these rights are an essential foundation for freedom, justice and peace. It seeks also to advance equality of opportunity, freedom of self-expression and access to human services.

In working to achieve its mission, ICSW advocates policies and programmes which strike an appropriate balance between social and economic goals and which respect cultural diversity. It seeks implementation of these proposals by governments, international organizations, nongovernmental agencies and others. It does so in cooperation with its network of members and with a wide range of other organizations at local, national and international levels. ICSW's main ways of pursuing its aims include gathering and disseminating information, undertaking research and analysis, convening seminars and conferences, drawing on grass-roots experiences, strengthening nongovernmental organizations, developing policy proposals, engaging in public advocacy and working with policy-makers and administrators in government and elsewhere.*

The International Federation of Social Workers recognizes that social work originates variously from humanitarian, religious and democratic ideals and philosophies; and that it has universal application to meet human needs arising from personal-societal interactions, and to develop human potential.

Professional social workers are dedicated to service for the welfare and self-fulfillment of human beings; to the development and disciplined use of scientific knowledge regarding human behaviour and society; to the development of resources to meet individual, group, national and international needs and aspirations; to the enhancement and improvement of the quality of life of people; and to the achievement of social justice.

History: The International Federation of Social Workers is a successor to the International Permanent Secretariat of Social Workers, which was founded in Paris in 1928 and was active until the outbreak of World War II. It was not until 1950, at the time of the International Conference of Social Work in Paris, that the decision was made to create the International Federation of Social Workers, an international organization of professional social workers.

The original agreement was that the IFSW would come into being when seven national organizations agreed to become members. After much preliminary work, the Federation was finally founded in 1956 at the time of the meeting of the International Conference on Social Welfare in Munich, Germany.**

International Definition of Social Work The social work profession promotes social change, problem solving in human relationships and the

*http://www.icsw.org/

**http://www.ifsw.org

empowerment and liberation of people to enhance well-being. Utilizing theories of human behaviour and social systems, social work intervenes at the points where people interact with their environments. Principles of human rights and social justice are fundamental to social work.

Commentary: Social work in its various forms addresses the multiple, complex transactions between people and their environments. Its mission is to enable all people to develop their full potential, enrich their lives, and prevent dysfunction. Professional social work is focused on problem solving and change. As such, social workers are change agents in society and in the lives of the individuals, families and communities they serve. Social work is an interrelated system of values, theory and practice.

Values*:* Social work grew out of humanitarian and democratic ideals, and its values are based on respect for the equality, worth, and dignity of all people. Since its beginnings over a century ago, social work practice has focused on meeting human needs and developing human potential. Human rights and social justice serve as the motivation and justification for social work action. In solidarity with those who are disadvantaged, the profession strives to alleviate poverty and to liberate vulnerable and oppressed people in order to promote social inclusion. Social work values are embodied in the profession's national and international codes of ethics.

Theory: Social work bases its methodology on a systematic body of evidence-based knowledge derived from research and practice evaluation, including local and indigenous knowledge specific to its context. It recognizes the complexity of interactions between human beings and their environment, and the capacity of people both to be affected by and to alter the multiple influences upon them including bio-psychosocial factors. The social work profession draws on theories of human development and behaviour and social systems to analyse complex situations and to facilitate individual, organizational, social and cultural changes.

Practice: Social work addresses the barriers, inequities and injustices that exist in society. It responds to crises and emergencies as well as to everyday personal and social problems. Social work utilizes a variety of skills, techniques, and activities consistent with its holistic focus on persons and their environments. Social work interventions range from primarily person-focused psychosocial processes to involvement in social policy, planning and development. These include counselling, clinical social work, group work, social pedagogical work, and family treatment and therapy as well as efforts to help people obtain services and resources in the community. Interventions also include agency administration, community organization and engaging in social and political action to impact social policy and economic development. The holistic focus of social work is universal, but the priorities of social work practice will vary from country to country and from time to time depending on cultural, historical, and socio-economic conditions.*

*International Association of Schools of Social Work/ International Federation of Social Workers. Definition of Social Work Jointly Agreed 27 June 2001 Copenhagen

SUMMARY

A number of aspects of international or global social work have been addressed in this chapter. Social workers, especially social workers in the United States and other affluent nations, have both unique opportunities and serious responsibilities in the global arena. For social work to fulfill its purposes as a profession, it must increasingly move into the international arena. In order to more fully understand human behavior and the social environment, it is essential that we become knowledgeable about international issues and people. If we are members of affluent groups and societies, we must recognize that our privilege is not shared by many others on the planet. In addition, we have the responsibility of using the benefits of our privileged status to advocate both locally and globally for social and economic justice in its fullest sense. As social workers we need to develop a true worldview that transcends national borders, belief systems, and ways of life.

Professional
Identity

Human
Rights
& Justice

Log onto **www.mysocialworklab.com** to watch videos on the skills and competencies discussed in this chapter. (If you did not receive an access code to **MySocialWorkLab** with this text and wish to purchase access online, please visit **www.mysocialworklab.com**.)

PRACTICE TEST

Diversity
in Practice

1. With reference to social welfare, Healy uses this term to refer to the comparative accounts of social welfare activities in many countries.
   a. international
   b. global
   c. worldwide
   d. international and global can be used interchangeably

Human
Rights

2. The history of international social work has been categorized in four phases. Which phase showed international social work becoming more social development oriented, comprehensive, and sensitive to the needs of the cultural and social contexts of different countries and regions?
   a. Phase 2
   b. Phase 4
   c. professional imperialism phase
   d. charity organization phase

3. _____ refers of the dominance of Western influences in social work and the development and export of social work education from the U.S. to other countries.
   a. Social welfare colonialism
   b. Indigenization of social work
   c. Social welfare globalization
   d. Professional imperialism

Policy
Practice

4. This approach for promoting human well being seeks to link social programs directly to economic development efforts and advocates suggest that social programs should contribute positively to economic development.
   a. comprehensive development
   b. social development
   c. socio-economic development
   d. global war on poverty

5. This is one of the most important documents guiding international social work organizations and has been used to develop principles and missions of social work organizations around the world.
   a. International Social Workers Code of Ethics
   b. Council on Social Work Education Core Competencies
   c. United Nations Universal Declaration of Human Rights
   d. International Red Cross Charter

6. _____ can be defined as an ideal condition in which all members of a society have the same basic rights, protections, opportunities, obligations and social benefits.
   a. social justice
   b. civil rights
   c. human rights
   d. ideal rights

7. _____ is a global nongovernmental organization whose basic mission is to promote forms of social and economic development which aim to reduce poverty, hardship, and vulnerability throughout the world. It represents national and local organizations in more than 80 countries throughout the world.
   a. International Red Cross (IRC)
   b. International Federation of Social Workers (ICSW)
   c. International Council on Social Welfare (IFSW)
   d. United Nations Development Program (UNDC)

8. The adoption of the Millennium Declaration in the year 2000 set an agenda for ending _____ by the year 2015.
   a. torture
   b. discrimination
   c. genocide
   d. world poverty

9. _____ refers to those rights that belong to us all just because we are human and to specific universal standards relevant to freedom and well being, personal and collective rights.
   a. social and economic justice
   b. human rights
   c. empowerment
   d. political justice

10. Social workers face several issues in their efforts to understand social work in a global context. Which of the following is not one of these issues?
    a. the universality of social work values
    b. the nature of social work itself, i.e. whether the profession should be committed to remedial, activist, or development forms of practice
    c. the profession's commitment internationalizing social work education and practice
    d. all of the above are relevant issues

Log onto **MySocialWorkLab** once you have completed the Practice Test above to take your Chapter Exam and demonstrate your knowledge of this material.

Answers

1) a 2) b 3) d 4) b 5) c 6) a 7) c 8) d 9) b 10) d

A Plague of Our Time: Torture, Human Rights, and Social Work

David W. Engstrom & Amy Okamura

Abstract

Social work provides services to refugees and immigrants, the groups most likely to have been tortured, and despite this, the professional literature contains little information on torture or torture treatment. In this article, the authors discuss the extent of torture worldwide, review the prevalence of torture survivors in the United States, and discuss populations most at risk and the effects of torture. In the heart of the article, they discuss treatment considerations and resources for social workers involved with torture survivors. Working with survivors requires knowledge about human rights violations; identification of symptoms of torture and survivors reluctant to reveal this part of their past; community context and treatment environments; skills in healing trauma; advocacy; and brokering necessary medical, mental health, legal, and social services.

Torture has been all too much a part of the human experience (Peters, 1985). Human rights organizations, the United Nations, and governments all document the pervasive and persistent use of torture worldwide. Despite the long history of torture as an instrument of extreme cruelty and political persecution, only within the last 20 years has a specialized body of knowledge emerged to assist in treating survivors of torture.

A significant portion of social work consists of providing social and mental health services to refugees and immigrants, the groups most likely to have suffered torture. Although mental health needs of refugees from war-torn countries has long been a concern of the profession, there has been little discussion on torture per se (Carlin, 1979; Kinzie, Fredrickson, Rath, Fleck, & Karls, 1984; Kinzie, Sack, Angell, & Manson, 1986; Levine, 2001; Lin, Tazuma, & Masuda, 1979; Owan, 1985; Westermeyer, 1987). Nevertheless, social workers are among the key professionals who work in torture treatment centers throughout the world. Yet, unlike other professions such as psychology, medicine, nursing, and law, there is remarkably little recognition of the existence of torture or the treatment of torture in the social

David W. Engstrom, PhD, is associate professor, San Diego State University School of Social Work, College of Health and Human Services, and is vice president of the board of directors, Survivors of Torture, International, a community-based torture treatment center in San Diego, California. Dr. Engstrom is also the author or editor of two books on refugees and immigrants to the United States: *Presidential Decision Making Adrift* (New York: Roman and Littlefield, 1997), a policy case study of the Mariel boatlift of 1980, and coeditor with Patora San Juan Cafferty of *Hispanics in the United States* (New Brunswick, NJ: Transaction Publishers, 2002). **Amy Okamura, MSW, LCSW,** has been lecturer, San Diego State University School of Social Work, College of Health and Human Services for 11 years and is a private practitioner affiliated with Survivors of Torture, International. Ms. Okamura has 34 years of experience in clinical and administrative practice with expertise in work with refugees and torture survivors. Correspondence regarding this article may be sent to the first author at engstrom@mail.sdsu.edu.

Families in Society: The Journal of Contemporary Social Services www.familiesinsociety.org Copyright 2004 Alliance for Children and Families work professional literature.[1] Nevertheless, social workers need to be informed about torture, both because it harms the lives of tens of thousands of people who might be or become social work clients and also because its effects are often missed. Torture is an affront to—indeed, an assault on—social workers' code of ethics and humanity's basic human rights.

In this article, we discuss the extent of the problem of torture worldwide and review the prevalence of torture survivors in the United States. We detail the traumatic effect of torture and provide guidelines for developing competence in providing social work services to survivors of torture. Because many survivors live in areas that have no specific torture treatment centers and because many survivors present for services in community clinics, hospitals, and social service agencies, we review treatment issues for social workers who find themselves working with survivors of torture.

Human Rights and Torture

Writing in 1958, the French philosopher Jean Paul Sartre called torture "a plague infecting our whole era" (p. 26). What was true decades ago is true today: Torture remains all too common an experience for far too many people. At the beginning of the new century, torture is not merely the aberrant behavior of a few rogue states. It is practiced on persons of all ages, races, religions, and genders. Despite the widespread use of torture, nations seldom publicly admit to practicing it; when they do, it is often couched in the language of means justifying the ends. For example, even before evidence of torture surfaced at Abu Ghraib prison in Iraq, the United States had used countries that routinely practiced torture to "interrogate" individuals suspected of links to Al Qaeda and other terrorist organizations, all in the name of the war on terror (Human Rights Watch, 2004; Brown & Priest, 2003).

Elimination of the use of torture has long been a primary aim of both international and country-specific human rights groups. To strengthen their moral campaign against torture, human rights groups point to a host of international standards prohibiting its use. Among the most important statements condemning torture is Article 5 of the 1948 United Nations' (U.N.) *Universal Declaration of Human Rights,* which proclaims, "No one shall be subjected to torture or to cruel, inhuman or degrading treatment or punishment" (U.N., 1948). Focusing on the action and behavior of nations, the 1975 U.N. *Convention Against Torture and Other Cruel, Inhuman or Degrading Treatment or Punishment* forcefully declares, "No State may permit or tolerate torture or other cruel, inhuman or degrading treatment or punishment" (U.N., 1975). Regional conventions, such as the *Inter-American Convention to Prevent and Punish Torture,* use similar language (Organization of American States, 1987). The existence of international human rights covenants and conventions demonstrates a worldwide consensus that torture is immoral and should be condemned. However, although such covenants and conventions are important symbolic documents, they do not compel nations to abolish the use of torture. Indeed, a number of signatories

---

[1]For example, from 1998 to 2002, PsycINFO reported 14 articles on psychology and torture; Medline listed 20 articles on physicians and torture and 10 articles on nursing and torture. During the same time range, Social Work Abstracts reported 5 articles, only 3 of which appeared in North American journals.

to the U.N.'s *Universal Declaration of Human Rights* have been identified as active practitioners of torture.[2]

There are many definitions of *torture.* Historian Edward Peters (1985, p. 3) stated that torture is a "torment inflicted by a public authority for ostensibly public purposes." The U.N.'s *Convention Against Torture* (1975) provided an international definition of torture:

> Torture means any act by which severe pain or suffering, whether physical or mental, is intentionally inflicted on a person for such purposes as obtaining from him or a third person information or a confession, punishing him for an act he or a third person has committed, . . . or intimidating or coercing him or a third person, or for any reason based on discrimination of any kind, when such pain and suffering is inflicted by or at the instigation of . . . a public official or other person acting in an official capacity. It does not include pain or suffering arising only from, or inherent in or incidental to lawful sanctions. (Article 1, ¶ 1)

Human rights advocates have criticized the U.N. definition because it ignores the use of torture by paramilitary groups and "militants and or other nonofficials" (Iacopino, 1998, p. 45). The often-cited 1975 Tokyo Declaration by the World Medical Association defines *torture* as "the deliberate systematic or wanton infliction of physical or mental suffering by one or more persons acting alone or on the orders of any authority, to force another person to yield information, to make a confession, or for any other reason" (World Medical Association, 1975).

Others have noted that official definitions tend to focus on the individual while ignoring the consequences of torture for communities and society itself. Sister Dianna Ortiz (2001), herself a torture survivor, regards torture as "an act of terrorism aimed at instilling a paralyzing fear not only in individuals but also in the family, the community, and society" (p. 14). Writing about the function of torture, Enrique Bustos (1990) stated, "Torture is used to obtain information, to punish, and to physically and psychologically annihilate. Opposition in the rest of society is intimidated, terrorized, and paralyzed" (p. 143). Torture is ultimately about the perverse use of power to coerce and oppress.

The Prevalence of Torture

Social workers need to be informed about torture, both because it harms the lives of tens of thousands of people who might be or become social work clients and also because its effects are often missed.

It is difficult to estimate the prevalence of torture. In part, this is because there are many and varied definitions of torture; more importantly, it is because governments actively deny practicing it and suppress information about it (Basoglu, 1992, p. 2; Fischman, 1998, p. 30). Amnesty International's reports of human rights violations are frequently used to document the global extent of torture. Amnesty International presented evidence that between 1997 and 2000, more than 150 countries had practiced torture or other forms of ill treatment. That human rights group further noted that 70 of those countries persistently practice torture (Amnesty International, 2000). Moreover, in 2001, Amnesty International documented the use of torture by 125 countries—almost two thirds of all countries and territories (Amnesty International, 2001). Torture is most associated with authoritarian regimes, but it exists in far too many democratic countries as well (Conroy, 2000). In the first half of 2004, evidence mounted that the United States and its coalition partners practiced torture in Iraq and Afghanistan, though these incidents were officially defined as the work of local soldiers acting on their own. More troubling, the condition under which the United States is

---

[2]For example, in its regional summaries, Amnesty International has identified 24 countries as practicing torture; 16 of them are signatories to the U.N. Convention Against Torture (Amnesty International, 2001).

justified to use torture as an instrument of state policy and to ignore international and domestic law against it has been explored in several Bush administration legal memorandums. For example, a legal memorandum from the Defense Department concluded that the prohibition against torture "must be construed as inapplicable to interrogation undertaken pursuant to his commander-in-chief authority" (Lewis & Schmitt, 2004). As of mid-2004, President Bush had declined to comment on whether U.S. law prohibits torture.

Though they have provided important information, the reports issued by Amnesty International were oriented toward documenting specific acts of torture and, to a lesser degree, the pervasiveness of it. They did not estimate the prevalence of torture. Additionally, data from Amnesty International depended on the ability of country-specific and international observers to identify and document cases of torture. This means that many cases go unreported.

As an egregious form of persecution, torture is most likely to have been experienced by refugees and applicants for political asylum.[3] No uniform or standard torture prevalence rate exists, because refugees and asylum seekers are subject to different forms and scales of state-sponsored violence. Persecution and violence are dynamic over time, even for a single, particular group. Nevertheless, researchers have developed torture prevalence estimates for refugees. Using data from torture treatment centers in Western countries, Ron Baker (1992) estimated that between 5% and 35% of refugees had been tortured. Assuming that Baker's estimate provides a reasonable low and high end, in 2000, somewhere between 600,000 and 3.4 million refugees worldwide were subjected to torture.

Since World War II, the United States has resettled more than 3.5 million refugees, with approximately 1.1 million of them arriving in the past 11 years (U.S. Immigration and Naturalization Service, 2003). The exact number of torture survivors among this refugee population is not fully known. Because of daunting methodological problems, only one randomized prevalence survey of torture has been fielded (Jaranson et al., 2004). The Center for Victims of Torture in Minnesota has produced the most frequently cited estimate of 500,000 torture survivors living in the United States (*Labor HHS Appropriations,* 2001).

The category of refugee does not embrace all of those exposed to torture. Refugee status denotes only those individuals recognized by the United States government as having a well-founded fear of persecution who are processed abroad for resettlement and whose plight is of special humanitarian concern. A large number of the world's refugee populations do not fit all three of those criteria. Individuals seeking asylum, in contrast, must present themselves to U.S. immigration officials at the border or in the interior. Asylum seekers also claim persecution but, unlike refugees, must undertake a burdensome and adversarial process to have their requests for asylum granted.[4] The United States has denied asylum to tens of thousands fleeing persecution by governments that remain our allies, despite evidence of widespread human rights abuse—including torture—by those very governments. Only those granted asylum are tallied in official data on refugees.

An unknown number of torture survivors enter the United States either legally through family- or occupation-based immigration categories or illegally by overstaying temporary visas or entering without inspection. Indeed, most of the people

---

[3]Early estimates of the prevalence of torture among refugees placed the range between 20% and 30% (Bojholm & Vesti, 1992, p. 299).

[4]The Immigration and Naturalization Service has historically approved only 24.6% of asylum cases (U.S. Immigration and Naturalization Service, 2002). Moreover, approval rates vary greatly by district office and immigration judges.

escaping from the civil wars of Central America entered the United States illegally. Of those, many decided to seek legal immigration status not through asylum but through other means. There is little data or literature linking immigrants to torture because most attention is focused on refugees and asylum seekers (Bouthoutsos, 1990, p. 129). Nevertheless, demographic profiles from torture treatment centers in the United States report considerable numbers of torture survivors originating from countries associated not with refugees but with immigrants.

Effects of Torture

> Torture is a corruption of the expected relationship between governmental authority and its citizenry; survivors know that they can neither trust the state nor rely on it to protect them.

The techniques of torture are generally classified as active infliction of physical pain, passive infliction of pain (such as being tied up), induction of extreme exhaustion and/or fear, combined physical and mental torture, and primarily mental torture (Suedfeld, 1990, p. 9). Torture survivors may be subjected to one or all of these types of torture; the intensity and duration may vary as well. Torture by physical means, such as beatings, rape, and electroshock, produce trauma to the body. (For a description of the common physical findings in torture survivors, see Piwowarczyk, Moreno, & Grodin, 2000, p. 540.) In addition, chronic health effects commonly result from deprivations of food, water, and shelter; inhumane conditions of imprisonment; and exposure to heat, cold, dampness, and human waste. Victims' emotional and psychological states are further eroded by threats to their lives and to their families' lives, threats of more brutal torture, isolation and sensory deprivation, deprivation of human contact (including interaction with fellow captives), and the lack of predictability or pattern in their handling and mistreatment. Nevertheless, because many torture survivors endure multiple forms of torture and experience "overlapping injuries, it may be difficult, particularly in the long term, to trace the symptoms and signs to particular forms of torture" (Basoglu, Jaranson, Mollica, & Kastrup, 2001, p. 37). This issue is especially salient for those working in health care.

Torture that is undertaken by psychological means, such as mock executions and witnessing violence done to others, is associated with a constellation of psychological effects and problems. Indeed, as an experienced clinician observed, torture is an assault "systematically designed to distort normal psychological mechanisms" (Fischman, 1998, p. 28). Experts note that "the commonly reported symptoms of torture survivors were anxiety; cognitive, memory, and attention problems; mood disturbance; sleeping difficulty; sexual dysfunctions; personality change; lack of energy; and behavioral disturbances" (Basoglu et al., 2001, p. 39). Researchers have suggested that the psychological symptoms resulting from torture are frequently categorized as posttraumatic stress disorder (PTSD), depression, anxiety, or other diagnoses. Some observers point out that because the trauma of torture is ongoing, there is nothing "post" about the traumatic stress (Basoglu, 1992, p. 7; Lira, 1998, p. 53).

The sequelae of torture go well beyond physical and psychological trauma. Torture experience interferes with the capacity and ability of survivors to function in social and economic spheres. This is perhaps the least researched and least understood consequence of torture (Basoglu et al., 2001, p. 45). Torture often renders survivors unable to work and thereby make a living. It isolates survivors from the community and creates in them a lasting attitude of distrust and fear (Chester, 1990).

Torture is a corruption of the expected relationship between governmental authority and its citizenry; survivors know that they can neither trust the state nor rely on it to protect them. This form of persecution frequently requires that torture survivors flee and seek asylum in countries where the culture and social structure are vastly different from those of their homeland (Gorman, 2001).

Even as survivors attempt to deal with the physical and emotional scars of torture, their lives are "further complicated by the demands of adjustment to a new country and dealing with the losses of homeland, culture, social ties, and former economic status" (Kinzie & Jaranson, 2001, p. 112). Indeed, flight and asylum seeking often produce additional trauma. The process of submitting an asylum application and having to constantly retell stories of torture to verify a "well-founded fear of persecution" can be enormously stressful to torture survivors, leaving them vulnerable, shaken, and mistrustful.

The effects of torture extend into the spiritual and existential domains. Because torture is such an awful assault on and betrayal of human dignity, some survivors are left searching for meaning, asking such questions as, "How could this have happened to me?" and "Why did God let me be so harmed?" Torture led Sister Dianna Ortiz (2002) to write, "God, I don't know who to turn to. I don't even believe in you but yet I talk to you. . . . I don't want to remember the details of this nightmare. Please, God, take away these memories" (p. 73). Left unattended, spiritual crises may further weaken survivors' bonds to family, friends, and community and contribute to alienation and despair.

In contrast, others' faith sustains them in the face of horror. Indeed, torture leads some to deeper spirituality, as they determine that their horrific experiences were not random but instead have meaning and purpose beyond the trauma.

The harm created by torture radiates from survivors to their family members. For some torture survivors, grief over the loss of family members (who may have been killed or disappeared) becomes a primary factor in their lives. Research has documented that spouses of torture survivors often suffer from PTSD, depression, and physical disorders (Allden, 1998). Torture survivors who were raped report long-term sexual dysfunction (Koss & Kilpatrick, 2001, p. 184). Children of torture survivors frequently experience anxiety, nightmares, depression, irritability, and excessive clinging to parents (Basoglu et al., 2001, p. 47). Parents whose children were tortured must also deal with the guilt stemming from their inability to protect the children. Moreover, "the family may have shared the extremely stressful experience of flight into exile" (Bojholm & Vesti, 1992, pp. 301–302).

Working with Survivors of Torture

Founded in 1977, the Canadian Centre for Victims of Torture, located in Toronto, Canada, was the first torture treatment center established in North America. Since 1985, the United States has witnessed the emergence of treatment centers specifically for survivors of torture. The National Consortium of Torture Treatment Programs now has 30 full and provisional members. These centers, operating from a multidisciplinary perspective, provide medical, mental health, case management, immigration, legal, and social services. Torture treatment programs are also a resource for referrals and consultations. Because these centers specialize in treating torture survivors, social workers are advised to refer clients to such a center whenever possible. The Torture Victims Relief Act of 1998 added significant resources to expand torture treatment programs in the United States, but even so, too few centers exist to assist survivors. Table 1 lists the names and locations of torture treatment centers in the United States.

Both globally and nationally, social workers have been at the forefront in creating and working in torture treatment centers. In an extensive review of torture treatment centers, van Willigen (1992) noted that social workers have been involved in providing counseling and social services to survivors of torture in Europe, Africa, Central and South America, and North America. Others have

Table 1   **National Consortium of Torture Treatment Programs**

Program Name	City, State
Full Members	
Center for Survivors of Torture (Asian Americans for Community Involvement)	San Jose, CA
Survivors International of Northern California	San Francisco, CA
Survivors of Torture, International	San Diego, CA
Institute for the Study of Psychosocial Trauma	Palo Alto, CA
Program for Torture Victims	Los Angeles, CA
Rocky Mountain Survivor Center	Denver, CO
Khmer Health Advocates	West Hartford, CT
Florida Center for Survivors of Torture	Clearwater, FL
The Marjorie Kovler Center	Chicago, IL
Boston Center for Refugee Health and Human Rights	Boston, MA
Harvard Program in Refugee Trauma	Cambridge, MA
International Survivors Center c/o International Institute of Boston	Boston, MA
Advocates for Survivors of Trauma and Torture	Baltimore, MD
ACCESS Psychosocial Rehabilitation Center	Dearborn, MI
Center for Victims of Torture	Minneapolis, MN
Center for Survivors of Torture and War Trauma	Saint Louis, MO
F.I.R.S.T. Project, Inc.	Lincoln, NE
Cross Cultural Counseling Center, International Institute of New Jersey	Jersey City, NJ
Bellevue/NYU Program for Survivors of Torture	New York, NY
Doctors of the World	New York, NY
REFUGE	New York, NY
Safe Horizon/Solace	New York, NY
Victims of Torture at Jewish Family Services	Columbus, OH
Amigos de los Sobrevivientes	Eugene, OR
Center for Survivors of Torture	Dallas, TX
Program for Survivors of Torture and Severe Trauma	Falls Church, VA
Provisional Members	
Catholic Social Services of Central and Northern Arizona	Phoenix, AZ
Center for the Prevention and Resolution of Violence	Tucson, AZ
Torture Treatment Center of Oregon	Portland, OR
Liberty Center for Survivors of Torture	Philadelphia, PA
Associate Members	
Center for Justice and Accountability	San Francisco, CA
Lutheran Immigration and Refugee Service	Baltimore, MD

Note. Information about organizations in the National Consortium of Torture Treatment Programs and how to contact them can be found at http://ncttp.westside.com/default.view

commented on the role of social workers in specific treatment centers in the United States, such as the Bellevue/New York University program (Keller, Saul, & Eisenman, 1998, p. 25) and the Indochinese Psychiatric Clinic in Boston (Allden, 1998). Gerald Gray, a social worker, founded Survivors International in San Francisco and recently created the Center for Justice and Accountability, an organization that takes legal action against torturers living in the United States. However, because the overwhelming majority of social workers who come into contact with torture survivors are not affiliated with treatment centers and because such a center may not be available in their locality, there are some basic things they need to know.

One of the first and most compelling issues for social workers is to recognize torture survivors when they come across their paths. The literature on torture treatment consistently notes that few social service and health care professionals are even aware of torture, and fewer still recognize its symptoms (Iacopino, 1998, p. 46). One study documented that although 1 in 15 foreign-born patients in an urban hospital had been tortured, none had been identified by their primary care physicians as torture survivors (Eisenman, Keller, & Kim, 2000). Because survivors seldom self-disclose (for a variety of reasons, discussed later), social workers must take greater responsibility in assessing the likelihood that a person has been subjected to torture. This requires that social workers, especially those working with immigrant and refugee populations, expand their assessment skills to include knowledge of the past and present political and human rights conditions of the countries from which their clients originate (Fabri, 2001).

The starting place for most social workers is to view human rights work as central to social work. A human rights perspective, according to Ife (2001, p. 1) provides social work with "a strong basis for an assertive practice that seeks to realize the social justice goals of social workers." Reports from Amnesty International, Human Rights Watch, and the U.S. State Department on human rights abuses can alert social workers to the groups most likely to be persecuted and to the types of torture that might have been employed. These reports can be easily accessed via the Internet and can provide information on past and present country conditions.[5] Other risk factors associated with torture include political and antigovernment activity in the country of origin, a history of arrest and detention, family members missing or killed, and/or membership in a minority group (Iacopino, 1998, p. 45). Social workers can communicate to their clients that they are aware of country conditions and use that as an opening for clients to broach the subject of torture. Social workers can also use a number of assessment instruments that are designed to measure the effects of torture and trauma, such as the Hopkins Symptom Checklist and the Harvard Trauma scale. Like all assessment methods, these instruments should be used with sensitivity: Survivors may have strong reactions to them, including the surfacing of troubling memories of awful events.

---

[5]The following are excellent sources to locate the human rights conditions of specific regions and countries: Amnesty International: http://www.amnesty.org; Human Rights Watch: http://www.hrw.org; U.S. State Department, Human Rights: http://www.state.gov/g/drl/ht/: U.S. State Department, Human Rights Country Report: http://www.state.gov/www/global/human_rights/hrp_reports_mainhp.html: United Nations Office of High Commissioner for Human Rights: http://www.unhchr.ch/

Torture is toxic. It affects not only survivors, families, friends, and communities, but also those who would be healers.

Helping torture survivors rebuild their lives requires that social workers recognize the political context of torture. This aspect differentiates torture from other human-induced traumas such as domestic violence and rape. Lira (1998) emphasized the "importance of incorporating political and cultural meaning into the therapeutic process. Put simply, a torture survivor is not simply another instance of posttraumatic stress disorder" (p. 54). As part of the treatment, social workers should reiterate and reinforce that the violence experienced by survivors falls well outside the norms of acceptable behavior. Torture is illegal and internationally condemned.

Moreover, social workers must avoid pathologizing torture survivors and instead acknowledge their resiliency in the face of efforts to crush them (Cariceo, 1998). The physical and psychological problems resulting from torture are normal responses to calculated and intentional harm. Pathologizing torture survivors serves only to extend the reach and efficacy of the torturers.

Recognition of the political context of torture first requires that social workers acknowledge and validate the stories of torture related to them. The stories may represent only fragments of memory, or the accounts may seem so outrageous as to be incredible—yet believing what the client says may be the most important of all interventions. As Fabri (2001) stated, "Many survivors have been instructed by their torturers that no one will believe them if they disclose what happened to them" (p. 452). Torture aims for silence. Believing breaks the silence. As professionals, social workers confer legitimacy on what is said by their belief in it; such legitimacy can lead to wider societal recognition that the torture described actually happened. The opposite may also occur: Fischman (1998) observed, "By minimizing their experience we may be revictimizing our patients" (p. 30).

One final point about torture and political persecution is in order. Survivors frequently have adverse reactions to health care professionals in the United States because physicians and mental health care providers in their country of origin participated in the act of torture. In all too many instances, the very professionals who are supposed to alleviate pain and trauma instead create it (Rubenstin, 1998, p. 18). Such a corruption of ethics and practice causes these survivors to associate doctors and mental health care providers with torture. Whether social workers are aware of it or not, survivors may transfer their experiences in their homeland and may avoid or resist social workers' efforts to help them.

During torture, people lose control over what is done to their bodies and minds. They are powerless to stop the violence; indeed, torture ends at the whim of the torturer. Iacopino (1998) stated, "Having experienced lack of control and helplessness [during torture], survivors may be reluctant to seek assistance because this process often involves a feeling of helplessness" (p. 46). This fact makes it imperative for social workers to pay special attention to assisting survivors to reclaim a sense of power and control. For some torture survivors, basic choices about where to sit in an office or how to be addressed by the social worker may be important; others may seek to regain control by being able to speak about their torture.

Torture creates profound issues of fear, trust, and safety. Because they have lived in repressive regimes, survivors may well have experienced chronic fear even before their torture. Certainly, after torture occurs, fear becomes a pervasive feature of survivors' lives. As noted before, resettlement and asylum create new sets of stressors and new causes for fear. Fischman (1991) suggested that "the therapist must provide a context in which the survivors' anxiety and fears can be contained and where they are able to develop trust and begin to address their torture-induced fears" (p. 181). To deal with fear, survivors must feel safe; to feel safe, they must have the capacity to trust. Indeed, as Fabri (2001) asserted, "The reconstruction of trust in another person is the first task of treatment" (p. 452). There is no clear recipe for how to establish trust, but certainly belief, active caring, consistency, and follow-through on what is promised are key ingredients.

Torture survivors experience guilt on a number of levels. For some, there is guilt over surviving when others did not. Others experience guilt from being forced to hurt others or from knowing that during torture, the survivor betrayed other people. Guilt may also come from a sense that one is burdening others with the stories of torture. Regardless of how guilt is mainfested, survivors need constant reminders that it is the torturers who bear full responsibility for the trauma and harm of torture. Survivors are victims and must not be blamed.

Hearing and believing the stories of torture may be the most significant therapeutic intervention. Paradoxically, though understandably, giving the account is often the most difficult thing for survivors of torture to do. To talk of the experience of torture is to revisit excruciatingly painful memories and sensations. As Iacopino (1998) observed, "The process of recalling or talking about one's torture experience nearly always results in re-experiencing the torture and worsening symptoms" (p. 46). Nevertheless, if they do not revisit that traumatic ground, torture survivors risk staying trapped by symptoms that impair their lives (Cienfuegos & Monelli, 1983). A climate of safety and trust are prerequisites for discussing the trauma of torture with survivors. Because of control and power issues, social workers should allow torture survivors who begin to disclose to do so at their own pace and in ways acceptable to the client, such as through nonverbal art or sand tray therapy. The process often takes a long time, but it should not be rushed. Additionally, social workers should recognize that retelling of the torture experience is not a universal in treatment: Survivors from some cultures may not find it helpful to discuss their torture trauma (Jaranson et al., 2001). Social workers should follow their client's lead and not presume that overt discussion is necessary. Much healing work can be done through focus on empowerment and rebuilding life without retelling the torture story.

Whether social workers are operating in the capacity of therapists, case managers, or social service providers, they must be aware that many simple, routine, and seemingly innocent acts may elicit traumatic responses. Bouthoutsos (1990) cloquently stated, "A problem unique to those refugees who have been tortured is their exquisite sensitivity to stimuli that would present no problem to the average refugee" (p. 130). Literature on torture repeatedly notes that a physical examination and the instruments used in it sometimes resemble the act of torture. For example, an EKG may trigger memories of electroshock; testing for reflexes may remind survivors of beatings. The same can be said of mental health and social service interventions. The direct questions of an eligibility assessment may flood survivors with unwelcome images of being interrogated. Waiting alone in a sterile office or dealing with a crowded waiting room may trigger memories of sensory deprivation or overstimulation. Clearly, social workers cannot anticipate and mitigate all the various stimuli that might cause torture memories to resurface, but certainly they need to be vigilant about quickly recognizing the signs of stress, anxiety, and panic when they occur. More importantly, by being more attuned to the reality that some of their clients may be torture survivors, social workers can reduce the likelihood that their work environment and professional practices may unintentionally harm them.

Because most torture victims arrive from non-Western countries, it is safe to say that most clients who seek services in the United States or other

> Because torture has a lasting effect on the body, mind, and social system, social workers must play a key role in linking survivors to a broad array of medical, mental health, legal, and social services.

Western-oriented countries will undergo an intercultural experience. A language difference is usually the first barrier, followed by the need to develop more complex cross-cultural understandings and behaviors necessary for communication. The acculturation tasks in an intercultural communication setting do not fall only to clients; they must be shared by service providers as well. It is important for English-speaking, Western-oriented service providers in today's multicultural and multilingual contexts to know how to structure services appropriate to the clientele. In work with survivors of torture, this knowledge is essential. The goals should be to reduce the degree to which a seeker or receiver of services must accommodate the lack of appropriate language interpretation services or the service providers' ignorance of conditions, political history, and culture in the client's country of origin.

The trend in both public and private health and mental health care is toward services that are time limited, symptom specific, and drug oriented. This is a challenge for practitioners who recognize that work with survivors of torture requires time to build relationships and trust; it also requires a contextual focus beyond the individual presentation. For example, it is difficult to involve a survivor client in talking therapy to recover from trauma or to discuss ways to be able to sleep better when the asylum-seeking client is distraught over family survival issues.

It is essential that treatment and social service programs hire and train bilingual and bicultural staff members, both professional and paraprofessional, who can provide a range of services to meet basic and longer term recovery needs (Engstrom & Okamura, 2004). All staff members, from the receptionist who answers the telephone and greets clients, to secretaries, case workers, supervisors, managers, and boards of directors, must be trained and equally committed to providing culturally responsive services. The physical context of services is also important in terms of its offer of comfort and welcome to multicultural clients. Training in intercultural communications—including a self-assessment of one's own cultural communications—is essential. This should not be a one-time-only event, but rather an ongoing strategy to keep service providers proficient in working with a variety of culturally different individuals and communities.

Because survivors of torture are often isolated and disconnected from social relationships, social workers must attend to the macro task of rebuilding social and community ties (Chambon et al., 2001). In work with survivors of torture, it is critical that social workers understand the development and organization of ethnic communities. Many such communities are made up families of previous arrivals who live near each other as well as children and adults who attend school with each other, establish businesses that serve the ethnic tastes and needs of community members, pool funds to establish places of worship, and develop intricate social networks. These are the strengths of individuals and families that emerge despite many years of hardship as people reach out to others with whom they share a language, customs, practices, values, and behaviors and naturally begin to repair what was lost and rebuild what they can in a new environment. The resiliency of the human spirit to survive losses and onslaughts against their humanity is evident in refugee families (Pipher, 2002). Relationships for strong collaborations with community leaders, associations, and groups must be developed and supported by social workers, as these sources provide the strength and resources for long-term recovery of torture survivors. Social workers must advocate for resources for refugee and immigrant families for health, mental health, and social services, as well as education, business, and community development. All of this requires keeping informed of global news and issues and accessing research data, as well as participating in research to advance the knowledge of improved practice.

Practice Implications

The code of ethics requires social workers to have the knowledge and skills necessary to practice competently with the populations they serve, as well as to promote social justice and human rights. Immigrant and refugee families are reshaping the demographic face of the United States, so social workers need a working understanding of immigration, immigration policies, and the acculturation process and stresses. This knowledge is a prerequisite to assisting survivors of torture because it reveals the context of their lives and the reality that they are dealing with issues other than torture. Additionally, social workers should remember that the refugee and immigrant communities where torture survivors often live have considerable cohesion and social capital on which to draw. These are communities of collective strength as their members, through their survival, have demonstrated remarkable capacities of resilience against tremendous hardships and trauma.

Social workers who serve immigrants and refugees are most likely to be in contact with torture survivors. It is imperative for them to recognize the reasonable probability that refugees and also immigrants from countries with histories of human rights abuses have been tortured. This, of course, means that social workers must know about human rights conditions internationally. Assessment questions that cover political and social group membership in the country of origin can be used to identify clients who might have been tortured. In the experience of one of the authors in assessing and treating hundreds of Southeast Asian refugee children, adolescents, and adults in a mental health clinic from the late 1970s to the 1990s, it was rare that a survivor would willingly answer a question related to having been tortured, much less raped. Social workers should be familiar with the psychological symptoms most often associated with torture so that they can continue to work effectively with the client without the expressed acknowledgement of the torture experience. Not every refugee with acute anxiety or sleep disturbance is a torture survivor, but combining awareness of common psychological symptoms with knowledge of human rights conditions certainly enhances social workers' assessment ability.

Social workers and their multidisciplinary teams in the health and mental health arenas are in a position not only to assess the effects of torture, but also to provide appropriate treatment services. At a minimum, those professionals should have training and supervision in dealing with trauma; better yet, they should have additional training in torture-specific trauma sequelae and interventions. Because torture has a lasting effect on the body, mind, and social system, social workers must play a key role in linking survivors to a broad array of medical, mental health, legal, and social services. This liaison role may require that social workers strongly advocate for survivors to access necessary services and that they intervene when barriers arise. It should be emphasized that survivors of torture often lack health care coverage, transportation, housing, and employment, and they may face language barriers as well; all these factors make it difficult for them to move down the path of recovery without assistance.

Even when refugee-serving agencies have developed expertise in refugee health and medical care screening and referral, created English-as-a-second-language programs, and established a variety of social service programs, it is vital that they expand their focus to include knowledge and accommodation of the emotional and mental health needs of their clientele. Training in the signs and symptoms of mental health problems, in understanding the effects of trauma, and in approaches for treating survivors of torture is important for appropriate referrals to specialists and treatment centers. Refugee-serving agency staff can be an important gateway for torture survivors to receive appropriate mental health services.

Torture is toxic. It affects not only survivors, families, friends, and communities, but also those who would be healers. Social workers who assist torture survivors risk vicarious or secondary trauma and burnout. Hearing stories of torture may result in social workers having intrusive thoughts or nightmares. Experienced clinicians note that working with torture survivors sometimes results in clinicians developing feelings of hopelessness, helplessness, despair, cynicism, and disbelief. Although quality supervision is reported as a means to deal with these issues, there is little research on what works best to protect professionals from secondary trauma (Lira, 1998, p. 55). Group support, meditation, participation in stress-reduction exercises, and use of spiritual sources of support are approaches that torture treatment professionals have used. It is key that social workers remain vigilant about vicarious trauma and keep themselves healthy if they are to render effective, ethical client service.

References

1. Allden, K. (1998). The Indochinese psychiatry clinic: Trauma and refugee mental health treatment in the 1990s. *Journal of Ambulatory Care Management, 21*(2), 20–29.
2. Amnesty International. (2000). *Campaign against torture: Medin briefing.* Retrieved July 21, 2004 from http://web.amnesty.org/library/index/ENGACT400162000
3. Amnesty International. (2001). *Amnesty International Report 2001.* Retrieved July 8, 2004, from http://web.amnesty.org/web/ar2001.nsf/home/home?OpenDocument
4. Baker, R. (1992). Psychological consequences for tortured refugees seeking asylum and refugee status in Europe. In M. Basoglu (Ed.), *Torture and its consequences* (pp. 82–105). New York: Cambridge University Press.
5. Basoglu, M., (1992). Introduction. In M. Basoglu (Ed.), *Torture and its consequences* (pp. 1–9). New York: Cambridge University Press.
6. Basoglu, M., Jaranson, J. M., Mollica, R., & Kastrup, M. (2001). Torture and mental health. In E. Gerrity, T. M. Keane, & F. Tuma (Eds.), *The mental health consequences of torture* (pp. 35–64). New York: Kluwer Academic/Plenum Publishers.
7. Bojholm, S., & Vesti, P. (1992). Multidisciplinary approach in the treatment of torture survivors. In M. Basoglu (Ed.), *Torture and its consequences* (pp. 299–309). New York: Cambridge University Press.
8. Bouhoutsos, J. C., (1990). Treating victims of torture: Psychology's challenge. In P. Suedfeld (Ed.), *Psychology and torture* (pp. 129–141). New York: Hemisphere.
9. Brown, N. L., & Priest, D. (2003, November 5). Deported terror suspect details torture in Syria. *The Washington Post,* p. A1.
10. Buston, E. (1990). Dealing with the unbearable: Reactions of therapists and therapeutic institutions to survivors of torture. In P. Suedfeld (Ed.), *Psychology and torture* (pp. 143–163). New York: Hemisphere.
11. Cariceo, C. M. (1998, June). Challenges in cross-cultural assessment: Counseling refugee survivors of torture and trauma. *Australian Social Work, 51*(2), 49–53.
12. Carlin, J. E. (1979). The catastrophically uprooted child: The Southeast Asian refugee child. In J. Noshpita (Ed.), *Basic handbook of child psychiatry* (Vol. 1, pp. 290–300). New York: Basic Books.
13. Chambon, A. S., McGrath, S., Shapiro, B. Z., Abai, M., Dremetsikas, T., & Dudriak, S. (2001). From interpersonal links to webs of relations: Creating befriending relationships with survivors of torture and war. *Journal of Social Work Research, 2,* 157–171.
14. Chester, B. (1990). Because mercy has a human heart. In P. Suedfeld (Ed.), *Psychology and torture* (pp. 165–181). New York: Hemisphere.
15. Cienfuegos, A. J., & Monelli, C. (1983). The testimony of political repression as a therapeutic instrument. *American Journal of Orthopsychiatry. 53,* 43–51.
16. Conroy, J. (2000). *Unspeakable acts. ordinary people: The dynamic of torture.* Berkeley, CA: University of California Press.

17. Eisenman, D. P., Keller, A. S., & Kim, G. (2000). Survivors of torture in a general medical setting: How often have patients been tortured, and how often is it missed? *Western Journal of Medicine, 172,* 301–304.
18. Engstrom, D. W., & Okamura, A. (2004). Working with survivors of torture: Approaches to helping. *Families in Society, 85,* 301–309.
19. Fabri, M. (2001). Reconstructing safety: Adjustments to the therapeutic frame in the treatment of survivors of political torture. *Professional Psychology: Research and Practice, 32,* 452–457.
20. Fischman, Y. (1991). Interacting with trauma: Clinicians' responses to treating psychological aftereffects of political repression. *American Journal of Orthopsychiatry, 61,* 179–185.
21. Fischman, Y. (1998). Metaclinical issues in treatment of psychopolitical trauma. *American Journal of Orthopsychiatry, 68,* 27–38.
22. Gorman, W. (2001). Refugee survivors of torture: Trauma and treatment. *Professional Psychology: Research and Practice, 32,* 443–451.
23. Human Rights Watch. (2004). *"Empty promises": Diplomatic assurances no safeguard against torture.* Retrieved June 13, 2004, from http://www.hrw.org/reports/2004/un0404/
24. Ife, J. (2001). *Human rights and social work.* New York: Cambridge University Press.
25. Iacopino, V. (1998). Commentary. *Journal of Ambulatory Care Management, 21*(2), 43–51.
26. Jaranson, J. M., et al. (2001). Assessment, diagnosis, and intervention. In E. Gerrity, T. M. Keane, & F. Tuma (Eds.), *The mental health consequences of torture* (pp. 249–276). New York: Kluwer Academic/Plenum Publishers.
27. Jaranson, J. M., Butcher, J., Halcom, L., Johnson, D. R., Robertson, C., Savik, K., et al. (2004). Somali and Oromo refugees: Correlates of torture and trauma history. *American Journal of Public Health, 94,* 591–598.
28. Keller, A., Saul, J. M., & Eisenman, D. P. (1998). Caring for survivors of torture in an urban, municipal hospital. *Journal of Ambulatory Care Management, 21*(2), 25.
29. Kinzie, J. D., Fredrickson, R. H., Rath, B., Fleck, J., & Karls, W. (1984). Post-traumatic stress disorder among survivors of Cambodian concentration camps. *American Journal of Psychitary, 141,* 645–650.
30. Kinzie, J. D., & Jaranson, J. M. (2001). Refugees and asylum-seekers. In E. Gerrity, T. M. Keane, & F. Tuma (Eds.), *The mental health consequences of torture* (pp. 111–120). New York: Kluwer Academic/Plenum Publishers.
31. Kinzie, J. D., Sack, W. H., Angell, R. H., & Manson, S. M. (1986). The psychiatric effects of massive trauma on Cambodian children: I. The children. *Journal of the American Academy of Child Psychiatry, 25,* 370–376.
32. Koss, M. P., & Kilpatrick, D. G. (2001). Rape and sexual assault. In E. Gerrity, T. M. Keane, & F. Tuma (Eds.), *The mental health consequences of torture* (pp. 177–194). New York: Kluwer Academic/Plenum Publishers.
33. *Labor HHS appropriations: Hearings before the House Appropriations Committee,* 107th Congress, 2nd session (2001) (testimony of John P. Salzberg).
34. Levine, J. (2001). Working with victims of persecution: Lessons from Holocaust survivors. *Social Work, 46,* 350–360.
35. Lewis, N. A., & Schmitt, E. (2004, June 8). Lawyers decided bans on torture didn't bind Bush. *The New York Times,* p. A1.
36. Lin, K. M., Tazuma, L., & Masuda, M. (1979). Adaptational problems of Vietnamese refugees: I. Health and mental health. *Archives of General Psychiatry, 36,* 955–961.
37. Lira, E. (1998). Commentary. *Journal of Ambulatory Care Management, 21*(2), 51–55.
38. Organization of American States, (1987). *Inter-American Convention to Prevent and Punish Torture.* Retrieved July 8, 2004, from http://www.oas.org/juridico/english/Treaties/a-51.html
39. Ortiz, D. (2001). The survivor's perspective. In E. Gerrity, T. M. Keane, & F. Tuma (Eds.), *The mental health consequences of torture* (pp. 13–34). New York: Kluwer Academic/Plenum Publishers.

40. Ortiz, D. (2002). *The blindfold's eye; My journey from torture to truth.* New York: Orbis.
41. Owan, T. C. (Ed.), (1985). *Southeast Asian mental health: Treatment, prevention, services, training, and research.* Washington, DC: National Institute of Mental Health.
42. Peters, E. (1985). *Torture.* New York: Basil Blackwell.
43. Pipher, M. (2002). *The middle of everywhere: Helping refugees enter the American community.* New York: Harcourt.
44. Piwowarczyk, L., Moreno, A., & Grodin, M. (2000). Health care of torture survivors. *Journal of the American Medical Association, 284,* 539–541.
45. Rubenstin, L. S. (1998). Treatment of torture survivors: An introduction. *Journal of Ambulatory Care Management, 21*(2), 18–19.
46. Sartre, J. P. (1958). Introduction. In H. Alleg, *The question* (pp. 13–36). New York: Braziller.
47. Suedfeld, P. (1990). Torture: A brief overview. In P. Suedfeld (Ed.), *Psychology and torture* (pp. 1–10). New York: Hemisphere.
48. Torture Victims Relief Act of 1998, Pub. L. No. 105–320, 112 Stat. 3016 (1998).
49. United Nations. (1948). *Universal declaration of human rights.* Retrieved July 8, 2004, from http://www.un.org/Overview/rights.html
50. United Nations. (1975), *Convention against torture and other cruel, inhuman or degrading treatment or punishment.* Retrieved July 8, 2004, from http://www.unhchr.ch/html/menu3/b/h_cat39.htm
51. U.S. Immigration and Naturalization Service. (2002). *Statistical yearbook of the Immigration and Naturalization Service, 1999.* Washington, DC: U.S. Government Printing Office.
52. U.S. Immigration and Naturalization Service. (2003). *Fiscal year 2001 statistical yearbook.* Retrieved July 8, 2004, from http://uscis.gov/graphics/shared/aboutus/statistics/IMM0lyrbk/IMM2001list.htm
53. van Willigen, I., (1992). Organization of care and rehabilitative services for victims of torture and other forms of organized violence: A review of current issues. In M. Basoglu (Ed.), *Torture and its consequences* (pp. 277–298). New York: Cambridge University Press.
54. Westermeyer, J. (1987). Prevention of mental disorder among Hmong refugees in the U.S.: Lessons from the period 1976–1986. *Social Science Medicine, 25,* 941–947.
55. World Medical Association. (1975). *World Medical Association declaration guidelines for medical doctors concerning torture and other cruel, inhuman or degrading treatment or punishment in relation to detention and imprisonment.* Retrieved July 20, 2004 from www.wma.net/e/policy/c18.htm

References

Chapter 1

Berman, M. (Winter 1996). "The shadow side of systems theory." *Journal of Humanistic Psychology, 36*(1).

Bloom, M., and Klein, W. (Eds.). (1997). *Controversial issues in human behavior in the social environment.* Boston: Allyn and Bacon.

Boulding, Kenneth E. (1964). *The meaning of the 20th century: The great transition.* New York: Harper-Colophon.

Capra, Fritjof. (1983). *The turning point: Science, society, and the rising culture.* Toronto: Bantam Books.

Collins, Patricia Hill. (1990). *Black feminist thought: Knowledge, consciousness, and the politics of empowerment.* Boston: Unwin Hyman, Inc.

CSWE. (2008). Educational Policy and Accreditation Standards Retrieved July 1, 2008, from http://www.cswe .org/CSWE/accreditation/

Council on Social Work Education (CSWE). (2001). *Handbook of accreditation standards and procedures* (5th ed.). Alexandria, VA: Author.

Gambrill, E. (July/August 1999). "Evidence-based practice: An alternative to authority-based practice." *Families in Society, 80(4).*

Gambrill, E., and Gibbs, L. (1996). *Critical thinking for social workers: A workbook.* Thousand Oaks, CA: Pine Forge Press.

Gibbs, L. G., Blakemore, J., Begun, A., Keniston, A., Preden, B., and Lefcowitz, J. (1995). "A measure of critical thinking about practice." *Research on Social Work Practice, 5*(2): 193–204.

Goldstein, Howard. (1990). "The knowledge base of social work practice: Theory, wisdom, analogue or art?" *Families in Society, 71*(1): 32–43.

Guba, Egon G., and Lincoln, Yvonna S. (1989). *Fourth generation evaluation.* Newbury Park, CA: SAGE Publications.

Gutierrez, L., Delois, K., and Linnea, G. (November 1995). "Understanding empowerment practice: Building on practioner-based knowledge." *Families in Society: The Journal of Contemporary Human Services.*

Helms, J. E. (1994). "The conceptualization of racial identity and other 'racial' constructs." In Trickett, E. J., Watts, R. J., and Birman D. (Eds.). (1994). *Human diversity: Perspectives on people in context.* San Francisco: Jossey-Bass.

Kuhn, Thomas S. ([1962] 1970). *The structure of scientific revolutions* (2nd ed.). Chicago: The University of Chicago.

Lather, P. (1991). *Getting smart: Feminist research and pedagogy with/in the postmodern.* New York: Routledge.

Lincoln, Y. S., and Guba, E. G. (1985). *Naturalistic inquiry.* Beverly Hills: Sage.

Logan, Sadye. (1990). "Black families: Race, ethnicity, culture, social class, and gender issues." In Logan, S., Freeman, E., and McRoy, R. *Social Work Practice With Black Families.* New York: Longman.

Lonner, W. J. "Culture and human diversity." In Trickett, E. J., Watts, R. J., and Birman D. (Eds.). (1994). *Human diversity: Perspectives on people in context.* San Francisco: Jossey-Bass.

Manchester, William. (1992). *A world lit only by fire: The medieval mind and the renaissance: Portrait of an age.* Boston: Little, Brown and Company.

Myers, Linda J. (1985). "Transpersonal psychology: The role of the afrocentric paradigm." *Journal of Black Psychology, 12*(1): 31–42.

National Association of Social Workers (NASW). (1982). *Standards for the classification of social work practice.* Silver Spring, MD: NASW.

National Center for Cultural Competence, G. U. (2004). Achieving Cultural Competence: A Guidebook for Providers of Services to Older Americans and Their Families Retrieved 2/22, 2009, from http://www.aoa.gov/ PROF/adddiv/cultural/CC-guidebook.pdf

Persell, Caroline Hodges. (1987). *Understanding society: An introduction to sociology.* New York: Harper and Row.

Pharr, Suzanne. (1988). *Homophobia: A Weapon of Sexism.* Inverness, CA: Chardon, Press.

Rank, M., and Hirschl, T. (1999). "The likelihood of poverty across the American adult life span." *Social Work, 44*(3): 201–216.

Reason, Peter, (Ed.) (1988). *Human inquiry in action: Developments in new paradigm research.* London: SAGE Publications.

Root, Maria P. P. (Ed.). (1992). *Racially mixed people in America.* Newbury Park, CA: Sage.

Sahakian, William S. (1968). *History of philosophy.* New York: Barnes and Noble Books.

Sands, R., and Nuccio, K. (1992). "Postmodern feminist theory in social work." *Social Work, 37:* 489–494.

Schutz, Alfred. (1944). "The stranger: an essay in social psychology." *American Journal of Sociology,* 49: 499–507.

Spickard, P. R. "The illogic of American racial categories." In Root, Maria P. P. (Ed.). (1992). *Racially mixed people in America.* Newbury Park, CA: Sage.

Trickett, E. J., Watts, R. J. and Birman, D. (Eds.). (1994). *Human diversity: Perspectives on people in context.* San Francisco: Jossey-Bass.

Van Den Bergh, N. (Ed.). (1995). *Feminist practice in the 21st century.* Washington, DC: NASW Press.

Witkin, S., and Harrison, D. (October 2001). "Editorial: Whose evidence and for what purpose?" *Social Work, 46(4).*

Chapter 2

(AIP), A. I. o. P. (2006). Physics Degrees Earned by U. S. Minorities Retrieved March 14, 2009, from http://www.aip .org/statistics/trends/highlite/ed/table13.htm

Alix, E. K. (1995). *Sociology: An everyday life approach.* Minneapolis: West.

AmeriStat. (2000). *Race and ethnicity in the census: 1860–2000,* [Web site]. AmeriStat Population Reference Bureau and Social Science Analysis Network. Available: http://www.ameristat.org/racethnic/census.htm [2000, 4/4/00].

Armas, G. (2000, March 13, 2000). Administration puts out new guidelines for multiracial categories. *Northwest Arkansas Times.*

Beaver, Marion. (1990). "The older person in the black family." In *Social work practice with black families.* Logan, Sadye, Freeman, Edith, and McRoy, Ruth (Eds.). New York: Longman.

Belenky, Mary F., Clinchy, Blythe M., Goldberger, Nancy R., and Tarule, Jill M. (1986). *Women's ways of knowing: The development of self, voice, and mind.* New York: Basic Books, Inc.

Bent-Goodley, T. B. (2005). An African-centered approach to domestic violence. *Families in Society, 86*(2), 197.

Berlin, Sharon B. (1990). "Dichotomous and complex thinking." *Social Service Review, 64*(1): 46–59.

Besthorn, F., and McMillen, P. (2002). "The oppression of women and nature: Ecofeminism as a framework for an expanded ecological social work." *Families in Society,* 83(3): 221–232.

Bottomore, Tom. (1984). *The Frankfurt school and critical theory.* London: Tavistock Publications.

Bowser, B. P., and Hunt, R. G. (Eds.). (1996). *Impacts of racism on white Americans* (2nd ed.). Thousand Oaks, CA: Sage.

Bricker-Jenkins, Mary, and Hooyman, Nancy R. (Eds.). (1983). *Not for women only: Social work practice for a feminist future.* Silver Spring, MD: NASW, Inc.

Bureau of the Census. (2000). *Census 2000, Frequently asked questions.* U.S. Bureau of the Census. Available: http://www.census.gov/dmd/www/genfaq.htm

Canda, E. R. (1989). "Religious content in social work education: A comparative approach." *Journal of Social Work Education, 25*(1): 36–45.

Capra, Fritjof. (1983). *The turning point: Science, society, and the rising culture.* Toronto: Bantam Books.

Carter, R. T., and Jones, J. M. (1996). "Racism and white racial identity merging realities." In Bowser, B. P. and Hunt, R. G. (Eds.) *Impacts of racism on white Americans.* (2nd ed.). Thousand Oaks, CA: Sage.

Cobb, A., & Forbes, S. (2002). Qualitative research: What does it have to offer to the gerontologist? *Journals of Gerontology, 57A*(4), 6.

Cole, E., & Omari, S. (2003). Race, class and the dilemmas of upward mobility for African Americans. *Journal of Social Issues, 59*(4), 785–802.

Collins, P. H. (1986). "Learning from the outsider within: The sociological significance of black feminist thought." *Social Problems, 33*(6): 14–32.

Collins, P. H. (1989). "The social construction of black feminist thought." *Signs, 14*(4): 745–773.

Collins, P. H. (1990). *Black feminist thought: Knowledge, consciousness, and the politics of empowerment.* Boston: Unwin Hyman, Inc.

Collins, P. H. (1996). What's in a name? Womanism, black feminism, and beyond. *Black Scholar, 26*(1), 9–17.

Cowley, A. S., and Derezotes, D. (1994). "Transpersonal psychology and social work education." *Journal of Social Work Education, 30*(1): 32–41.

Daniel, G. R. (1992). Beyond Black and White: the new multiracial consciousness. In Root, M. P. P. (Ed.). *Racially mixed people in America.* Newberry Park, CA: Sage Publications.

Dawson, Betty G. Klass, Morris D. Guy, Rebecca F. and Edgley, Charles K. (1991). *Understanding Social Work Research.* Boston: Allyn & Bacon.

Dean, Ruth G., and Fenby, Barbara L. (1989). "Exploring epistemologies: Social work action as a reflection of philosophical assumptions." *Journal of Social Work Education, 25*(1): 46–54.

Demo, D. H., and Allen, K. R. (1996). "Diversity within lesbian and gay families: Challenges and implications for family theory and research." *Journal of Social and Personal Relationships, 13*(3): 415–434.

Donadello, Gloria. (1980). "Women and the mental health system." In Norman, Elaine, and Mancuso, Arlene (eds.). *Women's issues and social work practice.* Itasca, IL: F. E. Peacock Publishers, Inc.

Easlea, Brian. (1990). "Patriarchy, scientists, and nuclear warriors." In Sheila Ruth (Ed.). *Issues in feminism.* Mountain View, CA: Mayfield.

Evans-Campbell, T., Fredriksen-Goldsen, K., Walters, K., & Stately, A. (2007). Caregiving exieriences among American Indian two-spirit men and women: Contemporary and historical roles. *Journal of Gay & Lesbian Social Services, 18*(3/4), 75–92.

Fernandes, F. (2003). A response to Erica Burman. *European Journal of Psychotherapy, Counselling & Health, 6*(4), 309–16.

Fong, R., Spickard, P. R., and Ewalt, P. L. (1996) "A multiracial reality: Issues for social work." In Ewalt, P. L., Freeman, E. M., Kirk, S. A., and Poole, D. L. (Eds.). *Multicultural issue in social work.* Washington, DC: NASW Press.

Guba, E. G., and Lincoln, Y. S. (1981). *Effective evaluation.* San Francisco: Jossey-Bass.

Guba, Egon G., and Lincoln, Yvonna S. (1989). *Fourth generation evaluation.* Newbury Park, CA: SAGE Publications.

Hartman, A. (1995). Introduction. In Tyson, K. (Ed.). *New foundations for scientific social and behavioral research: The heuristic paradigm.* Boston: Allyn and Bacon.

Heineman Pieper, M. (1995). Preface. In Tyson, K. (Ed.). *New foundations for scientific social and behavioral research: The heuristic paradigm.* Boston: Allyn and Bacon.

Helms, J. E. (1994). "The conceptualization of racial identity and other 'racial' constructs." In Trickett, E. J., Watts, R. J., and Birman D. (Eds.). (1994). *Human diversity: Perspectives on people in context.* San Francisco: Jossey-Bass.

Hillman, James. (1988). In Peter Reason (Ed.). *Human inquiry in action: Developments in new paradigm research.* London: SAGE Publications.

Imre, Roberta Wells. (1984). "The nature of knowledge in social work." *Social Work, 29*(1): 41–45.

Ivie, R. (2009). Women in Physics & Astronomy Faculty Positions. Retrieved March 14, 2009, from http://www.aip.org/statistics/trends/highlite/women3/faculty.htm

Kerlinger, Fred N. (1973). *Foundations of behavioral research.* New York: Holt, Rinehart and Winston, Inc.

Kich, George K. (1992). "The Developmental Process of Asserting a Biracial, Bicultural Identity." In Root, M. P. P. (Ed.). *Racially mixed people in America.* Newberry Park, CA: Sage Publications.

Lather, P. (1991). *Getting smart: Feminist research and pedagogy with/in the postmodern.* New York: Routledge.

Leigh, James. (1989). "Black Americans: Emerging identity issues and social policy." *The Annual Ellen Winston Lecture.* Raleigh: North Carolina State University.

Lincoln, Y. S., and Guba, E. G. (1985). *Naturalistic inquiry.* Beverly Hills: Sage.

Longres, J., and McLeod, E. (May 1980). "Consciousness raising and social work practice." *Social Casework, 61:* 267–276.

Manheim, Henry L. (1977). *Sociological research: Philosophy and methods.* Homewood, IL.: The Dorsey Press.

Maslow, Abraham H. (1962). *Toward a psychology of being.* Princeton: Van Nostrand.

McIntosh, Peggy. (1992). "White privilege and male privilege. A personal account of coming to see correspondences through work in Women's Studies." In Margaret Anderson and Patricia Hill Collins (Eds.). *Race class and gender: An anthology.* Belmont, CA: Wadsworth Publishing Co.

Miller, Jean Baker. (1986) *Toward a new psychology of women.* (2nd ed.). Boston: Beacon.

Miovic, M. (2004). An introduction to spiritual psychology: Overview of the literature, East and West. *Harvard Review of Psychiatry, 12*(2), 105–115.

Moustakas, Clark. (1981). "Heuristic research." In Peter Reason and John Rowan (Eds.). *Human inquiry: A sourcebook of new paradigm research.* New York: Wiley and Sons.

Murphy, Y., Hunt, V., Zajicek, A., Norris, A., & Hamilton, L. (In press). *Incorporating Intersectionality in Social Work Practice, Research, Policy, and Education.* Washington, DC: NASW Press.

Myers, L. J., and Speight, S. L. (1994). "Optimal theory and the psychology of human diversity." In Trickett, E. J., Watts, R. J. and Birman D. (Eds.). (1994). *Human diversity: Perspectives on people in context.* San Francisco: Jossey-Bass.

Pastrana, A. (2004). Black identity constructions: Inserting intersectionality, bisexuality, and (Afro-) Latinidad into black studies. *Journal of African American Studies, 8*(1/2), 74–89.

Reason, Peter (1988). "Reflections." In Peter Reason. (Ed.). *Human inquiry in action: Developments in new paradigm research.* London: SAGE Publications.

Reason, Peter. (1981). "Methodological approaches to social science by Ian Mitroff and Ralph Kilmann: An appreciation." In Peter Reason and John Rowan. (Eds.). *Human inquiry: A sourcebook of new paradigm research.* New York: John Wiley and Sons.

Reason, Peter, and Hawkins, Peter. (1988). "Storytelling as inquiry." In Peter Reason (Ed.). *Human inquiry in action: Developments in new paradigm research.* London: SAGE Publications.

Root, M. P. P. "Within, between, and beyond race." In Root, Maria P. P. (Ed.). (1992). *Racially mixed people in America.* Newbury Park, CA: Sage.

Rubin, A., and Babbie, E. (1997). *Research methods for social work.* (3rd ed.). Pacific Grove, CA: Brooks/Cole.

Ruth, Sheila. (1990). *Issues in feminism.* Mountain View, CA: Mayfield Publishing Co.

Scott, Joan W. (1988). *Gender and the politics of history.* New York: Columbia University Press.

Sermabeikian, P. (1994). "Our clients, ourselves: The spiritual perspective and social work practice." *Social Work, 39*(2): 178–183.

Sherman, Edmund. (1991). "Interpretive methods for social work practice and research." *Journal of Sociology and Social Welfare, 18*(4): 69–81.

Spickard, P. R. (1996). "The Illogic of American Racial Categories." In Root, M. P. P. (Ed.). *Racially mixed people in America.* Newberry Park, CA: Sage Publications.

Spickard, P. R., Fong, R., Ewalt, P. L., Freeman, E. M., Kirk, S. A., and Poole, D. L. (Eds.). *Multicultural Issues in Social Work.* Washington, DC: NASW Press.

Stewart, A., & McDermott, C. Gender in psychology. *Annual Review of Psychology, 55*(1), 519–44.

Swigonski, M. E. (July 1994). "The logic of feminist standpoint theory for social work research." *Social Work, 39*(4): 387–393.

Turner, Robert J. (1991). "Affirming consciousness: The Africentric perspective." In Joyce, E., Chipungu, S., and Leashore, B. (Eds.). *Child welfare: An Africentric perspective.* New Brunswick, NJ: Rutgers University Press.

Tyson, K. (1995). "Editor's Introduction" *Heuristic research. New foundations for scientific social and behavioral research: The heuristic paradigm.* Boston: Allyn and Bacon.

Tyson, K. (Ed.) (1995). *New foundations for scientific, social and behavioral research: The heuristic paradigm.* Boston: Allyn and Bacon.

Van Den Bergh, N. (Ed.). (1995). *Feminist practice in the 21st century.* Washington, DC: NASW Press.

Webster's New Universal Unabridged Dictionary (2nd ed.) (1983). In Edmund Sherman, "Interpretive methods for social work practice and research." *Journal of Sociology and Social Welfare, 18*(4): 69–81.

Weick, Ann. (1991). "The place of science in social work." *Journal of Sociology and Social Welfare, 18*(4): 13–34.

Westkott, Marcia. (1979). "Feminist criticism of the social sciences." *Harvard Educational Review, 49*(4): 424–430.

Zukav, Gary. (1980). *The dancing wu li masters: An overview of the new physics.* Toronto: Bantam Books.

Chapter 3

Alix, E. K. (1995). *Sociology: An everyday life approach.* Minneapolis: West Publishing.

Anderson, Ralph, and Carter, Irl. (1990). *Human behavior in the social environment: A social systems approach* (4th ed.). New York: Aldine de Gruyter.

Anderson, R., Carter, I., and Lowe, G. (1999). *Human Behavior in the social environment: A social systems approach.* 5th ed. New York: Aldine de Gruyter.

Asamoah, Yvonne, Garcia, Alejandro, Hendricks, Carmen Ortiz, and Walker, Joel. (1991). "What we call ourselves: Implications for resources, policy, and practice." *Journal of Multicultural Social Work, 1*(1): 7–22.

Bengston, V., and Allen, K. (1993). The life course perspective applied to families over time. In P. Boss, W. Dogherty, R. LaRossa, W. Schumm, and S. Steinmetz (Eds.), *Sourcebook of family theories and methods: A contextual approach.* New York: Plenum.

Bergen, D. (1994). *Assessment methods for infants and toddlers: Transdisciplinary team approaches.* New York: Teachers College Press, Columbia University.

Berman, M. (Winter 1996). "The shadow side of systems theory." *Journal of Humanistic Psychology, 36*(1): 28–54.

Besthorn, F., and McMillen, D. (2002). The oppression of women and nature: Ecofeminism as a framework for an expanded ecological social work (2002:229). *Families in Society, 83*(3), 221–232.

Bricker-Jenkins, Mary, and Hooyman, Nancy, (Eds.). (1986). *Not for women only: Social work practice for a feminist future.* Silver Spring, MD: National Association of Social Workers, Inc.

Bricker-Jenkins, Mary, Hooyman, Nancy, and Gottlieb, Naomi (Eds.). (1991). *Feminist social work practice in clinical settings.* Newbury Park, CA: SAGE Publications.

Brown, Edwin G. (1981). "Selection and formulation of a research problem." In Richard M. Grinnell, Jr, *Social work research and evaluation.* Itasca, IL.: F. E. Peacock Publishers, Inc.

Capra, Fritjof. (1983). *The turning point: Science, society, and the rising culture.* Toronto: Bantam Books.

Cowger, C. D. (1994). "Assessing client strengths: Clinical assessment for client empowerment." *Social Work, 39*(3): 262–268.

Cowley, A. S., and Derezotes, D. (1994). "Transpersonal psychology and social work education." *Journal of Social Work Education, 30*(1): 32–41.

Dawson, Betty, Klass, Morris D., Guy, Rebecca F., and Edgley, Charles K. (1991). *Understanding social work research.* Boston: Allyn and Bacon.

DeJong, P., and Miller, S. D. (November 1995). "How to interview for client strengths." *Social Work, 40*(6): 729–736.

Diller, J. (1999). *Cultural diversity: A primer for the human services.* Belmont: Brooks/Cole Wadsworth.

Gardner, H. (2000). "Technology remakes the schools." *The Futurist, 34*(2): 30–32.

George, L. (1996). Missing links: The case for a social psychology of the life. *Gerontologist, 36*(2).

Germain, Carel. (1979). *Social work practice: people and environments, an ecological perspective.* New York: Columbia University.

Germain, Carel. (1986). "The life model approach to social work practice revisited." In Francis Turner (Ed.). (3rd ed.). *Social work treatment.* New York: Free Press.

Germain, Carel. (1991). *Human behavior in the social environment: An ecological view.* New York: Columbia University Press.

Gingerich, W. J. (2000). Solution-Focused Brief Therapy: A Review of the Outcome Research. *Family Process, 39*(4), 477.

Gleick, J. (1987). *Chaos: The making of a new science.* New York: Penguin Books.

Goldstein, Howard. (1990). "The knowledge base of social work practice: Theory, wisdom, analogue, or art?" *Families in Society, 71*(1), 32–43.

Green, J. (1999). *Cultural awareness in the human services: A multi-ethnic approach.* (3rd ed.). Boston: Allyn and Bacon.

Gutierraz, L. M., DeLois K. A., and Glen Maye, L. (1995). "Understanding empowerment practice: Building on practitioner-based knowledge." *Families in Society: The Journal of Contemporary Human Services,* 534–543.

Henslin, J. M. (1996). *Essentials of sociology: A down-to-earth approach.* Boston: Allyn and Bacon.

Jones, G. C., and Kilpatrick, A. C. (May 1996). "Wellness theory: A discussion and application to clients with disabilities." *Families in Society: The Journal of Contemporary Human Service, 77*(5): 259–267.

Krippner, S. (Summer 1994). "Humanistic psychology and chaos theory: The third revolution and the third force." *Journal of Humanistic Psychology, 34*(3): 48–61.

Lee, M. Y. (2003). A solution-focused approach to cross-cultural clinical social work practice: Utilizing cultural strengths. *Families in Society, 84*(3), 385–395.

Leigh, L. (1998). *Communicating for cultural competence.* Boston: Allyn and Bacon.

Lum, D. (1999). *Culturally competent practice: A framework for growth and action.* Pacific Grove: Brooks/Cole.

Martin, Patricia Yancey, and O'Connor, Gerald G. (1989). *The social environment: Open systems applications.* White Plains, NY: Longman, Inc.

Miovic, M. (2004). An introduction to spiritual psychology: Overview of the literature, East and West. *Harvard Review of Psychiatry, 12*(2), 105–115.

Mullen, Edward J. (1981). "Development of personal intervention models." In Richard M. Grinnell, Jr. *Social work research and evaluation.* Itasca, IL: F. E. Peacock Publishers, Inc.

Newman, Barbara, and Newman, Philip. (1991). *Development through life: A psychosocial approach* (5th ed.). Pacific Grove, CA: Brooks/Cole Publishing Company.

Newsome, W. S., and Kelly, M. (2004). Grandparents raising grandchildren: A solution-focused brief therapy approach in school settings. *Social Work with Groups, 27*(4), 65–84.

Norman, J., and Wheeler, B. (1996). "Gender-sensitive social work practice: A model for education." *Journal of Social Work Education, 32*(2): 203–213.

Patterson, J. B., McKenzie, B., and Jenkins, J. (1995). "Creating accessible groups for individuals with disabilities." *The Journal of Specialists in Group Work, 20*(2): 76–82.

Persell, Carolyn. (1987). *Understanding society* (2nd ed.). New York: Harper and Row.

Pool, C. (1997). "A new digital literacy: a conversation with Paul Gilster." *Educational Leadership, 55:* 6–11.

Queralt, M., and Witte, A. (1998). "A map for you? Geographic information systems in the social services." *Social Work, 43*(5): 455–469.

Richards, R. (Spring 1996). "Does the lone genius ride again? Chaos, creativity, and community." *Journal of Humanistic Psychology, 36*(2): 44–60.

Saleebey, D. (1997). "Introduction: Power in the people." In D. Saleebey (Ed.). *The strengths perspective in social work practice* (2nd ed., pp. 3–19). New York: Longman.

Saleeby, D. (May 1996). "The strengths perspective in social work practice: Extensions and cautions." *Social Work, 41*(3): 296–305.

Saleebey, Dennis. (1992). *The strengths perspective in social work practice.* White Plains, NY: Longman, Inc.

Scannapieco, M., and Jackson, S. (1996). "Kinship care: The African American response to family preservation." *Social Work, 41*(2): 190–196.

Scott, Joan W. (1988). "Deconstructing equality-versus-difference: Or, the uses of poststructuralist theory for feminism." *Feminist Studies, 14*(1): 33–50.

Sermabeikian, P. (1994). "Our clients, ourselves: The spiritual perspective and social work practice." *Social Work, 39*(2): 178–183.

Shafritz, Jay M., and Ott, J. Steven. (1987). *Classics of organization theory.* Chicago: The Dorsey Press.

Stanley, D. (1996). *The Giants of Gaia.* Web Publication by Mountain Man Graphics: Australia. http://magna.com.au/~prfbrown/gaia_jim.html

Swigonski, M. E. (Summer 1993). "Feminist standpoint theory and the questions of social work research." *Affilia, 8*(2): 171–183.

Szasz, Thomas Stephen. (1987). *Insanity: The idea and its consequences.* New York: John Wiley and Sons, Inc.

Thyer, B. (2001). "What is the role of theory in research on social work practice?" *Journal of Social Work Education, 37*(1):9–25.

Trickett, E. J., Watts, R. J., and Birman, D. "Toward an overarching framework for diversity." In Trickett, E. J., Watts, R. J., and Birman, D. (Eds.). (1994). *Human diversity: Perspectives on people in context.* San Francisco: Jossey-Bass.

Tyson, K. (1995). *New foundations for scientific and behavioral research: The heuristic paradigm.* Boston: Allyn and Bacon.

Van Den Berg, N. (Ed.). (1995). *Feminist practice in the 21st century.* Washington, DC: NASW.

Walsh, R., and Vaughan, F. (1994). "The worldview of Ken Wilber." *Journal of Humanistic Psychology, 34*(2): 6–21.

Weaver, H. (1998). "Indigenous people in a multicultural society: Unique issues for human services." *Social Work, 43*(3): 203–211.

Weaver, H. N. (1999). "Indigenous people and the social work profession: Defining culturally competent services." *Social Work, 44*(3): 217.

Weick, Ann. (1991). "The place of science in social work." *Journal of Sociology and Social Welfare, 18*(4): 13–34.

Whitechurch, Gail G., and Constantine, Larry L. (1993). "Systems Theory." In Boss, P. G., et al. (Eds.). *Sourcebook of family theories and methods: A contextual approach.* New York: Plenum Press.

Williams, C. (2006). The epistemology of cultural competence. *Families in Society, 87*(2).

Chapter 4

Achenbaum, W. A., and Bengtson, V. L. (1994). "Re-engaging the disengagement theory of aging: On the history and assessment of theory development in gerontology." *The Gerontologist, 34*(6): 756–763.

Bergen, D. (1994). *Assessment methods for infants and toddlers: Transdisciplinary team approaches.* New York: Teachers College Press, Columbia University.

Berzoff, Joan. (1989). "From separation to connection: Shifts in understanding." *Affilia, 4*(1): 45–58.

Bloom, Martin. (Ed.). (1985). *Life span development* (2nd ed.). New York: MacMillan.

Chatterjee, P., and Hokenstad, T. (1997). "Should the HBSE Core Curriculum Include International Theories, Research, and Practice?" In M. K. Bloom, W. (Ed.). *Controversial issues in human behavior in the social environment.* Boston: Allyn and Bacon.

CSWE (2008). *Educational Policy and Accreditation Standards.* Alexandria, VA.

D'Augelli, A. R. (1994). "Identity development and sexual orientation: Toward a model of lesbian, gay, and bisexual development." In Trickett, E. J., Watts, R. J., and Birman, D. (Eds.). *Human diversity: Perspectives on people in context.* San Francisco: Jossey-Bass.

Erikson, Erik H. (1950) *Childhood and society.* New York: W. W. Norton and Company, Inc.

Erikson, Erik H. (1963). *Childhood and society.* (2nd ed.). New York: W. W. Norton and Company, Inc.

Erikson, Erik H. (1968) *Identity: Youth and crisis.* New York: W. W. Norton and Company, Inc.

Gardner, H. (1993). *Multiple intelligences: The theory in practice.* New York: Basic Books.

Gemmill, G., and Oakely, Judith. (1992). "Leadership an alienating social myth?" *Human Relations* 45(2):113–139.

Gilligan, Carol. (1982). *In a different voice: Psychological theory and women's development.* Cambridge: Harvard University Press.

Green, Michael. (1989). *Theories of human development: A comparative approach.* Englewood Cliffs, NJ: Prentice Hall.

Healy, William, Bonner, Augusta, and Bowers, Anna Mae. (1930). *The structure and meaning of psychoanalysis as related to personality and behavior.* New York: Alfred A. Knopf.

Helms, J. E. (1994). "The conceptualization of racial identity and other 'racial' constructs." In Trickett, E. J., Watts, R. J., and Birman, D. (Eds.). *Human diversity: Perspectives on people in context.* San Francisco: Jossey-Bass.

Herrnstein, R. J., and Murray, C. (1994). *The Bell Curve: Intelligence and class structure in American life.* New York: Free Press.

Jendrek, M. P. (1994). "Grandparents who parent their grandchildren: Circumstances and decisions." *The Gerontologist, 34*(2): 206–216.

Levinson, D., and Levinson, J. (1996). *The seasons of a woman's life.* New York: Knopf.

Levinson, Daniel. (1986) "A conception of adult development." *American Psychologist, 41*(1): 3–13.

Levinson, Daniel J., Darrow, Charlotte N., Klein, Edward B., Levinson, Maria H., and McKee, Braxton. (1978). *The seasons of a man's life.* New York: Alfred A. Knopf.

Loevinger, Jane. (1987). *Paradigms of personality.* New York: W. H. Freeman and Company.

Milillo, D. (2006). "Rape as a tactic of war: Social and psychological perspectives." *Affilia: Journal of Women and Social Work, 21*(2), 196–205.

Miller, Jean Baker. (1986). *Toward a new psychology of women.* Boston: Beacon.

Miller, Jean Baker. (1991). "The development of women's sense of self." In Jordan, J., Kaplan, A., Miller, J. B., Stiver, I., and Surrey, J. *Women's growth in connection: Writings from the Stone Center.* New York: Guilford Press.

Miller, R. L. (1992). "The human ecology of multiracial identity." In Root, Maria P. P. (Ed.). *Racially mixed people in America.* Newbury Park, CA: Sage.

Parks, E., Carter, R., and Gushue, G. (July/August 1996). "At the crossroads: Racial and womanist identity development in Black and White women." *Journal of Counseling and Development, 74:* 624–631.

Pharr, Suzanne. (1988). *Homophobia: A weapon of sexism.* Inverness, CA: Chardon Press.

Richards, R. (Spring 1996). "Does the lone genius ride again? Chaos, creativity, and community." *Journal of Humanistic Psychology, 36*(2): 44–60.

Spencer, Margaret Beale. (1990). "Development of minority children: An introduction." *Child Development, 61:* 267–269.

Spencer, Margaret B., and Markstrom-Adams, Carol. (1990). "Identity processes among racial and ethnic minority children in America." *Child Development*, 61: 290–310.

Steenbarger, Brett. (1991). "All the world is not a stage: Emerging contextualist themes in counseling and development." *Journal of Counseling and Development*, 70: 288.

Szasz, Thomas Stephen. (1961). *The myth of mental illness: Foundations of a theory of personal conduct*. New York: Harper and Row Publishers, Inc.

Tornstam, L. (Winter 1999/2000). "Transcendence in later life." *Generations*, 23(4): 10–14.

University of Arkansas Nursery School. (September 1996). *Play*. Typescript. Fayetteville, AR: Author.

Weick, Ann. (1981). "Reframing the person-in-environment perspective." *Social Work*, 26(2): 140.

Weick, A. (1991). The place of science in social work. *Journal of Sociology and Social Welfare, 18, 13–33*

Wheeler-Scruggs, K. S. (2008). "Do lesbians differ from heterosexual men and women in Levinsonian phases of adult development?" *Journal of Counseling & Development*, 86(1), 39–46.

Chapter 5

Abrams, L., and Gibson, P. (2007). "Reframing multicultural education: Teaching white privilege in the social work curriculum." *Journal of Social Work Education, 43*(1), 147–160.

Aldarondo, F. (2001). "Racial and ethnic identity model, and their application: Counseling U.S. biracial individuals." *Journal of Mental Health Counseling, 23*(3): 238–255.

Andrews, A., and Ben-Arieh, A. (1999). "Measuring and monitoring children's well-being across the world." *Social Work, 44*(2): 105–115.

Belanky, Mary F., Clinchy, Blythe M., Goldberger, Nancy R., and Tarule, Jill M. (1986). *Women's ways of knowing: The development of self, voice, and mind*. New York. Basic Books, Inc.

Bent-Goodley, T. B. (2005). "An African-Centered approach to domestic violence." *Families in Society, 86*(2), 197.

Burdge, B. J. (2007). "Bending gender, ending gender: Theoretical foundations for social work practice with the transgender community." *Social Work, 52*(3), 243.

Bureau, U. S. C. (2008). The 2008 HHS Poverty Guidelines. Retrieved from http://aspe.hhs.gov/poverty/08Poverty.shtml

Burgess, C. (2000). "Internal and external stress factors associated with the identity development of transgendered youth." *Journal of Gay and Lesbian Social Services, 10*(3/4), 35–47.

Carter, R. T., and Jones, J. M. (1996). "Racism and white racial identity." In Bowser, B. P., and Hunt, R. G. (Eds.). *Impact of racism on White Americans*. (2nd Ed.). Thousand Oaks, CA: Sage.

Cass, Vivienne C. (1984). "Homosexual identity formation: Testing a theoretical model." *Journal of Sex Research, 20*(2): 143–167.

Chodorow, Nancy. (1974). "Family structure and feminine personality." In Michelle Zimbalist Rosaldo and Louise Lamphere. (Eds.). *Women, culture and society*. Stanford: Stanford University Press.

Chodorow, Nancy. (1978). *The reproduction of mothering: Psychoanalysis and the sociology of gender*. Berkeley: University of California Press.

Collins, Patricia Hill. (1990). *Black feminist thought: Knowledge, consciousness, and the politics of empowerment*. Cambridge: Unwin Hyman, Inc.

Cross, W. E. (1971). "The Negro to Black experience: Towards a psychology of Black liberation." *Black World, 20*(9): 13–27.

D'Augelli, A. R. (1994). "Identity development and sexual orientation: Toward a model of lesbian, gay, and bisexual development." In Trickett, E. J., Watts, R. J., and Birman, D. (Eds.). *Human diversity: Perspectives on people in context*. San Francisco: Jossey-Bass.

Demo, D. H., and Allen, K. R. (1996). "Diversity within lesbian and gay families: Challenges and implications for family theory and research." *Journal of Social and Personal Relationships, 13*(3): 415–434.

Eliason, M. J. (1996). "Working with lesbian, gay, and bisexual people: Reducing negative stereotypes via inservice education." *Journal of Nursing Staff Development, 12*(3): 127–132.

Evans-Campbell, T., Fredriksen-Goldsen, K., Walters, K., and Stately, A. (2007). "Caregiving exieriences among American Indian two-spirit men and women: Contemporary and historical roles." *Journal of Gay and Lesbian Social Services, 18*(3/4), 75–92.

Fong, R., Spickard, P. R., and Ewalt, P. L. (1996). "A multi-racial reality: Issues for social work." In Ewalt, P. L., Freeman, E. M., Kirk, S. A., and Poole, D. L. (Eds.). *Multicultural issues in social work*. Washington, DC: NASW.

Food Research and Action Council, (2000). *Hunger in the U.S.* [Web site]. Food Research and Action Council. Available: http://www.frac.org/html/hunger_in_the_us/hunger_index. html [2000, 4/5/00].

Franklin, A. (1999). "Invisibility syndrome and racial identity development in psychotherapy and counseling African American men." *Counseling Psychologist, 27*(6): 761–793.

Gardner, H. (1983). *Frames of mind: The theory of multiple intelligences*. New York: Basic Books.

Gardner, H. (1993). *Multiple intelligences: The theory in practice*. New York: Basic Books.

Gates, G. (2006). *Same-Sex Couples and the Gay, Lesbian, Bisexual Population: New Estimates from the American Community Survey*. Los Angeles: Williams Institute on Sexual Orientation Law and Public Policy, UCLA School of Law.

Gibbs, Jewelle Taylor, and Huang, Larke Nahme, and collaborators. (1989). *Children of color: Psychological interventions with minority youth*. San Francisco: Jossey-Bass Publishers.

Gilligan, Carol. (1982). *In a different voice: Psychological theory and women's development*. Cambridge: Harvard University Press.

Gundry, L. K., Kickul, J. R., and Prather, C. W. (1994). "Building the creative organization." *Organizational Dynamics, 22*(4): 22–37.

Hammack, P. L. (2005). "An integrative paradigm." *Human Development, 48*(5), 267.

Harding, Sandra. (1986). *The science question in feminism*. Ithaca, NY: Cornell University Press.

Helms, J. E. (1994). "The conceptualization of racial identity and other 'racial' constructs." In Trickett, E. J., Watts, R. J., and Birman, D. (Eds.). *Human diversity: Perspectives on people in context*. San Francisco: Jossey-Bass.

Herbert, James I. (1990). "Integrating race and adult psychosocial development." *Journal of Organizational Behavior, 11:* 433–446.

Hopkins, N. (2008). "Identity, practice and dialogue." *Journal of Community and Applied Social Psychology, 18*(4), 363–368.

Hunter, S., and Sundel, M. (1994). "Midlife for women: A new perspective." *Affilia, 9*(2). "Is homosexuality biological?" (1991). *Science: 253,* 956–957.

Jacobs, James. (1992). "Identity development in biracial children." In Root, Maria P. P. (Ed.). *Racially mixed people in America.* Newbury Park, CA: Sage.

Jordan, Judith, Kaplan, Alexandra, Miller, Jean Baker, Stiver, Irene, and Surrey, Janet. (1991). *Women's growth in connection: Writings of the Stone Center.* New York: Guilford Press.

Keller, Evelyn Fox (1985). *Reflections on gender and science.* New Haven: Yale University Press.

Kich, George Kitahara. (1992). "The developmental process of asserting a biracial, bicultural identity." In Root, Maria P. P. (Ed.). *Racially mixed people in America.* Newbury Park, CA: Sage.

Kimmel, M. S., and Messner, M. A. (Eds.). (1995). *Men's lives.* (3rd ed.). Boston: Allyn and Bacon.

Kinsey, Alfred C. (1948/1998) *Sexual behavior in the human male.* Philadelphia: W. B. Saunders; Bloomington: Indiana University Press.

Kopels, S. (Fall 1995). "The Americans with Disabilities Act: A tool to combat poverty." *Journal of Social Work Education, 31*(3): 337–346.

Levy, B. (1995). "Violence against women." In *Feminist practice for the 21st century.* Van Den Bergh, N. (Ed.). Washington, DC: NASW.

Mallon, G. (2000). "Appendix A: A glossary of transgendered definitions." *Journal of Gay and Lesbian Social Services, 10*(3), 143–145.

Malone, M., McKinsey, P., Thyer, B., and Starks, E. (2000). "Social work early intervention for young children with developmental disabilities." *Health and Social Work, 25*(3): 169–180.

MayoClinic.com. (2009) Women's health: Preventing top 10 threats. http://www.mayoclinic.com/health/womens-health/WO00014

McCarn, S. and Fassinger, R. (1996). "Revisioning sexual minority identity formation: A new model of lesbian identity and its implications for counseling and research." *Counseling Psychologist, 24*(3): 508–536.

McQuaide, S. (1998). "Women at midlife." *Social Work, 43*(1): 21–31.

Miller, Jean Baker. (1976). *Toward a new psychology of women.* Boston: Beacon Press.

Miller, Jean Baker. (1986). *Toward a new psychology of women.* (2nd ed.). Boston: Beacon Press.

Miller, R. L. (1992). "The human ecology of multiracial identity." In Root, Maria P. P. (Ed.). *Racially mixed people in America.* Newbury Park, CA: Sage.

Myers, Linda J., Speight, Suzette, Highlen, Pamela, Cox, Chikako, Reynolds, Amy, Adams, Eve, and Hanley, C. Patricia. (1991). "Identity development and worldview: Toward an optimal conceptualization." *Journal of Counseling and Development, 70:* 54–63.

Nash, M., Wong, J., and Trlin, A. (2006). "Civic and social integration." *International Social Work, 49*(3), 345–363.

NOMAS. (1996). Available: http://www.spacestar.com/users/abtnomas/history.html

Ogbu, John U. (1978). "Caste and education and how they function in the United States." In *Minority education and caste: The American system in cross-cultural perspective.* New York: Academic Press.

Orlin, M. (1995). "The Americans with Disabilities Act: Implications for social services." *Social Work, 40*(2): 233–234. Reprinted with permission.

Parham, T. (1999). "Invisibility syndrome in African descent people: Understanding the cultural manifestations of the struggle for self-affirmation." *Counseling Psychologist, 27*(6): 794–801.

Parham, Thomas A. (1989). "Cycles of psychological nigrescence." *The Counseling Psychologist, 17*(2): 187–226.

Parks, E. E., Carter, R. T., and Gushue, G. V. (1996, July/August). "At the crossroads: Racial and womanist identity development in Black and White women." *Journal of Counseling and Development, (74):* 624–631.

PRB Reports on America Vol. 2, No. 1, February 2001, by Phyllis Moen, Population Reference Bureau, http://www.prb.org/Publications/ReportsOnAmerica/2001/TheCareerQuandary.aspx

Rank, M., and Hirschl, T. (1999). "The likelihood of poverty across the American adult life span." *Social Work, 44*(3): 201–216.

Rothblum, E. D. (1994). "Transforming lesbian sexuality." *Psychology of Women Quarterly, 18.*

Sanders Thompson, V. (2001). "The complexity of African American racial identification." *Journal of Black Studies, 32*(2), 155–165.

Schroots, J. (1996). "Theoretical developments in the psychology of aging." *The Gerontologist, 36*(2).

Scott, D., and Robinson, T. (2001). "White male identity development: The Key Model." *Journal of Counseling and Development, 79*(4), 415.

Seipel, M. (1999). "Social consequences of malnutrition." *Social Work, 44* (5): 416–425.

Sellers, R., Smith, M., Shelton, J., Rowley, S., and Chavous, T. (1998). "Multidimensional model of racial identity: A reconceptualization of African American racial identity." *Personality and Social Psychology Review (Lawrence Erlbaum Associates), 2*(1), 18.

Simon, Gregory E., Evette J. Ludman, Jennifer A. Linde, Belinda H. Operskalski, Laura Ichikawa, Paul Rohde, Emily A. Finch, and Robert W. Jeffery. (2008). "Association between obesity and depression in middle-aged women." *General Hospital Psychiatry* 30(1), 32–39. http://www.pubmedcentral.nih.gov/articlerender.fcgi?artid=2675189

Snyder, C., May, J. D., Zulcic, N., and Gabbard, W. (2005). "Social work with Bosnian Muslim refugee children and families: A review of the literature." *Child Welfare, 84*(5), 607–630.

Spencer, Margaret Beale, and Markstrom-Adams, Carol. (1990). "Identity processes among racial and ethnic minority children in America." *Child Development, 61:* 290–310.

Spickard, P. R. (1992). "The illogic of American racial categories." In Root, Maria P. P. (Ed.). *Racially mixed people in America.* Newbury Park, CA: Sage.

Spriggs, W. (2006). "Poverty in America: The poor are getting poorer." *Crisis 113*(1), 14–19. Retrieved June 1, 2009, from Academic Search Premier database.

Stack, Carol B. (1986). "The culture of gender: Women and men of color." *Signs, 11*(2): 321–24.

Stout, K. D. (1991). "A continuum of male controls and violence against women: A teaching model." *Journal of Social Work Education, 27*(3): 305–319.

Sue, D. W., Capodilupo, C. M., Torino, G. C., Bucceri, J. M., Holder, A. M. B., Nadal, K. L., et al. (2007). "Racial microaggressions in everyday life." *American Psychologist, 62*(4), 271–286.

Wastell, C. A. (1996). "Feminist developmental theory: Implications for counseling." *Journal of Counseling and Development, 74,* 575–581.

Worrell, F., Cross, W., and Vandiver, B. (2001). "Nigrescence theory: Current status and challenges for the future." *Journal of Multicultural Counseling and Development, 29*(3), 201.

Yeh, C. (1999). "Invisibility and self-construct in African American men: Implications for training and practice." *Counseling Psychologist, 27*(6): 810–819.

Chapter 6

Adi-Habib, N., Safir, A., and Triplett, T. *NSAF Survey Methods and Data Reliability: Report No. 1.*

Ainslie, Julie and Feltey, Kathryn. (1991). "Definitions and dynamics of motherhood and family in lesbian communities." In *Wider Families.* Binghamton, NY: Haworth Press.

Al-Krenawi, A., and Graham, J. (2000). "Islamic theology and prayer." *International Social Work, 43*(3), 289.

American Immigration Lawyers Association. (1999). *American is immigration.* [Web site]. American Immigration Lawyers Association. Available: http://www.aila.org/aboutimmigration.html [2000, 3/20/00].

Bailey, D., Skinner, D., Rodriquez, P., Gut, D., and Correa, V. (1999). "Awareness, use, and satisfaction with services for Latino parents of young children with disabilities." *Exceptional Children, 65*(3): 367–381.

Baker, B. (n. d.). *How many children are living in grandparent-headed households.* AARP.

Bengston, V. L., and Allen, K. R. (1993). "The life course perspective applied to families over time." In P. G. Boss, Doherty, W. J., LaRossa, R., Schuman, W. R., and Steinmetz, S.K. (Eds.). *Sourcebook of family theories and methods: A contextual approach.* New York: Plenum Press.

Billingsley, A. (1992). *Climbing Jacob's ladder: The enduring legacy of African-American families.* New York: Simon and Schuster.

Billingsley, Andrew. (1968). *Black families in white America.* Englewood Cliffs, NJ: Prentice Hall.

Boyd-Franklin, Nancy. (1993). "Race, class and poverty." In *Normal family processes,* Walsh, Froma. (Ed.). New York: Guilford

Carter, B., and McGoldrick, M. (1999). Eds. *The Expanded Family Life Cycle.* (3rd ed.). Boston: Allyn and Bacon.

Carter, Betty, and McGoldrick, Monica. (1989). *The changing family life cycle: A framework for family therapy* (2nd ed.). Boston: Allyn and Bacon.

Carter, Elizabeth, and McGoldrick, Monica. (1980). *The family life cycle: A framework for family therapy.* New York: Gardner Press.

CNN (Producer). (2009, May 27, 2009) "Lawmakers approve same-sex marriage in N.H., Maine." Podcast retrieved from http://www.cnn.com/2009/POLITICS/05/06/maine.same.sex.marriage/.

Demo, D. H., and Allen, K. R. (1996). "Diversity within lesbian and gay families: Challenges and implications for family theory and research." *Journal of Social and Personal Relationships,* 13 (3): 415–434.

Devore, Wynetta, and Schlesinger, Elfriede G. (1991). *Ethnic-sensitive social work practice* (3rd ed.). New York: Macmillan Publishing Company.

Duvall, Evelyn M. (1971). *Family development* (4th ed.). Philadelphia: J. B. Lippincott Company.

Duvall, Evelyn M. (1988). "Family development's first forty years." *Family Relations, 37:* 127–134.

Edelman, Marian Wright. (1987). *Families in Peril.* Cambridge, MA: Harvard University Press.

Elder, G. H. (1998). "The life course as developmental theory." *Child Development, 69*(1).

English, Richard. (1991). "Diversity of worldviews among African American families." In Everett, Joyce, Chipungu, Sandra, and Leashore, Bogart, eds. *Child welfare: An Africentric perspective.* New Brunswick, NJ: Rutgers University Press.

Feliciano, C. (2005). "U.S. Immigrant More Educated Than Nonimmigrants," retrieved September 27, 2009, from http://www.prb.org/CPIPR/NewReleases/Feliciano2005.aspx

Ferree, Myra M. (1990). "Beyond separate spheres: Feminism and family research." *Journal of Marriage and the Family, 52:* 866–884.

Fong, R., Spickard, P. R., and Ewalt, P. L. (1996). "A multiracial reality: Issues for social work." In Ewalt, P. L., Freeman, E. M., Kirk, S. A., and Poole, D. L. *Multicultural issues in social work.* Washington, DC: NASW.

Gebeke, D. (1996). *Grandparenting and stepgrandparenting: When grandparents become parents to their grandchildren.* [Web site]. North Dakota State University Extension Service. Available: http://www.ext.nodak.edu/extpubs/yf/famsci/fs561w.htm [2000, 3/20/00].

Hall, R., and Livingston, J. (2006). "Mental health practice with Arab families: The implications of spirituality vis-à-vis Islam." *American Journal of Family Therapy, 34*(2), 139–150.

Harrison, Algea, Wilson, Melvin, Pine, Charles, Chan, Samuel, and Buriel, Raymond. (1990). "Family ecologies of ethnic minority children." *Child Development, 61:* 347–362.

Harry, B. (2002). "Trends and issues in serving culturally diverse families of children with disabilities." *The Journal of Special Education, 36*(3): 131–138.

Hartman, Ann, and Laird, Joan. (1983). *Family-centered social work practice.* New York: Free Press.

Hernandez, M., and McGoldrick, M. (1999). "Migration and the life cycle." In B. Carter and M. McGoldrick. (Eds.). *The expanded family life cycle: Individual, family, and social perspectives* (3rd ed., p. 541). Boston: Allyn and Bacon.

Hetherington, E. Mavis, Law, Tracy, and O'Connor, Thomas. (1993) "Divorce, changes, and new chances." In *Normal family processes.* Walsh, Froma. (Ed.). New York: Guilford.

Hill, Reuben. (1986). "Life cycle stages for types of single parent families: Of family development theory." *Family Relations,* 35:19–29.

Hines, Paulette Moore, and Boyd-Franklin, Nancy. (1982). "Black families." In *Ethnicity and family therapy.* McGoldrick, Monica, Pearce, John, and Giordano, Joseph. (Eds.). New York: Guilford.

Ho, Man Kueng. (Ed.). (1987). *Family therapy with ethnic minorities.* Newbury Park, CA: Sage Publications.

Hodge, D. (2005). "Social work and the house of Islam: Orienting practitioners to the beliefs and values of Muslims in the United States." *Social Work, 50*(2), 162–173.

Hollingsworth, L. (1998). "Promoting same-race adoption for children of color." *Social Work, 43*(2): 104–116.

Jendrek, M. P. (1994). "Grandparents who parent their grandchildren: Circumstances and decisions." *The Gerontologist, 34*(2): 206—216.

Kennedy, Carroll E. (1978): *Human development: The adult years and aging.* New York: Macmillan Publishing Co., Inc.

Kennedy, M., and Agron, L. (1999). "Bridging the digital divide." *American School and University, 72*(2), 16–18.

Laird, Joan. (1993). "Lesbian and gay families." In *Normal family processes.* Walsh, Froma. (Ed.). New York: Guilford.

Langbein, L., and Yost, M. A. (2009). "Same-sex marriage and negative externalities." *Social Science Quarterly (Blackwell Publishing Limited), 90*(2), 292–308.

Leigh, James. (1989). "Black Americans: Emerging identity issues and social policy." *The Annual Ellen Winston Lecture.* Raleigh: North Carolina State University.

Logan, Sadye. (1990). "Black families: Race, ethnicity, culture, social class, and gender issues." In *Social work practice with black families: A culturally specific perspective.* Logan, Sadye, Freeman, Edith, and McRoy, Ruth. (Eds.). New York: Longman.

Logan, Sadye, Freeman, Edith, and McRoy, Ruth. (Eds.). (1990). *Social work practice with Black families: A culturally specific perspective.* New York: Longman.

Malone, M., McKinsey, P., Thyer, B., and Straka, E. (2000). "Social work early intervention for young children with developmental disabilities." *Health and Social Work, 25*(3): 169–180.

Martin, Joanne, and Martin, Elmer P. (1985). *The helping tradition in the black family and community.* Silver Spring, MD: NASW.

Mather, M. (2009). *Children in Immigrant Families Chart New Path.* Washington, DC.

McGoldrick, Monica, Pearce, John, and Giordano, Joseph. (Eds.). (1982). *Ethnicity and family therapy.* New York: Guilford Press.

Miller, Jean Baker. (1986). *Toward a new psychology of women.* (2nd ed.) Boston: Beacon.

Myers, Linda. (1985). "Transpersonal psychology: The role of the Afrocentric paradigm," *The Journal of Black Psychology.* 12(1):31–42.

National Telecommunications and Information Administration. (1999). *Falling through the Net: Defining the digital divide.* [Web site]. U.S. Department of Commerce. Available: http://www.ntia.doc.gov [2000, 4/8/00].

Park, J., Turnbull, A., and Turnbull III, H. (2002). "Impacts of poverty on quality of life in families of children with disabilities." *Exceptional Children, 68*(2): 151–170.

Pinderhughes, Elaine. (1982). "Afro-American families and the victim system." In McGoldrick, M., Pearce, J., and Giordano, J. (Eds.). (1982). *Ethnicity and family therapy.* New York: Guilford Press.

Piotrkowski, Chaya, and Hughes, Diane. (1993). "Dual-earner families in context." In *Normal family processes.* Walsh, Froma, ed. New York: Guilford.

Population Reference Bureau. (2008). *World Population Highlights.* Washington, DC.

Rehman, T., and Dziegielewski, S. (2003). "Women who choose Islam." *International Journal of Mental Health, 32*(3), 31–49.

Ronnau, J. P. and Marlow, C. R. (November 1993). "Family preservation, poverty and the value of diversity." *Families in Society: The Journal of Contemporary Human Services.* 74:538–544.

Ross-Sheriff, F. (2006). "Afghan women in exile and repatriation: Passive victims or social actors?" *Affilia: Journal of Women and Social Work, 21*(2), 206–219.

Rothenberg, D. (1997, 8/1/97). *Grandparents as parents: A primer for schools.* [Web site]. ERIC Clearinghouse on Elementary and Early Childhood Education. Available: wysiwyg://770/http://www.kidsource...ource/content2/grandparents.3.html [2000, 3/20/00].

Rounds, K. A., Weil, M., and Bishop, K. K. (January 1994). "Practice with culturally diverse families of young children with disabilities." *Families in Society: The Journal of Contemporary Human Services.* 75(1):3–14.

Scannapieco, M., and Jackson, S. (1996). "Kinship care: The African American response to family preservation." *Social Work, 41*(2):190–196.

Scanzoni, John, and Marsiglio, William. (1991). "Wider families as primary relationships." *Wider families.* Binghamton, NY: The Haworth Press.

Slater, Suzanne, and Mencher, Julie. (1991). "The lesbian family life cycle: A contextual approach." *American Journal of Orthopsychiatry, 61*(3):372–382.

Stack, C. (1974). *Allowrkin: Strategies for survival in a Black community.* New York: Harper and Row.

Staveteig, S., and Wigton, A. (2000). *Racial and ethnic disparities: Key findings from the national survey of america's families.* [Web site]. Urban Institute. Available: http://newfederalism.urban.org/html/series_b/b5/b5.html [2000, 4/8/00].

Visher, Emily, and Visher, John. (1993). "Remarriage families and stepparenting." In *Normal family processes.* Walsh, Froma. (ed.). New York: Guilford.

Walsh, Froma. (2003). *Normal family processes.* (3rd ed.) New York: Guilford.

Wilhelmus, M. (1998). "Mediation in kinship care: Another step in the provision of culturally relevant child welfare services." *Social Work, 43*(2): 117–126.

Zedlewski, S. (2003). "1999 Snapshots of America's families II: Economic Well-Being." Available: www.urban.org

Chapter 7

Anderson, Ralph, and Carter, Irl. (1990). *Human behavior in the social environment: A social systems approach* (4th ed.). New York: Aldine de Gruyter.

Attneave, Carolyn. (1982). "American Indians and Alaska Native families: Emigrants in their own homeland." In McGoldrick, Monica, Pearce, John, and Giordano, Joseph. (Eds.). *Ethnicity and family therapy.* New York: Guilford.

Brown, Beverly M. (1995). "The process of inclusion and accommodation: A bill of rights for people with disabilities in group work." *The Journal for Specialists in Group Work, 20*(2):71–75.

Brown, Leonard N. (1991). *Groups for growth and change.* New York: Longman.

Curran, D. J., and Renzetti, C. (1996). *Social Problems: Society in Crisis.* (4th ed.). Boston: Allyn and Bacon

Davis, L. E., Galinsky, M. J., and Schopler, J. H. (1996). "RAP: A framework for leadership of multiracial groups." In *Multicultural issues in social work.* Ewalt, P. L., Freeman, E., M., Kirk, S. A., and Poole, D. L. (Eds.). Washington, DC: NASW Press.

Davis, Larry. (1985). "Group work practice with ethnic minorities of color." In Sundal, Martin et al. (Eds.). *Individual change through small groups.* (2nd ed.). New York: The Free Press.

Davis, Larry, E. Galinsky, Maeda J., and Schopler, Janice H. (1995). "RAP: A framework for leadership in multiracial groups," *Social Work,* 40(2):155–167, appearing in Ewalt, P., et al. (1996). *Multicultural Issues in Social Work.* Washington, DC: NASW Press. Reprinted with permission.

Estrada, M., Brown, J., and Lee, F. (1995). "Who gets the credit? Perceptions of idiosyncrasy credit in work groups." *Small Group Research,* 26(1):56–76.

Garvin, Charles. (1985). "Work with disadvantaged and oppressed groups." In Sundel, Martin et al. (Eds.), *Individual change through small groups.* (2nd ed.). New York: The Free Press.

Gastil, John. (1992). "A definition of small group democracy." *Small Group Research,* 23(3): 278–301.

———. (1994). "A definition and illustration of democratic leadership." *Human Relations,* 47(8): 953–975.

Gemmill, Gary, and Oakley, Judith. (1992). "Leadership: An alienating social myth?" *Human Relations,* 45(2):113–139.

Hare, A. P. (1994). "Types of roles in small groups: A bit of history and a current perspective." *Small Group Research,* 25(3):433–448.

Janus, I. L. (1982). *Groupthink.* (2nd ed.). Boston: Houghton Mifflin.

Johnson, David, and Johnson, Frank. (1991). *Joining together: Group theory and group skills* (4th ed.). Englewood Cliffs, NJ: Prentice Hall.

Kanter, Rosabeth Moss. (1977). "Women in organizations: Sex roles, group dynamics and change strategies." In Alice Sargeant, *Beyond sex roles.* St. Paul: West.

Knouse, S. and Dansley, M. (1999). "Percentages of work-group diversity and work-group effectiveness." *The Journal of Psychology,* 133(5): 486–494.

Lewis, E. (1992). "Regaining promise: Feminist perspectives for social group work practice." *Social Work with Groups,* 13(4): 271–284.

McGoldrick, M., Pearce, J., and Giordano, J. (Eds.). (1982). *Ethnicity and family therapy.* New York: Gilford Press.

McLeod, P. L., Lobel, S. A., and Cox, T. H. (1996). "Ethnic diversity and creativity in small groups." *Small Group Research.* vl 27 (2):248–264.

Miranda, S. M. (1994). "Avoidance of groupthink: Meeting management using group support systems." *Small Group Research,* 25(1):105–136.

Napier, Rodney, and Gershenfeld, Matti K. (1985). *Groups, theory and experience* (3rd ed.). Boston: Houghton Mifflin Company.

Neck, C. P., and Manz, C. C. (1994). "From groupthink to teamthink: Toward the creation of constructive thought patterns in self-managing work teams." *Human Relations,* 47(8): 929–952.

Neck, C. P., and Moorhead, G. (1995). "Groupthink remodeled: The importance of leadership, time pressure, and methodical decision-making procedures." *Human Relations,* 48(5):537–557.

Oetzel, J. (2001). "Self-construals, communication processes, and group outcomes in homogeneous and heterogeneous groups." *Small Group Research,* 32(1): 19–54.

Patterson, J. B., McKenzie, and Jenkins, J. (1995). "Creating accessible groups for individuals with disabilities." *The Journal for Specialists in Group Work,* 20(2):76–82.

Sabini, J. (1995). *Social psychology.* (2nd Ed.). New York: W. W. Norton.

Sundell, Martin; Glasser, Paul; Sarri, Rosemary; and Vinter, Robert, Eds. (1985). *Individual change through small groups* (2nd Ed.). New York: The Free Press.

Thomas, D. (1999). Cultural diversity and work group effectiveness: An experimental study. *Journal of Cross-Cultural Psychology,* 30(2), 242.

Worchel, Stephen; Wood, Wendy; and Simpson, Jeffry A. (Eds.). (1992). *Group process and productivity.* Newbury Park, CA: SAGE Publications.

Chapter 8

Abrahamsson, Bengt. (1977). *Bureaucracy or participation: The logic of organization.* Beverly Hills: SAGE Publications.

Anderson, Ralph, and Carter, Irl. (1990). *Human behavior in the social environment: A social systems approach* (4th ed.). New York: Aldine de Gruyter.

Attneave, Carolyn. (1982). "American Indians and Alaska Native families: Emigrants in their own homeland," in McGoldrick, Monica, Pearce, John, and Giordano, Joseph. (Eds.). *Ethnicity and family therapy.* New York: Guilford.

Austin, M. J., & Claasen, J. (2008). Impact of organizational change on organizational culture: Implications for introducing evidence-based practice. *Journal of Evidence-Based Social Work,* 5(1/2), 321–359.

Barrett, F. (1995). "Creating appreciative learning cultures." *Organizational Dynamics,* 24(2): 36–49.

Burton, B., and Dunn, C. (1996). "Feminist ethics as moral grounding for stakeholder theory." *Business Ethics Quarterly,* 6: 133–147.

Colon, E. (1995). "Creating an Intelligent Organization." In Ginsberg, L. and Keys, P. (Eds.). *New management in the human services.* (2nd ed.). Washington, DC: NASW.

Dodge, R. and Robbins, J. (1992). "An Empirical Investigation of the Organizational Life Cycle." *Journal of Small Business Management,* 30(1): 27–37.

Etzioni, Amitai. (1964). *Modern organizations.* Englewood Cliffs, NJ: Prentice Hall.

Evans, K. G. (1996). "Chaos as opportunity: grounding a positive vision of management and society in the new physics." *Public Administration Review,* 56: 491–494.

Ginsberg, L. (1995). "Concepts of new management." In Ginsberg, L. and Keys, P. (Eds.). *New management in the human services.* (2nd ed.). Washington, DC: NASW.

Gortner, Harold F.; Mahler, Julianne; and Nicholson, Jeanne. (1987). *Organization theory: A public perspective.* Chicago: The Dorsey Press.

Grusky, Oscar and Miller, George (Eds.). (1981). *The sociology of organizations: Basic studies* (2nd ed.). New York: The Free Press.

Hendry, J. (1999). "Cultural theory and contemporary management." *Human Relations,* 52(5): 557–577.

Hodgetts, R. M., Luthans, F. and Lee, S. M. (1994). "New paradigm organizations: From Total Quality to Learning to World Class." *Organizational Dynamics,* 22(3): 5–19.

Howard, D. and Hine, D. (1997). "The population of organisations life cycle (POLC): Implications for small business assistance programs." *International Small Business Journal, 15*(3): 30–41.

Iannello, Kathleen P. (1992). *Decisions without hierarchy: Feminist interventions in organization theory and practice.* New York: Routledge.

Jawahar, I, and McLaughlin, G. (2001). "Toward a descriptive stakeholder theory: An organizational life cycle approach." *Academy of Management. The Academy of Management Review, 26*(3): 397–414.

Liedtka, J. (1996). "Feminist morality and competitive reality: a role for an ethic of care?" *Business Ethics Quarterly, 6:* 179–200.

Neugeboren, Bernard. (1985). *Organizational policy and practice in the human services.* New York: Longman.

Nixon, R., and Spearmon, M. (1991). "Building a pluralistic workplace." In Edwards, R. and Yankey, J. (Eds.). *Skills for effective human services management.* Washington, DC: NASW Press. Reprinted by permission.

O'Neil, D. A., and Bilimoria, D. (2005). "Women's career development phases: Idealism, endurance, and reinvention." *Career Development International, 10*(3), 168.

Ouchi, William G. (1981). *Theory Z.* New York: Avon Books.

Overman, E. S. (1996). "The new science of administration: chaos and quantum theory." *Public Administration Review, 56:* 487–491.

Patti, R. (Ed.). (2009). *The Handbook of Human Services Management* (2nd ed.). Los Angeles: Sage.

Pugh, D. S.; Hickson, D. J.; and Hinings, C. R. (Eds.). (1985) *Writers on organizations.* Beverly Hills: SAGE Publications.

Rifkin, J. (1998). "A civil education for the twenty-first century: preparing students for a three-sector society." *National Civic Review, 87:* 177–181.

Schein, Edgar. (1992). *Organizational culture and leadership.* (2nd ed.). San Francisco: Jossey-Bass.

Schneider, B., Brief, A. P., and Guzzo, R. A. (1996). "Creating a climate and culture for sustainable organizational change." *Organizational Dynamics, 24*(4): 7–19.

Shafritz, Jay M., and Ott, J. Steven. (1987). *Classics of organization theory* (2nd ed.). Chicago: The Dorsey Press.

Taylor, Frederick W. (1981). "Scientific management." In Grusky, Oscar, and Miller, George A., eds. *The sociology of organizations: Basic studies* (2nd ed.). New York: The Free Press.

Thomas, R. Roosevelt, Jr. (1990). "From affirmative action to affirming diversity." *Harvard Business Review,* March–April 1990: 107–117.

Thomas, R. Roosevelt, Jr. (1991) "The concept of managing diversity." *The Bureaucrat: The Journal for Public Managers.* Winter 1991–1992: 19–22.

Thomas, R. (1996). "Redefining diversity." *HR Focus, 73*(4): 6–7.

Westen, T. (1998). "Can technology save democracy?" *National Civic Review, 87:* 47–56.

Wheatley, M., and Kellner-Rogers, M. (1996). "Breathing life into organizations." *Public Management, 78:* 10–14.

Zhu, Z. (1999). "The practice of multimodal approaches, the challenge of cross-cultural communication, and the search for responses." *Human Relations, 52*(5): 579–607.

Chapter 9

Abrams, L., and Moio, J. (2009). "Critical race theory and the cultural competence dilemma in social work education." *Journal of Social Work Education, 45*(2), 245–261.

Aidala, Angela A. (1989). "Communes and changing family norms: Marriage and lifestyle choice among former members of communal groups." *Journal of Family Issues, 10*(3): 311–338.

Aidala, Angela A., and Zablocki, Benjamin D. (1991). "The communes of the 1970s: Who joined and why?" *Marriage and Family Review, 17*(1–2): 87–116.

Anderson, Ralph, and Carter, Irl. (1990). *Human behavior in the social environment.* (4th ed.). New York: Aldine De Gruyter.

Asamoah, Y., Healy, L. M., and Mayadas, N. (1997). "Ending the international-domestic dichotomy: New approaches to a global curriculum for the millennium." *Journal of Social Work Education, 33*(2), 389–402.

Beverly, S., and Sherraden, M. (1997). *Human capital and social work* (97–2). St. Louis: Washington University George Warren Brown School of Social Work, Center for Social Development.

Briggs, X. N. de Soyza. (1997). "Social capital and the cities: Advice to change agents." *National Civic Review, 86:* 111–117.

Bouvard, Marguerite. (1977). "The intentional community movement." In Roland L. Warren, ed., *New perspectives on the American community: A book of readings* (3rd ed.). Chicago: Rand McNally College Publishing Company.

Bricker-Jenkins, Mary, and Hooyman, Nancy R., (Eds.). (1986). *Not for women only: Social work practice for a feminist future.* Silver Spring, MD: National Association of Social Workers, Inc.

Campbell, Carlos. (1976). *New towns: Another way to live.* Reston, VA: Reston Publishing, Inc.

Collins, Patricia Hill. (1990). *Black feminist thought: Knowledge, consciousness, and the politics of empowerment.* Cambridge: Unwin Hyman, Inc.

Compete.com (2009). "Top twenty-five social networking sites—Feb 2009." Retrieved June 10, 2009, from http://social-media-optimization.com/2009/02/top-twenty-five-social-networking-sites-feb-2009/

CSWE (2008). "Educational policy and accreditation standards 2008 (July 1)." Retrieved from http://www.cswe.org/CSWE/accreditation/

Demo, D. H., and Allen, K. R. (1996). "Diversity with lesbian and gay families: Challenges and implications for family theory and research." *Journal of Social and Personal Relationships, 13*(3):415–434.

Ewalt, P., Freeman, Edith, and Poole, Dennis. (Eds.). (1998a). *Community building: Renewal, well-being, and shared responsibility.* Washington, D.C.: NASW Press.

Ewalt, P. (1998b). "The revitalization of impoverished communities." In P. Ewalt, E. Freeman, and D. Poole (Eds.). *Community building: Renewal, well-being, and shared responsibility* (pp. 3–5). Washington, DC: NASW Press.

Feagin, Joe R., and Feagin, Clairece Booher. (1978). *Discrimination American style: Institutional racism and sexism.* Englewood Cliffs, NJ: Prentice Hall.

Fellin, P. (1993). "Reformulation of the context of community based care." *Journal of Sociology and Social Welfare 20*(2):57–67.

Kanter, Rosabeth Moss. (1977). "Communes and commitment." In Warren, Roland L., *New perspectives on the American community: A book of readings.* Chicago: Rand McNally College Publishing Company.

Kuhn, Thomas S. (1970). *The structure of scientific revolutions* (2nd ed.). Chicago: The University of Chicago Press.

Lappé, F. M., and DuBois, Paul M. (1997). "Building social capital without looking backward." *National Civic Review, 86:* 119–128.

Logan, John R. (1988). "Realities of black suburbanization." In Warren, Roland L., and Lyon, Larry. *New perspectives on the American community* (5th ed.). Chicago: The Dorsey Press.

Longres, John. (1990). *Human behavior in the social environment.* Itasca, IL: F. E. Peacock.

Louv, R. (1996). "The culture of renewal, part I: Characteristics of the community renewal movement." *National Civic Review, 85:* 52–61.

Louv, R. (1997). "The culture of renewal, part 2: Characteristics of the community renewal movement." *National Civic Review, 86:* 97–105.

Lynn, M. (2004). "Inserting the 'race' into critical pedagogy: An analysis of 'race-based epistemologies.'" *Educational Philosophy & Theory, 36*(2), 153–165.

Mackelprang, R. W., and Salsgiver, R. O. (1996). "People with disabilities and social work: Historical and contemporary issues." *Social Work, 41*(1): 7–14.

Maton, K. I., and Wells, E. A. (1995). "Religion as a community resource for well-being: Prevention, healing and empowerment pathways." *Journal of Social Issues, 51*(2): 177–193.

Maybury-Lewis, David. (1992). "Tribal wisdom." *Utne Reader, 52:* 68–79.

McKnight, John L. (1987). "Regenerating community." *Social Policy, 17*(3): 54–58.

McKnight, John L. (1992). "Are social service agencies the enemy of community?" *Utne Reader, 52:* 88–90.

Myers, Linda J. (1985). "Transpersonal psychology: The role of the Afrocentric paradigm." *The Journal of Black Psychology, 12*(1): 31–42.

Naparastek, A., and Dooley, D. (1998). "Countering urban disinvestment through community-building initiatives." In P. Ewalt, E. Freeman, and D. Poole. (Eds.). *Community building: Renewal, well-being, and shared responsibility* (pp. 6–16). Washington, DC: NASW Press.

Netting, Ellen; Kettner, Peter; and McMurty, Steven. (1993). *Social work macro practice.* New York: Longman.

Page-Adams, D., and Sherraden, M. (1997). "Asset building as a community revitalization strategy." *Social work, 42*(5): 423–434.

Parrish, R. (2002). "The changing nature of community." *Strategies, 15*(2).

Porter, E. (2004). "A typology of virtual communities: A multidisciplinary foundation for future research." *Journal of Computer Mediated Communication, 10*(1). Retrieved from http://jcmc.indiana.edu/vol10/issue1/porter.html#s01

Reiss, Albert J., Jr. (1959). "The sociological study of communities." *Rural Sociology, 24:* 118–130.

Rubin, Israel. (1983). "Function and structure of community: Conceptual and theoretical analysis." In Warren, Roland L., and Lyon, Larry. *New perspectives on the American community.* Homewood, IL: The Dorsey Press.

Saleebey, D. (May 1996). "The strengths perspective in social work practice: Extensions and cautions." *Social Work, 41*(3): 296–305.

Sanderson, Dwight. (1988). In Warren, Roland L., and Lyon, Larry. *New Perspectives on the American community* (5th ed.). Chicago: The Dorsey Press.

Schiele, J. H. (2007). "Implications of the equality-of-oppressions paradigm for curriculum content on people of color." *Journal of Social Work Education, 43*(1), 83–100.

Schulman, M. D., and Anderson, C. (1999). "The dark side of the force: a case study of restructuring and social capital." *Rural Sociology, 64*(3): 351–372.

Solomon, Barbara. (1976). *Black empowerment: Social work in oppressed communities.* New York: Columbia University Press.

Sullivan, W. P. (1994). "The tie that binds: A strengths/empowerment model for social development." *Social Development Issues, 16*(3): 100–111.

Tönnies, Ferdinand. (1988). "Gemeinschaft and Gesellschaft." In Warren, Roland L., and Lyon, Larry. *New Perspectives on the American community* (5th ed.). Chicago: The Dorsey Press.

Utne, Eric. (1992). "I am because we are." *Utne Reader, 52:*2.

Wallis, A. D., Crocker, J. P., and Schecter, B. (1998). "Social capital and community building: part one." *National Civic Review, 87:* 253–271.

Walsh, J. (1997). "Community building in theory and practice: three case studies." *National Civic Review, 86:* 291–314.

Warner, M. (1999). "Social capital construction and the role of the local state." *Rural Sociology, 64*(3): 373–393.

Warren, Roland. (1977). *New perspectives on the American community: A book of readings* (3rd ed.). Chicago: Rand McNally College Publishing Company.

Warren, Roland L. (1978). *The community in America* (3rd ed.). Chicago: Rand McNally College Publishing Company.

Warren, Roland. (1988b). "The good community." In Warren, Roland L., and Lyon, Larry. *New perspectives on the American community* (5th ed.). Chicago: The Dorsey Press.

Warren, Roland and Lyon, Larry. (1983). *New perspectives on the American community.* Homewood, IL: The Dorsey Press.

Warren, Roland and Lyon, Larry. (1988). *New perspectives on the American community* (5th ed.). Chicago: The Dorsey Press.

Weber, Max. (1988). "The nature of the city." In Warren, Roland L., and Lyon, Larry. *New perspectives on the American community* (5th ed.). Chicago: The Dorsey Press.

Webster's II New College Dictionary. (1995). Boston: Houghton Mifflin Co.

Yosso, T. (2005). "Whose culture has capital? A critical race theory discussion of community cultural wealth." *Race, Ethnicity and Education, 8*(1), 69–91.

Chapter 10

Al-Krenawi, A., and Graham, J. (2000a). "Culturally sensitive social work practice with Arab clients in mental health settings." *Health and Social Work, 25*(1), 9–22.

Al-Krenawi, A., and Graham, J. (2000b). Islamic theology and prayer. *International Social Work, 43*(3), 289.

Asamoah, Y., Healy, L. M., and Mayadas, N. (1997). "Ending the international-domestic dichotomy: New approaches to a global curriculum for the millennium." *Journal of Social Work Education, 33*(2), 389–402. Retrieved from http://search.epnet.com/login.aspx?direct=true&db=aph&an=9706244126&loginpage=Login.asp

Gray, M., and Fook, J. (2004). "The quest for a universal social work: some issues and implications." *Social Work Education, 23*(5), 625–644.

Healy, L. (2001). *International Social Work: Professional Action in an Interdependent World.* New York: Oxford.

Healy, L. (2008). "Exploring the history of social work as a human rights profession." *International Social Work,* *51*(6), 735.

International Association of Schools of Social Work (IASSW). Available: http://www.iassw.soton.ac.uk/Generic/Mission .asp?lang=en

International Association of Schools of Social Work/ International Federation of Social Workers. Definition of Social Work Jointly Agreed 27 June 2001. Copenhagen.

International Council on Social Welfare (ICSW). Available: http://www.icsw.org/

International Federation of Social Workers. Available: http:// www.ifsw.org

Lundy, C., and Van Wormer, K. (2007). "Social and economic justice, human rights and peace: The challenge for social work in Canada and the USA." *International Social Work,* *50*(6), 727.

Mayadas, N. and Elliot, D. (1997). Lessons from International Social Work. Book chapter in Reisch, M. and Gambrill, E. *Social Work in the 21st Century.* Thousand Oaks, CA: Pine Forge Press.

Midgely, J. (1997). *Social Welfare in Global Context.* Thousand Oaks, CA: Sage Publications.

Rehman, T., and Dziegielewski, S. (2003). "Women who choose Islam." *International Journal of Mental Health,* *32*(3), 31–49.

United Nations Universal Declaration of Human Rights. Available: http://www.un.org/Overview/rights.html

U.N. Millennium Development Goals. Retrieved May 8, 2009, from http://www.undp.org/mdg/goal3.shtml

U.N. (2008). *The Millennium Develpment Goals Report 2008.* New York: United Nations.

Photo Credits

Index